The authors

Peter Madge is a money adviser and has worked for Citizens Advice Specialist Support since 1991. He is a consultant for the Money Advice Specialist Support Consultancy Service, and writes and delivers training and presentations on money advice issues. Peter is the Institute of Money Advisers Council member for South Wales.

John Kruse currently works as a money adviser for Redbridge Citizens Advice Bureau. He has been a debt counsellor for the last 22 years, specialising in bailiffs law. He is the author of several books and articles on the subject, and acts as a trainer and consultant to the Government, Council of Europe and many advice agencies.

David Malcolm is Head of Social Policy at the National Union of Students.

Paula Twigg is Manager of CPAG's Citizens' Rights Office.

Janet Wilson has delivered advice and training on all aspects of debt during her 15 years at Citizens Advice Specialist Support, including writing the Wiseradviser *Business Debt Handbook*.

Acknowledgements

The production of this eighth edition has been made possible by a number of other authors who have contributed their specialist expertise.

Janet Wilson, from Citizens Advice Specialist Support, has updated the chapter on business debts, Paula Twigg from CPAG has revised the chapter on maximising income, David Malcolm from the NUS has updated the chapter on student debts and John Kruse has revised the bailiffs chapter.

Thanks are also due to Martin Williams, Carolyn George and Keith Houghton for their valuable contribution.

I would also like to acknowledge the efforts of the authors of previous editions of this book, most notably Mike Wolfe.

Thank you to all my colleagues at Citizens Advice Specialist Support, particularly Marina Gallagher, Jane Phipps, Lorraine Charlton and Janet Wilson, and Jan Channing of Caerphilly County CAB for checking and making useful comments on the text.

I am grateful to Alison Key at CPAG for producing this edition. Thanks also to Paulette Storey and Paul Levay for producing the index, and to Paula McDiarmid for proofreading the text.

Peter Madge
Citizens Advice Specialist Support

The law covered in this book was correct on 1 October 2008 and includes Regulations laid up to this date.

Foreword

Over the last ten years or so, personal debt problems have become an increasingly important part of the work of many advice agencies. For the CAB service, debt enquiries have grown year on year, so that in 2007/08 Citizens Advice Bureaux dealt with around 1.7 million new problem debts. Debt became the single biggest issue on which bureaux gave advice.

For most of this time, the story has been dominated by the growth of consumer credit debt in what were otherwise relatively benign economic conditions for borrowers. An apparently ever-expanding credit market seemed to throw up too many cases of borrowers building up sometimes huge debts over multiple credit products and this fuelled concerns about the responsibility of some of the lending practices in the market.

But this is, of course, now old news. The unsustainable lending practices in mortgage markets on another continent have made the economic conditions of the last decade look like another planet. The 'nice decade' is apparently over and the fall-out from the ongoing credit crunch seems likely to write a new chapter in the modern history of personal debt problems in the UK.

Firstly, this combination of events seems to be accelerating trends we are already seeing in money advice caseloads. Between 2007 and 2008, consumer debt enquiries to the CAB service have actually been falling after a decade of continuous growth. Within this, the decline of problems with credit cards for some the poster boys of the past decade's over-indebtedness has been particularly notable. While this does not lessen the need for a rigorous and wide-ranging debate on responsible lending and better considered borrowing, recent initiatives by the credit industry to identify better borrowers for whom credit is becoming a problem are to be welcomed.

Over the same period we have been seeing a quite sharp increase in some of the key debts identified as priorities by money advisers. Mortgage arrears, fuel debts and council tax problems have all been on the rise, with the effects seemingly felt most by lower income households and those towards the margins of the pre-credit crunch mortgage market. Perhaps this is the consequence of households being squeezed by substantial increases in the cost of essential living expenses. Perhaps, and with little irony, the tightening credit market has left some households with reduced access to the credit they would previously have used to manage variable or persistently low incomes. As one money adviser recently put it, relatively cheap credit from mainstream providers has been a sort of second welfare state for many CAB clients over the last few years.

How this trend will play out over the next period is unclear and much will no doubt depend on where the economy goes from here. If the so-called secondary effects of the crisis in global finance markets spread out into greater levels of unemployment and reduced hours, and inflation continues to erode real wage levels, those of us concerned with personal debt could very quickly find ourselves in uncharted waters. Advisers will be aware that levels of both secured and unsecured debt are considerably higher than was the case in the 1990s and we have yet to find out what the combination of a significant recession and a mass consumer credit market might do to UK society.

Hopefully, we will not get the chance to find out any time soon. But if times get tougher we can be certain that the help available from high quality money advice services will be more important than ever. The tireless and dedicated work of money advisers provides the last, best hope for many of the families and individuals who find themselves in serious financial difficulties. This *Handbook* continues to be an essential resource for all those working in debt advice and will help advisers meet the challenges of the near future, whatever these may be. I congratulate the authors on another excellent publication.

David Harker
Chief Executive, Citizens Advice

Contents

How to use this *Handbook*

This *Handbook* is produced:

- as a guide and training aid for the new debt adviser;
- as a reference work for those who undertake debt advice alongside other sorts of advice work or other professional disciplines – eg, social workers and housing officers;
- for the specialist debt adviser as a first step in accessing primary legislation and Regulations;
- for the manager or purchaser of debt advice services to help understand and evaluate debt advice.

The subjects covered within debt advice are vast and could fill many volumes. In this *Handbook* much detail has deliberately been excluded in order to make it accessible to the reader and to make clear the structure of debt work.

With the increasing use of computers in advice agencies, most relevant legislation and court forms are now available online from www.opsi.gov.uk and www.hmcourts-service.gov.uk respectively and so are no longer included in the Appendices. The Civil Procedure Rules are available online at www.dca.gov.uk and many judgments of the higher courts are available in the legal/professional section of www.hmcourts-service.gov.uk. Most debt packages used in advice agencies now come with standard letters and forms and so these are no longer included in the Appendices. The Common Financial Statement is increasingly the standard form of financial statement sent out to creditors and this is available online at www.moneyadvicetrust.org together with supporting documentation.

The *Handbook* can best be used as follows.

Training aid

The **Introduction** and **Chapters 1 to 3** are written to assist those who are interested in debt advice and outline the processes and skills involved. These should be read by new debt advisers and those who have done some of this work and would like to think more about the structure behind their practical experience. The chapters can also be used by those who commission or manage debt advice as a means of clarifying the product with which they are dealing.

The new adviser should ensure that s/he is able to identify each type of debt (this is explained in **Chapter 4**) because this is fundamental to using the rest of the *Handbook*. Maximising income is a key part of the debt advice process and this is summarised in **Chapter 6**. The new adviser will also need to be familiar with the criteria to be used in prioritising debts (**Chapter 7**). S/he will find it useful to skim through the different strategies for priority and non-priority debts (**Chapters 7 and 8**). These can be examined in detail as they arise in the course of advising.

The debt adviser

Readers already familiar with the processes of debt advice may wish to use **Chapter 5** (minimising debts) and the strategy selection (**Chapters 7 and 8**) to help them think about the best strategy for a particular debt. This might include bankruptcy or an individual voluntary arrangement (these are discussed in **Chapter 12**). Court procedures are covered in **Chapter 9** (county court) and **Chapter 10** (magistrates' courts). If the client is threatened with bailiff action, the adviser should refer to **Chapter 11**. Specific debts are dealt with in **Chapter 13** (business debts) and **Chapter 14** (student debts). The index will enable you to find detailed information on a particular strategy, type of debt or court process. References can be accessed via the endnotes contained at the end of each chapter for those readers who want more in-depth information about a particular topic. Details of other useful reference material and organisations are in the Appendices.

Abbreviations

AA	attendance allowance
AO	administration order
APR	annual percentage rate
BRO	bankruptcy restriction order
BRU	bankruptcy restriction undertaking
CA	carer's allowance
CAB	Citizens Advice Bureau
CFS	Common Financial Statement
CSA	Child Support Agency
CTB	council tax benefit
CTC	child tax credit
DIUS	Department for Innovation, Universities and Skills
DLA	disability living allowance
DRO	debt relief order
DRP	debt repayment plan
DWP	Department for Work and Pensions
ERO	enforcement restriction order
ESA	employment and support allowance
EU	European Union
EWC	expected week of childbirth
FOS	Financial Ombudsman Service
FSA	Financial Services Authority
FTVA	fast-track, post-bankruptcy voluntary arrangement
GAP	guaranteed asset protection
HB	housing benefit
HE	higher education
HP	hire purchase
IB	incapacity benefit
IS	income support
IVA	individual voluntary arrangement
JP	Justice of the Peace
JSA	jobseeker's allowance
LLP	limited liability partnership
LSC	Legal Services Commission
MA	maternity allowance
MCOB	*Mortgages and Home Finance: conduct of business sourcebook*
MIG	mortgage indemnity guarantee
NI	national insurance
NINA	no income, no asset
NSEA	*National Standards for Enforcement Agents*
NUS	National Union of Students
OFT	Office of Fair Trading
PAYE	Pay As You Earn
PC	pension credit
PGCE	Postgraduate Certificate in Education
the Revenue	Her Majesty's Revenue and Customs
SAP	statutory adoption pay
SCIVA	straightforward consumer individual voluntary arrangement
SDA	severe disablement allowance
SFE	Student Finance England
SIVA	simple individual voluntary arrangement
SLC	Student Loans Company
SMP	statutory maternity pay
SPP	statutory paternity pay
SSP	statutory sick pay
VAT	value added tax
WTC	working tax credit

Introduction

Debt has always been an inevitable consequence of borrowing and is recognised by the credit industry as a necessary corollary of its lending. Lenders will always make provision in their accounts for debts that are to be written off. This *Handbook* is based on the assumption that debt is caused by lenders who predict it, but lend none the less.

While the causes of debt may not be individual, the effects are: bailiffs, disconnections, repossessions and imprisonment. Money worries are a significant cause of relationship problems, depression, anxiety and stress, with many of those in debt receiving treatment from their GP.

Mental health problems are both a cause and effect of debt and so it is good to see that the money advice sector and the credit industry have worked together under the auspices of the Money Advice Liaison Group to produce good practice guidelines for dealing with this particular situation.

What is debt advice

Debt advice is a series of tools and professional strategies that can be used to help clients with financial difficulties. Debt advice provides help to clients by:

- enabling them to maximise their income;
- explaining the implications of non-payment of each of their debts, and on this basis deciding which are priorities;
- assisting them to plan their budgets;
- helping them choose a strategy (usually to reduce or stop payments) that will minimise the effects of their debt on their financial, social or medical wellbeing by giving them impartial, independent and confidential advice which enables them to make an informed choice about the options available to them;
- preserving their home, fuel supplies and liberty;
- assisting by advice or representation with the implementation of whatever strategy is chosen.

Debt advice should be distinguished from 'budgeting advice' and 'financial education'. Budgeting advice can only be effective where there is enough money for a person's needs to be met. Very often, because of benefit levels or the escalation of credit charges, this is not the case. In these circumstances, budgeting advice is likely to be at best unrealistic and, more usually, patronising. Budgeting advice was often based on methods which were not, in any case, open to poor people (buy in bulk or travel to distant supermarkets) or entirely unrealistic for any but the leisured classes (bake your own bread or make your own jam).

Financial advice is not much use to a person who has no financial products and cannot even afford to meet her/his essential living expenses. On the other hand, debt advice should not reinforce financial exclusion; it should seek to promote financial inclusion. Debt advice does include a comprehensive check of a person's entitlement to state benefits, but it goes much further than welfare rights.

In the past, the words 'debt counselling' and 'money advice' have been used almost interchangeably to describe what we shall call 'debt advice'. We prefer this term to 'money advice' because this is often confused with benefit checking. 'Debt counselling', on the other hand, can appear to suggest that debt is a problem about which individuals merely need counselling. Counselling may sometimes be important in the early stages of debt advice, but is not a substitute for the work of the debt adviser. Debt advice is not just about making offers (token or otherwise) to the client's creditors. The processes described in this *Handbook* are not set in stone and advisers should not be afraid to step outside them in order to help their clients. Advisers should not assume that creditors and courts always get it right, but should examine their practices and their paperwork to protect their clients from inappropriate enforcement action.

Recent developments

The past few years have seen the emergence of a new type of 'debt client' – people with substantial amounts of credit debts, but also with substantial amounts of available income with which to repay them. At some stage, a debate may need to take place as to whether the debt advice described in this *Handbook* should be confined to those clients who are unable to meet their commitments instead of being available to everyone who has debts, regardless of whether or not they can service them.

But for those clients who do have financial products, and with the likelihood that more of them are going to have to consider using the equity in their homes to service their commitments, traditional debt advice may be falling short. There is a need for such clients to be given at least money guidance (the new name for generic financial advice) and the question is, how is it going to be provided and by whom?

Advice agencies providing debt advice are increasingly under pressure. As the free sector struggles to cope with the demand, it is no surprise to see a continuing rise in fee-charging agencies, who may offer free advice but whose solution is likely to be an individual voluntary arrangement, involving the client in the payment of costs. Although a simple form of an individual voluntary arrangement has been produced by the Insolvency Service and is soon to be implemented, there are no plans to introduce set fees. As now, the administration of these will be the monopoly of insolvency practitioners and so the extent to which market pressures will operate to reduce costs must be open to question. In spite of the welcome increase in liaison between debt advisers and the credit industry – which has enabled each to understand more about the other's position – advisers continue to see:

- irresponsible lending, including debt consolidation loans being made to clients who have no ability to repay them;
- credit cards being issued to people with no verification of their income and no checks that they will be able to afford to service their commitments;
- unsympathetic and negative attitudes on the part of some creditors and collectors towards people in debt, in clear breach of industry codes of practice;
- unacceptable and aggressive debt collection practices, a situation which Office of Fair Trading guidelines issued in July 2003 are starting to address;
- an increasing willingness on the part of creditors to take court action (including the use of bankruptcy proceedings) to recover or secure their debts;
- more applications for orders for sale being made by creditors who have charging orders and more courts being prepared to assist creditors obtain charging orders in the first place.

Not only clients, but some major financial institutions have fallen victim to the 'credit crunch'. Now that the Government has a stake in some of the creditors that advisers commonly encounter, it will be interesting to see what effect, if any, this has on the creditor practices outlined above.

Last year, the Government passed legislation (the Tribunals, Courts and Enforcement Act 2007) which, when implemented (there is no timetable for this), will see a harsher enforcement regime in the civil courts. After many hundreds of years, bailiffs are to be given powers of forcible entry. And, in breach of the fundamental principle of enforcement of judgment debts, creditors are to be allowed to obtain charging orders without the need for the debtor to have defaulted on the terms of the judgment (a rule change which some courts appear to be applying already). Does this mean an increase in orders for sale will not be far behind?

The Act also contains provisions for two court-based solutions to the problem of over-indebtedness: debt relief orders and reformed administration orders. Debt relief orders will be available for people who meet fixed criteria on the level of their debts, assets and available income. Access will only be via an 'approved intermediary', and the role of the intermediary is an issue the free money advice sector will need to resolve over the next couple of months. Reformed administration orders, on the other hand, will only be available to people with a maximum level of debt and a minimum level of available income, with composition of the debts only available after compliance with the terms of the order over a five-year period. People on low incomes are likely to find themselves excluded from administration orders in the future. Homeowners who are asset rich and income poor and people with a high level of indebtedness are also likely to find themselves excluded from both remedies.

Chapter 1

Debt advice: an outline

This chapter covers:

1. The adviser as a professional

Debt advice is a professional activity. There is a package of attitudes, skills and strategies that are necessarily part of any debt advice service. This guarantees consistency and quality assurance. Users of such services are misled if anything less than this package is offered.

Debt advice can be provided by specialists or by professionals whose job primarily involves other activities – eg, housing officers and social workers. It can be provided by paid or voluntary workers. Recent years have seen the growth of debt management companies that charge clients a fee for setting up and handling debt repayment programmes.

There is currently no qualification that recognises the profession of money advice or acknowledges the wide range of skills and knowledge which money advisers bring to the job. However, the draft National Occupational Standards for Legal Advice Qualifications and Assessment Framework (currently under consultation) recommends a Level 3 NVQ (aimed at generalist advisers) and a Level 4 NVQ (aimed at specialist advisers), including two knowledge units covering first-line and casework money and debt legal advice, LA41 and LA42 respectively. Further information can be obtained from Skills for Justice at info@skillsforjustice.com. Several awarding bodies have expressed an interest in developing related qualifications, which means it is possible that a generalist NVQ Level 3 and a specialist NVQ Level 4 in debt and money advice will be available some time after October 2008.

A professional debt adviser needs a mixture of skills, knowledge and attitudes, which together form the basis of good practice. The Institute of Money Advisers (the professional association for full-time, part-time or volunteer debt advisers in England, Wales and Northern Ireland who deliver or promote free, confidential, impartial and independent debt advice services) is currently working on a code to outline the main aspects of good practice.

In December 2001 the Office of Fair Trading (OFT) issued guidance on the minimum standards of service that debt management companies should provide, but made it clear that its principles applied equally to the free advice sector. The OFT subsequently issued a commentary to clarify the extent to which the guidance applies to the free sector.[1] It largely underlines what should be good practice and will be referred to where relevant below.

The Money Advice Trust is currently leading on a Money Advice Quality Model project with input from various advice sector bodies. This aims to develop a quality assurance scheme for money advice providers to complement the individual accreditation of money advisers.

An unambiguous role

In any situation where money is owed, there are two parties whose interests may conflict. Both parties will have a variety of legal remedies and defences, and well-established professionals know that they cannot advise both parties in such a situation. A debt adviser similarly needs to be clear that s/he is working only for the interests of the client. This is true even if the adviser's employment is funded by the finance industry or other creditors, such as a local authority, or if s/he works for an organisation that seeks to be impartial.

While impartiality may at different times require a worker to offer to assist both creditors and clients, it cannot mean that a debt adviser is working towards the best interests of both parties at the same time when there is an inherent conflict of interests.

The OFT guidance and commentary make clear that all advice must be in the best interests of the client and should take account of:

- the nature of the debt;
- the client's financial position;
- the powers of the creditor;
- whether interest or other charges have been frozen.[2]

A professional attitude

A debt adviser should be aware of experiences in her/his own past which may give her/him judgemental attitudes towards clients and/or creditors. Debt advisers must consciously rid themselves of any personal bias and adopt a professional approach to the work.

A professional adviser must also offer a high-quality, accessible service to all groups in society and should work towards understanding that debt can affect clients from different social groups in different ways.

A commitment to social policy

A professional debt adviser should not allow the same problem to affect adversely the lives of countless users, but will make known the lessons which can be learnt from her/his work to as wide an audience of policy makers as possible.

Sound knowledge of law and procedures

A professional debt adviser should be knowledgeable and imaginative about the ways in which the law can be applied to mitigate the effects of debt. S/he should be able to offer and explain each of these to any user.

A commitment to developing the service

A professional debt adviser should take regular opportunities to enhance her/his own skills through training, research and education, and should participate in offering this to others so that the practice of debt advice continues to be refined and developed.

A systematic approach

A professional debt adviser should apply a single systematic approach to each individual client. This does not, however, detract from the adviser's duty to ensure that any advice given is:

- in the best interests of that particular client;
- appropriate to her/his specific situation;
- realistic; *and*
- where an offer of payment is made, sustainable.

The ability to involve the client in informed choices

A professional adviser should always try to involve the client, ensuring that the client understands the implications of her/his situation and the steps the adviser proposes be taken. The adviser assists the client to make informed choices by giving her/him all her/his options and explaining their consequences before anything is done. The adviser should also manage the client's expectations of the adviser and agency.

Many advisers tend to put pressure on themselves to solve their clients' problems and client expectations can add to this. Whilst advisers should always do the best they can for their clients, there will be times when the options are limited because matters have simply gone too far and the adviser cannot make the problem go away. Advisers should not feel that they have somehow 'failed' the client as they are likely to need supporting through the situation.

Also, many debt cases involve very distressing facts and advisers need to feel that they can share and discuss these sorts of issues with colleagues and supervisors/managers.

2. The debt advice system

The debt advice system is a structured set of procedures and activities that must be worked through if a debt adviser is to provide the best possible service to someone with a multiple debt problem. It is designed to:
- maintain the client's home, liberty and essential services;
- advise the client about her/his rights and responsibilities;
- give the client the information s/he needs to make informed choices in dealing with the debt situation;
- empower the client, where possible.

A systematic approach is essential because of:
- the large amount of information and paperwork generated by most debt enquiries;
- the need to avoid overlooking a particular strategy;
- the need to keep detailed records of the agency's work – both to ensure effective advice and to enable case material to be used for evaluating the service and for social policy development;
- the need to train new workers in a clearly defined set of skills and knowledge;
- the need to guarantee consistency in spite of the diversity of clients using the service;
- the need to protect the adviser from the strain of having continually to 're-invent the wheel'.

A system should not be seen as a straitjacket, and it does not prevent the need for individuals to operate in a creative and flexible way in the best interests of the individual client. Different agencies will need to develop their own paperwork based on demand and resources, and any reporting requirements of funders – eg, the Legal Services Commission.

A debt adviser needs to perform a wide range of tasks in order to provide effective help to clients. This section provides a list of these tasks, in the order in which they should be performed.
- Explore the debt problem. This involves establishing the extent of the client's debts, and the reason(s) for the client's financial difficulties and whether these are temporary or long term. This includes finding out who the client's creditors are, how much is owed to each one and the action each creditor has taken to collect its debt (which may have involved passing the debt to a firm of debt collectors or even selling the debt to a debt purchaser, in which case it is necessary to see what action the collector/purchaser has taken[3]). In this *Handbook*, the word 'creditor' includes not only the original creditor but also, if the debt has been sold, the debt purchaser (unless stated otherwise).
- Emergencies, such as bailiffs' warrants, threats of disconnection of fuel supply or loss of the home are dealt with first. Where court action is involved, the

adviser can help the client to complete court forms and may represent clients at any hearings.

- The adviser must then check that clients are liable for each of their debts.
- All possible ways of increasing clients' income should then be explored, particularly by checking they are receiving all benefits to which they are entitled. There may also be some clients who are receiving benefits to which they are not entitled. The implications of this need to be discussed in full with the client, along with the effect this may have on their financial statement.
- A financial statement should then be drawn up, showing what income clients are receiving, their essential expenditure and whether there is any income available to make payments to their creditors. There may be instances in which a client's expenditure needs to be challenged. Should this be the case, the adviser must discuss the reasons for this.
- All possible options for resolving the debt problem should then be explored, discussed with clients, and a strategy (or strategies) agreed with them.
- The adviser should then negotiate with priority creditors – ie, creditors whose sanctions for non-payment include imprisonment, disconnection of essential services or loss of the home.
- The adviser should then negotiate with the remaining creditors (known as non-priority creditors) with a view to persuading them to accept the agreed strategy.
- Sometimes, the adviser may have to challenge creditors on whether they are entitled to recover what they are claiming from clients – eg, if clients are not liable for their debts.

Chapters 2 and 3 explain in more detail how to carry out these tasks. Chapters 7 and 8 discuss the strategies for dealing with priority and non-priority debts.

Information to clients

It is not necessary for an agency to have any written agreement with the client, but the adviser should provide the following information to the client at the outset, either verbally or, preferably, in writing.

- Adequate information about the service in plain language – ie, how the debt advice process operates.
- Warnings:
  - that creditors need not accept offers or stop interest or other charges;
  - that creditors may still continue to try to collect their debt and such action could incur additional costs, which will be added to the debt;
  - that the client's credit rating could be adversely affected;
  - about the importance of meeting priority commitments;
  - that correspondence from creditors should not be ignored;
  - about the implication of court action;

– about the possible consequences of missing pre-arranged appointments with their adviser.

If the agency uses a form of written agreement, it should:

- be clear and written in plain, intelligible language;
- set out the nature of the service to be provided by the agency, together with the amount to be repaid or an estimate (ie, the total amount the client is to pay under the strategy chosen to deal with her/his debts, although it may not be possible to provide this information to the client until later in the process, if at all);
- make clear that:
  – clients are not prohibited from corresponding or communicating with creditors;
  – the agency will deal appropriately and promptly with any correspondence it receives;
  – the agency will keep the client informed of the progress of her/his case, including sending the client copies of correspondence sent to, and received from, creditors.[4]

It is good practice for the adviser at the first interview to point out also:

- the agency's commitment to confidentiality;
- the steps the agency will take and the steps the client has agreed to, or is expected to, take her/himself;
- that the client should not incur any further credit commitments without prior discussion with the adviser;
- that the client should inform the agency of any change in her/his financial circumstances;
- that a successful outcome cannot be guaranteed.

Monitoring creditor practices

The effectiveness of pressure for change often depends on the ability of an agency to produce evidence in support of its recommendations. For this reason, case recording must not just be accurate and detailed, but must also be stored in a form which allows details of particular practices, and the hardship they cause, to be retrieved and patterns detected. In July 2003 the Office of Fair Trading (OFT) issued guidance to the credit industry on what it regards as unfair debt collection practices (see Chapter 2). Debt advisers should, therefore, keep a record of the collection techniques and tactics favoured by individual creditors. This will be useful in the future choice of strategy. In addition, they should note practices or situations that continually cause hardship to clients and should monitor which creditors are responsible for such situations, for use in their social policy work.

There are frequent changes in the law and procedures that affect debt, and agencies are often in a very good position to look closely at how these are working in practice. Agencies often carry out such exercises as part of a network of local and national debt services.

Credit reference agencies

There is no right to credit and most lenders decide credit applications on the basis of 'credit scoring' – ie, a system used to assess the probability of applicants meeting their financial commitments using information supplied on the credit application form, the lender's own records (where available) and data from credit reference agencies. Different lenders use different systems which should not only establish the likelihood of the applicant repaying but also whether s/he can afford to do so.

Credit reference agencies provide factual information about clients and their credit records. They do not:

- make the decision or express any opinion on whether clients should be granted credit and are unable to tell clients why they have been refused credit; *or*
- keep 'blacklists' or details of clients' credit scores.

Credit reference agencies usually keep details of:

- electoral roll entries;
- county court judgments (these are held for six years unless paid within one month, when any record is removed);
- bankruptcy orders, administration orders and individual voluntary arrangements (these are held for six years);
- credit accounts (a record is held until the account is paid off and then for a further six years);
- whether the client has defaulted on the credit agreement (a record is held for six years from the date the default was registered);
- mortgage repossessions, including voluntary repossessions (these are held for six years);
- aliases, associations and linked addresses – ie, any other names the client has been known by, previous addresses or correspondence addresses and whether the client shares financial responsibility for an account with another person;
- a warning from the Fraud Prevention Service (known as CIFAS). This is a fraud avoidance system developed to protect people whose names, addresses or other details have been used fraudulently by other people in order to apply for or obtain credit. It does not mean that the client is being accused of fraud, but any credit applications may be checked out to ensure s/he is in fact the applicant;
- information from the Gone Away Information Network – ie, on clients who have 'gone away' without informing their lenders of a forwarding address;
- previous credit searches by lenders in the past two years. Several searches within a short period of time may indicate attempted fraud or overcommitment.

Previously, a client's credit file could contain information about other people with the same or a similar surname who live or lived at the same address at the same time as the client concerned (known as 'third-party data'). From October 2004, a client's credit file should only hold information about her/him and any other person with whom s/he has a 'financial association' – ie, joint account holders or applicants, or people who inform the agency they have financial ties. Associations allow lenders to take account of information about anyone 'linked' to the client. Although the client can 'opt out' – ie, ask a lender only to take account of information about her/him, this does not prevent the lender carrying out checks to make sure that the opt-out is not merely intended to hide a partner's poor credit rating. If there is no financial association, the client should inform the agency so the link can be removed.

Guidelines from the Information Commissioner state that an account should not be recorded as in default unless the relationship between the creditor and the client has 'broken down' – ie, the client has been in arrears for at least three consecutive months on the contractual instalments or under an agreement to reschedule repayments, but should be recorded as in default if such payments have not been made in full for six months. Accounts which are subject to repayment arrangements or debt management plans should only be recorded as 'defaults' if the client:

- is only making token payments (see below); *or*
- defaults on the arrangement and the arrears are equivalent to three months' payments under the original contract; *or*
- is making reduced payments, but no agreed arrangement is in place.

A client who is making token or reduced payments can file a 'notice of correction' to record this fact.

A client who has been refused credit should be informed whether or not the lender used a credit reference agency and details of the agency should be provided on request.[5] A client has the right to obtain a copy of her/his file at any time by sending details of her/his full name and address (including any previous addresses in the past six years), together with a fee of £2 to the credit reference agency concerned.[6] If the client considers that any of the information on the file is wrong and that s/he is likely to be prejudiced as a result, the credit reference agency can be asked to correct or remove the information.[7] The client should write to the credit reference agency stating why the information is wrong and submitting any supporting evidence – eg, that a debt has been paid. The agency must respond in writing within 28 days stating either that it has corrected or removed the information, or done nothing. In the meantime, the information is marked 'account query' while the agency checks its accuracy. If the agency fails to remove the information or the client does not agree with the proposed correction, s/he can ask the agency to add her/his own 'notice of correction' to the file – eg, an explanation of how the debt arose. This must be no more than 200 words long and must be sent to the agency within a further 28 days. The agency must inform the client within 28 days if it accepts the notice. If it does not, the agency must refer the case to the Information Commissioner for a ruling.

A client can complain to the Information Commissioner if s/he believes inaccurate information is being held, but a 'notice of correction' is not appropriate – eg, it needs to be completely removed. If the information about the client's credit history is factually correct, however, it will not be removed just because s/he does not want it made public. Credit repair companies who claim to be able to 'clean up' people's credit reference files (in return for a fee) should be avoided, as the information they give may be misleading or worse.[8]

The Information Commissioner can be contacted at Wycliffe House, Water Lane, Wilmslow, Cheshire SK9 5AF, www.ico.gov.uk. The Information Commissioner's Office produces a useful leaflet, *No Credit?*, available free of charge or online.

3. **Administrative systems**

Good systems and time management are essential, particularly if the adviser is working under a Legal Services Commission contract.

Appropriate referrals

It is important to establish whether a case should be referred to a specialist or more experienced adviser, and if there is a mechanism in place for referring cases, if appropriate, to other organisations.

Key dates – eg, court hearings, should be recorded so they are not missed and adequate preparation can be made. It may be appropriate to keep a record of referrals to track the outcome.

Once a case is opened, a record should be made of the case, and the client's name and address, to ensure the file can be accessed in the future should the client return after the case is closed.

Files and cases

All documents relating to a case must be kept in an adequate file. All the papers should be kept in date order. Incoming letters could be stored on one side of the file and outgoing on the other. Also there could be dividers to separate each different creditor, so it is easy to access each debt and monitor its progress. Alternatively, papers relating to each creditor could be kept together with a separate sheet on the file to indicate the action on each debt.

Correspondence

The client should be kept informed of each stage of the case and given copies of correspondence from the creditor. Telephone conversations should be recorded on the file and names kept of the person spoken to and date. It is good practice to follow up the call with a letter from either the adviser or creditor, as appropriate, to confirm information discussed if it is relevant to the case. A financial statement should be prepared to give a clearer picture of the client's circumstances and whether s/he is in a position to present offers and at what rate (see p42).

Reviews

Each case should be regularly reviewed to check that replies have been received, where appropriate, that preparation for any court hearings has been carried out, and what the next step in the case should be. The use of a brought-forward diary system may be useful to ensure that important dates are noted and follow-ups are done regularly. There is no point keeping a file open if there is no further work to be carried out, or if the client has ceased contact and the adviser is carrying out work for the client without any confirmation that s/he is maintaining payments as agreed.

By managing the caseload, advisers will also have a clearer idea of how many additional cases, if any, they can take on.

Cases should also be reviewed, if possible, by other workers to check that the advice given is appropriate and correct.

Closure

At the outset, the adviser should give the client an indication of how long the case will remain open. This gives the adviser an idea of how many cases s/he is dealing with and when s/he will be able to take on additional ones. As the adviser is trying to empower the client, the aim should be that, once the work is done on the case, clients can continue with the work themselves, but possibly with the option of returning in the future should they feel unable to deal with matters themselves or if there is a change of circumstance.

If clients return for help when creditors are asking for a review of the finances it may be advisable to assist them with a new financial statement and then advise how to prepare an offer letter, with the intention that they act for themselves.

Client contact

As much information as possible on all the debts should be gained at the first interview and this should be recorded in a clear and concise manner. A *pro forma* could be used to record the information, which could also remind the adviser what to ask the client in order to establish the full facts of the case. Debt clients are known to reveal only debts that they are worried about. It is therefore important that the adviser goes through all the priority commitments, whether or not they are in arrears, and then moves on to the non-priority commitments. Advice could be given in each area on the consequences should s/he default. The adviser should be realistic about the outcome and be honest with the client at all times.

The adviser should check that agreements have been drawn up correctly and consider any applicable time limits.

It is a good idea to have standard letters held electronically to cut and paste the relevant facts of each individual case. The first letter after the interview should confirm all the advice given, setting out the creditors' powers and the client's options and consequences. The agreed action and the expected time scale should also be outlined.

The adviser should keep clients informed and involved at each stage, with the intention they will be able to deal with the case themselves once the case is closed. The client should also keep the adviser informed of any change in circumstances throughout the life of the case.

Once all the work is completed on the case the adviser should send out a closure letter, detailing the work carried out and the outcome, and giving general advice on how to deal with the various creditors in the future.

Notes

1. The adviser as a professional

1 DMG; *Note: application of debt management guidance to CABx and other independent advice agencies*, OFT, April 2002

2 For a discussion of this issue, see 'Quarterly Quarrel', *Quarterly Account* 4, IMA, Spring 2007

2. The debt advice system

3 The sale of a debt is known in law as an 'assignment' of the debt and the purchaser is known as an 'assignee'

4 paras 6-10 and 20-21 DMG

5 The lender must supply the details if the request is made in writing: s157 CCA 1974

6 s158 CCA 1974

7 s159 CCA 1974

8 *Credit Repair Promises Fall Short*, OFT, May 2000

Chapter 2

Key skills

This chapter covers:

1. Interviewing

This section is not a general guide to interviewing, but there are some features of an interview with a person in debt that are important to note.

- The debt adviser must immediately make it clear to the client that s/he will not be judged.
- The debt adviser must be aware of the ways in which preconceptions or personal attitudes affect the interview process. S/he must work to recognise any negative images s/he may have of borrowing, debt or debtors and eradicate them.
- It is important that the client is enabled to voice her/his emotions in order to get these out of the way and concentrate on remembering, thinking and decision making as the interview progresses. For example, many people in debt fear imprisonment. For the vast majority of debts this is not a possibility, but this fear must be voiced if progress is to be made. The client may also have problems which initially do not appear to be debt-related – eg, relationship issues. Clients need to be able to express whatever is important to them and their concerns so that they can concentrate on sorting out their debts.
- Because of the numerous threats from individual creditors, many clients feel hopeless about their situation. Advisers cannot afford to raise false expectations by dismissing these threats, but they should be positive and explain it is possible to do something.
- The debt adviser must anticipate problems the client may face. It is important that the client does not depart from decisions made as part of a strategy, but

the adviser is unlikely to be there when these decisions are tested. For example, an adviser and client may agree that, because the client has been paying creditors who call at the door and not paying her/his priority creditors, the best course of action is to withhold all payments to unsecured creditors until the arrears on the client's priority debts have been cleared. This decision will not be tested until an unsecured creditor calls, perhaps late at night, making threats. The client may find it difficult to stick to her/his earlier decision unless this possibility has already been explored with the adviser.

- Partners, or other people with whom the client lives, will usually need to be consulted if a good decision – ie, one which is likely to be adhered to, is to be made. Many of the decisions taken involve third parties who may not be at the interview. Even if the debt adviser considers that urgent action is required, this can generally be delayed long enough for the client to consult these people. Occasionally there will be compelling reasons for not consulting – eg, a fear of violence.
- A clear explanation of the tasks to be undertaken by the adviser and those expected of the client must be written down and a copy given to the client and one kept by the agency (see p5).
- Performing realistic tasks can reduce the sense of hopelessness and empower the client. Modest tasks, such as asking a particular creditor about arrears, can help the client feel involved in the processes that are being carried out on her/his behalf. While it is important for the adviser to offer expertise and services, s/he should not take over the client's life.
- The debt adviser must always be impartial and not assume s/he knows what is best for the client. All options open to the client must be considered before any course of action is agreed.

2. **Negotiation**

Negotiation is a process of communication between the adviser or client and creditor. It takes place over a period of time, after which an agreement is made that both sides find acceptable. A decision must be made about whether it is appropriate for negotiation to be carried out by the client or the adviser. Sometimes, it is more empowering for the debt adviser to support a client by providing, for example, a financial statement or *pro forma,* rather than negotiating her/himself. This support should usually be mentioned to the creditor and the client encouraged to remain in contact with the adviser. Some creditors have a policy of refusing to deal with advice agencies. If the client has authorised the debt adviser to negotiate with a creditor on her/his behalf, the Office of Fair Trading regards it as an unfair and improper business practice for a creditor to refuse to do so.[1] A creditor who refuses to negotiate with an adviser without a valid reason should be challenged.

A debt adviser must only represent the interests of the client and should ensure that s/he does not offer more than s/he can afford. Advisers should do their best to enable the client regain control of her/his financial situation as quickly as possible, as opposed to being tied into a repayment programme, which may take many years to complete (if ever).

A debt adviser is often in a powerful position in relation to creditors because no one in the credit industry wants to be accused (particularly publicly) of acting illegally or oppressively. If a debt adviser from a well-respected local or national agency contacts a creditor to negotiate on a client's behalf, it is likely that the creditor will want to reach a settlement. In some cases, the adviser's power is increased because debt advice is likely to lead to payment and, in others, because the creditor realises that a debt cannot profitably be pursued. This does not mean that creditors should routinely be expected to agree to each and every proposal that a debt adviser puts forward. On the other hand, if the debt adviser feels that the creditor is being unreasonable and/or unrealistic, s/he should consider referring the matter to a more senior person in the creditor organisation with a view to using the creditor's complaints procedure, if necessary.

Arguments should be supported by referring to any relevant code of practice. All negotiations should be conducted with the aim of resolving the debt problem and bearing in mind that the client's best interests are paramount.

Informal arrangements with creditors – eg, for reduced payments, are generally not long term and clients should be warned that creditors will invariably require a review at some stage.

3. Letter writing

Much negotiation begins with a letter. While emergency applications, particularly concerning priority debts (see p198), may have to be initiated on the telephone and confirmed in writing later, it is more effective to send a letter in the first instance so that full details can be enclosed. Important changes to agreements reached through negotiation should always be confirmed in writing.

It is sometimes more appropriate for the adviser to help the client prepare letters and a financial statement using standard forms, but for the letters to be sent from the client her/himself. Letters should refer to the agency that is advising. The client will receive the replies and must be encouraged to seek further advice, as required. In this way, the client regains control over her/his own affairs and, in the long term, may be more able to cope. In addition, the workload of the adviser may be reduced. The structure and content of the letter will be similar, whoever it is sent from.

Format of a letter

Letter writing needs to follow a basic format, explained below.

Use simple language

Write letters in simple, clear language. 'Thank you for your letter of 11 June' is just as meaningful as 'Your communication of 11 June is gratefully acknowledged.'

Assume nothing

Letters, particularly initial ones, will generally be read by a person who knows little or nothing about the situation in question. A letter should, therefore, contain all the background information needed to make a decision.

Holding letters

It will often be necessary to write an initial letter requesting information which the adviser needs in order to advise the client and identify the available options. Such information includes:

- copies of any agreement and of any default notice (see p239) or termination letter;
- a statement of account, showing full details of the outstanding balance;
- details of any court orders or other enforcement action.

The letter should also ask the creditor to put a hold on any further collection activity until the information requested has been supplied and the client has had an opportunity to put forward her/his proposals for resolving the matter. Any breaches of the *Debt Collection Guidance* by the creditor or debt collector should also be addressed in this letter (see p24).

Use a framework

As well as standard letters or phrases, new or unusual situations require individual letters. These are easier to write with a framework to follow.

- **Address.** The letter should begin with the address to which it is sent, which must appear on the adviser's copy as well as the top copy.
- **Client and references.** Next comes the full name and address, including postcode, of the client and all references or other identifying numbers. Major creditors may have borrowers of the same name and thus detailed identification is essential to avoid confusion.
- **Standard opening phrase.** This can usefully explain the agency's status. For example, 'The above has contacted us for advice about her/his financial affairs and we are now helping her/him to look at these as a whole.'
- **Outline the background.** Next, tell the story so far (although not necessarily in the holding letter as the adviser may not have all the details at this stage). It is essential to give all the necessary background and details. Go through the story in chronological order. Keep sentences short and to the agreed facts. Do not include demands or excuses.
  The statement of facts must include those on which the adviser is basing the strategy. Thus, if asking for a temporary suspension of payments and interest

charges, the adviser should ensure that s/he has explained there is at present no available income or capital, and has set out the client's future prospects.

- **Make the request.** The next stage of the letter should be the request. This needs to be clearly and simply phrased. Use bold type if possible. Do not be apologetic or circumspect – link the request to the facts outlined and make it appear to be an inevitable consequence of them.
  The letter should continue by stating in what period it is proposed to review this strategy. This may be expressed either:
  – as a fixed period; *or*
  – with reference to other factors – eg, 'We will be happy to review this when Mr Parkinson gets a job.'
- **Add any special reasons.** After outlining the request add the special reasons why this should be accepted. These may be obvious from the facts you have listed and it is not worth repeating them. If arrangements have broken down in the past or it is believed a creditor will be resistant to the suggestion, however, it is useful to list whatever special reasons you can.
- **Details of any offer.** If an offer of payment (or some other offer – eg, a withdrawal of a counterclaim) is being made, this should be clearly described – eg, 'The first payment of £. . . will be made on 27 August and following payments will be made on the 27th of each month.' The client should be advised to begin making the payments in accordance with the offer without waiting for confirmation from the creditor as some creditors are prepared to accept offers but do not notify that acceptance and then complain that the client has not kept to the payment arrangement.
- **Response expected.** Your letter could then suggest the kind of reply that you expect – eg, 'We would be grateful if you could confirm, in writing, that this will be possible and send a paying-in book.'
- **To whom should the creditor reply?** It is worth considering whether or not it is desirable for creditors to reply to the agency or to clients directly. If the volume of debt advice is great, it may be advisable to ask creditors to reply direct to their customer. It may be worth explaining why this is necessary.
  On the other hand, some creditors and collectors contact the client directly even when asked to reply to the agency, usually in an attempt to persuade the client to increase their repayment offer. This is a breach of the Office of Fair Trading's *Debt Collection Guidance* (see p24).
- **Ending.** The letter can end with a conventional politeness, such as 'We are very grateful for your help in this matter' followed by 'yours sincerely/ faithfully' (by convention the former is used when the letter is addressed to a named individual and the latter when it is addressed Dear Sir/Madam).

4. Court representation

Many debt advisers regularly represent clients at court hearings, but if the court has not had experience of representation by lay advisers, the advice agency will need to talk to its local courts to arrange this. For more details about the courts, see Chapters 9 and 10.

Type of hearing

Chambers

The majority of hearings at which advisers represent clients are in chambers.[2] This means that the hearing is usually held in private in the district judge's office, with only the client and her/his representative, the solicitor or representative acting for the creditor, and the district judge present. The district judge does not wear a wig or gown, and everyone remains seated throughout the hearing. Before a hearing the debt adviser is obliged to make known to the court and creditor all information and documents to be used at the hearing.[3] There is also a duty to reveal any application which will be made at a hearing as soon as this is known.[4]

The claimant or her/his solicitor presents her/his case to the district judge. The claimant is normally the creditor, except if the client has applied for something like a time order or the suspension of a warrant (see Chapter 9). After this, the other side gets the opportunity to speak. The client's representative has an opportunity to explain briefly the client's circumstances and make a proposal. A financial statement (see p42) is essential if making an offer of payment. The solicitor or agent is able to comment on the proposal and the district judge will make an order.

It is always worth introducing yourself to the creditor's representative at the court while waiting to be called and finding out what s/he has been instructed to ask the court for. The hearing will normally take five to ten minutes, but this can be reduced if the adviser has successfully negotiated with the creditor or solicitor prior to the hearing.

The court always needs to know what powers it has to make a decision, and if the district judge is unsure (or sceptical) s/he may ask an adviser to point out where in the Civil Procedure Rules 1998 or elsewhere the proposed order is sanctioned (see Chapter 9).

Open court

Some hearings (such as appeals to judges) occur in open court and an adviser may wish to represent the client. At present, there is no right of audience for lay advisers (except in the small claims procedure), but most courts welcome the assistance of a debt adviser. It is important to ask an usher or clerk to find out the views of the judge or magistrate in advance, if possible.

As the name suggests, hearings are held in public, and are more formal than hearings in chambers. A circuit judge, a district judge or magistrate hears the case. The judge may be dressed in a wig and gown. The court may be full of people waiting to have their cases heard, and solicitors or barristers waiting to represent. The creditor or a solicitor presents the case and may bring witnesses to cross-examine.

The client may be asked to speak on oath, but the adviser may be able to present the case without the client needing to speak. It is customary to stand when addressing the judge.

Many magistrates' courts do not allow lay representation, but the adviser may be able to be a 'McKenzie Friend' (adviser) (see p314). A refusal to allow lay representation should not be taken as final, but should be taken up with the chief executive or chair of the bench who could be referred to the positive experience of tribunals (eg, social security appeal tribunals) with lay representatives. The court clerk is likely to be a useful contact at the magistrates' court.

Techniques of representation

Planning

Plan everything to be said in advance. Make sure it is logical and clear. Use notes where necessary. Rehearse presentations if possible, particularly if you are a new representative. You should inform the court if you have not had time to obtain full instructions – eg, in the case of emergency hearings or court/duty desks. It may then be in the best interests of the client to request an adjournment, even if this involves the client in increased liability for the creditor's costs.

Be brief

Local courts operate to very tight timescales (hearings are often listed for five or ten minutes) and judges expect representations to be short and to the point. Avoid any repetition.

Summarise

A written summary of the case is often helpful and can be handed out at the beginning if it has not been possible to circulate it in advance (take copies for the judge and creditor's representative). This can then be amplified at presentation.

Prepare clear documents

Financial statements or other documents used to support a case should be clearly presented and photocopied for the judge and creditor's representative.

Tell the story

Explain the background to the case clearly and concisely in chronological order. Do not assume that the judge has read the papers.

Quote precedents and powers

Give clear references and explanations of any past cases cited in support of your case if it is unusual and the legal powers upon which it depends. Have references to the Civil Procedure Rules (see Chapter 9) and any caselaw on which you intend to rely (take copies for the judge and creditor's representative).

Admit ignorance

If stuck, it is better to admit this and ask for help rather than pretend otherwise. Provided your case appears reasonable, many judges will be helpful if they are asked. However, this should never be used as an alternative to thorough preparation of the case. The debt adviser should never pretend to be a solicitor or allow others to assume wrongly that s/he is one.

Use court staff

It is helpful before the hearing to tell the usher you wish to speak on the client's behalf. S/he will then inform the court clerk or the judge and tell you if there is anyone to represent the creditor.

Address

Address a district judge or magistrate as 'sir' or 'madam' and a judge as 'your honour'.

Look smart, be polite, speak clearly

Wear smart clothes (or apologise for your inability to do so – eg, if it is an emergency application). It is usually acceptable for lay representatives to dress less formally, but the dress prejudice of the judiciary should not be underestimated. Use standard English where possible; slang may not be understood and will almost certainly not further your case. Appear as confident as possible without being 'cocky'. Be respectful, but pleasant. Use eye contact and smiles to retain the attention of the judge.

Know your own limits

Do not attempt to represent in court without being aware of all the possible outcomes. Complex representation may require lay advisers or lawyers who are not specialists to refer to lay advocates, solicitors or barristers who are.[5]

5. **Changing social policy**

If a particular law, practice, structure or policy adversely affects many clients or affects vulnerable groups of clients, the adviser should work to change the policy.

When contacting individual creditors, the adviser should stress that this is a general social policy approach and not an attempt to re-open a case that has already been discussed.

Other organisations can be helpful. The ways in which creditors deal with debt may be controlled or overseen by one of a number of organisations.

Advisers should also pass on details to umbrella organisations, such as Citizens Advice, AdviceUK or the Institute of Money Advisers.

The Office of Fair Trading and trading standards departments

The Office of Fair Trading (OFT) is a central government body, which regulates trading or company practices and which has statutory responsibility for licensing those who require a licence under the Consumer Credit Act 1974 (see Chapter 4).

Trading standards (or consumer protection) departments are part of a local authority. They have certain statutory functions for weights and measures, and consumer safety. They also have a responsibility to investigate breaches of the Consumer Credit Act and to report to the OFT on problems encountered in their geographical area.

It is best to seek the help, first of all, of a local trading standards department with both gathering information about a trader's practices and putting these to the OFT.

The OFT can issue a number of different types of notice to traders before it actually revokes their consumer credit licence (without which they cannot operate in that field). The major one of these is a notice declaring it is 'minded to revoke' a particular trader's licence. In addition, the OFT and trading standards departments can use Part 8 of the Enterprise Act 2002 to require creditors to cease engaging in conduct which breaches consumer protection legislation and harms the interests of consumers generally. If the matter cannot be resolved informally, the court can be asked to make an order to prohibit the conduct concerned. A breach of the order is punishable as a contempt of court by imprisonment or a fine. Since 6 April 2008 the OFT has had new powers (see p51).

If a local trading standards department is not helpful in pursuing a particular company, it can be reported directly to the OFT (see p5). It is important that even relatively minor infringements or bad practice are routinely reported because it is generally the volume of reported cases on a particular issue or individual that gives rise to investigation by the OFT.

Advisers should remember that trading standards departments may also be able to assist in resolving individual cases. As the regulator, the OFT is not able to provide redress in individual cases.

Ofgem, Ofcom and Ofwat

The suppliers of fuel, telecommunications and water all have regulatory bodies (see Appendix 1), which have varying powers to investigate and comment on their activities. The fuel regulatory bodies have a responsibility to prevent unlawful price increases or disconnections. They can also be very useful in exercising pressure in other areas.

Trade associations

Many industries have trade associations. These are bodies that are regulated by their members, but impose certain agreed standards as a membership condition. A list of trade associations is in Appendix 1. Many have a code of practice or conduct, and all have some kind of complaints procedure, which can be used to resolve individual cases (see p26).

Trade associations exist primarily to protect their members. However, they can be a vital tool in changing the behaviour of an individual company. Trade associations do not want the good name of their other members affected by the poor behaviour of one company. The peer-group pressure they can exert, either through a complaints procedure or less formally, is probably much greater than the pressure an advice agency acting on its own could create.

Local councillors and MPs

Much debt is payable to local or national government. This includes council tax, income tax, VAT and rent. The statutory powers which the state has given itself in order to enforce these debts are considerable and thus they all become priority debts. However, as government debts, they are subject to scrutiny by elected members – ie, councillors or MPs. This can provide a powerful method of ensuring that the state's powers are not used in too draconian a fashion.

Elected members are often not aware of the measures being used by their officers to collect debts. For instance, many local councillors are unaware of the extent to which their authority uses private bailiffs and, once briefed by an advice agency, can make it a live political issue and change the way these debts are collected.

Ombudsmen

If the administration of debt collection by the state is poor and results in individuals experiencing hardship, complaints can be made to an Ombudsman (see Appendix 1).

The **Parliamentary Commissioner for Administration** investigates complaints of maladministration by any central government department. Complaints must be made via an MP. A simple statement, with dates and supporting evidence, should, if possible, be sent to the MP with a request that it be forwarded to the Ombudsman.

Complaints about local government matters are probably best made through a local councillor, but can also be made directly by a member of the public. Complaining to the Local Government Ombudsman (or in Wales, the Public Services Ombudsman for Wales) is important, even where the maladministration has been corrected in an individual case. Negative adjudications by the Ombudsman are disliked by local government officers and will usually lead to procedural changes to prevent a recurrence of the event complained about.

The **Local Government Ombudsman** often investigates a particular department or function of an authority – eg, council tax collection. The debt adviser should collect a few cases of maladministration and then discuss with staff at one of the Ombudsman offices whether they will investigate in such a way. A report on the workings of a department is much more powerful than a single case.

The **Adjudicator's Office** deals with complaints about the way things have been handled by Her Majesty's Revenue and Customs (but not about the amount of tax or VAT the client has been asked to pay). See Appendix 1 for address.

The **Financial Ombudsman Service** is the body that handles complaints between clients and finance firms (including banks and building societies) and, since 6 April 2007, firms with a consumer credit licence (including debt collectors and sub-prime lenders). See Appendix 1 for address and also p26.

Since 1 July 2006 (1 September 2007 in the case of mis-selling), complaints about gas and electricity suppliers can be referred to the **Energy Ombudsman**. A complaint must first be made to the supplier and it should be asked to put the account on hold while it deals with it. If, after 10 days, there has been either no response or an unsatisfactory response, the complaint should be escalated through the supplier's complaints procedure (refer to its code of practice for details). The case can be referred to the Energy Ombudsman either eight weeks after the complaint was made or after the supplier has issued a 'deadlock letter' – ie, negotiations have broken down and neither party will re-consider their position. The complaint must be referred to the Energy Ombudsman within either six months of the deadlock letter being issued or nine months of the complaint first being made.

Ombudsmen are not regulators and their primary role is to assist in the resolution of individual cases. They expect the client to give the creditor the opportunity to investigate her/his complaint and resolve the matter before referring the case to them.

Monitoring local courts

Court procedures should be monitored on a local basis by debt advisers. Having collected information about the way in which a particular court operates, it is important to decide whether pressure for change needs to be exerted upon the court secretariat or the judiciary, or both. The secretariat is made up of the people who process the administration of the court's work and who may also, by accepting or rejecting certain procedures, have a strong influence upon the types of decisions made by the court.

Neither judges nor magistrates are open to being lobbied by groups about individual decisions or types of decisions which they are required to take. However, particularly when an adviser works for a charitable organisation with a good reputation locally, it may be possible to arrange meetings with the chair of the bench – ie, the senior magistrate, or representatives of the judges in a county court to discuss ways in which the advice centre can assist the courts in their work or other issues of mutual concern. In practice, this means it is generally possible to discuss procedures and engage the decision makers in an analysis of the effects of their judgments.

In a magistrates' court, the chief executive will generally discuss procedural matters and policy issues (eg, when and how they use their discretion to allow the payment of fines by instalment), and any such matter should be discussed with her/him if its operation causes problems.

Local liaison groups

Some public services have liaison groups. These include local court users' groups and are set up, for example, by the Department for Work and Pensions and local authorities. The debt adviser should investigate groups that exist (and perhaps advocate their creation where they do not). S/he should use membership of these groups as a means of gaining credibility through networking, and changing policies and procedures that are unhelpful or oppressive. Some groups (for instance, court users' groups) may have existed for a long time with a fixed membership (perhaps solicitors, probation service and police). The debt adviser may have to invest time to secure membership, but this may be rewarded with a direct line of communication to powerful local decision makers.

Using the media

Discussion with the various bodies outlined above can often bring about useful changes that prevent continued injustice. However, it is often only when something becomes a live, public, political issue that real change can occur. It is important, therefore, to cultivate links with local and national media so that publicity can be gained for particular injustices.

When considering using the media, general advice work issues, such as confidentiality, will need bearing in mind. However, even if an individual client does not wish to have her/his case publicised, it may be acceptable for an anonymous description of the issues involved in it to be part of a media campaign. There is an almost endless demand from media organisations for examples of individuals who have suffered by being in debt. Many people do not wish to have their private affairs so publicly paraded, but for others this can be an important way of regaining a sense of power after the experiences they have faced at the hands of creditors. It is certainly the way to bring an issue to public debate.

6. **Dealing with harassment**

What is harassment

Many creditors harass debtors. Much of this goes unreported and unchallenged, and is expected by many clients. Section 40 of the Administration of Justice Act 1970 defines harassment as trying to coerce a person to pay a contract debt by making demands for payment that are calculated to subject a person to 'alarm, distress or humiliation, because of their frequency or publicity or manner'. In addition, any false representation that a type of non-payment is criminal or that the person is a court official or other publicly-sanctioned debt collector is also regarded as harassment.

Harassment can take place in writing or orally. It can include using obviously marked vehicles, calling repeatedly at anti-social hours, or visiting neighbours or places of work. Harassment occurs if a debt collector purports to be enquiring about a person but explains to neighbours why the enquiries are necessary. Harassment might also include posting lists of debtors in public. It includes abusive or threatening behaviour and all acts of violence. It is likely to involve a breach of the Office of Fair Trading's (OFT) *Debt Collection Guidance* (see below).

Since 26 May 2008 a breach of section 40 is no longer a criminal offence in relation to commercial transactions and now falls under the general umbrella of 'unfair commercial practices' (see p26).

Debt collection guidelines

The OFT's *Debt Collection Guidance* (OFT664) was published in July 2003.[6] Copies can be downloaded from www.oft.gov.uk or obtained free of charge by telephoning 0870 606 0321. This document, which is indispensable for debt advisers, sets out practices which the OFT considers to be unfair, and provides advisers with the basis for challenging unacceptable behaviour. The guidelines cover anyone who has a consumer credit licence – ie, lenders (both secured and unsecured), utilities and telephone companies, solicitors and bailiffs, and in-house as well as external debt collectors. Advisers can find out if a creditor has a consumer credit licence by telephoning the OFT's Consumer Credit Licensing branch on 020 7211 8608.

The guidelines do not apply to routine collection of repayments; they apply only once an account is 'in default'. An account is in default as soon as the client fails to meet the terms of the agreement, but it has been suggested that an account will only be 'in arrears' if either a default notice has been served, a default letter sent, default charges added to the account or a default registered with a credit reference agency.[7] If a creditor or collector is attempting to recover those arrears, advisers should argue that the guidelines apply and that the creditor or collector must comply with them. The guidelines state that creditors who employ external debt collectors must take responsibility for their conduct and the OFT expects creditors to investigate any complaints about such debt collectors and take appropriate action. If this does not happen, advisers should consider complaining not only about the debt collectors but also about the creditor.

Creditors and debt collectors are expected to abide by the spirit as well as the letter of the guidelines. They cover the following areas.

- It is unfair to communicate with clients, in whatever form, in an unclear, inaccurate or misleading manner – eg, if those contacting clients do not make clear who they are, who they work for, what their role is and the purpose of the contact.
- Those who contact clients must not be deceitful by misrepresenting their authority and/or the correct legal position – eg, by pursuing third parties for payment when they are not liable.
- It is considered to be oppressive to put physical or psychological pressure on clients or third parties – eg, by pressurising clients to pay in full, in unreasonably large instalments, or to increase payments when they are unable to do so.
- Dealings with clients must not be deceitful and/or unfair – eg, by contacting clients directly and bypassing their appointed representatives.
- Charges for debt collection should not be levied unfairly – eg, by claiming collection costs from the client in the absence of express contractual or other legal provision.
- Those making debt collection visits must not act in an unclear or threatening manner – eg, by entering a property uninvited or not leaving a property when asked to do so.
- In the case of statute-barred debt (see p124), although the debt still legally exists:
  - it is unfair to pursue it if the client has heard nothing from the creditor during the relevant limitation period (but not if the creditor has been in regular contact with the client before the debt became statute-barred);
  - it is unfair to mislead clients about their rights and obligations – eg, by falsely claiming that the debt is still recoverable through the courts;
  - it is unfair to continue to press for payment after a client has stated that s/he will not be paying a debt because it is statute-barred (this could also amount to harassment – see p24).

The guidelines state that it is an unfair practice to:

- fail to investigate and/or provide details as appropriate when a debt is queried or disputed;
- require an individual to supply information to prove s/he is not the client in question – eg, a driving licence or passport;
- continue with debt collection activity while investigating a reasonably queried or disputed debt.

Breaches of the guidelines should first be raised with the creditor and debt collector concerned. If the matter is not resolved, the client should use the complaints procedure to escalate the matter to the appropriate trade body (eg, the Finance and Leasing Association) or the regulator (eg, the OFT). Complaints can be made online to the OFT's Debt Collection Team at www.oft.gov.uk/advice_and_resources/resource_base/legal/cca/debt-collection.

Codes of practice

Many creditors have their own codes of practice. For example, all gas and electricity suppliers are required to have a code of practice on dealing with customers in financial difficulty. Other creditors subscribe to trade associations, which have codes of practice with which members should comply – eg, the Banking Code, the Finance and Leasing Association Code and the Credit Services Association Code. Some regulators – eg, the OFT, Ofwat and Ofgem, issue guidelines on how customers in debt should be dealt with. There is also guidance for bailiffs (*National Standards for Enforcement Agents*), produced by the (then) Lord Chancellor's Department.

All these codes set high standards, which creditors and collectors are expected to meet in their dealings with clients. The Banking Code even requires subscribers to ensure that when they sell a debt, the purchaser agrees to comply with its guidance on handling financial difficulties. However, creditors and collectors often fall short of the standards set in the relevant code of practice. Unfortunately, codes of practice are invariably voluntary in the sense that they cannot be directly enforced in the event of non-compliance. The only remedy is a complaint, which in some cases can be referred to an independent Ombudsman.

This *Handbook* refers to codes of practice where relevant. It will often be in a client's best interests to point out to a creditor or collector where there is non-compliance with a code of practice and request that it is complied with. In the case of collectors (and private bailiffs) it is also worth copying in the creditor. This does not mean that a complaint should be made in every case. The aim of a complaint should be to achieve a better outcome for the client than currently appears likely and so, if a complaint is likely to impede, rather than promote, negotiation, the adviser should discuss this with the client and consider deferring it.

Unfair commercial practices

Consumers are protected by the Consumer Protection from Unfair Trading Regulations 2008, which came into force on 26 May 2008. These apply to 'commercial practices' – ie, conduct by 'traders' (ie, businesses) directly connected to the promotion, sale or supply of goods and services to and from 'consumers' (ie, individuals acting outside the purposes of their business) whether before, during or after the transaction is entered into. Actions relating to enforcement and debt collection are, therefore, covered, but any breach of the regulations will not in itself make the debt unenforceable.

These Regulations also prohibit codes of practice promoting unfair commercial practices. Unlike breaches of other provisions, however, it is not a criminal offence to breach this.[8] As any breach is likely to take the form of a statement in the code of practice, the most likely remedy is altering the code of practice. In addition, according to the OFT, a business which has signed up to a code of practice may be in breach of the Regulations if it breaks a commitment in a code, which is capable of being verified and is not purely aspirational. A breach of a code of practice is, therefore, potentially illegal and can be used to add weight to a complaint.

The OFT and local trading standards departments enforce the Consumer Protection from Unfair Trading Regulations, but this does not necessarily mean that civil or criminal enforcement action must be taken in all cases. Unless enforcement action is seen as proportionate and appropriate, the OFT has said that securing voluntary compliance will be its response to complaints in the first instance.[9]

Dealing with harassment

Much debt collection activity takes place verbally over the telephone, at the client's home and sometimes at her/his place of work. Debt advisers, therefore, should always ask how demands were made and, in the case of verbal demands, exactly what was said, and check all written communications for evidence of inappropriate behaviour. It is important to take urgent action to protect the client from further contact. As with breaches of the OFT's *Debt Collection Guidance*, a letter of complaint should be sent immediately, outlining the facts as understood and warning the collector and creditor that if not resolved to the client's satisfaction, the complaint will be taken to the next level. In cases of violence or extreme harassment, the police and the local trading standards department should be informed as soon as possible.

The client should then be advised to have no further contact with the collector/creditor until the matter has been clarified. This may involve politely, but firmly, refusing her/him entry to property or not answering the telephone. The client should be advised to keep a diary recording details of any further attempted collection action. If possible, practical steps should be taken to ensure that friends, neighbours or relatives know about serious harassment and are able to provide a safe haven or support to the client. Some agencies give clients a sheet of their letterhead, and advise them to show this to any collectors/creditors who visit and tell them to contact the agency.

7. Budgeting advice

Although advice on budgeting is not debt advice, a debt adviser must use the procedures and skills described in other parts of this *Handbook* to assist clients deal with their debts. Budgeting advice is fraught with difficulties, but it can play a useful part in the debt advice process. Indeed, some people who present at advice agencies with financial difficulties may only need budgeting advice to resolve their problems and consequently should not be taken through the debt advice process.

It is important that advisers are able to identify such people. Many families living on a low income are expert at budgeting. Others, especially those whose circumstances have been changed radically, can find it helpful to discuss their budget. This gives the client an opportunity to consider her/his own priorities and find out about ways of paying for essential items. For example, s/he may be unaware of the possibility of having a budget account for gas, funded by weekly or fortnightly payments at a post office. Detailed budgeting information is privileged information between the client and the adviser and should not be given to creditors in detailed form, but summarised on the financial statement.

Pressure to spend can be difficult to deal with – spending can represent status, or give someone a greater sense of control, and some expenditure may be made because of problems in family relations.

There are particular problems when budgeting on a low income. Often, people on a low income only have access to the more expensive forms of credit. In the absence of credit, goods available are generally more expensive because it is impossible to buy enough to benefit from the lower unit prices charged for larger quantities. Similarly, access to the cheapest sources of goods may be denied if transport is not readily available to the large out-of-town stores. Budgeting on a low income often requires purchasing inferior goods because money is not available to buy more expensive ones which would last longer and thus be much cheaper in the long run.

Where poverty exists alongside other factors, such as disability, parenthood or the breakdown of a relationship, it is likely that budgeting is constrained by the time available, which in turn is constrained by the practical and emotional demands of these other situations.

The financial statement

Very often, the process of producing a financial statement (see p42) will enable people to see the sources of their financial problems. It will often be clear when all items of expenditure have been listed that these cannot be met from available income. Ideally, if there is a need to cut expenditure it will occur to the client her/himself. If this does not happen, the debt adviser may wish to suggest ways of budgeting and put to the client the likely results of such strategies. The adviser must be aware of vocabulary, body language and tone of voice, to avoid giving the impression that s/he is judging the client.

On the other hand, this exercise may establish that the client is able to meet all her/his contractual liabilities together with any accruing charges as well as maintaining her/his essential expenditure, and consequently does not need debt advice or any of the strategies discussed in this *Handbook*.

'Luxury items'

There are some items of expenditure which may, in comparison to the possible loss of other goods or services, be less essential.

- Cars are generally more expensive than is realised to purchase, run, maintain, tax and insure. If a car is not necessary for personal and family mobility or work requirements, the client may need to consider either selling it and acquiring a cheaper one, or doing without.
- In the past, telephones, particularly mobiles, have been considered a luxury. This is not always the case, and would certainly not be so if someone's health might require her/him to summon assistance in an emergency or, for instance, if someone has been subjected to racial abuse or marital violence and this could happen again. The telephone may also be an important social lifeline or a means of making emergency help available to another person outside the client's home. However, where no such factors exist, particularly if phone bills are large, the possibility of doing without or changing to incoming calls only could be considered. Where a mobile phone is used, the cost (which may be less than that for a landline on some tariffs and usage patterns) and appropriateness of this should be explained. Clients who are in receipt of income support, income-based jobseeker's allowance or the guarantee credit of pension credit may be able to benefit from a low-cost phone package available from BT. Known as BT Basic, the line rental of £13.50 a quarter includes £4.50 worth of free local, national and international calls every quarter to landlines (0845/0870 and premium rate numbers and calls to mobile phones are excluded). For more details, visit www.bt.com/btbasic.
- Videos and DVD players were often considered an extravagance and a cause of debt. In fact, the cost of a video or DVD player would never cause serious debt and its value as very cheap entertainment (particularly where people are housebound or have children) is very high. The sale of a video or DVD player will generally have a negligible effect on a client's current debt and ending a hire agreement is unlikely to do very much more.
- Cable or satellite television is more expensive than video or DVD. If a client has an agreement that has already run for its minimum period, the adviser could discuss whether satellite TV is more important than other items on which the money could be spent. On the other hand, it may well be part of a package, including the telephone, where the overall cost can be justified.

Non-dependants living with the client

A particular problem for a client can be the contribution made by non-dependants living in her/his household. The complexity of family budgeting is well demonstrated by a parent's wish to charge an adult son or daughter only a nominal amount for board. This may also be generated by a desire to keep the family together and can save money – eg, by reducing childminding costs. In some cases, challenging the amount being paid by a non-dependant could lead to family disruption.

Faced with this difficult situation, a client will need information and support in order to make decisions. For example, if housing benefit or housing costs in income support are being claimed, s/he will need to know by how much this is reduced by the non-dependant living with her/him. From the financial statement (see p42) a client can judge what might be a fair share of the total household expenditure to be attributed to the non-dependant.

Financial exclusion

Over-indebtedness and poverty often go hand in hand, particularly in deprived communities where many people are on a low income and financially excluded – ie, lack access to basic financial products such as bank accounts, ways of saving and affordable credit. In addition, financially excluded people can find themselves paying more for essential services, such as fuel, insurance and essential goods because they only have access to high-cost credit, provided by sub-prime lenders or, even worse, loan sharks.

Advisers may find CPAG's *Personal Finance Handbook* useful for more information on financial exclusion and financial literacy.

Credit unions

A credit union is one way of extending low-cost financial services to local communities. Credit unions are financial co-operatives owned and controlled by their members. Each credit union has a 'common bond' which determines who can become a member – eg, people living or working in a particular area. They offer savings facilities and affordable loans sourced from their members' savings. By law, a credit union cannot charge more than 2 per cent a month on the reducing balance of a loan (26.8 per cent APR), although the average is 1 per cent a month (12.7 per cent APR). Many now provide current accounts, bill-paying services through budgeting accounts and benefit payments direct to the claimant's credit union account, and savings accounts. Credit unions with access to the Growth Fund (supported by the Government's Financial Inclusion Fund) may be able to offer loans to people who are not yet savers with the credit union.

The Government's stated aim is to encourage credit unions to make loans which might otherwise be judged 'risky'.

Credit unions, together with advice agencies, offer a range of potentially complementary services which can assist in tackling financial exclusion and over-indebtedness. For example, a credit union can help clients gain access to financial services and manage their finances effectively, help and encourage them to save and budget, and may even be able to provide a loan to pay off debts. However, a loan – even at a much lower rate – is not always in a client's best interests and more effective assistance can be provided by money advice.

Advisers should ensure that the debt advice process does not reinforce financial exclusion by cutting clients off from mainstream products. There are, however, a number of issues for money advisers in referring clients to a particular credit union. In order to preserve independence, the adviser must make it clear that s/he is not an agent of the credit union and must not give clients unrealistic expectations of the assistance they can expect from a credit union. The adviser should also make it clear that a referral does not guarantee immediate access to financial services, such as a loan. Credit unions are not charities and should only lend to people who have the capacity to repay. Provided the referral is in the best interests of the client, the fact that s/he may be borrowing to pay off other debts should not be ruled out in all circumstances. Advisers should also bear in mind that affordable credit is not the only financial service offered by a credit union, and that access to current and savings accounts also promote financial inclusion.

If the client defaults on a loan, the credit union not only becomes one of the client's creditors but also a non-priority creditor. If not treated as a priority, the client is likely to lose the benefits of membership. If other non-priority creditors object to a credit union loan being given priority over their own debt(s), advisers should point out that, as part of its financial inclusion agenda, the Government has signalled that credit union loans should be given priority by allowing them to be repaid by deductions from benefits if a client defaults (see below). Advisers should also be aware that, as in the case of other financial institutions, credit unions are able to offset funds in savings and other accounts against debts.

From December 2006, credit unions can, in certain circumstances, apply to the Department for Work and Pensions (DWP) to have loans repaid to them through deductions from certain benefits.[10] In order to do this, the credit union must agree that no interest or other charges will be added to the debt following the application. In addition, the client must:

- have failed to make payments as agreed for a period of 13 weeks and not have resumed making those payments;
- have given written permission for the credit union to provide her/his personal data to the DWP;
- not already be having deductions made to pay another eligible lender (another credit union or certain other third sector lenders);
- not already be having deductions made to repay an overpayment of benefit or a social fund loan.

DWP guidance states that lenders must apply to the DWP to join the scheme and prove they have responsible lending criteria and practice.[11] They must also have taken other reasonable steps to collect the repayments (including writing to the client on three occasions, with the final letter notifying her/him that deductions from benefit will be sought).

Notes

2. **Negotiation**
1 para 13 DMG; para 2.8(c) DCG

4. **Court representation**
2 r39.2 CPR and Part 39 para 1 PD CPR
3 Part 1 CPR; Part 23 para 9 PD CPR
4 Part 23 paras 2.7 and 2.10 PD CPR
5 For further information see P Madge, 'Advocacy for Money advisers', *Adviser* 44

6. **Dealing with harassment**
6 See S Edwards, 'Debtors' Shield', *Adviser* 100
7 'Debt Collectors Warned', *CCA News*, Autumn 2003
8 Part 8 EA 2002 allows enforcers to apply to the court for an enforcement order to prevent domestic or Community infringements (ie, breaches of EU-derived legislation). Breach of an enforcement order is punishable as a contempt of court.
9 The OFT has published guidance on the CPRs, available at www.oft.gov.uk/advice_and_resources/publications/guidance/cprregs/oft931int
10 Sch 9 para 7C SS(C&P) Regs
11 Available at www.dwp.gov.uk/advisers/elds.asp

Chapter 3

Stages of debt advice

This chapter summarises the nine stages essential to debt advice and shows how the individual stages link together as a single process. It covers:

1. Creating trust

The adviser must create a trusting and safe environment in which the client can talk about her/his personal and financial affairs. This may take some time to develop but should start at the beginning of the process, when the adviser makes it clear that s/he will not judge and is on the client's side.

The adviser must explain what s/he will do and why. When collecting information, the adviser is not intruding unnecessarily into people's affairs but needs information to help the client decide upon a strategy and/or negotiate with creditors. It is, therefore, important to tell the client that such information is confidential and explain how the agency's confidentiality principles operate. Often, people seek advice about a specific debt and are reluctant to discuss other debts they are managing to pay or if they feel the creditor has been particularly helpful. However, it is often impossible to deal with a particular debt in isolation. This stage can include a discussion of the whole position.

2. Listing creditors and minimising debts

The first facts to gather are details of the debts and the creditors. If the adviser uses a factsheet for each client, much of this information can be included either by using tick boxes or recording the information only when relevant. This needs to show all debts, including those with no arrears or ones where the client has already negotiated lower payments.

A client may not have all the necessary information with her/him on the first visit to enable the adviser to complete the creditor list. It is, therefore, important to agree how the missing information will be collected, by whom and when. The client's credit reference file may be a useful information-gathering tool if the client has no, or incomplete, paperwork.

The creditors

Advisers should record the following.

- **The name, address and telephone number of each creditor.** Exact company names are important, as the proliferation of credit has led to a surprising number of creditors with very similar names.
- **Account/reference numbers.** Most creditors access their computers with a reference number and this must be included.
- **Letter references.** If the client has received correspondence from the company, any letter reference should be noted together with any contact details.
- **Agents' details.** Solicitors or commercial debt collectors are often used. Record details of these (and their references) separately. Record details of the one who has made most recent contact with the client. Check whether the collector has actually bought the debt (in which case s/he will now be the creditor) or whether the agent is acting on behalf of the original creditor (in which case s/he will be accountable to that creditor).

The debts

The following details must be noted.

- **Age of debt.** Find out when the credit was first granted. The length of time for which the agreement has run or a bill has been unpaid can be a factor in negotiation (and might even provide grounds for challenging the debt). For instance, a creditor is more likely to be sympathetic if payments have been made for some time than if a new agreement is breached. The legal position on some agreements depends on when they were made – eg, see p55 for credit agreements made before 6 April 2007. An old debt may also be 'statute-barred' – ie, unenforceable through the courts.
- **Reason for debt.** It is important to ask the reason for the debt. This is necessary – eg, to refute suggestions that the debt was unreasonably incurred.
- **Status of the debt.** Note the status of the debt. This should either be a priority or non-priority (Chapter 7 explains the criteria for making such decisions). If possible, check any documents or agreements to confirm this information, as clients can be unsure or may describe debts incorrectly – eg, 'hire purchase' is

often used to mean 'credit sale agreement', but has very different legal consequences (see p72).

- **The written agreement.** Check whether the debt is based on a written agreement and, if so, whether or not it has been seen and photocopied for future reference. Ensure agreements are checked for defects which may affect their enforceability. Obtain a copy from the creditor if necessary. Note the absence of a written agreement, which can render some agreements unenforceable. See Chapters 4 and 5.
- **Liability.** This means checking the client is actually responsible for the debt. Note in whose name(s) agreements were made and/or whose name(s) is/are on the bill (although this is not necessarily conclusive). This may either be the client alone, the client and a partner, or some other friend or relative who acted as a guarantor. This will ensure that all debts listed are properly minimised (see Chapter 5).
- **Payments.** Note the amount currently owing. State whether the figure is approximate or exact. Note contractual payments under any original agreement and any subsequent amendment to them. Note the existence of arrears in payments, although initially these need only be approximate. Note the payment method. Advice may be needed about coping with doorstep collectors or about changing or cancelling standing orders or direct debit arrangements. However, clients should not be advised to stop or reduce contractual payments to creditors unless it is clearly in their best interests to do so – eg, if the client has been making payments to non-priority creditors but not paying priority creditors (see Chapter 7). The date and amount of the last payment made are needed, especially for priority debts, to assess the urgency of any action.
- **Insurance cover.** Many people take out insurance (known as payment protection insurance) with a mortgage or credit agreement against, for instance, sickness, death and redundancy. Sometimes, such insurance is given by the creditor as part of the contract. Always check whether a particular debt is insured, so this important way of minimising the debt is not overlooked (see p107).

The threats

The adviser needs to know what the creditor has done to obtain repayment of the debt and what threat is posed to the client by the recovery action.

- **Warnings.** The first stage of recovery action is normally a reminder letter. The date of this should be recorded. Exact details of further action should be noted. For instance, regulated consumer credit agreements (see Chapter 4) may require a default notice to be served before any further action is taken. Other creditors must issue different warnings – eg, notice of proposed disconnection of fuel or notice of intention to seek possession of the client's home.

- **Court action.** If court action has begun, a claim form will have been issued. The date and type of claim should always be recorded. Courts work on a system of case numbers and it is essential to record these. Note if solicitors are now acting for the creditor. If they are, the adviser will need to deal with them rather than the creditor until further notice. If a date for a hearing has been set, this should be noted. In many cases, a court will already have made an order and details of the judgment, including its date, the payment or action ordered, and the time or amounts required, should be recorded (see Chapter 9 for further information, including what action should be taken if a judgment has been made).
- **Enforcement action.** After judgment, enforcement can mean bailiffs' action (see Chapter 11), a third-party debt (formerly garnishee) order, attachment of earnings order, or a charging order (see Chapter 9). Note if any of these have actually begun, with dates and full details.

Action to be taken

- **By the client.** Any action required of a client relating to a particular debt should be noted on the list – eg, 'get exact balance'. This section will normally be completed once the strategy has been decided.
- **By the adviser.** Record the action required on each debt. This can be crossed through when it has been carried out. If the case is a complex one and likely to involve a lot of work, the adviser should prepare a case plan, summarising the action(s) to be taken, who is responsible for any action and the timetable.

3. Listing and maximising income

The next stage is to list all possible income for the client (and her/his family where applicable).

Whose income to include

Creditors are likely to expect the income and debts of a couple (particularly if they are married or civil partners) to be dealt with together. There is no basis in law for this expectation (unless they are jointly and severally liable for the debt), and the client and adviser will be able to decide later how to present things. The overriding consideration must be the best interests of the client. As always, the final decision lies with the client.

A decision must eventually be made about whether to include the income of a partner or spouse or, rarely, someone else living as part of the same household as the client. This depends upon several factors.

- If all the debts are in the name of one person only (or are in the joint names of the client and a previous partner) and s/he has little or no income or property against which action could be taken, the other person may be unwilling to contribute out of her/his income.

- If one person has a number of debts and a partner also has a number of debts, it might be more convenient to deal with both partners' debts in one set of strategies.
- If only one person has sought advice without the knowledge of her/his partner, the adviser should find out why and encourage both partners to be involved. The person who seeks advice may not know details of her/his partner's income or may not want her/his partner to know about the debts.
- The type of debt. Many partners will wish to pool their income and help with each other's debts, irrespective of legal liability, if they themselves could face dire consequences (eg, eviction) if they failed to do so or where, for example, all members of the household have benefited from the debt being incurred. At this stage it is, therefore, important to note the income of all household members (if possible) so that a decision can be made later as to which will be used to implement any strategy.

Types of income to include

- All benefits (do not forget child benefit and tax credits). Note, however, that clients may decide not to use disability benefits (including disability living allowance and attendance allowance) to make payments to creditors. This view is supported by the Revised Determination of Means Guidelines[1] and the Money Advice Liaison Group's Good Practice Guidelines on dealing with clients with mental health problems.[2] It is based on the fact that disability benefits are designed to meet only the additional costs of disability, but they must still be included in any court forms (see Chapter 9). They should be included in the list of income even if they do not appear in the financial statement. Usually, however, they will be balanced by an identical item of expenditure, or mobility or care costs.

  If it is decided to exclude disability benefits from the financial statement, do not forget to exclude also any additional expenditure incurred from those benefits. The fact that the client is in receipt of disability benefits should always be disclosed to creditors, as the fact that s/he is a disabled person is likely to be a relevant factor. The decision whether or not to include/use disability benefits is ultimately for the client, not the adviser.[3]
- Earnings – ie, take-home pay from full-time and part-time work.
- Self-employed earnings, net of estimated tax and national insurance contributions.
- Regular maintenance/child support payments received. Include what and who it is paid for.
- Investment income – eg, from savings (if any).
- Contributions from other household members – eg, non-dependent children living with the client.

- Occupational pensions.

If income has recently been unusually high or low, this should be noted and the basis upon which income is assessed should be clear – eg, the average of five weeks' wage slips. Only include regular sources of income, as any offer of payment must be sustainable.

The Office of Fair Trading expects advisers to use appropriate means to verify the client's income (eg, wage slips) while recognising that advisers working at court duty desks or providing self-help advice will, in practice, be unable to do so.[4]

Note any impending changes/additions to income and circumstances, such as benefits recently claimed but not yet awarded, or if a member of the household is about to start or end paid employment.

Capital

The client may have capital or potential capital in the form of realisable property or other assets which it would be reasonable for her/him to use, and the adviser should make a separate note of any such items (see Chapter 8). Unless the circumstances are wholly exceptional, creditors are unlikely to accept that a client is unable to pay her/his debts if s/he has capital and may even refuse to accept nil or token offers of payment if they believe it would be reasonable to expect the client to dispose of an asset.

Maximising income

Follow the advice in Chapter 6 to maximise the client's income. Income from benefits that have been claimed but not yet paid should be listed only where this is advantageous to the client. The adviser should explain that a claim is pending if it is included.

4. Listing expenditure

The next stage of the debt advice process is to list everything on which the client is currently spending her/his income. Most people spend money on different items in different periods of time, and it is important to standardise everything to a particular period – generally weekly or monthly. Expenditure must include the following.

Housing

Costs include:

- rent/mortgage repayments;
- other secured loan repayments (there may be several);

- council tax;
- water charges;
- ground rent;
- service charges;
- an amount for household repairs and maintenance based on a full year's expenditure if possible;
- household insurance for both buildings and contents;
- any insurance linked to a mortgage, if not already included in mortgage expenses;
- the housing costs of any boarders, which can simply be the amount they pay for their board and lodging.

Fuel

Fuel costs include charges for electricity, gas and other fuels. Take an annual cost and divide it into weekly or monthly figures.

If payments to fuel suppliers include an amount for items other than fuel – eg, payment for a cooker, these need to be deducted and only the fuel expenditure listed here.

Furniture and bedding

Costs should be separately itemised. This item may require research by the client or discussion with others with whom s/he lives.

Launderette or other washing

Costs should be averaged out over the previous couple of months.

Telephone, television and licence

These costs should be converted into weekly/monthly figures.

Other household items, toiletries and food

The adviser should ensure that the individual circumstances of the client dictate the amount allowed for these items. Other household items, toiletries and food include:

- housekeeping;
- meals taken outside the home, such as school dinners or canteen meals;
- expenses related to children going to school or being given pocket money.

Clothing and shoes

These are often bought seasonally and so costs will have to be estimated annually and divided. It is important to include small items, like tights, in this category.

Health costs

Costs include:

- prescriptions;

- dentistry;
- optical charges.

These are often high and advisers should check entitlement to reduced or free treatment, or free prescriptions.

Religious and cultural activities

Costs include:

- donations that are an essential part of a person's membership of a religious community;
- classes for children in religious institutions (particularly mosques).

If a person is committed to such payments, they should be protected to ensure that debt does not further exclude individuals or families from community life and support.

Transport

Costs include:

- public transport;
- the cost of owning a car or motorbike. In this case, the amount spent on tax, insurance, repairs, MOT and petrol should be included. If a car is essential, for instance to travel to work, the cost of its hire purchase (but not any credit sale) agreement should be included with a note to explain why the item is essential.

Hire purchase

The hire purchase or conditional sale (see Chapter 4) costs of any items that are essential for the individual family to own, the loss of which would cause serious problems (eg, a washing machine) should be included.

Fines

Instalments payable on fines (see Chapter 10 for ways of reducing these) should be included.

Other costs

Other costs include:

- maintenance/child support payments;
- childminding costs;
- self-employment costs not taken into account when calculating the client's net income;
- spending for exceptional circumstances – eg, special diets or extra heating because of illness. Apparent 'luxury' items need to be explained. For example, for some people a telephone (land line and/or mobile) is an absolute necessity (eg, for health or safety reasons) and therefore counts as essential expenditure.

The Office of Fair Trading expects reasonable steps to be taken to verify the client's expenditure, but says that estimates or standard expenditure guidelines can be used where there is no better indication of the client's expenditure, provided they are appropriate. Although standard figures should not be used where actual figures or accurate estimates are available, they are useful as a 'benchmark' against which to test the client's level of expenditure and as a tool with which to challenge creditors who claim that the client's expenditure is too high.

At this stage, the adviser can discuss the overall income and spending with the client. Use Chapter 6 to increase income wherever possible, and discuss which, if any, items of spending could be reduced, either permanently or temporarily (see Chapter 5 for information on how to minimise debts). This should be done in a sensitive and non-judgemental way, and any items of high or unusual expenditure should be explained to creditors in a covering letter. Clients are not required, and should not be expected, to live on the breadline and are entitled to a reasonable standard of living. If the adviser knows that creditors are likely to challenge an item of expenditure and it cannot be justified, it is not judgemental to point this out to the client and explain that, as a consequence, creditors or the court are unlikely to accept the client's offer based on it.

Opening a new bank account

It may be necessary to advise the client to change the bank account into which wages are paid to prevent the bank (a non-priority creditor) taking control over income. If a client finds it difficult to open another account – eg, because of her/his credit reference details, s/he may find the Financial Services Authority's list of basic bank accounts useful.

First right of appropriation

If it is not possible to open a new bank account immediately, the client may have to consider exercising the 'first right of appropriation'. This gives an account holder the right to earmark funds paid into the account to be used for specific purposes. This process can also be useful as a temporary measure on overdrawn accounts. In order to exercise this right, the client should inform the bank in writing (before funds are paid in) specifically where they should be applied – ie, how much and to whom. The bank must honour such instructions, but it will continue to charge interest on the overdraft and may refuse to undertake further transactions.[5]

By this stage, it should be clear why the debts have arisen, and how the client's circumstances have led to financial difficulties. This information will be essential when negotiating with creditors.

5. Dealing with emergencies

The adviser must next identify any emergencies – ie, eviction, repossession, imprisonment, disconnection or bailiffs, and deal with these first (see the relevant sections of Chapters 7, 9, 10 and 11).

6. Dealing with priority debts

The next stage of the debt advice process is to deal with those debts that are described as priorities (see Chapter 7). This will ensure that the threat of homelessness, the loss of goods or services or the threat of imprisonment is lifted. It is essential that arrangements for dealing with these debts are negotiated at this stage so that any extra payments for priority debts can be included in the expenditure details before they become part of a financial statement (see below).

However, a financial statement may be needed when negotiating priority debts, and this stage of the process can therefore overlap with Stage 7.

Each possible strategy, along with its advantages or disadvantages, must be explained to the client. It may be necessary for the client to consult with a partner or other family members, and strategy information may need to be written down. Once agreed, the adviser implements the strategy by negotiation or court application and the client must then carry out her/his own agreed course of action – eg, start paying rent or set up direct debits. An orally agreed strategy must always be confirmed in writing with the creditor, and an acknowledgement confirming this must be requested. The client should be advised to start making any agreed payments immediately and not wait for confirmation from the creditor.

7. Drawing up a financial statement

A financial statement is a document, which can be presented to creditors and courts, that presents a clear picture of the individual (or family), her/his income and expenditure, details of her/his creditors and whether there is any surplus income with which to pay those creditors. It must be realistic and any offers made must be sustainable. It can also be a useful budgeting tool for the client. Advisers must be aware of what a court may consider reasonable for the client to spend on a particular item if it is being asked to agree to the client paying the debt at a particular rate, especially, for example, in possession proceedings where the client's home is at risk (see Chapter 9).

A financial statement based on the joint income and expenditure of the client and her/his partner should be fairly straightforward to prepare. A financial statement based on the income and expenditure of only the client needs more care. The financial statement should always reflect what actually happens in practice – eg, if the client actually pays all the household bills out of her/his own income and contributions from other members of the household, the financial statement should be drawn up on this basis. On the other hand, in many cases it is not possible to identify who actually pays what because all income is pooled. In such cases, expenditure should be apportioned proportionately to income.

A financial statement is a vital document because it summarises information in a standard form and allows the adviser to present this to the other side in a structured way. A carefully drawn up financial statement is probably the adviser's most important negotiating tool, as it forms the justification for any repayment proposal as well as for any request for non-payment.

Many agencies now use either the Common Financial Statement (see p44) or computer software which includes a financial statement as part of the package. For agencies who do not use either of these, it is useful to devise a standard format and to prepare blank statements, using a computer. The statement must be clearly and neatly presented, and must include all relevant information. Advisers should use all the facts discovered in the previous stages in this chapter when preparing the statement. Provided it is stored on computer, it is easy to amend the statement as circumstances change.

The statement should include:

- the basis on which it was prepared. For example, 'This financial statement has been prepared on the basis of information submitted by:
  Mr A Client
  123 High Street
  London';
- the members of the household whose income and outgoings are being considered together;
- a breakdown of all the income for the individual or household;
- a list of expenditure under the headings used in Stage 4 plus expenditure to deal with priority debts. Certain types of expenditure may best be combined – eg, cigarettes are probably most persuasively included in 'other household items, toiletries and food' rather than on their own. No expenditure is shown for debts other than those that have been defined as priorities;
- comparison of income and expenditure. In some cases, the financial statement will show there is more income than expenditure. Such excess of income over expenditure should be calculated in the financial statement and described as available income. If expenditure already equals or exceeds income, the available income should be stated as none. In many cases, expenditure will exceed income. This may be because amounts have been included that are not actually spent, but are what should be spent if the client was able to do so.

Whatever the reason, the adviser should be prepared to explain if challenged by creditors.

Common Financial Statement

The Common Financial Statement (CFS) is an initiative of the Money Advice Trust and British Bankers' Association. It was launched in November 2002 following a two-year pilot, and is incorporated into a number of software programmes and case management systems.

The CFS consists of:

- a budget form for completion by the adviser with the client. This contains a detailed checklist of income and expenditure as an aide memoir for advisers and clients so that income and expenditure items are less likely to be overlooked;
- a financial statement to which the summarised figures on the budget sheet are transferred and which is then sent to the creditor with the client's offer of payment (if any);
- trigger figures. This is a set of expenditure levels considered 'reasonable' for sample types of household. There are four trigger figure headings – telephone, travel, housekeeping and other – with a 'child multiplier' to take account of the actual number of children in a household;
- a specific car expenditure allowance;
- a licence agreement covering the use of the trigger figures to ensure that the CFS is only used in accordance with the published forms and guidance.

Members of the British Bankers' Association and the Finance and Leasing Association have agreed that, if the CFS is used:

- they will not query expenditure items falling within the trigger figure levels (advisers are expected to provide an explanation if expenditure is above these levels);
- offers made will be accepted so long as the guidelines have been followed;
- accounts transferred or sold to third parties for collection will remain subject to the CFS principles.[6]

The trigger figures are not 'budget' or 'standard' figures and, in many cases, the CFS will contain figures that exceed the trigger figure level. In such cases, the adviser should explain in the 'additional information' section on the CFS why the needs of the client are above the trigger figure level.

The budget forms and guidance documents can be viewed on the Money Advice Trust website at www.moneyadvicetrust.org. However, the trigger figures are now protected and not shown unless the adviser ticks a box accepting the licence terms. The Money Advice Trust then issues a 'licence key' enabling the adviser to view the trigger figures via the website. A licence number is also issued which appears on the CFS so that creditors know that the adviser is operating within the terms of the licence.

The advantage for advisers and agencies of using the CFS is that it is intended to be recognised and understood by all parties. It therefore provides a fast-track route to proposing repayment arrangements and means advisers can save time in securing acceptance of offers from creditors. However, feedback from advisers suggests that:

- not all collections departments are familiar with the CFS and reject financial statements prepared in line with the trigger figures;
- explanations for exceeding the trigger figures are not always accepted.

If a creditor who is signed up to the CFS does not accept the financial statement/ offer, the adviser should draw the creditor's attention to its commitment and to the fact that the adviser has followed the guidelines. If the offer is still not accepted, the adviser should consider making a complaint.

The commitment to accepting offers does not extend to freezing or reducing interest or other charges. This will have to be requested and justified when using the CFS as with any other financial statement. A payment arrangement that is not accompanied by a concession on interest/charges is not usually in the client's best interests (see p218).[7]

8. Choosing a strategy for non-priority debts

From the financial statement, the adviser knows whether or not there is any available income or capital and any likely changes in circumstances. This stage involves using these factors to decide a strategy for all non-priority debts (see Chapter 8). The starting point should be what the client wants, but s/he must be given the full range of available options so that s/he can make an informed choice of action. All advice given should be realistic and in the best interests of that particular client. If the chosen strategy is to offer payments to creditors, the client should be advised to start making any payments offered immediately and not wait for confirmation from the creditor. If the creditor does not confirm that interest/charges have been frozen, the creditor should be pressed for a decision. If the creditor refuses to freeze interest/charges, the adviser should ask for specific reasons and either urge the creditor to reconsider its decision or review the strategy with the client. If the adviser thinks the creditor is not treating the client 'sympathetically and positively' in line with a relevant code of practice, s/he should discuss with the client whether or not to complain.

By the end of this stage, the client will have made an informed choice of the strategy that is most likely to resolve the debt problem.

Mental health issues

The Office for National Statistics estimates that people with mental health problems are three times more likely to experience financial difficulties than other people.[8] According to research carried out for MIND, one in four people will experience a mental health problem during their life.[9] This does not mean that taking on borrowing will necessarily lead to debt problems, but there is a need to strike a balance between allowing access to financial services on the one hand, and treating people fairly on the other. When people with mental health problems do experience financial difficulties, it may be because:

- benefits provide their only source of income;
- their income fluctuates, possibly because of irregular work;
- they lack financial management skills;
- of communication difficulties, including a reluctance to discuss their condition;
- of relationship breakdown.

There is a clear link between debt and mental health issues. Being in debt can negatively affect a person's mental health, while living with a mental health problem increases the likelihood of falling into debt. Financial problems can, in turn, trigger fresh mental health issues or exacerbate existing ones. Many conditions have no physical signs, and fluctuations in the severity and effects of an illness are common. In many cases, creditors will not even be aware that there is a mental health issue until after payments have been missed and the collections process has reached an advanced stage. Even then, it may not be apparent whether a question of the client's capacity to conduct transactions arises (see p105). Money advisers and creditors are not trained to diagnose mental health problems and often do not understand the implications, but, once a creditor is aware of the issue, it should have procedures in place to take account of the situation, and should respond fairly and appropriately. There is also a need to bring health professionals involved in treating clients into the process to try and ensure a joined-up approach.

Existing codes of practice in the credit industry tend to set out an approach to dealing with clients with mental health problems, rather than guidance on dealing with the debts themselves.

Recognising that improvements need to be made in the way both money advisers and creditors deal with this issue, the Money Advice Liaison Group set up a working party consisting of representatives of stakeholders to propose good practice in this area. Its *Good Practice Guidelines* were published in November 2007 and its supporting guidance includes the following.

- Creditors should have procedures in place to ensure that people with mental health problems are treated fairly and appropriately.

- If creditors sell debts once a mental health issue has been advised, they should ensure that the debt purchaser agrees to comply with the guidelines and any relevant codes of practice.
- If a debtor has a serious mental health problem, creditors should only start court action or enforce debts through the courts as a last resort and only when it is appropriate and fair for lenders to do so.
- Creditors should be willing to write off unsecured debts when mental health problems are long term and unlikely to improve and if it is highly unlikely that the client will be able to pay outstanding debts.[10]
- Disability benefits – ie, disability living allowance and attendance allowance, should be recognised as being specifically awarded for meeting mobility and care requirements. Creditors should not expect these benefits to be included as disposable income in any financial statement. The decision whether to make such benefit income available for payment of her/his debts and, if so, how much is entirely the client's and s/he is perfectly entitled to treat the whole amount as non-disposable income if s/he wishes to do so.

Advisers should note that these guidelines only apply to the management of debt problems and not to the stage when the debt was incurred.

Much of the guidelines deals with obtaining evidence to demonstrate the effect of a client's mental health on her/his ability to deal with her/his debt problems. The Money Advice Liaison Group has produced a debt and mental health evidence form to assist advisers in this process. The form (together with guidance notes, which should be read before using it) can be downloaded from the Money Advice Trust's website at www.moneyadvicetrust.org.

The form can be used to request information from health and/or social care professionals who may be in the best position to provide evidence about the client's capacity to deal with money and debt issues. Its use is not compulsory. There are, however, a number of issues.

- The form does not specifically address the question of whether or not the client was able to understand the contract s/he originally entered into. This is relevant to the enforceability of the contract and, therefore, the client's liability for the debt and is a matter advisers should consider first of all (see p105).
- The client is required to give her/his written consent to the form being used to obtain information about her/him and may, of course, lack the mental capacity to provide that consent, an issue which the guidance recognises but does not resolve.
- The form is long, but there does not appear to be any agreement that it will be completed without requiring payment of a fee. This is always an issue when requesting any report from a professional, particularly if the report required is long and detailed. The Money Advice Liaison Group is aware of this issue and is seeking to address it.

9. Implementing and following up chosen strategies

Although some emergency work may have been done to prevent catastrophes, it is only when all the information is available and decisions have been made that the major work of implementing a debt advice strategy will begin. Implementation is by means of communication with creditors by letter, telephone, electronically or sometimes in person or via the courts. The strategy to be implemented may require different letters to a number of creditors or groups of creditors. This requires communication skills, both written and oral, as well as representational skills.

The implementation of debt advice strategies involves more than mere individual casework. In addition, the effectiveness of strategies used should be continually monitored and work should be done to change policies that are found to be oppressive.

If a strategy is rejected for no apparent reason, the adviser should contact the creditor(s) and specifically request the reason(s) for rejection. Creditors reject clients' proposals mainly because of the following.

- Insufficient information has been provided. Provide additional information/ evidence to enable the creditor to understand the client's financial situation.
- The creditor has conflicting or different information. Clarify the real position and either explain or point out that the creditor is incorrect – eg, the client's circumstances may have changed since the creditor obtained its information.
- The chosen strategy is inappropriate – eg, it is based on incorrect information. Consider the alternatives.
- The creditor's collection policies do not permit the proposal to be accepted. Either try to persuade the creditor to treat the client's situation 'sympathetically and positively' on an individual basis or consider whether it might be in the client's best interests to comply.
- The creditor's collection system cannot deal with the proposal – eg, the case cannot be transferred to the creditor's debt recovery section until there are at least three months' arrears. Deal with a more senior person who is authorised either to handle the proposal or to transfer the case to someone who can.
- The client has a poor payment record or history of broken payment arrangements. Point out that previous payment arrangements were unrealistic and that the current proposals are not only realistic but sustainable.
- Items on the financial statement are disputed. Either explain or justify, and use supporting evidence where available.
- The creditor wants more money. Ask the creditor where the extra money is to be found, given that other creditors are likely to object to having their payments reduced.

- The creditor is determined to take court action. Point out that parties are expected to act reasonably and to avoid unnecessary court proceedings. If the matter goes to court, it is the judge not the creditor who will decide the rate of payment (see Chapter 9).
- The creditor will not deal with the agency. Point out that this is a breach of both the Office of Fair Trading's (OFT) *Debt Management Guidance* and the *Debt Collection Guidance* (see p24), and so could be the subject of a complaint.

Some reasons for rejection could amount to a breach of a code of practice and so, where appropriate, advisers should find out what trade association a creditor belongs to and check with the relevant code of practice – eg, Banking Code or Finance and Leasing Association's Lending Code (see p21). Advisers should also familiarise themselves with OFT guidance, as discussed elsewhere in this *Handbook*. Complaints under a code or guidance can be made the subject of a complaint to the Financial Services Ombudsman (see p21) or the OFT. See Appendix 1 for details of these.

If a creditor rejects a client's proposal for repayment, the client should usually make the payments regardless. If the client decides not to pay, the adviser should be able to demonstrate there was a good reason for this and that it was in the client's best interests.

The remainder of this *Handbook* explains the practical knowledge and skills necessary to put into effect the strategy agreed by the client and debt adviser.

Notes

3. **Listing and maximising income**
   1 para 5.4.2
   2 para 11 Supporting Guidance
   3 See D Shields and M van Rooyen, 'In or Out?', *Adviser* 93
   4 para 22(b) DMG

4. **Listing expenditure**
   5 See J Wilson, 'First Right of Appropriation', *Adviser* 98

7. **Drawing up a financial statement**
   6 FLA members have not agreed to adopt the CFS in the case of either secured loans or where the loan relates to the purchase of an asset, such as a vehicle.
   7 For more information (including details of the current trigger figures), see the e-learning and library section at www.wiseradviser.org and see articles in *Adviser* 103

8. **Choosing a strategy**
   8 *The Social and Economic Circumstances of Adults with Mental Disorders*, ONS, 2002
   9 *In the Red: debt and mental health*, MIND, 2008
   10 The MIND report recommends that creditors should consider writing off debts if a person's mental health means s/he did not have mental capacity to contract, even though the creditor was unaware of this at the time.

Chapter 4

Types of debt

This chapter covers:

This chapter describes each type of credit or debt that might be encountered. It is vital to identify accurately each debt before attempting to deal with it. The chapter contains a brief outline of the Consumer Credit Act 1974, together with the amendments introduced by the Consumer Credit Act 2006, which govern most credit-related debts. Debts, therefore, fall into two groups – those covered by the Consumer Credit Act and others.

1. The Consumer Credit Act

The Consumer Credit Act 1974 is a wide-ranging piece of legislation that regulates almost all aspects of personal credit. It provides definitions of every type of credit agreement and is framed to cover every imaginable type of agreement. The Act brings together previous attempts to regulate credit and provides protection by:

- licensing traders (see below);
- regulating agreements (see p54);
- giving the right to cancel (see p59).

The courts have powers to provide relief to clients, specifically when the relationship between the client and the creditor is unfair to the client (see p115) and via time orders (see p283). Substantial reforms have been made by the Consumer Credit Act 2006 (see p61). However, many of the changes are not retrospective and do not affect agreements entered into or judgments made before the relevant provisions were implemented.

Licensing

The Consumer Credit Act 1974 requires most businesses that offer credit or lend money to consumers to be licensed by the Office of Fair Trading (OFT). This includes if credit is arranged to finance the purchase of goods or services. Licences may also be required by debt collectors, debt advisers and businesses that offer goods for hire or to lease. From 1 October 2008, businesses that administer agreements (but do not collect debts) for creditors or debt purchasers (known as 'debt administration'), or help clients locate and correct records about their financial standing (known as 'credit information services') also require a licence.

A licence must cover all categories of credit activities that the business carries out. Trading without a licence is a criminal offence and can result in a fine and/or imprisonment.

All professions or trades are 'businesses' for licensing purposes, even if they are non-profit-making, make no charge for their services, or the credit-related activities only comprise part of the overall activities of the business. However, businesses which only 'occasionally' carry out a licensed activity are not treated as carrying out that type of business and do not require a licence. What is 'occasional' depends on the facts of the case. A business does not require a licence to collect its own debts (including, from 1 October 2008, debts it has purchased), although the business may require a licence if it also undertakes other credit-related activities.

When considering whether or not to issue a licence, the OFT can take into account any circumstances that appear relevant, including evidence of:

- any past misconduct, such as criminal offences, particularly involving fraud, violence or dishonesty;
- the skills, knowledge and any relevant experience the people operating the business have in relation to the licensed activity;
- the practices and procedures the business proposes to operate; *and*
- evidence of business practices that appear to be deceitful or oppressive, or otherwise unfair or improper. These do not have to be unlawful and can arise in relation to the licensed business or otherwise. The OFT considers, in particular, any breaches of OFT guidance. This could include evidence of irresponsible lending (see p53).[1]

The OFT takes a targeted and 'risk-based' approach to consumer credit licensing and has identified a number of debt-related activities which it considers to be of higher potential risk to clients. These include:

- businesses offering debt adjusting/debt counselling on a commercial basis;
- credit repair; *and*
- debt collecting.

Businesses which apply for a licence to undertake any of these high-risk activities are required to provide a 'credit competence plan'. They are also likely to have an on-site inspection by the OFT and/or local authority trading standards officers.

The OFT has also identified the following types of credit activity as being of higher potential risk and consequently requiring greater levels of scrutiny:

- secured lending, broking and debt administration to sub-prime clients;
- lending and broking which takes place in the home; *and*
- credit reference agencies.

Businesses intending to carry out any of these activities are required to give further details to the OFT on a 'credit risk profile'. The OFT uses this information to consider the business's competence. The business may also have an on-site inspection by the OFT and/or local authority trading standards officers.

The OFT checks the information in the application with a number of different sources, including local authority trading standards officers. The OFT assesses fitness and competence in relation to each individual activity, and licences are only issued to cover those activities for which this assessment has proved satisfactory.

If the OFT receives evidence that raises sufficient doubts about an applicant's fitness to hold a consumer credit licence, the application is passed on to an independent OFT adjudicator. The adjudicator decides whether to issue a notice informing the applicant that the OFT is considering refusing the licence application.

Where there are insufficient grounds to consider refusing the application, but the OFT is nevertheless dissatisfied with certain aspects of the business's conduct, it may impose a requirement on the business to do (or stop doing) something to remedy the matter. The OFT has powers to impose a financial penalty of up to £50,000 if the business subsequently fails to comply with the requirement.

New licences last indefinitely. During the life of the licence, as well as asking for information from licence holders from time to time, the OFT receives information from other sources including:

- local authority trading standards officers;
- the Financial Services Authority;
- consumer bodies, such as Citizens Advice and AdviceUK;
- individual advisers;
- consumers;
- complaints data from the National Consumer Advice Service;
- Consumer Direct; *and*
- complaints data from the Financial Ombudsman Service.

Information from these and other relevant sources can raise doubts about a business's activities and trigger fitness investigations. If this occurs, the OFT may consider suspending, limiting or revoking the licence, or imposing a requirement. If concerns about conduct are serious, or there are concerns about the integrity of the business, the OFT may conclude it is not fit to hold a licence and will take action to revoke it. However, if the OFT considers it sufficient to ensure the business changes its conduct and does not have concerns about its integrity, it may take a different approach in the first instance and use one of the other enforcement tools.

The OFT is restricted in relation to the information it can reveal about its ongoing work. This, coupled with the fact that it cannot act on behalf of individual clients, can lead to frustration on the part of advisers and doubt as to whether passing information to the OFT is a worthwhile practice. Without information on which to build up a file of its business practices, however, the OFT is unable to act against the business.

For more information on licensing, see *Consumer Credit Licensing: general guidance for licensees and applicants on fitness and requirements* (OFT969), which can be found at www.oft.gov.uk/publications.

The OFT keeps a register of applications for, and holders of, consumer credit licences. The register can be found at www2.crw.gov.uk/pr/Default.aspx. This provides basic information on licence holders, including:

- the commencement date of a licence;
- type of activities covered;
- the authorised trading names and main business address of the licence holder; *and*
- details of any undertakings given, requirements imposed and/or subsequent financial penalties levied.

Unlicensed creditors cannot pursue their claims for debt through the county court without first applying to the OFT for an order to validate the agreement,[2] but in practice this rarely happens.

The OFT has published various guidance to the sector referred to elsewhere in this *Handbook*, particularly on debt management (see p2), non-status lending (see below) and debt collection (see p24), which identify activities that the OFT regards as unacceptable. Advisers should advise clients to complain to the creditor/debt collector about any examples of bad practice, refer them to the Financial Ombudsman Service where appropriate, and report them to the OFT.

Responsible lending

'Irresponsible lending' is now a specific business practice that the OFT can consider when deciding whether or not a business is fit to hold a licence. Lenders take different approaches to responsible lending, but the OFT says that they should undertake proper and appropriate checks on the client's creditworthiness, ability to repay the loan and to meet the terms of the agreement. These checks should take account of the type of agreement, the amounts involved, the nature of the lender's relationship with the client and the degree of risk to the client. The OFT plans to consult a wide range of stakeholders on lending practices, with the aim of producing guidance identifying practices and conduct that are inconsistent with the requirements of responsible lending. Until then, the OFT says that its

November 1997 *Non-Status Lending Guidelines* (OFT 192) continue to apply and should be followed where relevant. This document is available from www.oft.gov.uk.

The basic principle is that there should be responsible lending, with decisions subject to a proper assessment of the client's ability to repay and taking full account of all relevant circumstances. Paragraphs 38 to 41 of the *Guidelines* state that lenders should:

- carry out a proper assessment of the client's ability to repay taking full account of all relevant circumstances to ensure that the client does not take on a commitment s/he is unlikely to be able to fulfil;
- if brokers or other fees and/or insurance premiums are to be added to the loan, the assessment of ability to repay should be based on the total loan, including any fees and premiums;
- take account of any seasonal variations in the client's income, any likely changes in her/his income or employment and whether s/he is in financial difficulties;
- concentrate on the client's ability to repay a secured loan rather than on the amount of equity in the property (so-called 'equity-lending');
- ensure they have sufficient evidence of the client's income and other financial details, and take all reasonable steps to verify the accuracy of information provided in support of a loan application.

Regulated agreements

Most credit agreements that a debt adviser comes across will be regulated, although there are some important exceptions. A regulated agreement is an agreement which:

- provides credit of £25,000 or less if made before 6 April 2008 (£15,000 if made before 1 May 1998); *and*
- is made by the creditor with one or more individuals or clients. The credit must be given in the course of the creditor's business. If a client borrows money for a business, provided s/he is not a limited company, this will still be classed as lending to an individual. However, if the agreement was made on or after 6 April 2007, an 'individual' does not include partnerships consisting of more than three people and may also be covered by the 'business related' exemption (see below).

Agreements that are not regulated include:

- agreements providing credit of more than £25,000 made before 6 April 2008 (or £15,000 before 1 May 1998);
- 'small agreements' not exceeding £50 – eg, vouchers;
- 'non-commercial agreements' not made in the course of business – eg, between friends;
- some low-interest rate credit;

- agreements involving goods or services repayable in no more than four instalments in 12 months – ie, normal trade credit, for example payable in 30 days;
- mortgages taken out to purchase land or property;
- secured loans for home improvements where the mortgage for the purchase of the property was provided by the same lender;
- accounts involving goods or services repayable in one instalment – eg, charge cards (see p80);
- regulated mortgage contracts (see p87) made on or after 31 October 2004, even if the amount borrowed is within the consumer credit limit;
- agreements made on or after 6 April 2008 to a 'high net worth' individual (see below);
- agreements made on or after 6 April 2008 for more than £25,000 entered into 'wholly or predominantly' for the purpose of the client's business (see below).

The 'high net worth' exemption allows individuals to opt out of Consumer Credit Act regulation. It applies if the individual's net income is at least £150,000 a year or her/his assets are at least £500,000 (excluding her/his home and pension). The individual must sign a declaration of high net worth, supported by a statement from an accountant. The rationale for this exemption (asked for by the credit industry) is that such people have the resources to seek their own financial and legal advice and, if such exemption were not available, might seek finance involving less formality from outside the UK.

The business-related exemption .applies where an individual has been granted credit of more than £25,000 'wholly or predominantly' for the purpose of her/his business. If the agreement contains a declaration by the borrower that it has been entered into wholly or predominantly for business purposes, it will be presumed that this is the case. However, if the agreement either contains no declaration, or contains a declaration but the creditor either knows or reasonably suspects it is not true, the presumption will not apply and the issue will depend on the circumstances of the case.

The form of the agreement

The form of a regulated agreement is very important. If an agreement is not made in accordance with the Consumer Credit Act, it can only be enforced with special permission of the courts. In the case of some agreements made before 6 April 2007, it will be irredeemably (ie, completely) unenforceable.

Pre-contract information

If the agreement was 'executed' (ie, signed by both parties) on or after 31 May 2005, the creditor is required to provide specified information to the client before the agreement is made, except in the case of:

- secured loans (see p78); *and*

- distance contracts (see p60).

This information includes:

- the appropriate consumer credit heading describing the nature of the agreement;.
- the names and addresses of the creditor and the client(s);
- financial and related information, such as details of any goods or services, the amount of credit, total charge for credit, rate of interest and repayment details;
- statements of consumer protection rights and remedies.

There is no prescribed format, except that the information has to be headed 'pre-contract information', handed to the client before the agreement is made and must be capable of being taken away by the client to be studied. As there is no prescribed period for providing the information, the creditor can hand over the 'pre-contract information' document to the client and then immediately invite her/him to sign the actual agreement. It remains to be seen how far the pre-contract provisions will prevent clients from signing agreements which they have not read (or been given a proper opportunity to read). If the creditor does not comply with the pre-contract information requirements, the agreement will be improperly executed and the creditor will need the permission of the court to enforce it.[3]

Prescribed terms

All regulated agreements (except current account overdrafts) must be made in writing, must be signed by all the borrowers and must contain the following information.

- The amount of credit (or the credit limit). Some creditors confuse the 'amount of credit' with the total amount of the loan. The **'amount of credit'** is a technical term and is the amount borrowed less all the 'charges for credit' (see below). An item forming part of the charges must not be treated as credit even if time is allowed for its payment. Some creditors get this wrong, with serious consequences. For example, in *London North Securities v Meadows*, the clients borrowed £5,750 under a secured loan, including £750 for a premium for payment protection insurance, described in the agreement as 'optional'. The county court judge found that the insurance was not optional but required by the lender and so was a 'charges for credit' item. The amount of credit was, therefore, £5,000 and the agreement was completely unenforceable. The Court of Appeal upheld this decision, with the result that the lender was unable to enforce payment of the outstanding balance of the agreement and had to remove its legal charge from the Land Registry.[4] Arguably, the agreement does not need to use the phrase 'amount of credit', but this may not be the case where the agreement is ambiguous as to which figure is the amount of credit.[5]

- The rate of interest and whether it can vary (if the amount of interest is not fixed at the beginning).
- A notice of cancellation in the prescribed form (if the agreement is cancellable).
- A term stating how the client is to discharge her/his obligations to make repayments – ie, details of payments (how many/how much/how often). Many secured loans provide for the client to pay the creditor's legal fees in connection with drawing up documents and provide for payment of these to be made immediately or deferred to the end of the loan period. Interest usually accrues on this amount and is compounded monthly, so that by the end of the loan a substantial sum is likely to be due. Many agreements do not make the client's obligations in relation to such deferred fees clear and, as a result, the whole agreement could be irredeemably unenforceable.[6]

The above are 'prescribed terms' in the Consumer Credit Act. If the agreement was made before 6 April 2007 and any prescribed term is missing or stated incorrectly, or if the agreement has not been signed by all the borrowers, it is irredeemably unenforceable. So too is any security – eg, on a secured loan.[7]

What further terms the agreement should contain depends on whether it was executed before 31 May 2005 or on or after this date.

Agreements made before 31 May 2005

In addition to the prescribed terms described above, the agreement should also contain the following 'non-prescribed terms'.

- The appropriate consumer credit heading that describes the nature of the agreement.
- The names and addresses of the client and creditor, and a signature box.
- Details of any security to be provided as part of the agreement.
- A brief description of any goods supplied under the agreement.
- The cash price(s) of any goods or services.
- The amount of any deposit/part payment.
- The total charge for credit (where the amount of interest is fixed at the beginning). This includes not only the total interest (if any), but also other charges payable under the transaction – eg, brokers' fees and compulsory payment protection insurances. Where it is a condition of the loan that any arrears owed under a different credit agreement are paid out of the advance, payment of those arrears may be a charge for credit item if the client was in fact unaware that the lender was going to pay them. The arrears, however, are not a charge for credit item if payment of them was part of the purpose of the loan in question, or the client agreed that they could be paid out of the loan.
- The annual percentage rate (APR) (see p59).
- A statement about the rights of the client – eg, termination rights and paying off the account early (but see p120).

Agreements made on or after 31 May 2005

The agreement should not only contain the 'non-prescribed terms' listed below but should also set them out in a particular format in the following order.

- The appropriate consumer credit heading that describes the nature of the agreement.
- The names and addresses of the creditor and the client(s).
- Key financial information:
  - amount of credit or credit limit;
  - total amount payable (but only in the case of fixed interest rate agreements);
  - repayment details;
  - the APR.
- Other financial information:
  - description of any goods or services;
  - cash price(s) of any goods or services;
  - advance payments (where appropriate);
  - total charge for credit;
  - details of interest rates and whether these are fixed or variable.
- Key information:
  - description of any security provided;
  - list of default charges;
  - where applicable, a statement that the agreement is not cancellable;
  - examples of the amount required to settle the agreement early;
  - statements of consumer protection and remedies.
- Signature box.
- Cancellation box (where appropriate).
- If the client is purchasing optional insurance on credit under the agreement, a form of consent to taking out the insurance(s) to be signed by the client(s).[8]

If a non-prescribed term is missing or incorrectly stated, the creditor can only enforce the agreement with the permission of the court.

From 6 April 2007, the court has discretion to allow agreements made on or after this date to be enforced even if:

- there is no agreement signed by all the borrowers; *or*
- the agreement fails to contain a prescribed term or it is incorrect; *or*
- in the case of a cancellable agreement, the creditor has failed to comply with the provisions on cancellation notices.

Advisers should note these changes are not retrospective, so that improperly executed agreements made before 6 April 2007 can still be irredeemably unenforceable.[9]

The court must decide whether or not to allow the agreement to be enforced and, if so, on what terms. The court can refuse an enforcement order only if it considers it 'just' to do so, having regard to:

- prejudice caused to any person;
- the degree of culpability;
- the court's powers in relation to the agreement – ie, to reduce or discharge any sum payable by the client and/or to make a time order.

The court could allow the agreement to be enforced unconditionally – eg, if the client has 'suffered no prejudice' as a result of the creditor's failure to comply with the Act, allow it to be enforced subject to conditions, or refuse to allow it to be enforced at all – eg, if, had the agreement not been improperly executed, the client would not have entered into it.

Transitional agreements

If the agreement was provided to the client before 31 May 2005, but was not executed prior to that date *and* the agreement became an executed agreement no later than 31 August 2005, the agreement is governed by the rules on pre-31 May 2005 agreements. However, the creditor must have been required to provide pre-contract information to the client in the new format before the agreement was made. An agreement is 'executed' or 'made' when the last person who must sign it has done so.

Electronic communication

Since 31 December 2004 electronic communications can be used to conclude regulated agreements, and send notices and other documents. Documents may only be transmitted electronically if the client has agreed to this. Creditors can also make provision for clients to sign agreements electronically.[10]

Annual percentage rate

This is a way of expressing the charges that are added to a loan. These include not just interest but also setting-up charges, agent's and survey fees, and other associated costs. These are all added to the interest payable and then distributed across the period of the loan to give customers a standardised cost for a loan which they can compare with that charged by other lenders.

Costs that can be added only when a person defaults on a loan do not have to be shown in the APR.

The right to cancel: cooling-off period

A regulated credit agreement can be cancelled if it was signed somewhere other than the trade premises of the creditor or supplier of goods and following face-to-face negotiations with the creditor or supplier (including their agents or employees). Telephone calls do not count as face-to-face (but see p60).

A copy of the agreement must be given to the client immediately s/he signs it (whether or not it is cancellable). Unless the creditor has already signed it or signs at the same time, another copy must be sent within seven days,[11] with a notice of cancellation rights, where applicable. Otherwise, a separate notice of cancellation rights must be sent within seven days of the agreement being signed. The cooling-off period begins with the receipt of this second copy of the document/separate notice of cancellation rights, which will also have a notice of cancellation to be used if desired. Any such agreement must be cancelled within five days.

Cancellation must be in writing and, if posted, is effective immediately even if it is never received by the creditor. The client should, therefore, obtain proof of posting or send it by 'recorded signed for'. Cancellation is probably best made initially by telephone, but must be followed up immediately by a letter, fax or email. Under such circumstances, a letter need say no more than 'I hereby give you notice that I wish to cancel the regulated credit agreement signed by me on... [date]'.[12] It should be sent to the company providing the credit, with a copy to the company supplying the goods, if appropriate. Any goods already supplied under the agreement should be returned or await collection by the trader. Any deposit or advance payment for the goods must be refunded to the client.

Even if an agreement is not cancellable, the client can still withdraw from it if, when s/he signs, it has not yet been signed by the creditor and is not signed by the creditor on the same occasion. Withdrawal must be communicated to the creditor before the creditor can sign it. Withdrawal has the same effect as a cancellation.[13] Withdrawal can be verbal (if time is short) or (preferably) in writing.

In the case of unsecured credit agreements made on or after 1 October 2004 without face-to-face contact between the client and the creditor/intermediary, such as online, by post or on the telephone:

- the creditor must supply certain information to the client regarding her/his cancellation rights in good time before the agreement is entered into;
- the creditor must also supply the same prescribed information to the client in writing in good time before the agreement is entered into (the client can waive this requirement in certain circumstances, but the prescribed information must then be supplied immediately after the agreement is made);
- the client is entitled to cancel the distance agreement within 14 days:
  - starting on the day after the agreement was made if the written information referred to above was supplied on or before the date the agreement was made; *or*
  - starting on the day after all the written information referred to above was supplied to the client if this was not supplied before the agreement was made;
- the client may give notice of cancellation:
  - verbally (if the creditor has informed the client that notice may be given orally); *or*
  - by leaving the notice at the creditor's address (notice is given on the day it is left); *or*
  - by posting, faxing or emailing the creditor (notice is given on the day it is posted or sent); *or*

  - by sending it to an internet address or website which the creditor has indicated can be used for the purpose of giving notice of cancellation (notice is given when it is sent);
- if the credit agreement is a debtor-creditor-supplier agreement, cancellation of the credit agreement automatically cancels any secondary contract to be financed by the credit agreement, except if the secondary contract has been carried out at the client's express request before s/he gave notice of cancellation – eg, the client asked the supplier to fit double glazing, which was being financed by the credit agreement, and then gave notice of cancellation after the double glazing had been fitted;
- following cancellation, the supplier must refund any sum paid by the client in relation to the contract, less a proportionate charge for any services already supplied within 30 days. No charge may be made if the supplier began to carry out the contract prior to the expiry of the cancellation period without the client's consent. The client must repay any money received, and return any property acquired, in relation to the contract within 30 days.[14]

Reform of the Consumer Credit Act

The Consumer Credit Act 2006 removes the financial limit for regulation of consumer credit and consumer hire agreements, with effect from 6 April 2008. From this date, all such agreements are regulated by the Consumer Credit Act 1974 (unless specifically exempted), regardless of the amount of credit provided or the hire payments. However, where the borrowing or hire is wholly or predominantly taken out for the purposes of the borrower's or hirer's business, the £25,000 limit remains. Such agreements are not regulated if the amount of credit provided or the hire payments exceed this figure.

Post-contract information

Annual statements

From 1 October 2008, creditors of fixed-sum credit agreements with a term exceeding 12 months must provide annual statements to borrowers. If a creditor does not comply with this requirement, it will not be entitled to enforce the agreement during the period of non-compliance, and the client will not be liable to pay either any interest or any default sum (see p62) accruing during the period of non-compliance.

There is no corresponding sanction in the event of non-compliance for running-account credit agreements (where there is already a statutory duty to provide annual statements), but statements must contain warnings about the consequences of failing to make repayments or of only making the minimum repayments (which many statements already include). This applies to existing fixed-sum and running-account credit agreements, as well as new agreements.

Arrears notices

Once at least two payments have fallen due under the agreement and the account has gone into arrears by the equivalent of at least two repayments, the creditor is required to give the client notice of the sum(s) in arrears in a specified form within 14 days ('arrears notice'), and thereafter at six-monthly intervals until the client has cleared the arrears, any interest on the arrears and any default sum (see below). The arrears notice must be accompanied by an 'information sheet about arrears' produced by the OFT. The duty to send an arrears notice ends once the creditor has obtained a judgment in relation to the sums payable under the agreement. If a creditor does not comply with this requirement, it is not entitled to enforce the agreement during the period of non-compliance and the client is not liable to pay any interest or any default sum accruing during the period of non-compliance. These provisions apply to arrears arising after 1 October 2008 on both new and existing agreements.

Once an arrears notice is served, the client can apply for a time order (see p283), provided s/he has given 14 days' notice to the creditor of her/his intention to do so. The client's notice (which must be in writing, but not in any prescribed form) must state that s/he intends to apply for a time order and s/he wants to make a repayment proposal to the creditor, and must give details of that proposal (presumably, the proposed terms of the time order). The client can still apply for a time order following service of a default notice or during proceedings for enforcement of the agreement or any security, or to repossess any goods or land. In these situations, however, the client is not required to serve the 14-day notice. These provisions apply to new agreements and also to existing agreements.

Default sum notices

If the client incurs a 'default sum' (ie, any sum, other than interest, which becomes payable under the agreement as a result of a breach of the agreement), the creditor is required to give the client a notice in a specified form. Costs ordered by a court are not payable 'under the agreement' and so do not fall within the definition of default sum. If a creditor does not comply with this requirement, it cannot enforce the agreement during the period of non-compliance. The creditor cannot charge any interest on the default sum until the 29th day after the notice is given. After that date, it can only charge simple interest on the default sum (although the arrears themselves continue to accrue interest at the contractual rate, provided the creditor has given the appropriate statutory notices). If a creditor does not comply with this requirement, it cannot enforce the agreement during the period of non-compliance. These provisions apply to new agreements and also to existing agreements, but only in relation to default sums payable after 1 October.

Default notices

Before the creditor can terminate the agreement, demand early payment, recover possession of goods or land, or enforce any security, it must serve a 'default notice' on the client (see p239). From 1 October 2008, in addition to the information and wording previously required (see p239), the creditor must provide information on the client's right to terminate a hire purchase or credit sale agreement and the procedure involved (see p72). Where applicable, the notice must also contain a statement of the creditor's right to charge interest under the credit agreement after judgment. The creditor is also required to attach a copy of the information sheet about arrears produced by the OFT (see p64). Since 1 October 2006, default notices must give the client 14 days in which to comply, instead of the seven days previously required, regardless of whether the breach occurred before or after this date.

Interest after judgment

A creditor who wants to recover post-judgment contractual interest from the client is required to give her/him notice of its intention to do so in the prescribed form. The notice must be given after the judgment is made and further notices must be given at six-monthly intervals. The client is not liable to pay post-judgment interest for any period for which the creditor has not served the required notice(s).

It is not enough that the creditor 'wants' to claim interest after judgment. The agreement must specifically allow it to be claimed (see p254). On the other hand, the prescribed wording does not say that any such interest is not included in, and recoverable as, part of the judgment, but that the creditor must issue separate proceedings.[15] However, the intention appears to be that if the client either refuses to pay or cannot come to an agreement with the creditor, the creditor will have to sue for it separately. The client can then defend the proceedings if s/he challenges the creditor's right to claim post-judgment interest under the contract or the amount claimed, or the client can make an offer of payment through the court, if appropriate.

Until the judgment is made, the client only has a potential liability for post-judgment contractual interest and, even after the judgment is made, that liability is conditional on the creditor serving the appropriate notice(s). Therefore, once these provisions apply to a judgment, arguments that such interest should have been provided for in the judgment, if the creditor wants to be able to recover it, will no longer be available. If the client receives notice(s) of the creditor's intention to claim post-judgment contractual interest, s/he should consider applying for a time order and asking the court either to freeze, or reduce the rate of, interest/charges.

Some creditors have successfully argued in the past that time order applications cannot be made once there is a judgment, as there is no longer any 'sum owed' under the agreement as opposed to the judgment. However, the prescribed wording of the notices invites the client to apply, in effect, for a time order and so such arguments from creditors should no longer prevail.

These provisions do not apply to post-judgment statutory interest (although such interest can never be claimed if the judgment arises out of an agreement regulated by Consumer Credit Act 1974, regardless of the amount). They apply to agreements made before 1 October 2008, but only in relation to judgments made after that date.

Information sheets

The Consumer Credit Act 2006 requires the OFT to prepare information sheets to accompany arrears notices and default notices. From 1 October 2008, lenders are required to include a copy of the current information sheet with each relevant notice. The legislation says that the information sheet must be 'included' in the notice, so it is arguable that, if a notice is sent out but not an information sheet, the notice is invalid.

The OFT has produced an information sheet for each notice regardless of the type of agreement involved. The sheets are two sides of A4 in length and are available in Welsh as well as English, and can be made available in large print, audio tape and Braille. They set out some of the client's key rights, such as the right to terminate the agreement, apply for a time order or complain to the Financial Ombudsman Service. They also set out the effect of failure to pay, such as the effect on credit rating, additional interest and court action by the creditor. They include a list of sources of help, such as Citizens Advice Bureaux and National Debtline.

Joint liability

Under the Consumer Credit Act, when credit is provided as part of an agreement to supply goods or services, both the credit provider and the supplier of the goods or services are 'jointly and severally' (see p100) liable for ensuring that the goods or services are not sold as a result of misrepresentations and the contract is not broken.[16] This means that if goods or services supplied are not fit for their purpose or are of a sub-standard quality, the client has greater protection than cash buyers. In the absence of action by the original supplier (or if the supplier is in liquidation), the client can take action against the creditor and will have a valid defence or counter-claim against any action to recover money due under the agreement.

Linked agreements

The right to a cooling-off period (see p59) also applies to any sale linked to the supply of the credit. In other words, if someone ordered double glazing at home and at the same time applied for credit to a company recommended by the seller, s/he has the right to cancel the credit application and the order for double glazing.[17] In addition, the creditor is jointly and severally liable with the supplier for the refund of any deposit or advance payment following cancellation of the credit agreement.[18]

2. Consumer Credit Act debts

Bank overdraft

A bank overdraft is a type of revolving credit (see p78). The bank allows a customer with a current account to overdraw on the account up to a certain amount. Repayment of the overdraft is made as money is paid into the account.

The legal position

Bank overdrafts are regulated under the Consumer Credit Act, provided the credit is for no more than £25,000 if granted before 6 April 2008 (£15,000 before 1 May 1998). It is immaterial whether the overdraft is authorised or unauthorised. No written agreement is required. If the credit is granted on or after 6 April 2008, the agreement is regulated regardless of the amount, unless it is exempt (see p54). An overdraft may be either secured or unsecured.

Special features

Interest is charged usually on a daily basis and repayment in full can be requested at any time. When the agreed overdraft limit is reached, cheques drawn against the account will usually be stopped.

If the overdraft is not approved by the bank or the limit is exceeded, a higher rate of interest is usually charged and additional service charges may be made at the bank's discretion.

When a customer has both a current account with overdraft facilities and a loan account with the same bank, it is common for banks to require payments to the personal loan account to be made from the current account. This may be done even if there are no funds in the current account, so that the higher overdraft rate of interest will apply to the payments made to the personal loan account.

Similarly, if someone has her/his wages paid directly into a current account, they will always be applied initially to reduce any overdraft on that account even if debts such as mortgage arrears ought to be given a higher priority for repayment.

Emergency action may, therefore, be needed to ensure income is not swallowed up as it becomes available. It may be necessary to open a current account with another bank so that wages can be paid into the new account or, if this is not possible, exercise the 'first right of appropriation' (see p41).

Once the bank is aware the client is in financial difficulties, it should deal with the case 'sympathetically and positively' according to the Banking Code. The bank should be encouraged to take steps to avoid the situation getting worse – eg, by agreeing to stop internal transfers set up to service its own credit debts (usually irrevocable, so the client cannot cancel them without the bank's agreement), so that charges do not build up. The bank could also consider reducing its interest rate and charges, particularly if the unauthorised rate is being applied. A consolidation loan should not routinely be offered. Although the bank has the right to offset any credits received against any debt owed to it, the Banking Code says that the client should be left 'with sufficient money for reasonable day-to-day expenses taking into account individual circumstances'. In other words, banks should not use standard figures to assess a client's needs. **Note:** banks cannot transfer money from a joint account to a sole account in order to pay a sole debt.[19] In multiple debt cases, the bank should recognise the *pro rata* principle when considering a payment arrangement and that priority debts should take precedence over non-priority debts, which the bank's debt is likely to be unless it is secured on the client's home (see Chapter 8).

It may be possible to challenge any charges added to the account as a penalty (see p109).

Bill of sale

A bill of sale is also known as a 'chattel mortgage' and is a way of raising money by offering an item of personal property (commonly a motor vehicle) as security for the loan. The essential feature of a bill of sale is that the mortgaged goods remain in the possession and use of the client but ownership is transferred to the creditor, so the goods can be repossessed and sold if the debt is not repaid. Similar arrangements containing some, but not all, of these features are not bills of sale – eg, pawnbroking, where the goods are deposited with the creditor as security, but remain the property of the client (see p77).

However, bills of sale are increasingly used to finance the actual purchase of motor vehicles. With hire purchase (HP)/conditional sale, the dealer sells the vehicle to the creditor who then lets (HP) or sells (conditional sale) it to the client. With a bill of sale, the dealer sells the car to the client who then enters into a credit agreement with the creditor (likely to be regulated by the Consumer Credit Act) secured by a bill of sale. A bill of sale gives the creditor all the advantages of HP/conditional sale agreements – ie:

- security for the debt;
- the right to repossess the vehicle if the client defaults;
- provided there is a term to that effect in the bill of sale, the right forcibly to enter the client's property to repossess the goods without a court order.

From the creditor's point of view, a bill of sale also removes some of the disadvantages of an HP/conditional sale – ie:

- the client has no right to terminate the agreement and limit her/his liability to one-half of the total price;

- the vehicle is not protected from repossession without a court order once the client has paid one-third of the total price;
- a private individual (ie, someone who is not a motor dealer) who purchases the vehicle from the client without knowing it is subject to a bill of sale does not obtain ownership. S/he is, therefore, not protected from having the vehicle repossessed by the creditor as would be the case if the vehicle were subject to a HP/conditional sale agreement.

There are a number of formalities associated with bills of sale and, if the creditor fails to comply with them, the creditor risks it being void and so unenforceable (although this will not necessarily affect the underlying credit agreement, which will remain enforceable but as an unsecured debt).

The legal position

Bills of sale are regulated by two pieces of 19th century legislation which still represent the law: the Bills of Sale Acts 1878 and 1882. The formal agreement, known as the bill of sale, must be set out in the way specified by the Schedule to the Bills of Sale (1878) Amendment Act 1882. Where the bill of sale secures an agreement regulated by the Consumer Credit Act, there must be a separate agreement, which should itself comply with the Consumer Credit Act and the regulations. This includes the requirement for the agreement to refer to the bill of sale. If the agreement is improperly executed, the creditor will either need the leave of the court to enforce its security under the bill of sale or, if the agreement is irredeemably unenforceable, the creditor will be unable to enforce its security.

Special features

In order to be valid and enforceable a bill of sale must be:

- 'in accordance with' the statutory form set out in the Schedule to the Bills of Sale Act 1882. This means it must be to the same effect, but not necessarily word for word the same, as the Act (see below);
- registered at the High Court in London within seven days of being made and then re-registered every five years. A copy of the registered document is forwarded to the local county court. Anyone can search, inspect, make extracts from and obtain copies of the register on payment of the prescribed fee (currently £40). This can be done by personal visit to the court office.

To be 'in accordance with the statutory form' and, therefore, valid and enforceable a bill of sale must contain:

- the date of the bill of sale;
- the names and addresses of the parties;
- a statement of the 'consideration'. This is the amount paid by the creditor to, or on behalf of, the client and does not include any item forming part of the total charge for credit in a regulated agreement secured by the bill;

- an acknowledgment of receipt of the consideration by the client. This is obligatory, even though the money is not paid to the client but to a third party – eg, the supplier of the goods;
- an assignment by way of security of the goods;
- no description of the goods in the body of the bill; this must be in a schedule to the bill;
- a monetary obligation. This can include an obligation to insure the goods or maintain the security;
- a statement of the sum secured, the rate of interest and the instalments by which repayment is to be made. Interest is an essential part of a bill and must be stated as a rate, even if it is also expressed as a lump sum. This is an area where creditors have frequently gone wrong, as it is not just a question of importing figures direct from the credit agreement. Where, as is often the case, the interest rate under a regulated agreement is not variable, there was no requirement prior to 31 May 2005 to include the interest rate in the agreement, as opposed to the annual percentage rate (APR). In the case of these agreements, if the bill of sale quotes the APR instead of the interest rate, the bill will not be in accordance with the statutory form. Nor will the bill be in accordance with the statutory form if the sum stated to be secured includes the interest charged under the credit agreement, because this would involve double charging of interest. Arguably, a bill of sale which refers to the credit agreement for the statement of these terms (or any of them) is not in accordance with the statutory form;[20]
- any terms that are agreed for the 'maintenance' or 'defeasance' of the security. A 'defeasance' is a provision in a document which nullifies it if specified acts are performed. For example, on payment of all sums due under the bill, the security will be void – ie, in this context, discharged. 'Maintenance of the security' means the preservation of the whole security given by the bill of sale in as good a condition as when it was made. The following terms are included:
  - to insure the goods and produce receipts for premiums;
  - to repair the goods and replace worn-out goods;
  - to allow entry to inspect the goods;
  - to allow the creditor to enter the premises in which the goods are situated in order to seize them (the bill of sale may even permit forcible entry);[21]
- a proviso limiting the grounds of seizure. The bill of sale will be void if it contains a power to seize in events other than in the case of:[22]
  - default in repayments or in performance of any terms in the bill of sale necessary for maintenance of the security;
  - bankruptcy of the client;
  - fraudulent removal of the goods, or allowing them to be removed, from premises. In the case of a vehicle, this might include a sale without the lender's consent;
  - unreasonably refusing to produce the last receipt for rent, rates or taxes;

– the levy of execution on the goods or distraint for rent, rates or taxes;

- signature of the bill of sale by the client. A bill need no longer be sealed;[23]
- an attestation clause. This is essential and must be meticulously completed. The security will be unenforceable unless the client's signature is witnessed by at least one person who is not a party to the bill. The parties to the bill are likely to be only the creditor and the client but not the supplier of any goods financed by the bill;[24]
- the name, address and description of the witness. The name alone without address (which may be the business address and not necessarily a private address) and description (ie, the profession, trade or vocation of the witness) is insufficient;
- a schedule, in which reference is made to the goods comprised in the bill of sale. If the bill entirely omits a schedule it is totally void.

Clients often present themselves to an adviser with either a HP/conditional sale or an unsecured loan. In these circumstances, if the creditor is threatening to repossess the subject of the agreement – eg, the motor vehicle, the adviser should establish whether the debt is, in fact, secured by a bill of sale. If so, the adviser should check that the credit agreement is properly executed and that the bill of sale is validly drawn up and registered (the creditor can be asked to supply a copy of the bill of sale showing the court stamp). Emergency action may be needed if there is a risk of repossession of the goods. This is likely to be a priority debt (see Chapter 7).

If the agreement secured by the bill of sale is regulated by the Consumer Credit Act, the creditor must serve a default notice before being entitled to repossess the goods on the grounds that the client has defaulted under the bill of sale. In cases where the agreement is irredeemably unenforceable, the bill of sale cannot be enforced either. In cases where the agreement can only be enforced with the permission of the court, the bill of sale cannot be enforced until the creditor has obtained an enforcement order (see p58).[25]

Seized goods should not be removed from the premises where they were seized until five clear days have expired.[26] During this period, the client could apply for a time order if appropriate (see p283).

If a bill of sale is believed to be invalid and unenforceable, but the creditor will not accept this and threatens to go ahead with repossessing the goods, a rarely used procedure, known as applying to 'expunge' (ie, remove) the registration of the bill of sale must be used. This is, in effect, a declaration of unenforceability. As bills of sale are registered in the High Court, the application has to be made to the High Court under Part 8 Civil Procedure Rules, even though the bill of sale may be securing a regulated consumer credit agreement. Specialist advice is needed.

If the creditor has already repossessed the goods under an invalid or unregistered bill of sale, the creditor should be challenged and, while the client may still owe the balance outstanding under the loan agreement, it may be possible to persuade the creditor to write off the debt. Specialist advice may be needed.

Budget account

A budget account is a type of revolving credit (see p78) provided by shops. The client can spend up to an agreed credit limit and makes regular repayments.

The legal position

This type of account is regulated under the Consumer Credit Act, provided the credit is for no more than £25,000 if the agreement was made before 6 April 2008 (or £15,000 before 1 May 1998).[27] If the agreement was made on or after 6 April 2008, the agreement is regulated regardless of the amount, unless it is exempt (see p54).

Special features

Many large stores offer budget account facilities which, by requiring clients to pay a monthly amount even when they have not recently purchased anything, can be a powerful incentive to continue shopping at that store. Instant credit is often available, including interest-free credit (see p75) on larger purchases.

A report published by the Competition Commission in March 2006 confirmed that clients who obtain credit in this way pay a higher price for it than they should, and that clients are not clear about the terms on which the credit is provided. The Competition Commission also expressed concern about insurance offered in connection with the use of the credit.

These debts are non-priority debts (see Chapter 8).

Conditional sale agreement

A conditional sale agreement is a sale made on credit subject to conditions that give the client possession of the goods during the repayment period, but where the goods only become the client's property when the last payment has been made. Conditional sale agreements are mostly used for motor vehicles (and are very similar to HP agreements – see p72).

The legal position

Agreements are regulated under the Consumer Credit Act, provided the credit is for no more than £25,000 if the agreement was made before 6 April 2008 (or £15,000 before 1 May 1998).[28] If the agreement was made on or after 6 April 2008, the agreement is regulated regardless of the amount, unless it is exempt (see p54).

Special features

Conditional sale has a number of special features. These are the same as those for HP (see p72) and the two types of credit operate in the same way.

Credit card

A credit card (eg, Mastercard, Visa) is a form of revolving credit (see p78) and allows the client to buy goods or services from a trader by use of a four-digit personal identification number (PIN). The trader invoices the credit card company and the client receives a monthly account showing all transactions made during that period. A minimum monthly repayment is required – usually 5 per cent of the total balance or a nominal amount, such as £5. Interest is added to balances outstanding after a specified payment date, or immediately for cash withdrawals using a credit card.

The legal position

Transactions made by credit card are linked agreements under the Consumer Credit Act. Consequently, credit card companies can be held responsible for misrepresentation and for defective goods or services costing between £100 and £30,000 if the trader is unwilling to remedy the situation. This could include a claim for damages due as a consequence of the misrepresentation or other breach. This section of the Act came into force in 1977 and there are different views on whether it applies to credit cards taken out prior to 1 July 1977. This has not been tested by the courts, but both Mastercard and Barclaycard have told the Director General of Fair Trading that they would be willing to accept limited liability up to the actual cost of the goods or services purchased with pre-1977 cards. The House of Lords has recently confirmed that overseas transactions are covered.[29]

If an additional credit card is issued to another person (usually a member of the client's family) to enable her/him to use the client's account, the client is liable for all transactions incurred by the additional cardholder, including if the client has not specifically authorised the transaction in question.

Unless the credit card agreement is a joint agreement (signed by both the client and the additional cardholder), the additional cardholder has no liability under the agreement if the client fails to pay.

If the client withdraws the additional cardholder's permission to use the credit card, the client remains liable for any transactions incurred by the additional cardholder until the client informs the creditor that the second cardholder's permission has been withdrawn in accordance with the terms and conditions of the credit card agreement. Once that has been done, the additional credit cardholder is no longer an 'authorised person' and the client has no further liability for transactions incurred by the additional cardholder.

Special features

The use of a credit card is the cheapest way to obtain short-term credit (up to about six weeks) for specific items. This is because on most cards no interest is charged if the account is cleared at the first due date after a purchase is added to it. However, interest is charged immediately for cash withdrawals and there is often an annual charge for cardholders. Advisers should:

- check liability and that the goods purchased were as described and of satisfactory quality (see Chapter 5); *and*
- choose a strategy from Chapter 8, as this will not be a priority debt.

Credit sale agreement

Goods bought on credit sale are owned immediately by the client. Regular payments are due in accordance with a regulated agreement. The creditor is often the supplier of the goods and this type of credit is used extensively to sell furniture and cars, and by fuel suppliers to sell cookers and fires.

The legal position

The agreement is regulated by the Consumer Credit Act provided the credit is for less than £25,000 if made before 6 April 2008 (or £15,000 before 1 May 1998). If the agreement was made on or after 6 April 2008, the agreement is regulated regardless of the amount, unless it is exempt (see p54).

Special features

The creditor has no rights over the goods. S/he simply takes the goods, signs the agreement, and starts to make payments. Sometimes interest-free credit (see p75) is given in the form of a credit sale agreement.

Some credit sale agreements (particularly for cars) provide that:

- the client must not sell the goods during the lifetime of the agreement; *and*
- if the client does sell the goods, s/he must pay the proceeds to the creditor.

The OFT regards the restriction on the sale of the goods as an unfair contract term, which means a client will probably not be in breach of it if s/he does sell the goods. However, the OFT does not regard it as unfair for the creditor to require payment of the proceeds, although the creditor would need to serve the debtor with a notice under s76 Consumer Credit Act before being entitled to take action to enforce such a term.[30] If the client is unable to comply with such a notice, on the OFT view, the client would then be in default. For a fuller discussion of unfair contract terms, see p110.

Advisers should:

- check liability, including the enforceability of the agreement under the Consumer Credit Act 1974; *and*
- check that the goods purchased were as described and of satisfactory quality (see Chapter 5); *and*
- choose a strategy from Chapter 8, as this will not be a priority debt.

Hire purchase agreement

An HP agreement hires goods to the client for an agreed period. At the end of this period the client has the option to buy them (usually for a nominal amount). HP is predominantly used for motor vehicles. The creditor (who is the hirer) owns the goods, generally having bought them from the supplier who introduced the client to the hirer.

The legal position

HP agreements for up to £25,000 if made before 6 April 2008 (or £15,000 before 1 May 1998) are regulated under the Consumer Credit Act. If the agreement was made on or after 6 April 2008, the agreement is regulated regardless of the amount, unless it is exempt (see p54).

The contract is between the client and the hirer of the goods, rather than the supplier – ie, in the case of a car, between the client and the finance company, rather than with the garage. Therefore the hirer – ie, the finance company, is liable for compensation for misrepresentation (see p104) and faulty goods. The Consumer Credit Act treats HP and conditional sale in the same way and so what follows also applies to conditional sale agreements.

Special features

The goods belong to the hirer until the end of the agreement. The client must not sell them during this period without obtaining the hirer's permission. The client can choose to return the goods to the hirer at any time during the lifetime of the agreement. The client must first give written notice to the hirer of her/his wish to terminate the agreement. In order that there should be no doubt as to what the client is doing (particularly if the hirer is threatening to repossess the goods), the letter should refer to the client exercising her/his right to terminate the agreement and request instructions from the hirer on the return of the goods.[31]

The amount payable on return depends on the amount already paid.

- If less than half the total purchase price (as stated on the agreement) has been paid, the client must pay either half the total purchase price minus the payments already made or any arrears of payments which have become due by the termination date, whichever is greater.
- If more than half the total purchase price has already been paid, the client may return the goods and will owe nothing further except any arrears on payments due.
- If the client has not taken reasonable care of the goods, s/he is liable to compensate the hirer.

When clients inform hirers that they can no longer afford the repayments and wish to end the agreement, they are often advised to surrender the vehicle voluntarily. A 'voluntary surrender' is not the same thing as a termination. A voluntary surrender has the same legal consequences as if the hirer had terminated the agreement and repossessed the goods (see p74). Whilst hirers are under no duty to inform clients of their rights, they must not mislead them.

Hirers often put obstacles in the way of clients attempting to end their agreements – eg, claiming that the client cannot end the agreement if it is in arrears or that the sum due on ending the agreement must be paid as a pre-condition of ending the agreement. This is not correct; the right to end the agreement is unconditional. If the hirer challenges the client's right to end the agreement, specialist advice should be sought. It is not the creditor's responsibility to arrange collection of the goods if a client terminates the agreement and, if the creditor has to collect the goods because the client refuses to return them, the client is liable for any charges incurred. On the other hand, if the creditor insists on collecting the goods, the client should challenge any collection charges the creditor seeks to impose.[32]

If the client claims to have terminated the agreement, specialist advice should be sought if the creditor is nevertheless seeking to recover the total balance due under the agreement. The client will lose the right to terminate the agreement if the hirer has already done so or called in the balance due under the agreement.

If the client defaults on payments, the hirer can repossess the goods. It must obtain a court order, unless:

- the client gives permission (this must be free and informed in the sense that the client has not been misled about her/his rights); *or*
- less than one-third of the total purchase price has been paid and the goods are not on private premises.

If the hirer repossesses the goods (including 'voluntary surrender' cases where the client returns the goods without terminating the agreement in writing), the client is liable for the outstanding balance due under the agreement, less the sale proceeds of the goods.[33]

Advisers should:

- check liability, including enforceability of the agreement under the Consumer Credit Act 1974; *and*
- check that the goods purchased were as described and of satisfactory quality (see Chapter 5); *and*
- be prepared to take emergency action to prevent repossession and choose a strategy from Chapter 7, as this may be a priority debt.

Many HP/conditional sale agreements also incorporate credit agreements for insurance sold as part of the same transaction – eg:

- payment protection insurance to cover the repayments in the event of the client's unemployment, sickness, disability or death;
- mechanical breakdown insurance;
- vehicle recovery insurance;
- accident assistance insurance;
- extended warranties or guarantees; *and*

- guaranteed asset protection (GAP), also known as shortfall insurance, which covers any shortfall if, following an accident, the write-off value of the goods is less than the balance owed to the creditor.

A credit agreement for such insurance (known as the 'subsidiary agreement') is a different type of agreement to the HP/conditional sale (known as the 'principal agreement') and is treated as a separate agreement. It is, however, permissible to include a subsidiary agreement for such insurance (but not for any other insurance or products) in the same document as the principal agreement containing only the consumer credit heading and signature box for the principal agreement. Agreements made before 31 May 2005 should not have included credit for GAP in the subsidiary agreement and any such credit agreement is improperly executed and unenforceable without leave of the court.[34] Leave will usually be granted on condition that the cost of GAP and its associated credit charges are removed.

The consequences of this practice are as follows.

- There is no right for the client to terminate the subsidiary agreement and so termination of the principal agreement does not affect the client's liability under the subsidiary agreement. The client must deal with this separately – eg, settle the agreement early, complain about any mis-selling of the insurance or raise any unenforceability issues.
- In calculating whether the client has paid one-third or one-half of the total price in connection with protected goods and termination rights, only the payments due or made in relation to the principal agreement should be taken into account. Advisers should check the one-third and one-half figures in the agreement.
- If the client was required to take out payment protection insurance as a condition of making the principal agreement, it may be that both agreements are irredeemably unenforceable and specialist advice should be sought.

Interest-free credit

This is a type of credit sale agreement in which money is loaned to buy goods without any interest being charged. It is usually offered by larger stores. Some agreements offer interest-free credit provided the total balance is paid off within a specified period and, thereafter, become ordinary credit sale agreements.

The legal position

These agreements are regulated by the Consumer Credit Act, provided the credit is for no more than £25,000 if made before 6 April 2008 (or £15,000 before 1 May 1998), even though there is no charge for credit. If the agreement was made on or after 6 April 2008, the agreement is regulated regardless of the amount, unless it is exempt (see p54).

An agreement is exempt if it requires the credit to be repaid in no more than four instalments within 12 months of the making of the agreement and this is quite a common feature of this type of credit. However, if it is not exempt, it must contain all the details required by a regulated agreement (see p55) and details of the circumstances in which interest could become chargeable. Interest can be charged on late payments if the agreement contains a clause allowing it. This type of credit can be expensive if it is not repaid during the interest-free period.

Special features

Interest-free credit is offered as an inducement to buy particular goods in a particular place and, therefore, is a linked agreement (see p64). Advisers should:

- check liability, including enforceability under the Consumer Credit Act 1974; *and*
- check that the goods purchased were as described and of satisfactory quality (see Chapter 5); *and*
- choose a strategy from Chapter 8, as this will not be a priority debt.

Mail order catalogues

Mail order catalogues offer a way of buying goods by post and usually spread payment over a period of weeks by instalments. Payments are sometimes collected by an agent – often a friend or neighbour of the client. The arrangement is usually an on-going one.

The legal position

Catalogue debts are covered by the Consumer Credit Act whether or not there is a charge for credit, provided the credit is for no more than £25,000 if the arrangement began before 6 April 2008 (or £15,000 before 1 May 1998). If the arrangement began on or after 6 April 2008, the agreement is regulated regardless of the amount, unless it is exempt (see p54).

Some mail order companies provide goods on the basis that they are paid for in full on receipt. These agreements are not regulated by the Consumer Credit Act 1974. If in doubt about whether a catalogue debt is regulated, specialist advice should be sought.

Special features

Often clients do not receive an agreement to sign. This means that the client's liability for the debt is irredeemably unenforceable if the arrangement began before 6 April 2007 and enforceable only with the permission of the court if the arrangement began on or after this date.[35] In these circumstances, the client is not legally obliged to settle the debt if the arrangement began before 6 April 2007, although s/he may choose to do so.

Mail order purchases can be cancelled by returning the goods within seven days of receipt.

Catalogues are often particularly important to people on low incomes as the only way of affording essential items such as bedding or clothing and charges for their delivery. Advisers should:

- check liability by asking the creditor to supply a copy of the agreement signed by the client; *and*
- check that the goods were of satisfactory quality and as described (see Chapter 5);
- if the client decides not to challenge liability, choose a strategy from Chapter 8, as this will not be a priority debt unless the use of mail order catalogues is the only way in which the client can buy essential goods.

Pawnbrokers

Money is lent against an article left with the pawnbroker as security – a pledge. The goods can only be reclaimed (redeemed) if the loan is repaid with interest.

The legal position

Pawnbrokers must be licensed and lending is covered by the Consumer Credit Act, provided the credit is for no more than £25,000 if the agreement was made before 6 April 2008 (or £15,000 before 1 May 1998). If the agreement was made on or after 6 April 2008, the agreement is regulated regardless of the amount, unless it is exempt (see p54).

Special features

The pawnbroker must keep the goods for at least six months, during which time interest is charged on the money borrowed. If the goods are not redeemed, the client must renew the pledge to prevent the goods being sold. Advisers should:

- check liability, including enforceability of the agreement under the Consumer Credit Act 1974 (see also Chapter 5);
- choose a strategy from Chapter 8 (or Chapter 7 if the pawned item is essential).

Personal loan

A personal loan is a loan offered at a fixed or variable rate of interest over a set period.

The legal position

Personal loans are regulated under the Consumer Credit Act, provided the credit is for no more than £25,000 if the agreement was made before 6 April 2008 (or £15,000 before 1 May 1998). If the agreement was made on or after 6 April 2008, the agreement is regulated regardless of the amount, unless it is exempt (see p54).

Special features

Personal loans are widely available from banks, building societies and other finance houses, including small moneylenders. Some personal loans have fixed interest rates and the total interest charged is set at the beginning of the period of the loan. Repayments are then made in equal instalments. Sometimes, a personal loan is part of a linked transaction (see p64). The amount to be loaned may be paid direct to the supplier rather than the borrower. With smaller moneylenders, repayments are often collected at the door by a representative. Advisers should:

- check liability including enforceability of the agreement under the Consumer Credit Act 1974 (see also Chapter 5);
- choose a strategy from Chapter 8,, as personal loans are generally not a priority debt.

Revolving credit

Revolving credit is a type of personal borrowing in which the creditor agrees to a credit limit and the client can borrow up to that limit, provided s/he maintains certain previously agreed minimum payments. Revolving credit takes a number of different forms – eg, credit cards (see p71), budget accounts (see p70) and bank overdrafts (see p65).

Second mortgage (secured loan)

A second (or subsequent) mortgage allows a homeowner to take out a (further) loan, using the property as security. The lender takes a legal charge on the property giving rights of repossession similar to those of a building society or bank holding the first charge on the property (in some cases, the creditor may also hold the first charge). If a house is repossessed and sold, the proceeds will be distributed to meet claims of secured lenders in the order in which loans were given.

The legal position

Second mortgages for £25,000 or less taken out before 6 April 2008 (£15,000 prior to 1 May 1998) are regulated agreements under the Consumer Credit Act unless exempt. The most common reason for exemption is where the secured loan is taken out for the purpose of improving/repairing the home and the creditor is the same lender which granted the mortgage to buy the home. If the agreement was made on or after 6 April 2008, the agreement is regulated regardless of the amount, unless it is exempt (see p54).

Special features

Interest rates on second mortgages with finance companies are much higher than those charged by building societies or banks for first mortgages. Loans are often repayable over a much shorter term than for first mortgages and this, together with higher interest rates, means it is an expensive form of borrowing.

There are special rules for entering into secured loans under the Consumer Credit Act. The borrower must be given a copy of the agreement, which is not to be signed for seven days. S/he must then be sent a copy for signing and left for a further seven days. If the borrower does not sign, there is no agreement. The lender should not contact the prospective borrower during either of the seven-day 'thinking' periods unless asked to do so. If these rules have not been followed the loan is not enforceable without a court order.

Advisers should:

- consider whether emergency action is necessary; *and*
- check whether the agreement is enforceable under the Consumer Credit Act 1974;
- choose a strategy from Chapter 7, as this will be a priority debt.

Trading cheque or voucher

Finance companies may supply a voucher or cheque to the client to be used at specified shops in exchange for goods. Repayments, which include a charge for the credit, are then made by instalments to the finance company. The shop is paid by the credit company.

The legal position

Agreements are regulated under the Consumer Credit Act, provided the credit is for no more than £25,000 if the agreement was made before 6 April 2008 (or £15,000 before 1 May 1998). If the agreement was made on or after 6 April 2008, the agreement is regulated regardless of the amount, unless it is exempt (see p54). If the voucher is for £50 or less the creditor is not obliged to comply with the rules on p55.[36]

Special features

This is normally an expensive way of borrowing and limits the client to shopping in a limited number of outlets where prices may be high. This will not usually be a priority debt – see Chapter 8 for details of how to deal with it. If this is the only way in which the client can buy essential goods, see p211.

3. **Other debts**

Business debts

It will often be necessary to advise people with business debts (see Chapter 13). If a business is still trading but is facing financial difficulties, specialist advice should be sought from, for instance, an accountant, insolvency practitioner, local business centre or small firms advisory service as to the viability of the business.

The legal position

If the business has already ceased trading, debts should be dealt with like any other case of multiple debt, using the same criteria to decide whether they should be treated as priority or not (see Chapter 7).

Liability for the debts must be established and the adviser should check whether the client was a sole trader, in a partnership or a limited company. A sole trader is personally liable for all the debts; in a partnership, all partners are jointly and severally liable. In limited companies, only the directors can be held liable for any debts, and then only if they have personally guaranteed a loan or, under company law, if there has been wrongful trading or neglect of their duties as directors.

Charge card

A charge card (eg, Diners Card) is not a credit card. Purchases are made and the amount is charged to the account, but the balance must be cleared in full at the end of each charging period (usually monthly).

The legal position

Charge cards are exempt from the Consumer Credit Act because there is no extended credit.

Special features

In order to obtain a charge card it is necessary to pay an annual fee and show proof of a high income. This will not usually be a priority debt (see Chapter 8).

Child support payments

The Child Support Agency (CSA) collects payments from non-resident parents to parents with care on income support (IS) or income-based jobseeker's allowance (JSA). In addition, it may collect payments from other non-resident parents if the parent with care/applicant requests this. From 14 July 2008, parents with care who claim IS or JSA on or after this date are free to choose whether or not to use the CSA to calculate and collect maintenance for them. From 28 October 2008, all parents with care who are using the CSA and who are receiving IS or JSA can choose whether or not to continue using it.

The legal position

Child support payments are governed by the Child Support Acts 1991 and 1995, the Child Support, Pensions and Social Security Act 2000 and subsequent regulations and amendments.

The Child Support Scheme was reformed in April 2003. The main changes relate to how maintenance is worked out and internal case administration. In July 2008 the Child Maintenance and Enforcement Commission was launched. It is planned that this will eventually take over all the functions of the CSA.

Special features

Child support payments are worked out according to set rules. The pre-2003 scheme (old rules) is a complex and rigid formula, although sometimes a 'departure' from this is allowed. It is vital to check the calculation (although it is difficult to do this because it often requires information about the other parent and her/his family which may not be available to the client). Some debt advisers may need the assistance of a specialist to do this. The reformed scheme (new rules) is simpler to calculate, although variations from it may still be possible to reflect special circumstances.

The first step in enforcement is to make a deduction from earnings order. This is made, in practice, by a member of the CSA staff. The CSA should always attempt to contact the non-resident parent to make an agreement to pay the arrears as soon as a payment is missed without a reason, or where a deduction from earnings order is not appropriate or has failed.[37] If the non-resident parent has still not paid four months after making initial payment arrangements, the case will be passed to the CSA's specialist enforcement unit.[38] A liability order will be sought from the magistrates' court. The court must accept that the non-resident parent is liable and that the assessment is correct. (The CSA's appeal process should be used to raise such issues.) From 12 July 2006 the six-year limitation period on the CSA applying for a liability order has been abolished (although debts already over six years old on this date are unaffected).[39] Where still relevant, time begins to run on the date the maintenance assessment in question was notified to the non-resident parent.[40] The non-resident parent should be told that if s/he makes and keeps to an arrears agreement, the liability order will not be enforced.[41] Following the granting of the liability order, if the non-resident parent has not made or kept to an arrears agreement, distress may be used (see Chapter 10) or the powers of the county court used to make a charging order or third party debt order (see Chapter 9). If one of these fails, the CSA can apply to the magistrates' court to commit a person to prison (for a maximum of six weeks) or disqualify the person from driving (for a maximum of two years). The court must decide whether the parent has 'wilfully refused or culpably neglected' to pay (see p338).

For more information about the child support scheme, see CPAG's *Child Support Handbook* (see Appendix 2).

Council tax

This is a tax administered by local authorities, composed of two equal elements – a 'property' element and a 'people' element.

Property element

All domestic properties have been valued and placed in one of eight valuation bands in England and nine in Wales.

In England, the valuation is based on what the property would have sold for on the open market in April 1991. In Wales, properties were re-valued on 1 April

2003 and the new valuations took effect from 1 April 2005. It is assumed that the property was sold freehold (99 years' leasehold for flats), with vacant possession and in a reasonable state of repair. Under some circumstances, an appeal against this valuation can be made. Certain properties are exempt, and advisers should check to make sure that exemption has been applied for if appropriate.

Assuming the property is not exempt, the level of council tax is set annually by the local authority. Occupants of Band H properties in England pay three times as much as those in Band A. In Wales, properties in Band I pay four times as much as those in Band A.

People element

The tax assumes that two adults aged 18 or over live in each household. Nothing extra is payable if there are more than two adults. One adult living on her/his own receives a 25 per cent discount. If there are no adults there is a 50 per cent discount. If the latter applies, it may be that the property is exempt and advisers should check whether this is the case.

When counting the number of adults in the household, certain people can be disregarded. Once again, this should be checked. Additionally, in certain cases there are reductions for people with disabilities whose homes have been modified.

Liability

A council tax bill is sent to each domestic property. The person(s) nearest the top of this list will be liable for payment of the council tax:

- resident freeholder (owner);
- resident leaseholder;
- resident statutory/secure tenant (including a council tenant);
- other resident(s);
- non-resident owner.

If there is more than one person resident in the house who has the same interest in the property (ie, joint owners or joint tenants), they are jointly and severally liable. This means that all the people concerned can be asked to pay the full charge, together or as individuals.

Married couples and both heterosexual and same-sex couples who live together are jointly and severally liable. A single bill is sent, either in the name of one of the persons concerned, or in both names.

Bills should be issued less any discounts, deductions and council tax benefit, and must arrive at least 14 days before the first instalment falls due. The local authority must offer the option of paying by monthly instalments. As discount is not a benefit, provided a claim is made, the appropriate discount(s) can be backdated indefinitely.

Students and people who are 'severely mentally impaired' are disregarded and usually exempt. They cannot be jointly and severally liable either as members of a couple or with someone who is not exempt.

Since 18 November 2003 local authorities have had the power to write off or reduce council tax arrears in cases of hardship.[42]

Special features

This is a priority debt (see Chapter 7). For more detailed information, see CPAG's *Council Tax Handbook*.

Fines

Fines are the most common form of punishment imposed by the magistrates' or crown courts for criminal offences.

The legal position

Magistrates' courts can impose fines for criminal offences by a wide variety of legislation. They are bound to consider the means of the defendant 'as far as they are known to the court'.[43] Maximum amounts are laid down for each offence.

Special features

Fines should be distinguished from costs or compensation, which are often also awarded against defendants in criminal actions.

Advisers should consider emergency action if payment of fines is difficult for a client. This is a priority debt (see Chapter 7). Court procedures and enforcement are explained in Chapter 10.

Gas and electricity charges

Gas and electricity suppliers charge for their fuel in a number of ways. Prepayment meters, quarterly accounts, direct debit and online schemes are common payment methods. Clients have a choice of supplier, although a supplier to whom arrears are owed can usually object to a transfer.

The legal position

The industry is regulated by the Electricity Act 1989, the Gas Acts 1986 and 1995, the Competition and Services (Utilities) Act 1992, the Utilities Act 2000 and the Energy Act 2004 plus various statutory instruments and the licences granted to suppliers. The industry is regulated by Ofgem and there is an independent consumer organisation, Consumer Focus, which acts as a watchdog. Suppliers are required to operate codes of practice on the payment of bills and disconnection, including guidance for customers who may have difficulty in paying such bills. Advisers should obtain copies of the codes of practice of their clients' suppliers.

All suppliers are required to provide a range of free services (including quarterly meter readings) to clients who are on their Priority Services Register. This is available to clients who:

- have a disability; *or*
- are over pension age; *or*
- are chronically sick; *or*
- are visually impaired or have hearing difficulties.

For further information, see CPAG's *Fuel Rights Handbook*.

Clients may be able to obtain a grant to pay off fuel debts. The only suppliers who have energy trust fund schemes at the moment are British Gas and EDF Energy, and only clients who are customers of one of these suppliers can apply. Grants are available for electricity and gas bills and may also be available to pay off other essential household bills. Both of these schemes are administered by Charis.

Fuel bills may include payments for goods sold by the supplier – eg, cookers and freezers These non-fuel debts will generally be credit sale agreements (see p72). A client cannot have her/his fuel supply disconnected for arrears on a credit sale agreement.

Many bills are based on estimated meter readings. Under their licence conditions, suppliers are only required to obtain actual meter readings once every two years. If the estimated reading is different to the actual reading, the client should read the meter her/himself and ask for this reading to be used in order to avoid either an overpayment now or an underpayment which will have to be made good in addition to future consumption. The name and address of the client as well as the address to which fuel was supplied should be noted from the bill. The prioritisation of the debt will depend upon the customer's continued need for that fuel at her/his present address.

Fuel supplies may be disconnected if there are arrears and this is likely, therefore, to be a priority debt (see Chapter 7). In the case of electricity, the supply can only be disconnected at the address to which the bill relates. In the case of gas, the customer can be disconnected at her/his current address even though the arrears may relate to a previous address.[44]

Ofgem has published *Preventing Debt and Disconnection* (see Chapter 7).

Income tax arrears

Most income above certain fixed limits is taxable. Employees are taxed by direct deduction from their income by their employer (the Pay-As-You-Earn (PAYE) scheme). PAYE taxpayers will rarely owe tax on their earned income unless mistakes have been made in the amounts deducted. Self-employed people receive their earnings before tax is deducted and are responsible for paying their own tax directly to HM Revenue and Customs (the Revenue). Arrears are, therefore, more likely to occur with self-employment (see Chapter 13).

The legal position

Income tax is payable under the Taxes Management Act 1970 and the Income and Corporation Taxes Act 1988 and subsequent Finance Acts and regulations.

Special features

There are many ways of reducing liability for tax, unless it is deducted under PAYE. Self-employed people in particular will require detailed advice on how to complete their tax returns since the introduction of self-assessment in April 1997. They also need detailed advice on any arrears that the Revenue may be claiming. Self-employed people should seek specialised help either from an accountant, or from Business Debtline or TaxAid if they wish to challenge the amount of any arrears claimed (see Appendix 1).

It may be possible to negotiate remission (write-off) of a tax debt if the client's circumstances are highly unlikely to improve – eg, if s/he is permanently unable to work because of ill health or if s/he is elderly with no hope of increasing her/his income. If the client has ceased trading, income tax arrears are only usually a priority (see Chapter 7) if imprisonment is a real possibility, as the Revenue says that it will only go for committal in cases of fraud. If the business is continuing to trade, however, it is vital that the client pays any ongoing tax on time and makes arrangements to repay any tax debt, otherwise the Revenue can seize essential goods without a court order, and so close down the business.

Maintenance payments

Before April 1993, either the magistrates' court or county court made orders to require a parent or ex-spouse to make maintenance payments to the other partner for her/himself and/or any children.

From April 1993, child maintenance payment powers passed to the CSA (see p80) under the Child Support Act 1991, although arrears due under court orders made before this date may still exist. The only new court orders are applications not covered by child support regulations (eg, applications for additional maintenance over and above the maximum awarded on CSA assessment) and for spousal maintenance.

The legal position

Magistrates' courts not only make maintenance orders but also collect and review maintenance orders made by the county court, divorce registry or High Court.[45]

Special features

If a maintenance order is unpaid, the magistrates' court has powers similar to those used where fines are unpaid (see Chapter 10). Maintenance payable under a court order should be distinguished from voluntary maintenance payments, even those written as a legal agreement.

A spousal/child maintenance order is a priority debt (see Chapter 7).

Mortgage

Usually, the term 'mortgage' is used to describe a loan used for the purchase of a house. If repayments are not kept up, the lender has the right to recover the money lent by repossessing the property and selling it. A 'charge' is registered on the property to safeguard the rights of the lender.

The legal position

First mortgages from building societies and the major banks are exempt from regulation by the Consumer Credit Act (see p50). Most will be regulated by the Financial Services Authority (FSA) from 31 October 2004.

Special features

There are a variety of different mortgages.

- **Capital repayment mortgage.** The amount borrowed ('capital') is repaid gradually over the term of the mortgage. At the beginning, repayments consist of virtually all interest, but towards the end of the term of the mortgage they are virtually all capital.
- **Endowment mortgage.** Repayments cover the interest on the capital borrowed and separate payments are made to an insurance company for the endowment premium. The capital is repaid at the end of the term of the mortgage in one lump sum from the proceeds of the insurance policy. Endowment policies aim to pay off the mortgage capital when they mature and produce extra capital for the borrower to use as s/he wishes. However, there is no guarantee that the policy will pay off even the capital, let alone provide extra money. Any client with an endowment mortgage should contact the policy provider and enquire how much the policy is expected to produce on maturity and seek independent financial advice if a shortfall is predicted.
- **Pension mortgage.** The borrower pays interest only to the lender and a separate pension premium which attracts tax relief. When it matures, the cash available from this pension pays off the capital on the mortgage and the rest funds a personal pension plan.
- **Low start/deferred interest mortgage.** Reduced interest is charged for the first two to three years. In some schemes, interest accrues during the first few years, but payment is spread over the remaining term of the mortgage. They are only helpful for people who expect their income to increase in order for them to afford the rise in repayments after the first few years. These are sometimes known as 'discount rate mortgages'.
- **Fixed rate mortgage.** The interest rate is fixed for a number of years, either at the outset or during the life of the loan. They are obviously more attractive during a period when interest rates are rising.
- **Tracker mortgage.** These mortgages guarantee always to follow the Bank of England's base rate or some other rate up or down, maintaining the same differential between the rate charged and that set by the Bank of England.

- **Other types of mortgage** include 'capped rate' (where repayments do not exceed a set level (the 'cap') or 'collared rate' (where payments do not fall below a set level (the 'collar')).

A mortgage is a priority debt (see Chapter 7). See p287 for the position on a mortgage shortfall after repossession of a property.

Regulated mortgage contract

Since 31 October 2004 most mortgage lending (including arranging and administering mortgages) is regulated by the FSA, the regulator set up by the Government to look after the financial services industry under the Financial Services and Markets Act 2000.[46]

The legal position

Firms involved in these activities must be authorised by the FSA. If not, they will commit a criminal offence and any regulated mortgage contract will be unenforceable. To check whether a lender or intermediary is authorised, go to www.fsa.gov.uk/register and follow the instructions. However, the court can allow enforcement if satisfied that it is 'just and equitable' to do so.[47]

A mortgage is a regulated contract if it was taken out on or after 31 October 2004 and:

- the borrower is an individual;
- the loan is secured by a first mortgage on property;
- the property is at least 40 per cent occupied by the borrower or her/his family.

The purpose of the loan is not relevant. Secured loans that would have been regulated by the Consumer Credit Act 1974 if made before 31 October 2004 are now regulated mortgage contracts if they meet the above criteria.

The FSA has detailed rules covering:

- advising on and selling mortgages;
- financial promotions;
- disclosure requirements;
- calculating the APR;
- responsible lending;
- unfair or excessive charges;
- arrears and repossession (including mortgage shortfall debts).

Special features

Generally, lenders and intermediaries must conduct their business with integrity, consider the interests of clients and treat them fairly. The detailed rules are set out in the *Mortgages and Home Finance: conduct of business sourcebook*, available online at http://fsahandbook.info/FSA/html/handbook. It is not worth downloading this document as it is subject to frequent change and the adviser will need to insert the date at the top of the screen in order to ensure s/he is reading the version in force at the relevant date.[48]

Before the client is offered a mortgage, s/he must be provided with a 'Key Facts Illustration' a personalised illustration setting out specified information. Any mortgage offer subsequently made must incorporate this, updated as necessary. The offer must include a tariff of fees and charges the client could incur. Arrears charges must not be excessive, but should be a reasonable estimate of the cost of the additional administration required as a result of the client being in arrears. The lender must be able to demonstrate that it has taken into account the client's ability to repay the loan by keeping adequate records (but these need only be retained for a year). Lenders must operate a written policy setting out the factors it will take into account when assessing ability to repay. The policy should be written on the assumption that any regular payments will be made out of the client's income and, therefore, lenders should take account of the client's actual and/or reasonably anticipated income. Lenders should only rely on self-certification of a client's income where this is appropriate – eg, where proof of income is not readily available (there have been cases where non-status lenders, in particular, have accepted inflated income figures based on self-certification from clients in regular employment where proof of income was readily available).[49]

Lenders must deal fairly with clients in arrears and not only have a written arrears policy in place, but also follow it. This requires the lender to use reasonable efforts to reach agreement with the client over repayment, liaising with advisers and applying for repossession only where all other reasonable attempts to resolve the position have failed. Within 15 business days of the account falling into arrears (defined as the equivalent of two monthly payments) the lender must send the client a copy of the FSA's information sheet on mortgage arrears, together with a statement of account, including details of the arrears, charges incurred and the outstanding balance. This information must be provided at least quarterly and, even if a repayment arrangement is in place, the information must still be sent out quarterly if the account is attracting charges. Lenders must not put pressure on clients through excessive telephone calls or letters and must not contact them at unreasonable hours ('reasonable hours' are defined as 8am–9pm). Lenders must not use documents that look like court forms or other official documents containing unfair, unclear or misleading information designed to coerce the client into paying.

If a property is repossessed, the lender must market it as soon as possible and obtain the best price that might reasonably be paid, although the lender is entitled to take account of market conditions or other factors that might justify deferring a sale – eg, the repayability of a grant if the property is sold by a certain date. In the event of a mortgage shortfall, the lender should inform the client of this as soon as possible, but has six years in which to notify the client of its intention to recover the shortfall debt (in line with the position for pre-31 October 2004 mortgages to which the rules discussed on p127 still apply).

Breach of the above rules does not make any transaction void or unenforceable.[50] Lenders and intermediaries must have a written complaints policy and the client will be able to complain to the Financial Ombudsman Service if the matter cannot be resolved with the lender or intermediary.[51]

Tax credit overpayments

Child tax credit (CTC) and working tax credit (WTC) are means-tested credits administered by the Revenue. People with children (this includes some young people) can qualify for CTC. WTC provides financial assistance to people in low-paid work. Entitlement to WTC does not depend on the presence of a child in the claimant's household.

Overpayments of tax credits can arise because initial awards are usually based on annual income over the previous tax year – 6 April to 5 April (although they can be based on an estimate of the current year's income). Some changes in circumstance must be reported during the year and are taken into account by the Revenue. However, in many cases (including where income changes), it is optional to report changes in circumstances. However, such changes are taken into account at the end of the tax year when awards are finalised.

For further information about tax credits, see Chapter 6 and CPAG's *Welfare Benefits and Tax Credits Handbook*.

The legal position

If there is likely to be an overpayment during a tax year, or the Revenue realises during the year that an award is too high (sometimes referred to as an 'in-year' overpayment), it can revise an award and reduce payments for the remainder of the year.[52] From November 2006, there are maximum amounts by which an award can be reduced.

Overpayments that come to light when an award is finalised at the end of the year are sometimes referred to as 'end of year' overpayments.[53] In the case of joint claims by couples, each partner is jointly and severally liable to repay any tax credit overpaid during the year. The Revenue must issue an overpayment notice stating the amount to be repaid and the method of repayment it intends to use.[54] Recovery can be:

- by reducing an ongoing tax credits award. There are maximum amounts by which an award can be reduced.[55] This is the method the Revenue prefers; *or*
- from the person(s) overpaid, in one lump sum or by equal instalments over 12 months; *or*
- through the PAYE system.

Former partners could be asked to repay different amounts, but the Revenue says it will only do this where there is a difference in the partners' abilities to pay.

Interest can be added to an overpayment if the Revenue considers the overpayment was due to the claimant's fraud or neglect.[56] The interest is recovered using the same methods as for overpayments.

Note that penalties can be imposed in some circumstances – eg, if someone makes an incorrect statement or supplies incorrect information and this is done fraudulently or negligently. Different procedures apply for the recovery of penalties.

Special features

All overpayments are recoverable, whatever the cause, although the Revenue has the discretion not to recover and can decide to write off an overpayment. It has a code of practice on the recovery of tax credit overpayments, *What Happens if We Have Paid You Too Much Tax Credit?*, available at www.hmrc.gov.uk/leaflets/cop26.pdf.

The code of practice was changed from 31January 2008 and the decision on whether to recover any overpayments notified to the claimant on or after this date should be made according to the principles in this amended version. The code of practice says that the Revenue will not pursue repayment if:

- the overpayment was caused by the Revenue failing to meet its 'responsibilities'; *and*
- the claimant has met all of her/his 'responsibilities'.

See CPAG's *Welfare Benefits and Tax Credits Handbook* for details about these 'responsibilities' and the 2007/08 edition for recovery of overpayments decided before 31 January 2008.

There is a right of appeal against Revenue decisions about entitlement to tax credits. It is, therefore, vital to check that entitlement has been correctly calculated (ie, that there has been an overpayment), appealing any incorrect decisions within the time limit.

There is *no* right of appeal against a decision to recover an overpayment. However, such a decision can be disputed. It is best practice to use the Revenue's official dispute form (TC846). The Revenue suspends recovery when it receives this, pending its decision on whether to write off any of the overpayment. If a claimant is appealing an incorrect decision (see above) it is important to dispute recovery at the same time to ensure that recovery is suspended pending the outcome of the appeal.

An additional means of challenging recovery of an overpayment is to use the Revenue's complaints procedure and/or to complain to the Independent Adjudicator (see Appendix 1). The only legal challenge to a decision to recover an overpayment would be by judicial review.

If the Revenue is recovering an overpayment by reducing tax credits payments on a continuing award, and this is causing the claimant hardship, a claimant can ask for 'additional payments'. These effectively limit the reduction in payments to set maximums, thereby extending the length of time given to recover the overpayment. The code of practice says that the Revenue will not usually make 'additional payments' if an award is being reduced because it found out during an enquiry or an examination that the claimant provided wrong information.

If clients refuse to pay or do not keep to any payment arrangement, the Revenue will consider taking legal proceedings to recover the debt. This is likely to be a non-priority debt unless the client is entitled to an ongoing tax credit award, or pays income tax through the PAYE system.

National insurance contributions

National insurance (NI) contributions are a compulsory tax on earnings and profits above certain levels (set annually).

The legal position

National insurance contributions are payable under s2 Social Security Act 1975, as amended by the Social Security Contributions and Benefits Act 1992.

Special features

Employed people pay Class 1 NI contributions directly from their wages and thus arrears do not build up. Class 2 contributions must be paid by self-employed earners unless they have a certificate of exception on the grounds of low income. Self-employed people have to pay Class 2 NI contributions by monthly direct debit or quarterly bill. In addition, self-employed people may have to pay Class 4 contributions, calculated as a percentage of their profits above a certain level (set annually). After the year end, the Revenue sends out demands to self-employed people from whom it has not received the required Class 2 contributions.

If a self-employed person has also employed someone else, s/he may be liable for Class 1 NI contributions for the employee, as well as Class 2 and perhaps 4 for her/himself.

Demands for payment should be distinguished from the notice sent to people whose contribution record is insufficient to entitle them to use it towards a retirement pension or bereavement benefits. In such cases, the Revenue sends a notification giving the insured the opportunity to make up the deficit for a particular year with voluntary (Class 3) contributions. This is not a demand for payment.

If the client has ceased trading, arrears of contributions are only usually a priority (see Chapter 7) if imprisonment is a real possibility, as the Revenue says it will only go for committal in cases of fraud. If the business is continuing to trade, however, it is vital that the client pays any ongoing contributions on time and makes arrangements to repay any arrears, otherwise the Revenue can seize essential goods without a court order and so close down the business. In addition, if contributions remain unpaid, the client's eventual entitlement to retirement pension will be affected.

Rent

Rent is payable by tenants to landlords in exchange for the use of their property. A landlord may be either a private individual or property company, or a public sector landlord, such as a local authority or housing association.

The legal position

Rent is payable under a tenancy agreement (whether written or oral). For more details, see the *Manual of Housing Law* (see Appendix 2).

Special features

After the termination of a tenancy (eg, because a notice to quit is served), a tenant is allowed to remain in possession of the home because of protection given by legislation. In these circumstances, the landlord may refer to the money due in exchange for possession of the home as 'mesne profits'. For practical purposes, this is the same as rent. Similarly, where a person is a licensee rather than a tenant what s/he pays will not strictly be rent, but will be a charge for use of the property. Arrears of payment due under a licence are treated in the same way as rent when giving debt advice.

Rent due for a person's current home is a priority debt (see Chapter 7).

Social fund repayments

Social fund loans (budgeting loans and crisis loans) are available to claimants who need to borrow money for essential items. Budgeting loans are only available to those getting IS, income-based JSA or pension credit (PC). Social fund loans are normally repaid by a direct deduction from the claimant's weekly benefit. However, when a person stops getting benefit before having repaid the entire loan, s/he will still owe money to the social fund.

For further information about social fund loans, see Chapter 6 and CPAG's *Welfare Benefits and Tax Credits Handbook*.

The legal position

Social fund repayments are required by s78 Social Security (Administration) Act 1992. The *Social Fund Guide* lays down the procedures that the Department for Work and Pensions (DWP) uses to collect loans from claimants.

Special features

The DWP tells the client how the loan is to be repaid. Claimants on IS, income-based JSA or PC have a fixed proportion of their benefits deducted, depending on their other commitments. The debt adviser should consider asking for these deductions to be reduced (or, if the client is no longer in receipt of benefit, the loan rescheduled), especially if the DWP was unaware of the financial problems. **Note:** deductions from benefit can be made even where an order for bankruptcy or sequestration has been made.[57] See CPAG's *Welfare Benefits and Tax Credits Handbook* for further details (see Appendix 1).

The DWP can take court action to recover the money if no arrangement is made. If the client is unable to afford repayment, it may consider writing off the debt. The debt should be treated as a normal unsecured loan and is not a priority unless the client is in receipt of a benefit from which deduction can be made (see Chapter 8).

Business rates

This is a charge levied on most commercial property by local authorities. It is based on a national valuation and fixed amounts are charged across England and Wales in proportion to this.

The legal position

The rate is payable under the Local Government Finance Act 1988.

Special features

Arrears are recovered through a liability order in the magistrates' court. If bailiffs are used by a local authority after it has obtained a liability order, there is no exemption for tools, books, vehicles or goods which are necessary for use in the client's business (as there is for council tax arrears).[58] Once a business ceases trading, it may be able to claim local discounts or reliefs from business rates and advisers should check with the local authority what is available. If the business is renting premises under a lease, it will continue to be liable for the business rates for as long as the lease exists.

Local authorities have power[59] to reduce or write-off arrears of business rates in situations of severe hardship. This is most appropriate in cases of business failure and should always be sought before considering payment.

This may or may not be a priority debt, depending on the risk of loss of essential goods by the client.

Value added tax

Value added tax (VAT) is a tax charged by the Revenue on most transactions of businesses with an annual taxable turnover of more than a certain limit, set annually. A business must be registered for VAT unless its turnover is below the limit.

The legal position

VAT is payable under the Finance Act 1972 and the VAT Act 1983, and subsequent regulations and amendments. Its scope and level are reviewed each year and changes are often made to the Act following the Budget.

Special features

VAT is a tax on the value added to goods and services as they pass through the registered business. Thus, although VAT is payable on purchases, this amount can be offset against the tax on the business's own sales. For example, if the total purchases in a year were £100,000 and the total sales were identical, there would be no value added and no tax payable.

A debt adviser will generally encounter VAT debts after a business has ceased trading and the partner or sole trader is left responsible for VAT (see Chapter 13). Some goods are exempt and the calculation of the amount of VAT is complicated. Help should normally be sought from an accountant specialising in VAT. If VAT is overdue, a surcharge, which will be a percentage of the VAT owed, will be added to the debt. This amount can be appealed.

If the client has ceased trading, VAT arrears are only usually a priority (see Chapter 7) if imprisonment is a real possibility, as the Revenue says it will only go for committal in cases of fraud. If the business is continuing to trade, however, it is vital that the client pays any ongoing VAT on time and makes arrangements to repay any VAT debt, otherwise the Revenue can seize essential goods without a court order and so close down the business.

Water charges

Water companies charge for water, sewerage and environmental services on the basis of either a meter or the rating system, which was abolished as the basis of a local tax in April 1990 in England and Wales. Under the rating system, every dwelling was given a rateable value. Each year, water companies set a 'rate in the pound', which converts this rateable value into an annual charge. For example, a rate of 20p in the pound converts a rateable value of £300 to an amount of water rates payable of £60.

If a water meter is installed, a client pays for the actual amount of water used. Charges are per cubic metre at a rate set by the water company. A standing charge is also payable. There may also be installation and inspection charges. Separate charges are levied for sewerage and environmental services. These charges are based either on the rateable value of the property or on the amount of water used as recorded by the meter.

The legal position

Water charges are payable under the Water Industries Act 1991. Water companies will initially use county court action to recover arrears. They have no discretion to waive charges if there is an ongoing supply.

Special features

Bills for water charges are sent out in April. Payment can be made in eight to ten instalments or weekly/monthly in cases of financial hardship. It is important to check that the bill refers to a property in which the client actually lives, or lived, and that the dates of occupation and name(s) shown on the bill are correct. The occupier of the property is the person liable to pay the bill. If there is a meter, bills are issued every three or six months based on meter readings carried out by the company's staff or the client. If this is not possible, an estimated bill will be issued. Bills should be checked and queried if they seem too high as there may be a hidden leak or the meter may be faulty.

Since 30 June 1999 water companies cannot disconnect for arrears of domestic water charges and, therefore, this is a non-priority debt (see Chapter 8), but the realistic cost of current water charges must be in the financial statement to avoid ongoing enforcement action.[60]

Ofwat guidelines, *Dealing With Water Customers in Debt,* available from www.ofwat.gov.uk, set out the following principles, which companies should include in their own codes of practice.

- Companies should be proactive in attempting to contact clients who fall into debt as early as possible and at all stages of debt management.
- Companies should provide clients with a reasonable range of payment frequencies and methods. The entire range of options should be properly and widely advertised to ensure that clients can select the arrangement which best suits their circumstances.
- Paperwork sent to clients should be written in plain language and in a courteous and non-threatening style, but should clearly set out the action the company will take if the client fails to make payment or contact the company, along with the possible consequences for the client.
- When agreeing payment arrangements, the client's circumstances (including her/his ability to pay) should be taken into account wherever possible.
- Clients whose accounts have been passed to collectors should receive the same treatment as if the account had remained with the water company and the potential consequences should be no more severe than if the service was provided by the water company – ie, the collector should comply with its own industry codes of practice as well as the water company's code of practice (although the guidelines recognise this may not be possible if the debt is sold, which should only be done where all other debt recovery methods have been attempted, they seem to assume that such clients will be 'won't pays' and so not entitled to the same level of 'service').
- Some water companies use local authorities or housing associations as 'billing agents' to bill and collect water charges from their tenants. The guidelines state that service standards should be agreed and notified to the tenants, but do not spell out what those standards should be. If the water charges are collected as part of the rent, the guidelines state that where eviction for non-payment of rent (including unpaid water charges) is a possibility, alternative solutions should be found (although it may well be that such provisions in a tenancy agreement could be challenged under the Unfair Terms in Consumer Contract

Regulations 1999). In such situations, specialist housing advice should be sought.

Advisers should be aware that there are vulnerable groups schemes (now known as the WaterSure scheme) available in England and Wales for clients on low incomes. Many water companies have set up trust funds to assist clients with payment of arrears of water charges. Advisers should check their local company's website for details of any scheme operating in their area.[61]

Traffic penalties

A number of traffic penalties, particularly parking charges and certain other fixed penalty notices, are recovered by local authorities using the county court under Part 75 Civil Procedure Rules.

The legal position

It is important to distinguish between traffic penalties registered in the magistrates' court for enforcement – which are recoverable as fines and are, therefore, priority debts (see p83) – and penalty charges recoverable through the Traffic Enforcement Centre at Northampton County Court.[62] Once the penalty charge has been registered in the county court, it is passed to private bailiffs for collection. If the bailiff is unable to collect the debt, the local authority can then use other county court enforcement methods (see Chapter 9).

If the client claims s/he is not liable to pay the penalty – eg, s/he was not the owner of the motor vehicle at the time, s/he should complete either the form of statutory declaration (PE 3) or the witness statement (TE 9) which accompanies the court order registering the charge. This must be returned to the court before the end of the period of 21 days beginning with the date of service of the order. The court can extend this time limit where it considers it reasonable to do so.

Special features

A traffic penalty enforced through the county court does not have the sanction of imprisonment for non-payment, but the county court has no power to suspend bailiff action by applying on an N245 (see p303), nor does the court have power to make an instalment order to prevent enforcement action.

This will not be a priority debt unless the client is at risk of losing essential goods.[63]

Notes

1. **The Consumer Credit Act**

1 s25(2A)(e) and (2B) CCA 1974, as amended by s29 CCA 2006
2 s40 CCA 1974
3 Consumer Credit (Disclosure of Information) Regulations 2004 No.1481
4 *London North Securities v Meadows* [2005] EWCA Civ 956 (*Adviser* 107 and 108 abstracts)
5 See *Ocwen v Hughes & Hughes* [2004] CCLR 4 and *Central Trust v Spurway* [2005] CCLR 1
6 See *McGinn v Grangewood Securities* [2002] EWCA Civ 522 (*Adviser* 92 abstracts); *London North Securities v Williams*, Reading CC, 16 May 2005, unreported (*Adviser* 112 abstracts). Even if the prescribed term is present, it is unlikely that the agreement will contain the more detailed non-prescribed repayment obligations which will make the agreement improperly executed and enforceable with leave of the court only on such terms as it thinks fit; see *Hurstanger Ltd v Wilson* [2007] EWCA Civ 299 (*Adviser* 122 consumer abstracts)
7 ss113 and 127(3) CCA 1974 and Sch 6 Consumer Credit (Agreements) Regulations 1983 No.1553
8 Consumer Credit (Agreements) (Amendment) Regulations 2004 No.1482
9 For a summary of pre-6 April 2007 unenforceability arguments, see A Leakey and B Say, 'Unenforceable Agreements', *Adviser* 117 and for a discussion of the position post-6 April 2007, see G Skipwith, 'Consultancy Corner 1', *Adviser* 124
10 Consumer Credit Act 1974 (Electronic Communications) Order 2004 No.3236
11 s63 CCA 1974
12 s69(7) CCA 1974
13 s57 CCA 1974
14 Regs 7–13 and 29 and Schs 1 para 13, and 2 para 5 Financial Services (Distance Marketing) Regulations 2004 No.2095. These only apply where the client is a 'consumer' – ie, the transaction must not be for the purposes of the client's business.
15 Regs 34-35 and Sch 5 CC(IR) Regs 2007
16 s75 CCA 1974
17 ss57(i) and 69(i) CCA 1974
18 s70(3) CCA 1974

2. **Consumer Credit Act debts**

19 For a discussion on various aspects of bank transfers, see J Wilson, 'Consultancy Corner', *Advisers* 107 and 108. See also the report of a complaint to the Financial Ombudsman Service in *Adviser* 107 abstracts
20 *Lee v Barnes* [1886] 17 QBD 77
21 *Re Morritt ex p Official Receiver* [1886] 18 QBD 222, CA
22 s7 Bills of Sale Act 1882
23 s1(1)(b) Law of Property (Miscellaneous Provisions) Act 1989
24 Although a party may not attest the bill, a party's agent, manager or employee may do so; *Peace v Brookes* [1895] 2 QB 451
25 s113 CCA 1974
26 s13 Bills of Sale Act 1882
27 s8 CCA 1974
28 s8 CCA 1974
29 *Office of Fair Trading v Lloyds TSB & others* [2007] UKHL 48 (*Adviser* 125, consumer abstracts)
30 A creditor is required to give seven days' notice of its intention to enforce a term of the agreement allowing it to demand early payment of any sum in cases where this right arises even though the client is not in default.
31 The OFT has produced a leaflet, *Hire Purchase: making the right choice*, which includes a section on the client's right to terminate.
32 See P Madge, 'Take it Back', *Adviser* 106
33 *First Response v Donnelly*, Durham CC, 16 October 2006 (*Adviser* 122, consumer abstracts). For a discussion on challenging this approach to creditor termination, see C Meehan and P Madge in *Adviser* 125 and 127
34 Creditors could avoid this by including two principal agreements in the same document, each containing its own consumer credit heading and signature box.

35 s127(3) CCA 1974 (repealed with effect from 6 April 2008, but not retrospectively by s15 and Sch 3 para 11 CCA 2006
36 ss14 and 17 CCA 1974

4. **Other debts**

37 CSA, *Debt Enforcement Guide*, Chapter 3
38 CSA, *Client Charter 2006*
39 Reg 3(5) Child Support (Miscellaneous Amendments) Regs 2006 No.1520
40 *R (on the application of Sutherland) v Secretary of State for Work & Pensions* [2004] EWHC 800 (Admin)
41 CSA, *Debt Enforcement Guide*, Chapter 4
42 s76 LGA 2003 and see 'Complaint against Redcar and Cleveland BC', *Adviser* 126, money advice abstracts
43 s35 MCA 1980
44 Sch 6 para 2(1)(b) EA 1989; Sch 2B paras 3 and 7(1) GA 1986
45 s1 MOA 1958
46 See R Rosenberg, 'Mortgage Day: the final countdown', *Quarterly Account* 73, IMA, Winter 2003/04
47 s28 FSMA 2000
48 In October 2008 the Council of Mortgage Lenders issued industry guidance on arrears and possessions to assist lenders to comply with MCOB 13 and their duty to treat customers fairly. It can be found at: www.cml.org.uk
49 see MCOB 11.3
50 s151(2) FSMA 2000
51 See P Bristow, 'One-stop Complaints Shop', *Adviser* 107, and S Quigley, 'Removing the Barriers', *Adviser* 109
52 s28(5) TCA 2002
53 s28(1) TCA 2002
54 s29 TCA 2002
55 Reg 12A TC(PC) Regs
56 s37 TCA 2002
57 *Mulvey v Secretary of State for Social Security* [1997] SC 105 (HL); *R v Secretary of State for Social Security ex parte Taylor and Chapman, The Times*, 5 February 1996 (HC); s78(3A) and (3B) SSAA 1992
58 Reg 14(1A) Non-Domestic Rating (Collection and Enforcement) (Local Lists) Regulations 1989
59 s49 LGFA 1988
60 s1 and Sch 1 Water Industry Act 1999
61 *Adviser* 105 contains a series of articles on dealing with water debt. See also, J Guy, 'Maximising Income: using utility trust funds', *Quarterly Account* 4, IMA, Spring 2007
62 Part 75 CPR
63 See P Madge 'No Waiting' *Adviser* 68 and T Redmond, 'Parking Complaints', *Adviser* 108

Chapter 5

Minimising debts

This chapter covers:

Advisers must check that the client is legally liable to pay the debts claimed by her/his creditors. In general, a debt will be owed only if:

- there is a valid contract between the client and creditor; *or*
- money is owed because of particular legislation; *or*
- the client has been ordered by a court to make payments to someone else, or to the court itself, and there are no grounds to challenge the court order.

Sometimes, nothing will be payable because a contract has not been made in the correct way or the rules governing the ways in which public authorities can demand money have not been complied with. In other cases, it may be possible to reduce the amount owed because the law says that a term of the contract is 'unfair', or (in the case of credit agreements) there is an 'unfair relationship' (see p115) or there has been irresponsible lending (see p53). Even if the adviser has established that a debt does exist, it is still possible that the client is not liable to pay it, either because liability actually falls on someone else, or because the contract is not enforceable – eg, the creditor is outside the time limit for taking court action to recover the debt.

The adviser must also check that the amount of any debt is correct by checking the accuracy of calculations and that all payments made by the client have been credited to the account. This will usually involve asking the creditor to provide a statement of account.

1. Using the law of contract to challenge or reduce liability

A contract is an agreement between two parties (ie, individuals, companies, or a mixture of these) that becomes binding (ie, legally enforceable) because it specifies that goods or services are to be exchanged by one party in return for a 'consideration', usually money, from the other. The most common situation in which an amount of money claimed under a contract may not be due, or may be reduced, is when one party has not kept to her/his side of the bargain – eg, the supplier has sold defective goods.

There are also important ways in which consumer, housing or other legislation can reduce the amount a client owes. These are listed below.

'Joint and several liability'

If more than one client enters into a credit agreement, they are each liable for the whole amount of the debt. This is known as **'joint and several liability'**. If relevant, the agreement must be signed by all parties in the form required by the Consumer Credit Act (see p55). If all the clients have not signed such an agreement and it was made on or before 6 April 2007, none of them is liable because the agreement is 'irredeemably unenforceable' (see p56).

Joint and several liability can also apply to rent arrears on joint tenancies, arrears on joint mortgages, water and sewerage charges and to council tax on properties which are jointly owned/occupied by heterosexual and same-sex couples.

Guarantors

A creditor will sometimes ask for a guarantee before agreeing to lend money or provide services. The guarantor agrees to make the necessary payments should the actual customer or borrower fail to do so, and is bound by the terms of the guarantee s/he has given. If these terms are part of a regulated consumer credit agreement, they are governed by the Consumer Credit Act. A guarantee must be in writing and signed by the guarantor. Sometimes, creditors ask for people to act as second purchasers. They are asked to sign the original agreement as purchasers and become jointly and severally liable for the debt. Guarantors should be given copies of the original agreement and also any notices required to be sent to the client on default.

If the creditor has not properly explained to a guarantor that s/he is equally liable for the total debt, there may be a way of challenging liability if it can be shown that the guarantor has been either misled or coerced. In any case, if there is a non-commercial relationship between the client and the guarantor – eg, they are cohabitees, the creditor is required to take reasonable steps to satisfy itself that the guarantor understands the transaction and the risks s/he is taking by entering into it. The creditor can either do this itself or require the guarantor to see a solicitor. If the creditor fails to take either of these steps, but the guarantor has seen a solicitor anyway, the creditor cannot assume the solicitor has advised the guarantor appropriately when no such advice was in fact given.

If the creditor fails to take these steps and the guarantor's consent to the transaction has been improperly obtained, the creditor may be unable to enforce the guarantee.[1] This commonly arises where one of a couple applies for a loan for her/his own purposes – eg, to pay off debts or fund a business, which the creditor requires to be in joint names so that it can be secured on jointly-owned property or so that the income of the other person can be taken into account as part of the creditor's lending process. If it appears the agreement was only given to a joint loan because the first borrower used 'undue influence' (see p104) by saying, for instance, 'we'll lose our home if you do not sign', or by misrepresenting the effect of the transaction, the second borrower may be able to escape liability. S/he should always seek specialist help.

Agents

An agent sells goods or collects money on behalf of someone else – eg, an agent may show or distribute mail order catalogues to her/his friends and neighbours, take orders and pass them on to the supplying company. S/he collects money from the customers over a number of weeks, and is liable to pay any money collected, regardless of whether or not the creditor can enforce the agreement against the customer – eg, because s/he has not signed a contract. An agent is obliged to create a separate account for each customer. If s/he does not do this, s/he can become liable for money not paid by customers for whom s/he has failed to create an account. If there is a separate account, the agent will not be liable for money that customers do not pay.

An agent may lose commission with which s/he has already been credited (and thus her/his own personal account may go into arrears) if someone does not keep up the payments on items bought and supplied. However, an agent is not liable for the customer's default (except in the situation discussed above).

When advising an agent about liability, it is important to check whether the amount owed includes other customers' debts. If so, provide the creditor with a clear breakdown of the accounts, and the names and addresses of customers in arrears and ask the creditor to invoice them separately. Specialist advice will be required if a client has not obtained signed agreements from her/his customers or has received payments but not accounted for these to the creditor.

The wrong person

An account may be sent to the wrong person or the wrong address, and the person who receives the request for payment is not actually liable. If there is any doubt about this, check any documents relating to the debt and ask the creditor to produce original invoices, agreements and details of goods or services supplied. Full initials and addresses are obviously important in this process, as are reference numbers.

Using the wrong name, however, does not invalidate a debt and, if a name is shown incorrectly, particularly if it has always been inaccurate but both parties know who is intended, the debt can still be valid.

Forged signatures

If a signature on an agreement has been forged, the person whose name has been forged is not liable for any debt arising from that agreement. A signature may have been forged with knowledge. For example, a person who wants a loan but has reached her/his credit limit with a particular creditor may use a relative's name to obtain the loan, receive the money and make repayments. The relative knows and agrees to this. In such cases, the adviser should proceed as though the signature was valid and the beneficiary of the loan should continue to maintain repayments.[2]

A partner or close relative's signature may be used without her/his consent – eg, if a young person obtains credit by using her/his parent's name and signature without the knowledge of the credit company or the parent. If there is any accusation of fraud, the client should obtain legal advice. Fraud is a serious criminal offence and a solicitor specialising in criminal law may be required. In some cases, the use of a more creditworthy relative's name may have been sanctioned by the credit company. If a representative of a creditor has allowed a false name to be given knowingly, that representative may be either conniving with a fraud or, if the signing occurred on her/his advice, creating a situation in which the creditor accepts that the borrower is allowed to use another name. A broker is not usually regarded as a representative of the credit company for this purpose.

The debt adviser should advise the person whose name has been used that s/he does not owe the money because s/he has not signed the agreement. The adviser should be aware of the possible repercussions for the actual signatory and should explain these to the person being advised as s/he may prefer to accept liability for the debt rather than risk, for instance, a prosecution of the actual signatory and/or a breakdown in family relationships.

Liability after the death of a client

An individual's debts usually die with her/him, although creditors may be entitled to make a claim against the deceased's estate – ie, money, personal possessions and property. It is possible, however, that creditors will attempt to hold partners or close relatives responsible for an individual's debts, particularly if they lived with the deceased, although this could involve a breach of the Office of Fair Trading's (OFT) *Debt Collection Guidance*.[3]

If someone is dealing with a deceased's estate s/he has no personal liability for any debts that cannot be paid from the deceased's own property. Possible exceptions to this rule include:

- debts for which someone had joint and several liability with the deceased (see p100);
- if the deceased's estate has been handed over to beneficiaries without first paying her/his creditors (including if the person handling the estate is also the only beneficiary). If a client in this situation is being held personally liable by the deceased's creditors, the adviser should seek specialist advice;
- a mortgage remaining on a property, even if this passes to a new owner by inheritance (although it may be paid off by an insurance policy on death);
- taking over a tenancy from the deceased by succession, which may involve taking over rent arrears if these cannot be paid by the estate. A tenant by succession can lose her/his home if s/he does not pay off arrears;[4]
- for heterosexual and same-sex couples, joint liability for council tax. Although a person's liability ceases at the date of death, the estate and the surviving partner remain liable for any arrears.

The deceased's share in a jointly owned property is not part of her/his estate and passes directly to the other co-owners, regardless of whether the deceased made a will or died intestate. It is, therefore, not available to creditors unless, for example, a creditor has obtained a charging order on the beneficial interest of one of the owners (see p263), one of the joint owners was made bankrupt, or the ownership of the property was originally set up in unequal shares because, for instance, one of the parties contributed a lump sum to the purchase. The joint owners are now said to be 'tenants in common' as opposed to 'joint tenants'. The effect of this is that each of them has a potential estate against which her/his creditors (including unsecured creditors) can make a claim on that person's death. Joint owners should be advised to seek financial advice on the most appropriate method of protecting themselves against potential claims on the estate by a co-owner's creditors, which could result in the loss of their home.

Even if the co-owners are not tenants-in-common, since 2 April 2001, if a creditor presents a bankruptcy petition against the deceased and an order is made, the court can require the surviving owner(s) to pay the value of the deceased's share on the date of death to the trustee. The petition must be presented within five years of the death. It is advisable for a client faced with this possibility to make a payment arrangement with the creditor(s) rather than risk a sale of the property. Advice should be sought from a specialist.[5]

When a person has died and someone continues to live in her/his home and use services for which the dead person previously paid (eg, fuel and water), the survivor should open a new account in her/his own name as soon as possible after the death. In this way, s/he is stating a willingness to pay for future goods or services used and also demonstrating that s/he was not previously liable. It is important to ensure s/he does not agree to take responsibility for the deceased person's debt when s/he opens the new account (although the deceased person's estate, of which the house may be part, will be liable).

Some debts are paid off on death by insurance policies. Many mortgages and some consumer credit agreements will be covered, and advisers should check these.

Money owed by under-18-year-olds

If a client was under 18 (a 'minor') at the time a contract was made, check whether it was for 'necessaries'. If not, a court may decide the contract is not enforceable.

'Necessaries' are defined as 'goods suitable to the condition in life of a minor and her/his actual requirements at the time of sale and delivery'. Examples include fuel, clothes and possibly mobile phones. The client is expected to have paid no more than was 'reasonable' for such goods. Young people under 18 are often asked to provide a guarantor who is liable to pay if the client cannot (see p100). If there was no guarantor and the goods were not 'necessaries', the client need not pay and the creditor is unable to use the court to claim repayments. However, a court could order any goods to be returned if the supplier has suffered loss.

Advisers should also bear in mind that if the client specifically informed the creditor that s/he was 18 or over on the date of the contract, although s/he may not be liable for the debt, s/he could be prosecuted for fraud if s/he attempts to challenge liability.

Contracts made under 'undue influence'

If a contract has been made under 'undue influence' – ie, if a person has taken unfair advantage of her/his influence over another person, it may not be enforceable. Undue influence may be actual – eg, if a person has been subjected to oppression. It may also be presumed – ie, if a person is persuaded to enter into a contract by someone on whom s/he relies for advice and guidance and the transaction is explainable only on the basis that undue influence was used, because it puts the person at a substantial disadvantage.[6] This issue can often arise with guarantees (see p100).

Misrepresentation of the terms of the contract

If one party misrepresents the terms of a contract to another – ie, inaccurately explains the transaction, the latter party may be able to avoid the transaction. For example, if a creditor persuades a client to sign a legal charge by stating that a secured loan does not put her/his home at risk, the loan may not be enforceable as the client would have the right to cancel the legal charge.

The client can seek compensation for any loss suffered as a consequence of a misrepresentation. As it is difficult to prove oral misrepresentation, it is important that the adviser obtains copies of all relevant correspondence. Alternatively, if the misrepresentation can be established, the creditor may decide not to pursue the debt for fear of bad publicity.

In the case of agreements regulated by the Consumer Credit Act 1974, if the finance is arranged through the supplier or dealer, the lender is jointly and severally liable with the supplier/dealer for any misrepresentations made by the supplier/dealer in relation to both the goods or services supplied and the credit agreement (see Chapter 4).

Capacity to make a contract

A contract is only valid if someone has the 'capacity' to make it. The Mental Capacity Act 2005 (fully in force since 1 October 2007) contains the following principles.

- A person lacks capacity in relation to a contract if, at the time the contract is entered into, s/he is unable to make a decision for her/himself about the contract because of an impairment of, or a disturbance in the functioning of, her mind or brain (the impairment or disturbance may be permanent or temporary).
- A person is assumed to have capacity unless it is established that s/he does not.
- A person should not be treated as unable to make a decision merely because s/he makes an unwise decision.
- A person is unable to make a decision for her/himself if s/he is unable to:
  - understand the information relevant to the decision, including information about the reasonably foreseeable consequences of deciding one way or another;
  - retain that information (the fact that s/he is only able to retain the information for a short period does not prevent her/him from being able to make the decision);
  - use or weigh up that information as part of the process of making the decision; *or*
  - communicate her/his decision, whether by talking, using sign language or any other means.

This means that if someone is unable to understand the nature and effect of the transaction, particularly the responsibilities involved, because of, for example, the influence of alcohol or drugs, mental ill health or a learning disability, the contract may not be enforceable *provided* the creditor either knew or ought to have known of the person's incapacity.

Advisers sometimes assume that, because a client has mental health or learning difficulties, any agreement s/he has entered into is automatically unenforceable.

This cannot just be assumed and medical evidence will usually be necessary to establish the client's inability to understand the transaction in question. In many cases, the client's lack of capacity can be established, but not the creditor's knowledge or presumed knowledge. However, it will often be possible to ask the creditor to write off the debt, either because there is evidence of inappropriate lending and/or the client's situation is such that setting up a debt repayment programme is not a realistic strategy.[7] For further information on dealing with clients with mental health issues, see p46.

A client who 'lacks capacity' for the purposes of the Mental Capacity Act 2005 is a 'protected party' where county court proceedings are concerned and can only take part in those proceedings through another person, known as a 'litigation friend'. A creditor can issue a claim and it can be served on a client who is a protected party even if s/he does not have a litigation friend, but any further steps taken before a litigation friend has been appointed – eg, entering default judgment or taking enforcement action, is of no effect unless the court subsequently ratifies it.[8] This means that the court could set aside the judgment and the enforcement action.

Specialist advice should be sought if the enforceability of a contract on the grounds of incapacity is being considered or if someone who appears to lack capacity is involved in court proceedings.

Housing disrepair

In many cases where there are rent arrears, landlords have not always fulfilled their obligations in connection with repairs. The amount of rent arrears claimed by the landlord can then be reduced by either a 'set-off' or a 'counterclaim' by the tenant. A 'set-off' is money spent by the tenant to carry out repairs required by law and is, therefore, owed to the tenant by the landlord. A 'counterclaim' is money claimed by the tenant as compensation for a failure to repair and the resultant loss.[9] Specialist housing advice should be sought.

Faulty goods and services

If a client owes money on faulty goods or unsatisfactory services, s/he may be able to avoid paying all or part of the bill. A client may be able to obtain a refund on goods that are not of satisfactory quality or not as described.[10] The goods must be rejected immediately or very soon after purchase. Similarly, services should be carried out with reasonable care and skill and within a reasonable time.[11] In addition, faulty goods or services may entitle the purchaser to claim for whatever expenses s/he has incurred as a result of the fault. Dangerous goods should be reported to the local trading standards department.

Insurance

Many loans are covered by insurance against sickness and unemployment, known as payment protection insurance. If the terms of the insurance policy are met, it will make repayments towards contractual instalments. Advisers should always check to see if repayments of a credit debt (secured or unsecured) are covered by insurance. Some policies only provide cover for a set period of time and, in the case of joint agreements, for only one of the parties, often the first person named in the agreement.

Payment protection insurance is often paid for with a single premium, which is then funded as part of the credit agreement and so interest is charged on it. If the client defaults, s/he can still claim under the policy because the premium has already been paid. Alternatively, the insurance is paid for through the monthly repayments under the credit agreement, but is not part of the credit provided under the agreement. If the client defaults, the policy often provides for it to lapse after, say, three missed payments.

In some cases, insurance companies refuse to pay – eg, if the client has an illness that started before the insurance policy began (a 'pre-existing condition') or was not actually employed when the policy was taken out. Some policies only provide cover for people under 65 or exclude certain situations altogether – eg, voluntary redundancy. In other cases, delays in processing claims result in creditors applying default interest/charges and/or threatening enforcement action.

Payment protection insurance is invariably purchased at the same time as the credit agreement is entered into. Financial Services Authority (FSA) rules state that before agreeing to take out the insurance, clients must receive a policy summary containing its 'main characteristics' – ie, duration, price, benefits and 'significant' exclusions and limitations. In this context, something is significant if it would affect the client's decision whether or not take out the policy.[12]

There is considerable evidence of payment protection insurance being mis-sold. A study by Citizens Advice found cases in which people who were unemployed or who had mental health problems were persuaded to take out insurance even though they would never have been able to claim under the policy.[13] Clients often report that they were told that the finance was conditional on insurance being taken out. Mis-selling also often accompanies irresponsible lending.

If the client suggests that taking out a single premium insurance policy was a condition of being given the finance, the whole agreement may be unenforceable (see p56).

Many insurance contracts in which the premium is payable by a single up-front payment contain terms preventing clients from receiving a refund if they repay the loan early ('nil refund' terms) or decide to cancel the policy before the end of the repayment period. The FSA view is that nil refund terms may be unfair under the Unfair Terms in Consumer Contracts Regulations 1994/1999. In cases where a refund is allowed, but this is not calculated on a *pro rata* basis, this may be considered an unfavourable term that should have been drawn to the client's attention at the outset. The FSA expects firms to provide partial refunds if the client cancels the insurance for any reason, unless the policy is very near its end or a claim has already been paid out.

The adviser must check the terms of the policy and the client's circumstances carefully, investigate any evidence of mis-selling and negotiate with the creditor and/or the insurance company as appropriate. If the client's complaint is about the way the claim has been handled, s/he must first use the insurance company's complaints procedure and can then complain to the Financial Ombudsman Service (see Appendix 1). If the policy has been mis-sold, the adviser should seek either a refund of the premium or a reduction of the debt by the amount of the premium plus interest/charges. Again, any complaint must first of all be made to the creditor before being taken to the Ombudsman.

Inaccurate calculations

Advisers should not assume that the amounts owed by clients have been accurately calculated. They must check the client's own records of payments and that all payments have been credited to the account, and, if in doubt, request a full statement to confirm this.

The adviser should also request that any recovery action be suspended while the matter is being investigated. It may be necessary to contact a regional or head office if negotiations with the local branch are unsuccessful. If the creditor is not being co-operative in supplying information and the debt is regulated by the Consumer Credit Act 1974, the adviser should write to the creditor asking for a full statement of account under sections 77 and 78 of the Consumer Credit Act and enclose a payment of £1. If the creditor fails to comply with the request within 12 working days (in effect, two weeks), the debt will be unenforceable until the information is supplied.[14] See p112 for more information about using sections 77 and 78.

Mistaken payments

A client's bank account may be mistakenly credited with money to which the client is not entitled. Although the creditor or bank has made a mistake, generally, a client is legally required to repay money which does not belong to her/him. However, a client does not have to repay money if s/he has 'changed position' through believing in good faith that the money was hers/his. Spending the money on ordinary day-to-day living expenses or repaying a debt is not a change of position, but buying something that s/he would not otherwise have bought is.

It must be unfair for the client to have to repay the money. It is not unfair if:

- the client has acted in bad faith – eg, was aware of the mistake; *and/or*

- full or partial repayment is possible because all or some of the money is still in her/his possession.

The bank should not pay the money back to the party that made the mistaken payment into the account without the client's permission.[15]

Similar issues arise where creditors mistakenly understate how much a client owes on a mortgage or other loan. Some people consider the creditor must accept the figure it has mistakenly quoted, rather than the correct, higher, figure. If the debt is regulated by the Consumer Credit Act 1974 and the creditor has provided a figure to the client under the provisions of the Act, the creditor is bound by the information supplied (although a court can grant such relief to the creditor as it feels is just).[16] Otherwise, the 'change of position' principles explained above apply. If a client is required to repay money or pay an additional amount, the adviser should argue that s/he should be allowed to (re)pay by affordable instalments without the addition of any (further) interest or other charges.

Default charges

Many credit agreements (as well as mortgages and secured loans) make provision for the creditor to add charges to the client's account in certain circumstances. These are sometimes referred to as arrears charges or penalty charges. Usually, the amount of the charge is fixed. Often, such charges accrue interest while they remain unpaid. Examples of situations in which charges are imposed include late payment, exceeding a credit limit, dishonoured cheques and unauthorised overdrafts. All these situations involve a breach of contract by the client and the charges are supposed to reflect the damages or financial loss for the creditor from this. The courts will only enforce such provisions if they are seen as a genuine attempt to estimate in advance the loss the creditor will face for the additional administration involved in the client's breach of contract. The provisions are then enforceable as 'liquidated damages'. Otherwise, it may be possible to challenge the charges either as:

- a 'penalty' at common law; *or*
- an unfair term under the Unfair Terms in Consumer Contracts Regulations 1994.

In *Dunlop Pneumatic Tyre Co Ltd v New Garage and Motor Co* the House of Lords gave the following guidance to help establish whether a charge is liquidated damages (enforceable) or a penalty (unenforceable).[17]

- It will be a penalty if the sum stipulated for is 'extravagant and unreasonable' in amount in comparison with the greatest loss which could conceivably be proved to have followed from the breach – ie, the sum claimed is disproportionately higher than the costs and expenses reasonably incurred by the creditor.

- It will be a penalty if the breach consists only in not paying a sum of money and the amount of the charge exceeds the amount of the unpaid sum.
- It may be a penalty when a single lump sum is made payable by way of compensation on the occurrence of one or more of several events, some of which may occasion serious and others but trifling damage – ie, the same charge is payable regardless of the seriousness of the breach.

Although the case is nearly a hundred years old and the language is rather archaic, the above still represents the law on penalties today. If:

- the client is a 'consumer' – ie, is not making the contract in the course of business; *and*
- the agreement was made on or after 1 July 1995; *and*
- the contract is in the creditor's standard form – ie, it has not been individually negotiated,

a term is unfair where, 'contrary to the requirements of good faith, it causes a significant imbalance in the parties' rights and obligations arising under the contract to the detriment of the consumer'.[18]

An unfair term is not 'binding' on the client and so cannot be enforced against her/him by the creditor, although the remainder of the agreement is unaffected provided it is capable of continuing without the unfair term.[19] Examples of unfair terms include those:[20]

- requiring clients who fail to fulfil their obligations to pay a disproportionately high sum in compensation;[21]
- that irrevocably bind clients to terms with which they had no real opportunity of becoming acquainted before the conclusion of the contract.[22]

Complaints about unfair terms can be made to the OFT (or to the FSA in relation to activities which it regulates), which can investigate the complaint and require the creditor to amend its contract terms to remove any unfairness or potential unfairness.

In *Calculating Fair Default Charges in Credit Card Contracts* (OFT 842), the OFT suggests a threshold figure of £12, above which a default charge will usually be presumed to be unfair, whilst recognising that a figure below this level might be unfair in individual circumstances. This apparently contradictory statement means the OFT will not take regulatory action over an unfair charge if the figure involved is less than £12, but this does not prevent individual challenges by clients. The document states that its principles apply to similar default terms in other agreements, including mortgages, current accounts and store cards. It is available from www.oft.gov.uk under 'News and Publications'.

If an adviser believes that a default charge is a penalty/unfair term, s/he should first check the relevant terms of the agreement and, if the agreement allows the creditor to levy the charge(s) in question, write to the creditor:

- pointing out that the default charges do not reflect the creditor's actual or anticipated loss in the particular circumstances of the client's breach of contract and are, therefore, a penalty and irrecoverable at common law;
- stating that the default charges are also an unfair term contrary to paragraph 1(e) Schedule 1 to the Unfair Terms in Consumer Contracts Regulations 1994/1999 because they require the client to pay a disproportionately high sum in compensation for her/his failure to perform the obligations under the contract;
- requiring the creditor either to refund these charges to her/his account or else justify the level of default charges.

If the client is not satisfied with the creditor's response, s/he could consider either issuing a county court claim for a refund, or taking the matter through the creditor's complaints procedure to the Financial Ombudsman Service (see p21) or part-defending any court action taken by the creditor.[23]

Following a well-publicised series of successful claims by clients through the county court and the Financial Ombudsman Service for repayment of what were alleged to be excessive bank charges on unauthorised overdrafts, a Mr Berwick finally lost a case in Birmingham County Court. The bank argued that the charges had not been imposed for breach of contract and so were not penalties. It further argued that the charges were the price paid for the bank's services and so could not be assessed for unfairness under the Unfair Terms in Consumer Contracts Regulations 1994. Unfortunately, Mr Berwick was unable to produce his terms and conditions, and so was unable to establish that he was being charged a penalty. The judge also agreed with the bank that charges for a service could not be assessed for unfairness.[24]

Following this decision, the OFT began a test case in the High Court against a number of lenders. In a preliminary decision, the judge decided that, as none of the terms and conditions produced by the OFT contained a prohibition on going overdrawn, the banks' charges were not a penalty. However, the charges were not imposed in exchange for a service but because the account had gone overdrawn, and so the OFT could assess them for unfairness.[25] Advisers should note that this decision (which the lenders are appealing) does not mean that unauthorised overdraft charges are unfair. This has yet to be decided, and cases pending in the county court, complaints to lenders and the Ombudsman remain on hold. Cases and complaints, however, must still be brought within the appropriate time limits. The FSA has recommended that banks continue to deal with complaints where the client alleges s/he has been caused financial hardship.

Note: *Calculating Fair Default Charges in Credit Card Contracts* can still be used in other situations referred to in it, such as credit card charges, where there are express terms and conditions about making the minimum monthly payment and not exceeding the credit limit.

2. Using the Consumer Credit Act to challenge or reduce liability

The Consumer Credit Act (see p50) regulates the way in which most credit agreements can be set up. It gives the borrower certain rights and, if these are denied, a court may decide that the agreement is unenforceable and, therefore, the creditor will not be able to require repayment.

Requests for information

In order to check the client's liability for the debt and the amount the creditor is claiming to be due, advisers often need to contact the creditor for information. Creditors are required to provide certain information within 12 'working days' – ie, excluding weekends and bank holidays. If they do not, the agreement is unenforceable unless and until they do provide it.[26] In some circumstances if it occurred before 26 May 2008, a failure to provide the information is also an offence.

The client is entitled to request that the creditor provide:

- a copy of the executed agreement (a 'true copy' but not necessarily a photocopy – see p113);
- a copy of any other document referred to in the agreement – eg, a bill of sale but not a default notice;
- a statement of account containing prescribed information (not just the amount of arrears).

The request must be in writing and must include the prescribed fee of £1 per credit agreement. It is recommended that advisers use either first-class post or 'recorded signed for'.

When to make a request

- To obtain information which the adviser has been unable to get voluntarily and which is required to deal with the client's case.
- To prevent enforcement action from being commenced while the adviser is investigating liability.
- To halt enforcement action already taking place to enable the adviser to investigate liability.

Possible responses

- No reply. Send a reminder after 14 days pointing out that the agreement is now unenforceable unless and until the creditor complies with the request.
- No reply and the creditor contacts the client for payment. Point out that not only is the agreement unenforceable until a statement/copy of the agreement is provided, but an offence has been committed (if 12 working days plus one

month has elapsed since the request was made and that period expired before 26 May 2008). Consider reporting any offence to trading standards and complaining about any breaches of the Office of Fair Trading's (OFT) *Debt Collection Guidance*.[27]

- The creditor says the request must come from client personally. People can usually act through agents and the Consumer Credit Act does not require the debtor to act in person in this situation. As creditors have been known to raise this as an issue, it may be advisable for the client to sign the request.
- The debt has been sold and the new creditor ('debt purchaser') says it does not have the information and does not have to provide it because they are not the 'creditor'. The definition of 'creditor' in s189 Consumer Credit Act 1974 includes someone to whom the original creditor's rights and duties under the agreement have passed – eg, by assignment. Some debt purchasers argue that they only purchase the rights, not the duties, and so do not fit within the definition of 'creditor'. They also argue (correctly) that, so long as the client has had notice of the assignment, the debt purchaser is entitled to enforce the agreement, including by issuing court proceedings. But the 'right' to enforce the agreement carries with it the 'duty' to comply with the Consumer Credit Act (which is not a liability under the agreement). In addition, the right to enforce is not an absolute right because, if the client had a defence to any claim brought by the original creditor – eg, that the agreement is unenforceable, the client also has a defence to any claim brought by the debt purchaser.
- The creditor says it does not have to comply with the request because, for example, the loan repayment period is over or the account has been terminated. However, s77(3) Consumer Credit Act 1974 says that the duty to comply with a request does not apply where no sum is, or will or may become payable by the client and so by implication does apply if a sum is, will be or may become payable by the client, which is the case if the creditor is demanding payment.
- The creditor does not provide a photocopy but only a *pro forma* agreement with no client signature. The rules say that the creditor must supply a 'true copy', which can omit any signature and so this does comply with the Act. However, not supplying a photocopy is an indication that the creditor does not have the original with the client's signature.[28]
- The creditor complies with the request. Check the agreement to see whether any other documents are referred to in it, which could help the client's case, and ask for copies. The adviser should now be in a position to deal with the client's case.

Obtaining information

There are other arguments that can be put to creditors/debt purchasers who fail or refuse to supply copies of agreements. Both the OFT's *Debt Collection Guidance*[29] and Credit Services Association's Code of Practice[30] place obligations on creditors, debt collectors and debt purchasers to provide information and any failure to comply could be a breach of the Consumer Protection from Unfair Trading Regulations (see p26). If court action is threatened, the pre-action protocols require the parties to act reasonably in exchanging information (see p235) and, if a claim is defended, the creditor (whether the original creditor or a debt purchaser) will have to produce any 'relevant documents'.[31]

Advisers should note that the real issue here is not whether the creditor/debt purchaser is able to produce a copy of the agreement, but whether a properly executed agreement complying with the Consumer Credit Act 1974 has ever actually existed. Failure to comply with sections 77 and 78 is only a temporary defence to a county court claim in that the creditor can always comply by producing a 'true copy' and, in the meantime, the court is likely to stay the case – ie, halt the case from proceeding further pending compliance. If a client does not dispute the existence of a properly executed agreement, but the adviser is considering defending a claim on the grounds that the original creditor/debt purchaser/collector failed to produce a copy of the agreement, the adviser should seek specialist advice.

Unlicensed creditors

If a creditor enters into a regulated agreement (see p54), but does not hold a current consumer credit licence, s/he cannot enforce that agreement without permission from the OFT. S/he also commits a criminal offence.[32] If a creditor appears to be unlicensed – eg, because the company is clearly new, badly organised and unprofessional, its documentation is of a poor standard, or the adviser has not heard of it before – the adviser can check whether it has a licence by searching the Consumer Credit Register online at http://www2.crw.gov.uk/pr/Default.aspx. Creditors who are not licensed will sometimes withdraw at this point when the need for a licence is pointed out to them. In the meantime, the client should be advised that s/he need not pay and informed of her/his rights concerning harassment (see p24) and under the OFT's *Debt Collection Guidance* (see p24).

Early settlement of a credit agreement

If a regulated agreement is ended early by the client, s/he should pay less than the total amount that would have been payable if the agreement had run to its full term.[33] A formula (the 'Rule of 78') is contained in the Early Settlement Regulations 1983 as a means of ensuring that creditors can recoup costs associated with setting up an agreement and, therefore, a lower percentage rebate is given for settlement during the earliest parts of a credit agreement.

Note: the Rule of 78 has been replaced with a formula for agreements made on or after 31 May 2005.[34] The Rule of 78 continues to be used for pre-31 May 2005 agreements:

- until 31 May 2007 if the agreement was for a term of ten years or less;
- until 31 May 2010 if the agreement was for a term of more than ten years.

Extortionate credit

People who have financial problems, are on low incomes or are otherwise vulnerable are particularly susceptible to exploitation. The Consumer Credit Act 1974 contains provisions enabling a court to re-open a credit agreement which it finds to be an 'extortionate credit bargain'. A credit bargain is extortionate if it requires a borrower to make payments which are 'grossly exorbitant' or which otherwise 'grossly contravenes ordinary principles of fair dealing'.

However, it has long been recognised that these provisions have not been effective. Few cases reach the courts and even fewer have been successful. From 6 April 2007, the extortionate credit provisions were replaced with the unfair relationship provisions (see below).

Unfair relationships

The Consumer Credit Act 2006 introduced the concept of an 'unfair relationship'.[35] This enables a borrower to challenge a credit agreement on the grounds that the relationship between the creditor and the borrower in connection with the agreement (or a related agreement) is unfair to the borrower. These provisions are in addition to the Financial Ombudsman Service's new 'consumer credit jurisdiction' (see p121).

The provisions in the Act attempt to address situations where the creditor has taken 'unfair advantage' of the borrower or there has been 'oppressive' or 'exploitative' conduct (but not where the borrower has simply made a 'bad bargain'). They replace the extortionate credit provisions and have applied since 6 April 2007 (see below if the agreement was made before this date). The provisions apply equally to regulated and non-regulated agreements, including exempt agreements, and regardless of the amount of credit involved, except where the agreement is exempt because it is a regulated mortgage contract (see p87) and so regulated by the FSA.

An order may be made on a client's application, either as a stand-alone application or as part of court proceedings relating to the credit agreement or a related agreement. If the client alleges that the credit relationship is unfair, the onus of proof is on the creditor to show that the relationship is not unfair. It is not sufficient merely to assert that the relationship is unfair: the facts in support of the allegation must be set out.

What is an unfair relationship

The Consumer Credit Act 2006 does not define an unfair relationship. However, it does set out in general terms, factors that may give rise to an unfair relationship. These are:

- the terms of the credit agreement or a related agreement;
- the way in which the creditor has exercised or enforced its rights under the agreement (or a related agreement);
- anything done (or not done) by or on behalf of the creditor either before or after making the agreement (or a related agreement).

In some cases, unfair contract terms may be sufficient in themselves to give rise to an unfair relationship, but the court can also look at:

- the way agreements are introduced and negotiated;
- the way in which agreements are administered; *and*
- any other aspect of the relationship it considers relevant.

The Act includes both acts and omissions – eg, a failure to take certain steps which in the interests of fairness the creditor might reasonably be expected to have taken.

It also includes actions or lack of action on behalf of the creditor – ie, on the part of employees, associates and agents such as brokers and debt collectors, including:

- pre-contract business practices such as misleading advertisements, mis-selling products, high-pressure selling techniques, 'churning' (see p117) and irresponsible lending;
- post-contract actions, such as demanding money the borrower has not agreed to pay and aggressive debt-collection practices;
- failing to provide key information in a clear and timely manner or to disclose material facts.

Although OFT guidance (OFT 854), available at www.oft.gov.uk, does not define an 'unfair relationship', it outlines the OFT's opinion on what it means for the purpose of exercising its regulatory powers. Until there are some court decisions, it should be the starting point for advising clients.

Definitions

A '**related agreement**' is:

- a credit agreement consolidated by the main agreement; *or*
- a linked transaction in relation to the main agreement (or a consolidated agreement); *or*
- a security provided in relation to the main agreement (or a consolidated agreement or a linked transaction).

For example, payment protection insurance is likely to be a linked transaction.

An agreement is 'consolidated' by a later agreement if:

- the later agreement is entered into, in whole or in part, for purposes connected with debts owed under the earlier agreement; *and*

- at any time before the later agreement is entered into, the parties to the earlier agreement included the client under the later agreement and either the creditor or an associate or former associate.

This addresses the practice (known as '**churning**') of creditors entering into successive agreements with a client (often before the earlier agreement has been paid off) and which usually involves not only re-financing the earlier agreement, but also providing extra finance, charging additional fees and selling further payment protection insurance, and which may, in itself, give rise to an unfair relationship. The purpose of the provisions is to enable the court to look at the whole course of dealings between the parties (ie, the relationship).

An agreement is not a related agreement if the later agreement is with a different creditor, unless the new creditor is an 'associate' or 'former associate' of the original creditor. The fact that the earlier agreement has been paid off by the later, consolidating, agreement does not mean that the earlier agreement cannot be challenged, since an application can be made even though the relationship has ended (although there are transitional arrangements for pre-6 April 2007 agreements – see p119).

Under the extortionate credit provisions, the courts decided that only the transaction in question could be challenged and that the agreement could only be considered at the time it was made. The unfair relationships provisions are much wider.

In place of the list of specific factors found in the extortionate credit provisions (prevailing interest rates, the debtor (eg, age, experience, business capacity, state of health, degree of financial pressure) and the creditor (eg, degree of risk having regard to the value of any security), the court must take into account all matters it thinks relevant, including matters relating to the individual client and creditor. This means that a term or practice may not be unfair in a particular case because of the client's knowledge or experience, but may be unfair in another client's case if s/he is more vulnerable or susceptible to exploitation. There is also an expectation that clients will act honestly in providing accurate and full information to enable the creditor to assess risk.

The provisions apply to completed agreements – ie, there is no longer any sum which is or may become payable (subject to transitional provisions – see p119) and also where a judgment has been made.

Identifying potential unfair relationship situations

Possible examples of unfairness include:

- compounding default interest and charges, resulting in a very large debt;
- mis-selling subsidiary insurance products, such as payment protection insurance, including selling inappropriate products, aggressive selling and misleading borrowers into believing that a product is compulsory, or in a client's interests, when it is not;

- applying post-judgment interest to a debt without having informed the client;
- misleading clients about their legal rights – eg, misrepresenting a client's right to terminate voluntarily a conditional sale or hire purchase agreement or dishonestly obtaining a client's consent for protected hire purchase goods to be repossessed without a court order;
- draconian and/or unreasonable use of enforcement rights or powers – eg, in respect of bills of sale, agreements secured on land, and the use of charging orders and orders for sale for unsecured debts;
- unreasonable use by creditors of the power to vary interest rates – eg, increasing them as base rates rise, but not reducing them as base rates fall;
- charging unjustified, or unjustifiable, default charges – ie, unlawful penalties;
- breaching the OFT's licensing provisions and guidance – eg, the *Debt Management Guidance*, the *Non-status Lending Guidelines* and the *Debt Collection Guidance*, or the FSA rules and guidance;
- breaching trade associations' codes of practice – eg, the Banking Code, the Finance and Leasing Association Code and the Credit Services Association Code;
- unfair practices under the Consumer Protection Regulations;
- exploiting vulnerable clients and clients with little financial knowledge or experience;
- agreements with excessive costs, such as where charges are much higher than those applicable generally in the particular market sector or those payable by clients in similar situations, including excessive interest rates – eg, the high rates charged under bills of sale;
- failing to disclose relevant information or giving false, partial or misleading information to clients;
- applying unreasonable pressure on clients to sign agreements, particularly in face-to-face situations, and not giving clients sufficient time to read and consider the terms of an agreement or to take independent advice where appropriate;
- secret commissions – eg, an undisclosed fee paid by a creditor to a broker who has also received a fee paid by the client;
- irresponsible lending, including irresponsible consolidation of debts ('churning');
- replacing irredeemably unenforceable agreements with new agreements after 6 April 2007;
- 'coin-slot' hire purchase agreements, where each time a further item is purchased a modifying agreement is entered into, creating obstacles to the client terminating the agreement and returning certain items whilst continuing the agreement in respect of the remaining items.

Whichever factors are being relied on must have the effect of making the relationship unfair 'as a whole'. There is currently no caselaw to indicate how the courts will interpret this phrase.

Remedies

If the court determines that the relationship is unfair to the borrower, it can:

- require the creditor, or any associate or former associate, to repay (in whole or part) any sum paid by the client by virtue of the credit agreement or any related agreement; *and/or*
- require the creditor, or an associate or former associate, to do, not to do, or to cease anything specified in the order in connection with the agreement or a related agreement; *and/or*
- reduce or discharge any sum payable by the client by virtue of the agreement or a related agreement; *and/or*
- set aside (in whole or part) any duty imposed on the client by virtue of the agreement or a related agreement; *and/or*
- alter the terms of the agreement or any related agreement.

Where security is provided in relation to a credit agreement or linked transaction, any surety can also apply to the court under the unfair relationships provisions. In addition to the above orders, the court can order the return to a surety of any property provided by her/him for the purposes of security.

Relevant dates

The unfair relationships provisions have applied since 6 April 2007 to credit agreements entered into on or after this date.

From 6 April 2008, the new rules have applied to agreements made before this date, unless the agreement was paid off in full by then. Such agreements remain subject to the extortionate credit bargain provisions in the Consumer Credit Act 1974. Advisers who are considering arguing that there is a case of extortionate credit should seek specialist advice.

The court's powers to make an order under the unfair relationship provisions are not limited to matters arising after 6 April 2007. The court can also take into account matters arising before this date. In considering a current agreement (whenever it was made), the court can take into account a related agreement made before 6 April 2007, but cannot make an order for repayment of any sum paid under a related agreement if that agreement ceased to be in operation before 6 April 2007.

In practice, the OFT anticipates that most consumers are likely to seek out-of-court resolution of disputes rather than initiate court proceedings, which may be costly and time-consuming. Nevertheless, the unfair relationship provisions are an important additional protection for clients, and may be especially useful for people facing court proceedings for enforcement or repossession, or where the restrictions on the Ombudsman granting a remedy for conduct before 6 April 2007 mean that the client has no option but to resort to the unfair relationship provisions and their retrospective effect in order to challenge the creditor or defend the claim. However, it should be viewed very much as a remedy of last resort – at least until there is some caselaw. Advisers who are considering taking advantage of these provisions should seek specialist advice.

Procedural irregularities

The Consumer Credit Act 1974 specifies procedures that must be followed for a regulated agreement to be properly executed.[36] Further provisions are contained in regulations (see p54).

An improperly executed regulated agreement is enforceable only by court order.[37] Such an order can only be made where the court has considered both the creditor's culpability for the improper execution and its effect on the client.[38]

If a creditor has an unenforceable agreement with a client, it should apply to the court for permission to enforce it. The court can allow enforcement on such terms as it thinks fit – eg, reduce the amount owed by the borrower, make a time order and reduce (see p283) or freeze interest/charges.[39]

The court has no power to order enforcement if the agreement was made before 6 April 2007 and:

- the agreement has not been signed by the client(s); *or*
- the agreement has been signed, but does not contain certain prescribed information (see p55 for details);
- in the case of a cancellable agreement, the client was not given a copy of the agreement before the creditor took court action, or told of her/his cancellation rights.[40]

If a creditor has an unenforceable agreement with a client, it should apply to the court for permission to enforce it. The court can allow enforcement on such terms as it thinks fit – eg, reduce the amount owed by the borrower, make a time order (see p283) and reduce or freeze interest/charges.[41]

If a loan is secured, the creditor cannot enforce the security in order to recover more than it could under the agreement. This means that if the agreement is unenforceable, then so is any security.[42]

A creditor may sue a client for payment of a debt without informing the court that the agreement is unenforceable. If this happens and judgment is entered against the client, s/he may be able to get the judgment 'set aside' (see p298). Specialist advice should be sought.

Mail order catalogues

Mail order catalogues are a common example of a situation where creditors do not obtain a signed agreement from the client in accordance with the Consumer

Credit Act 1974. Catalogue debts are usually regulated by this and so a request under section 78 could be made for a copy of any agreement (see p112). If the information is not sent within 12 working days, the agreement is unenforceable unless and until the information has been supplied. If the company has already started legal action in the county court, the debt could be disputed on the reply to the claim (see Chapter 9).

The above may be a useful tactic in any other case where the adviser suspects the client may not have signed a regulated agreement.

3. **Using the Financial Ombudsman Service**

The Financial Ombudsman Service (FOS) has been able to consider complaints against banks and building societies since December 2001 and against all other holders of consumer credit licences since 6 April 2007 (known as its 'consumer credit jurisdiction'). This means debt collectors, sub-prime lenders and debt purchasers are likely to be covered. Advisers should remember that the FOS is not a regulator (the relevant regulators are the Financial Services Authority and the Office of Fair Trading). The role of the FOS is to decide individual disputes between clients and businesses in accordance with its rules. In other words, the FOS is a form of alternative dispute resolution.

Businesses which fall within FOS jurisdiction are required to have in place, to publicise and to operate written complaints procedures. The FOS cannot consider a complaint unless the business has had an opportunity to deal with it. The first step, therefore, is always to complain in writing to the business. On receipt of a complaint, the business should:

- acknowledge the complaint promptly;
- keep the client informed of progress; *and*
- send a 'final response' in writing within eight weeks.

A final response is one which:

- either accepts the complaint and offers redress; *or*
- does not accept the complaint, but offers redress anyway; *or*
- rejects the complaint and gives reasons for this; *and*
- informs the client that if s/he remains dissatisfied s/he has a right to refer the matter to the FOS within six months, and encloses a consumer leaflet.

If no final response has been received after eight weeks, the client can refer the complaint to the FOS, provided it is within its jurisdiction (see p122). Even if it does not contain referral rights, provided a letter is clearly the business's last word on the matter, the FOS will accept the complaint even if less than eight weeks have elapsed.

Unless the circumstances are exceptional or the business does not object, a complaint must be made within:

- six months of the date of the final response (this time limit must have been made clear in the final response otherwise it will not apply);
- six years of the matter complained of taking place or, if later, three years of the client reasonably becoming aware s/he might have grounds for complaining.

The FOS does not consider complaints about the way businesses reach their commercial decisions and, in consumer credit cases, cannot consider complaints about events which occurred before 6 April 2007, although it can 'take account' of them. This means that if the complaint is about, for example, excessive charges added to an account before 6 April 2007 which the client did not find out about until after this date, the FOS cannot provide a remedy. On the other hand, if the complaint relates to excessive charges added to an account after 6 April 2007, the FOS can look at the agreement to see what it says, even if it was made before 6 April 2007. Banks and building societies within FOS jurisdiction before this date are not subject to this restriction, even if the complaint against them relates to a consumer credit agreement.

The FOS will not determine whether or not a relationship is unfair. It decides disputes on the basis of what is 'fair and reasonable'. It is there to resolve disputes: it is not on anyone's 'side'. The FOS looks at the relevant legislation, regulations, any official guidance, relevant codes of practice and standards, and good industry practice at the time of the conduct complained about. This means it can take into account the same issues that a court would consider, but can come to a different conclusion. The FOS has an inquisitorial remit and so conducts its own enquiries rather than just relying on what the parties tell it.

A complaint to the FOS should contain the following information:

- the client's details;
- details of the business complained about;
- reference/account numbers;
- copies of the final response (if any) and of any other relevant documents – eg, the agreement and correspondence;
- a summary of the complaint. This should set out the 'story' in the client's own words, if possible, rather than take the form of a legal-type submission (this can be done later in the process, if necessary);
- how the client wants the business to address the issue (the FOS does not grant a remedy just because a business has broken rules (that is the job of a regulator); there must be some consumer detriment (not necessarily financial – eg, distress, inconvenience, injury and damage to reputation);
- letter of authorisation (if the adviser is submitting the complaint on behalf of the client).

The complaints form is available online at www.financial-ombudsman.org.uk/consumer/complaints.htm. It must be printed off and posted. If the FOS accepts the complaint, it will attempt to resolve the dispute through mediation – ie, assisting the parties come to an agreement. If not, an adjudicator will form a preliminary view, which will be circulated to the parties. If they accept this, the dispute is settled. If they do not, the case is referred to an Ombudsman for determination. If the Ombudsman upholds the complaint, the business can be ordered to:

- pay compensation for financial loss (up to a limit of £100,000); *and/or*
- pay compensation for non-financial loss (this tends to be a few hundred pounds maximum); *and/or*
- take appropriate action to remedy the issue complained about – eg, remove excessive charges from an account.

FOS decisions are binding on the business, but not on the client, who can still take the matter to court if s/he remains dissatisfied (there is no appeal against a FOS decision). If the business fails to comply with the decision, it can be enforced through the courts. Advisers should seek specialist advice if this becomes necessary.

More information can be found on the FOS website (www.financial-ombudsman.org.uk), including technical and non-technical information and guidance. Informal guidance on FOS practice and procedure is available by telephoning 020 7964 144 or emailing technical.advice@financial-ombudsman.org.uk.[43]

4. Time limits for action

There are time limits in which to take court action to recover debts.[44] These are mainly contained in the Limitation Act 1980, although some debts have their own limitation period – eg, council tax. These time periods are known as **'limitation periods'**. Most limitation periods run from the date the 'cause of action accrued' – ie, the earliest time at which court action could be taken against the client.[45] The following are some of the most common limitation periods advisers will encounter.

- **Unsecured borrowing:** six years from default unless repayable 'on demand' when the time period does not start until the date of the demand.
- **Interest:** six years from default in payment. Each amount of interest charged to an account has its own six-year limitation period.
- **Fuel debt:** six years from the date of the bill.
- **Telephone charges:** six years from the date of the bill.
- **Water charges:** six years from the date of the bill.
- **Council tax:** six years from the date of the bill (demand notice).

- **Rent arrears:** six years from the date the rent became due. Each amount of rent due has its own six-year limitation period.
- **Possession of land** – ie, by a mortgage or secured lender or landlord: 12 years from default in payment.
- **Mortgage shortfall:** see p125.

Once the relevant limitation period has expired, a debt is said to be '**statute-barred**'. When calculating the limitation period, the date the cause of action accrued is ignored. For example, if the client defaulted on 30 November 2000, a six-year limitation period would have ended on 30 November 2006. If the limitation period has already started, but the law requires the creditor to serve a notice on the client before taking court action – eg, a default notice, the creditor cannot claim that the limitation period only starts when the notice is served, as otherwise the creditor could defer the start of the limitation period indefinitely.[46] (**Note**: if a loan is repayable 'on demand' – eg, an overdraft, until the demand is made there is no cause of action.) Limitation periods are only relevant to when the creditor must take the initial court proceedings. Time ceases to run when court proceedings are issued. If the creditor obtains a judgment, the law relating to limitation periods does not apply to the enforcement of that judgment.

A limitation period that has already started can be repeatedly re-started by an 'acknowledgement' or 'part-payment'.

Acknowledgements

In this context, an acknowledgement means that the client has, in effect, admitted liability for what is being claimed. No amount needs to be specified. An acknowledgment must be in writing and signed by the client (or her/his agent). The debt must be acknowledged either to the creditor or agent. This means the client cannot acknowledge a debt on the telephone and letters from the creditor to the client cannot re-start the limitation period. On the other hand, an adviser could inadvertently acknowledge a debt when writing to a creditor on behalf of the client.

An admission of part of a debt coupled with a denial of liability for the balance is not an acknowledgment of the disputed balance. The phrases 'outstanding amount' and 'outstanding balance' have been held to be acknowledgments.[47] An acknowledgment by one co-debtor only re-starts the limitation period against that debtor and not any co-debtors. Once a debt becomes statute-barred, it cannot be revived by any subsequent acknowledgment.

Part-payment

In order to re-start the limitation period, a payment must be made by the client (or a co-debtor) or agent, to the creditor or agent and must be in respect of the particular debt in question. For this purpose, the Department for Work and

Pensions (DWP) is treated as the client's agent when making payments of mortgage interest to lenders.[48]

A payment of interest re-starts the limitation period for the capital, but not the interest. **Note**: once the capital is statute-barred, so is any claim for interest, even if that interest was added to the account less than six years ago. Similarly, a payment of rent arrears does not re-start the limitation period for any other rent outstanding. Writing off part of a debt does not count as a payment. Once a debt has become statute-barred it cannot be revived by any subsequent payment (although the client cannot recover the payment, as the effect of a debt being statute-barred is only to prevent court action; the debt still legally exists and can be recovered by any other lawful method).

Advisers should note the difference between payments by co-debtors (which re-start the time limits against every other debtor) and acknowledgments by co-debtors (which only re-start the time against the acknowledger).

If a client receives a claim form for a debt which is statute-barred or partly statute-barred – eg, in the case of rent or interest, and the client wishes to avoid a judgment being made against her/him, s/he must defend the claim on the ground that the debt is statute-barred.[49] Although the client must raise a limitation defence, once s/he has done so, the onus switches to the creditor to prove that the claim is not statute-barred.

Mortgage shortfalls

Mortgage shortfall debts raise particular issues. If a property has been repossessed by the lender and the outstanding balance due under the mortgage is more than the proceeds of sale, this is known as a 'mortgage shortfall'.

Mortgage indemnity guarantees

Most, but not all, mortgage lenders have a normal lending limit of 70-80 per cent of the property value. If a borrower wants to borrow a higher proportion, say 95-100 per cent, these lenders will ask the borrower to pay for an insurance policy to protect the lender against a mortgage shortfall. This is the mortgage indemnity guarantee (or indemnity insurance or building society indemnity). The insurance premium is usually, but not always, paid as a lump sum of several hundred pounds at the time of purchase. Advisers should note that the mortgage indemnity guarantee (MIG) is to protect the lender, not the borrower. The only value to the borrower is that s/he will not be given the amount of mortgage s/he requires without agreeing to pay the insurance premium.

The MIG will not pay the full shortfall. The amount paid will be a proportion of the shortfall relative to the lending risk. There will, therefore, still be a shortfall owing to the lender.

However, the insurance company that provides the MIG can pursue the borrower for the money paid towards the mortgage shortfall under a process known as 'subrogation'. In some cases, the borrower may receive a demand for money from the insurer, even though the lender has agreed not to pursue the shortfall. Alternatively, some insurers appoint the lender to collect a client's liability on their behalf. In this case, the lender will contact the client to ask for payment of the entire shortfall. Commonly, the borrower can expect to receive a demand from the insurer and the lender for their respective proportions of the shortfall. Claims cannot be ignored and must be dealt with.

Challenging mortgage shortfall debts

Provided the loan remains secured, the lender has 12 years in which to take action to recover the principal amount (ie, the capital sum borrowed) and six years to recover arrears of interest. The position is complicated by the fact that the limitation period starts again every time the borrower or her/his representative acknowledges the debt (see p124). The limitation period for the principal (but not the interest) also starts again every time the borrower, a joint borrower or agent makes a payment into the account (including payments of mortgage interest by the DWP[50]). Once the limitation period has expired, it cannot be started again by further payments or acknowledgements.

In 1997 a judge in the Court of Appeal suggested that it was 'seriously arguable' that the six-year limit applied to the principal as well as to the interest.[51] After a period of considerable uncertainty, the Court of Appeal and House of Lords have now resolved the issue.

- The limitation period for the principal sum borrowed is 12 years from the date when the sum became payable under the terms of the mortgage deed, usually after the borrower has failed to pay two or three monthly instalments.[52]
- The limitation period for the interest is six years from the date when the lender had the right to receive that interest.[53]
- The fact that the mortgage deed contained an express provision under which the borrower agreed to pay any shortfall to the lender does not give the lender a fresh right of action starting on the date of sale.[54]
- The position is the same if the loan is regulated by the Consumer Credit Act 1974[55] or if the mortgage deed contains no covenant allowing the lender to call in the mortgage on default but it has, nevertheless, repossessed and sold the property.[56]
- The proceeds of sale will be treated as appropriated first to arrears of interest and then to capital.[57]

In the majority of cases, the shortfall will be made up of capital only because the interest will have been paid from the proceeds of sale and the whole debt will be subject to a 12-year time limit. This should, however, be checked with the lender.

As a concession, if:

- the lender is a member of the Council of Mortgage Lenders or subscriber to the Mortgage Code (or the MIG insurer is an Association of British Insurers member); *and*

- no contact about the shortfall has been made by the lender/insurer with the borrower before 11 February 2000,

lenders and insurers have agreed not to pursue the claim unless the borrower is contacted within six years of the date of sale of the property.

'Contact' includes letters or telephone calls received but ignored by the borrower, but should not include letters sent to a previous address, unless these have been forwarded, and does not include failed attempts to trace the borrower. This concession does not apply if the borrower was contacted before 11 February 2000 or had entered into a payment arrangement with the lender/insurer prior to that date, even if the contact was made more than six years after the property was sold.

Strategies

A mortgage shortfall debt is, in many ways, no different from any other unsecured debt, since once the property has been sold, it is no longer a priority debt. The strategies, tactics and principles of good money advice described throughout this *Handbook* still apply. However, the debt is often disproportionately high compared with the borrower's normal income and lifestyle. It can be very distressing for borrowers to be faced with such a huge debt.

Some lenders will already have a county court judgment for money. This does not prevent the borrower from using any of the strategies detailed, but in addition the adviser may need to protect the borrower's interest by applying to vary or suspend the judgment. This will be essential if the lender is attempting to enforce it (eg, by attachment of earnings) as the Limitation Act does not apply to enforcement action. Borrowers who have acquired assets, particularly another property, may be especially vulnerable. If possible, the borrower should try to resolve the shortfall debt before acquiring further assets such as a house or flat.

It is not unusual for borrowers to fail to give the lender details of their new address. Some may hope they will not be found. The Council of Mortgage Lenders has indicated that its members will vigorously pursue borrowers with shortfall debts, using tracing agents if necessary.

Before entering into negotiations, always check whether the Council of Mortgage Lenders/Association of British Insurers concession (known as 'the CML Agreement') applies. Go to the Consumer Information section under 'Debt Following Mortgage Possession' at www.cml.org.uk, and then use the preceding paragraphs to check the account and, if appropriate, note any points which may be used to challenge the extent of the debt.

It may be necessary to contact the lender to obtain information (taking care not to acknowledge the debt and re-start the limitation period). The information required may include:

- copies of any letters written by the lender to the client (which could confirm whether or not the CML agreement applies);

- a copy of the lender's 'completion statement' following the sale of the property (which will confirm the breakdown of the shortfall);
- a full statement of account (which will confirm when the last payment was made into the account by any of the borrowers); *and*
- copies of any letter(s) received by the lender from the client (which could be acknowledgements).

Additional information may also be required and advisers may wish to seek specialist advice if unclear how to proceed.

Otherwise consider the following strategies.

- **Write-off.** A total write-off is likely to be the most appropriate strategy where it can be demonstrated that the client has no available income or assets and that the position is unlikely to improve (see p214). In other cases, pressure should be brought (perhaps by using publicity or local politicians) to highlight the unfairness of seizing a person's home and also expecting repayment of the shortfall.
- **Bankruptcy** (see Chapter 12). Personal bankruptcy will legally and finally end the shortfall debt recovery process. It will usually be appropriate when the lender/insurer insists on pursuing the claim, but the borrower has no property or assets, little income and needs the peace of mind and fresh start that follows bankruptcy.
- **Individual voluntary arrangements** (see Chapter 12). An individual voluntary arrangement is usually only appropriate where the shortfall is modest and in proportion to other unsecured debts, and the borrower can afford substantial repayments and/or owns a home that would be at risk in bankruptcy proceedings, or if the lender obtained a charging order (see p258).
- **Full and final settlement.** Most lenders and insurance companies will agree to accept a smaller sum than the full outstanding shortfall debt. How much will be acceptable varies according to individual circumstance. Settlements in the region of 10 per cent to 50 per cent are not uncommon. For more information about full and final settlements, see p219. Advisers should ensure that any full and final settlement covers the claims of both the lender and any insurer.
- **Instalment payments.** Many lenders will accept modest monthly payments towards a substantial debt, where personal circumstances show this to be reasonable. The borrower may find it daunting to be asked to pay, say, £20 a month towards a debt of £35,000 because s/he cannot see an end. On the other hand, many lenders see token payments as recognition that the borrower is being responsible about the shortfall. Debt advisers should suggest that provided the borrower keeps up the payments for, say five years, the lender should accept this in full and final settlement and agree to write off the balance. For more information about partial write-offs, see p216. If the borrower has other non-priority debts and the mortgage shortfall is to be

included in a *pro rata* payment arrangement, the debt adviser should attempt to agree a total figure that the lender is prepared to accept for inclusion in the financial statement, on the basis that the balance will be written off on completion of the payment arrangement.

When preparing a strategy, bear in mind that if there was an MIG, there may be two separate demands to negotiate, one from the lender and one from the MIG insurer.

5. **Reducing gas and electricity charges**

Debts for the supply of gas or electricity will usually be priority debts (see Chapter 7). CPAG's *Fuel Rights Handbook* provides full details and legal references for advisers dealing with complex fuel debts (see Appendix 2)

Arrears of gas or electricity payments may arise as a result of high bills. While high bills may be caused by high consumption, price increases or previous underpayments, they may also be caused by estimated bills based on wrong assumptions about the amount of fuel used.

Note: it is possible to reduce charges by changing supplier. If there are arrears, the old supplier may object to the transfer unless the arrears are paid. This does not apply if the debt does not exceed £100. If the transfer goes ahead without objection, the arrears cannot be transferred to the new supplier.

Clients can also take steps to help save energy and reduce fuel bills. The Energy Saving Trust offers free advice on ways to reduce fuel consumption and should be aware of grants that are available locally to help cover the cost of energy efficiency measures. It has a freephone number (0800 512 012), which directs callers to their local office.

Estimated bills

If the bill is estimated and the estimated reading is higher than the actual reading, it is possible to reduce the amount owing. The bill will explain (often by means of an 'E' next to a reading) whether an estimated reading has been given. Suppliers are required to read meters at least once every two years. Clients can read their own meters and provide the supplier with their reading and so should never be disconnected on the basis of an estimated bill. The adviser should ask the client to read the meter and request an amended bill.

Liability for electricity and gas bills

Electricity

A person is liable to pay an electricity bill if:

- s/he is the owner/occupier of the premises supplied with electricity and s/he gave written notice requesting a supply of electricity; *or*

- s/he requested a supply of electricity over the phone; *or*
- s/he has signed a contract for the supply of electricity; *or*
- no one else was liable for the bill or their liability has come to an end (see below) and s/he has, in practice, been supplied with electricity.

A person is not liable to pay an electricity bill if:
- s/he has not a made a contract with a supplier (either in writing or, for example, over the phone); *and*
- someone else is liable to pay the bill and their liability has not come to an end (see below).

A person is no longer liable to pay an electricity bill if:
- s/he has terminated any contract in accordance with its terms (but s/he is still liable if s/he continues to be supplied with electricity); *or*
- s/he ceases to be the owner/occupier of the property, starting from the day s/he leaves the property, provided s/he has given at least two days' written notice of leaving; *or*
- written notice was not given prior to her/him leaving the property, on the earliest of:
  - two working days after s/he actually gave written notice of ceasing to be an owner/occupier; *or*
  - on the next day the meter is due to be read; *or*
  - when someone else either requires/requests a supply, or signs a contract for the supply, of electricity to those premises.

Clients should be advised to arrange for a final reading of the meter before leaving the property, if possible, and should, at least, read the meter themselves in order to be able to check their final bill.

Gas

A person is liable to pay a gas bill if:
- s/he was a British Gas 'tariff customer' before 1 March 1996 and has continued to be supplied with gas after that date; *or*
- the liability of the former tariff customer has ended or been terminated and s/he has continued to occupy the premises supplied with gas; *or*
- s/he entered into a contract for the supply of gas on or after 1 March 1996 by requesting a supply of gas (it is not necessary for the request to have been made in writing) and is being supplied under the terms of that contract; *or*
- her/his contract has come to an end or been terminated, but s/he has continued to be supplied with gas; *or*
- s/he is a new owner/occupier of premises on or after 1 March 1996 and has been supplied with gas, but has not entered into a contract for that supply (s/he has a 'deemed contract' for the supply of gas).

A person was a 'tariff customer' of British Gas if:

- s/he was the owner/occupier of premises supplied with gas; *and*
- s/he gave written notice requiring a supply of gas; *or*
- no one else was liable for the bill or their liability has come to and end (see below) and s/he was in practice supplied with gas.

The liability of a tariff customer ended when:

- s/he left the premises, provided s/he gave at least 24 hours' written notice that s/he intended to leave; *or*
- in a situation where written notice was not given before s/he left the premises, on the earliest of:
  - 28 days after s/he actually gave written notice that s/he had left; *or*
  - on the next day when the meter should have been read; *or*
  - on the day when someone else required a supply.

A person currently liable under an actual or deemed contract will remain liable until:

- s/he terminates the contract by giving 28 days' notice (but if s/he still occupies the premises and continues to be supplied with gas, s/he will still be liable to pay for the gas supplied); *or*
- s/he ceases to occupy the premises, provided s/he has given at least two working days' notice that s/he intended to leave; *or*
- if notice was not given before s/he left the premises, the earliest of:
  - 28 days after s/he informed the supplier that s/he has left the premises; *or*
  - the next date the meter was due to be read; *or*
  - the date when another person requires a supply of gas.

The notice does not necessarily have to be in writing. Clients should be advised to arrange for a final reading of the meter before leaving the property, if possible, and should, at least, read the meter themselves in order to be able to check their final bill.

The 'beneficial user' argument

Before privatisation, suppliers argued they were entitled to obtain payment from anyone who had actually used a supply. This was known as the 'beneficial user argument'. Some county courts agreed with the suppliers; others did not. The higher courts were never called on to rule about its validity.

Liability for electricity is now a matter of contract and if either there is no contract or someone else's liability under a contract has come to an end without a new contract being entered into, the user of the supply will be liable. In the case of gas, all supply is now either under the terms of a contract or 'deemed contract' so where there is no actual contract, the users is liable.[58]

Suppliers still take the view that, because there is a legal liability to pay for all fuel consumed, everyone who has lived in the property over the relevant period is jointly and severally liable. However, the law of contract does not presume that someone who is not a party to the contract is jointly and severally liable.

If a supplier is demanding payment from someone other than the person(s) named on the bill, the supplier's code of practice should be consulted and the complaints procedure used, where appropriate. This issue may come before the Energy Ombudsman at some stage for a ruling.

'Backbilling'

From July 2007 suppliers cannot recover fuel charges more than 12 months old if the supplier has:

- billed on estimated readings and has failed to use the readings provided either by the client or an official meter reader;
- billed on the basis of a four-digit reading when there is a five-digit meter at the premises;
- made a refund based on estimated rather than actual meter readings;
- failed to act on a query raised by the client about her/his bill or the meter.

If the client pays by direct debit, in addition to being unable to recover arrears that have arisen in the above situations, the supplier cannot recover any fuel charges more than 12 months old unless:

- the account has been correctly set up, payments taken and statements issued; *and*
- the supplier has reassessed the client's direct debits within the previous 15 months to ensure that her/his fuel consumption is covered (unless the client has failed to respond to a request from the supplier for a meter reading in order to carry out the reassessment); *and*
- it has been made clear on the statements that fuel consumption has been based on estimates.

Suppliers can recover charges more than 12 months old if estimated bills have been sent to the client, but s/he has not provided her/his own reading to the supplier, nor tried to challenge the bill in any other way.

Social tariffs

A 'social tariff' is a reduction on the standard tariff, which most suppliers offer to vulnerable or disadvantaged clients. Each supplier's scheme is different and, if the client does not qualify for a social tariff from her/his current supplier but would qualify with a different supplier, it will usually be in the client's best interests to switch suppliers.

Social tariffs are not advertised and have to be applied for by name.

Advisers should check the websites of their local suppliers to see what social tariffs are available, so they can identify clients who could take advantage of them.

Non-fuel items

Clients may owe money for items other than fuel, such as repairs or credit sale agreements. The client cannot be disconnected for such items. The adviser should reduce repayments by arranging to pay for fuel costs only and treating non-fuel items alongside other non-priority debts.

Meter faults

If a gas or electricity meter is registering fuel consumption at too high a rate, the client will receive a bill that is higher than it should be. According to the industry, meter faults are rare but, if the client believes a meter is faulty, the fuel supplier will check the accuracy of the meter if requested to do so.

See CPAG's *Fuel Rights Handbook* for more details (see Appendix 2).

Meter tampering

Tampering with a meter in order to prevent it registering or to reduce the amount it is registering is a criminal offence. Accusations of tampering usually follow a visit to the client's home by a meter reader who has noticed and reported something unusual about the meter. The supplier should write to the client informing her/him of an investigation into suspected tampering. If the meter is considered to be in a dangerous condition, it may be rendered unusable pending the investigation. The investigation should be carried out in accordance with the code of practice and advisers should obtain a copy of this from the supplier.

If a client is threatened with prosecution, s/he should be referred to a solicitor.

See CPAG's *Fuel Rights Handbook* for more details (see Appendix 2).

Notes

1. **Using the law of contract to challenge or reduce liability**

1 *RBS v Etridge (No.2)* [2002] HLR 37 (HL); see also G Skipwith, 'Banks, Solicitors, Husbands and Wives', *Adviser* 95
2 Ombudsman's complaint 47/1, *Adviser* 113
3 Para 2.4(f) states it is an unfair practice to pursue third parties for a debt when they are not liable.
4 *Sherrin v Brand* [1956] 1 QB, 403
5 Clients should be referred to *Land Registry Public Guide* 18, which can be downloaded from the Land Registry website at www.landregistry.gov.uk/assets/library/documents/public_guide_018.pdf
6 *RBS v Etridge (No.2)* [2002] HLR 37, HL; see also G Skipwith, 'Banks, Solicitors, Husbands and Wives', *Adviser* 95
7 See *Ombudsman News* 50, November/December 2005 for details of some complaints which illustrate the FOS approach (also abstracted in *Adviser* 114).
8 r21.3(4) CPR. See also C Bradley, 'The MCA 2005 and Litigation Issues', *Adviser* 127
9 *Defending Possession Proceedings*, Legal Action Group
10 s14 SGA 1979
11 s13 SGSA 1982
12 Insurance Code of Business 6.4
13 *Protection Racket*, Citizens Advice, September 2005
14 ss77-79 CCA 1974
15 *Crantrave Ltd v Lloyds Bank* (*Adviser* 87 abstracts); see also P Madge, 'Consultancy Corner', *Adviser* 101
16 s172 CCA 1974
17 *Dunlop Pneumatic Tyre Co Ltd v New Garage and Motor Co* [1915] AC 79, HL
18 Reg 5(1) UTCC Regs
19 Reg 8 UTCC Regs
20 Sch 2 UTCC Regs
21 Sch 2 para 1(e) UTCC Regs
22 Sch 2 para 1(i) UTCC Regs
23 See 'Penalty Charges on Credit Cards and Current Accounts', *Quarterly Account* 78, IMA, Winter 2005/06; G Skipwith, 'Penalty Shoot-out', *Adviser* 113
24 *Berwick v Lloyds TSB* (*Adviser* 123, consumer abstracts)
25 *Office of Fair Trading v Abbey National & others* [2008] EWHC 875 (*Adviser* 128, consumer abstracts)

2. **Using the Consumer Credit Act to challenge or reduce liability**

26 ss77 and 78 CCA 1974
27 For example, para 2.8(k) (not ceasing collection activity whilst investigating a reasonably queried or disputed debt).
28 Reg 3 Consumer Credit (Cancellation Notices and Copies of Documents) Regulations 1983, No.1557
29 para 2.8(i)
30 para 4(r)
31 r31.8 CPR
32 ss39 and 40 CCA 1974
33 ss94 and 95 CCA 1974
34 Consumer Credit (Early Settlement) Regulations 2004, No.1483
35 ss19–22 and Sch 3 paras14 –17 CCA 2006
36 ss60-64 CCA 1974
37 s65 CCA 1974
38 s127(1) CCA 1974
39 *National Mortgage Corporation v Wilkes* (*Legal Action*, October 1991)
40 s127(3) and (4) CCA 1974
41 *National Mortgage Corporation v Wilkes* (*Legal Action*, October 1991)
42 s113 CCA 1974

3. **Using the Financial Ombudsman Service**

43 For further information, see B Philbey, 'The FOS and Consumer Credit Complaints', *Quarterly Account* 4, IMA, Spring 2007; S Quigley, 'Ombudsman Takes on Consumer Credit Cases', *Adviser* 121

4. **Time limits for action**

44 For a discussion of tactics when dealing with statute-barred debts, see C Wilkinson, 'Consultancy Corner', *Adviser* 109, including a suggested response letter to a demand for payment.
45 *Reeves v Butcher* [1891] 2 QB 509
46 *Swansea CC v Glass* [1992] 2 All ER 680
47 *Bradford & Bingley v Rashid* [2006] UKHL 37 (*Adviser* 117 abstracts)
48 *Bradford & Bingley v Cutler* [2008] EWCA Civ 74 (*Adviser* 128 money advice abstracts)
49 para 13.1 PD 16 CPR
50 *Bradford & Bingley v Cutler* [2008] EWCA Civ 74 (*Adviser* 128 money advice abstracts)
51 *Hopkinson v Tupper,* 30 January 1997, CA, unreported (*Adviser* 63 abstracts)
52 s20(1) LA 1980
53 s20(5) LA 1980
54 *Bristol & West plc v Bartlett,* 31 July 2002, CA, unreported (*Adviser* 94 abstracts). For a full discussion of the issues, see P Madge, 'Out of the Blue', *Adviser* 61 and P Madge, 'About Face', *Adviser* 94.
55 *Scottish Equitable v Thompson* [2003] EWCA Civ 225 (*Adviser* 98 abstracts)
56 *West Bromwich Building Society v Wilkinson* [2005] UKHL 44, HL (*Adviser* 111 abstracts)
57 *West Bromwich Building Society v Crammer* [2002] EWCA 2618 Ch (*Adviser* 97 abstracts)

5. **Reducing gas and electricity charges**

58 Sch 2B para 8 GA 1986 as inserted by GA 1995; Sch 4 para 3 EA 1989 as inserted by UA 2000

6

Chapter 6

Maximising income

This chapter covers:

1. Introduction

The purpose of maximising income is to ensure that a person's income is raised as high as possible. This includes ensuring that:

- a client receives all the benefits and tax credits to which s/he is entitled, and that these are paid at the correct amount;
- tax liability is as low as possible;
- all possible income streams have been explored.

Maximising income is not the same as increasing it. Maximisation means that income is not only increased, but that it cannot be increased any more.

If a debt adviser is not a welfare rights specialist, s/he should consult with colleagues who are, or refer cases to someone who is able to undertake this work.

The debt adviser's approach to income maximisation must be systematic in order to be comprehensive. Advisers must be familiar with the benefits and tax credits system and the books on income maximisation listed in Appendix 2. Many terms are not described fully here and the adviser who is unfamiliar with them should consult the relevant CPAG *Handbooks*.

This chapter cannot explain all the ways in which income can be maximised. Instead, it describes some common ways of increasing income for particular groups of people in debt. Many of the suggestions are appropriate for groups other than those under which they are described. Many people fit into more than one category, so the adviser should check all the categories that could be relevant.

This chapter assumes general advice knowledge. It does not explain everything about each benefit or allowance, but highlights issues which can give rise to extra income.

It does not cover students. For information on the income sources available for students, see CPAG's *Student Support and Benefits Handbook* (England and Wales) and *Benefits for Students in Scotland Handbook*.

2. Overview of benefits and tax credits

When deciding which benefits and/or tax credits someone should claim, check to see if s/he:

- is entitled to any earnings-replacement benefits, such as contribution-based jobseeker's allowance (JSA);
- can get any benefits because of her/his circumstances – eg, because s/he has a disability and/or children;
- qualifies for any means-tested benefits or tax credits to top up her/his benefit and/or other income.

Qualifying for some non-means-tested benefits may give the client an entitlement to, or a higher amount of, means-tested benefits or tax credits. If getting one of the non-means-tested benefits qualifies the client for another benefit the client should claim the other benefit at the same time in order to get maximum backdating. Remember that when a client makes a claim for a benefit or tax credit s/he should ask for the claim to be backdated, where applicable.

The following table gives an overview of the possible benefits and tax credits to which a client may be entitled depending on her/his circumstances. It may be that more than one circumstance applies to a client – eg, a client may have a child, a disability, a mortgage and work part time, in which case, the adviser should refer to each circumstance that applies.

Whatever category a client fits into, the following benefits may also be payable if s/he does not have enough money to live on. These can be paid in addition to other benefits and tax credits, or on their own:

- income support (IS) or income-based JSA if not in full-time paid work;
- income-related employment and support allowance if s/he has 'limited capability' for work;
- working tax credit (WTC) if in full-time paid work;
- pension credit (PC) whether in or out of full-time paid work.

Circumstance	*Potential benefits and tax credits*
Bereaved	Bereavement payment
	Widowed parent's allowance
	Bereavement allowance
	Funeral expenses payment
Carer	Carer's allowance
Responsible for a child	Child tax credit
	Child benefit
	Guardian's allowance
	Statutory maternity pay
	Statutory paternity pay
	Statutory adoption pay
	Maternity allowance
	Health benefits
	Cold weather payment
Disabled	Disability living allowance
	Attendance allowance
	Industrial injuries benefits
	Cold weather payment
Incapable of work or limited capability for work	Incapacity benefit
	Non-contributory incapacity benefit
	Employment and support allowance (from 27 October 2008)
	Statutory sick pay
	Severe disablement allowance
	Cold weather payment
Have a mortgage	Income support
	Income-based jobseeker's allowance
	Income-related employment and support allowance
	Pension credit
	Council tax benefit
Not enough money to meet certain needs	Community care grant
	Budgeting loan
	Crisis loan
Pensioner	State retirement pension
	Pension credit
	Winter fuel payment
	Cold weather payment

Pregnant	Statutory maternity pay
	Maternity allowance
	Sure Start maternity grant
	Health benefits
Tenant	Housing benefit
	Council tax benefit
Unemployed and seeking work	Contribution-based jobseeker's allowance
	Income-based jobseeker's allowance

3. Parents

Child benefit

Child benefit is paid to people who are responsible for a child or qualifying young person.[1] In this chapter the term 'child' is used to refer to both a child and a qualifying young person. People count as responsible for a child if they have a child living with them, or if they contribute to the cost of supporting the child at a rate of at least that of child benefit. Advisers must always check that a client with children is receiving the correct amount of child benefit. Child benefit can continue until the child reaches 20, provided certain conditions are met, such as the child being on (or enrolled to start on) a course of full-time non-advanced education or approved training before s/he is 19.

Family premium in means-tested benefits

Family premium is included in a person's applicable amount for housing benefit (HB) and council tax benefit (CTB) if s/he has a dependent child living with her/him.[2] A higher amount – a baby addition – is paid in HB and CTB is there is at least one child under the age of one in the family.

Child tax credit (CTC) has replaced the family premium (and all other amounts for children) in the applicable amounts for income support (IS) and income-based jobseeker's allowance (JSA), but claimants who had not been awarded CTC before 6 April 2004 continue to get these amounts in their IS or income-based JSA until they are awarded CTC. The Government intends to transfer such claimants onto CTC, but at the time of writing there is no date for when this will happen.

Child support

Some parents who receive child support may be eligible to have part or all of it disregarded for the purposes of calculating means-tested benefits and tax credits (see p147).

Child tax credit

CTC is paid to people who have responsibility for a child(ren) under 16 (or 20 if in full-time non-advanced education or approved training).[3] It is an income-based credit payable whether or not the claimant is in work. It is administered by HM Revenue and Customs (the Revenue).

Parents who work 16 hours or more a week may be entitled to both CTC and working tax credit (WTC). A claim for both CTC and WTC is made on one form. Both CTC and WTC are awarded for the tax year, so a claim made in July will run until 5 April. They are based on a person's or couple's gross annual income. The Revenue uses the previous tax year's income to make an initial award for the year (although it can use an estimate of income for the current tax year instead). At the end of the tax year, the Revenue finalises the award by comparing the actual income over the year of the award (current year) with that of the previous year. This could result in an underpayment, which the Revenue will pay back in a lump sum, or an overpayment that may have to be repaid. Some changes of circumstances have to be reported and taken into account during the year and carry a potential penalty if not reported. Other changes can wait to be reported at the end of the year, but may result in under- or over-payments. Advisers should bear this in mind when giving advice about whether and when to report a change during the year. For more details of how the annual system works, see CPAG's *Welfare Benefits and Tax Credits Handbook*.

CTC is paid in addition to child benefit and can also be paid with most other benefits, but it counts as income for HB and CTB (except for those aged 60 or over). People entitled to IS, income-based JSA, pension credit (PC), or income-related employment and support allowance (ESA) are automatically passported to maximum CTC. They need to make a separate claim for CTC.

Working tax credit

WTC is an income-based credit for certain people working 16 hours or more a week.[4] One of the routes to entitlement is having responsibility for a child(ren). WTC can also help with eligible childcare costs (see below).

Note: some people aged 25 or over without children can also claim WTC but have to work 30 or more hours a week.

Childcare costs

The following people can receive a childcare element as part of their WTC award and/or have some childcare costs disregarded from their earnings for the purposes of calculating HB and CTB:[5]

- lone parents who work 16 hours or more a week;
- couples if both partners work 16 hours or more a week;
- couples if one partner works 16 hours or more a week and the other is incapacitated, or in hospital or prison;

- for HB/CTB only, couples if one partner works 16 hours or more a week and the other is aged 80 or over.

Parents can only get help with 'relevant childcare' costs. Generally, this means childcare provided by a registered childminder, school scheme or similar specified schemes. The childcare element of WTC is 80 per cent of the actual cost of childcare, up to a maximum of 80 per cent of £175 for one child (£140) or 80 per cent of £300 for two or more children (£240). The childcare element applies up to the week of 1 September following the child's 15th birthday, or 16th if the child is disabled.

Up to £175 of eligible childcare costs for one child, or up to £300 for two or more children, are disregarded as earnings in the calculation of HB and CTB. The disregard only applies up to the day before the first Monday in September following the child's 15th birthday, or 16th if the child is disabled.

For further details, see CPAG's *Welfare Benefits and Tax Credits Handbook*.

Maternity, paternity and adoption payments

Future changes

The Government plans to increase the payment period of statutory maternity pay and statutory adoption pay to a maximum of 52 weeks and to introduce an 'additional statutory paternity pay' – the maximum period for which is expected to be 26 weeks, in the year after the birth or adoption. The date for these changes has not yet been set, but it is unlikely they will apply to people whose baby is born before April 2010 or who expect a child to be placed with them before that date.

Sure Start maternity grant

This is a lump-sum payment from the social fund to help with costs associated with having or adopting a baby.[6] It is targeted at families on a low income and does not have to be repaid. Claimants have to be in receipt of IS, income-based JSA, PC, CTC at a rate that exceeds the family element, WTC that includes a disability or severe disability element, or income-related ESA. Claims must be made within a strict time limit.

For details, see CPAG's *Welfare Benefits and Tax Credits Handbook*.

Statutory maternity pay

Employees whose average gross weekly earnings are equal to or above the national insurance (NI) 'lower earnings limit' and who have worked for the same employer for at least 26 continuous weeks by the end of the 15th week before the expected week of childbirth (EWC) are normally entitled to statutory maternity pay (SMP) from their employer (provided they have given the employer the required notice and information).[7] SMP is paid for a maximum of 39 weeks. It is paid at a higher rate for the first six weeks (90 per cent of the employee's average weekly earnings) and then at a standard lower rate of £117.18 (in 2008/09), or 90 per cent of the employee's average weekly earnings, if that is lower, for up to a further 33 weeks.

SMP does not depend on a woman deciding to return to work (although there are certain notifications she needs to give about her expected date of childbirth – see CPAG's *Welfare Benefits and Tax Credits Handbook*).

If an employer refuses to pay SMP, see CPAG's *Welfare Benefits and Tax Credits Handbook* for how to challenge this.

Statutory paternity pay

Employees whose average gross weekly earnings are equal to or above the NI 'lower earnings limit' and who have worked for the same employer for at least 26 continuous weeks by the end of the 15th week before the EWC or the week in which the claimant or partner has been notified of a match with a child for adoption are normally entitled to statutory paternity pay (SPP) in respect of a child their partner has given birth to or for a child who is adopted. They must give the employer the required notice and information.[8]

To get SPP for a birth, the claimant must have been continuously employed by the same employer from the end of the 15th week to the date the child is born. To get SPP for adoption, the claimant must have been continuously employed by that same employer from the end of the week in which s/he was notified of a match to the date the child is placed with her/him for adoption.

SPP is paid for two weeks either at a standard rate of £117.18 (in 2008/09) or at 90 per cent of the employee's average weekly earnings, whichever is the lowest.

Statutory adoption pay

Employees whose average gross weekly earnings are equal to or above the NI 'lower earnings limit' and who have worked for the same employer for more than 26 continuous weeks by the end of the week in which they were notified of the adoption placement are normally entitled to statutory adoption pay (SAP) from their employer.[9] They must give the employer the required notice and information.

SAP is paid for up to 39 weeks either at a standard rate of £117.18 (in 2008/09) or at 90 per cent of the employee's average weekly earnings, whichever is the lowest.

Contractual maternity, paternity or adoption pay

Some employers have maternity, paternity or adoption pay schemes, which are much more generous than SMP, SPP and SAP. These should be included in the statement of terms and conditions of employment.

Maternity allowance

Women who do not qualify for SMP, perhaps because they are self-employed or unemployed, may be entitled to maternity allowance (MA).[10] This is a benefit available to women who have been employees or self-employed for at least 26 weeks out of 66 weeks before the baby is due and whose average weekly earnings are at least equal to the MA threshold of £30 a week (in 2008/09). MA must be claimed from the Department for Work and Pensions (DWP) and is payable for up to 39 weeks either at a standard rate of £117.18 (in 2008/09) or at 90 per cent of the claimant's average weekly earnings, whichever is the lowest.

The earliest a claim for MA can be made is after the 15th week before the EWC (although payment cannot begin until the 11th week before the EWC, unless the baby is born before then). In some cases it may be worth delaying a claim (if practicable) if it means the claimant will have higher average earnings. Increases for adult dependants can also be paid with MA. For further details, see CPAG's *Welfare Benefits and Tax Credits Handbook*.

Healthy Start food and vitamins

The Healthy Start scheme provides vouchers for free vitamins and food, which can be used to buy milk and fresh fruit and vegetables.[11] The scheme is for pregnant women and those who have children under four. People have to be in receipt of, or in a family where someone is in receipt of, IS, income-based JSA, income-related ESA or CTC (but not with WTC) and have a gross annual income that does not exceed £15,575 (in 2008/09).

Asylum seekers in receipt of asylum support who are pregnant or have a child under three should receive an additional payment to help them buy healthy food.

Children under the age of five are also entitled to free milk for each day they are in daycare, provided they are there for two hours or more each day.

There may be other health benefits to which a parent is entitled (see p155).

For further details see CPAG's *Welfare Benefits and Tax Credits Handbook*.

Housing benefit

Housing benefit (HB) is a means-tested benefit, paid by local authorities to tenants.[12] Check that all clients who are tenants are getting HB.

Some non-dependants living with the claimant can affect the amount of HB paid. It is, therefore, vital that the correct details of the non-dependant's income are disclosed to ensure the maximum HB entitlement is paid. Claims can be backdated for a maximum of six months if a claimant can show continuous 'good cause' for claiming late. Claimants or their partners not in receipt of IS, income-based JSA or income-related ESA who are aged 60 or over can get HB backdated for up to three months without needing to show 'good cause', provided they show they qualified during that period. Changes in circumstances should be reported immediately to avoid underpayments and overpayments.

Eligible rent

'Eligible rent' for HB purposes is generally the rent the claimant has to pay, less any ineligible charges – eg, charges for fuel, meals and water included in the rent. Most claimants living in privately-rented accommodation are also subject to rent restriction rules, which could mean that the 'eligible rent' is restricted to a lower level than the rent the claimant pays. The rules do not apply to local authority tenants.

There are currently three rent restriction schemes: pre-January 1996; local reference rent; and local housing allowance. See CPAG's *Welfare Benefits and Tax Credits Handbook* for details of which scheme applies to the claimant.

The local housing allowance is the latest scheme and, apart from some exceptions, applies to new claims for HB (or to HB claimants who move) on or after 7 April 2008. A claimant's HB is calculated using a flat-rate 'local housing allowance' (or if lower, the claimant's rent plus £15). The local housing allowance is set by the rent officer according to the area in which the claimant lives and the size of her/his household. If the claimant's rent is lower than her/his HB, s/he can keep the difference.

Some claimants may be better off under this scheme. According to DWP guidance,[13] it is possible for claimants to withdraw their current HB claim and make a fresh claim under the local housing allowance rules. The DWP's view is that there should be at least one week's gap between one claim and the next. Advisers should do a full HB calculation and consider whether a claimant will be better off under the new rules before advising anyone to take this action.

If a claimant needs help to cover the rent because HB only meets part of it, s/he may be able to get a discretionary housing payment (see p168).

Housing costs

These are included as part of the applicable amount in IS, income-based JSA and income-related ESA, and as part of the appropriate minimum guarantee in PC, if a person has housing costs as a result of owning or buying her/his home.[14] There are strict rules about what and how much can be covered. There are also long waiting periods, which depend on when the housing costs began. Some claimants, however, qualify for help immediately – eg, people over 60.

Council tax benefit

Council tax benefit (CTB) is paid by local authorities to people who are liable for council tax and are on a low income.[15] It is means tested and can be paid whether or not a person is in work. It is not the same as a council tax discount (see p149) or disability reduction (see p157), which are applied before CTB is calculated. It is important to check that any relevant discount or reduction has been applied to the council tax liability. It is also important to check whether a person is entitled to a second adult rebate. This is not means tested (but see p145).

Claims for CTB can be backdated for a maximum of six months if a claimant can show continuous 'good cause' for claiming late. Claimants or their partners not in receipt of IS, income-based JSA or income-related ESA who are aged 60 or over can get CTB backdated for up to three months without needing to show 'good cause', provided they show they qualified during that period.

A person cannot get both second adult rebate and council tax benefit. If someone is entitled to both, a calculation should be done to check which one s/he would be better off claiming. The amount of the second adult rebate depends on the income of a second adult who lives with the claimant. The second adult must be over 18 and not liable for council tax on the property, and must not be disregarded for the purpose of a council tax discount. For details, see CPAG's Council Tax Handbook.

Starting work

Parents starting full-time work may be entitled to one-off lump-sum payments, such as a child maintenance bonus (p148), a job grant (see p165), extended payments of HB/CTB or mortgage interest run-on (see p165).

Earnings disregards

Some of the money a claimant or her/his partner earns can be disregarded when calculating income for HB, CTB, IS, income-based JSA, income-related ESA and PC.[16] There are standard amounts that apply to different groups of claimants – eg, a lone parent qualifies for a higher disregard than a single person with no children. There are also additional earnings disregards for HB and CTB if a claimant or her/his partner is working sufficient hours (16 or 30 depending on the circumstances).

Tax allowances

The married couple's allowance was abolished from 6 April 2000 and now only applies to those who were aged 65 or over before 6 April 2000 (see p162). Those eligible have to be married or in a civil partnership and be living together.

The children's tax credit was abolished on 6 April 2003 and replaced by CTC (see p140).

A backdated claim for any allowance can be made for up to six years, so the adviser should check if a client has not received an allowance to which s/he is entitled.

Education maintenance allowance

Education maintenance allowances are means-tested payments for young people aged 16, 17 or 18 still in further education.[17] The payments are made direct to the young person and are conditional upon regular course attendance. They are payable for two to three years. The young person may receive a weekly allowance of £10, £20 or £30, depending on the household income. S/he may also receive bonuses if s/he remains on her/his course and does well against learning objectives set out in her/his education maintenance allowance contract. A further bonus may be payable if s/he returns to study for a second year.

Education maintenance allowances do not count as income for any benefits or tax credits the parent may get get. They are also unaffected by any income the young person earns from part-time work.

For further details, see www.direct.gov.uk, or www.wales.gov.uk.

Free school meals

Children are entitled to free school meals if their family receives:[18]

- IS or income-based JSA;
- income-related ESA;
- CTC (but not if also receiving WTC) and their gross annual income is £15,575 or less (in 2008/09);
- the guarantee credit of PC.

Also entitled are 16–18-year-olds receiving the above benefits and tax credits in their own right and asylum seekers in receipt of support provided under Part VI of the Immigration and Asylum Act 1999.

School clothing grants

Local authorities have a discretionary power to give grants for school uniforms or other clothing needed for school (eg, sportswear). Policies vary enormously across the county. Some school-governing bodies or parents' associations also provide help with school clothing.

School transport

Local authorities have a duty to provide free transport for a pupils under 16 if it is considered necessary to enable her/him to get to the 'nearest suitable school'. This might be because the pupil lives beyond walking distance or if s/he cannot walk because of a disability.

Social services payments

Social services departments are empowered to give direct financial assistance, or assistance in kind (eg, food parcels) to families with a child(ren) who has been assessed as being in need.[19] These payments are known as Section 17 payments. Local authority practice, however, differs widely.

4. Lone parents

Higher rate of family premium in housing benefit and council tax benefit

The higher rate of family premium included in housing benefit (HB) and council tax benefit (CTB) for lone parents, was abolished for new claimants from 6 April 1998. Existing claimants continue to receive this if:

- they remain entitled to HB and CTB; *and*
- they have not ceased to be a lone parent; *and*
- they do not become entitled or cease to be entitled to income support (IS) or income-based jobseeker's allowance (JSA); *and*
- a disability premium has not become applicable.

Child support

Note: from 10 June 2008, a new body (the Child Maintenance and Enforcement Commission) was created to replace the Child Support Agency (CSA). It is not expected, however, to start dealing with applications until 2010. From 14 July 2008 a parent with care will no longer have his/her IS or income-based JSA reduced for failing to co-operate with the CSA.

Child support is disregarded as income for child tax credit, working tax credit, pension credit and, from 27 October 2008, HB and CTB. From 27 October 2008, £20 of child support is disregarded as income for IS and income-based JSA (prior to this date, the disregard was £10 and only in respect of some child support agreements) and for income-related employment and support allowance. From April 2010, the Government plans that child support will be disregarded for all means-tested benefits.

For more details on child support, see CPAG's *Child Support Handbook*.

Tax credits

A lone parent should be entitled to child tax credit if her/his income is low enough (see p140). If a lone parent works 16 or more hours a week, s/he may also be entitled to working tax credit (WTC) (see p140).

Childcare costs

Lone parents who work 16 hours or more a week and need to pay for childcare may be able to get a childcare element in their WTC (see p140) and/or a disregard in HB/CTB.[20]

See CPAG's *Welfare Benefits and Tax Credits Handbook* for further details.

Health benefits

A lone parent may qualify for help with some NHS charges (see p155) and may also) be eligible for Healthy Start food and vitamins (see p143).

Starting full-time work

Lone parents whose entitlement to certain benefits stops because they start full-time work, or increase their hours or pay, may be entitled to the following bonuses.

Job grant

Lone parents who stop getting certain benefits when starting full-time work may be entitled to a job grant of £250 (in 2008/09).[21] See p165.

Extended payments of housing benefit, council tax benefit and mortgage interest run-on

Lone parents who stop getting certain benefits as a result of starting to work full time may be entitled to up to four weeks' extended payments of HB and CTB (see p165) and/or up to four weeks' IS mortgage interest run-on.[22] There may still be an entitlement to HB and CTB after this period, depending on whether the means test is satisfied.

In-work credit

Lone parents who move into full-time work having been in receipt of IS or JSA for 12 months or more may be entitled to an in-work credit of £40 a week (£60 in London) for the first year in work.

Child maintenance bonus

Future changes

The child maintenance bonus is being phased out. It is expected to be withdrawn at the time the child maintenance premium is extended to all parents with care on IS or income-based JSA by the end of 2008.

A lone parent who comes off IS/income-based JSA as a result of starting full-time work may be entitled to a child maintenance bonus.[23] For each week her/his IS/ income-based JSA is reduced by an amount of child maintenance, s/he will receive £5, or the actual reduction if this is less (subject to a maximum of £1,000).

A lone parent who qualifies for a child maintenance premium is not be entitled to a bonus, although some claimants can claim the bonus they have already accrued.[24]

See CPAG's *Welfare Benefits and Tax Credits Handbook* for further details.

Earnings disregards

The earned income used to calculate HB and CTB for lone parents not on IS, income-based JSA, income-related ESA or the guarantee credit of PC should be reduced by a £25 disregard.[25] The earned income used to calculate IS, income-based JSA and PC should be reduced by a £20 disregard.[26]

Tax allowances

There are no longer additional income tax allowances for children.

Council tax discount

A lone parent is entitled to a 25 per cent discount on her/his council tax bill if s/he is the only adult living in the property (some adults are ignored – see p157).

For further details, see CPAG's *Council Tax Handbook*.

5. Sick and disabled people

Attendance allowance

Attendance allowance (AA) is a non-means-tested benefit.[27] It is not taxable and does not count as income for the purposes of calculating means-tested benefits and tax credits.

It is a benefit for people who are aged over 65 when they claim and who need either attention from another person in connection with their bodily functions, or supervision in order to avoid substantial danger to themselves or others.

There are two rates of benefit, the higher of which requires a claimant to need attention or supervision during both the day and the night.

A claimant who is terminally ill (ie, who has a progressive disease from which it would not be unexpected for her/him to die within six months) should be awarded the higher rate of AA immediately. This is known as a claim under the 'special rules'.

Advisers should always check the correct rate is awarded and, where appropriate, advise clients on how to seek to change their award. Advisers should be aware that when trying to claim a higher rate, there is a risk that the award may be taken away altogether. The debt adviser should obtain specialist help, if necessary, but should never assume that a claimant is receiving the correct rate.

Entitlement to AA may give rise to an entitlement to some means-tested benefits (or for these to be paid at a higher rate), so a full benefit check should be carried out.

For further information, see CPAG's *Welfare Benefits and Tax Credits Handbook*.

Disability living allowance

Disability living allowance (DLA) is a non-means-tested benefit. It is not taxable and does not count as income for the purposes of calculating means-tested benefits and tax credits.

DLA consists of a care component,[28] payable at three different rates, and a mobility component,[29] payable at two different rates. It is paid to eligible people who claim when they are under the age of 65. The mobility component is for people who have difficulty getting around. The care component is for people with attention and/or supervision needs. Once DLA is awarded, a claimant can continue to qualify after s/he turns 65.

A claimant who is terminally ill (ie, who has a progressive disease from which it would not be unexpected for her/him to die within six months) qualifies automatically for the higher rate care component. This is known as a claim under the 'special rules'.

Advisers should always check the correct component and rate is being awarded and, where appropriate, advise claimants on how to get their award changed. Advisers should be aware that when trying to claim a higher rate of one of the components, there is a risk that the component already being paid may be taken away or paid at a lower rate. The debt adviser should obtain specialist help, if necessary, but should never assume that a claimant is receiving the correct rate.

Entitlement to DLA may give rise to an entitlement to some means-tested benefits (or for these to be paid at a higher rate), so a full benefit check should be carried out.

For further information, see CPAG's *Welfare Benefits and Tax Credits Handbook*.

Employment and support allowance

Employment and support allowance (ESA) is a benefit for people who have 'limited capability for work' because of illness or disability, and who are not entitled to statutory sick pay (SSP).[30] It replaced incapacity benefit (IB) and income support (IS) on the grounds of disability for people who claim on or after 27 October 2008. People who get IS on these grounds include: those incapable of work; disabled students; deaf students; and those registered blind.

A claim made for IB or IS on the above grounds on or after 27 October 2008 but backdated to before that date, can be treated as a claim for IS or IB. Advisers should, therefore, check whether a person would be better off on these benefits than ESA when advising about a claim made on or after 27 October that could be backdated to before this date.

There are two types of ESA. Contributory ESA is paid if a person satisfies the national insurance (NI) contribution conditions. It is not means tested. There are no age-related or dependant additions. Some young people may be able to get contributory ESA without satisfying the NI conditions. This is known as ESA in youth. Income-related ESA is means tested and has no NI contribution test. It is possible to receive contributory ESA (including ESA in youth) topped up with income-related ESA.

A basic allowance of ESA is paid during an initial 'assessment phase' of 13 weeks (for income-related ESA this could be higher if, for example, the applicable amount includes premiums). Thereafter, claimants are paid an additional component – either a work-related activity component if not assessed as having 'limited capability for work-related activity' or a support component if assessed as having 'limited capability for work-related activity'.

The person's capability for work is assessed under a 'work capability assessment'. Some people are treated as having limited capability for work and do not have to undergo this. This list is more restricted than the list of exempt groups for IB (see below). It includes those who are terminally ill, receiving or recovering from certain types of chemotherapy, and hospital inpatients. Advisers should check if the claimant has a severe uncontrolled or uncontrollable life-threatening disease or if, because of the claimant's illness, there would be a substantial risk to the mental or physical health of any person were the claimant found to have limited capability for work. In these cases, the claimant can satisfy the test without having to score the required points.

Incapacity benefit

Changes from October 2008

A new claim for IB made on or after 27 October 2008 will be treated as a claim for ESA (see above) unless the linking rules apply which enable a person to re-qualify for IB. It is expected that existing IB claimants will continue to receive IB until the Government decides to transfer them to ESA – at a date yet to be set. IB can be backdated for up to three months, so an IB claim made on or after 27 October 2008 can be treated as a claim for IB if it is backdated to a date before then. Advisers should, therefore, check whether a person would be better off on IB than ESA when advising about a claim made on or after 27 October 2008 that could be backdated.

IB is payable (subject to NI contributions, unless the claimant became incapable of work in youth) during the first 28 weeks of illness to people who cannot get SSP, and thereafter to others who are incapable of work.[31] There are three rates depending on the length of time a person is incapable of work – the longer the period the higher the rate. There are also age-related additions, paid with the long-term rate only, for people who become incapable of work under the age of 45.

Increases for adult dependants can also be claimed. Advisers should check whether an IB claimant would be better or worse off claiming an increase for an adult dependant who is part of their family – it could result in the loss of a means-tested benefit (such as IS) because IB and any such increases count in full as income for means-tested benefits. The loss of passports that IS brings, such as free school meals and health benefits, could mean a person is left with a lower income. However, even if a person has not claimed an increase, the Department for Work and Pensions (DWP) can treat her/him as having this extra income (known as 'notional income') and re-assess the means-tested benefit accordingly. For further details, see CPAG's *Welfare Benefits and Tax Credits Handbook*.

A person's capacity for work is assessed under a 'personal capability assessment' (but see below). Some people are exempt from this. These include people with a severe and progressive immune deficiency state, severe mental illness, severe learning disability, progressive neurological or muscle wasting disease, people getting the highest rate care component of DLA, or people registered blind. Sometimes people with these (and/or the other diseases that make a person exempt) are unaware that they are exempt. Their doctor's diagnosis may not also be specific enough or may not concur with the DWP Medical Service doctor. In these cases, specialist help is required. People who are terminally ill should always be exempt.

Future changes

The Government plans to apply the ESA test for incapacity for work (the 'work capability assessment' – see p151) to existing IB claimants aged under 25 from 2009, and to all existing claimants from 2010.

In addition to checking whether an exemption applies, an adviser should also check whether a client can be 'deemed' to be incapable of work. There are several situations when this can apply, one of which is being a hospital inpatient.

For further information, see CPAG's *Welfare Benefits and Tax Credits Handbook*.

Industrial injuries benefits

If an employed client has an injury or prescribed industrial disease caused during the course of her/his employment, s/he may be entitled to an industrial injuries benefit.[32] S/he must have lost 'a faculty' and be 'disabled' as a result of this. Receipt of this benefit may mean s/he becomes entitled to a means-tested benefit (or to be paid at a higher rate), so a full benefit check should be carried out.

For more details, see CPAG's *Welfare Benefits and Tax Credits Handbook*.

Working tax credit

Working tax credit (WTC) is an income-based credit for people working 16 hours or more a week.[33] One of the routes to entitlement is a physical or mental disability that puts a person at a disadvantage in getting a job. In order to qualify via this route, a claimant must satisfy other qualifying conditions, such as being, or previously being, in receipt of a qualifying benefit. Those in receipt of IB (at the higher rate short-term or long-term rate), ESA or severe disablement allowance (SDA) prior to receiving WTC can go straight back onto that benefit if they stop working within a set 'linking period' – currently 104 weeks.

Some people can claim or continue to receive WTC during the first 28 weeks of a period of incapacity for work.[34] Having access to WTC at this time may be particularly important to those with children who need help with childcare costs.

Claimants whose disability results in a reduction in their earnings or hours to 75 per cent or less of those for a person without that disability doing the same job can work more than 16 hours a week and remain eligible for IS or income-based jobseeker's allowance (JSA).[35] These claimants may also be entitled to WTC, but as WTC is taken into account as income when calculating IS and income-based JSA, a claim for WTC may result in them no longer being entitled to IS or JSA. If this happens, any housing benefit (HB), council tax benefit (CTB) or passported benefits could also be affected. It is worth checking, therefore, whether someone would be better off claiming WTC.

Note: some people aged 25 or over without a disability can also claim WTC but have to work 30 or more hours a week.

Premiums and additional amounts in means-tested benefits

Carer's premium or carer's additional amount

This is included in the applicable amount (or appropriate minimum guarantee of pension credit (PC) in means-tested benefits if the claimant gets carer's allowance (CA), or would do but is getting an 'overlapping' benefit, such as state retirement pension, instead.[36] Some people who do not live as part of the same household as an AA/DLA claimant may not realise they are eligible for CA for the care they provide. The possibility of receiving a premium or additional amount may make a claim for CA beneficial. Note, however, that receipt of CA may prevent the person being cared for from receiving the severe disability premium (or PC additional amount) – see p154.

Disabled child premium in housing benefit and council tax benefit

This premium is payable if a child receives DLA (at any rate) or is blind.[37]

Note: this premium is no longer payable in IS and income-based JSA. People with disabled children have an allowance for disabled children in their child tax credit (CTC). Those getting IS or income-based JSA before 6 April 2004 continue to get disabled child premium until they have been awarded CTC.

Disability premium

This is added to the applicable amount for people who are registered blind, or who are receiving a 'qualifying benefit'.[38] These include DLA, the long-term rate of IB, the disability or severe disability element of WTC, or an NHS invalid car (or private car allowance because of disability).

Note: there is no disability premium in PC or ESA.

With the introduction of ESA, the disability premium will no longer be available on grounds of incapacity for work in any new claims for IS or income-based JSA made on or after 27 October 2008. The only exceptions are claims backdated to before this date or those that satisfy the linking rules or, in the case of JSA, for couples where the partner is getting IB or, for joint-claim JSA, when one member has an incapacity or limited capability for work.

The disability premium is also not available in new claims for HB and CTB made on or after 27 October 2008 if the claimant has a 'limited capability for work' (see p150).

In general, if someone is already getting the premium included in these benefits on 27 October 2008 it will continue as long as the usual rules for the benefit and the premium are satisfied.

The means-tested element of ESA (income-related ESA) does not include a disability premium. Claimants (or their partners) who are assessed as having a limited capability for work who are also entitled to HB and CTB will not have a disability premium included in their HB or CTB on *any* ground, but will instead have either a work-related activity component or a support component included in their HB/CTB applicable amount. This means there are better-off issues to consider. For example, in a couple where one person is assessed as having a limited capability for work and the other gets DLA it may be better for the person getting DLA to become the HB and CTB claimant if this would mean they would qualify for a disability premium and thus be better off. Claimants may be able to get backdated medical certificates from their GP in order to get the premium paid from the earliest possible date.

Severe disability premium or severe disability additional amount

This is included if a person receives a 'qualifying benefit' (AA, the middle or highest rate care component of DLA, constant attendance allowance, exceptionally severe disablement allowance (or equivalent war pension)), has no non-dependant over 18 normally living with her/him, and no one gets CA for looking after her/him.[39] For couples to get the couple rate, both partners must be getting a qualifying benefit and no one must be getting CA for either of them. For couples to get the single rate, one must be getting a qualifying benefit and the other partner must be blind, or both partners must get a qualifying benefit and only one has a carer getting CA for looking after her/him. In all these cases, there must not be a non-dependant over 18 normally living with them.

Enhanced disability premium

Note: there is no equivalent of this premium in PC. This premium is also not payable for a disabled child in income-related ESA. It is no longer payable for a disabled child in IS and income-based JSA, except to those who were getting IS or income-based JSA before 6 April 2004 who have not yet been awarded CTC.

The premium can be paid in addition to the disability and severe disability premiums if a claimant or her/his partner is under 60 and receives the highest rate care component of DLA.[40] For HB and CTB only, it can also be paid for each of the claimant's child(ren) who receives the highest rate care component of DLA. This is payable to all HB and CTB claimants who have children who qualify and is not restricted to those under the age of 60.

Change claimant

In the case of couples, the choice of which partner makes the claim can affect a couple's entitlement to the disability premium and severe disability premium. **Note**: some couples have to make joint claims for income-based JSA (see CPAG's *Welfare Benefits and Tax Credits Handbook*).

The disability premium may be part of a claimant's applicable amount for IS, HB and CTB (but only if included in these claims on 27 October 2008) if s/he has been continuously incapable of work or treated as incapable of work for 364 days (196 days if terminally ill). To qualify for this premium through this route, the person incapable of work must be the claimant. For income-based JSA, the claimant must be capable of work. For the other routes to qualify for this premium, it does not matter which partner is the claimant, including for income-based JSA. See also p154 for couples claiming HB/CTB where one has limited capability for work and the other gets DLA.

For severe disability premium, in couples where only one partner gets a qualifying benefit and the other is blind, the person who gets the qualifying benefit must be the claimant for IS, income-based JSA, income-related ESA, HB or CTB. For PC, either partner can be the claimant.

For further details, see CPAG's *Welfare Benefits and Tax Credits Handbook*.

Health benefits

People can get free prescriptions, dental treatment, optical treatment, optical vouchers, sight tests, fares to hospital, wigs and fabric supports if they are in receipt of:

- IS;
- income-based JSA;
- guarantee credit of PC;
- income-related ESA;
- CTC, or CTC and WTC, or WTC that includes a disability or severe disability element, and they have a gross annual income of less than £15,050 (in 2008/09)

Other people qualify for free or reduced-cost treatment on the grounds of age, pregnancy (and for one year after childbirth), certain illnesses and disabilities and low income. Certain war pensioners also qualify.

It is important to check whether a client requires, or is likely to require, any health benefits and to claim in advance (particularly if the claim is made on low-income grounds, which may take some time to settle). The claim on low-income grounds is made on Form HC1 or HC1(SC) if the claimant is in a care home or is a 16/17-year-old care leaver. Forms are available from Jobcentre Plus offices or NHS hospitals or online from the Prescription Pricing Division website at www.ppa.nhs.uk.

Those who do not qualify for free prescriptions and who need them frequently can purchase a pre-payment certificate, which reduces the overall cost. The form for England is FP95 and is available from www.ppa.nhs.uk. Prescriptions are free in Wales. Someone who becomes entitled to free prescriptions may be able to claim a refund of the cost of the pre-payment certificate. For further details about refunds, see www.ppa.nhs.uk. For further details, see CPAG's *Welfare Benefits and Tax Credits Handbook*.

Working during periods of incapacity

Most claimants getting benefits based on their incapacity for work will not be able to do *any* work while claiming these, unless it is 'permitted work'. This allows a claimant to do some paid work, some of which is subject to a limited period.[41]

For further details, see CPAG's *Welfare Benefits and Tax Credits Handbook*.

Starting work

Extended payments of housing benefit and council tax benefit

Claimants whose entitlement to IB, SDA or ESA (income-related or contributory) ends as a result of starting full-time work may be entitled to a four-week extension of HB and CTB. They may still be entitled to HB and CTB after this time, depending on whether the means test is satisfied.

Job grant

IB and SDA count as qualifying benefits for a job grant (see p165). At the time of writing, it was also expected that income-related ESA would also count as a qualifying benefit.

Earnings disregards

For some sick and/or disabled claimants, £20 can be disregarded from earned income for the purposes of calculating IS, income-based JSA, income-related ESA,

PC, HB and CTB. Higher disregards apply to IB and ESA in certain cases of 'permitted work'. There is also an additional earnings disregard for HB and CTB if the claimant (or her/his partner) is working 16 hours or more a week and one (or both) of them gets a qualifying benefit (or a qualifying premium, component or element in that benefit or tax credit), or is registered blind, or has been incapable of work for 364 days (196 days if terminally ill). For details, see CPAG's *Welfare Benefits and Tax Credits Handbook*.

Tax allowances

A person who is registered blind can claim a blind person's allowance for the whole tax year. This is in addition to the personal allowance. Any unused allowance can be transferred to her/his spouse or civil partner. Where both spouses or civil partners are registered blind, they can claim an allowance each.

A backdated claim can be made for up to six years for any allowances so the adviser should check to see if their client has not received an allowance to which s/he is entitled.

Housing benefit

HB is paid to tenants on low incomes. Claimants who are sick and/or disabled may qualify for premiums/components in their HB applicable amount, which will increase their potential to receive HB.

Council tax benefit

A client who is liable to pay council tax may qualify for CTB (see p144). Claimants who are sick and/or disabled may qualify for premiums/components in their CTB applicable amount, which will increase their potential to receive CTB.

Council tax discounts

A disabled person may be entitled to a disability reduction in her/his council tax if the property in which s/he lives has features that are essential or of major importance because of her/his disability. An application must be made in writing to the local authority.

A single disabled person who has a carer living with her/him may be deemed to be the only adult in the property and so entitled to a 25 per cent discount on her/his council tax bill. If the carer has left a property which was her/his main residence unoccupied to live with the disabled person, the unoccupied property should be exempt from council tax for an indefinite period. This applies whether the property was rented or owner-occupied. Equally, a property left unoccupied because the person who lived there now lives somewhere else because s/he needs to be cared for is exempt from council tax.

See CPAG's *Council Tax Handbook* for more details.

Carer's allowance

CA is paid to people who spend regular and substantial time (35 hours a week or more) caring for someone who is in receipt of AA, the middle or highest rate care component of DLA, or constant attendance allowance for industrial or war disablement.[42] This includes if the claimant is caring for a member of her/his family – eg, a child. A carer cannot get CA if s/he is in full-time education or is employed and earning more than a set amount a week.

Advisers should note the following.

- Those getting CA may be entitled to a carer premium if they claim IS/income-based JSA, income-related ESA, HB or CTB, or to a carer's additional amount if they claim PC. This will mean they are entitled to a more generous earnings disregard when calculating these benefits. CA is, however, taken into account in full as income for these benefits.
- CA overlaps with other 'earnings replacement' benefits, such as retirement pension, which means that a claimant may not get any CA if the benefit with which it overlaps is higher than CA. In this situation, however, the claimant retains an underlying entitlement to CA and can, therefore, still qualify for a carer's premium or a carer's additional amount (see p153).
- If someone cares for a person who is not a member of her/his household, s/he can still claim CA if s/he meets the conditions.
- CA recipients receive Class 1 national insurance contribution credits.

Note: receipt of CA prevents the cared-for person from receiving a severe disability premium with her/his IS, income-based JSA, income-related ESA, HB and CTB, or a severe disability additional amount with her/his PC. Therefore, careful consideration must be given, and if necessary specialist advice sought, to ensure that the client is aware of all the implications.

For further details, see CPAG's *Welfare Benefits and Tax Credits Handbook*.

Civil compensation for damages

Personal injury claims can be made against an individual or organisation if they have been negligent in causing damage, either by doing something or by failing to do something. Injury caused by negligence can be an issue in road traffic accidents or accidents at work, in the street or other public places. Damages for personal injury can be substantial, but can be reduced by the amount of social security benefit paid as a consequence of the injury.

Refer to a solicitor

If the claimant wants to take legal action to claim compensation for personal injury, s/he should normally do so within three years of the injury becoming known. The law in this area is, however, very complex. If it is possible that a client might have a claim for compensation, s/he should be referred without delay to a solicitor or advice agency specialising in personal injury work. Some solicitors offer a free interview to personal injury claimants to examine the likelihood of a claim succeeding, usually through a personal injury referral scheme, such as Accident Line. Legal action for compensation can be costly. Publicly-funded legal services are only available for certain categories of personal injury claims and only then if the person is financially eligible and the case is deemed as having sufficient merit by the Legal Services Commission. If a person is not eligible for publicly funded legal services, solicitors might help on a 'conditional fee' basis if it is likely the person will win because their costs will be awarded from the damages. Clients should seek advice from an experienced adviser before entering into a 'conditional fee agreement'.

If the injury occurred at work, the client should contact her/his trade union, if a member.

For more information contact:

- The Solicitors Regulation Authority for details of the Personal Injury Accreditation Scheme on 0870 606 2555 or www.sra.org.uk;
- The Association of Personal Injury Lawyers on 0870 609 1958 or www.apil.com;
- Accident Line on 0800 192 939 or www.accidentlinedirect.co.uk;
- The Motor Accident Solicitors Society on 0117 929 2560 or www.mass.org.uk.

6. Retired people

Retirement pension

A few months before retirement age (men aged 65, women aged 60, although note that pensionable age for women will be increased from 60 to 65 between 2010 and 2020), the Department for Work and Pensions (DWP) normally sends out a claim form (BR1). The final award of retirement pension is calculated from a person's national insurance (NI) contributions throughout her/his working life. If s/he is awarded only a reduced retirement pension, the situation should be examined carefully. In some cases, this is correctly based on an incomplete contribution record (because, for example, of periods spent not working, abroad or in prison). However, in some cases employers have deducted NI contributions and have not paid these to the National Insurance Fund. In such cases, any available evidence (which may not be as formal as P60s or pay slips) should be gathered to support someone's claim that s/he did pay contributions in a particular period.

A claim for retirement pension can be backdated up to 12 months.

There are different types of pension, the most common being a Category A pension,[43] based on a person's own contribution record. People who are divorced or who have had a civil partnership dissolved may be entitled to a Category A pension[44] based on their former spouse or civil partner's contribution record.

Women with an incomplete record of their own might be able to claim a Category B pension,[45] based on the contribution record of their current husband. However, married men and civil partners cannot currently qualify for a Category B pension on this basis – the earliest they can qualify is from 6 April 2010 or, in the case of male civil partners, from 6 April 2015. A person might also qualify for a Category B pension, based on the contribution record of their late spouse or civil partner.[46]

There is also an addition payable with retirement pension for dependants. **Note:** the child dependency increases were abolished from 6 April 2003 with the introduction of child tax credit (CTC) and no new claims for this increase for children can be made. Those entitled on 5 April 2003 retain their entitlement for as long as they continue to meet the transitional protection rules.

For further details, see CPAG's *Welfare Benefits and Tax Credits Handbook*.

Pension credit

Pension credit (PC) is a means-tested benefit made up of two elements – a guarantee credit and a savings credit. The guarantee credit tops up a person's income to a guaranteed level. The claimant must be 60 or over.[47] The savings credit rewards people who have made provisions above the basic state pension, through things like savings, private pensions or earnings. The claimant or her/his partner must be 65 or over.[48]

Couples where one partner is 60 or over and the other is under 60 can choose whether the person under 60 claims income support (IS) or income-based jobseeker's allowance (JSA) for both of them, or the person 60 or over claims PC for both of them. A couple is likely to be better off claiming PC because the rules on the treatment of income and capital are more generous for PC than they are for IS or income-based JSA and there is no bar on working full time for PC. Furthermore, in order to benefit from the more generous rules for housing benefit (HB) and council tax benefit (CTB) for those 60 or over the claimant or her/his partner must not be in receipt of IS or income-based JSA.

Men aged between 60 and 65 have a choice about whether to claim PC or income-based JSA. Again, the different rules on these benefits must be considered, although in most cases the man will be better off on PC.

There is no restriction on the hours a PC claimant can work, so it might be possible for a person to get both PC and working tax credit (WTC). WTC counts as income, however, when calculating PC, as do earnings (subject to certain disregards). PC claimants who have responsibility for a child should claim CTC.

Sometimes people do not make a claim for benefit if they think they are only going to get a small amount. However, it is worthwhile making a claim for PC because even if a person only gets a small award of the guarantee credit s/he will be passported to maximum HB and CTB, as well as other benefits, such as health benefits and the social fund. Even if a person does not get the guarantee credit but gets the savings credit s/he will have access to payments from the social fund.

Pensioner premiums

A claimant who is 60 or over can no longer claim IS. The pensioner premiums below only apply to IS claimants under 60 who have a partner who is 60 or over. Couples in this situation will usually be better off on PC (see p160). The premiums below also do not apply to HB and CTB. HB and CTB claimants who are (or who have a partner who is) 60 or over do not lose out as they get a higher personal allowance instead (unless they are getting IS, income-based JSA or income-related employment and support allowance (ESA), in which case they are passported to full HB and CTB).

Pensioner premium

This is paid to people aged 60 to 74 years old and to people aged 75 to 79, when it is sometimes referred to as enhanced pensioner premium.[49] A higher pensioner premium is paid to people aged 80 or over and others (see below).

The pensioner premiums are paid at the same rate, with a higher amount for a couple. It is important to identify entitlement to the higher pensioner premium as this brings more generous earnings disregards and may help to satisfy entitlement to WTC (as one of the WTC disability element qualifying conditions).

Higher pensioner premium

This is added to the applicable amount for:[50]

- people aged 80 and over;
- people eligible for the pensioner premium who receive one of the qualifying benefits described under disability premium (see p153);
- anyone getting the disability premium just before her/his 60th birthday who has continued to be eligible for it ever since. Qualifying via this route is more complicated than the others and it should always be checked.

For further details, see CPAG's *Welfare Benefits and Tax Credits Handbook*.

Housing benefit and council tax benefit

Retired people on a low income may qualify for HB and/or CTB. Those not in receipt of IS, income-based JSA or income-related ESA can benefit from the different rules that apply to claimants age 60 or over. Under these the income and capital rules are more generous, so a couple (or a man aged between 60 and 65) has a choice about whether to claim IS/income-based JSA/income-related ESA or PC. They are likely to be better off choosing PC and will then have their HB and CTB assessed under the more beneficial rules.

The rules on restricting a claimant's eligible rent for HB purposes are the same as described on p144. Note that the rules that applied before January 1996 give some claimants protection if a member of their household is 60 or over. See also discretionary housing payments on p168.

Housing costs

The stringent waiting periods for IS, income-based JSA and income-related ESA housing costs payments do not apply if the claimant's partner is 60 or over. There is no waiting period for PC.

Winter fuel payments

People aged 60 or over are entitled to a winter fuel payment of £250 or £400 if aged 80 or over (in 2008/09) in what is known as the 'qualifying week'.[51] This is the week beginning on the third Monday in September. Only one payment is made per household. The payments are automatic for anyone who got a payment the previous year or who is in receipt of retirement pension or any other social security benefit (other than child benefit, HB and CTB) in the qualifying week.

If someone is not entitled to an automatic payment, a claim must be made before the 31 March following the qualifying week. The payment is meant to assist older people with their fuel costs at a time of year when they are likely to be highest. Where possible, a claim should therefore be submitted before the qualifying week to ensure payment is received as early as possible. Payments are aimed to be made before Christmas.

Claim forms are available from the winter fuel payment helpline 08459 151 515 (textphone 08456 015 613), although a written claim does not have to be on the designated form.

Earnings disregards

For IS, income-based JSA, income-related ESA, PC, HB and CTB, some of the money a claimant or her/his partner earns can be disregarded when calculating income for these benefits. These are standard amounts that apply to different groups of claimants – eg, £20 of earned income can be disregarded if a claimant or a claimant's partner gets attendance allowance.

Tax allowances

A higher personal allowance can be claimed by those aged 65 to 74, and an even higher amount by those aged 75 or over. This age-related personal allowance is reduced once a person's income exceeds a certain limit, but can only be reduced up to the rate of the basic personal allowance.

People aged 65 or over before 6 April 2000 may still be entitled to a married couple's allowance. Those eligible have to be married or in a civil partnership and be living together. It is paid in addition to the personal allowance (but see below). Any unused married couple's allowance can be transferred to the other spouse or civil partner. Alternatively, spouses and civil partners can elect to transfer the whole of the minimum allowance to the other partner or share it between them. This allowance is reduced once the income of the person claiming the allowance exceeds a certain limit. However, the age-related personal allowance is reduced to the level of the basic personal allowance before any reduction is applied to the married couple's allowance. So, for example, if the claimant's income does not reduce the age-related personal allowance to the basic level, the married couple's allowance is not reduced.

A backdated claim can be made for up to six years for any allowances, so the adviser should check to see if the client has not received an allowance to which s/he is entitled.

7. Unemployed people

Jobseeker's allowance

Jobseeker's allowance (JSA) is a benefit payable to unemployed people who are available for and actively seeking work.[52] JSA may be income-based (means tested) or contribution-based (paid if national insurance contribution conditions are satisfied). Contribution-based JSA is paid for a maximum of 182 days and can be topped up by income-based JSA, if the means test is satisfied.

Sanctions[53]

JSA can be 'sanctioned' (ie, reduced) in certain situations. These include where it is decided that the claimant has left her/his job voluntarily, or lost it through misconduct, or has failed to apply for or accept a job, or has refused to carry out a 'jobseeker's direction'. The sanction period varies. In some cases, it can last for up to 26 weeks.

Consideration should be given to challenging such decisions. In particular, the 26-week period of disqualification should be seen as a maximum to be used only in the most serious cases.

Hardship payments

Claimants who have been sanctioned (and certain other claimants, such as those who have had their JSA suspended because they did not satisfy the labour market conditions) may be able to claim a hardship payment from the Department for Work and Pensions (DWP), provided they are in a 'vulnerable group' or can show they would experience hardship without such a payment.[54] Hardship payments are reduced-rate payments of income-based JSA. The payments are subject to a means test. If payments are refused, the claimant can challenge the decision by requesting a revision and/or appealing. A claimant does not have to seek a revision before appealing but because of the time it takes for an appeal to be heard the matter may be resolved quicker via a revision.

For further details, see CPAG's *Welfare Benefits and Tax Credits Handbook*.

Tax rebate

A person who is unemployed or is laid off may be entitled to a tax rebate at the end of the tax year. However, this will be reduced or may be cancelled out if s/he receives JSA, as this is taxed. In some cases, where HM Revenue and Customs has delayed paying the tax rebate it must pay interest on it.

Notice pay

An employee is entitled to be paid during the notice period if s/he works during that period or cannot work because of illness, pregnancy or childbirth, or because s/he is on adoption, parental or paternity leave or holiday, or the employer does not wish her/him to work. An employee who is dismissed without being given the correct notice is entitled to be paid her/his normal wages 'in lieu' of notice, unless the dismissal is due to gross misconduct. Notice rules are laid down in the law and these depend on length of service. Some employees may be entitled to a longer period of notice under the terms of their contract with the employer. The contract may be written or unwritten.

For further details, see www.direct.gov.uk/notice.

Redundancy payments

An employee who has two years' continuous service and is not in an excluded occupation, and who loses her/his job through redundancy might be entitled to a statutory redundancy payment. If a statutory redundancy payment has not been made or is not for the correct amount, the employee can apply to an employment tribunal. There is a strict six-month time limit from the date of termination for making such an application. A person in need of advice in this situation should be referred to an employment law adviser.

Some workers may be entitled to a larger redundancy payment under the terms of their contract.

For further details, see www.direct.gov.uk/redundancy.

Guarantee payments

If an employer fails to provide work for (lays off) an employee, then, in most cases, s/he must pay a guarantee payment for five days of lay-off in any period of three months. Guarantee payments can be enforced through an employment tribunal. Specialist help should be sought. An employee who is dismissed for seeking to enforce this right is entitled to claim unfair dismissal to an employment tribunal, regardless of the length of her/his service.

Guarantee payments are taken into account as earnings for means-tested benefits.

For further details, see the guidance on guarantee payments on the Department for Business Enterprise and Regulatory Reform's website at www.berr.gov.uk/employment/employment-legislation/employment-guidance.

Private pensions

Clients who are members of an employer's (occupational) pension scheme or a private pension plan may be entitled to take benefits from these plans before the normal retirement age if, for instance, they become permanently incapable of work. Benefits available from pension schemes should be closely examined and independent financial advice should be sought before making a decision to take benefits early from a private scheme.

Starting work

Claimants starting full-time work may be entitled to one-off lump-sum payments – child maintenance bonus (p148), a job grant (see below) or extended payments of housing benefit (HB)/council tax benefit (CTB) and mortgage interest run-on (see below).

Job grant[55]

People who start full-time work may be entitled to a job grant of £100, or £250 if they have children (in 2008/09). They must have been in receipt of the following benefits for 26 weeks and stopped getting them as a result of starting full-time work:

- income support (IS);
- income-based JSA;
- incapacity benefit (IB);
- severe disablement allowance (SDA);
- income-related employment and support allowance (ESA) (expected at the time of writing);
- specified allowances under the New Deal or Jobcentre Plus schemes.

The work must be expected to last five weeks or more.

Mortgage interest run-on

People who start full-time work after having received housing costs in their IS, income-based JSA or income-related ESA for the previous 26 weeks may qualify for an extra four weeks of such housing costs payments.[56]

Extended payments of housing benefit and council tax benefit

Claimants who have been on IS, income-based JSA, ESA (income-related or contributory), IB or SDA for the previous 26 weeks whose entitlement ends because they start work or increase their hours may be entitled to a four-week extension of HB and CTB.[57] There may still be an entitlement to HB/CTB after this period, depending on whether the means test is satisfied.

For further details, see CPAG's *Welfare Benefits and Tax Credits Handbook*.

8. Other help

This section covers ways of maximising income that apply to several types of client and which have not been covered above.

Social fund

There are two sections to the social fund – the regulated and the discretionary.[58] Maternity grants, funeral expenses, winter fuel payments and cold weather payments are part of the regulated social fund so have specific regulations. If the claimant satisfies these, s/he will be entitled to a payment.

Budgeting loans, community care grants and crisis loans are part of the discretionary social fund. Decisions are largely at the discretion of local Department for Work and Pensions (DWP) officials.

For all the social fund payments, except crisis loans, a claimant must be in receipt of a qualifying benefit (and in the case of budgeting loans have been in receipt of a qualifying benefit or tax credit for 26 weeks) in addition to satisfying other conditions of entitlement. In some cases, someone can claim if her/his partner is in receipt of the qualifying benefit or tax credit.

If s/he is refused a grant or a loan from the discretionary social fund, or s/he does not consider the amount offered to be sufficient, the decision can be challenged by asking for a review. If the claimant is still dissatisfied, s/he should ask for a further review by a social fund inspector. If the decision concerns the regulated social fund, s/he should seek a revision and/or appeal to an appeal tribunal. For further details, see CPAG's *Welfare Benefits and Tax Credits Handbook*.

Bereavement benefits

There are three main types of bereavement benefits, all of which are based on the national insurance (NI) contributions of the claimant's late spouse or civil partner. These are:

- bereavement payment (a lump-sum payment of £2,000);[59]
- widowed parent's allowance – a weekly benefit paid to widows, widowers or surviving civil partners who have children, or widows or surviving civil partners who are pregnant at the time their husband or civil partner dies;[60]
- bereavement allowance – a weekly benefit paid for up to 52 weeks to widows, widowers or surviving civil partners who were 45 or over when their spouse or civil partner died.[61]

These benefits do not depend on NI contributions if a spouse or civil partner dies as a result of an industrial accident or disease. The contribution conditions are different for each benefit.

Bereavement allowance and widowed parent's allowance cease when the claimant re-marries or enters a new civil partnership, and are suspended during any period of cohabitation. The exact circumstances should be examined to see whether or not a couple's relationship actually consists of cohabitation.

Problems can arise if the DWP doubts the existence or validity of a marriage.

For further details, see CPAG's *Welfare Benefits and Tax Credits Handbook*.

Benefit overpayments

If an amount of benefit to which a claimant is not entitled has been paid, this is an overpayment. The rules on overpayments of housing benefit (HB) and council tax benefit (CTB) differ from those for other benefits. For benefits other than HB and CTB, an overpayment is recoverable if the DWP can show it has been caused by claimant misrepresenting or failing to disclose a material fact.[62]

Overpayments of HB/CTB are recoverable unless caused by official error, no relevant person caused the official error and no relevant person could reasonably have been expected to realise s/he was being overpaid.[63]

If it appears that the overpayment is not a recoverable one or the amount of the overpayment is incorrect, the claimant should challenge the decision by seeking a revision and/or appeal.

Even if a recoverable overpayment has occurred, the adviser should always check the amount being recovered in detail. Ensure, for example, that the correct earnings disregards and any offsets have been applied on a weekly basis. If a claimant's circumstances have altered during the period of overpayment, the calculation may be complex. Rates of recovery of overpayments are negotiable and the adviser should always consider this. There are maximum weekly amounts that can be recovered by deduction from benefits. There is a discretionary power to waive recovery in exceptional circumstances.

For further details, see CPAG's *Welfare Benefits and Tax Credits Handbook*.

Tax credit overpayments

The rules for tax credit overpayments differ from those for benefits. All overpayments of tax credits are recoverable, even those caused by official error.[64] However, HM Revenue and Customs (the Revenue) does not have to recover an overpayment and must exercise its discretion when deciding whether to do so. The Revenue has a Code of Practice (COP26) on overpayments. In this, it states that an overpayment may be written off in whole or in part if the Revenue has failed to meet its 'responsibilities' (these are set out in the Code of Practice) or if recovery would cause hardship. COP26, *What Happens if We Have Paid You Too Much Tax Credit?* is available at www.hmrc.gov.uk.

Most overpayments are recovered through a reduction in an existing tax credit award and there are maximum rates of recovery depending on the level of the award. The client should check whether the Revenue has applied the maximum rate and, if so, try to negotiate a lower reduction rate. If an overpayment is being disputed, the Revenue suspends recovery.

Payments for war injury

There are a number of different schemes providing benefits for those disabled, or for the dependants of those killed, in either the First World War or any conflict since 3 September 1939. Some of these schemes only cover members of the armed forces but there are others that apply to auxiliary personnel, civil defence volunteers, merchant mariners and ordinary civilians. Who qualifies and what payments they can receive are complicated. For who may be eligible, contact the Veterans Helpline on 0800 169 2277 or write to the Service Personnel and Veterans Agency, Norcross, Thornton Cleveleys, Lancashire, FY5 3WP or email veterans.help@spva.gsi.gov.uk

Discretionary housing payments

Discretionary housing payments are not part of HB or CTB but can be paid to HB and CTB claimants to help them meet their rent or council tax.[65] They are paid by the local authority from a cash-limited budget. There is no 'right' to the payments and it is up to the local authority to decide whether to make them, how much should be paid and how far they can be backdated. There is no right of appeal, but applicants can ask the local authority to review its decision. Any further challenge would have to be made by judicial review. These payments are disregarded as income for income support, income-based jobseeker's allowance, income-related employment and support allowance, HB, CTB and tax credits. A claim must be made to the local authority.

For further details, see CPAG's *Welfare Benefits and Tax Credits Handbook*.

Equal pay rules

The equal pay rules mean that a woman should not be paid less than a man for work of equal value or for the same work. Where a working woman is in debt, it is always worth checking whether these rules might help increase her income. The Equal Pay Act is specifically about ensuring equal pay between men and women. However, if a person is being paid less than others doing similar work because of their age, gender, disability, race, religion and belief, or sexual orientation, it could constitute unlawful discrimination. Specialist help will be necessary to pursue a claim. For further details, contact the Equality and Human Rights Commission Helpline on 0845 604 6610 (England) or 0845 604 8810 (Wales), or see www.equalityhumanrights.com.

National minimum wage

Most employees are entitled to be paid at a rate equivalent to at least the national minimum wage. An employee who is entitled to the national minimum wage and being paid less than this can complain to the national minimum wage helpline or to an employment tribunal. For more information, contact the helpline on 0845 6000 678 or visit www.direct.gov.uk.

Tax reliefs

Tax reliefs are amounts that are deducted from taxable income in recognition of money necessarily spent by the taxpayer in working. They can be claimed in addition to a personal allowance and can be backdated for up to six years. Tax reliefs for the self-employed should be calculated by a specialist adviser.

For employed people, it is possible to claim relief on any money that is spent to enable a job to be done, but which is not paid for by the employer. The expenses have to 'wholly, exclusively and necessarily' incurred in order to do the work.

Tax reliefs should be claimed on a tax return form, accompanied by a covering letter and any supporting evidence – eg, an itemised phone bill.

Items for which tax relief can be claimed include:

- membership of professional bodies;
- special clothing for work;
- using heating/lighting or the telephone at home for work;
- buying tools.

Another form of tax relief is the 'rent a room' scheme. This enables someone to let out a main room in their home and not pay tax on the rental income, provided the rent stays below a certain level. Even if the client cannot benefit from this scheme, there are other forms of tax relief that may be applicable if s/he lets out property. Moreover, because expenses such as repairs, heating and lighting (that can be claimed under normal letting) cannot be claimed under the 'rent a room' scheme, a person may not be better off joining this scheme – specialist advice should be given.

Charities

There are thousands of charities that can provide payments to individuals in need. Some are open to all and others are for certain groups only, such as armed service personnel or people with certain disabilities. Many have a committee that sifts applications and meets on a cyclical basis. Some of the very large charities receive thousands of applications in a year and may place limits on people from whom they are prepared to accept applications – eg, from social workers only.

It is worthwhile investigating less well known charities to approach, in addition to major charities. These are either locally based or specialise in helping particular people. Some charities expect a person to have exhausted other statutory provision before approaching them – eg, the social fund. The organisation turn2us has a website (www.turn2us.org.uk) with an A-Z of all the charities that can provide financial help and applications for support can in many cases be made directly from the website.

The publication *A Guide to Grants for Individuals in Need* provides a list of local and national charities, advises on the most appropriate charity and gives guidance on how to make a successful application.

Most charitable payments are ignored for means-tested benefits if they are made regularly. Most that are made irregularly are treated as capital – this will only affect the benefit if it takes the claimant above the capital limit.

Trade unions

Many trade unions have central hardship funds for members or ex-members. Unions may also be involved in various benevolent funds and charities associated with particular industries. If someone has been a member of a union it is worth approaching the union to enquire about possible lump-sum payments or, in some cases, ongoing support.

Notes

3. **Parents**

1 s141 SSCBA 1992
2 **HB** Sch 3 para 3 HB Regs; Sch 3 para 3 HB(SPC) Regs
CTB Sch 1 para 3 CTB Regs; Sch 1 para 3 CTB(SPC) Regs
3 ss3, 7, 8 and 42 TCA 2002; regs 3-5 CTC Regs; reg 3 TC(Imm) Regs; reg 3 TC(R) Regs
4 ss3, 10 and 42 TCA 2002; regs 4-8 WTC(EMR) Regs; reg 3 TC(Imm) Regs; reg 3 TC(R) Regs
5 s12 TCA 2002; regs 3,13 and 14 WTC(EMR) Regs
HB Regs 27 and 28 HB Regs; regs 30 and 31 HB(SPC) Regs
CTB Regs 17 and 18 CTB Regs ; regs 20 and 21 CTB(SPC) Regs
6 Reg 5 SFM&FE Regs
7 ss164–171 SSCBA 1992
8 ss171ZA–171ZK SSCBA 1992
9 ss171ZL–171ZT SSCBA 1992
10 s35 SSCBA 1992
11 Reg 3 HSS&WF(A) Regs
12 s130 SSCBA 1992
13 HB/CTB Bulletin G10/2008
14 **IS** Sch 3 IS Regs
JSA Sch 2 JSA Regs
PC Sch 2 SPC Regs
ESA Sch 6 ESA Regs
15 s131 SSCBA 1992
16 **IS** Sch 8 IS Regs
JSA Sch 6 JSA Regs
PC Sch 6 SPC Regs
ESA Sch 7 ESA Regs
HB Sch 4 HB Regs; Sch 4 HB(SPC) Regs
CTB Sch 3 CTB Regs; Sch 2 CTB(SPC) Regs
17 s14 Education Act 2002
18 s512 Education Act 1996; Sch 14 para 117 IAA 1999
19 s17 Children Act 1989

4. **Lone parents**

20 s12 TCA 2002; regs 3,13 and 14 WTC(EMR) Regs
HB Regs 27 and 28 HB Regs; regs 30 and 31 HB(SPC) Regs
CTB Regs 17 and 18 CTB Regs ; regs 20 and 21 CTB(SPC) Regs
21 s2(2) ETA 1973

22 **HB** Schs 7 and 8 HB Regs; Sch 7 para 3 HB(SPC) Regs
CTB Schs 6 and 7 CTB Regs; Sch 5 CTB(SPC) Regs
23 Reg 3 SS(CMB) Regs
24 Reg 4 SS(CMPMA) Regs
25 **HB** Sch 4 para 4 HB Regs; Sch 4 para 2 HB(SPC) Regs
CTB Sch 3 para 4 CTB Regs; Sch 2 para 2 CTB(SPC) Regs
26 **IS** Sch 8 para 5 IS Regs
JSA Sch 6 JSA Regs
PC Sch 6 SPC Regs

5. **Sick and disabled people**
27 s64 SSCBA 1992
28 s72 SSCBA 1992
29 s73 SSCBA 1992
30 ss1 and 20 WRA 2007
31 s30A SSCBA 1992
32 s94 and Sch 7 SSCBA 1992
33 s10 TCA; regs 4 and 9 WTC(EMR) Regs
34 Reg 6 WTC(EMR) Regs
35 Reg 6(4)(a) and Sch 1B para 8 IS Regs; reg 53(h) JSA Regs
36 **IS** Sch 2 para 14ZA IS Regs
JSA Sch 1 para 17 JSA Regs
PC Sch 1 para 4 SPC Regs
ESA Sch 4 para 8 ESA Regs
HB Sch 3 para 17 HB Regs; Sch 3 para 9 HB(SPC) Regs
CTB Sch 1 para 17 CTB Regs; Sch 1 para 9 CTB (SPC) Regs
37 **HB** Sch 3 para 16 HB Regs; Sch 3 para 8 HB(SPC) Regs
CTB Sch 1 para 16 CTB Regs; Sch 1 para 8 CTB(SPC) Regs
38 **IS** Sch 2 para 11 IS Regs
JSA Sch 1 paras 13 and 14 JSA Regs
HB Sch 3 para 12 HB Regs
CTB Sch 1 para 12 CTB Regs
39 **IS** Sch 2 para 13 IS Regs
JSA Sch 1 paras 15 and 21 JSA Regs
PC Sch 1 para 1 SPC Regs
ESA Sch 4 para 6 ESA Regs
HB Sch 3 para 14 HB Regs; Sch 3 para 6 HB(SPC) Regs
CTB Sch 1 para 14 CTB Regs; Sch 1 para 6 CTB(SPC) Regs
40 **IS** Sch 2 para 13A IS Regs
JSA Sch 1 paras 15A and 21A JSA Regs
ESA Sch 4 para 7 ESA Regs
HB Sch 3 para 15 HB Regs; Sch 3 para 7 HB(SPC) Regs
CTB Sch 1 para 15 CTB Regs; Sch 1 para 7 CTB(SPC) Regs
41 Regs 16-17 SS(IFW) Regs; regs 40-45 ESA Regs
42 s70 SSCBA 1992

6. **Retired people**
43 s44 SSCBA 1992
44 s48 SSCBA 1992
45 s48A SSCBA 1992
46 ss48B, 48BB, and 51 SSCBA 1992
47 ss1(2) and (6), 2 and 4(2) SPCA 2002; regs 2-4 and 6 SPC Regs
48 ss1(2), 3 and 4(2) SPCA 2002; regs 2-4 SPC Regs
49 **IS** Sch 2 paras 9 and 9A IS Regs
JSA Sch 1 paras 10 and 11 JSA Regs
50 **IS** Sch 2 para 10 IS Regs
JSA Sch 1 para 12 JSA Regs
51 Reg 2 SFWFP Regs

7. **Unemployed people**
52 ss1-3A JSA 1995
53 ss19, 20 and 20A JSA 1995
54 Regs 140-146H JSA Regs
55 s2(2) ETA 1973
56 Reg 6(5)–(8) IS Regs
57 **HB** Regs 72-73D HB Regs; regs 53-53D HB(SPC) Regs
CTB Regs 60-61D CTB Regs; regs 44-44D CTB(SPC) Regs

8. **Other help**
58 SFM&FE Regs; SFCWP Regs; SFWFP Regs; Social Fund Directions; ss138-140 SSCBA 1992
59 ss36 and 60 SSCBA 1992
60 ss39A and 60 SSCBA 1992
61 ss39B and 60 SSCBA 1992
62 s71 SSAA 1992
63 **HB** Reg 100 HB Regs; reg 81 HB(SPC) Regs
CTB Reg 83 CTB Regs; reg 68 CTB(SPC) Regs
64 ss28 and 29 TCA 2002
65 s69 CSPSSA 2000; reg 2(1) DFA Regs

7

Chapter 7

Dealing with priority debts

This chapter covers:

1. Deciding on priorities

After dealing with any emergencies and checking the client is liable for the debts, advisers need to identify which debts must be dealt with first – ie, which debts are priority debts. The criteria for deciding which debts are priorities are for the most part 'objective' – the severity of the legal remedies available to creditors determines the degree of priority. If non-payment would give the creditor the right to deprive the client of her/his home, liberty, or essential goods and services, that debt will have priority. For a discussion of other debts which may need to be treated as priority, see Chapter 8.

Clients often believe that priorities must be decided on the basis of the amount owed, or that any debt that is subject to a court order should be a priority. The existence of a court judgment does not automatically give priority status to a debt and there are millions of judgments given by courts in England and Wales each year for debts that remain unpaid. These debts would only become a priority if the enforcement methods open to a creditor through a court posed a serious threat to the client's home, liberty or essential goods.

Recognising priority debts

Using the criteria outlined above, the following are priority debts.

Secured loan

Mortgages and all other loans secured against a client's home are priorities because non-payment can lead to possession action by the lender and homelessness. One of the strategies outlined in this chapter must be adopted immediately for any secured loan in arrears. If the lender has already begun possession proceedings, see Chapter 9.

Rent arrears

Rent arrears are a priority because they can lead to possession action by the landlord and homelessness. If the landlord has already begun possession proceedings, see Chapter 9.

A client who is a tenant may find that water charges are paid as part of the rent so that the client could be evicted for non-payment. In such cases, water charges should be considered as a priority. If a client is threatened with possession proceedings for non-payment of water charges, see Chapter 4.

Council tax

Council tax arrears are a priority because non-payment could lead to the loss of essential goods as a result of bailiff action or, ultimately to imprisonment. If the magistrates' court has issued a liability order (which allows the council to use bailiffs) or the client is facing a committal hearing or a committal warrant has been issued (which could result in imprisonment), see Chapter 10.

Fines, maintenance and compensation orders

Unpaid fines, maintenance and compensation orders are a priority because non-payment could lead to a loss of essential items to bailiffs or, ultimately, to imprisonment. If the client is in arrears with any of these debts, even if no bailiff or other enforcement action has been taken, see Chapter 10.

Charges for utilities

Payment for gas and electricity are priorities because suppliers have powers to disconnect for non-payment of bills. Such sanctions do not apply to arrears on non-fuel items (eg, cookers or the cost of central heating installation) purchased from gas and electricity suppliers, and thus debts for such items are not a priority.

Until the passing of the Water Industry Act 1999, water companies also had powers to disconnect for debt and so were considered priorities. This is no longer the case and attempts by water companies to retain priority status should be resisted as this would be inequitable to other creditors. A realistic amount for current consumption of water must be included in the financial statement, but not for arrears. Help with arrears may be available from one of the water industry's trust funds or the WaterSure scheme may be able to help with high bills (see Chapter 4).

If disconnection is threatened, make immediate contact with the supplier to challenge this and discuss ways of paying for the supply (see p199).

TV licence

A colour TV licence costs £139.50 a year. Payment plans are available to spread the cost. Although not a debt as such, because it is a criminal offence to use a television without a licence (for which the usual penalty is a fine), if a client either does not have a licence (but does have a television) or is behind with a payment plan, this should be treated as a priority.

Some people qualify for a concession on the cost of the TV licence – eg, clients who are aged 74, have sight impairments, or who are living in residential care. A person aged 75 or over is entitled to a free licence.

Tax and VAT

These debts are a priority if the client is continuing to trade because HM Revenue and Customs (the Revenue) can seize goods from the client to cover unpaid tax without requiring a court order, or could make the client bankrupt and put her/him out of business. If the client has ceased trading, each case must be looked at on its merits. If:

- bailiffs are involved, see Chapter 11;
- action has been started in the magistrates' court, see Chapter 10;
- action has been started in the county court, see Chapter 9.

See also Chapter 13.

Hire purchase and conditional sale agreements

Some hire purchase or conditional sale agreements will need to be treated as priority debts if they are for goods that are essential for the client to retain – eg, a car for work in the absence of suitable public transport, because the creditor has powers to repossess the goods if payments are not kept – see Chapter 4.

National insurance contributions

Class 4 national insurance contributions for self-employed earners are a priority because they are assessed and collected by the Revenue along with unpaid income tax.

2. The general approach to priority debts

Once identified, priority debts must be dealt with quickly and effectively. General rules about how this should be done are listed below. There are also specific ways of dealing with particular types of debts.

Immediate contact should be made with the creditor. If it is not possible to make a definite offer of payment immediately, ask for more time – eg, 14 or 28 days and ask the creditor either to take no further action or suspend any existing action during this period. If possible, the client should be advised to pay at least the current instalments in the meantime.

Generally, it is not appropriate to make offers to priority creditors on a *pro rata* basis (see p225) and it will be necessary for advisers to negotiate with them individually. It must first be decided whether to make payment:

- either as soon as possible; *or*
- over as long a period as possible.

The following should be taken into account.

- If the debt is accruing interest or charges it may be in the client's best interests to pay it off quickly.
- It might be in the client's best interests to pay off a small priority debt as soon as possible.
- The creditor's collection policies – eg, the local authority's policy may be to send council tax liability orders straight to the bailiffs, which will increase the debt.
- The creditor may insist on arrears being cleared before the next bill is due to be delivered or payment made.
- If the client is currently earning above her/his average, it may be in her/his best interests to make higher payments while s/he can.
- If capital or lower-cost finance is available, the debt can be cleared more quickly.
- The client's age or state of health may lead to a reduction in income. It could be in her/his best interests to make a payment before this happens.
- If the client is considering moving, it may be necessary to make a payment before doing so.
- If the client has any non-priority debts, s/he will usually need to make some provision for these (see Chapter 8).

Advisers should also further prioritise the debts in the light of:

- what the client wants;
- the existence of more than one priority debt;
- the severity of the sanction available to the creditor;
- the potential consequences of using a particular strategy;
- the stage the recovery process has reached.

Although the decision to give one debt priority over another is to some extent a subjective one, advisers should always discuss with the client the range of options available and the possible consequences.

Advisers should work through the following list of tasks.

- In the case of secured loans and hire purchase/conditional sale agreements, check whether the client has payment protection insurance to cover the repayments in the event of sickness or incapacity, unemployment, accident or death. If the client does have insurance and her/his situation is covered by the policy, advise the client to make a claim. If the claim is refused, consider whether this can be challenged and/or also whether the policy may have been mis-sold (see p107). If the client's situation is not covered by the policy, also consider whether the policy may have been mis-sold – eg, the client's circumstances were such that s/he could never have made a claim. If the agreement is regulated by the Consumer Credit Act 1974 and the client says that taking out payment protection insurance was a condition of being granted the credit, the agreement may be unenforceable (see p57).

- In the case of secured loans and hire purchase/conditional sale agreements, investigate whether the lender complied with its duty to assess the client's ability to repay either under the Banking Code, the Financial Services Authority's *Mortgages and Home Finance: conduct of business sourcebook* (MCOB) or any other applicable code of practice. Irresponsible lending is now a matter the Office of Fair Trading is required to take account of when considering whether a lender is a 'fit person' to hold a consumer credit licence.
- Consider whether the client has any other grounds for challenging either the debt or the creditor's conduct (see Chapters 4 and 5).
- Telephone the creditor as soon as possible, even if the adviser does not have all the necessary information on which to base a strategy. This may help prevent further action and alert the priority creditor to the involvement of an independent agency.
- If necessary, take emergency action to prevent the immediate loss of home, liberty, essential goods or services (see p198).
- Negotiate the amount, manner and time of repayments.
- Ensure the client is clear about whom to pay, when to pay and how much to pay.
- Encourage the client to seek further assistance from the adviser if s/he is facing practical difficulties with repayment arrangements.
- Monitor the initial strategy with the client. If the client's circumstances change or the original strategy is unsuccessful, the adviser and the client must decide whether to adopt a new strategy or whether the details of the original strategy can be modified.

Consider carefully the amount of income included as 'available' to the client. The fact that a debt is priority may influence the way in which a partner's income is treated. A partner may not wish to pool her/his income and liabilities if only non-priority debts have been accrued (and there is no need to – see p36). However, where serious consequences, such as loss of home, could be experienced by the client's partner, s/he may wish to contribute towards repaying a debt for which s/he is not legally liable. This situation can also occur when a debt arose whilst someone was with a previous partner.[1]

Points to note

- Although many priority creditors have their own collection policies which act as guidelines for their officers, these can always be negotiated.
- It may be necessary to contact someone in a position of authority within the relevant organisation before policies can be changed.

- Accounting periods, such as local authority financial years or other periods between quarterly bills, should not be taken as absolute dates by which current liabilities must be met.
- Secured lenders often argue that arrears should be repaid in short periods. However, in an important decision the Court of Appeal suggested that a reasonable period to clear arrears might be the whole of the remaining term of the mortgage.[2] Thus, if a possession action were started half-way through a 30-year mortgage, it would be possible for the court to suspend an order on payment of an amount which would repay the mortgage together with the arrears over the next 15 years. On the other hand, if the secured loan is regulated by the Consumer Credit Act, the client may be able to apply for a time order (see p283). If the loan is a regulated mortgage contract (see p87), the lender should have complied with section 13 MCOB. This requires the lender to use reasonable efforts to come to an agreement with the client on payment of the arrears over a reasonable period (in appropriate cases, the remaining term of the mortgage) and repossessing the property only as a last resort where there is no other realistic alternative.

The client should be advised to:

- start making payments immediately the strategy has been decided, as this will encourage the creditor to accept the arrangements; *and*
- where possible, set up a direct debit or standing order to ensure a payment arrangement is kept.

Creditors should be asked to confirm the agreed strategy in writing. They may often require a financial statement (see p42), list of debts and written proposal from the adviser before providing such confirmation.

'Negative equity'

Negative equity occurs when the value of a client's property falls below the amount due under her/his mortgage or other loans secured on it. This means that, even if her/his property were sold, the client would not be free of debt and would still owe an amount (the negative equity) to the creditor. If a client wants to sell a property in negative equity, s/he will need the permission of any secured creditors who are not going to be repaid out of the sale proceeds. Section 13.3 MCOB requires Financial Services Authority-regulated lenders to treat clients 'fairly'. If a creditor unreasonably refuses to agree to a sale, the court can overrule it.[3] In this situation, the adviser should seek specialist advice.

The strategies that follow depend on the housing market. If houses cannot be sold easily, creditors may not want to repossess and a sale by the client could be undesirable or impossible. However, advisers should not necessarily rely on this, as lenders will sometimes decide to cut their losses and repossess regardless.

If possible, it is important to reach an agreement to avoid such a situation. Section 13.3 MCOB says that, where a payment arrangement cannot be made, the lender should consider allowing the client to remain in the property in order to sell the property.

Negative equity will affect whether some of the following strategies apply. However, in most circumstances, the approach remains the same, either because a lender is prepared to ignore the negative equity or because it becomes an unsecured and non-priority debt (see Chapter 8).

The 'mortgage shortfall' on the sale of the property

For what to do where there is a 'mortgage shortfall' or a claim from a mortgage indemnity insurer, see Chapter 5. These debts, though non-priority at present, need to be dealt with because they represent a potential future problem if an attachment of earnings order, bankruptcy or charging order were to be used at a future date.

3. Strategies for dealing with priority debts

'Interest-only' payments (for mortgages and secured loans)

A large proportion of secured borrowing is repaid by means of monthly payments that combine interest with a repayment of capital. In such cases, a client can reduce the payments if the creditor will agree to accept payment of the interest alone without any capital repayment. Creditors will need to be persuaded that a request to make interest-only payments is not just a delaying tactic or an excuse for being unable to pay anything. If a client can afford to pay the interest which is accruing on an agreement, advisers are not asking for anything that is either out of the ordinary or generous.

Payments towards the capital can be resumed if the client's financial circumstances improve in the future. Some creditors are prepared to wait until property is sold for the capital to be repaid. Creditors will need to be satisfied either that the arrangement is a temporary one and that the client will be able to resume making the full contractual payments or that repayment of the capital by some other method is adequately assured.

When applicable

Paying interest only is applicable where payment of the interest and capital cannot currently be afforded. Interest-only payments cannot be used for:

- any agreement where the total interest has already been added at the beginning of the loan period and the whole amount secured against the property, because no interest is accruing on a daily basis (but see reduced payments on p180); *or*

- an endowment mortgage, because payments are already for interest only and the capital is repaid in a lump sum at the end of the period of the loan by an endowment insurance policy (see p86).

Advantages

- It is easily accepted by priority creditors.
- It prevents further action.
- It may avoid a bad credit rating.

Disadvantages

- The debt may take longer to clear than it would if full payments were maintained, or if a reduction in capital or charges could be negotiated and so the client may pay more in the long run.
- The Administration of Justice Act 1973 requires the arrears to be cleared in a 'reasonable time'.[4] Although the court could use its powers to order an adjournment or a suspended possession order to allow payments of interest only,[5] this would only be possible for a short period (eg, six months), after which time an increased payment would be necessary to clear the arrears in a reasonable time (see p183). Similarly, the court could not make a time order on this basis as it would not provide for payment of the loan (see p192).

Useful arguments

- Most building societies or other secured lenders have policies that allow local managers to accept interest-only payments for a fixed period (perhaps six months). These can often be arranged over the telephone (although any such arrangement must be confirmed in writing and a financial statement may be required).
- For clients in receipt of income support (IS), income-based jobseeker's allowance (JSA) or income-related employment and support allowance (ESA) that does not yet cover the whole mortgage interest, many creditors will accept half the interest until the client becomes eligible to have the full interest met by the Department for Work and Pensions (DWP).

Checklist for action

- Telephone/write to the creditor to propose the strategy and request written confirmation that the strategy is accepted.
- Explain the cause of the client's inability to pay – through a change of circumstances or economic factors such as high interest rates.
- Advise the client of how much to pay and when.
- Consider direct payments for clients on IS/income-based JSA/pension credit (PC) (see p194).
- Consider advising the client to set up a direct debit or standing order to ensure payments are kept up.

Reduced payments

A creditor can be asked to renegotiate the contract that has been made so that a client can afford the payments. There are three principal ways in which payments can be reduced.

- Ask the creditor to charge a lower rate of interest, either for a period of time (eg, the next year) or for the rest of the loan, even if interest has already been added to the amount payable over the whole period of the loan.
- Ask the creditor to agree to reduce the amount outstanding on a loan so that future payments (perhaps of interest only) are affordable by the client.
- Ask the creditor to allow repayments to extend over a longer period, thereby reducing the capital portion of the repayments. There would need to be enough equity to allow this – the amount of equity can be calculated by deducting the total amount of all loans secured on the property from the market value of the property.

When applicable

- If the client cannot possibly meet her/his original contractual obligations.
- If interest rates have risen significantly since the contract was taken out, or if the interest originally charged was significantly higher than available elsewhere or if, despite a general fall in interest rates, a high rate of interest continues to be charged. This is particularly true where a time order would be appropriate (see p283).
- If the outstanding balance includes capitalised arrears of interest/charges, particularly where these have accrued at a high rate.
- If the property against which the loan is secured is worth less than the capital outstanding, some lenders will reduce their capital outlay rather than continue to chase something which is effectively no longer a fully secured debt.
- If there is another secured loan against the same property, the first mortgagee may reduce the amount outstanding on its loan in order that the client can borrow enough to be able to pay off the second mortgagee and then have one remaining loan. This might be a likely option if the second mortgagee is considering repossession, and the first mortgagee wishes to continue with the business it has with its customer.
- If adverse publicity would be attracted by a repossession.
- If the property market is slow and, therefore, repossessed properties are unlikely to be saleable.

This strategy is not applicable to endowment mortgages.

Advantages

- It reduces the amount payable and protects the client's home and essential goods.

Disadvantages

- It will be difficult to gain agreement to this as a long-term strategy from creditors, particularly if the loan is more than fully secured.
- The lender may only defer interest and so the client may be faced with substantially higher payments at the end of the arrangement, which may lead to further default in the future.
- Repaying an interest-bearing debt over a longer period may result in additional interest being paid, unless the payments are sufficient to cover this or the rate of interest is reduced accordingly.
- It is sometimes better to allow the home to be lost if it will end indebtedness and ensure appropriate rehousing by a local authority or housing association (see p231). The local authority may argue, however, that the client has made her/himself intentionally homeless and, if the sale results in the client having equity, this could affect entitlement to certain benefits.
- If the capital outstanding is to be reduced, it may require changes to the legal charge (see p209), which is registered on the property. The client will be liable for the costs associated with this.

Useful arguments

- If a time order would be possible (see p283), a creditor may prefer to negotiate changes voluntarily rather than have them imposed by the court, especially if adverse publicity is likely to be attracted by a case.
- Point out any failure by the creditor to prevent the build up of arrears, to send the client regular statements of account or to inform the client of the need to increase payments to cover the ongoing arrears/charges. Reference can be made to paragraph 46 of the Office of Fair Trading (OFT) *Guidelines for Non-status Lending* (whose principles of good practice apply to all lending), which points out that lenders should monitor the accrual of default charges carefully to prevent an excessive build-up of arrears and should also notify the client on a monthly basis of the amount of arrears and the amount of any interest or other charges, including default charges. If the alternative for the creditor is repossession of a house, point out that the strategy being offered may be cheaper, as possessing and reselling a property is a time-consuming, and, therefore, expensive way of making a profit.
- In the case of regulated mortgage contracts, the Financial Services Authority's (FSA) *Mortgages and Home Finance: conduct of business sourcebook* (MCOB) requires the lender to contact the client within 15 days of the account falling into arrears and to provide her/him with prescribed information including the likely charges that will be incurred should the arrears not be cleared. Any failure to comply with MCOB could be pointed out to the lender if this has contributed to the build-up of arrears. From 1 October 2008, additional post-contract information requirements will be imposed on creditors under agreements regulated by the Consumer Credit Act 1974 (see p50).

- In all cases, point out mis-selling of any part of the loan, such as payment protection insurance, or failure to assess the client's ability to repay, in order to support arguments to reduce the amount outstanding and for reduced payments. For example, mis-selling of payment protection insurance may give rise to an argument for a rebate of some or all of the premium (see p107) or that the loan agreement itself is unenforceable (see p57).
- Payments are more likely to be maintained if set at a lower level, affordable by the client.
- The sums already paid by the client have given the creditor a more than adequate return on the loan.

Checklist for action

- Telephone/write to the creditor to propose the strategy and request written confirmation of its acceptance.
- Advise the client of how much to pay and when.
- Consider a time order in Consumer Credit Act cases (see p283).

Capitalise arrears

Where arrears have built up (particularly on a repayment mortgage), a creditor can be asked to add these to the capital outstanding and simply charge interest on the new capital amount. This can then be rescheduled over the remaining period of the mortgage, although it may be possible to extend the repayment period.

When applicable

- This strategy is particularly useful when there is an improvement in the client's circumstances following a period in which arrears have built up. For example, if a client has recently become employed after a period of unemployment or returned to work after a long strike or period of sickness, provided her/his payment record was previously satisfactory, most creditors will agree to capitalise the arrears.
- Creditors will only capitalise arrears if the market value of the property is significantly greater than the amount of capital currently outstanding. They will not usually do so if it would lead to the capital outstanding being more than the value of the property.

Advantages

- It regularises the situation.
- It prevents further action.
- It can avoid a bad credit rating as the client will no longer have arrears.
- The repayments are affordable.

Disadvantages

- The repayments on the loan will be increased if the loan is to be repaid within the original contractual period.
- The debt may take longer to pay off, in which case the client would pay more.
- If interest charges rise, the effect is greater than when capital was less.
- Interest is in effect paid on the arrears throughout the term of the mortgage.
- For IS/income-based JSA/PC claimants, the DWP will not usually meet the cost of additional interest because arrears have been capitalised.

Useful arguments

- Some creditors will only consider capitalising arrears after a trial period in which a client makes regular repayments, particularly where there is little prospect of an improvement in circumstances. The adviser can, therefore, suggest that the lender reviews the strategy after an agreed period in which the client is able to demonstrate that s/he is able to maintain the repayments.

Checklist for action

- Telephone/write to the creditor to propose the strategy and request written confirmation that this is agreed.
- Advise the client of any change in repayments.
- Advise clients on IS/income-based JSA/PC to notify the DWP of changes in repayments.

Scheduled payment of arrears

On secured loans

Arrears may be repayable over a period of time. This may be a set amount each month, calculated to repay the arrears over a period of time acceptable to the creditor/lender and/or court. Proposals to clear arrears over three years are regularly accepted. The court has said that it is acceptable to repay arrears over the amount of time remaining until the end of the loan.

However, advisers should be imaginative in their suggestions for repayment schedules. Staggered offers, where initially a smaller amount is offered towards the arrears, followed by increased payments, are very useful for repayment in anticipation of improved circumstances. Such arrangements may be made directly with the creditor or may need to be ratified by the court if proceedings have already started.

If there is no spare income immediately available, so that only the normal contractual payment can be met, creditors can sometimes be persuaded to accept no payments towards the arrears for several months, particularly if there is plenty of equity (see p209) in the property. In extreme circumstances, they may be persuaded to accept no payments at all for one or two months where inability to pay is clearly temporary.

Many creditors have their own internal rules about the time period over which they will spread the repayment of arrears for secured borrowing, but these periods can generally be increased by contacting regional or head offices when necessary. Most lenders are subject to codes of practice which require them to treat clients 'sympathetically and positively' and, if an adviser feels a creditor is allowing a policy to stand in the way of its duty to consider every case individually, s/he should consider using the complaints procedure and referring the matter to the Financial Ombudsman Service, where appropriate.

On rent, fuel and council tax

Creditors will use various criteria to decide whether the repayments are acceptable, including the level of arrears, the client's previous payment record and the likelihood of the client remaining as a tenant, consumer or council tax payer in the same location.

When applicable

- After there has been an improvement in financial circumstances.
- After a debt adviser has helped the client to prioritise payments of debts.

Advantages

- Provided the income is available to repay both contractual payments and something towards the arrears, this should be readily acceptable to creditors.
- It prevents further action.

Disadvantages

- It increases the client's outgoings at a time when financial shortage may not be over.
- In the case of loans, interest will accrue not only on the capital outstanding but also on the unpaid arrears so that, unless the creditor agrees to freeze interest and other charges, the repayments will continue beyond the original contractual period (sometimes, on unregulated agreements, at a penalty rate which is higher than that normally charged. Check the agreement to find out if this is the case).

Useful arguments

- Creditors will need to understand why payments have not been made in the past and why they are now possible.
- Advisers must explain any changes of circumstances and the fact that the client has now reorganised her/his financial affairs to give priority to these debts.
- Advisers should explain to creditors that ability to pay needs to be the guiding factor in deciding on repayment of arrears. Point to any relevant code of practice which supports this. A carefully drawn up financial statement will be the adviser's most useful tool.

- The strategy is considered appropriate by a reputable money advice agency.
- If the creditor/court is reluctant to accept that payments will be made, the arrangement can be made subject to a review after a set period – eg, six months, so that the creditor's position is not prejudiced.

Checklist for action

- Telephone/write to the creditor to propose the strategy and request written confirmation of the repayment schedule.
- Advise the client of how much to pay and when.
- If necessary, make the appropriate application to court.

Change to repayment mortgage

An endowment mortgage is a secured loan on which only interest is payable, accompanied by an endowment life assurance policy which will pay off the capital borrowed either at the end of the agreed term or on the death of the borrower (whichever is the sooner).

There are many potential problems with endowment mortgages. In broad terms, they are only to the borrower's advantage where the return on the investment made by the insurers on the stock market exceeds the cost of borrowing money. These general problems affect all endowment mortgages. The FSA estimates that as many as 500,000 households have endowment policies that will not cover their loans.[6]

For the borrower in debt there is a particular problem because it is essential that the full amounts of both the endowment insurance payments and the interest on the loan itself are repaid on, or shortly after, the due date. The creditor relies on the insurance company to repay the capital amount lent at the end of the loan period and, if payments to the insurance company stop, the creditor is likely to call in its loan on the basis that its security is at risk, unless acceptable proposals for repayment of the capital at the end of the loan can be made. If, on the other hand, payments to the creditor are not kept up, the amount outstanding on the loan rises and is likely to become more than the amount which will be produced by the insurance policy at its maturity. Thus, endowment mortgages are less flexible than repayment ones.

To have flexibility to capitalise arrears, extend the period of a loan or negotiate repayment of arrears over several years, an endowment mortgage needs to be changed to a repayment mortgage. For some clients, the creditor will do this automatically once the endowment premium is significantly in arrears.

However, to cease paying, surrender or sell an endowment policy is a major financial decision and should not be taken without specialist advice from an independent financial adviser.

When applicable

- A client is in arrears with an endowment mortgage, or likely to go into arrears, and therefore a renegotiation on the terms of the mortgage is necessary.
- A client is unable to maintain the payments on the endowment policy.
- A client is facing a substantial period of low income and needs to achieve more flexibility.
- The endowment policy has been running for several years – in which case it may be beneficial to cash it in or sell it and use the lump sum to pay off arrears. Advice from a number of independent financial advisers should always be taken before surrendering an endowment policy. Some insurers charge significant fees for early surrender and, in addition, the value of the policy depends on the state of the stock market. The surrender value of a policy is frequently much less than the amount of the payments made into it to date. A sale of the policy instead usually produces a better return. But, even if changing to a repayment mortgage, it is better if possible to keep the endowment policy (without making any new payments into it) until it matures.
- The client can afford the new repayments.

Advantages

- Increased flexibility in the long term.
- Ensures that the home is not lost.
- Possible reduced monthly outgoings.

Disadvantages

- There may be an arrangement fee to convert the mortgage to a capital repayment type.
- The client will have to arrange separate life insurance cover.
- Some or all of the money already invested in the endowment policy may be lost (especially if it is relatively new).
- If a policy is 'assigned' to the lender, the surrender/sale value may be taken by it in full (although negotiation is possible).
- Possible increased monthly outgoings.

Useful arguments

- Creditors may be sympathetic if this is the only way of paying the mortgage as it does ensure that the loan is repaid.

Checklist for action

The client should get independent advice from a specialist in this field (but not from a broker who was involved in setting up the endowment mortgage as s/he may be motivated by the knowledge that s/he will probably lose commission if a recently taken out endowment policy is cancelled).

If after taking financial advice, the client decides on this course of action, do the following.

- Telephone/write to the creditor to propose the strategy and request details of new instalments and the surrender/sale value of the endowment policy.
- Advise the client of how much to pay and when.
- If disposing of the endowment policy, ensure the full surrender value of the policy is paid to the client. Selling it rather than merely surrendering may produce a larger sum.
- Advise the client to take advice to arrange new life assurance cover for the mortgage, if necessary.
- Advise clients on IS/income-based JSA/PC to notify the DWP of changes in repayments.

Mortgage rescue schemes

Also known as 'sale and lease-back', these are schemes that allow a owner-occupier who is unable to meet the mortgage repayments and possibly facing repossession to sell her/his home and remain in the property as a tenant. Typical features of such schemes are as follows.

- Companies offer to pay 75–80 per cent of the 'market value', which might not cover the mortgage or other loans secured on the property.
- There is no independent valuation.
- The tenancy is invariably an assured shorthold tenancy, giving only six months' security of tenure and the market rent might be higher than the mortgage repayments.
- There is an option to buy back the property at full market value (sometimes with a time limit).

Such schemes are not regulated by the FSA (although Citizens Advice, Shelter and the Council of Mortgage Lenders have jointly called on the Government to address this). If the client is the victim of misselling, s/he may have little redress. Although tenants can qualify for housing benefit (HB) to assist with their rent, as a former owner, the client may not qualify unless s/he was facing imminent eviction, and, even if s/he does qualify, the amount of HB payable might be restricted. If the client goes bankrupt in the five years following the transaction, the trustee in bankruptcy may challenge the arrangement as a transaction at an under-value. This might put the client's home at risk if the new owner decides to sell it to pay off the trustee.

Even where mortgage rescue schemes are offered by housing associations or local authorities, some of the issues referred to above are still present. Clients should only consider such schemes as a last resort and be advised to take independent financial advice before committing themselves.[7]

Sale of the property

There are a number of circumstances in which it may be advisable to sell a home in order to repay priority creditors.

When applicable

There are circumstances in which the loss of a home may be inevitable and indeed the best option.

- A client has somewhere else to live as well as the home in question.
- A client has considerable equity in the home but now the property is too large or in the wrong place for her/his current requirements and a more suitable home could be purchased at a lower price.
- Repossession is inevitable. For example, if the client's available income is too low to make an acceptable repayment proposal, a better price may be paid to an owner-occupier than a mortgagee in possession. This can give a client equity, but her/his need for a suitable home must be paramount (see disadvantages on p189).

This strategy, although superficially tempting, is not generally applicable merely to repay priority debts. When other circumstances make the sale of the home inevitable or even desirable, however, clearing the debts can be achieved in this way and there may even be sufficient capital to make a full and final offer to non-priority creditors (see p219). As it is such a major decision, it is important that the client and her/his family reach it for themselves. The debt adviser must ensure that the advantages and disadvantages of this strategy are understood and that the client has time to consider all the implications.

For former local authority tenants who have exercised their right to buy, it is worth checking if the local authority or a housing organisation to whom their stock is now transferred operate a 'buy back' scheme, whereby the owner sells the home back to the local authority and remains as a tenant. Check whether the client is still within the discount repayment period. If so, a proportion of the purchase price will have to be repaid to the local authority.

Advantages

- It is easily accepted by priority creditors and courts. Time may be given for the sale to go through if necessary.
- It prevents further action.
- It may avoid a bad credit rating.
- It may release capital for other purposes.
- A better price will generally be achieved by a voluntary sale than by a financial institution selling the property after it has repossessed it.
- It is an alternative to bankruptcy proceedings either as part of an individual voluntary arrangement (see Chapter 12) or an informal arrangement with creditors.

- It may avoid court costs if the strategy is agreed prior to repossession action (see p272).
- It can be seen by the client as an opportunity for a fresh start.

Disadvantages

- The client is forced to move home. This is costly and disruptive.
- Unless the client actually has a buyer, it may be seen by the creditor and the court as a way of delaying possession/eviction proceedings.
- If rehousing by a local authority is required, it may be difficult to persuade it that the client has not made her/himself intentionally homeless.
- It may not be possible to find alternative suitable housing.
- The client may lose money if the housing market is depressed and s/he has only recently bought the property.

The client or adviser must explain the circumstances to the local authority in advance and gain its approval of the strategy, in writing, and its acceptance that homelessness is inevitable rather than intentional. For further details, see *Manual of Housing Law* (Appendix 2).

Useful arguments

- Creditors prefer to avoid repossessing and selling property and so can be persuaded of the advantages of not having to sell an empty property. A property is likely to sell more quickly if inhabited.
- The loan will be repaid in full. If it is not and the creditor is unreasonably refusing to agree to a sale, the court can override the creditor's objections.[8]

Checklist for action

- Ensure that the client has suitable alternative accommodation.
- Inform the creditors of the proposed strategy.
- Advise the client to put the house on the market. If a quick sale is required, the client should explain this to the estate agent.
- Discuss with the client how much to pay, if anything, towards the mortgage until the house is sold, particularly if there is negative equity.

Refinancing

Refinancing means taking out a loan or other credit agreement to repay an existing debt.

When applicable

When a priority debt (often a second mortgage) has terms that are very expensive, then it can be worth refinancing it. It is common for possession of homes to be sought by second mortgagees (who may have lent money for double glazing or other home improvements) from clients who had always managed to pay their first mortgage. The repayments on a medium-term loan from a finance company may be greater than those on a standard building society mortgage – a client could typically be required to pay as much each month on a home improvement loan of £10,000 as s/he was required to pay on her/his main mortgage of £50,000.

In these circumstances, the first mortgagee will generally be sympathetic to the client and will not want to lose her/his business simply because s/he has become unable to repay the high rate of interest charged by the second mortgagee.

Even though possession action is not threatened, it may be obvious that a client's financial problems are caused by excessive repayment on a particular priority debt. Refinancing may, therefore, be more appropriate than asking the creditor to capitalise arrears as this could result in higher repayments than if the loan were refinanced.

Refinancing should be used when a cheaper form of borrowing is available to replace a priority debt. A variety of credit products can be used – eg:

- an unsecured loan;
- an additional advance from an existing secured lender;
- a secured loan from a new lender;
- a re-mortgage;
- a transfer of balances to a credit card (some credit card companies offer 0 per cent interest for a temporary period on balances transferred from other creditors).

It should only be considered if:

- the client's monthly outgoings will be reduced; *and*
- the client can afford the new repayments; *and*
- the client will also be able to meet her/his essential expenditure and any other financial commitments.

When refinancing is not applicable

Many advertisements for refinancing or debt consolidation also promote the 'feel-good factor' by suggesting that people can borrow money to pay for a holiday, a new car, a kitchen or just for extra spending money in addition to paying off their debts. Many people do this and, for those in financial difficulties, the effect is to exacerbate their problems. The 'churning' of loans – ie, where debts are consolidated and then consolidated again, can be very expensive because of the way the interest is apportioned, the amount of capital paid off is small and so the debt increases. The client may also pay for a new payment protection insurance each time. Indeed, the churning of loans could give rise to an unfair relationship (see p115).

Advantages

Clients can benefit from refinancing or consolidating their debts on more advantageous terms – ie:

- lower interest rates;
- lower monthly payments;
- having to deal only with one creditor.

Disadvantages

Refinancing or debt consolidation is often seen as an easy way of obtaining more credit or as a short-term solution to debt problems. The possible long-term implications may not always be understood and, without clear information on the costs involved, problems can occur – eg:

- costs of settling existing loans – eg, early settlement charges, and finding and arranging new loans – eg, broker's fees, can be significant;
- clients can pay more for their credit overall and have a larger debt for a longer period if the new loan is spread over a longer period of time.

A report published by the OFT in March 2004 (*Debt Consolidation* OFT 705) found that most consumers did not 'shop around' for new finance; many were unaware of alternative solutions to their debt problems – eg, negotiating with their creditors or getting help from the free debt advice sector; and most did not take proper account of the length of the term of the new loan or the total cost of the repayments. The study also identified potentially unfair practices – eg, creditors requiring existing customers to take out consolidation loans as a way of dealing with their debt problems and inappropriate selling of payment protection insurances on such loans – eg, to borrowers who were unlikely to be able to claim on it.

Useful arguments

- If the first mortgagee is being asked to refinance a second secured loan, whenever possible emphasise the client's good payment record.
- Point out the business advantages to the creditor of refinancing the loan rather than allowing another secured lender to take possession.
- If they will not agree immediately, it is worth advising creditors to review their decision after three to six months of regular payments.

Checklist for action

- Advise the client to take independent financial advice and obtain full details of the refinancing, including new monthly instalments, arrangement fees, interest rates and annual percentage rate.
- Inform the existing creditor of the proposed action.

Refinancing should be distinguished from rescheduling existing repayments, which does not involve taking on (further) credit.

Time orders

A time order is granted by the county court and sets new repayment terms and possibly lower interest rates/charges for an agreement if the court believes that the original terms should be altered (see p283 for further details).

When applicable

- A time order can only be granted for loans, credit cards, overdrafts and any other type of agreement regulated by the Consumer Credit Act 1974.[9]
- Time orders are most likely to be granted if the borrower's circumstances have changed during the period of the loan. Time orders will usually be granted if the change in circumstances is expected to be temporary but can be made for a longer period where the court accepts that it is 'just' to do so.[10]

Advantages

- The agreement of the creditor is not required if the courts can be persuaded that an order should be made.
- Any possession order will be suspended by the court on the terms of the time order.
- Once made, the creditor can take no further action as long as payments are maintained.
- It can reduce interest rates/charges (possibly retrospectively) and set payments at an affordable level.

Disadvantages

- Time orders are difficult to get and, because they are still rarely applied for, many judges are not familiar with the principles. The court is required to draw a distinction between the 'deserving' and the 'undeserving' client.
- The client will have to wait until the creditor issues an arrears notice (on or after 1 October 2008) or a default notice, or takes court action before applying for a time order.
- Creditors' costs may be added to the debt.

Useful arguments

See Chapter 9.

Checklist for action

See Chapter 9.

Voluntary charge

Most unsecured debts are not priorities. However, very occasionally it may be advisable to offer to turn an unsecured debt into a secured one. This is achieved by offering the creditor a 'voluntary charge' secured on the client's property.

Many advisers routinely dismiss creditors' requests for a voluntary charge without considering whether it would be in the client's best interests to agree.

When applicable

Although often requested by creditors, a voluntary charge is only very rarely in the client's best interests. The only circumstances in which it may be advisable are the following.

- It is the only means of stopping the Revenue from taking action to commit a person to prison.
- It is the only means to stop someone issuing undesirable bankruptcy proceedings. **Note:** although many creditors threaten bankruptcy proceedings, including issuing a statutory demand (see Chapter 12) this very rarely results in an actual petition for bankruptcy.
- It is essential to the client that no county court judgment is made – eg, because s/he would lose her/his job if this happened. **Note:** a time order may be a more appropriate way of stopping a county court judgment.
- The creditor refuses to accept any other strategy and if the creditor obtains a county court judgment it is likely the court will make a charging order (see p258).
- The creditor has an automatic right to impose a charge – eg, Community Legal Service-funding debts, which incur higher costs than a voluntary charge.
- It is known that when a person's current home is sold s/he will not need the proceeds of sale – eg, if s/he is terminally ill. In this situation, a voluntary charge could reduce the stress of lengthy negotiations with creditors.

It is essential that the client seeks legal advice before signing a voluntary charge in order to safeguard her/his position should the creditor decide to enforce the charge and apply for an order for sale. As a minimum, the adviser should ensure that the charge document is worded so that the creditor's right to do so is removed altogether (or it is at least restricted) in order that that the property cannot be repossessed and sold against the client's wishes. In addition, the client must ensure almost always that the creditor will agree to freeze interest so that the charge is against a fixed sum that will not swallow up the equity.

Agreement also needs to be reached about whether any instalments are required by the creditor in addition to the charge. All these issues need to be agreed before a voluntary charge is made, and must be part of a written agreement.[11]

Advantages

- A voluntary charge is likely to satisfy a creditor and therefore mean that no further action is taken.

- Once their capital outlay is secured by a voluntary charge, many creditors will agree to add no further interest/charges until the property is sold and to accept the client's repayment offer or even no (or only token) payments.
- Lenders can be persuaded to agree not to enforce their charge – ie, not to force a sale but to wait for payment until the client sells the property (or re-mortgages).

Disadvantages

- By changing the status of a debt, a client is potentially putting her/his house under threat.
- There may be costs incurred by the client seeking legal advice to ensure a watertight agreement is drawn up.
- If the client has a partner who is a co-owner of the property, the partner will have to sign the charge document and make her/himself liable for the debt.
- The creditor may still insist on payments being paid in addition to the charge.

Useful arguments

From the client's point of view the voluntary charge is only ever the lesser of two evils. To the creditor, the adviser may need to argue the following.

- In practice, it is the only way the creditor will get any money.
- Making people bankrupt does not often produce money, but a voluntary charge will do so.
- If house prices increase, so too will the equity against which the charge is made.

Checklist for action

- Consider whether any other strategy would be more appropriate – eg, a time order.
- Advise the client to obtain full details of the terms of the charge in writing from the creditor.
- Ensure the client receives legal advice about the agreement before signing.
- Check that interest is frozen and all the other terms are acceptable.

Deductions from benefits

Certain priority arrears can be deducted from a claimant's IS, income-based JSA, income-related ESA and PC at a set weekly amount and paid directly to creditors.[12] If this is done, the creditor concerned can demand that payments for current liabilities also be met in full from benefit. Deductions can also be made from contribution-based JSA and some other benefits in limited circumstances. See CPAG's *Welfare Benefits and Tax Credits Handbook* for further information.

Deductions from benefits are commonly used to pay off arrears of gas and electricity charges as an alternative to disconnection, or rent arrears as an alternative to eviction. In some circumstances, direct payments can be made without the claimant's consent – eg, for council tax arrears and fines.

When applicable

- Deductions from IS, income-based JSA or PC can be made to pay for rent arrears, residential accommodation charges, hostel payments, fuel, water charges, council tax arrears, community charge arrears, fines, repayments of eligible loans and child support maintenance. Deductions can also be made for the cost of home loans, loans for repairs and improvements and other housing costs, and paid to the lender.
- Deductions from benefit are useful if the alternative is either the disconnection of a fuel supply, or an impending eviction.
- Because of the statutory maximums on the amount that can be deducted for arrears, they are often a cheaper method of paying off arrears than a repayment schedule, or than token or slot meters that have been recalibrated to recover arrears along with current consumption. Gas and electricity suppliers often seriously overestimate current use and request an amount from the DWP far in excess of the amount actually required to cover consumption. If they do, advise the client to take daily or weekly meter readings. It is the appropriate decision maker at the DWP who decides how much to deduct for current consumption, so the client can ask for a lower deduction to be made based on her/his own readings. If the DWP refuses, the client can appeal to an appeal tribunal.
- Some gas and electricity suppliers insist on installing a token meter to cover current consumption and will only collect arrears through deductions from benefit.
- For an IS, income-based JSA or income-related ESA claimant, full help with the cost of home loans is not usually available until s/he has been claiming for a period. There are no waiting periods for full help for PC claimants. See CPAG's *Welfare Benefits and Tax Credits Handbook* for further details. The housing costs element of IS/ESA/JSA/PC is usually paid automatically to the creditor under the mortgage payment scheme as soon as the claimant qualifies for full help, even if there are no arrears. Lenders may agree to adjourn a claim for possession if they are receiving payments direct from the DWP. If they have already obtained a possession order, they can be asked not to enforce it so long as deductions from benefit are paid.

Advantages

- If the client fits the criteria for deductions from benefit, it is a simple and quick way to ensure that no further action is taken by the creditor and that arrears are paid at a relatively modest rate – £3.05 per debt per week in 2008/09 – particularly if money is owed to several creditors (but see p196).
- Creditors are assured of payments.

Disadvantages

- Only certain debts can be paid for in this way (and council tax/community charge only at the request of the local authority, fines at the request of the magistrates' court and eligible loans at the request of the lender). If the client has more than one such debt, deductions might not be made for all of them. If this happens, there is a set order of priority.[13]
- By reducing subsistence-level benefits, they reduce the flexibility with which a claimant can juggle her/his weekly budget.
- Fuel suppliers may demand a large amount for current consumption.
- If the client is likely to cease claiming benefit in the near future (even if only for a temporary period), payments will have to be replaced with another strategy. The client may be faced with a demand for the full amount when her/his benefit ends.
- The DWP often pays amounts collected on a quarterly basis. This can mean long delays for creditors in receiving their money.
- If the client is getting help with her/his mortgage (or loans for repairs or improvements) via IS/income-based JSA/PC, payment is usually made directly to the lender under a mortgage payment scheme. If the client's lender is participating in this scheme, no amount for mortgage arrears can be deducted from benefit and paid to the lender.

Checklist for action

- Telephone the creditor to find out how much is required and, if the client can afford this amount, try to obtain the creditor's agreement to payments by deductions from benefit.
- Assist the client in her/his request for the DWP to arrange deductions.

Gas and electricity pre-payment meters

Both electricity and gas companies must provide a pre-payment meter to a customer to prevent disconnection of her/his supply, if it is safe and practicable to do so.[14] If someone has arrears on fuel bills, a pre-payment meter will collect money not just for the fuel used, but also towards the arrears. For a discussion of the different types of meters available, see CPAG's *Fuel Rights Handbook*.

When applicable

- Pre-payment meters allow arrears to be collected over a period of time, and are therefore a way of avoiding disconnection.

Advantages

- A client continues to have some access to fuel supplies and will not be pressed further for the debt.
- Pre-payment meters can assist budgeting.

Disadvantages

- A pre-payment meter is often a do-it-yourself disconnection kit, because it may not be possible to keep it running at all times.
- In some cases, the amount of money recovered towards the arrears varies in relation to the amount of fuel used and thus, in winter, not only does a client have to spend more money on fuel, s/he also has to contribute more towards her/his arrears.
- With token meters the client has to remember to buy enough tokens. There may be costs incurred (eg, bus fares) in buying tokens/cards or charging credit keys, or it may be difficult for the client to get to a charging point or point of sale (eg, in the case of illness), and such places may be closed.
- Fuel is more expensive per unit if paid for in this way. It should, therefore, be considered as a last resort.
- A pre-payment meter is not always technically possible. This applies where gas appliances have pilot lights that could go out when the pre-payment ends and are not protected by a fail-safe device when payment is resumed.
- Coin meters have to be positioned somewhere safe, which normally means they cannot be placed in buildings that do not have inside meters.

Useful arguments

Fuel suppliers are required to offer pre-payment facilities if this is the only means of avoiding disconnection. However, it may be necessary to argue with a fuel supplier about the level at which the arrears will be collected through the pre-payment meter. If a client is on IS/income-based JSA/PC, the amounts deducted by the DWP from benefit should be used as a maximum level of recovery (currently, £3.05 a week).

Checklist for action

- Check exactly what type of meters are available locally.
- Contact the fuel supplier to request installation of a meter.
- Advise the client to monitor fuel consumption to check the calibration of the meter. This will involve taking a meter reading each week and comparing the number of units with the amount paid.

See also Chapter 5.

Remittance of debts

Both the magistrates' court (in respect of fines, community charge and council tax) and the local authority (in respect of business rates and council tax) have powers to remit (ie, write off) amounts owing in cases of hardship. The Revenue can also remit taxes.

Advantages

- It reduces or removes the debt.

Disadvantages

- The client will often need to attend a means enquiry (see Chapter 10).
- The magistrate will need to consider whether there has been 'wilful refusal or culpable neglect' and may therefore look at other alternatives to remittance, such as imprisonment (see Chapter 10).

Useful arguments

- **Business rates.** The closure of a business may adversely affect the amenities or employment prospects of an area. Only 25 per cent of the cost of relief is borne by the authority; the remainder is borne by central government.
- **Fines.** Magistrates need to see how the client's circumstances have changed since the fine was imposed or that the client's financial situation was not taken into account when the fine was originally set. Guidelines state that fines should be paid in a reasonable period, and that two to three years would be exceptional.
- **Council tax.** Local authorities have complete discretion and should be encouraged to use it in all cases of hardship which fall outside the exemption, discount and benefits rules.
- **Tax.** The Revenue will need to see that there is no means of clearing the debt and little likelihood of further liability.

Checklist for action

- Write to the creditor to request remittance.
- Enclose a financial statement.

4. Emergency action

The necessity for debt advice very often arises as a result of a priority creditor threatening to take immediate action against someone's gas, electricity, property or liberty. In such circumstances, a debt adviser must always be prepared to take emergency action. In some cases, enough information and time will be available to use one of the strategies outlined above. In other cases, neither time nor information is immediately available and, therefore, action by the creditor needs to be halted or delayed. This may be possible by a telephone call to a creditor explaining that the client has approached the agency seeking advice and assistance, and indicating when an offer will be made. However, this is unlikely to be the case, particularly when adjournments or delays have already been granted. In such situations, other emergency action will have to be taken.

To prevent fuel disconnection

The legislation governing the supply of gas and electricity states that supplies should not be disconnected while there is a genuine dispute about the amount due.[15] When there is any question about the amount claimed, such a dispute should immediately be registered with the relevant supplier and confirmed in writing. The supplier should be asked not to disconnect the supply until the dispute has been resolved.

Before being offered a pre-payment meter, the consumer should have been offered some form of repayment option to pay the arrears and cover the ongoing consumption. If this breaks down, some suppliers automatically offer a pre-payment meter as the only remaining option. Advisers should consider offering an explanation about why the arrangement broke down – eg, it was unrealistic in the first place, and urge the supplier to enter into a new arrangement based on a financial statement.

Prior to disconnecting, the supplier is required to:

- comply with its code of practice (including information about reconnection);
- fit a pre-payment meter where it is safe and practical to do so;
- provide seven days' notice of the date of disconnection;
- obtain a warrant of entry if the client refuses access;
- give a further seven days' notice of intention to use it.

A warrant of entry is granted by the magistrates' court and allows the supplier to enter the client's home (by force if necessary) in order to disconnect the supply. Although the supplier must give the client written notice that it intends to apply for a warrant, it does not have to give the client notice of the actual application. Advisers can, however, phone the court in advance of an application, ask to speak to the magistrate who would deal with any application and make representations on behalf of the client – eg, that s/he is a vulnerable person and the supplier has unreasonably refused to agree to a repayment arrangement.

The client cannot be disconnected if:

- the bill is genuinely disputed;
- the debt is owed to a different supplier (a supplier who wants to retain the power to disconnect should object to the supplier being switched);
- the debt is due from a previous occupier and the client has agreed to take over the supply;
- the debt is for administration costs and does not relate to fuel consumption;
- a repayment plan has been agreed;
- the client has agreed to have a pre-payment meter fitted (the meter should be calibrated to recover the arrears at the rate the client can afford taking account of her/his ability to repay);

- it is between 1 October and 31 March, and the supplier either knows or has reason to believe there is a child under 18 living in the property or someone of pension age living either alone or with others over pension age;
- at any time, someone living in the property is either severely disabled or chronically sick.

Clients in the last two categories are likely to be on the Priority Services Register.

No one who is prepared to have a pre-payment meter or who is eligible for direct payments from her/his benefits or who can afford to pay for current consumption plus a payment towards the arrears should ever be disconnected. Energy trust funds or other charities may be able to help with payment of bills or to prevent self-disconnection – ie, where clients do not use gas or electricity because they cannot afford to pay for it. In the case of pre-payment meters, self-disconnection can be due to arrears being recovered at too high a rate. Suppliers can always be asked to confirm how arrears are being recovered and asked to recalibrate the meter where appropriate.

If negotiations with the fuel supplier are proving unsuccessful, the adviser should contact Consumer Focus or the Energy Ombudsman (see Appendix 1), who have the power to intervene when disconnection is threatened. See also CPAG's *Fuel Rights Handbook* for more information.

To prevent loss of the home

When a possession order has already been granted and is followed by a warrant of possession (see p297), an immediate application may need to be made to the court on Form N244 to suspend the warrant. If the eviction is not due to take place for several days, the debt adviser should attempt to negotiate directly with the lender (or the lender's solicitor) or the landlord, to obtain a binding agreement that the property will not be repossessed. If this is not possible or appears unlikely, or the eviction is due to take place that day or the following day, Form N244 needs to be submitted to the court. Form N244 must state the grounds of the application and, if possible, include an offer of payment. The fee is £35 (see p237 for applying for a remission). For further information about a warrant of possession and how to complete Form N244, see Chapter 9.

In the case of local authority or registered social landlord tenants, there will usually be an internal procedure that must be followed before a warrant is applied for, which may involve considering representations from the tenant. The adviser should check that procedure has been complied with and challenge the landlord if it has not.[16]

Such an application will always stop county court bailiffs executing a warrant (ie, carrying out its instructions) until the court has heard the application, although the court is usually very quick in arranging a hearing. The success of an application depends largely on:

- whether several arrangements have already been made but not kept to;

- the adviser's and the client's ability to present the case;
- how many previous warrants have been suspended;
- how long the client has been seeking help from an advice agency;
- the client's ability to pay.

If it is too late to make the application to the court because the bailiffs are already on their way to carry out the eviction, the adviser should ring the creditor immediately and negotiate, on the doorstep if necessary, with the bailiff for more time. Bailiffs normally have a mobile telephone with them and so can be contacted right up to the point of eviction.

To prevent seizure of goods by magistrates' court bailiffs

Bailiffs working for the magistrates' court cannot act without the authority of a distress warrant. This is a document issued by the court allowing the bailiffs to take goods belonging to the client, that can then be sold and the money used to pay for the unpaid debt.

If a distress warrant has been issued by a magistrates' court because of arrears in the payment of fines and bailiffs are about to seize goods, there is some doubt as to whether magistrates are entitled to hear an application to give further time to pay (see p321). Occasionally, bailiffs will agree to give a debt adviser a few days in which to produce an offer of repayment. This is always worth trying, but success is limited.

See Chapter 11 for details of bailiffs' powers.

Council tax

Private bailiffs (see p341) are used by a local authority after a liability order has been granted to collect the amount owing. Different local authorities give different instructions to their bailiffs. In some areas a clear code of conduct exists, preventing the seizure of goods from people on benefit or in certain other circumstances. An adviser must know what rules (if any) her/his own local authority uses. If an action by bailiffs breaches these, the relevant section of the local authority should be contacted immediately so that its order to the bailiffs can be withdrawn.

Even where there is no clear policy, the adviser should contact the local authority and ask it to consider withdrawing the warrant from the bailiffs or, if that is not possible, instructing the bailiffs to accept a lower payment offer. Bailiffs themselves may occasionally agree to delay action, but this is unlikely. There may be no need for the client to let the bailiffs in. See p347 for the rules about bailiffs' powers to enter property.

In appropriate cases, the local authority could be asked to write off council tax arrears.

Council tax and bankruptcy

Many local authorities now use bankruptcy proceedings to recover council tax arrears from homeowners. There is no government guidance on this. However, local authorities should bear in mind the principles of proportionality and reasonableness in deciding whether to use bankruptcy, particularly the client's potential liability for substantial 'trustee in bankruptcy' costs. Charging orders are likely to be a more proportionate recovery method in relation to the sums involved and should not be rejected purely on the basis that the court might not order a sale in the event of payment not being forthcoming.

The Local Government Ombudsman has made the following points.

- Whilst it cannot be said that bankruptcy should never be used, it should only be used as a 'last resort' and local authorities should have a policy to this effect.
- Local authorities should send out letters containing clear and detailed warnings of the potential consequences of bankruptcy for the client in terms of not only the costs of the petition itself and possible loss of the home but also the far greater costs that would be incurred if a bankruptcy order was made.
- The policy should also deal with charging orders and require their use to be considered as an alternative to bankruptcy. Charging orders should not be rejected on the grounds that they do not provide a practical recovery method.[17]
- Councils must consider the issue of proportionality.[18]

Advisers should, therefore, study their local authority's collection policy to ensure that it complies with the Ombudsman's recommendations and point out any shortcomings. Advisers should also use the recommendations to challenge any inappropriate use of bankruptcy proceedings by local authorities.

Advisers should also bear in mind that, before the local authority can take bankruptcy proceedings, it must have a liability order for the amount in question and be able to prove the existence of that liability order to the satisfaction of the court. The local authority's own computer records are not sufficient for this purpose; it must either be able to produce a sealed copy of the liability order or a statement from the magistrates' court that an order was made.[19]

Advisers should seek specialist advice if a client has received either a statutory demand or a petition from the local authority, or if a bankruptcy order has been made on the local authority's petition.

To prevent seizure of goods by county court bailiffs

If a creditor has instructed the court to issue a warrant of execution for an unpaid county court judgment, the client can make an application to the county court to suspend the execution of the warrant. This is done on Form N245. See p303 for details of how to do this and Chapter 11 for details of county court bailiffs' powers.

If the bailiff is threatening to seize goods subject to a hire purchase/conditional sale agreement or bill of sale, specialist advice should be sought.

To prevent seizure of goods by enforcement officers from the High Court

Enforcement officers enforce High Court judgments (including county court judgments transferred to the High Court for enforcement). Prior to 1 April 2004 this task was carried out by sheriffs' officers. They are private bailiffs authorised by the court to enforce debts in the High Court. See Chapter 11 for details of the powers of enforcement officers.

If an enforcement officer is threatening to seize goods, specialist advice should be sought.

To prevent seizure of goods by tax bailiffs

Officials from HM Revenue and Customs have the powers of bailiffs to take and sell goods to pay for unpaid tax debts.[20] If they are unable to gain access to a property they can apply for an order to force entry. Normally a private bailiff accompanies the collector on such visits.

It is possible to negotiate with the collector directly and either suggest a repayment arrangement or submit a late return if the client does not agree with the amount of the debt and is out of the normal time limit for appealing (see Chapter 13). If the client has no goods, the collector is likely to seek an alternative means of enforcement, such as court action or bankruptcy.

To prevent imprisonment

Magistrates' courts have the power to imprison people who refuse to pay financial penalties, maintenance, community charge, council tax or rates. See Chapter 10 for the exact circumstances in which they can use this power and the arguments to deploy against them.

Warrant with bail

When a client has failed to attend a court hearing, or sometimes just failed to keep up the payments, a warrant can be issued for her/his arrest by magistrates. In most cases this will be a warrant with bail which requires the client to surrender her/himself and be given a time and date for a court hearing.

Warrant without bail

Occasionally (usually where previous warrants have been ignored) a warrant without bail is issued. This requests the police to arrest the client and hold her/him in custody until a court hearing can be arranged (within 24 hours). Such warrants have a very low priority for the police and are often left for weeks or months before being discovered when the adviser rings the court.

If a warrant without bail has been issued the client should report to the court at a time, depending on local circumstances, when it is likely not to be busy so that s/he will not be held in the cells for too long. This may be after lunch if the court sits then or first thing in the morning before other prisoners have been brought from police stations. Some courts demand that people surrender themselves to the police station rather than the courts, but there is no legal foundation for this and advisers should ensure that police and other court staff accept a client's surrender in court buildings.

Committal hearing

Most magistrates' courts do not imprison people until they have been given a number of opportunities to pay by instalments (see Chapter 11). Whenever someone is brought before court after the issue of an arrest warrant, s/he should be represented, if possible. S/he cannot lawfully be imprisoned if legal representation has not been made available to her/him. If a solicitor (perhaps from the duty solicitor scheme) is to provide representation, an advice agency should brief her/him first and provide a full financial statement, as it is common for unrealistic offers to be made by solicitors, which then cause the client to be brought back before the court and treated with even less sympathy because s/he has broken a previous undertaking to pay. In some courts, probation officers are able to obtain adjournments so that they can produce a statement of the client's means for the courts. For further information about committal hearings, see p335.

After imprisonment

If magistrates have imprisoned someone for debt, it is possible that they have done so improperly, in which case an application for judicial review should be made immediately. An application for bail pending a hearing can also be made (to a High Court judge in London). The applications will always have to be made by a solicitor or barrister specialising in this field. The most likely improprieties are procedural irregularities (eg, the court failed to consider the question of wilfulness/culpability/alternatives to imprisonment) or unreasonableness (eg, the court expected someone on income support to pay £20 a week towards a fine), natural justice (eg, legal representation was denied to the client) or acting *ultra vires* (eg, the resolution setting council tax was not signed by the appropriately authorised officer of the council).

5. Penalties for non-payment of priority debts

Debt	*Ultimate penalties*
Mortgage arrears	Repossession/eviction
Rent arrears	Eviction
Council tax arrears	Imprisonment
Unpaid fine/maintenance	Imprisonment
Gas/electricity arrears	Disconnection
Income tax/VAT arrears	Goods seized
	Bankruptcy
Hire purchase arrears	Goods repossessed

Notes

2. **The general approach to priority debts**
   1 See P Madge, 'Till Debt Do Us Part', *Adviser* 71
   2 *Cheltenham & Gloucester BS v Norgan* [1996] 1 All ER 449
   3 s91 LPA 1925

3. **Strategies for dealing with priority debts**
   4 s8(2) AJA 1973
   5 s36 AJA 1970
   6 FSA Press Release, 3 November 1999; see *Your Endowment Mortgage: time to decide*, FSA, February 2002, available at www.fsa.gov.uk, and 'Complaint to Financial Ombudsman Service', *Adviser* 115 abstracts
   7 For further discussion, see M Mackreth 'Home Buy-back Schemes: rescue or rip-off?', *Adviser* 123 and V Smith, 'Sale and Leaseback Schemes', *Quarterly Account 9*, IMA, Summer 2008
   8 *Palk v Mortgage Services Funding,* 31 July 1992, CA (*Adviser* 34, abstracts)
   9 s129 CCA 1974
   10 *Director General of Fair Trading v First National Bank* [2001] UKHL 52 (*Adviser* 89, abstracts)
   11 For a further discussion, see J Wilson, 'Consultancy Corner', *Adviser* 95
   12 Reg 35 and Sch 9 SS(C&P) Regs
   13 See CPAG's *Welfare Benefits Handbook 2002/03*, p1023
   14 Condition 18 electricity supply licence conditions; condition 19 gas supply licence conditions

4. **Emergency action**
   15 Sch 6 EA 1989; Sch 2B GA 1986
   16 See B Fisher, 'Eviction Appeal Panels' and D Durden, 'A Landlord's Perspective', *Adviser* 114
   17 Complaint against Wolverhampton CC, 06/B/16600 (*Adviser* 128 money advice abstracts). See also Complaint against Camden LBC, 07/A/12661 (*Adviser* 129 money advice abstracts), where the local authority revenue department's failure to make internal enquiries resulted in bankruptcy proceedings against a vulnerable person.
   18 Complaint against Wolverhampton CC, 06/B/16600 (*Adviser* 128 money advice abstracts). See also Complaint against Camden LBC, 07/A/12661 (*Adviser* 129 money advice abstracts), where the revenue department's failure to make internal enquiries resulted in bankruptcy proceedings against a vulnerable person. The Ombudsman said: 'The dire

and punitive consequences of bankruptcy, involving a multiplication of the original debt many times over and frequently incurring the loss of the debtor's home, must be a factor to be taken into account in deciding that the 'last resort' is indeed appropriate.'

19 *Smolen v Tower Hamlets LBC* (*Adviser* 126, money advice abstracts)

20 s61 TMA 1970

Chapter 8

Dealing with non-priority debts

This chapter covers:

1. The criteria

The majority of a client's debts are likely to be non-priority ones. Non-priority debts are those where non-payment will not result in the loss of the client's home, liberty, essential goods or services. They vary from an unpaid bill of a few pounds to a loan of several thousand pounds. Non-priority debts will not usually include any of the debts listed in Chapter 7.

Advice given to a client on non-priority debts should take account of:

- the nature of the debt;
- the client's financial position;
- the powers of the creditor;
- whether interest or charges on the debt have been frozen or reduced.[1]

All available options should be discussed with the client, who must agree to the strategy chosen. It is not usually an appropriate option for the client to do nothing, although there are some occasions when doing nothing is in the client's best interests – eg, if a debt is about to become 'statute-barred' it is not in the client's best interests to acknowledge the debt and so start time running again (see p123). Doing nothing, however, usually leaves the client uncertain as to the status of the debt.

Occasionally, a client will have not only a large amount of non-priority debt but also a high disposable income. It is not usually in her/his best interests to put such a client through the debt advice process discussed in this *Handbook*.[2] S/he may just need some budgeting advice. It is probably not in any client's best interests for an adviser to contact creditors (except when dealing with an emergency), even by sending out holding letters, until the extent of the debt problem has been investigated, as some creditors may react inappropriately – eg, by terminating facilities and registering defaults with credit reference agencies.

A number of criteria are important when deciding which strategy will be the most appropriate for dealing with each of these debts. They are as follows.

Availability of income

Once the financial statement (see p42) has been produced, the adviser will know whether there is any income left over for non-priority debts after payments have been arranged with priority creditors and all the other essential items of expenditure have been met. In many cases, there will not be enough income, even to meet essential expenditure, but in others a significant amount may be available.

In the case of credit debts, check whether the client has payment protection insurance to cover the repayments in the event of sickness or incapacity, unemployment, accident or death. If the client does have payment protection insurance and her/his situation is covered by the policy, advise the client to make a claim. If the claim is refused, consider whether this can be challenged and/or whether the policy has been missold. If the client's situation is not covered by the policy, again consider whether the policy may have been missold – eg, the client's circumstances were such that s/he could never have made a claim. If the agreement is regulated by the Consumer Credit Act 1974 and the client says that taking out payment protection insurance was a condition of being granted the credit, the agreement may be unenforceable (see p57).

Availability of capital

It should have been established at the initial interview whether a client has any significant capital or savings available. These can include:

- bonds, savings certificates and shares;
- money put aside for specific items – eg, a holiday;
- capital that will become available in the near future – eg, expected redundancy pay and proceeds from the sale of a house or business;
- legacies under a relative's will.

Realisable assets

A client may have assets which are reasonable to realise. These will be valuable items that could be sold to raise money – for example, antiques or works of art, cars and life assurance policies with a considerable surrender value. Such a list should only include items of a non-essential nature. For example, a recently acquired and fairly new car that is only used for weekend trips may be a realisable asset, while one that is necessary for work is not. The client must be adequately advised about her/his options before coming to a decision about disposing of assets – eg, to ensure that a car is not subject to a hire purchase or conditional sale agreement, or that sale or surrender of an insurance policy is in the client's best interests. The client should be advised to obtain independent financial advice.

Equity in the home

The equity in a person's home is the total value of the property less the amount required to pay any loans or debts secured against it, including any 'charges' and the costs of a sale. 'Charges' include mortgages and secured loans, charging orders and statutory charges owed to the Legal Services Commission in connection with publicly funded legal work. For example, to calculate the equity on a property saleable for £45,000:

Deduct solicitor's fee on sale	£200
Deduct estate agent's fee	£700
Deduct first mortgage (building society)	£25,000
Deduct second mortgage (after early settlement discount)	£15,000
Total deductions	**£40,900**

Total equity = £45,000 – £40,900 = £4,100

If the property is jointly owned, the equity is shared in proportion to the amount each person owns (usually equally).

In many cases, there may be no equity in the property (see p177) and the amount owed may exceed the value of the property, particularly if the client has defaulted on a high-interest, non-status secured loan. In other cases, however, it is likely that the 'equity position' will be favourable, particularly if the property has no outstanding mortgage.

It is important to establish whether or not there is equity at an early stage since many creditors now seek to secure their debts – eg, by obtaining a charging order (see p258), whilst others seek preferential status by resorting to threats of bankruptcy (see p391). For this reason, advisers should stress to clients the urgency of dealing with any court papers. Whilst advisers should make it clear to clients that enquiries about equity do not necessarily mean they should sell their house, they should bear in mind that, unless the circumstances are wholly exceptional, creditors are unlikely to agree to, for example, writing off a debt (see p214) where there are realisable assets or equity in the home. A creditor may accept, for example, a token offer (see p223) on the basis that the amount due will be repaid out of the sale of the asset/property in due course.

Change of circumstances

It is important to know whether the client's current circumstances are likely to change. For example, if a client's income was until very recently quite high, but has now been reduced by a period of illness that is not expected to last very long, this must be taken into account. Similarly, if someone is about to retire or begin a new job with higher wages, these factors are vital to the strategy selected.

The amount owed

The choice of strategy is affected by the amount owing. Some strategies cost money to set up – eg, a voluntary charge (see p192), and would be too expensive for a small debt. In addition, large companies often have policies to write off small amounts owed if they are not paid after a final warning. Very large debts may also be written off in appropriate cases. Debt advisers should not assume that very large debts 'simply must be paid'. Creditors do write off sums of several thousand pounds.

It will sometimes be obvious to a debt adviser, particularly where a small debt is concerned, that a large company has already written off an amount owed because it has not communicated with the client for several years and the client has not been contacted by a collection agent acting on behalf of the creditor. In such circumstances, it is probably best to take no action and assume that the creditor has decided not to pursue the debt. However, there has been a tendency for some creditors to sell on debts where there has been no contact for many years (a practice which the Office of Fair Trading regards as unfair).[3] **Note:** if there has been no contact for more than six years, the debt is probably unenforceable (see p123).

Type of debt

Some debts that are not priority debts (see Chapter 7) do not fit into the usual debt advice process and so cannot be treated as straightforward non-priority debts (see p211). Separate strategies may need to be made for such debts.[4]

Repayment period

In the case of instalment arrangements, the shorter the repayment period, the more likely it is that the strategy will have a successful outcome. The longer the repayment period the more likely the client's circumstances are to change – and possibly deteriorate – and the more disheartened the client is likely to become. Advisers should, therefore, consider whether it is in the client's best interests to propose open-ended repayment arrangements or whether s/he should request there should be a time limit on the repayment period (see p216).[5]

Enforcement issues

If a debt is legally unenforceable, the client will be in a strong negotiating position as s/he can decide whether or not to repay the debt, and, if so, on what terms (see Chapter 5). This may make income available for payment of other debts. On the other hand, if the creditor is in a position to take enforcement action – or has already done so – the client could be at risk of losing her/his home or essential goods – eg, a creditor may have obtained a charging order over the client's home where there is substantial equity but little available income with which to make a reasonable offer. This debt may have to be treated as a priority debt as the creditor could apply for an order for sale in these circumstances (see p262).

Even where a debt is legally enforceable, it may be possible to persuade the creditor to write off some or all of the debt. Advisers should point out:

- any mis-selling of any part of a loan, such as payment protection insurance; *or*
- failure by a lender to assess the client's ability to repay; *or*
- 'churning' of loans (see p117).

2. The general approach to non-priority debts

If the suggested strategy is to be accepted by creditors, it is important that it is based on a consistent set of criteria and that all creditors are treated alike. Treating all creditors alike does not mean that a particular creditor should not be challenged where, for instance, the debt is unenforceable, or the creditor is adopting unacceptable lending or debt collection practices. The credit industry is competitive and individuals within it are likely to reject any strategy that appears to favour a competitor. The strength of a debt adviser's negotiating position lies in the ability to present a strategy that is empirically based and businesslike, and in line with the way courts treat creditors and clients. Thus, all offers to creditors must be made on the same basis, using the same criteria when making choices with regard to their debts. Where appropriate, creditors may need reminding of their obligations under the relevant industry code of practice – eg, to treat cases of financial difficulty sympathetically and positively, and also under the Office of Fair Trading's (OFT) *Debt Collection Guidance* – eg, not to pressurise clients to make payments which they are unable to afford, to sell property or increase their borrowing.[6]

If a debt has a special importance to the client, there may need to be an exception to this. Some debts that *may* need to be treated differently are as follows.

- **Debts created by a loan from a family or community member, or an employer.** These may, on strict legal criteria, be no different from money owed to a finance company. However, if failure to repay this debt will lead to serious financial or personal problems elsewhere in the family (eg, if a loan has been taken out to consolidate the client's non-priority debts which is secured on a family member's home) or at work (eg, dismissal), it may be necessary to give it priority over other non-priority debts. However, if there is any possibility of the client becoming bankrupt in the foreseeable future, the adviser should consider the implications of preferring such debts (see p411).

- **Unsecured debts that have been guaranteed** (see p100). These may need to be given priority in order to protect the guarantor, family or work relationships.
- **Mail order catalogues**. These are essential to someone on a low income as a way of budgeting for essentials such as household items and clothing, provided they maintain a low balance.
- **Bill paying services** (also known as budgeting accounts), perhaps through a credit union (see p30) or a commercial lender. The client makes monthly payments to the credit union or lender, who in turn pays various agreed household bills on the client's behalf. These bills are likely to be for essential expenditure in terms of including them on the client's financial statement and, if they fall into arrears, will then be priority debts. It may, therefore, be in everyone's best interests to maintain these payments if that means there will be more money available for other non-priority creditors.
- **A debt incurred through the fraud** of the client or her/his partner or a relative, where s/he could face prosecution if the debt is not paid.
- **Debts which do not fit into the usual debt advice process** – eg, credit union loans (see p30), mortgage shortfall (see p125) and traffic penalties (see p96).
- **'Loan sharks'**. This expression tends to refer to illegal moneylenders who make loans at extortionate rates and enforce payment through violence or threats of violence. Once involved with a loan shark, people often find themselves permanently in debt, with late payment resulting in substantial penalties being added to the debt. Besides not having a consumer credit licence, loan sharks are often involved in other criminality and sometimes coerce their victims into committing criminal offences as a way of repaying their debts.

  Clients rarely admit to being indebted to a loan shark and often use money intended for essential expenditure in order to make their repayments. They may even claim that money is being used to repay a 'family friend'.

  If an adviser discovers a client is a loan shark victim, it is likely s/he will be reluctant to report the matter, fearing for her/his own safety or that of her/his family. As ever, the decision as to the next step is the client's but it should be an informed one. The adviser could refer the client to a regional illegal money-lending unit, attached to a trading standards department. These can offer the client support and arrange to meet her/him at a safe venue (in the presence of the adviser, if necessary) to discuss what remedies are available, what action can be taken and the protection that can be provided.

Debt management plans

A 'debt management plan' is an informal arrangement, under which the client agrees to repay her/his creditors. The term is invariably used to describe an arrangement made on the client's behalf by a third party who also manages the plan. The arrangement usually involves an equitable distribution of the client's available income (after priority payments) (see p225). The client makes a single regular payment (usually monthly) to the third party, who may be:

- a debt management company. This negotiates the debt management plan, collects the payments from the client and distributes them to the creditors in return for a fee paid by the client (often referred to as 'fee chargers');
- the Consumer Credit Counselling Service or Payplan. These can arrange a debt management plan and distribute the payments to the client's creditors, but do not charge the client a fee. They are paid by the creditors through deducting a percentage of the money recovered. For this reason, they are part of the free money advice sector. Both have minimum criteria for setting up a plan and can also help clients to set up individual voluntary arrangements.

Debt management companies have individual consumer credit licences and from 6 April 2007 fall within the Financial Ombudsman Service's consumer credit jurisdiction. If a client is dissatisfied with the service provided, s/he should consider making a complaint.

3. The strategies

This section describes the recommended strategies for non-priority debts. They are not mutually exclusive. The adviser may use several strategies to deal with each debt – eg, a moratorium of three months followed by a partial write-off and the freezing of interest/charges with instalments by equitable distribution. Alternatively, different strategies (or combinations of strategies) may be needed for individual debts – eg, some requests for write-offs, some token offers and one voluntary charge.

Strategy selection often is not a single process, but may be done initially and reviewed later. The criteria described here should be equally applicable to initial or review strategies. The strategy chosen for each debt will need to be reviewed:

- if a creditor refuses to accept a particular strategy; *or*
- at the end of the time agreed by the creditor. For example, the creditor may agree to accept no payments for six months and then review the position; *or*
- if the client's financial circumstances change.

Often strategies will not be accepted on first application, and debt advisers should always urge creditors several times to accept a realistic strategy. Second and third letters can be strengthened by details of how other creditors have come to agree to a particular strategy. If the adviser considers a creditor is not complying with its obligations under a relevant code of practice – eg, is not treating the client 'sympathetically and positively', s/he should consider using the creditor's complaints procedure and threaten to refer the case to the Financial Ombudsman Service to resolve the matter in a 'fair and reasonable' way.

Clients should not routinely be advised to stop payments to all their non-priority creditors while negotiations are taking place. In many multiple debt cases it will be appropriate for the client to reduce payments to non-priority creditors or even stop them altogether. If the client is able to maintain contractual payments to non-priority creditors (while still servicing her/his essential commitments, including priority debts), s/he should be advised to do so. If s/he is unable to do so, the adviser should point out that the client's default will be registered with credit reference agencies and may eventually lead to court action by the creditor, but that it is still in the client's best interests not to make those payments because there is no, or very little, available income after meeting essential expenditure and payments to priority creditors. A long period without any payments at all to creditors is undesirable, unless a strategy involving non-payment has been proposed in the meantime. On the other hand, a short period where no payments are made may be inevitable while the adviser works out a strategy with the client.

Request a write-off

A write-off should be requested if:

- there is no available income or capital and a client's circumstances are unlikely to improve in the foreseeable future (or may even worsen); *or*
- the debt is uneconomical for the creditor to collect – eg, small amount is owed or the *pro rata* payment would be less than £1 a month (see p225); *or*
- there is some available income, but this will not repay the debt within a reasonable time (see also partial write-offs on p216); *or*
- the client's circumstances are exceptional and unlikely to improve – eg, s/he has a terminal illness or mental health problems that affect her capacity to make a contract (see p105)

A write-off means the creditor agrees not to collect any further payments and removes the account from its records. The client makes no further payments. If the debt is large, any realisable assets or equity in the client's home must be considered. It is likely that, if the creditor took court action and the client could not make payment as ordered by the court, the creditor could either apply for a charging order against the equity in the home (see p238) or ask the court to make a bankruptcy order (see p391) so that goods owned by the client or the home could be sold.

The question of write-offs has generated much discussion among debt advisers. Every creditor recognises the need to write off some debts (and makes provision for this in its accounts and the interest rates it sets). Advisers, exposed to a society whose prevalent moral code is one which lays emphasis on the importance of repaying one's debts, may well have personal anxieties about requesting a write-off. These should not be allowed to prejudice advice. Clients, too, may be anxious about the consequences of this strategy, so the adviser may need to explain the reasoning behind the suggestion and that it is being proposed to the creditor as the most economic and realistic solution available. However, the decision whether or not to request a write-off is ultimately one for the client. A client who initially says s/he wants to pay something may change her/his mind in the light of creditors' responses to her/his financial difficulties and so the possibility of proposing this strategy to creditors should be kept under review.

Advantages

- It removes the financial and emotional stress caused by that debt.
- It enables the client to make a fresh start.
- It acknowledges that further action against the client is not appropriate.

Disadvantages

- Creditors will not agree easily to write off debts, particularly if the debt has been incurred recently.
- When creditors write off debts, they often report this to a credit reference agency. This is an agency that collects evidence, such as county court judgments or evictions, and sells details of individuals who have experienced these to creditors. If a debt is reported as written off, it may be difficult for a client to get credit in the future. For more details on credit reference agencies, see p7.
- Many creditors never formally agree to write off a debt, even when they have received a request to do so. They will take no further action on it and at some point will write it out of their accounts. This can mean that the client is left uncertain as to whether or not the creditor has agreed to her/his request, and s/he can be vulnerable either to a change of company policy or to pursuit of a debt if her/his circumstances improve.

Useful arguments

- The circumstances of the client will need to be outlined carefully and attention drawn to the fact that the client has no property or goods of significant value, no income except benefits/low wages and there is no prospect of improvement in the foreseeable future. This will help creditors to see that court action is unlikely to be successful. Explain that if bankruptcy were pursued, the outcome would be the same. Medical evidence confirming, for example, the nature of any disability or that the client is unable to work may also be persuasive.

- Inform the creditor of the total amount of debt owing to all creditors to show the hopelessness of the client's situation.
- Most creditors have a set of criteria for deciding when to abandon debt recovery, which will be determined by the cost of recovering the money. The adviser should suggest that writing off a debt is likely to be the most economic solution for the creditor. For example, the Banking Code suggests that a write-off should be considered where the client's financial and personal circumstances are exceptional and unlikely to improve. The creditor must give reasons for refusing a write-off request and advisers should press for these to be provided as this may enable the adviser to ask the creditor to re-consider its position.
- Creditors may be more willing to write off a debt after repeatedly withholding action on the account for three or six months (see p222).
- It will be easier to get smaller debts written off.

Checklist for action

- Write to the creditor(s) proposing the strategy and request written confirmation that the strategy is agreed.
- Advise the client to stop paying.
- A creditor may not initially accept a write-off. The adviser should ask the creditor to reconsider after, say, three to six months, and repeat the request at subsequent reviews.

Partial write-off

If there is some money available to meet a creditor's demands, but this will not pay off the whole debt in a realistic period of time (in line with what a court would consider reasonable), creditors can be asked to reduce the balance owing immediately or to accept agreed instalments for a set period of years, after which the balance will be written off.

Partial write-off should be seen as a means of coming to an arrangement similar to an individual voluntary arrangement and which accords broadly with what a court would order if an income payments order in bankruptcy application were being considered. A period of at least three to five years, but no more than seven to ten years should be suggested. A request should also be made that further interest is stopped (see p218). Partial write-off is appropriate when:

- there are no realisable assets or substantial equity that could be charged;
- the client's circumstances are such that s/he cannot repay the whole debt within a reasonable period of time;
- there is no expectation of capital or extra income becoming available soon.

Advantages

- It reduces the amount owed and gives the client a realistic target to aim for and, therefore, a framework in which s/he can regain a sense of control over her/his financial affairs.
- The client repays less money.

Disadvantages

- When creditors write off debts they often report this to credit reference agencies and it may, therefore, be difficult for a person to get credit in the future.
- It may be difficult to get all creditors to agree to the strategy.

Useful arguments

- It can be argued that the creditor will receive more than if the client were made bankrupt, and thus it is quicker, cheaper and less stressful to the client for the creditor to limit demands to that amount now.
- A partial write-off is also very similar to a composition on an administration order (see p370) or an individual voluntary arrangement (see p234) and so creditors are only being asked to take a similar course of action to that taken by the courts, but on an informal basis. Again, as there are no attendant court/supervisor costs, the creditor is likely to see a higher return than in an administration order or individual voluntary arrangement.
- The creditor may be persuaded that it is better to go for something shorter term and realisable, rather than longer term but potentially expensive to collect and unlikely to be paid. Unless creditors reduce their demand to something the client can pay in the foreseeable future, the client is likely to lack the motivation to keep up with payments. It is unrealistic for both sides to set up repayment schemes which will last more than about five years and the likelihood is that such money will eventually be written off.
- If the creditor refuses to agree to this strategy initially, it is worth requesting it again after, say, 12 months of regular payments if there is still no improvement in the client's circumstances.

Checklist for action

- Agree with the client the amount of income available to creditors.
- Calculate offers and decide a payment period (two or three years).
- Write to the creditor(s) proposing the strategy, with details of the offers and requesting written confirmation that this is accepted.
- Advise the client to start making payments. Consider direct debits or standing orders if the client has a current account.
- Unless the arrangement is time-limited, ensure that interest is stopped. If not, consider advising the client to withhold payments until agreement is given to stop interest.

- Consider whether any steps need to be taken to ensure that the arrangement is legally binding on creditors (see full and final settlements on p219).

Freeze or reduce interest

If a client is unable to pay the contractual payments due under an agreement, adding interest and other charges, especially if s/he is not even repaying any capital due, will only increase the total balance and the debt will never be repaid. This fact has long been recognised by the county court where statutory interest is not charged after judgment on debts regulated by the Consumer Credit Act (but see p254 for when interest can be charged after a judgment).

Whenever a repayment schedule of less than the original contractual payments is envisaged, or if no payment can be afforded at present, a request should be made to stop (or freeze) all interest and any other charges accruing on the account. This strategy should always be used in conjunction with another strategy.

The request to stop interest should be made in most cases immediately the client contacts a debt adviser. However, the adviser must explain to the creditor why it is considered necessary – eg, the payments the client is likely to be able to afford will not cover the ongoing interest.

Advantages

- Realistic repayment schedules can be created under which debts will be repaid in a known time.
- All payments made reduce the debt. The client can see that s/he is repaying her/his debts.

Disadvantages

- Creditors may not accept the strategy, particularly if there is substantial equity in a property or the client has realisable assets which it is reasonable to expect her/him to use.
- It is not appropriate for loans where all interest is added at the beginning of the loan and there are no default interest/charges. In these cases, a partial write-off may achieve the desired result.

Useful arguments

- If a county court judgment were awarded, in practice interest would be stopped for all regulated consumer credit agreements (see p54).
- Excessive default charges – ie, charges which are more than any actual or anticipated loss which the creditor has or may face as a result of the loss, are almost certainly unenforceable either as a penalty at common law or as an unfair contract term, and so the creditor should either reduce them or remove them altogether and should consider doing so retrospectively (see p109).
- It is a necessary incentive to the client because otherwise s/he will not be prepared to lose valuable income in pursuit of a completely hopeless goal.

- Many other creditors are being asked (or have agreed) to stop interest and, therefore, fairness demands that this creditor does too.
- Make any offer of payment conditional upon interest stopping.

The Banking Code suggests that creditors should consider such requests on a case-by-case basis and that the seriousness of the client's situation may make it appropriate. On the other hand, creditors often complain that advisers 'automatically request creditors to freeze interest in all cases'. Requests to freeze interest should be appropriate and justified, and, in cases where a creditor believes the level of the client's repayments warrants it, the creditor may refuse to freeze interest, but may instead agree to reduce it. If the loan is regulated by the Consumer Credit Act, an application for a time order may be appropriate (see p283).

Checklist for action

This strategy should always be used with another strategy.

- Write to the creditor and include a request to freeze interest and other charges, together with some justification for the request.
- Request written confirmation that this has been done.
- If the strategy is not successful initially, ask the creditor to reconsider. It may be useful to provide evidence of other creditors' agreement to freeze or reduce interest and other charges.

Offering a reduced lump sum in full and final settlement

If there is available capital or saleable assets, or if the client will have such assets in the near future – eg, because s/he intends to sell a house for reasons unrelated to the debt, or a third party, such as a friend or relative, has a lump sum s/he is willing to give to the creditor, the creditor may accept an offer of an amount less than that which is actually due as early settlement. This is particularly likely if there is little or no available income and the client's financial position is unlikely to improve or may even worsen. Creditors are likely to recognise that acceptance of a cash lump sum makes commercial sense. When the client's income is low and unlikely to improve, it could be an attractive alternative to waiting to see if they get more over a long period. If there is more than one creditor, lump sums should usually be apportioned between them in proportion to the amount owing to each.

Ask the client if there are essentials s/he needs to purchase, or essential repairs that need to be carried out, before the lump sum is allocated to creditors.

The key to using this strategy successfully is to ensure that the lump-sum payment is not made until the creditor has agreed in writing to accept this in full and final settlement of all the money owed. Ideally, no payments should be made until all creditors have agreed and offers can – initially at least – be made on this basis, but advisers should be prepared to adopt a flexible approach to prevent the whole strategy from failing. For example, creditors who are reluctant to accept may be persuaded by knowing that other creditors have already agreed to accept it.

There is no set amount that needs to be offered and, in fact, a promise by a creditor to accept part-payment is not a legally binding contract unless the client has provided what the law regards as fresh 'consideration' for the creditor's promise to forgo payment of the balance. The Financial Ombudsman Service, however, may take the view that a creditor who goes back on its word is not behaving 'fairly and reasonably' unless the client misrepresented her/his true financial situation.

There will be a legally binding agreement if either:

- an arrangement is made with all the client's unsecured creditors; *or*
- the funds are made available by a third party (eg, a relative) and the offer is made by her/him on the client's behalf; *or*
- the agreement is embodied in a formal document known as a 'deed'. The client will need to be referred to a solicitor if s/he wants a deed drawn up – eg, if there is any doubt about the trustworthiness of a particular creditor.

Advantages

- The client pays less than s/he would if repaying over a longer term.
- The client has the opportunity of a fresh start.
- It is a more immediate and convenient solution than setting up a repayment schedule over a number of years.

Disadvantages

- The client loses the advantage of having a lump sum which could have been used for other purposes.
- Once aware of the existence of a lump sum, the creditor may attempt court action to obtain all the money for itself.

Useful arguments

- Contact the creditor before the money is available and suggest that this is the only chance that the client will have of paying a substantial amount and that because the client wants to pay her/his debts, s/he is prepared to hand all (or if there are several debts to be treated in this way, a proportionate share) of the money over to the creditor.
- It is worth pointing out that the creditor is not going to get more by refusing the offer and taking enforcement action, and that acceptance of the offer makes more commercial sense than the client continuing to make small payments over a long period of time. Such an arrangement may have to be made with senior staff in a creditor organisation and the adviser should ensure s/he is writing or speaking to senior credit control managers.

Checklist for action

- Write to the creditor(s) with details of the offer and request acceptance in full and final settlement to be confirmed in writing.
- If the money is coming from a third party, it should be made clear that the offer is being made by her/him on behalf of the client.
- Consider specialist legal help to draw up the agreement.
- Once written confirmation is received, advise the client (or third party) to send the payment(s).
- Any covering letter sent with a cheque should explain exactly what it is for and state that it is in 'full and final settlement'. Cashing a cheque sent 'in full and final settlement' is never binding on a creditor unless it has previously agreed to accept it on this basis (although cashing a cheque is strong evidence of acceptance unless it is accompanied by a swift rejection of the offer).
- If money is being made available from the sale of a house, it may be necessary to obtain a solicitor's undertaking that the money will be paid to the creditor once the house is sold.

In the unlikely event of a creditor threatening to go back on a full and final settlement if the client has made the payment, specialist advice should be sought.

Offering payment of a lump sum with instalments

When a client has capital or assets together with stable available income, but there are substantial arrears, the threat of further action often can be avoided by paying a single capital sum towards the arrears and then paying instalments towards part or all of the contractual payments. This often needs to be linked to another strategy, particularly freezing interest/charges (see p218), a partial write-off (see p233) or administration order (see p370). This is different from paying a capital sum in full and final settlement in that the payments will have to continue.

Advantages

- The creditor is no longer pressing.
- Weekly income has been maintained to a greater extent than otherwise.

Disadvantages

- The flexibility to use the capital sum elsewhere is lost.

Useful arguments

- If this tactic is being used to prevent imminent court action, the adviser can argue that the creditor will obtain its money more quickly than by going to court, and more money will be available to repay the debt as there will be less costs. An agreement such as this will have to be made in writing.

Checklist for action

- Contact the creditor proposing the strategy and request acceptance in writing.
- Calculate the instalments (see p225).
- Once written confirmation is received, advise the client to send payment of the capital sum, followed by regular instalments. Set up a direct debit or standing order for these if possible.
- Ensure that interest is stopped. If not, consider advising the client to withhold instalments until agreement is given to stop interest.

Holding tactics (moratorium)

It may sometimes be important for the adviser to gain time for the client when:

- there is some available income, but this is immediately required to deal with priority debts;
- there is no available income, but shortly there will be;
- available assets are being sold;
- the full situation is not yet known.

There are two types of holding tactic (also known as a 'moratorium'):

- **Asking creditors to suspend collection or enforcement action.** It may be useful to request a short delay if the adviser needs to check a credit agreement or its enforceability. Some agencies write automatically to all creditors asking them to withhold action for a short period when their advice is first sought. This is not necessary if a strategy can be formulated quickly or if the debt adviser will be asking the creditor to write off the debt or to accept no payments for three months. It is wasteful of resources to employ this device automatically and can increase the stress faced by the client, as it lengthens the time before agreement with creditors about a long-term strategy is reached, and may lead to creditors routinely refusing requests. If a delay is needed because balances are required before a strategy can be implemented, ask the client to obtain these where possible.

  If a debt is queried or disputed, the creditor (or debt collector) should investigate/provide details (as appropriate) and should cease collection activity in the meantime.[7]
- Asking creditors to accept no payments for a specified period. If no money is available at present to pay any non-priority debts, the creditor should be asked to accept no payments for three or six months and then review the situation.

This is invariably a temporary strategy and so will be subject to review, usually after three or six months. It will always be used with another strategy – eg, asking a creditor to withhold for three months and then follow this with a request for a write-off. This can be useful where it is known that the creditor is unlikely to accept a write-off immediately. If a request is made to a creditor to withhold any action and accept no payments, the creditor must always be asked, at the same time, to stop interest/charges in order to prevent the debt increasing even further.

The length of time for which the adviser requests no payments will depend on:

- any known future changes in the client's financial position which might allow payments to begin;
- the length of time needed to repay priority debts;
- the stress faced by the client and how much breathing space s/he needs.

If the creditor agrees to withhold action and collect no payments for six months, it gives the client a substantial period of relief.

However, as this strategy can never be a permanent solution, it means that a request for a six-month delay prolongs the process of reaching one.

Advantages

- Time can give the adviser space to gather all the necessary facts and work out the best strategy.
- It removes the immediate pressure from the client, and enables payments to be made for priority debts.
- It gets creditors used to the idea that there are problems, but does not leave them in the dark.
- Almost as a matter of routine, many creditors will accept a request from a debt advice agency to withhold action for a short period.

Disadvantages

- It does not actually solve anything. Some creditors will refuse to stop interest and thus the debt grows while no action is taken.
- It can create extra work for the adviser.

Useful arguments

- Explain that considerable debts have arisen and outline the client's circumstances.
- Explain that time is required for professional debt advice.

Checklist for action

- Telephone/write to the creditor to explain the situation and request written confirmation that the account is held in abeyance. Enclose a financial statement if requesting that more than a month's payments is withheld, unless a client receives means-tested benefits.
- Ensure that interest/charges will be stopped.
- Advise the client not to make payments.

Token payments

When there is no available income, assets or capital and the situation is unlikely to change, but it is impossible to get agreement to any other strategy, payment by instalments of a nominal or token nature may be necessary. This will sometimes satisfy either the pride or the administrative systems of a creditor and may be the only way to prevent it from taking further action.

Clients initially seeking advice often want to make token payments rather than withholding payments or asking creditors to write off, out of fear or ignorance of enforcement action, or because of previous harassment by creditors, or because they want to make some payment, however small, towards their debts. The adviser must ensure that clients do not make payments they cannot afford or at the expense of making payments towards priority debts. It should be stressed that a nominal payment need not be more than 50p a month (although it is usually £1).

The strategy need not be used for all creditors and should only be offered as a last resort where the creditor has refused to either write off the debt or accept no payments, or to freeze interest/charges and where court action by the creditor would be undesirable. The creditor must be asked to agree to take no further action and to stop interest in return for token payments being made. Token payments do not resolve the client's debt problems and so it is necessary to review the strategy at a later date to choose a more suitable long-term option.

If a creditor has already taken court action, but there is no available income and the court is unwilling to order no payments (see p222), the client will need to make a token offer to pay by instalments (eg, £1 a month) in order to prevent further enforcement action (see Chapter 9 for more details).

Advantages

- Paying a token amount may be the only way to obtain a creditor's agreement to take no further action and stop interest/charges.
- The client feels s/he is paying something towards her/his debts and creditors can see the habit of payment being re-established.

Disadvantages

- It uses up income that is not really available.
- It encourages creditors to take an unrealistic view of people's ability to pay.
- It can be expensive for the client as it may cost as much in postage and other charges to make the payment as the payment is worth.
- The debt will never be repaid at this rate and it hangs over the client.
- Creditors can continue to apply pressure on clients to pay more, particularly where money is paid to a collector who comes to the home.

Useful arguments

- A request for payments may be made by the creditor after the adviser has made it clear there is no (or only a nominal amount of) available income as shown by the financial statement. The adviser should explain that, in fact, the only payment possible is a token payment because the client is cutting back on essential spending, such as food or fuel, in order to make the payment.

- If creditors are threatening court action, draw their attention to any recent low judgments awarded by the local county court in similar cases and suggest that even if they go to the trouble of going to court, they will get no more than a nominal amount (or a general stay).

Checklist for action

- Telephone/write to the creditor and await written confirmation of the strategy.
- Ensure that further action, and interest and other charges, are stopped.
- Advise the client to make payments. Ask for a payment book if this facilitates payments without cost.
- Review at an agreed date with the client.

Token payments are essentially a short-term strategy. The Banking Code recommends that offers of token payments may be accepted where there is no available income for non-priority creditors but there is a realistic prospect of the client's circumstances improving. This guidance reflects not only the difficulty of persuading creditors to accept no payments at all but also the belief of creditors that, firstly, people can always find some money and, secondly, that something will turn up. All advice must be in the best interests of the client and it is not generally in the client's best interests to make payments at a higher level than s/he can afford. But if a creditor will not agree, for example, to freeze interest/charges unless token payments are made, the adviser must consider whether it is nevertheless in the client's best interests to make those payments.

Equitable distribution of available income (*pro rata* payments)

If there is available income, a number of debts, and no capital or realisable assets, this income should be distributed among all the non-priority creditors in a fair way. Apportioning the available income fairly is best done by a method known either as 'equitable distribution' or '*pro rata* payments', where the amount of each instalment is directly proportionate to the total amount owing to that particular creditor. Thus, if there are ten creditors, of whom five are owed £1,000 and the rest are owed £500, those owed the larger debt will be paid twice as much each week or month.

Some creditors seek a distribution that is proportionate to the payments due under their agreement rather than the capital outstanding. This is popular with those creditors that lend smaller amounts over short periods at very high rates of interest. Such arrangements should be rejected because:

- this is not the way in which a court would define an equitable offer if an administration order (see p233) or other insolvency procedures were being considered;

- the creditors owed large sums are unlikely to agree to it and may go to court and obtain an order for repayments based on capital outstanding;
- short-term lenders of small sums have already allowed for the high risk associated with such lending and this is reflected in the rates of interest charged.

The adviser must calculate the amount due to each creditor per week or month. The calculation is based on the following formula:

Amount owed to creditor ÷ total amount owed x total income available for distribution

Example

The client owes money to three creditors:

Creditor A	£1,000
Creditor B	£800
Creditor C	£250
Total amount owing	**£2,050**

The client's total available income is £12 a month

Calculation:

Creditor A	1,000 ÷ 2,050 x 12 = £5.85 a month
Creditor B	800 ÷ 2,050 x 12 = £4.70 a month
Creditor C	250 ÷ 2,050 x 12 = £1.45 a month
Total repayments to creditors	**= £12.00 a month**

(amounts may be rounded up or down for convenience, but not if this results in payments which the client cannot afford)

If the adviser does not use the common financial statement or some other computer-based financial statement which automatically calculates *pro rata* offers, this sum must be worked out for each creditor. Even if the exact balances are not known, it may be worth calculating a distribution on the basis of good estimates as the weekly variation will probably be very small and may be acceptable to creditors.

If the calculation gives rise to a very low payment to a particular creditor (eg, less than £1 per month) the adviser may wish to include in the offer letter a request that, in view of the high collection costs for such a small sum, the creditor should consider writing off the debt (see p214). When calculating the amount of available income on offer to creditors, the adviser should ensure some leeway in the financial statement to cope with unexpected events (eg, short periods of sickness) so that payments can still be maintained.

The Office of Fair Trading (OFT) points out that advisers should not assume that *pro rata* offers to non-priority creditors on outstanding balances are always in the client's best interests, and that clients should not usually be advised to make payments that do not cover ongoing interest or other charges. Instead, they should take into account that some loans may lose the benefit of a reduced rate of interest and consider paying off loans with a higher rate of interest before loans with a lower rate.[8] Although this appears to conflict with the principles of money advice discussed elsewhere, unless the client has sufficient available income to be able to maintain the contractual payments on these debts, as well as servicing her/his other debts, it will be in the client's best interests to offer *pro rata* payments, provided this is accompanied by a request for any ongoing interest and any charges to be stopped so that each payment made by the client actually reduces the debt. On the other hand, if the creditor refuses to stop interest or reduce it sufficiently, *pro rata* payments will almost certainly not be in the client's best interests and the creditor must be urged to reconsider, or the strategy reviewed with the client.

Advantages

- Equitable distribution is widely accepted by the credit industry (many creditors think it is the only strategy that money advisers should use).
- It ensures that all non-priority debts are dealt with together.
- It is based on court practices. This is how money is distributed to creditors when an administration order is granted (see p233).

Disadvantages

- A client may be left with little financial flexibility and money only for basics.
- Unless coupled with a partial write-off (see p216), many debts may take years to clear.
- If the payments do not cover ongoing interest/charges the debt will never be repaid.

Useful arguments

- The strongest argument in favour of this strategy is its fairness. It can be presented as a businesslike response to a difficult situation, ensuring that every creditor will be treated in a way which will give them the maximum possible amount.
- It is exactly what would happen if a court were to grant an administration order or in bankruptcy and is the kind of order which a court should make every time it makes an instalment order. The creditor cannot expect to do better.

- Some creditors will argue against the stopping of interest, particularly if the capital sums on which the equitable distribution is based include some where interest was added at the beginning of the loan. This is a reasonable argument and does lessen the fairness of this method. However, it ignores the fact that interest is often lower if applied at the start of the loan. It may be possible to discuss with creditors whose claim is for an amount which includes interest added to the beginning of the loan the option of claiming only that part of the interest due by the date of the equitable distribution.
- This strategy has often been used successfully where it can be shown that the person is starting to pay her/his creditors and wishes to treat them all fairly. In addition, consideration should be given to asking for a partial write-off where offers will be paid for two or three years only (see p216 for details).
- If the creditor subscribes to the British Bankers' Association/Money Advice Trust common financial statement (see p44), it has been agreed that the offer will normally be accepted (but not necessarily that interest/charges will be frozen). Non-acceptance would suggest the creditor has other information about the client, which it should be asked to disclose.
- Many creditors now have strict criteria for automatically accepting repayment offers based either on a minimum payment or percentage of the debt or repayment over a maximum period in exchange for concessions on interest/charges. However, the Banking Code guidance makes clear that creditors should consider other repayment offers, in line with their commitment to treat all customers 'fairly' and those in financial difficulty 'sympathetically and positively'.

It is usual to send to each creditor details of the amounts owed to all creditors, together with the offers made. This should not be done if the client wishes confidentiality to be maintained. However, it will be helpful for the creditors to know that they have been given the whole financial position of the client as they would in an administration order or bankruptcy. If the creditor has already obtained a court order that is higher than the offer calculated, the client should consider applying to the court on Form N245 to vary the order if s/he cannot obtain the creditor's written agreement to accept the offer made and to take no further action to enforce the debt (see Chapter 9 for how to do this).

Checklist for action

- Agree with the client the amount of income available for creditors.
- Calculate offers to creditors. Consider a partial write-off where the suggested repayment period will not clear the debts within a reasonable time (see p216).
- Write to the creditors with offers. Suggest a write-off where offers are low.
- Ensure that interest and other charges are stopped.
- Advise the client to make payments (consider direct debit or standing order if the client has a current account). Ask for a payment book if this allows payment

without cost. The client should not wait until all the creditors have accepted before starting to make payments.

- Consider whether a referral to a non-fee-charging debt management company might be in the client's best interests – ie, s/he would have to make one monthly payment for distribution among her/his creditors (see p225).

Debt consolidation

Debt consolidation involves the client either taking out a new loan or increasing existing borrowing in order to pay off multiple debts. Debts can be consolidated by:

- an unsecured loan. These are likely to be small and so of limited potential;
- a further advance from an existing mortgage or secured lender, also secured on the client's property;
- a secured loan from a lender other than the existing mortgage provider, in addition to the existing mortgage;
- a re-mortgage with a new lender to replace any existing mortgage or secured loan;
- the transfer of balances to a credit card (including the use of credit card cheques).

Advantages

- Multiple agreements are replaced by a single agreement. The client only has to deal with one creditor.
- The consolidation loan is likely to be on better terms than the agreements it replaces, such as lower interest rates and monthly repayments.
- Where the balance transfer is on the basis of a low interest rate and the client can settle the balance before any balance transfer offer expires, the flexibility of a credit card enables consolidation to take place without incurring any additional costs.
- The client's credit rating can be improved or the creditors prevented from registering defaults by the debts being repaid.

Disadvantages

- Debt consolidation often involves replacing unsecured non-priority debts with a secured priority debt with the client's property at risk if s/he defaults.
- Loans to clients with impaired credit ratings (non-status loans) are likely to be at higher rates of interest than those available to people with a clean credit record (status loans).
- There are usually costs associated with switching debts – eg, brokers' fees and early settlement charges.
- Many debt consolidation loans are sold with payment protection insurance, which increases the amount borrowed.

- Although debt consolidation tends to involve lower monthly payments, it is often over an extended period, increasing the total amount payable by the client.
- Many debt consolidation loans are refinanced before running their full term (a process known as 'churning'), which means that the client often has to borrow more as most of the repayments on the original loan will have been interest rather than capital and there will be early settlement charges. There may also be further costs – eg, broker's fee and new payment protection insurance, which will often be added to the new loan.

Debt consolidation loans are the subject of extensive advertising, particularly on television. Much of this advertising encourages people to borrow extra cash for a holiday, buy a new car, improve their home or just have more spending money as well as paying off their debts. For people in financial difficulties, this is likely to make the situation worse. There is some evidence of financial institutions offering consolidation loans to their customers as the only solution to their financial difficulties and solely to clear debts owed to them, so placing them in an advantageous position over the client's other creditors.

Advisers are reminded that paragraph 2.6(b) of the OFT's *Debt Collection Guidance* states that it is an unfair practice to pressurise a client into taking on further borrowing in order to raise funds to pay off debts. Clients who are not in arrears and can meet their monthly commitments have the option of either carrying on with their existing agreements or refinancing them individually on more advantageous terms. But for the average client, struggling to meet her/his commitments, the other options discussed in this *Handbook* are likely to be more suitable.

Equity release loan

An equity release or lifetime mortgage enables a property-owning client to release equity from her/his home. It is secured on the client's property and is a way of raising capital to repay debts. The term of the loan is the client's lifetime, at the end of which all the capital becomes due. The interest is rolled up and the client is not required to pay anything while s/he is alive. These loans are only available to clients over 60 and the older the client is the more s/he can borrow (depending on the amount of equity in the property). The interest rate is usually fixed (currently at about 7 per cent per annum). If at the time of death there is a shortfall because there is no longer equity, the lender must write the outstanding balance off and cannot pursue it from other funds the client may have in her/his estate.

This type of loan may involve the conversion of unsecured borrowing into secured borrowing and is only appropriate if there is plenty of equity in the property. It will be most useful if the client is finding it particularly stressful owing money to a number of different creditors, or if creditors are proving difficult to negotiate with. Clients must always be advised to obtain independent financial advice.

Advantages

- The loan prevents further action by the creditors.
- It may be a means of releasing equity from the house to use for other purposes, such as insulation or heating, which in turn can reduce living costs.

Disadvantages

- The equity in the home is reduced by the value of the loan and will be steadily eroded by the accruing interest.
- On the client's death, the property will have to be sold to repay the loan, which may result in dependants who lived with the client being left homeless.

Checklist for action

- Advise the client to obtain independent financial advice.
- Ensure the client obtains full details about the terms and conditions and the cost of the loan before signing any agreements.
- Inform creditors of the proposal and ask them to take no further action to enable the loan to be set up.

Sale of the home

When there is no available income, capital or realisable assets other than a home, sale may be considered (see p188). It should not be considered if the financial situation is likely to improve or if the sale of the home would result in homelessness. It is only appropriate as a way of dealing with non-priority debts if there is sufficient equity to satisfy most creditors' demands and to cover the costs of selling and moving, and when the stress of debts is creating unacceptable problems for the household.

The sale of a house is often recommended to people who are in debt as an easy way out of the situation, but it should be remembered that courts rarely order a property to be sold to satisfy unsecured borrowing and only, of course, after a charging order (see p258) has been made and an order for sale subsequently applied for (see p262), or a bankruptcy order made. It is generally much worse to be homeless than to be in debt. If, however, an expensive house can be sold and a more modest one, which would nonetheless satisfy the client's needs, can be bought, this can be an acceptable way of coping with a debt problem and perhaps having money left over for other purposes as well.

A client may have been advised (sometimes by family or friends) that s/he has no alternative other than to sell her/his house and s/he will, therefore, approach an adviser at a stage where this process has already begun. By examining the other strategies outlined here, it should be possible to demonstrate that the sale of the house in these circumstances is not the only option and would not be ordered by the courts. The state of the housing market may also mean that this strategy is not easily achievable.

If a local authority or housing association re-houses people following a sale of their home, it will normally only do so where it is clear that the sale is the only means to prevent eviction. Some local authorities still consider that the sale of a house makes someone intentionally homeless and, therefore, not eligible for re-housing under homelessness legislation. However, the code of guidance for local authorities states that a person should not be treated as intentionally homeless if her/his house was sold because of financial difficulties, and advisers should draw attention to this if necessary.[9]

Advantages

- It can clear the debts.
- It may raise capital for other purposes.
- The client may see it as providing the opportunity for a fresh start.

Disadvantages

- It releases equity held in the property to satisfy unsecured creditors in a way a court would be unlikely to order.
- It may not be possible to find alternative suitable housing.
- Moving house is a major disruption and costs a lot of money.
- The client may lose money if the housing market is depressed.
- The sale may take a long time or, in the midst of a recession, prove impossible, and the benefits of choosing this strategy may be lost.

Useful arguments

- Creditors will receive a lump sum, either paying the debt in full or partially in full and final settlement (see p219).

Checklist for action

- Discuss the pros and cons of selling a house with the client.
- Telephone/write to creditor(s) to inform them of the strategy and obtain written confirmation that they will take no further action.
- Ensure the house is put on the market with a reliable estate agent.
- Ensure suitable alternative accommodation is available.
- Once it has been decided to put the house on the market, letters should be written informing the creditors of this and asking them to withhold interest charges or any other action until sale prices are available. Creditors may require a letter from an estate agent, and if a confirmation of a request to sell a property is available, this can be photocopied and sent. They may also want a letter from the client's solicitor confirming her/his share of the proceeds of sale will be forwarded directly to them.

4. Court-based strategies

General stay

If a court order has been made, or is about to be made, for an instalment order and there is no available income, capital or assets, the county court can make an order for a general stay of judgment or enforcement. See p302 for an explanation of the court's power to make such an order and how the adviser can help the client make an application for no instalments.

Voluntary charge

Occasionally, but only as the 'lesser of two evils', it is advisable to turn an unsecured loan into a secured one in order to prevent any further action being taken. This is a very high-risk strategy and should not be undertaken lightly. It is described in detail in Chapter 7.

Administration order

If a client already has at least one county court (or High Court) judgment against her/him and her/his total debts do not exceed the limit for an administration order (currently £5,000), s/he can apply to the county court for the court to 'administer' payments to all her/his creditors. The client makes one monthly payment to the court, which will divide it equitably among all creditors. See p370 for details.

Bankruptcy

Bankruptcy is a legal procedure in which the inability of a client to pay her/his debts is acknowledged and the majority of unsecured creditors can no longer pursue their debts, which are eventually written off. A third party (known as the trustee in bankruptcy) takes over the handling of the client's financial affairs for the benefit of her/his creditors. The trustee will distribute a proportion of any available income and/or capital resources to creditors. Bankruptcy may be a suitable strategy for a client if:

- debts have arisen which creditors will not write off;
- s/he does not own a home or has little or negative equity;
- s/he does not have any available assets or capital;
- s/he has a low available income in comparison to the amount of debt, which means it would take many years to repay her/his creditors;
- s/he does not intend to be in business on her/his own in the next few years.

See Chapter 12 for further details, including the advantages, disadvantages, consequences and procedures involved in bankruptcy.

Individual voluntary arrangements

Individual voluntary arrangements are a means whereby a client can protect her/himself from further action by creditors by entering into a legally binding arrangement with them, supervised by an insolvency practitioner. They are often described as an informal bankruptcy and should be considered before bankruptcy itself. See Chapter 12 for further details.

Time order

An application for a time order may be appropriate either to prevent the creditor from obtaining a judgment or to freeze interest or other charges. See p283 for further details.

Notes

1. **The criteria**
    1 *Commentary on Debt Management Guidelines*, OFT, para 15
    2 See J Phipps, 'It's Debt Jim, but not as we know it', *Adviser* 88
    3 *Debt Collection Guidance*, OFT, July 2003, para 2.14
    4 See D Shields and M van Rooyen, 'Square Peg Debts', *Adviser* 99
    5 See J Kruse, 'The Death of Pro Rata?', *Adviser* 115

2. **The general approach to non-priority debts**
    6 *Debt Collection Guidance*, OFT, para 2.6(b) and (f)

3. **The strategies**
    7 *Debt Collection Guidance*, OFT, para 2.8(i) and (k). The Credit Services Association's Code of Practice contains similar provisions (para 4(r))
    8 *Debt Collection Guidance*, OFT, para 22(e)-(g)
    9 *Homelessness Code of Guidance for Local Authorities*, Department for Communities and Local Government, July 2006, s11.18

Chapter 9

The county court

This chapter covers:

1. Introduction

The majority of cases involving debt are dealt with by a network of around 225 county courts throughout England and Wales. Cases are heard by district judges and circuit judges, assisted by part-time judges, with some decisions being delegated to court staff (see p248). Judges are drawn from the ranks of experienced barristers and solicitors. The county court was originally intended to provide a cheap and simple system for the recovery of small debts, but its jurisdiction has gradually been increased. More than two million court actions are entered in the county courts every year (2,015,000 in 2007).

The county courts derive their powers from the County Courts Act 1984, as amended, in particular, by the Courts and Legal Services Act 1990 and the Civil Procedure Act 1997. Since 26 April 1999, the Civil Procedure Rules 1998 govern the procedures in the county court.

The Civil Procedure Rules include pre-action protocols. These are codes of practice that the parties are expected to follow prior to commencing court action. There is no protocol for debt cases. There is a protocol for possession claims for rent arrears, with a protocol for mortgage possessions coming into force on 19 November 2009 (available at www.civiljusticecouncil.gov.uk) and a consultation taking place on a general protocol. Regardless of whether there is a protocol relating to the specific type of case, the parties are expected to act reasonably in their pre-action conduct in exchanging relevant information and documents and generally in avoiding the necessity of court proceedings.[1]

Parties to a potential dispute should follow a reasonable procedure, intended to avoid litigation. This should usually include:

- the creditor writing to give details of the claim;
- the client acknowledging the claim letter promptly;
- the client giving a detailed written response within a reasonable period; *and*
- the parties conducting genuine and reasonable negotiations, with a view to settling the claim without court proceedings.

The Civil Procedure Rules are available online at www.dca.gov.uk/civil/procrules_fin/index.htm and are published in *The Civil Court Practice*.[2] This is an expensive two-volume publication (plus a separate volume containing prescribed forms) which, like its predecessor, is known as the 'Green Book' and is published annually with supplements. In addition to the rules, the Green Book contains annotations and commentary, tables summarising various common procedures, details of court costs and fees, the pre-action protocols and excerpts from relevant legislation.

The Department for Constitutional Affairs and the Courts Service are the government agencies responsible for the courts. The Courts Service publishes various leaflets and guides to court procedure and these are available free from court offices and www.hmcourts-service.gov.uk. There is also a Courts Charter, a series of leaflets covering all the courts and offices run by the Courts Service, which sets out the standards of performance court users can expect and how to complain. All forms of discrimination should be challenged and taken up with the court as part of the debt adviser's social policy work.

The court manager and her/his staff are responsible for carrying out the court's administrative functions – eg, issuing proceedings, processing applications and fixing hearing dates. It is a good idea for debt advisers to establish a working relationship with their local court. Many courts operate users' groups and/or court desks for unrepresented parties. Debt advisers have no right to represent their clients in courts (as opposed to tribunals) except at hearings allocated to the small claims track, but judges have increasingly recognised the value of such representation and rarely refuse to allow debt advisers to speak on behalf of their clients. However, only legal representatives[3] can sign court forms on behalf of clients.

There is an increasing emphasis on the use of alternative dispute resolution, with some courts offering the services of local court-based mediation schemes. The objective is to encourage parties to a dispute to use some form of alternative dispute resolution and, even after a county court claim has been issued, the court can 'stay' (ie, halt) the proceedings to enable the parties to attempt to settle their dispute by mediation or other means. Although the courts have no power to compel parties to do so, when deciding the amount of any costs to be awarded, they can take into account the efforts made before and during the proceedings to resolve the dispute (see p252).

Advisers are reminded that the Financial Ombudsman Service is a form of alternative dispute resolution and if a complaint has been, or could be, referred to the Ombudsman, the court may agree to stay the proceedings.[4]

Court fees

Most steps taken in court proceedings attract a fee to cover administrative costs, which must be paid to the court before the step can be taken. The fees are set annually by statutory instrument and details can be obtained from any court office or the Courts Service website (see leaflet Ex50).

A client who is not being funded by the Legal Services Commission for the proceedings can claim a full or partial remission if one of the following applies.

- If s/he is in receipt of income support, working tax credit with no child tax credit, income-based jobseeker's allowance, or the guarantee credit of pension credit, the client can get a full remission of the fees. To qualify, the client must be the person receiving the benefit and not the claimant's partner. Partners of benefit claimants must claim remission under one of the other grounds.
- A client will get a full remission of the fees if her/his 'gross annual income' (including that of any partner) is below a certain limit. The calculation is based on all income received from any source, excluding certain benefits and other payments but including tax credits, and takes into account whether or not the client has children.
- A client may qualify for full or partial remission on the basis of the amount of her/his disposable monthly income (including that of any partner). To calculate entitlement, the client's net monthly income from all sources, excluding certain benefits and other payments but including tax credits, is subject to a list of deductions to arrive at her/his disposable monthly income. No fee is payable if the client's disposable monthly income is less than £50. Above this figure, her/his contribution to the fee is assessed according to a fixed table.
- If none of the other grounds apply, the court has discretion to allow full or partial remission of a fee if, because of exceptional circumstances, the client would face undue financial hardship in paying the fee. Guidance suggests the client must satisfy the court that paying a fee would seriously impact on her/his day-to-day life – eg, if s/he has financial commitments that are not taken into account under the other grounds, but which are likely to have serious consequences if not paid on time.

Note: tax credits are taken into account in full as income but childcare costs are only taken into account in assessing monthly disposable income and not gross annual income. Also, while a client may be included in her/his partner's benefit entitlement, s/he cannot rely on the partner's receipt of benefit to claim remission. Disability living allowance and attendance allowance are both disregarded in the calculation of income, but there is no allowance for the costs of disability.[5]

The application should be made on Form EX160 (available from www.hmcourts-service.gov.uk), together with evidence of eligibility (see below). The Courts Service publishes an accompanying leaflet (EX160A) (also available from the website) and detailed guidance has been issued to court staff on assessing applications, *Guidance for Administering the System of Fee Concessions* (available from any court office). The guidance makes clear that joint litigants are jointly and severally liable for payment of the fee. If one joint litigant qualifies for full or partial remission, the other must pay the full fee, unless s/he also qualifies for full or partial remission.

If the client has no money with her/him to pay the fee and does not apply for remission, the court may nevertheless process the court action in an emergency (ie, where the interests of justice would be compromised if a delay occurs) – eg, to suspend an eviction the following day. The client must undertake to apply for fee remission within five days and to pay the fee if this application fails. If the client fails to do so, the matter is referred to the district judge who may revoke any order made in the court action.

A refusal of full or partial remission can be appealed to the court manager in writing within 14 days. The letter should state why the client believes the decision is wrong and can include further information and evidence. The court manager should notify the decision on the appeal within 10 days. There is a further right of appeal to the area director, again within 14 days. There is no further appeal, and because fee remission is an administrative matter, the judiciary is not involved.

If the application is not made at the same time as the court action is taken, any fee can be refunded retrospectively provided an application is made within six months of the fee being paid. This time limit can be extended for good cause. Remission cannot be applied for in the case of consolidated attachment of earnings orders (see p266) or administration orders (see p370).

2. Types of court action

The person or organisation bringing court action is called the 'claimant'. The person or organisation against whom court action is brought is called the 'defendant'. Most forms used in court proceedings are prescribed and can be identified by their number and title in the bottom left-hand corner. It is important for debt advisers to familiarise themselves with these. The forms debt advisers most commonly encounter are available online at www.hmcourts-service.gov.uk/HMCSCourtFinder/FormFinder.do.

Cases can be classified as follows.

- Money-only claims – eg, for repayment of an amount due under a loan, overdraft or credit card agreement (see p239).

- Claims relating to agreements regulated by the Consumer Credit Act 1974 which are not for money only – eg, for possession of goods supplied under a hire purchase agreement (see p270).
- Claims relating to land – eg, for possession of a house by a mortgage lender (see p272).
- All other claims – eg, a claim for the return of goods supplied under an agreement not regulated by the Consumer Credit Act 1974. These differ from money-only claims in that, if the client does not respond to the claim, the creditor must make a formal application to the court for judgment and submit supporting evidence. The court will decide whether the creditor is entitled to judgment.

3. **Action to recover money only**

Court proceedings start when the court issues a 'claim form' at the request of the creditor (claimant). In order for a claim form to be issued in the High Court, not only must the creditor expect to recover more than £15,000, but it must be able to justify the matter being dealt with by a High Court judge. This will rarely be possible in the ordinary debt case and so there should be no reason for creditors to issue proceedings in the High Court.[6]

Debts regulated by the Consumer Credit Act 1974

The High Court cannot deal with claims related to secured or unsecured agreements regulated by the Consumer Credit Act 1974, or actions linked to such agreements, regardless of the amount of the claim.

If an adviser encounters a case involving a regulated consumer credit agreement (or any other case) being dealt with in the High Court, s/he should seek specialist advice.

Default notice

A default notice is a form which must be issued by a creditor for all debts regulated by the Consumer Credit Act 1974 before court action can start for early payment of money due under an agreement and/or to repossess goods or land. It is usually required in debt cases where arrears are claimed along with the money which would become due if the agreement ran its course. It is not required if the time allotted to an agreement is already over but arrears remain, or if only arrears are claimed.

The default notice must contain details of:

- the type of agreement, including the name and address of creditor and client;
- the terms of the agreement which have been broken;
- for fixed-sum credit, the early settlement figure;

- the action needed by the client – eg, to pay arrears in full by a certain date;
- the action the creditor intends to take if the client is unable to comply with the default notice – eg, refer to debt collection, start court action, repossess goods or land.

A default notice served on or after 1 October 2008 must contain the following further information.

- If the notice relates to a hire purchase or conditional sale agreement, information regarding the client's right to terminate the agreement (including the amount of the client's liability if s/he does exercise the right to terminate) (see p73).
- Where applicable, a statement that the client may have to pay post-judgment contractual interest in the event of the creditor obtaining a judgment (see p63).
- A copy of the current Office of Fair Trading (OFT) information sheet on default.

The client must be given at least 14 days to carry out the required action, and if the default notice requests payment it must contain a statement about time orders (see p283) and about seeking advice from a Citizens Advice Bureau, solicitor or trading standards department.

If a default notice is not complied with, a creditor can:

- terminate the agreement;
- recover any goods or land which form part of the agreement;
- demand earlier payment of money due under an agreement.

Creditors will not always automatically initiate court action if a default notice is not complied with, and even if the time limit has expired it is always worth negotiating with a creditor in order to prevent possible court action. Clients often claim not to have received default notices and so advisers should bear in mind that a default notice is treated as served for this purpose if it is sent by post to the client's last known address.[7]

The venue

Claims for the recovery of money only can be started by creditors in any county court. This may not be near to where the client lives. Large creditors which issue county court claims in bulk and prepare claims on computer can use the Claim Production Centre or County Court Bulk Centre at Northampton County Court, which charges a lower court fee (see p237). The court that issues the claim (the originating court) deals with the matter by post unless it is transferred to another court. The case will automatically be transferred to the client's 'home court' (ie, the county court for the district in which the client lives) if:[8]

- the client defends the action (see p251); *or*
- there is a request for redetermination of a decision by the court (see p249); *or*

- the district judge decides that a request for an instalment order should be dealt with at a hearing; *or*
- there is an application to set aside a default judgment (see p298); *or*
- there is an application by a creditor to increase the amount payable under a judgment (see p301); *or*
- there is a request for reconsideration of a decision by the court relating to a client's application to vary the amount payable under a judgment or to suspend a warrant of execution (see p303).

If the client's defence is that s/he paid the debt before the claim was issued, this will be checked with the creditor before the case is transferred. In County Court Bulk Centre cases, all defences are checked with the creditor before the case is transferred. Automatic transfer is only available if the defendant is an individual. If automatic transfer does not apply, the court has the discretion to transfer the case if:

- it would be more convenient or fair for a hearing to be held in some other court; *and/or*
- the facilities available at the court where the case is currently being dealt with are inadequate because a party or witness has a disability.

The claim form

The claim form (N1) must contain a concise statement of the nature of the claim and a 'statement of value'. This states the amount the creditor is claiming and whether s/he expects to recover:

- not more than £5,000;
- more than £5,000 but not more than £15,000; *or*
- more than £15,000.

The amount claimed includes the court fee paid by the creditor to issue the proceedings and, if a solicitor has been instructed, an amount for the solicitor's costs. The court fee and solicitor's costs vary with the amount claimed. The claim form must state the amount of any interest included and whether the creditor is seeking interest after judgment (see p254).

Details of the court of issue and of the unique reference number allocated to the case appear in the top right corner of the claim form.

The claim form must be served on the client within four months of issue. This will usually be done by the court and will be by first-class post. The claim form is deemed to have been received on the second business day after it was posted – ie, if posted on Monday it is deemed to have been received on Wednesday (Saturdays, Sundays, Bank Holidays, Christmas Day and Good Friday are not counted).[9] In Claim Production Centre or County Court Bulk Centre cases, the claim form is deemed to be served five days after issue.

Particulars of claim

The claim form must be accompanied by 'particulars of claim' or these must be sent to ('served on') the client by the creditor within 14 days of the claim form being served. The particulars of claim must include a concise statement of the facts relied on by the creditor (including the details of any contract) and must be verified by a 'statement of truth' – ie, that the creditor believes the facts stated are true. A copy of any written agreement should (but not must) be attached (this is not required where the claim form and particulars of claim are issued by the Claim Production Centre or County Court Bulk Centre).[10]

If the claim form includes particulars of claim, it must be accompanied by:

- a response pack, including an acknowledgement of service (N9);
- a form for admitting the claim (N9A);
- a form of defence and counterclaim to be used if the client disputes the claim (N9B);
- notes for the client on replying to the claim form (N9C).

If the particulars of claim are served separately from the claim form, the forms must be served with the particulars of claim. This may be important as the client's time for responding to the claim runs from the date of service of the particulars of claim.

Responding to the claim form

The client must respond to the claim form/particulars of claim within 14 days of service – ie, the response must be received on or before the 16th day after the date of posting (or within 19 days of issue if issued by the Claim Production Centre or County Court Bulk Centre). S/he can:

- send ('file') a defence or counterclaim to the court (see p251); *or*
- file an acknowledgement of service within the 14-day period if s/he is unable to file a defence in time or wishes to dispute the court's jurisdiction – eg, if a creditor has issued proceedings for an amount due under a regulated consumer credit agreement in the High Court rather than, as required, in the county court (see p239). Once an acknowledgement of service has been filed, the client must file the defence within 28 days of the date of service of the claim form/particulars of claim; *or*
- send ('serve') an admission to the creditor, admitting the whole of the claim (see p243). There is no provision for filing an acknowledgement of service where the client admits the whole claim, but the client may still send the admission to the creditor outside the 14-day period provided the creditor has not requested a default judgment (see p251); *or*
- file an admission and defence, admitting part of the claim but disputing the balance or making a counterclaim (see p251).

Electronic communication

The Civil Procedure Rules enable the parties to file documents at court by fax. A document is not treated as filed until it is actually delivered by the court office's fax machine, so it is good practice for advisers to telephone the court and check it has been received. A fax delivered after 4pm is treated as filed the following day. Fax should not be used for routine or non-urgent documents or, unless it is unavoidable, to deliver documents which attract a fee and documents relating to a hearing less than two hours ahead.[11]

Parties to a claim in a court or court office which has published an email address for the filing of documents on the Courts Service website can send a document listed on the website to the court by email. This is not possible if a fee is payable for the particular step in the proceedings. Documents that can be filed by email include acknowledgement of service, partial admission, defence and allocation questionnaire.[12]

If a claim has been issued electronically using either the money claims online procedure or the Claim Production Centre/County Court Bulk Centre, clients can file an acknowledgement of service, part admission and defence electronically online (the claim form contains a password to enable her/him to access the case). A document is not filed until the transmission is received by the court (the time of receipt is recorded electronically). If a transmission is received after 4pm, the document is treated as filed on the next day the court office is open.

All parties to a claim can be served with documents, including the claim form, electronically if they have given prior written consent to accept electronic service and a fax number or email address to which they should be sent. A fax number or email address included on a letterhead, claim form or statement of case is sufficient.[13]

The admission and statement of means form

The admission and statement of means form (N9A) provides the creditor and the court with information about the client's financial circumstances, and allows the client to admit the amount owing and make an offer to pay the debt. See p251 if the client only agrees that part of the amount claimed is due.

The statement of means accompanying any admission is a vital document. It may be all the creditor knows of the client's ability to pay. Apart from any information provided by the creditor, it is the sole basis for the court's decision about the rate of payment if the creditor does not accept the offer made by the client (see p248).

Using financial statements

Much of the information required on Form N9A is contained in the financial statement and list of creditors (see Chapter 3). Courts may be willing to accept a financial statement attached to Form N9A, together with a list of creditors with balances and offers (if there are any) instead of the client completing Form N9A in full. **Note:** there must always be an offer of payment in Box 11. This saves time, and modification of court forms is permitted by the Civil Procedure Rules, provided all essential information is included.[14] It may not be acceptable to the court, however, as it needs to extract certain information from the specific boxes on the form. Debt advisers should check with the court before submitting financial statements without fully completing Form N9A. If in doubt, complete the form and attach a financial statement.

Completing Form N9A

Note: this section is also relevant to completing Form N245 (Application to Suspend a Warrant of Execution or Reduce an Instalment Order) and Form N56 (Reply to Attachment of Earnings Application). See pp303 and 265.

Form N9A does not always fit the circumstances of the particular client. Advisers should be prepared to amend it as necessary in order to give the creditor and the court as complete and accurate a picture as possible of the client's situation. In addition, the headings in the income and expenditure sections do not always reflect the headings on a financial statement. Also, where a couple pool their income, it is often not possible to say who is paying for what because the couple just do not live that way. In such a case, the partner's income should be shown as 'other income'.

- **Personal details.** This section should show the name, address and date of birth of the client. If there are joint defendants and separate N9As are completed, it should be made clear whether the offer made is a joint one.
- **Dependants.** This information is needed to explain the level of expenditure. A heterosexual or same-sex partner should be included on the form as a dependant even if s/he has an independent source of income. If a partner does not wish to be considered as a dependant, this fact should be noted either in the box or in an accompanying letter. S/he must, however, be included on the form because s/he is a member of the household and her/his presence may affect the level of instalment payments.
- **Employment.** Every employment status of the client should be shown (s/he may have more than one). If the client feels the standard boxes do not accurately describe her/his status, an additional description can be inserted. Take-home pay is entered in the income section. Courts do not take account of information provided by self-employed clients in Section 3 when determining a rate of payment and the question about annual turnover for self-employed people appears unnecessary. The information may, however, influence the decision the creditor makes on whether or not to accept the offer of payment. However, if the information is not easily available, it will be sufficient to indicate employment status only. Details of any tax or national insurance arrears should be included in Sections 8 or 9. Other business debts should be included in Sections 8, 9 or 10, although the N9A is not really suitable for a business which is still trading to make payment. Guidance to court officers

suggests that, where a client is still trading, unless the creditor is prepared to accept the client's payment offer, the papers should be referred to the district judge.

- **Bank account and savings.** Court officers are instructed to see whether sums are available to pay either a large lump sum towards a debt or a regular amount. They should ignore any amounts that are less than one-and-a-half times a client's monthly income or seven times her/his weekly income.
  If the amount shown is more than the ignored amount and some, or all, of the money in an account is needed to pay a priority creditor, it is important that the money is not shown as being available for a non-priority debt. So, if the amount is intended to meet the expenses detailed in Section 7 this should be made clear, as otherwise the court officer will assume it is available to pay the debt. If the client has a joint bank account, only her/his share of any savings need be declared.
- **Property.** This section provides background information to the creditor and may indicate whether the debt could ever be enforced by a charging order in the event of default on the judgment (see p258). The client could fit into more than one category – eg, rented and council property, so could tick either or both boxes.
- **Income.** This section requires details of the client's income from all sources (including any disability or incapacity benefits, and benefits paid for children). See p36 for how to treat clients who are couples to help decide whether to show joint income and expenses (see notes to Section 7) on the form.
  The decision is further complicated by the instruction at the top of Section 7. If, for example, a partner (or any other member of the household) pays all fuel bills, those items should not be included as an expense unless that person's contribution is included in 'Others living in my home give me'. Court officers are instructed to convert all figures to either weekly or monthly amounts for consistency and so the form should be completed in the same way.
- **Expenses.** Unless joint income and expenditure figures are being used, only include items of expenditure actually paid for by the client out of her/his income disclosed in Section 6 (see notes for Section 6). A major problem with this section is the absence of many categories of essential expenditure. These can be added in the space marked 'Others' and need not be limited to the three lines given – eg, telephone or mobile phone bills, insurance premiums and childcare costs. Always explain what 'other' expenditure is and use a covering letter to explain its importance if necessary. The expenses figure at the end of Section 7 should be accurate and the items a court may consider 'non-essential' should be included, where possible, in one of the named categories listed on the form. If disability/incapacity benefits, or benefits paid in respect of children cannot be fully accounted for in Section 7, a note should be added to explain that these payments are intended to meet the costs associated with disability, incapacity or bringing up children and are not intended to be used for payment

of unrelated debts. But this must only be done with the client's agreement following discussion; it is not the adviser's role to decide how clients spend their money.

Travelling expenses need to cover either fares or vehicle running costs plus petrol. Mail order catalogues are often used to budget for clothing, bedding and small household items and so expenditure for these items can be listed in that section if the client pays for these items this way.

Section 7 should include details of payments to meet the regular cost of ongoing services provided by priority creditors, including water charges (but any arrears of water charges should appear in Section 10, regardless of the instruction in Section 8).

Expenditure figures need to reflect accurately the actual spending as far as possible.[15]

- **Priority debts.** This section requires information about offers which have already been accepted to prevent action by priority creditors in pursuit of arrears. Thus, it is desirable before submitting Form N9A that arrangements with priority creditors have been made. If an arrangement has not yet been made with one or more priority creditors, state the total arrears outstanding to that creditor and amend the form by adding, for instance, 'payment to be arranged' or 'offering £x a month'. Otherwise, if the total arrears figures are given, court officers are advised to assume repayment of arrears in three months, except for hire purchase and mortgage arrears which might be spread over one to two years. If offers have been made, but a reply is awaited, they should be included on the form. Include priority business debts, such as VAT or income tax, here.

  Clients may be uncertain about what proportion of payments to priority creditors are to cover arrears. In this case, to save time, total payments, including arrears, could be entered in Section 7 'Expenses' and a note written in Box 8 to indicate this.
- **Court orders.** Only existing court orders should be listed, except the one subject to the present action. Use a separate sheet or financial statement if there is not enough room on the form.
- **Credit debts.** This section requires details of payments already arranged with other non-priority creditors who have not obtained a court order. The three spaces provided for such debts are unlikely to be adequate and another sheet may be needed. Only the amounts currently being paid should be included, but an accompanying financial statement is useful information to indicate the level of indebtedness and offers made to other creditors, as well as indicating how the offer on the N9A has been calculated.
- **Offer of payment.** If there is available income, an offer should normally be made on a *pro rata* basis, but some offer should always be made even if it is only a nominal figure – eg, 50p or £1 a month.

When the N9A has been completed, it should be photocopied and either sent by 'recorded signed for' to the address shown on the back of the claim form (Form N1) or a receipt requested if it is delivered by hand. A copy should be kept on file.

The creditor's response

When the creditor receives Form N9A it decides whether to accept or reject the offer of payment. If the creditor accepts, it requests the court to enter judgment on Form N205A/225 for the sum claimed to be paid as offered and the court sends the client a copy (N30(1) Judgment for Claimant (Acceptance of offer)). The creditor is not required to send a copy of the N9A to the court when accepting the offer and so the court has no information on the client's ability to pay the judgment.

If the client fails to comply with the terms of the judgment, the creditor can decide whether to use one or more means of enforcement in order to obtain payment (see p256). Some creditors request orders for immediate payment (or 'forthwith') as a matter of course so they can take enforcement action quickly.

If the client does not 'request time to pay', the creditor may specify the terms of the judgment (s/he could specify immediate payment) and the court enters judgment accordingly. If the creditor does not specify any terms of payment, the court enters judgment for immediate payment.[16] A 'request for time to pay' is defined as a 'proposal about the date of payment or a proposal to pay by instalments at the times and rate specified in the request'.[17] Thus, if the client wishes to avoid a judgment for immediate payment, s/he must make an offer of payment on the N9A – however small – in order to trigger the next step in the procedure.

If the creditor rejects the offer, s/he must inform the court and supply reasons for the refusal and a copy of the N9A. The court then enters judgment for the amount admitted and 'determines' the rate of payment.

'Judgment' is the formal term for the court's decision in a case. Prior to judgment, the creditor is trying to establish that the client owes the money. After judgment, liability cannot be denied unless the client appeals (see p307) or applies to set the judgment aside (see p298).

The court can order the client to pay:

- by monthly instalments; *or*
- in one instalment – eg, within 14 or 28 days; *or*
- immediately ('forthwith'). This means the client is inevitably unable to comply with the order and is automatically in arrears with the judgment.

If a client is unable to pay at the rate ordered by the court, s/he can take action to change the terms of the judgment (see p301).

How courts calculate instalment orders

If the amount involved is not more than £50,000, the rate of payment may be 'determined' by a court officer. S/he must do so without a hearing. The Courts Service provides guidance on how to do this.[18] This has been out of print for many years, but it is now possible to obtain copies from the Courts Service to refer to when completing the N9A. It is not available online. The following is a summary. The total income (Box 6) is the starting point. To this may be added any savings (Box 4). From this total income the following are deducted:

- expenses (Box 7);
- priority debts (Box 8);
- court debts (Box 9);
- credit debt repayments (Box 10).

Court officers are instructed to use common sense when assessing essential items of expenditure and to allow a reasonable amount for items not listed in Box 7, but which are essential to the client's household – eg, payments for a vehicle or childminder to enable the client to work, or the cost of travelling to and from work. Although court officers are not expected to assess whether any of the amounts are too high, 'frivolous' and 'non-essential' items will be disregarded. These are specified as:

- children's pocket money;
- money for gambling, alcohol or cigarettes;
- money for newspapers or magazines (unless essential to the client in her/his work);
- holiday money.

The guidance does, however, give the court officer discretion to allow £15 a week for 'sundries' (presumably per household).

The client should be allowed sufficient resources and time to pay priority debts, although court staff are instructed to make certain assumptions about what is a reasonable period for clearing such arrears. Although court officers are instructed to take a common-sense approach to credit debts, the guidance also states that 'there is no logical reason why these debts should take precedence over a county court judgment'.

The guidance reminds court officers that creditors must state reasons for rejecting offers. Rejecting an offer because of the amount of the debt or the length of time it has been outstanding or because the offer is 'too low' is not sufficient unless the creditor can demonstrate inaccuracies in the information provided by the client.

The resulting figures are then transferred to a 'determination of means calculator' (EX120) and the court officer works out the rate of payment based on the amount of 'disposable (available) income'. In some courts, the creditor is expected to complete the EX120 electronically, but this does not mean the creditor decides which figures to allow or disallow or what order is made. The guidance states that if the disposable income is:

- higher than the offer but lower than the figure the creditor is prepared to accept, the instalment order should be for the amount of disposable income;
- higher than the figure the creditor is prepared to accept, the instalment order should be for the amount the creditor is prepared to accept;
- lower than the offer, the instalment order should be for the amount the client has offered unless this is 'unrealistically high';
- nil or a negative figure, either the instalment order should be for the amount the client has offered (unless unrealistically high) or the matter should be referred to the district judge for advice or a decision.[19]

The guidance recognises that the N9A is designed for individual rather than business debts and that, unless a business has provided information about its financial position, it will be difficult for court officers to make a decision on the rate of payment. If the creditor has indicated the terms on which s/he will accept payment by instalments, the court officer can enter judgment accordingly. Otherwise, s/he is instructed to refer the matter to the district judge.

If the amount involved is more than £50,000, the rate of payment must be determined by a district judge who may decide the matter with or without a hearing. In some courts, claims for less than £50,000 are referred to the district judge for determination. In carrying out the determination, the district judge must take into account:

- the client's statement of means;
- the creditor's objections;
- any other relevant factors (increasingly this includes the fact that the client is a homeowner but the instalment offer is so low that it will not pay off the judgment within a reasonable period).[20]

The district judge is not required to follow the guidelines issued to court staff. If the district judge decides to hold a hearing, the case will be automatically transferred to the client's home court.

When the court has decided on the rate of payment, it notifies both the creditor and client of the order made (N30(2) Judgment for Claimant (Determination Without a Hearing)). Either party can apply to the court for a reconsideration of this decision (known as 'redetermination' – see below).

Redetermination by a district judge

If the rate of payment has been decided without a hearing, either the creditor or the client can ask for the amount to be reconsidered (redetermined) by a district judge within 14 days of service of the order. No court fee is payable.[21] The client can request a redetermination regardless of whether the original determination was made by a court officer or the district judge (provided there was no hearing).

District judges are not bound by the determination of means guidelines and can make whatever order they think fit. If there is available income, the N9A should be carefully completed so that a decision can be made from the form alone, and the decision is more likely to be upheld by a district judge if the creditor asks for a redetermination. This is particularly important where large amounts are owed or a creditor feels particularly aggrieved for some other reason – eg, no payments have so far been made on an agreement. However, there is an increasing trend for district judges to reject low or nominal offers of payment and make an order for immediate payment to enable the creditor to enforce it, if possible, usually by way of a charging order (see p258). Such offers may be seen as unrealistic and the creditor may not be regarded as being unreasonable in refusing to accept an offer of payment which will take many years to pay off the judgment, if ever. If the client has property, assets or savings, they may be at risk. On the other hand, if the client's financial difficulties are temporary, it is worth pointing this out to the court as, in these circumstances, the district judge may be more willing to make an instalment order at a low rate on the basis that it will be reviewed.

A client whose position is unusual may benefit from the wider discretion of a district judge if, for instance, payment could be made from money which s/he expects to receive in time or if s/he is seriously ill and likely to gain sympathy. All such arguments should be made clearly, and the application should be made by letter (or on Form N244 – see p305) giving reasons why the matter should be reconsidered. The court will arrange for the case to be transferred to the client's local court.

If the original determination was made by a court officer, the redetermination may take place without a hearing unless one is requested. If the original determination was made by a district judge, the redetermination must be made at a hearing unless the parties agree otherwise. There is usually no indication on the judgment who carried out the original determination. Although the adviser can establish this by a phone call to the court office, it is usually better to ask for a hearing so that the client's case can be put to the district judge in person. The decision is one for the client, not the adviser. The request should always refer to redetermination under Rule 14.13 Civil Procedure Rules, specify whether or not a hearing is required and set out why the original determination should be reconsidered – eg, the client cannot afford to pay the judgment at the rate ordered by the court but can pay at the rate of £x a month in accordance with the attached financial statement. If the client asks for the matter to be dealt with without a hearing, the request could be accompanied by a witness statement from the client setting out her /his case.[22] If the determination was made by a district judge at a hearing, there is no right to request a redetermination. If circumstances change, either party can apply for a variation in the rate of payment ordered (see p301).

Default judgment

If the client fails to reply to the claim form (including a 'nil' or no offer of payment – see above), the creditor can request the court to enter judgment in default on Form N205A/225. Default judgment cannot be entered if the client has, within the specified time limits:

- filed a defence; *or*
- filed an acknowledgement of service; *or*
- filed or served an admission together with a request for time to pay (even if this is outside of the time limit).[23]

The creditor must specify the date by which the whole of the debt is to be paid (which may be immediately) or the rate at which it is to be paid by instalments. If none is specified, the judgment will be for payment immediately.[24]

A debt adviser who thinks that default judgment has been entered, or is about to be, should check with the court of issue. If it has not been entered, the client can still respond (see above). However, if judgment has already been entered s/he should apply either to vary it (see p301) or set it aside (if appropriate, see p298).

If the creditor does not apply for judgment within six months of the expiry of the client's time for responding to the claim, the action is 'stayed' and the claimant must apply to the court for permission to proceed with it.[25]

After judgment, if the amount required is not paid within a month, details are entered in the Register of Judgments, Orders and Fines. This information is publicly available and is used by many credit reference agencies. Entries are cancelled six years after the date of judgment.

Completing the defence and counterclaim form

Form N9B provides the client with an opportunity to explain the circumstances and facts of any dispute, which should be stated clearly and in sufficient detail. A defence should be submitted where there is one – eg, if the debt has already been paid. It is not a defence that the client cannot afford to pay the debt. In these circumstances, the client should follow the admission procedure described above. A counterclaim can be made if the client has lost money because the creditor has failed to carry out her/his legal obligations, although a court fee is payable (unless the client is able to obtain remission – see p237).

The N9B should be returned to court within 14 days of service. If the defence cannot be prepared within this time, the client should return the acknowledgement of service (N9) to the court. S/he will automatically have a further 14 days in which to file a defence – ie, 28 days from the date of service of the claim form/particulars of claim. The client may need to obtain specialist consumer or legal advice before completing the N9B.

Where some of the claim is admitted and time is required to pay that amount, but some is disputed, both Forms N9A and N9B should be completed and returned to court (not the creditor).

Challenging costs

This procedure may be used to challenge the creditor's costs if it is felt that paragraph 4 of the protocols Practice Direction (see p235) has not been complied with. This imposes a general obligation to act reasonably in negotiations and avoid unnecessary court action (see p235). The client needs to show that:

- s/he has made reasonable attempts to avoid court action; *and*
- issuing proceedings was not a proportionate response by the creditor to the client's attempt to settle the matter.

Examples of where this might be successfully argued include if:

- the client has made a payment arrangement with the creditor prior to the issue of proceedings and has complied strictly with that arrangement;
- the client has made what the adviser regards as a reasonable payment offer but the creditor has unreasonably demanded higher payments – eg, other creditors have accepted offers made on the same basis and the creditor is unable to demonstrate where any additional payments are to come from;
- the creditor has not warned the client that it intends to take court action by sending her/him a 'letter of claim' (also called a 'letter before action'), setting out details of the debt and warning the client that, unless payment is made within a stated period – eg, 21 days, court action will be taken without further notice;[26]
- the creditor has acted unreasonably – eg, refused to negotiate or breached a code of conduct;

The court is required to take account of the conduct of both parties and also to assess the reasonableness of any offer made.

Advisers should beware of substituting what they consider reasonable for what a district judge is likely to consider reasonable, as it is the client who will have to pay any additional costs incurred. As a general rule, district judges do not consider it unreasonable for a creditor to seek a judgment which the client appears to be unable to pay. On the other hand, the district judge may well consider it unreasonable for a creditor to refuse an offer of payment, issue proceedings and then accept the same offer made on an N9A. The protocols Practice Direction says that the court 'is likely to look at the effect of non-compliance on the other party when deciding whether to impose sanctions'. If the court decides the default has made no difference to the client's position, it is unlikely to deprive the creditor of its costs.[27]

If the debt is disputed on grounds other than that it was paid before the issue of the claim form (see p241), the case will be automatically transferred to the client's home court on the filing of the N9B and the court will send both parties an allocation questionnaire on Form N149 (small claims track) or N150 (other cases). This must be returned to the court in 14 days, together with a fee of £35 payable by the creditor if the case is on the small claims track (unless the claim is for £1,500 or less) or £200, if the case is on one of the other tracks (see below). On receipt of the questionnaire the court will:

- allocate the case to a track (see below); *or*
- set a hearing date to consider allocation; *or*
- make orders on the future conduct of the case ('case management directions'); *or*
- summarily dispose of the case (see below); *or*
- if requested on the questionnaire by both parties, suspend further action for up to one month to enable the parties to try and settle the case.

Tracks

The **'small claims track'**[28] is the normal track for cases with a financial value of not more than £5,000. On allocating the case, the court gives standard directions for its future conduct and fixes a hearing date at least 21 days ahead. The case is normally heard in private by a district judge. Debt advisers have the right to represent clients at the hearing. Even where the value of the claim is more than £5,000 the parties can still agree to the case being allocated to the small claims track. The court will not usually allow more than a day for the hearing and so cases which are likely to last longer may not be considered suitable for this track by the court.

The **'fast track'**[29] is the normal track for cases with a financial value of no more than £15,000, which the court estimates can be tried in a day. On allocating the case, the court gives case management directions and sets a timetable in which those steps are to be taken. At the same time, the court also fixes either a hearing date or a period within which the hearing is to take place. The hearing of the case should take place within 30 weeks.

The **'multi-track'**[30] is the normal track for all other cases – ie, cases with a higher financial value that cannot be heard in a day or more complex cases requiring individual directions. On allocating the case, the court either gives case management directions with a timetable in which those steps are to be taken (although no trial date or period is fixed) or fixes a hearing to consider the issues in the case and the directions that will be required.

Summary disposal

One of the key features contained in the Civil Procedure Rules is the duty of the court to actively manage cases, with greater scope to act on its own initiative. The court can strike out the particulars of a claim or defence if:

- no reasonable grounds are disclosed in the particulars of the claim (eg, 'money owed £1,000') or defence ('I do not owe the money') for either bringing or defending the claim; *or*
- it is an abuse of the court's process – eg, where it raises issues which should have been dealt with in a previous case involving the same parties; *or*
- the court is satisfied either that a case has no real prospects of success on the facts or is bound to succeed or fail on a point of law and there is no other compelling reason for the matter to go to trial. To have a 'realistic prospect of success' the case must be a convincing one and not be merely arguable. Where there are significant factual issues between the parties, summary disposal is not appropriate.[31]

If either the particulars of claim or defence are struck out (literally deleted), this means that it cannot be relied on and the party will be unable to proceed. The court can then enter 'summary judgment' for the other party.[32] The court can take this step either on its own initiative or on the application of a party. Courts are now more proactive in this area than in the past and debt advisers should, therefore, exercise great care in the preparation of defences and counterclaims. Defences which lack detail are likely to be struck out – ie, the defence must set out the relevant facts and reasons for disputing the claim.

Interest

In most cases dealt with by a debt adviser, no interest is chargeable after a county court judgment. This is important, not only because it means that any payments the client is able to make will reduce the amount outstanding, but also because, if the creditor knows that interest charges will have to stop once the matter is taken to court, s/he may be persuaded to stop charging interest once a client begins to experience difficulties in repaying.

The court can include in any judgment simple interest, at such a rate as it thinks fit, from the date the debt fell due to:

- in the case of a debt paid before judgment, the date of payment; *or*
- in the case of debt for which judgment is entered, the date of judgment ('discretionary interest').[33]

Discretionary interest must be claimed specifically by the creditor in the particulars of claim and included in the 'amount claimed' figure on the N1 claim form. It cannot be claimed in addition to any other interest, nor can it be awarded to run after the date of judgment. Provided the creditor restricts her/his claim to the rate of interest payable on judgment debts (currently 8 per cent a year – see p255), the claim for interest can be included in a default judgment or judgment on admission. Such a claim is not subject to the Limitation Act 1980, but the client can ask the court to reduce the amount of interest included in the judgment where there has been a long delay in starting the proceedings with no satisfactory explanation for that delay.

- As a general rule, interest should be allowed from the date the right to sue for the relevant payment arose.
- The existence of and need to investigate a genuine dispute does not prevent interest running.
- If the creditor has been guilty of excessive delay in making or pursuing the claim, either the starting point or the rate of interest can be adjusted in favour of the client.[34]

If a client wants to challenge a claim for discretionary interest, s/he must file a defence (see p251).

Some judgments carry simple interest from the date of judgment to the date of payment at the rate specified from time to time (currently 8 per cent a year since 1 April 1993, 15 per cent prior to this date). This is known as **'statutory interest'**.[35]

Since 1 July 1991 county court judgments for £5,000 or more have carried statutory interest unless:

- under the terms of the judgment, payment is either deferred to a specified date or is to be made by instalments. Interest does not accrue until either the specified date or the date the instalment falls due; *or*
- the judgment arises out of a consumer credit agreement regulated by the Consumer Credit Act 1974; *or*
- a suspended possession order is made; *or*
- an administration order or attachment of earnings order is in force.[36]

Interest ceases to be due when enforcement proceedings (other than charging orders) are started, but if these do not recover any money, interest accrues as if the proceedings had never started. It seems that, if the client defaults under the terms of the original judgment and then obtains a variation or suspension of the judgment (see p301), interest does not accrue.

The above covers most debts with which debt advisers are likely to be involved. Loan agreements, however, contain provisions for lenders to charge interest on the amount borrowed and additional interest in the event of default by the client ('contractual interest'). The general rule is that once the lender obtains judgment, the right to any further contractual interest ceases. However, an agreement may contain a clause stating that the creditor can continue to charge contractual interest after a judgment is made. The House of Lords has ruled that such a clause is 'fair'.[37] Following the judgment in *Forward Trust v Whymark*,[38] which allowed lenders to obtain judgment for the outstanding balance of a loan without giving credit for any early settlement rebate, many lenders issue proceedings for the full sum owed (including interest pre-calculated to the end of the agreement). Other lenders (where the interest rate is variable) limit the claim and the judgment to the principal amount outstanding plus accrued interest to the date of judgment, while reserving the right to issue separate proceedings for the ongoing interest.

Clients who are paying off the judgment can be confused and alarmed to receive statements showing the debt increasing and demands from the creditor for additional payments. The judgment is satisfied once the amount sued for (plus costs) has been paid. Creditors who claim to be able to 'add' contractual interest to the judgment should be challenged. If creditors wish to include ongoing contractual interest in a judgment, they should seek a judgment for the amount of interest to be decided by the court.[39] Although the House of Lords in the *First National Bank* case declared that judgments should take account of accruing contractual interest so that courts could consider making time orders (see p283), they declined to decide whether the current rules actually allow such judgments to be made. To avoid this, the client could apply for a time order in Box 11 of the N9A as follows: 'I ask the court to (1) make a time order in the terms of my offer and (2) amend the loan agreement in consequence so that no further contractual interest accrues after the date of judgment.'[40]

If a judgment is made on or after 1 October 2008 in relation to a regulated consumer credit agreement and the creditor wishes to pursue a claim for post-judgment contractual interest, the creditor is required to serve a notice on the client stating its intention to charge interest after judgment and informing the client of her/his right to apply for a time order (known as the 'first-required notice'). This notice cannot be given until after the judgment has been made.

Subsequently, the creditor must serve further notices, containing details of the interest charged, at six-monthly intervals. The creditor cannot charge post-judgment contractual interest for any period prior to the service of the first required notice or during any period in respect of which the creditor has failed to serve a subsequent notice. Although these provisions only apply to judgments made on or after 1 October 2008, they apply to regulated agreements whenever made (provided the agreement contains a provision specifically allowing the creditor to charge interest after judgment).[41] Default notices served on or after 1 October 2008 must contain a statement of the creditor's right to claim post-judgment contractual interest (see p63).

If a creditor threatens to pursue additional interest by taking further proceedings, the debt adviser should obtain specialist advice.[42]

Enforcing a judgment

Once judgment has been given, it is the responsibility of the creditor (and not the court) to collect payments. It is, therefore, important for the client to record all payments made and obtain receipts. If the client fails to pay in accordance with the judgment, the creditor can attempt to enforce payment through the court by:

- a warrant of execution (see p257);
- a charging order (see p258);

- an attachment of earnings order (see p264);
- a third-party debt order (see p267).

Debt advisers should explain to clients that, provided they keep to the terms of the judgment, the creditor cannot take enforcement action however unhappy it may be with the terms of the judgment. The adviser should also emphasise that, if the judgment states that a certain payment should be made each month, it is important this amount is paid every single month by the date stated in the judgment. If payments are made in advance in a lump sum to cover future months and no payments made in the following months, the client will have defaulted on the terms of the judgment and the creditor can take enforcement action against her/him. For example, a judgment states that payment must be made at the rate of £2 a month. The client pays £6 to cover three months. If no payment is made in the second month, the client will have defaulted.

The creditor can use any available method of enforcement, and can use more than one method either at the same time or one after the other.[43] However, while an attachment of earnings order is in force, the creditor cannot take any other type of enforcement action against the client unless the court gives permission.[44]

See p298 for how to prevent enforcement.

Warrant of execution

The warrant of execution is a document that allows the county court bailiff to take and sell goods belonging to the client to pay a judgment debt plus the court fees and costs. If the client does not keep to the payments ordered by the court, the creditor can ask the court to issue a warrant of execution once a payment is missed. The warrant can be for the whole amount of the judgment outstanding or just the arrears, which must be at least £50. Goods can be taken unless the amount shown on the warrant plus costs are paid. Certain goods are exempt from seizure (see p353). The client has an opportunity to apply for the warrant to be suspended (see p302). A creditor who wishes to issue a warrant more than six years after the date of the judgment must obtain the prior permission of the court. Ordinarily, the delay will itself justify the refusal of permission unless the creditor can explain the delay and show that the circumstances take the case out of the ordinary.[45]

A county court judgment may be transferred to the High Court for enforcement by execution against the client's goods if the judgment is between £600 and £5,000. It must be transferred to the High Court for enforcement if it is for more than £5,000. Judgments relating to agreements regulated by the Consumer Credit Act 1974 cannot be transferred to the High Court regardless of the amount of the judgment.[46] If an adviser comes across a judgment which has been transferred to the High Court for enforcement, s/he should seek specialist advice.

Even though the numbers are declining slightly, warrants of execution remain the preferred enforcement method for most creditors. In 2007, 310,178 warrants were issued.

Charging order

A charging order is a court order that secures the amount owed under the judgment, usually against the client's interest in a property, in which case an entry is made on the Land Register to this effect. Charging orders are governed by the Charging Orders Act 1979.

When the property is sold, the judgment debt, together with court fees/costs plus any statutory interest (but not contractual interest),[47] must be repaid out of the balance of the proceeds of sale after payment of any prior mortgages or charges. A charging order can only be made if judgment has been entered and the client has defaulted. Even if only one instalment under a judgment has been missed, the creditor can apply for a charging order, unless the client has applied for a variation, obtained an instalment order and maintained the payments (see p248).[48]

The effect of a charging order is to turn an unsecured debt into a secured one. Many creditors request the court to make judgments for immediate payment simply so that they can apply straight away for a charging order. Some district judges regard this as reasonable, especially in cases of nominal offers or where it appears that the client's offer of payment will not clear the debt for many years. Advisers should, therefore, follow the admission procedure as far as redetermination (see p249), if necessary, in order to demonstrate to the district judge that the client's offer is a reasonable one and that a charging order should not be made (see p260).

Although the client can apply for a variation at any time, if, in the meantime, the creditor applies for a charging order and obtains an interim order, the variation may not prevent the charging order being made (see below).

Although charging orders are normally made against a person's home (including a part-share in a home) or business premises, they can also be made against shares or the client's interest under a trust.

Charging orders are increasingly sought by creditors (the number of applications have doubled since 2005). In 2007, 131,637 charging order applications were issued – a rise of more than 45 per cent from 2006.

Interim charging order

The creditor must first apply to the court to obtain an interim charging order on Form N379. This must be sent either to the court which made the judgment or, if the case has subsequently been transferred to a different court, to that court. Northampton County Court Bulk Centre does not deal with charging order applications and so the creditor must arrange for the case to be transferred to a court of its choice.

The application must demonstrate either that the client is in arrears with instalment payments due under a judgment or that the judgment is a 'forthwith judgment'. The creditor must also provide details of the client's interest in the property to be charged, and details and addresses of all other creditors if this information is known to the creditor – eg, if the adviser has previously sent the creditor a financial statement containing details of the clients other debts.[49] Provided the papers are in order, the court sends the client a copy of Form N379 and the interim charging order, together with notice of the date and time of the hearing at which the court will consider making the order final. These must be sent at least 21 days before the hearing. Copies are also served on any joint owner and creditor the court directs, so they have the opportunity to object.[50]

The creditor also applies to the Land Registry to register a 'notice' or 'restriction' on the property. This is a warning that an application is about to be made for a final charging order and means that if the client attempts to dispose of the property, or her/his interest in it, the creditor will be informed and can object to the transaction. The Land Registry sends a copy of the registration to the client as soon as it is received. This effectively 'blocks' any transfer or sale of the property made with the intention of avoiding the charge.

Once an interim charging order has been made against shares or other securities, a 'stop order' comes into force. This stops the sale or transfer of the shares and also prohibits the client from taking dividends or other income from them.

Final charging order

The second stage in the charging order process is for the creditor to obtain a final charging order. At the hearing, the district judge decides whether to make the interim charging order final, or to discharge it. S/he should take into account both the personal circumstances of the client and whether any creditors would 'be likely to be unduly prejudiced by the making of the order'.[51]

If the client wishes to object to the final order being made, s/he can apply to have the hearing transferred to her/his local court.[52] The client must also file at court and serve on the creditor written evidence stating the grounds of objection not less than seven days before the hearing.[53] Any relevant documents (including a financial statement) should be attached. In many cases, debt advisers will want to present a defence but, in practice, most district judges appear to make final charging orders automatically. If the client wants to defend the charging order, the following arguments could be used.

- Some creditors believe they can apply for a charging order at any time, so check if any of the instalment payments due under a judgment have been missed. If not, the court cannot grant a charging order.[54]
- Check if an application to vary the judgment was submitted and the variation order granted before the interim order was made. If it was, so long as the new payments have been maintained, the application for a charging order should

fail. However, a variation order made after the date of the interim order does not bar making a final order.[55]

- Once a request for redetermination has been received by the court, the original determination is no longer of any effect as it must be replaced by a new judgment – ie, it is only a final judgment if no application is made for redetermination, which is the end of the process. There is no rule preventing creditors from applying for charging orders pending a redetermination request or hearing. In fact, this frequently happens.[56] If the client has applied for redetermination, courts usually list the redetermination hearing and the charging order hearing together. The application for redetermination should be dealt with first regardless of which application was actually filed first because it is the judgment made on redetermination (N30(3)) which will be enforced. If the client's application for redetermination is successful and an instalment order is made, this is *not* a variation but a new judgment. As the client will not have defaulted, the court has no jurisdiction to make the charging order and the creditor's application should be dismissed. In the past, district judges have usually accepted this argument (but see 'hybrid orders' below). However, if the original determination is confirmed and the client has not paid in accordance with that determination, the Civil Procedure Rules would seem to enable the court to deal with the final charging order application immediately rather than require the creditor to start all over again.[57]
- Check whether other creditors have been notified of the charging order application, as the charging order could unduly prejudice their rights and, therefore, should not be made final. If the court was not given details in the charging order application of other creditors of which the creditor in question was aware (eg, because they had been included on a financial statement), it could be argued that the creditor has not complied with the rules and the client has been denied a fair hearing, as prejudice to creditors is one of the matters which the Charging Orders Act specifically requires the court to take into account. Alternatively (and more usually), the district judge may adjourn while other creditors are notified. If none of the creditors lodges an objection, this 'prejudice to other creditors' argument may fail.
- The client is technically insolvent and thus a charge in favour of one creditor prejudices the rest. This will be the case if there was insufficient equity in the property to cover all the debts in full and there either is, or is about to be, an arrangement to distribute the proceeds of sale on a *pro rata* basis among the client's creditors.[58]
- The debt is small compared with the amount of equity in the property.[59]

Hybrid orders

'Hybrid orders' were made for several years by the district judges at Northampton County Court in County Court Bulk Centre cases where the creditor had rejected the client's offer on Form N9A and asked the court to make an immediate judgment expressly for the purpose of obtaining a charging order. A judgment was made without a hearing on Form N24 stating:

'1. Judgment against defendant payable forthwith.
2. The claimant may apply for a charging order at once.
3. Apart from a charging order, all other execution is stayed as long as the defendant pays £x per month (as offered on N9A). [This is not an instalment order, but merely a stay (or halt) of any other type of enforcement action by the creditor. Provided the client complies, s/he is protected from multiple enforcement action by the creditor.]
4. Any party affected by this order may apply within seven days after service to vary, amend or set it aside.'

Similar types of order are now made by a number of district judges at redetermination hearings with one crucial difference: paragraph 1 is an instalment order. It is arguable that the court cannot override statutory rules by making an instalment order on the one hand and giving leave to the creditor to issue a charging order on the other in the absence of default under the instalment order. If an adviser comes across a hybrid order, s/he should seek specialist advice.

Once s93 Tribunals, Courts and Enforcement Act 2007 is in force (no date has yet been set, but it is not expected to be before 2010), the fact that an instalment order has been made and the client has not defaulted will no longer prevent the court from making a charging order. **Note:** at the time of writing, these provisions were not yet in force.

Conditions attached to a charging order

A charging order can be made either with or without conditions.[60] A client could apply at the hearing for a condition to be imposed to prevent the charging order being used as a basis for an order for sale, or for it only to be used as such in certain circumstances – eg, after the youngest child of the family ceases to be in full-time education. If a court is determined to impose a charging order, such conditions can mitigate the worst effects of its decision. Debt advisers should point out to the court that when making a final charging order, it should consider the possibility of enforcement by the creditor and should either attach conditions or suspend it on terms (see below).

Enforcement of a final charging order may be suspended on payment of instalments.[61] The client can apply for these payments to be suspended or varied if her/his circumstances change. Some district judges say that they cannot suspend the charging order or they cannot consider the application at the final charging order hearing. The county court's power to suspend an order is in s71(2) County Courts Act 1984 and because the court should attempt to deal with as many aspects of the case as it can at the same hearing, the court should be asked to deal with the application at the same time.[62]

Because a charging order is an indirect method of enforcement – ie, it only secures payment but does not actually produce any money at the time, a creditor may decide to use another method(s) of enforcement as well. It is, therefore, good practice to apply for a variation of the judgment as well as suspension of, or the attachment of conditions to, the charging order.[63]

If the client is going to ask the district judge to attach conditions to the final order or to suspend it on terms, written evidence in the form of a witness statement should be submitted together with a financial statement. If a final order has already been made, it is still possible to make an application to the court to vary or discharge the order if it seems the court did not consider the client's circumstances at the time the order was made or the circumstances have since changed. A co-owner or a joint occupier who is a spouse or civil partner can also apply.[64]

After a charging order has been made, the creditor can wait until the property is sold, in which case it will be paid out of the proceeds of sale. Alternatively, it can apply to the court for an order for sale (see below).

Some creditors argue that a charging order allows them to enforce payment of accrued contractual interest even though it forms no part of the judgment. If a creditor tries to argue this, the debt adviser should seek specialist advice.

Order for sale

Note: an application for an order for sale is both serious and legally complex. Specialist advice should always be sought.

An order for sale is a court order to sell a property that is the subject of a charging order so that the debt can be paid out of the proceeds. It is only possible after a charging order has been made final and if any conditions or terms attached to the order have not been met. **Note:** once s93 Tribunals, Courts and Enforcement Act is implemented, the court will not be able to make an order for sale if there has been no default in payment under an instalment order (including a variation order) or, if there has been default, the arrears have been paid.

The Charging Orders Act requires a district judge to use her/his discretion to decide whether to order a sale.[65] It is an extreme sanction and would be a draconian step to satisfy a simple debt and is likely only to be used in cases where clients' failure to pay has been intentional or where a sale is the only realistic way in which the debt will be paid. In the past, applications for orders for sale have been very rare, but advisers report that numbers appear to have increased.

The creditor must apply using the procedure under Part 8 Civil Procedure Rules. This requires a hearing in all cases. The application is made to the court that made the charging order, which may not be the client's local court. The client should complete and return the acknowledgement of service not more than 14 days after service of the claim form, together with a request for transfer to the client's local court (where appropriate) and any written evidence, indicating that s/he intends to oppose the order for sale and her/his reasons for doing so. It is vital that clients attend and are represented at this hearing. Strictly, where the judgment debt is in excess of £30,000, the application for an order for sale should be heard in the High Court, but the High Court can transfer all these cases to the county court.[66]

All the circumstances should be considered, including the size of the judgment debt and the value of the property. In particular, the amount of any equity in the property should be checked. Even if a sale is ordered, the court can suspend the order on terms (eg, payment by instalments) or postpone the order for sale until a future date – eg, when the youngest child of the family reaches 18. The debt adviser will need to discuss with the client a way of ensuring that the charging order creditor is paid and this debt must now be treated as a priority (see Chapter 7). A full financial statement should be completed and an offer of payment made if possible. If not, the adviser should consider whether there are any exceptional circumstances that could be used to prevent an order being made. Always re-check income maximisation, especially payment of interest by the Department for Work and Pensions (DWP) for home improvement loans.

If the court accepts the client's offer of instalments, the adviser should ask the court to adjourn the application for an order for sale on condition that the client makes the payments. If an order for sale is made and not suspended, the client is normally given 28 days to pay the debt or leave the property. If this does not happen, the creditor can apply for a warrant of possession (see p297).

Joint ownership of property and orders for sale

A charging order can be made against a client's 'beneficial interest' (her/his share) in a property. If a client owns only a part share of a property, a charging order can still be made but it will apply only to her/his share.

If a charging order is made, the creditor becomes a party with an interest in the property and can apply for an order to sell the property so that the creditor's interest can be realised.[67] The court is required to take into account:

- the intentions of the owners at the time of the original purchase – ie, the purpose for which the property was bought. For example, it may be that a court should not order the sale of an asset, which was bought for a specific purpose, until the need for it has ceased to exist. If this is a correct interpretation, a family home should not be sold until all members of the family have ceased to need it;
- the welfare of any child who occupies the property as her/his home;
- the interests of any secured creditor.[68] In one case, the Court of Appeal ordered the sale of a property where there was sufficient equity to pay only part of the debt and the client was apparently unable to make any offer of payment.[69]

The personal circumstances of the client and other occupiers should be explained to the court in detail. Point out:

- it is not equitable (or fair) for a whole family or group of occupants to be evicted for the debt of one of their members;
- any special factors – eg, age, disability, illness, need for stability at work or school, availability of alternative housing, effect on children;
- the history of the loan.

If an application for an order for sale is made, a claim form is sent to all co-owners of the property. This may include someone who owes no money to the creditor who has obtained the charging order. However, because that person owns part of the property against which the debt is secured, the court must treat her/him as a joint defendant in the case. This means s/he is entitled to be heard at the hearing of the application and to put forward her/his own case, if necessary.

If a divorce petition has been served, any application for a charging order (or order for sale) should normally be considered along with the finances and property of the couple.[70]

One important side effect of a charging order on a jointly-owned property is that it 'severs' any joint tenancy. This means that, if either of the joint owners dies, her/his share no longer passes automatically to the survivor but, instead, is dealt with as part of the deceased's estate. One of the consequences of this is that any creditors of the deceased will have an estate against which to claim (see p103).

Attachment of earnings order

An attachment of earnings order requires an employer who is paying wages, statutory sick pay or an occupational pension to a client to deduct some of it and make payments to the court to meet the debt. It cannot be used to attach state benefits or tax credits. Attachment of earnings orders are governed by the Attachment of Earnings Act 1971 and can be made either by the magistrates' or the county courts. The following information relates to county court judgments, not to magistrates' court fines or attachment of earnings orders made under liability orders.

The county court can make attachments to cover default on any judgment debt (including High Court judgments, which must be transferred to the county court for enforcement[71]) or administration orders.

In 2007, the number of applications for attachment of earnings orders fell slightly for the second year to 82,019.

A creditor can request an attachment of earnings order for any unpaid judgment debt over £50. The client receives a notice of the application (Form N55), together with Form N56 to complete, showing a statement of her/his means. **Note:** the time limit for returning the N56 is only eight days. If s/he does not return Form N56, the court can order the client to complete a statement of means and the client's employer can be ordered to supply a statement of earnings. This must always be filled in and returned to the court, as failure to do so can lead to a summons for a personal appearance. Failure to comply can lead to imprisonment.

Suspended attachment of earnings order

The N56 is similar to the N9A (see p243), except there is provision to include a partner's income. There is also space on the form to request a suspended attachment of earnings order be made. This allows the client to agree to make regular payments. A request for a suspended order should always be considered. A client may decide to make a request where an attachment order could lead to the client's dismissal by her/his employer.

A court officer uses the information supplied on the N56 together with a formula contained in the protected earnings calculator (EX119), to make an attachment of earnings order and set a 'protected earnings rate' in accordance with the determination of means guidelines (see p248). This is an amount that the court considers is the minimum the client, and any dependants, need to live on. The income support level is considered the minimum required plus housing costs, essential work-related expenses and other court orders. If, after taking into account any partner's income or other sources of income, the client has less than this amount (the protected earnings rate), the order will not be made. The guidance instructs court officers to disregard disability living allowance and attendance allowance when calculating income. The guidance suggests that deductions (the 'normal deduction rate') are set at between 50 per cent and 66 per cent of the client's 'disposable income' – ie, the difference between the client's net earnings and the protected earnings rate. It also recommends that a suspended attachment of earnings order should only be made if the client requests one, but that the request should be granted unless an attachment of earnings order is already in force. If the client does not give sufficient information on Form N56, the court officer will refer the matter to the district judge to make an order.

Both the client and the creditor have 14 days to give notice to the court that they object to the terms of the attachment of earnings order, whether the order has been made by a court official or a district judge. If an objection comes from either side, a hearing will be arranged in the client's local court at which the district judge can make any order s/he thinks appropriate. An objection can be made by letter stating the grounds – eg, if the protected earnings rate or the normal deduction rate do not leave the client with sufficient income for essential expenditure.

Disadvantages of an attachment of earnings order

There are two principal problems with an attachment of earnings order. Firstly, it reduces a client's flexibility to manage her/his own affairs, and secondly, it may endanger her/his employment because it notifies the employer of debts. Employers (eg, security firms or those where money is handled) may have a policy of dismissing anybody against whom a judgment is made. If this happens, the client should seek the advice of an employment specialist.

An attachment of earnings order tells the employer the total amount due under the judgment(s) concerned, and gives the normal rate to be deducted each week or month and states the protected earnings rate. The employer can only make deductions from any earnings in excess of the protected earnings rate. If the client's earnings are insufficient to enable the full, or any, deduction to be made, any resulting shortfall cannot be carried forward to the next pay day.

Even if the principle of an attachment is accepted, the adviser could argue against the normal deduction figure suggested. An offer could be made on a *pro rata* basis if the client has more than one non-priority debt. A good financial statement is the basis of this argument, showing how repayment of priority creditors represents essential expenditure and that amounts to cover these should be included in the protected earnings rate.

If an attachment order is made, a fee (currently £1) can be added to each deduction by the employer to cover administrative costs. If a client leaves a job s/he must notify the court within seven days of any new employment and income. Failure to do so is an offence which could be punishable by a fine. If the client becomes unemployed or self-employed, s/he should write to the court immediately.

A county court attachment of earnings order does not take priority over an attachment of earnings order made to recover fines, maintenance or local taxes or a deduction from earnings order made to recover child support arrears, even if made earlier. The combined effect may be to reduce the client's resources to a very basic level. In such a case the client should be advised to apply to vary the attachment of earnings order on Form N244 (see p301).

A court can also decide to make an administration order (see p370), when considering attachment of earnings, if the total indebtedness is below the administration order limit.[72] The court should always consider this if there are other debts. If attachment of earnings is to be accepted by the client, converting it to an attached administration order can simplify repayments.

An attachment of earnings order prevents the creditor from enforcing the debt by a warrant of execution, charging order (and, arguably, an order for sale) or third-party debt order (see p267) without first obtaining the permission of the county court.[73]

Consolidated attachment of earnings order

If:

- there are two or more attachment of earnings orders for debt; *or*
- one attachment of earnings order is in force and a second one is applied for; *or*
- one attachment of earnings order is in force and the client has at least one other county court judgment,

the client can ask the court to consolidate these two debts and all other debts on which there is a judgment. The court can also make such an order on its own initiative.[74]

No procedure is specified, but the client should provide the court with details of the other judgments and a financial statement. There is no limit on the number of judgments or the amount owed. The advantage of this procedure is that there is only one protected earnings rate and one deduction figure. Some clients welcome this opportunity to save, making several payments each month themselves.

Third-party debt order

Formerly known as a 'garnishee' order, a third-party debt order instructs someone (the 'third party') who owes money to the client (eg, a bank holding her/his savings) to pay it instead to the creditor. A third-party debt order may only be given to a creditor who has already obtained a judgment that is not being complied with.[75] The procedure is contained in Part 72 Civil Procedure Rules.

In 2007, 6,474 applications for third-party debt orders were made, almost the same as in the previous two years.

The order is given in two stages. An interim third-party debt order is made on application by the creditor on Form N349 either to the court which made the judgment or, if the proceedings have since been transferred, to the court being used. This temporarily prohibits the third party from making any payment which reduces the amount s/he owes the client to less than the amount specified in the order – ie, the balance of the debt plus the costs of the application. However, it should be noted that any funds paid into the account following service of the interim order are not affected.

This is followed by a final order after a hearing in front of a district judge, which must be not less than 28 days after the making of the interim order. If the client wishes to object to the making of the final order, s/he can apply to have the hearing transferred to her/his local court. The client (and also the third party) must file at court and serve on the creditor any written evidence in the form of a witness statement setting out the grounds of objection not less than three days before the hearing. When making a final order, the district judge has a full discretion and should consider the position of both the client and any other creditors (if known).[76] If, for instance, an attempt is made to seize a person's only monthly income, the debt adviser should argue this would be unreasonable and would cause hardship to the client and her/his family, as well as preventing payments to other (possibly priority) creditors.

If the third party is a bank or building society, on receipt of the interim order it must carry out a search for all accounts held in the name of the client, freeze them and give details to both the court and the creditor within seven days. The bank or building society is entitled to deduct £55 from the client's account balance towards its costs and expenses of responding to the order, regardless of the amount in the account. Similarly, the bank or building society is required to inform the court within seven days if the client has no account. If the bank or building society claims to be entitled to any of the money in the account, it must inform the court within seven days and state its grounds. The court cannot make a third-party debt order in relation to a joint account if the other account holder is not liable for the debt under the judgment.

Hardship payment order

If, because of an interim order, a client finds her/his account frozen and s/he or her/his family is experiencing 'hardship in meeting ordinary living expenses' as a result of not being able to withdraw money from the account, s/he can apply to her/his local county court for a hardship payment order. The client must produce written evidence to prove both her/his financial position and the need for payment. Applications are made on Form N244 (see p305). The fee is £75 (full or partial remission can be applied for). Two days' notice of the hearing must be given to the creditor, but the court can dispense with this in cases of 'exceptional urgency'. The court can permit the bank or building society to make one or more payments out of the account either to the client or some other specified person.[77]

The DWP cannot be the third party in an application by the creditor in respect of unpaid benefits (but benefit payments already paid into the client's account can be made subject to a third-party debt order). Also, an order cannot be made in respect of a debt owed jointly to the client and another person where the judgment is against the client alone. However, a third-party debt order could be used if, for example, a client had told a creditor that an amount of capital would shortly be due from an endowment insurance policy in her/his sole name. The creditor could obtain a third-party debt order against the insurance company after the amount became due but before it had been paid out. For this reason, it is important for a debt adviser not to reveal details of future money available to a client if it is required to pay priority creditors or to be shared among a number of creditors.

Bailiffs

Chapter 11 discusses bailiffs' powers in detail.

Orders to obtain information

Formerly known as 'oral examinations', an order to obtain information from a judgment client (or information order) is an order for the client to attend the court, in person, to be interviewed by a court official about her/his means or any other matter about which information is needed to enforce a judgment. It is not a way of enforcing a judgment, but more an information-gathering process. It can be used at any time, not just when payments have been missed. The procedure is contained in Part 71 Civil Procedure Rules.

In 2007, 27,148 information orders were made, continuing the year-on-year decline in numbers.

A creditor who has obtained a judgment against someone can apply to court on Form N316 for an information order requiring that person to attend a hearing at her/his local court before either a district judge (if there are 'compelling reasons') or, more usually, a senior court official. The order is on Form N39 and must be served personally on the client at least 14 days before the hearing. Within seven days of service the client can require the creditor to pay her/his reasonable travel expenses to and from the court. These are likely to be added to the judgment and so ultimately paid by the client, but it is always worth the client requesting travel expenses from the creditor because if they are not paid, the client cannot be committed to prison for non-attendance at the hearing. The N39 contains a list of documents which the client is required to bring to court – eg, pay slips, rent book, credit agreements, outstanding bills. The creditor can ask the court to add further documents to the list.

At the hearing, the court officer asks the client a set of standard questions contained on Form EX140 (available from www.hmcourts-service.gov.uk). This is a 12-page questionnaire designed to find out what money, goods, property or other resources the client has to satisfy the judgment, in order for the creditor to decide what action to take next. The creditor can ask additional questions. The client must answer on oath. The client must attend the hearing. If s/he does not appear, refuses to take the oath or to answer any questions, or possibly if s/he fails to bring any document listed on Form N39 to the hearing, the court can make a suspended order committing her/him to prison unless s/he attends a further hearing and complies with the other terms of the original order – ie, produces documents and takes the oath. If s/he again fails to comply, s/he will be arrested and brought before the judge to decide whether or not s/he should be committed to prison. In practice, the client will not be sent to prison provided s/he co-operates in the process, and cannot be committed if s/he requested travel expenses for the first hearing and these were not paid by the creditor.

The adviser can help a client who has been served with an information order by providing a financial statement and a list of other debts and capital resources (including any equity in a house) in accordance with the information required by Form N39, together with a letter of explanation if the client is unable to obtain any of the required information. The adviser can also help by going through the questions on Form N39 with the client prior to the hearing.

An information order will almost certainly be followed by further action if any is possible – eg, the creditor may apply for an attachment of earnings order or a charging order. It is therefore important to pre-empt this if possible by submitting the above information to the creditor, implementing the most appropriate strategy for all the debts, and agreeing this with the creditor who has requested the information order before the hearing, which may no longer need to take place. If this cannot be agreed, nevertheless, it may be appropriate to offer the strategy to all the other creditors and this fact (along with any responses available) can be reported at the hearing. If the client has defaulted, an application for variation of the judgment should be made to prevent enforcement. The court can also treat the hearing as an application for an administration order (see p370).[78]

4. Action to recover goods on hire purchase or conditional sale

A court order is required to repossess goods on hire purchase or conditional sale if more than one-third of the total cost has been paid (see p73) or if the client has paid less but has refused to allow the creditor to enter private property in order to take back the goods. The creditor must first serve a default notice (including, in the section on what action may be taken, that goods can be repossessed). See p239 for further information about the default notice. In these cases the so-called 'Consumer Credit Act procedure' applies.

- The claim must be started in the county court for the district in which the client either lives or carries out her/his business (or did when s/he made her/his last payment).
- The court fixes a hearing date when it issues the claim form (N1) and notice of the hearing date is given when the claim form is served.
- The particulars of claim (containing the information prescribed by paragraph 7, Part 7B Practice Direction, Civil Procedure Rules) must be served with the claim form.
- The claim form/particulars of claim are accompanied by Forms N1(FD) (Defendant's Notes for Guidance), N9C (Admission and Statement of Means) and N9D (Defence and Counterclaim). There is no acknowledgement of service.

The response

The client is not required to file either an admission or a defence, although s/he should do so as the court can take account of a failure to do so when deciding on its order for costs in the case – eg, if an unnecessary hearing has to take place as a result. The creditor cannot request a default judgment. The N9C enables the client to admit the claim and make an offer on which the court can make an order for the return of the goods suspended, so long as the client makes payments in accordance with her/his offer (a 'time order').[79] The statement of means is similar to the N9A. The client should complete Form N9C by:

- indicating whether or not s/he still has the goods in her/his possession;
- admitting liability for the claim; *and*
- offering to pay the unpaid balance of the total price (this figure is contained in the particulars of claim).

The admission should be returned to the court, not sent to the creditor. A copy is sent by the court to the creditor. If the creditor accepts the amount admitted and the offer of payment, it informs the court, which enters judgment accordingly and sends a copy to the client (N32(2) HP/CCA). No one need attend the hearing. If nothing is heard from the court, the client should attend the hearing. If the creditor does not accept the amount admitted or offer of payment, or the client does not respond, the hearing proceeds.

Negotiating prior to the hearing

An adviser should always try to negotiate with the creditor to reach an agreement before the court hearing. Most creditors prefer to receive payments rather than repossess the goods. Resuming the contractual payments will often be enough to persuade the creditor to withdraw or adjourn the court action. If no agreement can be reached, the hearing will take place and the client should attend, with a financial statement indicating her/his ability to pay. A court is unlikely to accept a long-term substantial reduction in payments – eg, £20 a month when the contractual agreement is for £120, but may accept a short-term reduction – eg, £20 a month for three months, then £120 a month. Unless a time order application is made (including completing Form N9C – see above) or the hearing is adjourned, the court appears to have no power to make an order for payment of less than the contractual instalments.

If the agreement is regulated under the Consumer Credit Act 1974, a default notice must have been issued in the correct format (see p239).

Decisions the court can make

The court has a general power to adjourn for a short period if required, but will only exercise this power if it has compelling reasons (see p308). If the client can make an offer of payment in respect of the balance of the total price which the court finds acceptable, it will award possession but suspend the order provided the payments are maintained.[80] If there is no acceptable payment offer, the court will order that the goods be returned. The judgment will be on Form N32(1) and give the date for delivery – ie, for the client to return the goods. If the goods are no longer in the possession of the client, the court cannot order their return.[81] The creditor will have to obtain a judgment for the total balance due under the agreement.

Alternatively, the client could make an application for a time order once the default notice (or from 1 October 2008, the arrears notice) has been issued (see p239 and p283).

If the client fails to make payments or return the goods as ordered, the creditor does not need any further court order and may repossess the goods provided it is possible to do so lawfully – eg, without trespassing on private land. Otherwise, the creditor can ask the court to issue a warrant of delivery (see p272).

Note: returning the goods to the creditor is not the end of the matter. The creditor will sell the goods and set the proceeds of the sale against the remaining balance due under the agreement. There may well be a shortfall that the client will be liable to pay. The creditor must apply to the court for a further hearing date to obtain an order for payment of the money.[82]

If the client's circumstances change, s/he can apply to vary the order.

Unless the client is merely disputing the amount s/he has already paid, the adviser should obtain specialist advice on any other potential defences. If the client disputes the claim, the court will either:

- deal with the case at the hearing; *or*
- allocate the case to a track and make directions; *or*
- give directions to enable it to make a decision on allocation (see p253).

Warrant of delivery

A **'warrant of delivery'** is a document that allows the county court bailiff to seize goods which are the subject of a hire purchase or conditional sale agreement if the court has ordered the goods be returned to the creditor. It is issued by the court following a request from the creditor if the client does not return the goods described in the judgment to the creditor as ordered by the court or is in breach of a suspended return of goods order (see p271). The warrant may allow the client to pay the value of the goods as an alternative to allowing them to be taken by the bailiffs. The client can apply for this warrant to be suspended and for delivery of the goods to be postponed (see p303). It is always worth approaching the creditor to negotiate an agreement before applying back to the court.

5. Action to recover property

A landlord or a mortgage lender can start an action in the county court for possession of a tenant's or owner occupier's home by completing a claim form (N5) and particulars of the claim (Form N119 for tenants and N120 for mortgagees). The creditor cannot request a default judgment or apply for summary judgment in this type of action. There must be a hearing to consider the merits of the claim. The procedure is contained in Part 55 Civil Procedure Rules. Possession claims are normally brought in the county court for the area where the property is situated. A claim may only be brought in the High Court in 'exceptional circumstances' and an adviser who encounters a possession claim or order made in the High Court should seek specialist advice.

A residential occupier cannot be forced to leave her/his home against her/his will unless a court order and warrant has been obtained.

This section only covers possession actions taken on the grounds of unpaid rent or payments due under a mortgage (or other secured loan). This *Handbook* cannot cover details of all the law in both these areas and advisers should refer to specialist books (see Appendix 2) and be prepared to refer to a housing specialist where necessary.

Mortgage possession actions continue to increase. In 2005 there were 114,764 actions, resulting in 70,964 possession orders and 14,600 properties taken into possession. In 2007 this had risen to 137,607 possession actions, 95,187 possession orders and 27,100 properties taken into possession. The figures continue to show an upward trend. The Council of Mortgage lenders forecasts that 45,000 properties will have been taken into possession in 2008.

There is a downward trend in rent possession actions, falling from 165,714 in 2005 to 146,818 in 2007, with the number of actual possession orders falling from 112,869 to 106,510.

Negotiating prior to the court hearing

The debt adviser should always try to negotiate with a creditor and reach a satisfactory agreement before going to court. This is preferable to relying on the decision of a district judge and avoids the possibility of things 'going wrong' at the hearing. In addition:

- tenants are usually ordered by the courts to pay landlords' costs;
- most mortgages allow the creditor to charge all her/his costs to the client in connection with default and repossession;
- it is important to avoid unnecessary court hearings or delays;
- ideally, both parties will apply for the matter to be adjourned generally (that is, without a future hearing date) on the agreed terms.

Often creditors insist on a suspended possession order (see below) being made rather than agreeing to the case being adjourned on the basis of the agreed terms. This puts the home at risk, but it may result in a better order for the client than if the matter had been left to the discretion of the district judge. If the creditor agrees to a suspended possession order, the debt adviser should check that the solicitor representing the creditor has been informed and obtain written confirmation of the terms of the proposed suspended order so this can be produced at the hearing if there is any dispute. See Chapter 7 for possible strategies.

If the agreement to clear the arrears was made before the landlord/lender issued court proceedings and the client has not defaulted under the agreement, the adviser should ask the court to adjourn the matter and disallow the landlord's/lender's costs. This is because the Civil Procedure Rules and paragraph 4 of the protocols Practice Direction requires people to act reasonably in trying to avoid the necessity for court proceedings (see p235).

In the case of social landlords, if the payment agreement is made before the issue of proceedings, the landlord should agree to postpone the issue of proceedings, provided the client keeps to the agreement. If the payment arrangement was made after the issue of proceedings, the landlord should agree to an adjournment.

Mortgages and secured loans

If the loan is a regulated agreement under the Consumer Credit Act (see Chapter 4), a default notice (see p239) must first be issued. If the mortgage was made on or after 31 October 2004, it may be regulated by the Financial Services Authority (FSA) (see p87). If so, the lender is required by the *Mortgages and Home Finance: conduct of business sourcebook* (MCOB) to deal 'fairly' with borrowers in arrears and have a written arrears policy and procedures. These should include:

- using reasonable efforts to come to an agreement with the client over the repayment of the arrears;
- liaising with an adviser or agency if the client arranges this;
- allowing a reasonable time for repayment of the arrears, bearing in mind the need to establish a practical repayment plan in the client's circumstances (in appropriate cases, arranging repayments over the remaining term of the mortgage);
- granting the client's request for a change to the payment date or method of payment (unless the lender has a good reason for not agreeing to this);
- where no reasonable repayment arrangement can be made, considering allowing the client to remain in possession of the property to effect a sale;
- repossessing the property only where all other reasonable attempts to resolve the position have failed.[83]

The lender should also have given the client certain prescribed information (see p87). In addition, many mortgage lenders have their own policies – eg, a special letter may be sent warning borrowers of impending court action, or the mortgagee will not seek possession until payments of mortgage interest are three months in arrears.

The mortgage arrears pre-action protocol (which comes into effect on 19 November 2008) makes clear that starting a possession claim should be the last resort and should not be started when the parties are actively pursuing a settlement, such as the options discussed above.

The possession claim form (N5) includes the date and time of the hearing. It must be accompanied by a 'particulars of claim' (Form N120), although the lender can use its own particulars of claim provided it contains details of:[84]

- the identity of the property to be recovered;
- whether the claim relates to residential property;
- the ground(s) on which possession is claimed;
- the mortgage or charge;
- every person in possession of the property (to the best of the lender's knowledge);

- whether any charges or notices have been registered under the Family Law Act 1996 or Matrimonial Homes Acts 1967-1983;
- the state of the account between the borrower and lender, including:
  - the amount of the advance, any periodic payments and any repayment of interest required to be made;
  - the amount which would have to be paid, taking into account any allowance for early settlement, to redeem the mortgage at a stated date not later than 14 days after the commencement of proceedings, including solicitor's costs and administrative charges;
  - if it is a regulated consumer credit agreement, the total amount outstanding under the terms of the mortgage;
  - the rate of interest payable originally, immediately before any arrears accrued and at the commencement of proceedings;
  - a schedule of arrears, showing all amounts due and payments made together with dates and a running total of the arrears either for the previous two years or from the date of default, if later;
  - details of any other payments required to be made as a term of the mortgage (such as insurance premiums, legal costs, default interest, penalties, administrative and other charges), whether any of these payments are in arrears and whether or not they are included in the periodic payment;
- whether or not the loan is a regulated consumer credit agreement and the date(s) on which the appropriate notices under the Consumer Credit Act have been served;
- such relevant information as is known by the lender about the borrower's circumstances and, in particular, whether s/he is in receipt of benefits and whether direct mortgage payments are being received from the Department for Work and Pensions (DWP);
- any previous steps taken by the lender to recover either the money secured under the mortgage or the property itself, including dates of any court proceedings and the terms of any orders made;
- the history of arrears (if longer than two years). This should be stated in the particulars and a schedule of the arrears should be exhibited to a witness statement, which should be served separately and at least two days before the hearing.

All the above requirements on the particulars of claim are covered in paragraphs 1 to 9 on Form N120.

The lender may also include a money-only claim arising out of an unsecured loan agreement. Although the lender can obtain a money judgment in respect of such a debt, it cannot be included in any possession order.[85] The lender will not normally be seeking an order for costs, as the mortgage normally allows for these to be added to the outstanding balance automatically.

The particulars of claim must be verified by a statement of truth.

'Possession claims online'

Certain specified county courts can now operate a scheme known as 'possession claims online', which enables lenders to issue claims for possession electronically via www.possessionclaim.gov.uk.

The particulars must contain the same information referred to above with one exception. If the lender has already provided the client with a schedule of arrears showing all amounts due and payments made, together with dates and a running total of the arrears either for the previous two years or from the date of default, if later, the particulars of claim may contain a summary of the arrears stating:

- the amount of the arrears on the date of the lender's pre-action letter;
- the dates and amounts of the last three payments (or, if less than three payments have been made, the dates and amounts of those payments); *and*
- the arrears on the date possession proceedings are issued.

In the case of mortgages (where MCOB applies), the lender should be able to take advantage of this provision, as both the pre-action schedule and the letter should have been provided under section 13.4.4 of the MCOB. However, if the lender only includes the summary information in the particulars of claim, it must serve a full arrears history on the client within seven days after the issue of the claim and verify this by witness statement or verbally at the hearing.

Proceedings are issued by reference to the property's post code supplied by the lender and, if this is not the client's local court, s/he can ask the court to transfer the case.[86]

Before 'possession claims online' was introduced, courts could send out information with possession claims containing details of local advice agencies and the availability of a court helpdesk. This is not possible under 'possession claims online'. The EX104 leaflet accompanying the claim form served on the client, however, makes clear the availability of free advice locally and of a court helpdesk where there is one.

Replying to the claim

The hearing (which takes place in private) will normally be fixed for not less than 28 days or more than eight weeks after issue of the N5. The claim form and particulars of claim must be served on the borrower not less than 21 days before the hearing. Not less than 14 days before the hearing, the claimant must send a notice to the property addressed to 'the occupiers' containing details of the claim. The purpose of this is to alert anyone living at the property who is not the borrower but who may be in a position to oppose the claim for possession. There is no acknowledgment of service.

There is a form of 'defence' (N11M) which is supposed to be completed and filed at court within 14 days of service but which may be filed at any time before the hearing. The questions are straightforward, although they are not cross-referenced to the numbered paragraphs in the particulars of claim. It is not a defence as such, but a reply to the claim. It is not essential to respond, but it is advisable to do so, as any delay caused by the borrower's failure to file the defence may involve her/him in further liability for costs. Although there will be a hearing, it is helpful if the district judge has been prepared for the borrower's circumstances and argument by submitting a well-completed reply form. A copy of the form will also be sent by the court to the lender.

In the case of 'possession claims online', the claim is accompanied by a covering letter containing details of the user name and password to access the website where the client can complete and file the form online. The website contains a User Guide, although most of the information is only relevant to lenders and there is no guidance on how to complete Form N11(M).

Form N11(M) should be completed as follows.

- **Question 1** requests details of the client's personal circumstances including the client's date of birth.
- **Question 2** relates to paragraphs 2 to 4 on Form N120, which should be confirmed as correct, or details of any disagreement given.
- **Question 3**. Check the level of arrears as carefully as possible. The court may not make an order if it is unsure that the arrears figure is correct.
- **Question 4** needs completing only in cases where possession is sought (perhaps partly) on grounds other than arrears.
- **Questions 5 and 6** are primarily addressed to borrowers whose loans are regulated agreements. Question 5 asks whether they want the court to consider whether the terms of the loan agreement are 'fair'. This appears to be applicable to the unfair relationship provisions of the Consumer Credit Act 1974 (which do not apply to mortgage contracts regulated by the FSA, as well as to unfairness, for example, under the Unfair Terms in Consumer Contracts Regulations (which apply to all agreements, not just Consumer Credit Act regulated agreements). Although one of the main principles of FSA regulation is that lenders must treat their customers fairly, it is not clear to what extent a court could address a breach of the FSA's rules as a defence to possession proceedings (see p87). Question 6 asks whether the borrower intends to apply for a time order (see p283). An application may be made either on this form (which does not attract a fee) or by notice of application (Form N244) (which attracts a fee, but full or partial remission is available – see p237).[87] As there is only room to tick a box on the N11(M), any applications will need to be supported by written evidence in the form of a witness statement, setting out the grounds.
- **Question 7**. If the arrears have been paid in full by the date of the hearing, the case should be adjourned.[88]
- **Question 8**. If an agreement has been reached, details should be included. In this case, the reply should ideally be accompanied by a letter requesting a general adjournment. If the lender agrees, it should also write to the court indicating its agreement to a general adjournment. If the agreement has been

running since before the action started, the borrower may argue there was no need to take court action, and ask for the matter to be adjourned generally and challenge any costs the lender seeks to charge.[89] Send proof of payments. Alternatively, include a written request from the lender that an order be made and suspended on payment of whatever sum has been agreed.

- **Question 9** should be completed in the affirmative if agreement has not been reached. Note that borrowers who fail to ask the court to consider instalments might later find this used against them if a local authority is considering the question of the intentionality of their homelessness.
- **Question 10** asks for the amount, in addition to the contractual payments, being offered. This question may not be relevant as it is not always necessary for the client to be able to afford the contractual payments for the court to make a suspended possession order. For the position if the client is applying for a time order, see p283; for other cases, see p280.
- **Questions 11-13** relate to income support (IS) and income-based jobseeker's allowance (JSA). It is important to check with the Department for Work and Pensions what payments have been made before attending court, so that any misunderstandings with the lender can be resolved. Remember to convert weekly benefit amounts to calendar monthly amounts to compare with monthly mortgage payments.
- **Questions 14-25** relate to dependants (and non-dependants), bank accounts and savings, income and expenditure, priority debts, court orders and credit debts similar to those required on Form N9A (see p244) and should be filled in similarly.
- **Question 26**. The borrower should not answer 'yes' to Question 28 ('If an order is made will you have somewhere to live?') unless the accommodation is absolutely certain. The date given, even in such cases, should always be realistic.
- **Question 27** is important because it gives the borrower the opportunity to explain:
  - any breaches of the FSA rules, especially the principle of treating clients fairly and any breaches of MCOB itself;[90]
  - the circumstances in which the loan was made if relevant – eg, to refinance unsecured borrowing in response to high pressure selling;
  - why the arrears arose;
  - what circumstances were beyond her/his control;
  - why it would cause particular hardship if eviction were ordered.

Written evidence may be given at the hearing and should be filed at court and served on the other side at least two days before the hearing date. Evidence of the arrears (including interest on the arrears) should be up to the date of the hearing, by reference to a daily rate, if necessary. If the claim cannot be dealt with on the hearing date because there appears to be a substantial dispute, the district judge should give directions, including track allocation.

Powers of the court in dealing with possession action

If a court is considering an action for the possession of a private house, it has wide-ranging powers in relation to the protection it can potentially give borrowers with mortgages and secured loans not regulated by the Consumer Credit Act 1974.[91] These include:

- adjourning the proceedings; *or*
- suspending a possession order; *or*
- postponing the date for the delivery of possession.

If an agreement is regulated under the Consumer Credit Act 1974 (see Chapter 4), the court should consider making a time order. This can be specifically requested by the client. See p283.

Adjournment

The court has a general power to adjourn any proceedings for a short period.[92] For example, if the borrower needs more time to seek money advice or the lender is required to clarify the arrears, the court may adjourn the matter, commonly for 28 days. The court may attach terms to the adjournment – eg, that basic instalments are paid or that no further interest is added to the loan. The court can also adjourn the proceedings for a short time to enable the borrower to pay off the mortgage in full – eg, by sale of the property, or otherwise satisfying the lender.[93]

The court sends out a written notice giving the date and time of the next hearing. If the property is about to be sold or the arrears cleared in full in some other way, the court may adjourn with 'liberty to restore'. There will not be another hearing so long as the expected action happens. However, if the expected action fails, the lender can ask for a hearing to be restored.

Advisers may wish to argue that the matter should be adjourned, rather than a suspended possession order granted, in one of the following ways.

- **Adjourn with liberty to restore** – eg, because the arrears have been, or are about to be, paid in full, or the property is in the process of being sold or an agreement to pay the arrears has already been agreed.
- **Adjourn for a fixed period** (eg, 28 days) for the borrower to get further advice or for the lender to produce correct particulars of claim.
- **Adjourn generally** because there is a repayment plan agreed and working.

Terms may be attached to an adjournment, commonly that basic payments be maintained. An adjournment is preferable because no further action, including enforcement, can be taken without a further court hearing. For borrowers who are vulnerable because of age or disability, this can be a valuable tactic.

Suspended possession orders

Under s36 Administration of Justice Act 1970 and s8 Administration of Justice Act 1973, a court can suspend possession so long as the mortgage arrears can be cleared in a 'reasonable period'.[94] The terms of the order will usually be for basic instalments plus £x towards the arrears. However, a number of court cases show this is not always necessary. In one case, an order was made for payment of £250 for one month and £500 for two months with a review thereafter on the basis that the client had good prospects of obtaining employment within that period. In another case, the client offered £150 a month until mortgage interest became payable by the DWP, which would cover the current payments. Although the arrears would increase meanwhile, they would be cleared within three-and-a-half years. The court made an order accordingly. In each case, the court held that the test was not whether the client could pay the contractual payments now but whether s/he would, within a reasonable period, be able to clear the arrears and pay the contractual instalments.[95]

In 1996, in the case of *Cheltenham and Gloucester v Norgan*,[96] the Court of Appeal said that a starting point for 'reasonable period' should be the remaining period of the mortgage. This valuable precedent strengthens the money advice case for setting repayments at a level the client can afford. In exceptional cases a 'reasonable period' could be longer than the remaining mortgage.[97] The decision also guides the court on points it should take into consideration, including the means of the borrower and the value of the lender's security. On the whole, the judiciary appears satisfied that for a long-term agreement, such as a mortgage, the security is safe. A clear financial statement is an essential tool. Identify the basic mortgage instalment separately from the payment towards the arrears to demonstrate to the court that the client is able to afford the contractual mortgage payments as well as being able to pay off the arrears within the period being requested. Tactically, advisers should still look for an affordable sum rather than spreading the arrears over as long a period as possible, just in case further difficulties arise in the future. Do not be intimidated by creditors and solicitors who say they want the arrears cleared in a shorter fixed period – eg, three years. The court will make its own decision and it should be familiar with the *Norgan* case.

If the arrears cannot be paid by instalments and the mortgage can only be repaid out of the proceeds of sale of the property, the *Norgan* decision does not apply. In *Bristol & West Building Society v Ellis,* however, the Court of Appeal held that in such cases the 'reasonable period' for a suspended order could be the time it will take to effect the sale.[98] What is a reasonable period depends on the circumstances of each case. Factors the court could take into account are:

- the extent to which the balance of the mortgage as well as the arrears are secured;
- where there is little equity and the value of the security is at risk, only a short period of suspension might be appropriate;

- where there has already been delay and/or there is negative equity or insufficient evidence of the property's value, an immediate possession order might be appropriate.

A court should grant either a deferred or suspended possession order if the proceeds of the sale will fully cover the mortgage to allow the borrower to remain in her/his home while it is sold.[99] In a county court case decided a few years ago, the judge stayed a warrant of possession for three months to allow the client to sell the property, pointing out that there would be no prejudice to the lender in view of the amount of equity.[100]

Creditors have challenged suspended orders made to allow time for sale of properties in negative equity. The Court of Appeal has held that if the mortgage cannot be cleared from the proceeds of the sale, the court has no jurisdiction to suspend the order under the Administration of Justice Acts.[101] It is beyond the court's powers to suspend a possession order in any other circumstances, although the court recognised that there might be occasions when it is necessary to adjourn the proceedings for procedural reasons.[102]

However, in the case of *Cheltenham & Gloucester v Booker*,[103] the Court of Appeal confirmed the court's jurisdiction to postpone giving possession to the lender for a short period to enable the client to sell the property.

Order for possession

If there is no real chance of clearing the arrears or the mortgage, the court will make a possession order, usually effective in 28 days. If the client has special reasons – eg, ill health or a new home not yet available, the court may extend this to 56 days. At the end of the specified period, the creditor can apply back to the court for bailiffs to execute a 'warrant of possession' (also known as a 'warrant of eviction'). See p297. The order points out that if the borrower does not leave the property, the lender can ask the court to instruct the bailiff to evict her/him without a further hearing (although it also points out that the borrower can apply to the court to postpone the eviction).

A warrant of possession allows the county court bailiff to evict the occupants from their home. The homeowner or tenant will receive notification that a possession warrant has been obtained on Form N54. It states the exact date and time the bailiffs will carry out the eviction. The bailiffs are empowered physically to remove the occupants from their home, if necessary, and hand over possession of the property to the landlord or mortgage company. This is usually followed by the creditor's agent changing the locks to prevent the occupier moving back in. The N54 informs the borrower that:

- a possession warrant gives the bailiff authority to remove anyone still in the property when the eviction takes place;
- the borrower should act immediately to get advice about the eviction or re-housing from an advice agency, solicitor or local housing department;

- the borrower can apply on an N244 (see p305) for the court to suspend the warrant and postpone the date for eviction;
- the borrower must attend the hearing of the application or it may simply be dismissed, incurring further costs;
- if the borrower can pay off any arrears, s/he should contact the borrower or the borrower's solicitor immediately.

The N54 must also contain details of the bailiff and the borrower or the borrower's solicitor.

When dealing with a warrant of possession, the debt adviser should either negotiate directly with the lender or landlord or help the client make an application to the court to suspend the warrant (see p304 for how to do this). County court bailiffs acting for a mortgage company or landlord who has issued an eviction warrant can change the locks and evict the client if no application has been made to suspend the warrant. They can use necessary reasonable force to carry out the eviction.

Granting a possession order should not, however, be seen as the end of the line. Even when this has occurred, creditors still do not want to repossess homes unnecessarily and it may be possible to negotiate terms directly with the creditor, which are more acceptable than those imposed by the court. Such variations should at least be agreed in writing and the court asked to vary the relevant order, with the consent of the other party if possible (see p301).

Arguing against a possession order

In some cases, the situation when the loan was made is relevant. In particular, if a borrower was badly advised to take out a new secured loan by a financial adviser (perhaps the lender itself), the court should be acquainted with the facts – eg, if there has been irresponsible lending (see p53). The early history of the loan can be vital in enlisting the sympathy of the court.

If mortgage interest should have been paid by the DWP but has not been, or if a claim is pending, this should be brought to the court's attention. Similarly, if penalties have followed slow payments from the DWP these should be challenged (and compensation sought from the DWP with the help of an MP if necessary).

If the loan is regulated by the Consumer Credit Act, the adviser should check whether the agreement has been drawn up correctly and, if not, whether this makes it irredeemably unenforceable or enforceable only if the court gives permission (see p55).

Debt advisers sometimes agree to a suspended possession order on the ground that this is a technicality and does no more than safeguard the lender's position. This is a very dangerous view and means that any future default in payment or the accruing of further mortgage arrears puts the borrower at serious risk of losing her/his home. If a suspended order is clearly going to be made, the amount of instalments towards arrears should be set at a level that provides some leeway for the borrower faced with an unexpected and essential item of expenditure.

It is unnecessary to argue against a possession order if a time order is made instead (or as well), in which case the order for possession should be suspended as long as the time order is complied with. A time order should, therefore, always be considered (see below) in cases of regulated agreements.

For agreements made after 1 July 1995, so-called 'arrears charges' and 'fines', and interest penalties on early settlement are also possible areas where the terms of a loan could be challenged under the Unfair Terms in Consumer Contracts Regulations 1994-1999 to reduce the amount payable by the borrower. It may also be possible to challenge the lender's legal charges on the grounds that they were unreasonably incurred and/or unreasonable in amount.[104]

Time orders

A **'time order'** is an order under ss129-136 Consumer Credit Act 1974 by which the court reschedules the payments under a credit agreement regulated by the Consumer Credit Act 1974. A time order provides for the client to pay any sum owed under a regulated agreement by instalments, payable at whatever frequency the court thinks 'just', having regard to the means of the client and/or any surety.[105] In the case of possession action, the 'sum owed' is the outstanding balance of the loan. The provisions of the Administration of Justice Acts 1970 and 1973 (see p280) do not apply to regulated agreements[106] and debt advisers should challenge district judges who still insist on making orders for payment of contractual instalments plus arrears instead of time orders.

Lenders often argue that courts can only make time orders in cases of 'temporary financial difficulty', but this no longer appears to be the case. Although time orders extending over a long period are generally regarded as undesirable, the House of Lords has confirmed that the court has the discretion to make whatever order it considers 'just' in the circumstances of the case.[107]

In *Southern and District Finance v Barnes*, the Court of Appeal made it clear that a court 'must first consider whether it is just to make a time order' in all possession cases involving regulated agreements.[108] This accords with the Consumer Credit Act 1974's grant of discretion to award a time order in such cases 'if it appears to the court just to do so'.[109] To use this discretion properly the court must consider the justice of an order in each case. The circumstances and terms of the loan, the reasons for default and the borrower's payment record are relevant circumstances.

Some creditors argue that, once judgment has been entered, the court no longer has the power to make a time order as there is no longer any 'sum owed' under a regulated agreement' – ie, the debt is now owed under the judgment. However, s129(2)(c) Consumer Credit Act 1974 says that a time order can be made 'in an action . . . to enforce a regulated agreement' and s130(1) specifically allows the court to make a time order where the debtor has made an instalment offer in response to a county court claim. Finally, none of the House of Lords judgments in the *First National Bank* case suggest that the court cannot make a time order in relation to a judgment debt. If an adviser comes across a case where the creditor is denying that the court has the power to make a time order, specialist advice should be sought.

When a time order is appropriate

A client can apply for a time order if money is owed under a regulated agreement and

- the creditor has served:
  - a default notice; *or*
  - a notice of intention to recover goods or land; *or*
  - a notice requiring payment early due to default; *or*
  - a notice seeking to terminate an agreement; *or*
- enforcement action has been taken by the creditor (including an application for an enforcement order); *or*
- from 1 October 2008, an arrears notice has been served by the creditor and the client has given the creditor 14 days' notice of her/his intention to apply for a time order and made a repayment proposal.[110]

A time order application is generally appropriate where:

- current circumstances make payments impossible, but the borrower's income is likely to increase – eg, if there is short-time working, a period of unemployment, benefit disqualification, a reduction in IS during the early months of a claim or illness. A time order can still be considered, however, if there is no foreseeable improvement in circumstances;
- the original agreement was harsh on the borrower and s/he was disadvantaged in negotiations or ignorant of its implications. In these circumstances, the court may be sympathetic to using a time order in the interest of justice;
- an application might persuade the creditor to negotiate realistically and reduce the payments due under a regulated agreement.

Time order applications can be made in relation to both secured and unsecured debts. In *Director General of Fair Trading v First National Bank*, the House of Lords recommended that a time order application could be made where a creditor was continuing to charge contractual interest after judgment. This can be done by adding in Box 11 of the N9A: 'I ask the court to make a time order in the terms of my offer and amend the loan agreement in consequence so that no further contractual interest accrues after the date of judgment.'

If the applications are granted, the client's full liability to the creditor will be discharged on completion of the payments ordered. If a hearing is required, the court should transfer the hearing to the client's local court on its own initiative.[111]

Although regulated mortgage contracts (see p87) are generally exempted from the Consumer Credit Act 1974 provisions, s16(6D) says that s126 (secured loan must be enforced by court order) and 'related provisions' apply to a regulated mortgage contract which meets all the other conditions for being a regulated agreement (see p54). According to the FSA, the 'related provisions' include the time orders. Advisers should seek specialist advice if they are considering using this argument.[112]

The application

Application can be made by the client after receiving a relevant notice using Form N440. A fee of £150 is payable (see p237 for details about how to apply for full or partial fee remission). The borrower will be the claimant and the lender will be the defendant. This can be useful when a lender is demanding very high payments towards the arrears, or in other ways pressurising the borrower, but does not start court action itself and refuses to negotiate. It is much more common for an application for a time order to be in response to a claim for possession. Application can be on Form N244 or in the borrower's defence form (N11M).[113]

The application must show it is just to both lender and borrower and indicate the terms of the time order that are required. Include:

- the circumstances of the borrower at the time s/he took out the loan, the situation now and her/his likely prospects for the future;
- the purpose of the loan;
- the borrower's payment history;
- the amount of the loan, the interest rate charged and any extra charges because of the default;
- the value of the security;
- the payments that can be made now, and if and when these can be increased in the future, including a financial statement;
- the implications the time order will have on any changes required to the original agreement, particularly the extra time required and the reduction in interest rate required.

The scope of the order

The court is required to be just to both parties and it will, therefore, consider the borrower's position. Was s/he able to afford the agreement when s/he entered into it? Is the cause of the arrears a temporary one? Will s/he be able to afford to resume at least contractual payments at a foreseeable future date? Positive responses to these questions suggest it is just to the borrower. The court will also consider if there is adequate security for the lender and how the interest rate charged compares with other lenders.

Example

A couple took a secured loan at 28 per cent APR to pay for double glazing and maintained payments for 18 months. The wage earner then had a serious accident and was unable to work. He should be fully recovered in about nine months when he will resume employment and contractual payments. The loan is secured against the couple's home, which has adequate equity. On these facts a court should grant a time order.

'The sum owed'

A time order can be made for 'the sum owed'. This phrase has been the subject of much dispute, but has now been clarified by the Court of Appeal. It means 'every sum which is due and owing under the agreement'. Where possession proceedings have been brought, this is the total indebtedness, and this was confirmed in the *Barnes* case. In the case of unsecured regulated loans, it will also usually be the total amount due.

The amount due (and subject to a time order) is therefore the sum of:

- the amount borrowed;
- the total charge for credit (early settlement rebates should not be applied to this);
- any default interest properly charged up to the hearing date;
- *less* all payments made to date.

The lender should make clear to the court the total sum owed and the present arrears as well as the contractual instalments. The debt adviser should, if possible, check these calculations. The lender should also be asked to confirm in writing:

- if the borrower makes the contractual payments plus £x towards the arrears, how much s/he will still owe at the end of the loan repayment period; *and*
- the monthly payment the borrower needs to make to repay the loan by the end of the contractual period.

How much to offer

The offer of payment will be according to the borrower's ability to repay and personal circumstances. In *Barnes*, an order was made for £25 a month for six months, then nearly £100 a month for the remaining 174 months.

Varying other terms

Having decided the instalments and their timing, the court is left 'inevitably', according to the Court of Appeal, with the need to amend either the rate of interest or the length of the loan. It can do this provided it is 'just to both parties and a consequence of the term of the order'.[114] It is, therefore, important for the debt adviser to demonstrate that a reduction in interest is a necessary consequence of a reduction in payments in order to prevent a loan running for too long. This may simply be a reduction in interest on the arrears, or a reduction in interest on the arrears and principal during the period of reduced payments, or a longer-term reduction. The court does not have the facilities to calculate interest charges. Advisers may consider approaching their local trading standards office for assistance with calculating interest rates or asking the court to include in the order that the lender adjusts the interest rate for payments to be completed in a fixed period.

Until *London North Securities v Meadows* it was thought that s136 could not be used to deal with interest that had already accrued.[115] However, there is no logical reason to restrict the wording of the section to amendments that only operate in the future.

Reviews

A time order can be varied or revoked by the court on the application of creditors or clients.[116] This power to review should be sufficient to persuade district judges who resist time orders that one can safely be granted because it can later be reviewed.

Policy

Time orders are unpopular with the credit industry. Some lenders prefer to negotiate out of court rather than have a time order, so the threat of an application can be part of the negotiating tactics.

Although *Barnes* clarified the court's powers in relation to time orders, it suggested that:

> If, despite the giving of time, the client is unlikely to be able to resume payments by at least the amount of the contractual instalments, no time order should be made.

However, the House of Lords decision in the *First National Bank* case suggests that the fact that the borrower's difficulties are not temporary is not necessarily an obstacle to making a time order: '. . . the broad language of s129 should be so construed as to permit the county court to make such an order as appears to it just in all the circumstances' (including any amendment to the loan agreement – eg, freezing/reducing interest as it considers just to both parties).[117]

After repossession for mortgage default

A warrant of possession is executed on the date and time stated in the warrant. A court bailiff comes to the property accompanied by a locksmith and a representative from the lender. The bailiff may use force to enter the property and evict all occupants. If opposition is expected, the bailiff may be accompanied by a police officer to prevent a breach of the peace (not to enforce the eviction). The locksmith will change the locks. Any of the borrower's property left in the home will therefore be locked inside. The borrower can ask the lender for access to the home to remove her/his property within a reasonable period, usually two weeks.

Once a warrant has been executed there is no further jurisdiction to suspend unless:

- the original possession order itself is set aside; *or*
- the warrant has been obtained by fraud; *or*
- there has been oppression or abuse of process in its execution. Court staff providing misleading information could amount to 'oppression', but unless there has been 'fault' on the part of the lender or the court, there will be no abuse of process.[118]

Otherwise, the property will be sold by the lender. What follows is a brief summary of the responsibilities of the lender (called the 'mortgagee in possession').

- The lender must take proper care of the property. This includes making essential or emergency repairs (eg, mending a leaking pipe) and may include simple maintenance (eg, mowing the lawn, painting the windows), but not include improvements (eg, refitting the kitchen).
- The lender must sell the property at the best price reasonably possible. Most lenders get at least two valuations to ensure the price is fair and sell through an estate agent in the usual way. Sale by auction is usually considered to achieve a fair market price, although a reserve price is set.
- The lender should sell the property as soon as possible. The lender is not under an obligation to delay the sale in the hope of obtaining a better price. The lender has to balance the need to prevent the debt increasing with market factors.
- The lender must account to the borrower for money received and charged in respect of the property (the account). See below.

After the sale of the property the lender will balance the payments and proceeds of the sale against the outstanding mortgage (the 'account'). The sale proceeds are applied first of all to any arrears of interest and are usually sufficient to extinguish these so that any shortfall is likely to consist of the capital borrowed.

There is no duty on the lender to give details of the sale. If the mortgage is less than the payments and proceeds of sale, the balance should be paid to the borrower as soon as reasonably possible. If the mortgage is more than the payments and proceeds, the borrower should be informed as soon as possible and asked to make up the difference, usually referred to as a 'mortgage shortfall' debt. In order to recover any debt, the lender must produce an account to show all payments made and proceeds of the sale versus the amount of the mortgage and its other costs to show the balance outstanding. The borrower is bound by law and contract to repay the mortgage and all the costs associated with recovering the debt. Once the property has been sold, the shortfall debt will be unsecured. Although the lender should inform the borrower of the amount of the shortfall as soon as possible after the sale, inevitably the borrowers will have moved and, in the absence of a forwarding address, it may take some time to trace her/him. It is not unusual for borrowers to remain unaware of the shortfall debt for several years.[119]

To lose a home is not necessarily the end of the line for the borrower. Many lenders do not take any action immediately following a forced sale because they recognise the borrower is likely to have financial problems that caused the arrears and therefore could not afford to pay anything anyway. However, many lenders keep records of repossessed borrowers and are likely to attempt to recover any shortfall at a later date when either the borrower's situation is known to have improved or the general economic situation is better. It is also possible that such lenders could sell these debts at a later date to companies whose standards of collection are more draconian than those of the original mortgage lender. If the lender decides to recover the shortfall from the borrower, it must inform her/him of this decision within six years of the date of sale.

It is, therefore, vital that the debt adviser advises any borrower whose home is sold by a secured lender that there may be future attempts by the lender to recover this money. For more details on dealing with mortgage shortfall debts, see p125.

Implications for the future

In 1991 the Council of Mortgage Lenders established a possessions register. Subscribers report repossessions to two credit reference agencies, Experian and Equifax. The information contained on the register includes:

- details of the lender and the borrower, the property and the mortgage;
- the date of possession and whether it was a voluntary possession or under a court order;
- whether or not any outstanding shortfall debt has been paid; *and*
- the borrower's current and previous addresses (where known).

These details remain on the register for six years from the date of possession and are then removed. Borrowers can ask to see their credit reference in the normal way. As with all credit, no one has a right to a mortgage and lenders will have their own individual policies on whether or not to offer a mortgage to someone who has been previously repossessed. The Council of Mortgage Lenders has indicated that someone's past credit history does not necessarily stop them from taking out a new mortgage but, if they have an outstanding shortfall debt, this will be taken into consideration by the prospective lender.

Rented property

Rent arrears pre-action protocol

Since October 2006 social landlords (ie, local authorities, housing associations and housing action trusts) have been required to follow certain steps before issuing claims for possession based on rent arrears alone. The aim of the protocol is to reduce homelessness by encouraging social landlords to work with their tenants to deal with rent arrears. The protocol does not apply to the private-rented sector. The protocol requires the following.

- The landlord should contact the client as soon as reasonably possible to discuss the reason for the arrears, the client's financial circumstances (including any entitlement to benefits) and repayment of the arrears by affordable amounts based on the client's ability to repay. The landlord should also advise the client to seek advice from the free money advice sector.
- The landlord must provide comprehensible rent statements on a quarterly basis.
- If the landlord is aware the client is under 18 or particularly vulnerable (eg, has mental health issues or a disability), the landlord should take appropriate steps to ensure the client's rights are protected.
- If there is an outstanding housing benefit (HB) claim, the landlord should work with the client to resolve any problems and, in most circumstances, should not issue possession proceedings.
- After service of the statutory notice seeking possession, the landlord should continue to try and contact the client to discuss the matter and, if an arrangement is made for payment of the current rent and an amount towards the arrears, the landlord should agree to postpone the issue of proceedings so long as the client complies with the agreement.
- At least 10 days before the possession hearing, the landlord must provide the client with an up-to-date rent statement, confirm the details of the court hearing and of the order the landlord is seeking and advise the client to attend the hearing.
- If, after the issue of proceedings, an arrangement is made for the payment of the current rent and an amount towards the arrears, the landlord should agree to adjourn the hearing so long as the client complies with the agreement.
- If the client fails to comply with any payment arrangement, the landlord should warn her/him of its intention to start, or continue with, possession proceedings and give the client a clear time limit within which to bring her/his payments up to date.

Courts should take into account the conduct of both landlord and client when considering whether the protocol has been followed and what orders to make. If the landlord has unreasonably failed to comply, the court may:

- order the landlord to pay the tenant's costs; *and/or*
- adjourn, strike out or dismiss the claim (unless it is brought on a mandatory ground).

If the tenant has unreasonably failed to comply, the court may take this into account when considering whether it is reasonable to make a possession order.

According to Shelter, during the first 18 months or so that the protocol has been in force, landlords and courts have paid little attention to its provisions.

Advisers should be prepared to bring the terms of the protocol to the attention of landlords and district judges and point out it is not a voluntary code of practice but part of the county court rules of procedure. Advisers can download a copy from: www.justice.gov.uk/civil/procrules_fin/contents/protocols/prot_rent.htm.

The claim form

The particulars of claim, on Form N119, in a possession action for rented property must include:[120]

- what land is to be recovered;
- whether the claim relates to a dwelling house;
- full details of the tenancy agreement;
- the grounds on which possession is claimed;
- details of every person living in the property (to the best of the landlord's knowledge);
- the amount due at the start of proceedings;
- a schedule showing all amounts of rent due and payments made over the previous two years (or from the date of first default if within the two-year period);
- the daily rate of rent (and any interest);
- any previous steps the landlord has taken to recover the arrears, including dates of any court proceedings and the dates and terms of any order made;
- any relevant information known about the tenant's circumstances, including whether s/he is in receipt of benefits and whether any deductions from benefit are being paid to the landlord.

If the landlord has used 'possession claims online' (see p276), particulars must contain the same information referred to above with one exception. Where, prior to the issue of proceedings, the landlord has provided the client with a schedule of arrears showing all amounts due and payments made together with dates and a running total of the arrears either for the previous two years or from the date of default, if later, the particulars of claim may contain a summary of the arrears stating:

- the amount of the arrears on the date of the landlord's notice of seeking possession;
- the dates and amounts of the last three payments (or, if less than three payments have been made, the dates and amounts of those payments); *and*
- the arrears at the date of issue of the possession proceedings.

As a notice of seeking possession is a statutory requirement in the case of secure and assured tenancies, most landlords should be able to take advantage of this provision. However, if the landlord only includes the summary information in the particulars of claim, it must serve a full arrears history on the client within seven days after the issue of the claim and verify this by witness statement or verbally at the hearing.

Replying to the claim

The reply is on Form N11R.

- **Question 1** requests details of the client's personal circumstances including date of birth.
- **Question 2** relates to paragraphs 2 and 3 of Form N119 and should either be confirmed as correct or details given of any disagreement.
- **Question 3** asks about the service of the 'notice seeking possession' or equivalent. The debt adviser should always ensure this has been done in the prescribed manner. See Appendix for further help with this.
- **Question 4** asks the tenant to check the rent arrears as stated by the landlord. This should be done carefully.
- **Question 5** only needs completing where possession is sought on grounds other than rent arrears – eg, nuisance.
- **Question 6** asks for any counterclaims that the tenant may have. There are a series of counterclaims or 'set-offs' that can be made by a tenant when a landlord claims possession.
  - Under a tenancy created before 15 January 1989, a landlord may be charging more than the fair rent set by the rent officer. In such cases, not only is the excess over the fair rent not recoverable or counted as arrears for the purposes of seeking possession of the property, but the tenant can claim back all the overpaid money for up to two years.[121]
  - A counterclaim can be made for disrepair if a landlord has failed to keep her/his statutory obligations to repair the exterior or main structure of the property or facilities for the supply of water, gas, electricity or removal of sewage. The tenant can claim the rent arrears should be reduced by an amount to compensate her/him for this loss, which can be done by completing the defence part of the reply to the possession claim form. However, in order to safeguard their rights, tenants should either pay the rent or open an account into which to pay it. In one case, a county court judge still made an order for possession because of rent arrears despite awarding an amount for damages for disrepair that was greater than the actual arrears. The decision to order possession was subsequently overturned by the Court of Appeal.[122]

  Consider seeking the advice of a specialist housing adviser if a landlord has failed in some contractual obligation – eg, has not provided furniture as agreed or redecorated a property as regularly as promised. In such cases, it is often wise to refer the matter to a solicitor before proceeding.
- **Question 7** is self-explanatory and asks for details of payments made since the claim form was issued.

- **Question 8.** If an agreement has been reached, details should be included and the reply should ideally be accompanied by a letter requesting a general adjournment and the landlord should be asked to write separately if the landlord can be persuaded to agree to this course of action rather than to an order suspended on payment of whatever sum has been agreed. If an unrealistic offer was previously made (perhaps under pressure) and broken, this should be made clear. If the landlord is a social landlord, the adviser should refer to the rent arrears pre-action protocol to check whether the landlord has complied with it (see p289).
- **Question 9** should be completed in the affirmative where agreement has not been reached. Note that tenants who fail to ask the court to consider instalments might later find this used against them if a local authority is considering the question of the intentionality of their homelessness.
- **Question 10** asks for the amount in addition to the rent that is being offered. If money is not yet available for the arrears, the court can be asked (probably on a separate sheet) to make an order suspended on payments of £x extra each week or month, with the first payment on a specified date in the foreseeable future. Alternatively, a token offer could be suggested for the first months followed by something more realistic.
- **Questions 11-15** are self-explanatory and relate to IS or HB. In preparation for any hearing, it is important for the debt adviser to know the up-to-date position on these (particularly if rent is paid directly to a landlord or if non-dependant deductions vary with the movement of non-dependants). If the landlord is a social landlord and is aware that an HB claim is pending, the adviser should refer to the rent arrears pre-action protocol (see p289).
- **Questions 16-27** relate to dependants (and non-dependants), bank accounts and savings, income and expenditure, priority debts, court orders and credit debts similar to those required on Form N9A (see p243) and should be completed in the same way.
- **Question 28.** The client should not answer 'yes' to this ('If an order is made will you have somewhere to live?') unless the new accommodation is absolutely certain. The date given, even in such cases, should always allow for 'slippage'.
- **Question 29** is important because it gives the client the opportunity to explain:
  - why the arrears arose;
  - what circumstances were beyond her/his control;
  - why it would cause particular hardship if eviction were ordered;
  - why an expensive property was rented (if applicable).

  If the landlord is a social landlord, any breaches of the rent arrears pre-action protocol can be pointed out here (see p289).

What counts as rent arrears

In many cases, particularly when the local authority is landlord, some of what is claimed as rent arrears may not, in fact, be so. For example, amounts of overpaid HB that an authority wishes to recover may be added to a tenant's rent account as though they were arrears. In fact, even where such an amount has properly become payable (and the tenant has been given the rights of appeal),[123] such amounts do not constitute unpaid rent. They can be included in a tenant's rent account, provided they are clearly distinguished from rent that is owed to the authority, but should not appear on a claim form as rent arrears. However, in non-local authority tenancy cases, where HB has been paid direct to the landlord and the local authority has exercised its right to recover any HB overpayment direct from the landlord, the amount recovered can be treated as rent arrears.[124]

In some cases, tenants may also have amounts of rates (from before April 1990), water charges, rent arrears from a previous tenancy or other non-rent charges included in their rent arrears. These amounts should not appear on a claim form, unless they are specifically included in the rent for the client's home. Where the tenancy agreement provides not only for water charges to be collected by the landlord but also for them to be treated as rent, it may be possible to argue that this is an unfair term within the meaning of the Unfair Terms in Consumer Contracts Regulations because it creates the possibility of the client being evicted on the basis of arrears of water charges. As an unfair term is unenforceable, this would be a full or partial defence to the possession proceedings, depending on whether the arrears also include any 'true' rent.

The powers of the court in dealing with a possession action

There are a number of grounds on which possession may be sought when rent is unpaid and these differ slightly according to whether the tenant has a private or public landlord and whether her/his tenancy began before or after 15 January 1989. A debt adviser must be certain about the status of the client's occupancy before giving advice about a possession claim. For example, some occupiers who consider themselves tenants may, in fact, be licensees.

A client may receive a possession claim form on grounds that are not connected to a debt. This *Handbook* does not cover these matters. For a detailed explanation of all the grounds upon which possession might be sought, see *Defending Possession Proceedings* (see Appendix 2), or consult Legal Action Group or a specialist housing advice service such as Shelter.

The court's role in every case of arrears, except those of some assured tenants who are more than 13 weeks in arrears (see p297), is to decide whether or not it is 'reasonable' to make an order for possession and whether or not to suspend this on particular terms (usually payment of the normal rent plus an amount towards the arrears). This means that, as long as the tenant keeps to the payment ordered by the court, the landlord cannot regain possession of the property. In the case of tenants who are in receipt of IS, income-based JSA or pension credit (PC), offers of the direct deduction rate of £3.05 a week may be accepted by the court. If the tenant does not attend the hearing or there is no request for time to pay the arrears from her/him, the order may be made absolutely – ie, for possession to be given up in a certain period of time (minimum 14 days, maximum 42 days, but usually 28 days).

Since 25 March 2002 the court has been able to award fixed costs (instead of assessed costs) in all cases where a possession order is made and not just in cases where the possession order is suspended.

Arguing against a possession order (rent)

An outright possession order is not necessarily a breach of the tenant's human rights under Article 8 (respect for family and private life).[125]

A variety of arguments can, however, be used to demonstrate that it is 'unreasonable' to make a possession order. Note, however, that courts take into account the view that a landlord is entitled not only to the increase in capital value of her/his property but also to revenue from rent. A debt adviser should argue that the existence of an agreement to clear the arrears or even a reasonable offer coupled with an ability to pay the ongoing rent makes a possession order unnecessary (and, therefore, unreasonable).

Arguments can be based on the tenant's circumstances (eg, s/he has children, or is sick or disabled) or her/his finances (eg, s/he has been dependent on benefits for some time). If an improvement in circumstances can be shown – eg, s/he has just got, or is about to get, a job, this will probably help convince the court that it is unreasonable to make a possession order. Other arguments could be based on the position of the landlord – eg, the landlord's identity was unknown or s/he had failed to collect rent or arrange for an agent to do so.

Any defence the tenant offers may be assisted if s/he has begun to pay the contractual rent and something towards the arrears by the time the hearing takes place. Such payments should have been recorded by the landlord or, if the landlord has refused to accept payments prior to the court hearing, the money should have been paid into a separate account. Proof of payment made should be taken to the hearing.

If a tenant should have been getting HB but was not, or is waiting for the outcome of a claim, this can be a powerful argument for saying it is unreasonable to make an order, particularly if it is a social landlord. In addition, the rent arrears pre-action protocol says that the landlord should make every effort to establish effective ongoing liaison with the HB department and should also offer to assist the client with her/his HB claim, in particular, if s/he has:

- provided the local authority with all the evidence required to process her/his HB claim;
- a reasonable expectation of eligibility for HB; *and*
- paid any other sums due to the landlord that will not be covered by the HB claim.

The landlord should not only refrain from issuing possession proceedings on the grounds of rent arrears but should also (with the client's consent) make direct contact with the HB department.

The adviser should ask the court not to make a possession order or award costs against the client if arrears are solely due to unpaid HB and the proceedings have been issued in breach of the rent arrears pre-action protocol, as possession action was unnecessary (see p289).

If the landlord is not a local authority, the tenant can ask the court to consider making a third-party costs order against the local authority – ie, for the local authority to pay the landlord's costs. This can only be done if the local authority is:

- made a party to the proceedings for the purposes of costs only; *and*
- given a reasonable opportunity of attending the hearing for the court to consider the question.[126]

This obviously requires action to be taken prior to the possession hearing itself. A threat to seek an order for costs may prompt the local authority to expedite the HB claim and clear the arrears. Otherwise, if possible, the client should obtain a letter from the local authority explaining when HB will be paid and take this to the hearing.

Debt advisers sometimes agree to a suspended possession order on the ground that this is a technicality and does no more than safeguard the landlord's position. This is a very dangerous view. Until recently it was thought that, provided the client did not default on the standard form of suspended possession order in rent arrears cases (N28), any secure tenancy would continue. In *Harlow District Council v Hall* the Court of Appeal held that, once the date for possession specified in the order had passed (usually after 28 days) the tenancy ended and the client became a 'trespasser' and, consequently, lost many of the rights of a secure tenant. However, an order under which the date for possession was either deferred or postponed so long as the conditions imposed by the order on the payment of the arrears and current rent were complied with would not have that effect.[127]

Following a suggestion from the Court of Appeal, the standard form of suspended possession order in rent arrears cases is now the N28A. It is, in fact, not a suspended possession order, but a postponed possession order. It does not set a date for possession, but allows the landlord to apply to the court to fix a possession date in the event of the client defaulting on the order. However, the landlord must first give the client 14 days' notice of intention to apply and invite her/him to bring the arrears up to date or provide an explanation for their non-payment. The landlord's application can be dealt with without a hearing, although the court could list it for a hearing. If the court grants the application, a date for possession will be fixed (usually the next working day). The landlord still needs to issue a warrant of possession if the tenant does not leave the property voluntarily and the client can still apply to suspend the warrant (see p297).[128]

Assured tenants

The Housing Act 1988 created a new mandatory ground on which a court must make a possession order. This applies only to assured tenants (eg, of housing associations and private landlords) and thus to no one except previously protected shortholders, whose tenancy began before 15 January 1989. It requires a court to grant a possession order to a landlord if at the date of the hearing at least eight weeks' or two months' rent (three months' if paid quarterly) is unpaid. The landlord has to prove there was two months' rent in arrears (or three months' if paid quarterly) both at the time when the notice of seeking possession was served and at the date of the hearing, which need be only two weeks later.

There is no requirement for the court to consider reasonableness when this ground is used. Therefore, even if delays in the payment of HB caused the arrears, this could nonetheless lead to a possession order being granted, as the court has no power to adjourn where the mandatory ground has been made out except for procedural reasons or in exceptional circumstances.[129] In such a case, the adviser should pressure the local authority to make an emergency payment before the hearing and, if it fails to do so, local politicians and the local government Ombudsman should be informed. This ground will fail if the arrears are reduced by the date of the hearing to even a nominal amount (eg, £1) below two or three months' rent. It may sometimes be worthwhile borrowing money, particularly from family or friends, to ensure the tenant does not become subject to this mandatory ground. See also Chapter 6 for ways of maximising income.

Warrant of possession

Advisers should carefully check the wording of any suspended possession order to see whether it provides for the order to cease to have effect once the borrower/tenant has paid the arrears in accordance with its terms. In such a case, if the borrower/tenant then falls into arrears again, the lender/landlord will need to obtain a further order and will not just be able to issue a warrant of possession. Suspended orders on Form N28 (rent arrears) or N31 (mortgage arrears) do not contain such a provision, so the lender/landlord will only need to apply to the court for a further order if more than six years has elapsed since the date of the possession order.[130] However, the new form of suspended order (rent arrears) (N28A) (see above) does provide for the order to cease to be enforceable once the arrears are paid.

A warrant of possession gives county court bailiffs the power to evict the occupiers and change the locks (see Chapter 11). It is issued by the court following a request from the lender or landlord if the borrower/tenant has not voluntarily left the property by the date ordered by the court at a possession hearing or has not kept to the terms of a suspended order for possession. In order to prevent eviction, an application must be made for the warrant to be suspended (see p304).

The notice of eviction (Form N54) informs the tenant/borrower about this (see p281).

6. Preventing enforcement

Setting aside judgment

If a judgment is set aside, its effect is cancelled and the client and creditor are put back to the position they were in before judgment was obtained. This includes cancelling any enforcement action by the creditor.[131]

Part 13 Civil Procedure Rules deals with setting aside and varying the amount of (but not the rate of payment) a judgment entered in default. The following are 'mandatory grounds' for setting aside a default judgment – ie, the court 'must' do so if:

- judgment was entered before the client's time for filing an acknowledgement of service or a defence had expired (see p242); *or*
- the client served an admission on the creditor together with a request for time to pay before the judgment was entered (see p242); *or*
- the client paid the whole of the claim (including any interest or costs due) before judgment was entered. If the client paid the whole of the claim before the claim form was issued, s/he should have filed a defence – see p251.

The following are 'discretionary grounds' for setting aside a judgment – ie, the court may do so where:

- the client has a real prospect of success in the claim; *or*
- the court is satisfied that there is some other good reason why the judgment should be set aside/varied or the client allowed to defend the claim; *or*
- there has been an error of procedure, such as a failure to comply with a rule or practice direction.

Note: provided the claim form was served in accordance with the Civil Procedure Rules, the fact that the proceedings only came to the client's attention after judgment was entered is not a ground in itself for it to be set aside, even if the client alleges s/he did not receive the claim form. If the claim form was issued before 1 October 2008, provided it:

- was sent by the court to the client's usual or last known address; *and*
- has not been returned by the Post Office as undelivered,

it is treated as having been served in accordance with the Civil Procedure Rules.[132]

After 1 October 2008, the claim form is treated as having been served in accordance with the Civil Procedure Rules even if it is returned undelivered to the court, provided it was sent to the client's 'relevant address'. This is the client's usual or last known address unless:

- the creditor has reason to believe it is no longer the client's current address; *and*
- the creditor is able to establish the client's current address; *or*
- the creditor is unable to establish the client's current address, but considers there is an alternative place or method of service.

If the creditor has reason to believe that the client's usual or last known address is not her/his current address – eg, because letters have been returned marked 'gone away', the creditor is required to take reasonable steps to find out the client's current address. If the creditor is able to establish the client's current address, the claim form must be served at that address. Provided this is the client's current address, the claim form will be treated as having been served even if the client does not actually receive it or it is returned to the court.

If the creditor is unable to establish the client's current address, it must consider whether there is an alternative place or method of service and, if so, must ask the court to authorise service at that place or by that method. The creditor must be able to satisfy the court that the claim form is likely to reach the client if it is served at the place or by the method proposed. For example, if the adviser contacts the creditor stating that s/he is acting for the client, but is not authorised to disclose the client's current address, the creditor could ask the court to authorise the claim form to be sent to the adviser's agency. The Civil Procedure Rules also suggest that leaving a voicemail message stating where the document is could be an alternative method of service, provided the creditor can satisfy the court that the client uses that telephone number and is likely to receive the message. If the court agrees to the creditor's request, it will make an order specifying:

- the method or place of service;
- the date the claim form is treated as served; *and*
- the period the client will have to respond to the claim form.

The claim form will be treated as having been served by the alternative method or at the alternative place, even if it does not reach the client or is returned to the court. If the creditor is both unable to establish the client's current address and there is no suitable alternative place or method of service, the client's usual or last known address is still the relevant address (even though it is unlikely that the claim form will come to the client's attention) and a claim form sent to that address will be treated as having been served even if it does not reach the client or is returned to the court.

If the claim form is treated as served under one of the above rules, unless one of the mandatory grounds applies (see p298), if the client wants to apply for a set aside, one of the discretionary grounds will have to be relied on (see p298).[133]

On the other hand, if the claim form has not been properly served, the client can apply to have the judgment and any enforcement action set aside. In the usual case, the court can only refuse a set aside either if there has been no prejudice to the client or possibly if the client has been guilty of 'inexcusable delay', in making the application.[134]

If the application is made on a discretionary ground, the court must take into account whether or not the client acted promptly in making the application. When applying for a judgment to be set aside, the client should always try to find an argument based on the facts or law of the case (eg, 'I do not owe the money because the goods supplied under a linked agreement were of unsatisfactory quality'), rather than personal circumstances (eg, 'I did not know how to reply to the claim form'). Although not strictly required by the Civil Procedure Rules, the client should explain why s/he failed to respond to the claim form – eg, whilst failure to receive the claim form may not be a set-aside ground in itself, it could be a valid explanation for failing to respond. The onus is on the client to show the defence is a 'convincing' one as opposed to merely 'arguable'.

Unless the client wishes to defend the claim or the creditor has already taken enforcement action (which would also be cancelled), it may be preferable for the client to apply to vary or suspend the terms of payment of the judgment (see below). Applying to set aside a judgment does not automatically prevent or delay any enforcement action by the creditor. The application to set aside should also contain an application for a stay of enforcement pending the hearing, quoting Rule 3.1(2)(f) Civil Procedure Rules. Application is made on Form N244 and must be supported by the client's statement in Section 10 of the form. A fee of £75 is payable (see p237 for applying for full or partial fee remission). The case will be transferred to the client's local court.

If the client is seeking to set aside a county court judgment transferred to the High Court for enforcement, it seems that the application must still be made to the county court.[135] However, an adviser faced with this situation should seek specialist advice.

If the client has admitted the debt and judgment was entered on the basis of an N9A, the correct application is for permission to withdraw the admission under Rule 14.1(5) and defend the claim under Rule 3.1(2)(m). The N244 must also contain a request for transfer to the client's local court (where appropriate) (see p240) plus a request for a stay of enforcement.

IfIf there has been a hearing in the county court, the client can apply to have the order set aside and the matter re-heard if s/he did not attend the hearing and an order was made in her/his absence. The court will want to know why the client did not attend and whether there has been a miscarriage of justice. The court is unlikely to order a re-hearing if the client deliberately failed to attend or if the court is satisfied that there is no real prospect of the original order being changed.[136] The court will not allow an application for a re-hearing purely on the grounds that the client did not receive notice of the hearing date without enquiring as to why s/he did not receive it. On the other hand, the court should not refuse an application for a re-hearing just because s/he failed to provide the creditor or lender with a forwarding address. In general:

- if the client is unaware that proceedings are imminent or have been served, s/he will have a good reason for not attending any hearing;
- if the client knows of the existence of proceedings but does not have a system in place for receiving communications about the case, s/he is unlikely to have a good reason for not attending any hearing.[137]

Varying payments due under an order for money

If the decision on the rate of payment was made by the court, the procedure on p249 should be followed. If judgment was either entered in default or on acceptance of the client's offer of payment, the following procedures apply.

If the creditor believes s/he can persuade the district judge that the client can afford to increase her/his payments, s/he can apply for the rate of instalments to be increased. Application is made on an N244 (see p305) and the case is automatically transferred to the client's home court for a hearing (the determination procedure on p248 does not apply).[138]

Once an order for payment has been made, either in default or on acceptance of the client's offer of payment, the client can apply to the court that made it to have it varied at any time. S/he does not need a particular reason for making this application, although it will normally be because a change in circumstances means the original instalment order can no longer be afforded or because the original order was made in ignorance of some material fact. In the case of default judgments for immediate payment, a successful application for variation prevents the creditor from taking subsequent enforcement action, so long as the client complies with the terms of the variation order.

The variation can include changes either to the amount of instalments or their frequency and is made on Form N245, which is very similar to Form N9A (see p244 on how to complete this). The N245 should be sent to the court that made the judgment (if it is also being used to apply to suspend a warrant of execution, it should be sent to the enforcing court – see p303). If the N245 is being used to apply to suspend a warrant of execution, an application for variation should be made at the same time by ticking both boxes. A fee of £35 is payable to cover both applications (see p237 for details about full or partial remission).

The court sends a copy of the N245 to the creditor and if s/he does not respond within 14 days the variation *must* be granted in the terms applied for.[139] If the creditor objects within 14 days, a court officer will use the determination of means guidelines to decide what the order should be.

Once the variation order has been made, either the creditor or client has 14 days to apply to the court for a reconsideration if they do not agree with the terms (see p249). The case will automatically be transferred to the client's local court and a hearing arranged. At the hearing, the district judge can make whatever order s/he thinks just. When helping a client to apply for a variation order, it is helpful to send a letter to accompany the N245, with a copy to the creditor, outlining the reasons for the application, especially if this is the first contact the debt adviser has had with the creditor.

Not all courts follow the above rules for dealing with an N245. For example, some have failed to follow up the application, because for instance the creditor has applied for a charging order, or they have allowed considerably more than 14 days for the creditor to send objections. Advisers should keep a copy of the N245. Clients may wish to ask the court for a receipt or, if the N245 is to be posted, send it by special delivery or obtain a certificate of posting. Advisers should follow up applications which are not dealt within 21 days of the N245 being posted to, or filed at, the court.

If the order for payment was made by a court officer or the district judge without a hearing and the client is out of time to apply for redetermination, or it was made by the district judge at a hearing, the client can only apply to vary the order on the grounds of a change of circumstances (including information not previously before the court). The application is made on an N244 (see p305).[140] A fee of £35 is payable (see p237 for applying for full or partial fee remission). The case will not be automatically transferred to the client's local court and so an application for this will have to be included in the N244, quoting Rule 30.2(1) Civil Procedure Rules.

If the order for payment of the judgment was made in the High Court either in default or on acceptance of the client's offer of payment, the adviser should seek specialist advice.

Suspensions and stays

Applications on an N245 must include an offer of payment. If even a nominal sum cannot be found, the client can apply for the judgment to be 'suspended' or 'stayed' (see also p243 on N9A). A suspension is usually on terms – eg, so long as payments are made – and a stay is usually until an event occurs – eg, until a particular date. In practice, the terms seem to be interchangeable. Application should be on Form N244 (see p305). Applications are more likely to be accepted if there are compelling reasons – eg, serious mental or physical ill health or the client is in prison. A fee of £40/£75 is payable, depending on whether or not a hearing is requested, although the court might be persuaded to charge the lower fee of £35 on the basis that the application is 'to vary a judgment or suspend enforcement' (see p237 for details about full or partial fee remission). The case will not automatically be transferred to the client's local court and so an application for this will have to be made in the N244, quoting Rule 30.2(1) Civil Procedure Rules.

Suspension of a warrant of execution (for money)

If payments ordered under a judgment are missed and the creditor applies to the county court for bailiffs to enforce the debt, the client will receive a notice from the court warning that a warrant for the seizure of goods has been issued and giving a date after which it will be executed. Bailiffs may call at the home to try and take goods to sell (see p345 for details of the powers of county court bailiffs). Form N245 should be completed in order to suspend the warrant. The client should not only tick the box requesting 'suspension of the warrant' but also the box requesting 'a reduction in the instalment order' (even if the current terms of the judgment are for immediate payment). **Note**: the bailiffs can continue to attempt to seize goods until the application has been heard and a decision given. The N245 should be sent to the enforcing court, which will be the client's local court. A fee of £35 is payable, which covers both applications (see p237 for details about applying for full or partial fee remission).

The client could apply to have the matter stayed (see above). However, in order to prevent seizure of goods an offer of payment must be made on the N245, but this need only be a token amount (eg, £1 a month) if the client is realistically unable to afford payments. The debt adviser should write to the creditor and explain the client's circumstances. If payments cannot be afforded explain why such enforcement is not appropriate.

An offer of payment may not be appropriate when the client has no goods that could be seized (see p353 for excluded items) and there are no other methods of enforcement open to the creditor (eg, charging orders and attachment of earnings orders – see pp258 and 266). In these circumstances, the debt adviser should ask the creditor to consider writing off the debt.

Once the court receives Form N245, a copy is sent to the creditor, who has 14 days to agree to the client's proposal or not. If the creditor agrees with the proposal, the warrant is suspended and the client is ordered to pay the amount offered. If the creditor does not agree to suspension on any terms, a hearing will be arranged at the client's local court, where the district judge will decide whether or not to suspend the warrant and on what terms. If the creditor agrees with a suspension but not the proposed terms, the determination procedure described above for varying an order will be followed.

In some cases, county court judgments may (and in others, must) be enforced in the High Court. Once the adviser is aware that High Court bailiffs (known as enforcement officers) have been instructed, s/he should seek specialist advice.

Suspension of a warrant of delivery (hire purchase or conditional sale)

If the client wants to keep goods that are the subject of a hire purchase or conditional sale agreement, an application can be made on an N244 (see p305) to suspend the warrant. A financial statement should be supplied. The N244 should be sent to the enforcing court. A fee of £35 is payable (see p237 for details about full or partial fee remission). An offer of payment must be made that will realistically repay the agreement and arrears. A court is unlikely to agree to very small payments compared with the original contractual sum. If this is not possible, the debt adviser should try and re-negotiate with the creditor the payments due under the agreement, or consider a time order (see p283).

Varying the terms of a suspended or postponed possession order

If the repayments under a suspended order, or any other terms of an order, require a change, the borrower can apply back to the court for the order to be changed or varied. Application is on Form N244 (see p305). A fee of £35 is payable (see p237 for details on applying for full or partial fee remission). It is always better to apply to vary an order if circumstances have changed, rather than be served with a warrant and have to apply to suspend it. For example, if the borrower is on maternity leave, and therefore has a reduced income for a period, she could apply for a reduction in payments, or if the borrower unexpectedly finds employment s/he can apply for a possession order to be suspended because s/he can now make payments.

Suspension of a warrant of possession

Following the issue of a warrant, a notice of eviction on Form N54 will be sent or delivered from the court, stating a date and time when the bailiffs will evict the client from her/his property (see p281). The client can apply for a warrant of possession to be suspended at any time before the date and time specified on the warrant, although it is preferable to apply as early as possible.

An N244 should be completed (see p305), showing:

- how the client's circumstances have changed since the possession order (see p281) was made;
- that the equity or rental revenue of the creditor is not threatened by a suspension;
- a well-supported offer of payment, and a lump sum (or first payment) if possible;
- if the client does not wish to remain in the property, that arrangements are in hand for sale of the property or re-housing, but that this will take time.

Form N244 should be accompanied by a financial statement. A fee of £35 is payable (see p237 for details on applying for full or partial fee remission). If possible, take the form to the court rather than post it as there will be little time available.

If the lender or landlord issued the possession action using possession claims online and the client wants to make her/his application online, any court fee must be paid either by debit card or credit card. The possession claims online website contains a list of organisations through which the client can claim full or partial fee remission online. Otherwise, the N244 must be filed, and any application for fee remission must be made, in person.

A hearing will be granted almost immediately and the client must attend. A debt adviser should always try to negotiate directly with the creditor prior to the hearing and ensure that if an agreement has been reached, the details are communicated to the solicitor or agent who will be representing the creditor at the hearing. If possible, arrange for confirmation in writing so the client can take this to the hearing in case there is any dispute. If no agreement can be reached, the matter must be presented clearly before the district judge using similar arguments to those covered on pp279–281 (mortgages) and pp289–297 (rent). It may be necessary to ask for the payment order to be varied (reduced) to a level the client can afford at the same time.

In theory, there is no limit to the number of applications that can be made to suspend a warrant, but if the client persistently applies and then fails to make payments, the application may be refused and s/he may be told s/he cannot make any further applications without leave of the court. In this case, assuming that the application is realistic, the client must ask for leave of the court to apply, on an N244, before continuing on the same application to explain the reasons. The court will usually consider granting leave to apply first then, if granted, continue in the same hearing to consider the application for suspension.

If the application is refused, the eviction will usually take place on the date and time on the warrant. The client may ask for a short suspension, say two weeks, to find alternative accommodation. Alternatively, in mortgage cases, if repossession is granted, the borrower could ask to stay in the property while the mortgagee sells it (see p281).[141] After the execution of a warrant (eviction), no order for suspension can be made unless:

- the possession order itself is set aside (see p298); *or*
- the warrant was obtained fraudulently; *or*
- there had been an abuse of the process or oppression in the execution of the warrant.[142] It appears that 'oppression' is not limited to conduct by the creditor but can extend to conduct by the court – eg, misleading information from court staff on the procedure for suspending a warrant.[143]

Applications: Form N244

Part 23 of the Civil Procedure Rules deals with applications. Form N244 is prescribed for making applications. There are guidance notes to help complete the form, available from www.hmcourts-service.gov.uk.

- **Section 1** should be completed with details of the client's name (unless s/he has a solicitor acting for her/him).
- **Section 2** should usually indicate that the client is the defendant (unless, s/he has a solicitor acting for her/him or, exceptionally, s/he is the claimant).

- **Section 3** asks what order the client is seeking and why s/he is seeking the order. This information must be supplied.[144] The following are suggested wordings for some common applications.
  - **Redetermination/reconsideration:** The judgment be paid by instalments of £x per month because I cannot afford to pay at the rate determined.
  - **Variation:** Payment of the judgment debt be varied to £x per month because my circumstances have changed and I can no longer afford to pay at the rate ordered.
  - **Suspension:** Payment of the judgment debt be suspended under section 71(2) of the County Courts Act 1984 on the ground that I am no longer able to pay it because. . .
  - **Stay of enforcement:** Any enforcement proceedings against me be stayed until further order (Rule 3.1(2)(f) Civil Procedure Rules).
- **Section 4** asks whether a draft of the order being applied for has been attached. This will not usually be required unless the application is being made by consent.
- **Sections 5 and 6** ask for information about the application. The client must indicate whether or not s/he wants the court to deal with the application with or without a hearing or at a telephone hearing. If a hearing is requested, the court will fix a time and date and notify the parties at the same time as it serves the N244. Debt advisers should use their experience to estimate hearing times, but can just leave the box(es) blank. If no hearing is requested, the application is referred to a district judge to consider whether the application is suitable for consideration without a hearing. There is no advantage in asking the court to deal with the application without a hearing since the district judge may disagree and order a hearing anyway and the other party can apply to set aside or vary any order made without a hearing.[145] Debt advisers should only ask the court to deal with an application without a hearing if the application is one that will not automatically be transferred to the client's local court, and should also ask the court to exercise its discretion to transfer the case to the client's local court if it decides that a hearing should take place, quoting Rule 30.2(1). If it is not going to be possible (or will be extremely difficult) for the client to attend a hearing in person, it is possible to ask the court to arrange a telephone hearing. The N244 should indicate whether the client is seeking a telephone hearing (if it is the creditor or lender's application, the client can request a telephone hearing in writing).[146]
- **Section 7** should contain details of any hearing date already allocated for the case.
- **Section 8** should usually specify a district judge for the hearing.
- **Section 9** should usually specify the other party/ies as the persons to be served with the application.

- **Section 10** should indicate whether the client is relying on a witness statement, her/his statement of case – ie, the claim form, particulars of claim or defence, or the evidence set out in the box on the N244 in support of the application. Evidence is required in certain cases (eg, set-aside applications) and the court can always ask for evidence of facts in support of an application. The client will not usually have served a defence and so any facts that the client wishes the court to consider should be set out in the box and any written evidence referred to and attached – eg, a financial statement. The client should sign the statement of truth (see particulars of claim on p242) at the foot of the box. There is no need for a financial statement to contain a statement of truth.
- **Section 11** should be signed and dated and the details of the client's address completed.

Applications should be made as soon as the debt adviser realises that one is going to be necessary. Applications can be made at a hearing that has already been fixed (eg, for an application by the creditor) and can be made without using an N244, but the creditor and the court should be informed (if possible in writing) as soon as possible.[147]

Administration order

If the client has a judgment (either a county court or High Court judgment) and her/his total debts do not exceed £5,000, s/he should consider applying for an administration order (see p370).

Appeal to a judge

If a client disagrees with a judgment or order made by a district judge and none of the applications discussed above is applicable, the client must appeal if s/he wishes to challenge the judge's decision. The client may appeal to a circuit judge against any decision made in a county court by a district judge (unless it was made by consent) on the grounds that the decision was:

- wrong – eg, the district judge wrongly decided a legal issue or wrongly exercised her/his discretion by reaching a decision which no reasonable judge could have made; *or*
- unjust – ie, there was a serious procedural or other irregularity in the proceedings before the district judge.[148]

An appeal must be made on a point of law, not on such things as a change in the client's circumstances. If new evidence becomes available, this may be a ground for appeal where the court considers it would be in the interests of justice to hold a re-hearing.[149]

The client must obtain permission to appeal:

- verbally from the district judge at the end of the hearing; *or*

- if permission was refused or not applied for, to the circuit judge in the notice of appeal.

Permission will only be given if:
- the court considers that the appeal would have a real prospect of success; *or*
- there is some compelling reason why the appeal should be heard (the Civil Procedure Rules contains no guidance on when this might apply).

The district judge must give written reasons for granting or refusing of permission to appeal on Form N460.

Time limits

The notice of appeal must be filed:
- within the time specified by the district judge when granting permission verbally; *or*
- within 21 days of the date of the decision being appealed.[150]

An appeal must be made on a Form N161 (N164 in small claims cases). A fee of £120 (£100 on the small claims track) is payable (see p237 for details about applying for full or partial fee remission).

If an adviser has identified possible grounds of appeal, specialist advice/assistance will almost always be required.

Adjournments

An adjournment is a court order to delay a hearing either for a specified amount of time or indefinitely. The county court can, at any time, either adjourn or bring forward the date of a hearing. It can decide to do this itself or because one or both of the parties have applied.[151]

An application for an adjournment on the grounds of illness should be accepted, provided it is backed up by a sick note, unless there is evidence that the illness or medical evidence is not genuine. Similarly, if an important witness cannot be present, a district judge should adjourn a hearing. It is reasonable to grant an adjournment if there would otherwise be a miscarriage of justice. Thus, for example, if a client comes into an advice agency at 10am to ask for representation at a possession hearing a quarter of an hour later, it should be argued that there are (or may be) legal points which the court will need to hear and which cannot be adequately presented without further preparation. However, there will need to be some explanation of why the client has left it until the last minute to obtain advice or representation.

It is not a sufficient reason to adjourn a hearing simply because one (or even both) of the parties is not yet ready. Judges will often be impatient or suspicious of applications to adjourn which they believe are merely means to prolong an action in which they believe the creditor should succeed.

A district judge should consider the merits of an adjournment, whether or not one or both parties are requesting one. However, it is clearly much easier to get an adjournment if the creditor agrees and it is always worth contacting it or its representative before applying for one.

It is important, if possible, to attend court to make the application in case it is not granted. One of the main aims of the Civil Procedure Rules is to avoid delays in hearing cases. Judges can, therefore, be expected to be more reluctant to adjourn cases than previously. In a recent case, the Court of Appeal upheld the trial judge's refusal to grant an adjournment on the basis of the unavailability of an expert witness on the ground that another expert should have been instructed.[152] If the adjournment is being sought precisely because no one is available to represent the client and it is not opposed by the creditor, a letter (or fax) should be sent to the court explaining that this is the case and that no one will be attending. In such circumstances, if a court did proceed to make a decision other than to adjourn, an application should be made to set it aside (see p298) on the grounds that both sides had not been properly heard.

A matter can be adjourned either:

- to the next available date after a certain period (eg, 28 days); *or*
- generally, with liberty to restore.

Notes

1. **Introduction**

1 para 4 Protocol PD CPR
2 Published by Butterworths.
3 Barristers, solicitors and their employees, and people authorised by the Lord Chancellor to conduct litigation under s11 CLSA 1990
4 In *Derbyshire Home Loans v Keaney* (*Adviser* 124 abstracts), Bristol County Court stayed possession proceedings for two months to enable the borrower to pursue a possible complaint in view of the lender's failure to respond to his proposals.
5 For further details, see S Edwards, 'Fee or Free?', *Adviser* 125

3. **Action to recover money only**

6 Part 7 para 2 PD CPR
7 s176(2) and (3) CCA 1974; *Lombard North Central v Power-Hines* [1995] CCLR 24
8 r2.3(1) CPR
9 r6.14 CPR; *Anderton v Clwyd County Council* (*Adviser* 93 abstracts)
10 Parts 7C para 1.4 and 16 para 7.3 PD CPR
11 Part 5A PD CPR
12 Part 5B PD CPR. For further information, see www.hmcourts-service.gov.uk.
13 rs6.3(d) and 6.20(1)(d) and Part 6A para 4 PD CPR
14 Part 4 para 1.2 PD CPR
15 For a discussion on drafting separate financial statements, see P Madge, 'Till Debt Do Us Part', *Adviser* 71
16 r14.4(6) CPR
17 r14.9(2) CPR
18 *Determination of Means: guidelines for court staff,* Lord Chancellor's Department, revised April 2006
19 r3.2 CPR
20 Part 14 para 5.1 PD CPR

21 Advisers should refer court staff who query this to item 3.4.5, 'What Happens Next?' in *Determination of Means: guidelines for Court Staff,* Lord Chancellor's Department, revised December 1998
22 For more information about the use of witness statements and how to draft them, see G Smith, 'Keep Your DJ Happy', *Adviser* 109
23 r12.3 CPR
24 r12.5 CPR
25 r15.11 CPR
26 *Phoenix Finance Ltd v Federation International de l'Automobile, The Times*, 27 June 2002
27 See P Madge, 'Using the Overriding Objective', *Adviser* 96
28 Part 27 CPR
29 Part 28 CPR
30 Part 29 CPR
31 *ED&F Man Liquid Products Ltd v Patel* [2003] EWCA Civ 472 (*Adviser* 101 abstracts)
32 Parts 3 and 24 CPR
33 s69 CCA 1984; s35a SCA 1981
34 *Adamson v Halifax plc* [2002] EWCA Civ 1134 (*Adviser* 115 abstracts); *Socimer International Bank v Standard Bank* [2006] EWHC 2896 (Comm) (*Adviser* 121 abstracts)
35 s17 JA 1838
36 CC(IJD)O 1991
37 *Director General of Fair Trading v First National Bank* [2001] UKHL 52, 25 October 2001, unreported (*Adviser* 89 abstracts)
38 *Forward Trust v Whymark* [1989] 3 All ER 915, CA
39 rs12.6, 12.7 and 14.14 CPR. In the *First National Bank* case the House of Lords assumed the creditor could take further court action, but the point was not argued and so the issue remains unclear, at least so far as pre-1 October 2008 judgments are concerned.
40 s130(1) CCA 1974 allows the court to make a time order without hearing evidence of the client's means in cases where the creditor accepts the client's offer and this should also 'include' exercising its powers under s136.
41 s130A CCA 1974, as inserted by s17 CCA 2006
42 For further discussion of these issues, see P Madge, 'Interest After Judgment Under Regulated Consumer Credit Agreements', *Legal Action,* December 1990; P Madge, 'A Point of Interest', *Adviser* 59; P Madge, 'No Further Interest', *Adviser* 79; P Madge, 'Full Circle', *Adviser* 89; R Rosenberg, 'Interest After Judgment: is it the end of the road?', *Quarterly Account* 62
43 r70.2(2) CPR
44 s8 AEA 1971
45 r5 CCR 26; Sch 2 CPR; *Patel v Singh* [2002] EWCA Civ 1938 (*Adviser* 105 abstracts)
46 Order 8(1A) HCCCJO, as amended
47 See also P Madge, 'Charging Interest', *Adviser* 76
48 *Ropaigealach v Allied Irish Bank*, [2001] EWCA Civ 1790 (*Adviser* 90 abstracts)
49 Part 73 para 1.2 PD CPR
50 r73.5 CPR
51 s1(5) COA 1979
52 Part 73 para 3 PD CPR
53 r73.8 CPR. 'Written evidence' is a person's evidence set down in writing and signed to the effect that the maker of the statement believes the facts stated are true. See Part 32 PD CPR for the formalities of witness statements. Unless specifically required, an affidavit should not be used in preference to a statement.
54 *Mercantile Credit Co Ltd v Ellis, The Times*, 1 April 1987, CA, confirmed in *Ropaigealach v Allied Irish Bank,* [2001] EWCA CIV 1790 (*Adviser* 90 abstracts)
55 *Ropaigealach v Allied Irish Bank,* [2001] EWCA Civ 1790 (*Adviser* 90 abstracts)
56 Arguably, if the charging order application was made after the client applied for redetermination, the court had no jurisdiction to make an interim order as there was no judgment on which the client could default.
57 See P Madge, 'Charging On', *Adviser* 115
58 *Rainbow v Moorgate Properties* [1975] 2 All ER 821
59 See S Oyebitan and J Wilson, 'Where Now?', *Adviser* 97
60 s3(1) COA 1979
61 s71(2) CCA 1984 gives the county court power to suspend or stay any judgment or order on such terms as the court thinks fit.

62 r1.4(2)(i) CPR. Also, if a date has already been fixed for a hearing, any other applications should be dealt with at that hearing; Part 23 paras 2.8 and 2.10 PD CPR.
63 Alternatively, an additional term or condition could be requested in the witness statement submitted for the final charging order hearing that all other enforcement action is stayed provided the client pays instalments as ordered.
64 s3(5) COA 1979; r73.9 CPR
65 s3(4) COA 1979
66 *National Westminster Bank v King* [2008] EWHC 280 (Ch) (*Adviser* 128 abstracts)
67 Under s14 TLATA 1996
68 s15 TLATA 1996. These provisions do not apply if the client is the sole owner of the property, even if it is the family home; *Wells v Pickering* [2000] EWHC 2540 Ch (*Adviser* 96 abstracts)
69 *Bank of Ireland v Bell*, [2001] 2 FLR 809, CA
70 *Harman v Glencross* [1986] 1 All ER 545, CA
71 r70.3 CPR
72 s4(2) AEA 1971
73 s8(2) AEA 1971
74 rs18-22 CCR 27; Sch 2 CPR
75 *Mercantile Credit Co Ltd v Ellis, The Times,* 1 April 1987, CA
76 *Rainbow v Moorgate Properties* [1975] 2 All ER 821
77 r72.7 CPR
78 r2 CCR 39; Sch 2 CPR

4. Action to recover goods on hire purchase or conditional sale

79 s130(1) CCA 1974
80 s135 CCA 1974
81 s135(2) CCA 1974
82 Part 7B para 3.3 PD CPR

5. Action to recover property

83 In October 2008, the Council of Mortgage Lenders issued industry guidance on arrears and possession to assist lender to comply with MCOB 13 and their duty to treat customers fairly. It can be found at www.cml.org.uk.
84 Part 55para 2 PD CPR
85 Part 55 para 1.7 PD CPR
86 r30.2(1) CPR
87 Part 55 para 7.1 PD CPR
88 *Halifax Building Society v Taffs*, CA (*Adviser* 81 abstracts)
89 See C Evans, 'The New Rules are Working!', *Adviser* 79
90 For a discussion on how this might be applied in mortgage possession proceedings, see N Clayton, 'Mortgage Conduct of Business Rules and Mortgage Repossessions', *Quarterly Account* 8, IMA, Spring 2008
91 s36 AJA 1970 and s8 AJA 1973
92 r3.1(2)(b) CPR
93 See *Birmingham Citizens Permanent Building Society v Caunt* [1962] 1 All ER 163
94 These powers are unlikely to apply to 'all monies charges' securing a debt repayable on demand – eg, a bank overdraft, since the client will have to pay the whole outstanding balance within a 'reasonable period'; see *Habib Bank v Taylor* [1982] 1 WLR 1218, CA
95 *Royal Bank of Scotland v Elmes*, Clerkenwell CC (*Legal Action*, April 1998, p11); *Halifax plc v Salt & Bell*, Derby CC, 29 December 2007 (*Adviser* 127 abstracts)
96 *Cheltenham and Gloucester v Norgan* [1995] 28 HLR 443, CA
97 See for example, *Abbey National v Padfield*, Bristol CC, 26 July 2002 (*Adviser* 96 abstracts)
98 *Bristol & West Building Society v Ellis* [1996] 29 HLR 282, CA
99 *Target Home Loans v Clothier* [1993] 25 HLR 48, CA
100 *Cheltenham & Gloucester plc v Frasca*, Gloucester CC, 16 June 2003 (*Legal Action*, April 2004 p15)
101 *Cheltenham & Gloucester Building Society v Krausz* [1996] 29 HLR 597, CA
102 *State Bank of New South Wales v Harrison*, [2002] EWCA Civ 363 (*Adviser* 95 abstracts)
103 *Cheltenham & Gloucester v Booker* [1996] 29 HLR 634, CA
104 For a general discussion of the court's powers, see M Robinson, 'Mortgage Possession in the County Court', *Adviser* 123
105 s129(2)(a) CCA 1974
106 s38a AJA 1970
107 *Director-General of Fair Trading v First National Bank* [2001] UKHL 52, HL (*Adviser* 89 abstracts)
108 *Southern and District Finance v Barnes, The Times,* 19 April 1995, CA
109 s129(1) CCA 1974
110 s129(1) CCA 1974, as amended by s16 CCA 2006

111 r3.1(2)(m) CPR
112 PERG 4.17.2(G) (in the Regulatory Guides section of the FSA Handbook)
113 Part 55 para 7 PD CPR
114 s136 CCA 1974
115 *London North Securities v Meadows*, Liverpool CC, 28 October 2004, unreported (*Adviser* 107 abstracts); decision confirmed on appeal, [2005] EWCA Civ 956, CA (*Adviser* 111 abstracts)
116 s130(6) CCA 1974
117 See P Madge, 'Full Circle', *Adviser* 89 for a full discussion of the implications of the *First National Bank* decision.
118 *Cheltenham & Gloucester BS v Obi* [1996] 28 HLR 22, CA (*Adviser* 65 abstracts)
119 For a full discussion of this issue, see D McConnell, 'No Equity?', *Adviser* 53
120 Part 55 para 2 PD CPR
121 ss44 and 57 RA 1977
122 *Trevantos v McCullogh* [1991] 19 EG 18, CA
123 CPAG's *Welfare Benefits Handbook 2002/03*
124 Reg 93(2) HB Regs, as amended by SI 1997/65 from 7 April 1997
125 *Lambeth LBC v Howard*, 6 March 2001, CA (*Adviser* 88 abstracts)
126 r48.2 CPR; Part 19 contains the procedure for adding parties
127 *Harlow District Council v Hall* [2006] EWCA Civ 156 (*Adviser* 115 abstracts). For a full discussion of the implications of this case, see R Latham, 'Tolerated Trespassers: the problem and the solution', *Legal Action*, May 2006. The position is the same in the case of assured tenancies; *White v Knowsley Housing Trust* [2007] EWCA Civ 404
128 Part 55 para 10 PD CPR. For a discussion of the background to, and implications of, the new procedure, see J Gallagher, 'The Tolerated Trespasser: an endangered species?', *Quarterly Account* 4, Spring 2007
129 *North British Housing Association v Matthews* [2004] EWCA Civ 1736 (*Adviser* 109 abstracts)
130 r 17(6) CCR 26; Sch 2 CPR

6. **Preventing enforcement**

131 r70.6 CPR
132 *Adam v Akam* [2004] EWCA Civ 1601, CA (*Adviser* 108 abstracts)
133 rs6.9, 6.15 and 6.18 and Part 6 para 9 PD CPR. The rules allow the creditor to take steps to effect service at an alternative place or by an alternative method and ask the court to validate it retrospectively. Provided the court makes the order, the claim form will be treated as served.
134 *Nelson v Clearsprings Management Ltd* [2006] EWCA Civ 1252 (*Adviser* 119 abstracts)
135 s42(6) CCA 1984, which says that the county court's powers to set aside a judgment continue to apply.
136 r23.11 CPR
137 *Estate Acquisition and Development v Wiltshire* [2006] EWCA Civ 533 (*Adviser* 118 abstracts)
138 r10(3) and (4) CCR 22; Sch 2 CPR
139 r10(7) CCR 22; Sch 2 CPR
140 Part 14 para 6 PD CPR
141 *Cheltenham & Gloucester Building Society v Booker*, [1996] 29 HLR 634, CA
142 *Hammersmith & Fulham LBC v Hill*, *The Times*, 25 April 1994, CA; see also *Cheltenham & Gloucester Building Society v Obi* [1994] 28 HLR 22, CA
143 *Hammersmith & Fulham LBC v Lemeh*, 3 April 2000, CA (*Adviser* 83 abstracts); *Lambeth LBC v Hughes*, 8 May 2000, CA (*Adviser* 84 abstracts)
144 r23.6 CPR
145 Part 23 para 2.4 PD CPR
146 Part 23A para 6 PD CPR
147 Part 23 paras 2.10 and 3(5) PD CPR
148 r52.11(3) CPR
149 r52.11(1)(b) CPR
150 r52.4 CPR
151 r3.1(2)(b) CPR
152 *Rollinson v Kimberley Clark Ltd*, *The Times*, 22 June 1999, CA

Chapter 10

The magistrates' court

This chapter covers:

The magistrates' court is best known as the first tier of the criminal justice system. Its decisions are made by magistrates. Magistrates have traditionally been lay volunteers – ie, unpaid and not legally qualified, although it is increasingly common for them to be full time and paid, particularly in London and urban areas. Paid magistrates are called district judges (previously, stipendiaries) and are either barristers or solicitors. Lay magistrates depend on their legally qualified clerks in much of their decision making. A justices' clerk, who is a qualified barrister or solicitor, is present at all hearings to direct the way the hearing proceeds and to advise the magistrates on the law and procedure, on the penalties available and any guidance on their use, but should not otherwise take any part in the proceedings.

The administration of magistrates' courts in England and Wales is the responsibility of Her Majesty's Courts Service (the Courts Service), part of the Ministry of Justice (formerly the Department for Constitutional Affairs). The Courts Service operates through a structure of seven areas and 42 regions, each headed by a director who manages delivery of local services. A justices' chief executive makes arrangements for the efficient and effective administration of the individual magistrates' court. This includes allocating responsibilities to the justices' clerks and other magistrates' court staff, such as issuing summonses, timetabling hearings, collecting payments (eg, fines) and conducting means enquiries. S/he is required to arrange for the justices' clerks to discuss matters of law (including practices and procedures) in order to ensure the advice given to the magistrates themselves is consistent. The chief executive and the justices' clerk may be, and often is, the same person.

Each Courts Service area has an enforcement manager. Fines officers are court staff with powers to enforce fines. Since the implementation of the Courts Act

2003, many decisions regarding fines enforcement that used to require court hearings (such as applications for further time to pay and deciding the enforcement action in cases of default) are now dealt with by fines officers.

This chapter looks at how the magistrates' court operates as a creditor, or collector of other people's debt, and discusses how the debt adviser should proceed when advising on such debts as:

- financial penalties – eg, fines;
- local taxes – eg, council tax;
- maintenance;
- civil debts, particularly Crown debts.

The law on fines enforcement is in the Magistrates' Courts Act 1981, the Courts Act 2003, the Fines Collection Regulations 2006 and Part 52 of the Criminal Procedure Rules. From April 2004, a new fines collection scheme was tested in a series of local and national pilots. The final scheme has been in place since July 2006.

In relation to the court itself, the debt adviser's role is predominantly to prepare a financial statement and list of debts for the client to take to court hearings and perhaps a letter explaining her/his circumstances.

The adviser may represent the client or act as a 'McKenzie Friend' (ie, a person who accompanies the client to the hearing, advises her/him, suggests what s/he should say and makes notes of the proceedings). Advisers should check local practice to see whether they are allowed to represent clients. Sometimes, the adviser will need to liaise with probation staff or solicitors, particularly in respect of unpaid fines. It will be helpful to establish links between the advice agency and the probation service so that once the adviser has produced the financial statement and details of debts, the client can be put in touch with the probation service for assistance and support at the court hearing. Probation officers and assistants are normally based at the court. Some advice agencies now staff help desks at their local magistrates' courts.

If a committal warrant has been issued for the client to be imprisoned (see p328), it is usually advisable to obtain good legal representation for her/him. Free legal representation is now available at committal hearings.

1. Financial penalties

A fine is the most common penalty imposed by magistrates' courts in criminal cases. Magistrates can also make costs and compensation orders (see p331). These are all known as 'financial penalties'. The client may be required to complete a means enquiry form (available from the court office), although many clients who plead guilty and ask the court to deal with the matter in their absence do not provide information about their means. When setting financial penalties the court must take account of the offender's financial circumstances. The court will also take into account any mitigating circumstances, and there is a reduction for a guilty plea. If the court has officially requested the client to supply a statement of her/his financial circumstances and s/he has failed to do so, it can 'draw an adverse inference' about her/his ability to pay – ie, assume s/he has the means and fine accordingly.[1] In cases where both a fine and compensation cannot be paid, the court should order compensation (see p331) rather than a fine. Costs are at the discretion of the court, but are usually ordered and fixed at the time.

When imposing a financial penalty the court can order:

- immediate payment; *or*
- payment within a fixed time; *or*
- payment by instalments.

Magistrates' courts are discouraged from inviting applications for time to pay and will usually ask the client how much can be paid immediately. The court can search the client for any money that could be used to meet the financial penalty, but this power is rarely used.

The court can only order imprisonment in default of immediate payment if:

- the offence is imprisonable and the client appears to have sufficient means to pay immediately; *or*
- the client is unlikely to remain long enough in the UK to enable other enforcement methods to be used; *or*
- the client is already serving a prison sentence (known as 'lodging' the financial penalty); *or*
- the client is sentenced to imprisonment by the court for the same, or another, offence.

Financial penalties should generally be capable of being paid within 12 months. This is not a fixed rule, but the period should not exceed two to three years.[2] If the client is unable to do this, it suggests that either there has been a change of circumstances since the penalty was imposed or that it was fixed without adequate financial information.

Some years ago, the High Court expressed concern at the level of fines imposed on benefit claimants. Recognising that income support is only sufficient for the necessities of life and a small but regular payment towards financial penalties might be possible over a short period of time, but contingencies might occur which would stretch a tight budget to breaking point, Lord Justice Staughton recommended that fines on people of limited means should be less, so they could be paid in a matter of weeks.[3] In either case, the debt adviser should consider asking for all or part of the financial penalty to be remitted – ie, totally or partially written off at a means enquiry (see p327). However, when making an application (either for further time to pay or remission), the adviser should bear in mind not only that financial penalties are a priority debt, but that they were imposed as a punishment and this affects the court's attitude to their recovery. Non-payment of a fine can be viewed as an attempt to avoid punishment, and so the Government has set itself the aim of making fines collection more effective, with the stated aim of improving public confidence in the criminal justice system.

The revised fines enforcement scheme attempts to remove the need for hearings by giving fines officers an increased role in deciding on the level of instalments and the enforcement step(s) to be taken. Once the fine has been imposed, obtaining a hearing before the magistrates is likely to happen only if the client appeals against a decision of the fines officer or if the fines officer refers the matter to the magistrates following a number of unsuccessful attempts to enforce the fine.

Payments are applied by the court in the following order:

- compensation orders;
- costs;
- fines.

This will be relevant to any term of imprisonment the client is ordered to serve if s/he defaults on payment and also to the question of remission. It is also relevant to the collection of Crown Court fines in the magistrates' courts, since the Crown Court will already have fixed the term of imprisonment the client is to serve for defaulting on the payment of the fine, but not of any costs or compensation. Although the sentence can be reduced proportionately by part payment or remission, the magistrates have no power to vary the actual sentence.

Problems can also arise if a client has more than one fine or compensation order. Courts do not always make it clear to clients how their payments will be applied, which can lead to enforcement action being taken on one matter, even though regular payments are being made in respect of another. Financial penalties can be paid either:

- consecutively, with the client allowed to clear the oldest first with no enforcement action taken on later ones; *or*
- concurrently, and payments credited to each outstanding financial penalty.

The client should be advised to request whichever method is in her/his best interests.

Debt advisers are likely to be concerned with the client's difficulty in paying financial penalties after they have been imposed, rather than with the conditions attached on the day of sentence. Advisers may, therefore, find themselves being required to negotiate with the fines officer or the bailiffs concerning unpaid financial penalties.

Re-opening a case

A magistrates' court may vary or even rescind a sentence or other order imposed or made by it (but not a sentence or order made by the Crown Court) if it appears to be in the interests of justice to do so.[4] Although discretionary, this could be a speedy and effective means of cancelling or reducing a financial penalty that has been wrongly imposed or is demonstrably too high, as there is no time limit on making the application and the client does not have to show any change of circumstances since the financial penalty was imposed.

In addition, if the case was dealt with in the client's absence and s/he had no knowledge of the summons or the proceedings, s/he can make a statutory declaration to this effect, which will result in the conviction being rendered void and the financial penalty being set aside. There will be a new hearing and so this option needs to be carefully considered.[5] The statutory declaration must be delivered to the magistrates' court within 21 days of the proceedings first coming to the client's knowledge. There is discretion to extend the time limit if the court decides it was not reasonable to expect the client to comply with it.

If either of these options is being considered, the client should be referred to a solicitor. If neither of the above applies and the client maintains her/his innocence of the offence(s), s/he should be referred to a solicitor for a possible appeal or application for judicial review. There are quite short time limits.

Enforcement procedure

Collection order

A magistrates' court that is either imposing a new financial penalty or enforcing payment of an unpaid financial penalty must make a collection order, unless it is impracticable or inappropriate to do so – eg, if the court has no information about the client's financial situation. The collection order sets out:

- a breakdown of the sum due – ie, the amount of the fine and/or compensation order and/or costs;
- whether the client is an 'existing defaulter' – ie, has already defaulted on payment of another financial penalty and, if so, whether that default can be disregarded;
- whether an attachment of earnings order or application for deductions from benefits has been made and, if so, the repayment terms that apply if the order or application fails ('reserve terms'). If not, the payment terms;
- which fines office will deal with the case; *and*
- the consequences of default.

The client is an existing defaulter

If the client is an existing defaulter and has failed to show the court there was an adequate reason for the default, the court must:

- make an attachment of earnings order if the client is in employment, provided it is not impracticable or inappropriate to do so; *or*
- apply to the Secretary of State to make deductions from benefits if the client is in receipt of income support (IS), income-based jobseeker's allowance (JSA),

income-related employment and support allowance (ESA) or pension credit (PC), provided it is not impracticable or inappropriate to do so.

If a fixed penalty has been registered in the magistrates' court for enforcement, the client is deemed to have no adequate reason for default so that the first enforcement condition will be satisfied automatically. If the client is in employment and entitled to a relevant benefit, the court can either make an attachment of earnings order or a request for deductions from benefit, but cannot do both.

There is no guidance on the meaning of 'impracticable or inappropriate'. It could include situations where the court has no information about the client's financial circumstances or where, for example, there is an existing council tax attachment of earnings order and the client would be left with insufficient income to meet essential expenses if another order were made. In the case of deductions from benefits, it could include a case where deductions were already being made from the client's benefit for debts with a higher priority.

If the court is satisfied the client has shown an adequate reason for her/his default, an attachment of earnings order or application for deductions from benefits can still be made, but only if the client consents, unless the financial penalty consists solely of (or includes) a compensation order. If it does, the court must make an attachment of earnings order or an application for deductions from benefits, unless it is impracticable or inappropriate to do so.

Attachment of earnings orders made in the magistrates' courts are not made in the same way as those made in the county court (see p264). Instead, fixed deductions are made from the client's net earnings using the percentage deductions in the table below.

Net earnings			
Monthly	*Weekly*	*Daily*	*Deduction rate*
Up to £220	Up to £55	Up to £8	0%
£220.01 to £400	£55.01 to £100	£8.01 to £15	3%
£400.01 to £540	£100.01 to £135	£15.01 to £20	5%
£540.01 to £660	£135.01 to £165	£20.01 to £24	7%
£660.01 to £1,040	£165.01 to £260	£24.01 to £38	12%
£1,040.01 to £1,480	£260.01 to £370	£38.01 to £53	17%
£1,480.01 and over	£370.01 and over	£53.01 and over	17% of this threshold and 50% of the remainder

Attachment of earnings orders for fines take priority over existing attachment of earnings orders for payment of judgment debts or administration orders, but have equal priority with other attachment of earnings orders – eg, for council tax arrears. Employers are required to deal with such priority orders in date order. The client's net earnings are calculated after making the deductions due under previous orders. If the client has more than one fine, they can be collected through a consolidated attachment of earnings order and so the client should be advised to contact the fines officer and ask for this to be arranged.

The court can apply to the Secretary of State for Work and Pensions to deduct payments towards a financial penalty from the client's IS, PC or JSA. The amount that can be deducted is £5 a week. Fines have low priority, however, and deductions can only be made in respect of one application at a time. If the client is likely to experience hardship as a result of the deduction being made, the adviser should consider making written representations to the Secretary of State not to enforce the court's application.

If a client does not want an attachment of earnings order or deductions from benefit, the adviser should check whether s/he has any outstanding financial penalties before a magistrates' court hearing and, if so, either advise her/him to bring her/his payments up to date or to provide the court with an explanation of the default and of the possible adverse financial consequences of any attachment of earnings order or request for deductions from benefits.

The client is not an existing defaulter

The collection order sets out the terms on how payment of the financial penalty is to be made (see p317). An attachment of earnings order or request for deductions from benefits can only be made if the client consents, unless the financial penalty consists solely of (or includes) a compensation order. If it does, the court must make either an attachment of earnings order or an application for deductions from benefits, provided it is not impracticable or inappropriate to do so. Where appropriate, clients should be advised to resist pressure to agree to such a course of action in favour of voluntary payments.

Varying the terms of a collection order

The client will be sent a copy of the collection order. Providing s/he has not defaulted on the payment terms, s/he can contact the fines officer and ask to vary the order on the ground that there has been a change in her/his circumstances since the collection order was made (or last varied), or that s/he is making further information available regarding her/his circumstances. This could be useful if there has been no change of circumstances, but the client did not provide full information about her/his financial circumstances on a previous occasion. The fines officer can require the client to provide a statement of her/his financial circumstances in connection with the request. It is an offence not to comply with such a requirement. There is no limit to the number of times a client can ask for variation. There is right of appeal against the fines officer's decision to the magistrates' court within 10 working days (see p325).

The attachment of earnings order fails

If the attachment of earnings order or application for deductions from benefits fails – eg, the client leaves her/his employment or the Department for Work and Pensions (DWP) is unable to comply with the request because of prior deductions, the fines officer must send the client a 'payment notice' informing her/him:

- the order (or request) has failed;
- the reserve terms in the collection order now have effect;
- what s/he must do to comply with the reserve terms;
- of her/his right to apply to vary the reserve terms.

The client can contact the fines officer and ask to vary the order on the grounds that there has been a change in her/his circumstances since the reserve terms were set (or last varied), or that s/he is making further information available regarding her/his circumstances. The fines officer can require the client to provide a statement of her/his financial circumstances in connection with the request. It is an offence not to comply with such a requirement. There is no limit to the number of times the client can ask for a variation, provided the fines officer has not issued a 'further steps notice' (see below). There is right of appeal against the fines officer's decision to the magistrates' court within ten working days (see p325).

The client defaults on the collection order

The client will be in default on the collection order if s/he fails to comply with the payment terms (or, if they have taken effect, the reserve terms). The fines officer may refer the case back to the magistrates' court or decide to enforce payment her/himself. Providing there is no outstanding request to the fines officer to vary the reserve terms or appeal to the magistrates about a previous decision of the fines officer on a request to vary the reserve terms, the fines officer can send a 'further steps notice', setting out which of the following steps the fines officer intends to take:

- issue a warrant of distress (see p321);
- register the financial penalty in the Register of Judgments, Orders and Fines (see p323);
- make an attachment of earnings order or request deductions from benefits (see p318);
- make a clamping order (see p323);
- apply to have the financial penalty enforced in the High Court or the county court (see p325).

There is a right of appeal against the fines officer's decision within ten working days (see p325). Advisers should always contact the fines officer immediately if there are arrears on an order as it may be possible to agree a new payment arrangement, particularly where the financial penalty can still be paid within the original period allowed by the court.

Distress warrants

The court can issue a distress warrant against the client's money and goods if s/he fails to pay as ordered by the court.[6] Although there is now more emphasis on the use of attachment of earnings and deductions from benefits, distress warrants are frequently the first enforcement method used. This is because many financial penalties are imposed in the offender's absence, with the court having no information about her/his means.

No hearing is required before a distress warrant is issued, although the court can postpone its issue if it wishes.[7] There is no requirement to hold a means enquiry before issuing a distress warrant,[8] but if there is evidence the client has sufficient assets to pay the debt, the magistrates should use distress rather than committal.[9]

The Courts Service has national contracts with a handful of private bailiffs firms to execute distress warrants. Since 18 July 2005, bailiffs collecting financial penalties (but not other debts) can use reasonable force, if necessary, to enter and search any premises if it is reasonably required.[10] This power, however, is rarely used.

Information about the bailiffs' contracts is available at: www.justice.gov.uk/foi-private-enforcement.htm. Bailiffs should not attempt to levy distress without referring back to the magistrates' court if the client:

- is in a hospital or nursing home;
- appears to have a severe physical, or any mental, disability;
- is an elderly person who has difficultly dealing with her/his affairs;
- has a long-term sickness, or serious or acute illness or frailty which has resulted in a recent period of hospitalisation, or s/he is housebound;
- has had a recent bereavement of a close/immediate family member;
- is heavily pregnant (no period of weeks is suggested and so it is a matter for the bailiff's discretion);
- has a genuine communication problem (there is no definition of this and so is a matter for the bailiff's discretion);
- produces evidence to show the 'account' has been paid (once the warrant is with the bailiffs, the court will not accept any payment from the client and will refer any offers of payment to the bailiffs); *or*
- claims to have made a statutory declaration to set aside the conviction (see p316).

The bailiffs should refer back to the court if they have doubts about the identity of the client or in any other circumstances if the bailiff considers it would be 'prudent' to do so (no examples or guidance are provided, but the *National*

Standards for Enforcement Agents include lone parents and unemployed people in its list of potentially vulnerable people).

The bailiff may not seize bedding or clothes belonging to the client or any member of the client's family, or the tools, books, vehicles or other equipment which the client personally needs to use in her/his employment, business or vocation. Rule 52.8(6) Criminal Procedure Rules 2005 lays down a more restrictive list of exempt goods than applies to most other debts. In addition, under their contract, bailiffs must not seize goods that:

- may be necessary to maintain the 'core of life' (this is not defined and so is left to the bailiff's discretion, but examples include the only cooking facility, and an item of heating or storing food); *or*
- are clearly identifiable as 'children's items'; *or*
- are tools, books, vehicles and other items of equipment that are necessary for the client to use personally in her/his job or business (broadly mirroring the statutory requirements).

Under their contract, bailiffs are given a timescale for collecting financial penalties, and the financial penalty must be paid before the bailiffs can take their own fees. The bailiffs' fees are laid down in the contract between the bailiffs' firms and the Courts Service. The scales can be viewed at www.dca.gov.uk/rights/dca/inforeleased/ir061124.pdf.

Full payment of both the financial penalty and costs is expected within 60 days of the first visit to the client or 90 days from the issue of the warrant. This means the bailiffs may refuse the client's offer of instalments and press for payment at a rate the client clearly cannot afford. A client may, therefore, want to ask the court for further time to pay after a distress warrant has been issued. Whether or not this can be done is a 'grey' area.

Although the High Court has held that the magistrates' court is not able to suspend or cancel such a warrant after it has been issued,[11] it has been pointed out in another High Court case that magistrates may be able to review the situation under s142 Magistrates' Court Act 1980 on the basis that it is 'in the interests of justice to do so' (see p316).[12] The Government's view is that this can only be used to correct an error in the actual sentence or order and cannot be used to affect the way the sentence (in this case, the financial penalty) is enforced. The contract only allows the court to withdraw a warrant if there is evidence that the client is vulnerable and that enforcement would either not be in the interests of justice or might bring the process into disrepute.

The bailiff will return the warrant to the court if:

- the bailiff is unable to make contact with the client after a minimum of three visits; *or*
- the bailiff is unable to obtain payment; *or*
- there are insufficient goods, or all the goods are in one or more of the categories listed above; *or*

- the client is identified as being in one of the categories listed on p322.

For more details on bailiffs, see Chapter 11.

Registration of the financial penalty

Registration in the Register of Judgments, Orders and Fines means that information about the client's default is available to credit reference agencies and may affect the client's ability to obtain credit. The entry must be cancelled:

- if the financial penalty is paid within a month of being registered;
- if the client's conviction is set aside or reversed;
- if the financial penalty has been remitted in full;
- five years after the date of the client's conviction.

Clamping orders

Before the magistrates' court or the fines officer can make a clamping order, they must be satisfied that:

- the client has the means to pay the financial penalty; *and*
- the value of the vehicle(s) is likely to exceed the amount of the financial penalty plus the likely charges due and estimated costs of sale.

It is not clear exactly what is meant by 'has the means to pay'. The natural meaning of the words is that the client must be in a position to pay the financial penalty immediately. As a client will always have at least ten days' warning of the possibility of a clamping order being made, s/he will have the opportunity to either remedy the default or demonstrate that one or both of the conditions is not satisfied.

A copy of the order must be sent to a clamping contractor who, if payment is not made, is required to execute the order on or after the date specified within a period of 60 days (which can be extended by the court to 90 days). The copy sent to the clamping contractor must be accompanied by details of the client's last known address, the vehicle and, if known, the likely whereabouts of the vehicle to be clamped.

The clamping contract is part of the contract agreed between the Courts Service and bailiffs' firms. The scales of charges can be viewed at www.dca.gov.uk/rights/dca/inforeleased/ir061124.pdf.

Vehicles may be clamped at any place (including on any highway or road) to which the public has access or on any private land to which access may be had at the time of clamping without opening or removing any door, gate or other barrier. The contractor may enter any such place (with a vehicle if necessary) in order to clamp a vehicle, release it from clamping or remove it for storage.

A vehicle cannot be clamped if:

- it is not registered in the client's name under the Vehicle Excise and Registration Act 1994;

- a current disabled person's badge is displayed on it, or there are reasonable grounds for believing it is used to carry a disabled person;
- it is used for police, fire or ambulance purposes;
- it is being used by a doctor on call away from her/his usual place of work, and a British Medical Association badge or other health emergency badge showing the doctor's address is displayed on it.

The contractor must ensure that members of staff engaged on clamping operations are dressed in an identifiable uniform with an identification card attached to the uniform in a prominent position. In the event of a complaint by the client in connection with the clamping, removal or storage of a vehicle, the contractor must give her/him a leaflet about the company's complaints procedure.

The contractor's office where payment of the fine and the charge(s) due is made must be readily accessible from the place where the vehicle is clamped during all hours when the contractor undertakes clamping and for at least two hours thereafter. Once the fine and charge(s) have been paid in full, the vehicle must be released from clamping or storage within:

- four hours of the time of payment, if payment is made at or to the contractor's office or the court; *or*
- two hours of the time of payment, if payment is made to a member of the contractor's staff.

Payment must be accepted by cash, cheque (up to the amount specified on the payer's debit card or cheque guarantee card) or credit card (up to the credit limit for which the card is valid). If full payment is not made, it will first be applied towards payment of the charges and the balance towards the financial penalty.

Unless released, the vehicle must remain clamped for up to a maximum of 24 hours, after which the contractor removes the vehicle to secure premises for storage. The contractor must notify the client and the fines officer of the vehicle's new location. If this does not result in payment, the contractor must refer the matter back to the court.

If the fine has not been paid in full and ten clear working days have elapsed since the date the vehicle was clamped, the fines officer must apply in writing to the court (and send a copy of the application to the client) for an order to sell the vehicle. **Note:** although either the magistrates' court or fines officer can make a clamping order, only the magistrates can order the actual sale of the vehicle. The application must not be listed for hearing until 21 days have elapsed.

When considering whether or not to order the sale of the vehicle, the magistrates' court must consider the history of the case, in particular whether the clamping order was justified, reasonable and proportionate. If the court decides the vehicle should not be sold, it may direct the vehicle to be released, either with or without liability for payment of the charges due. If the court makes an order for sale, the fines officer must send a copy of the order for sale to the contractor who will arrange for the vehicle to be sold by an agent or by auction (unless the client makes full payment in the meantime).

When the vehicle has been sold, the contractor must first deduct from the net proceeds of the sale the charges due for the clamping, removal and storage. The fines officer will then deduct an amount sufficient to discharge the client's liability in respect of the fine from the remaining balance, and must send the client a cheque for any balance remaining within ten working days of the date of sale of the vehicle, accompanied by a written statement of account.

If the net proceeds of sale are not sufficient to meet the amount of the fine and charges due, the net proceeds of sale must first be put towards meeting the charges due and then, if a balance remains, towards discharging the client's liability in respect of the fine. The fines officer must then seek to recover the outstanding amount of the fine under the collection order and the powers available under it, including the power to refer the case to the magistrates' court.

Complaints about making the clamping order and its content must be made to the fines officer. Complaints about its execution or the removal or storage of the vehicle must be made to the contractor's senior manager. If the client is dissatisfied with the outcome of the complaint, s/he has ten working days to ask for the matter to be referred to the magistrates' court. A hearing will be arranged at which the magistrates can make whatever decision it thinks fit.

High Court and county court orders

The fines officer may apply to the High Court or a county court for orders only available in these courts – eg, a third-party debt order, charging order or appointment of receiver.[13] Such an application is unlikely to be made unless the fines officer believes that none of the other available collection methods are likely to be successful, but a High Court/county court remedy is.

Powers of magistrates' court on appeals and referrals

The client can appeal to the magistrates' court within ten working days (ie, excluding Saturdays and Sundays, Christmas Day and Good Friday and bank holidays) against a fines officer's decision:

- on an application to vary the terms of a collection order;
- on an application to vary reserve terms;
- to issue a further steps notice.

On an appeal, the magistrates' court may:

- confirm or vary the payment terms (or any reserve terms);
- confirm, quash or vary a further steps notice;
- discharge the collection order and exercise any of its standard powers (see below).

On a referral to the magistrates' court by the fines officer, the magistrates can:

- confirm or vary the payment terms (or any reserve terms);
- discharge the collection order;
- exercise any of the powers referred to in this chapter.

By discharging the collection order the court retains the control of the collection and enforcement process itself rather than delegating it to the fines officer. The 'standard powers' given to the magistrates are much wider than the powers given to fines officers, although some of the powers can be exercised by both.

If a fines officer refers the case to the magistrates' court either instead of issuing a further steps notice or after taking any of the steps listed in it, the magistrates may increase the fine (but not any other part of the financial penalty) by 50 per cent, provided the magistrates are satisfied that the client's default on the collection order is due to her/his 'wilful refusal or culpable neglect'. The increase is enforced as if it were part of the fine.

To ensure the client attends a referral hearing, the fines officer may issue a summons directing her/him to attend the magistrates' court at a specified time and place. If the client fails to attend, the court will issue a warrant for her/his arrest by a civil enforcement officer. The warrant is either with or without bail – ie, the client is either bailed to attend court, or is arrested and brought before the court. If an adviser discovers a client is subject to a warrant without bail, s/he should advise her/him to surrender her/himself to the court on a day when the court is sitting to deal with fine defaulters, and prepare a financial statement for the client to take with her/him.

Standard powers of magistrates' courts

The following are the standard powers available to the magistrates' court, some of which can be exercised by the fines officer without referring to the magistrates. Others can only be exercised by the magistrates themselves – eg, the power to imprison or detain fine defaulters and to remit (write off) fines. Magistrates can:

- issue a distress warrant (see p321);
- issue a summons/warrant for arrest (see p328);
- make an attachment of earnings order (see p318);
- apply for deductions from benefits (see p319);
- search a client (see p315);
- apply for enforcement in the High Court or county court (see p325);
- order a means enquiry (see p327);
- remit a fine (see p327);
- fix a return date (see p327);
- issue a money payments supervision order (see p328);
- imprison a client aged 21 or over (see p328);
- order a client to be detained (see p329);
- issue an attendance centre order for clients aged 18 to 21 (see p330);
- issue an unpaid work order (see p330).

Means enquiry

Before the court can take certain types of enforcement action it must enquire into the client's ability to pay the financial penalty and reason for default at a hearing at which the client is present. For example, unless a person was sentenced to a term of imprisonment in default of immediate payment, there must be a means enquiry before imprisonment can be considered.[14] The client can be questioned by the magistrates' clerk.[15]

Clients are often required to complete a means enquiry form, which may be similar to a debt adviser's financial statement. Magistrates may have little knowledge of the benefits system and of many items of ordinary expenditure, and advisers should ensure that a full financial statement is prepared and given to the magistrates, even if this means adding considerably to the court's own form. This should include explanations of any essential expenditure that the debt adviser believes may be questioned by the court. In addition, magistrates may not take into account items of expenditure, which the client has prioritised over payment of the financial penalty, but which the magistrates regard as non-essential. Magistrates usually take account of expenditure on housing (including fuel), clothing and food for the client and her/his dependants, water charges and council tax. However, there is no consistent approach and debt advisers should establish the local practice. Information should also be made available about the reason for non-payment, the financial position at the time of the previous order and future prospects, as appropriate.

Following a means enquiry, the court has the power to do the following.

Remitting fines

To remit a fine means that the fine is cancelled, either in full or in part. Provided that circumstances have changed since the fine was imposed or the court did not take the client's financial circumstances into account when setting the fine, it can remit all or part of the fine.[16] If information is available at the means enquiry that was not before the court at the earlier hearing(s), the debt adviser should argue that this should be regarded as a change of circumstances.

Debt advisers should always argue for a full remission of a fine if a person is on benefit or in serious debt (although the court may take into account the client's financial position at the time the financial penalty was imposed (or warrant suspended) and any other resources available to her/him). The magistrates should be urged to consider full or partial remission if the guidelines on the time for payment of a financial penalty have not been observed.

The magistrates do not have the power to remit costs and can only remit compensation orders in limited circumstances (see p331).

Fixing a return date

Magistrates may also order payment of the amount due by a certain date or fix an amount to be paid periodically and give a date when the client must return if s/he has not paid either the amount due or all the instalments. If the client fails to appear, a warrant of arrest can be issued. Debt advisers should try to ensure that the order is one with which the client can realistically comply or, if s/he defaults, that they can show this was not due to the client's 'wilful refusal' or 'culpable neglect' (see p338).

Money payments supervision orders

The court can also make a money payments supervision order, appointing someone to 'advise and befriend the defendant with a view to inducing him to pay the sum adjudged to be paid' – ie, supervise the client during the payment of the financial penalty.[17] This is normally a probation officer or a fines officer. The court is not required to hold a means enquiry before making an order, nor is the client's consent required, but since the client's co-operation is essential to the working of the order it is normally required. As a matter of good practice, the money payments supervision order should specify the terms of payment.

Imprisonment

If a client falls into arrears with payment of a financial penalty the court may order her/his imprisonment.[18] There is a similar power to detain under-21-year-olds in a young offenders' institution, but there are additional restrictions.[19] The minimum term of imprisonment is five days and the maximum term that can be imposed by a magistrates' court is 12 months.

The court can only issue a warrant to imprison someone:

- if a distress warrant is returned to the court by the bailiffs because there are insufficient goods or money to cover the amount owing; or
- instead of issuing a distress warrant.[20]

Once a distress warrant has been issued, imprisonment cannot be considered unless the warrant is returned with an endorsement stating there were no goods. Debt advisers should consider asking solicitors to argue that if a warrant has been returned because the bailiffs were unable to gain access to the client's property, imprisonment is not an option open to the court, but this argument has not been tested in the higher courts.

There must also be a means enquiry,[21] at which the court must be satisfied:

- if the original offence was punishable by imprisonment, that the client appears to have sufficient means to pay the sum forthwith; or
- that the default is due to the client's 'wilful refusal' or 'culpable neglect' (see p338); and
- that all other methods of obtaining payment have been considered or tried, but have been either inappropriate or unsuccessful (including a money payments supervision order (see above)) or unpaid work order, if available (see p330).

The Divisional Court has stressed to magistrates the mandatory nature of this second part of the requirement.[22] In practice, the court will often assume that if a person has paid nothing this is deliberate. Debt advisers should encourage solicitors and other representatives to argue strongly that it is impossible to find money from a client's low income, even for priorities like financial penalties. However, even if the court is 'satisfied' that the client had the means to pay, a prison sentence will be quashed unless the court can demonstrate it has considered all the non-custodial alternatives discussed above. Over the past few years there has been considerable publicity over the number of wrongful committals. This has generally been due to inadequate means enquiries and/or failure to follow the above rules.

Any term of imprisonment must be proportional to the size of the financial penalty (the period is determined by a statutory scale and depends on the amount of the financial penalty outstanding) and a stay in prison can be avoided by immediately paying the outstanding balance. Any costs of unsuccessful bailiff action can be added to the amount the client must pay to obtain her/his release. The length of any period of detention (whether actual or suspended) can be reduced by paying a proportion of the outstanding balance.[23] The financial penalty and any costs are wiped out if the prison sentence is served.

If the court decides to impose a period of imprisonment, it can be postponed in certain situations – eg, if the client keeps to a payment arrangement.[24] This is known as a 'suspended committal'. The conditions can be varied if, for example, the client's circumstances change and s/he can no longer comply with the terms of the suspended committal. A suspended committal order cannot be combined with any other enforcement order, since by implication they have all been considered inappropriate, and any attempt to do so could be challenged on the basis that no period of imprisonment should have been imposed in the first place. If the client fails to comply with the conditions of postponement, another hearing must be held before s/he can actually be sent to prison. The client must be given the opportunity to attend the hearing in order to make representations on why the committal warrant should not be issued. This will involve attempting to persuade the magistrates that circumstances have changed since the previous hearing (including new facts). The court can still consider remission at this stage. Although the rules state that notice of the hearing is deemed to be served if sent by special or recorded signed for delivery to the client's last known address, the High Court quashed a sentence of imprisonment where a notice of hearing had been returned to the court as undelivered. The High Court said that the magistrates should have adjourned the hearing until the client had actually been served with notice of the hearing.[25]

Short local detention

Instead of imposing imprisonment, the magistrates can order the client to be detained for the remainder of the day, either in the court building or at a police station up until 8pm. S/he must be released in time for her/him to get home on the same day. The magistrates can also order the client to be detained overnight at a police station until 8am the next morning.[26] This is not imprisonment and so the restrictions on imprisoning clients do not apply, but (as with imprisonment) the financial penalty is wiped out (see p328).

It might be appropriate to ask the magistrates to consider this option if they have ordered the financial penalty to be paid immediately, the client is unable to do so and the magistrates are not prepared to allow her/him time to pay.

Attendance centre order

If the court has an attendance centre available to it and the client is less than 25 years old, the magistrates can order her/him to attend the centre for between 12 and 36 hours.[27] Attendance can be required for two to three hours at a time, usually on Saturday afternoons.

Unpaid work order

The magistrates' court can allow defendants over 18 liable to pay a fine (but not amounts due as compensation or costs) to discharge it by doing unpaid work, if it appears to the court that the amount owed cannot be collected by any of the other available methods.[28] The court makes an unpaid work order. This means that, in some cases, the courts make unpaid work orders rather than remit fines. Piloting of this scheme began on 21 September 2004 and will continue until 31 March 2009. Advisers should check the position with their local courts.

An unpaid work order may be made either on the application of a fines officer or on the court's own initiative if:

- it appears from the information about the client's financial circumstances that the following methods of fine collection are likely to be impracticable or inappropriate:
  - warrant of distress;
  - application for enforcement by the High Court or a county court;
  - supervision order;
  - attachment of earnings order;
  - deductions from benefits;
  - a collection order; *and*
- the court is satisfied that the client appears suitable to carry out the work; *and*
- the client consents to an unpaid work order being made.

An unpaid work order requires the client to work for a specified number of hours in accordance with instructions given by a fines officer.

The number of hours to be worked is calculated by dividing the sum owed by the prescribed hourly sum (currently £6) and rounding up to the nearest hour.

The client must work where, when and for the specified number of hours as instructed by the fines officer. The fines officer must ensure that, so far as is practicable, the instructions given should not conflict with the client's religious beliefs and not interfere with her/his work or education. DWP guidance advises that the work should not affect a claimant's benefit entitlement or her/his ability to be available for, seek, or take up work. If the work is completed before the specified date, the liability to pay the amount due is discharged.

Any existing orders relating to enforcement must be revoked when an unpaid work order is made. The client may discharge her/his liability by paying the fine for which the order was made and can also reduce the number of hours to be worked by paying part of the fine (fractions of an hour are disregarded). Payment of the amount to be discharged through work must not be enforced, however, unless the order is revoked.

The unpaid work order may be revoked or varied at any time by applying to the fines officer. If the client has failed, or is failing, to comply, but has a reasonable excuse, or a change in circumstances means the client is unlikely to be able to comply, the court may revoke the order or may allow the client more time to do the work.

If an unpaid work order has been revoked and it appears to the magistrates' court that the client has performed at least one hour of work, the court must specify the number of hours that have been worked, rounding down to the nearest hour. The client's liability to pay is then reduced by the amount corresponding to this number of hours (calculated using the prescribed hourly sum).

The amount of fine outstanding following the revocation of an unpaid work order (reduced as above if applicable) may be enforced against the client, but the magistrates' court may nevertheless allow time for payment or direct payment by instalments.

Transfer of fines

If a client moves to a different magistrates' court's area but still has a financial penalty to pay at the magistrates' court where s/he used to live, it may be advisable to apply to the original court for a fine transfer order to the new local court.[29] This should make payments easier to arrange.

2. Compensation orders

A magistrates' court can impose a compensation order alongside a fine or other sentence and must give reasons for not making an order in cases where it is empowered to do so.[30] The compensation order is intended to be a simple way for the injured party in a criminal case to get compensation without having to sue in the county court. Compensation orders are often made in cases such as criminal damage or petty theft. They are collected by the court and paid to the victim. The powers to remit a fine (see p327) do not apply to compensation orders. The only circumstances in which a compensation order could be altered are:

- if a person appeals against either the conviction or the compensation order. A solicitor is needed for this and there are strict time limits; *or*
- if subsequent civil proceedings demonstrate that the loss in respect of which the order was made was less than stated in the order; *or*
- if a compensation order is made for stolen goods which are later recovered; *or*
- if the defendant has experienced a substantial reduction in her/his means, which was unexpected at the time the order was made and they seem unlikely to increase for a considerable period.[31]

Compensation orders are difficult to change. If someone is appearing in a criminal court on a charge that might result in a compensation order, the debt adviser should advise her/him to take a clear statement of means with her/him. A representative should also be prepared to argue that, in view of the client's other debts, s/he should not have a compensation order awarded against her/him. The court must consider a client's financial statement and debts when making a decision.[32]

Costs awarded along with a fine or compensation order are treated in exactly the same way as the compensation order – ie, they cannot be remitted by the court.

3. **Council tax and community charge**

Magistrates' courts have two distinct roles in relation to the collection of council tax and community charge. These are:

- to decide about the issue of a liability order;
- to decide about committal to prison.

Both should already have taken place in any remaining community charge cases.

Issuing a liability order

The court can issue a liability order against an individual at the request of a local authority. The local authority cannot apply for a liability order after a period of six years beginning with the date on which the tax became due. The duty to pay does not arise until the demand notice is served – ie, the bill.[33] The client is summonsed to attend a hearing. The summons must be served at least 14 days before the hearing date. The summons will have been properly served by:

- delivering it to the client; *or*
- leaving it at the client's usual or last known place of abode; *or*
- posting it to the client's usual or last known place of abode; *or*

- leaving it at, or posting it, to an address given by the client as an address at which service of the summons will be accepted.

This means the client does not necessarily have to actually receive the summons.[34] The order states that an amount of tax is due from the client, that s/he has not paid it and is therefore liable. Issues concerning liability for, or exemption from, the tax cannot be raised at the hearing, but must be dealt with through the appropriate appeals procedure, although the court will probably adjourn if an appeal is pending.[35] Failure by the local authority to follow the rules on billing and reminder notices can be raised as a defence, as can the fact that the demand has actually been paid.

If the client is disputing liability, the adviser should consider an appeal to a valuation tribunal. This can determine appeals about banding, whether the client is liable for the council tax, entitlement to a discount or exemption, and the amount of council tax claimed to be due. The tribunal cannot consider wider issues, such as whether the council sent out the council tax bill at the correct time.[36] An appeal must be made to the local authority in the first instance.[37]

Although the fact that a claim for council tax benefit or rebate is pending is not a defence, the magistrates could adjourn the matter. However, the Local Government Ombudsman has repeatedly found local authorities guilty of maladministration where council tax arrears wholly or mainly arose as a result of their failure to determine council tax benefit claims (and the client has provided the information requested or a reasonable excuse for any delay).

If payment is made after the liability order has been applied for, the local authority can ask for an order for payment of its reasonable costs.[38] The magistrates cannot be asked to allow time to pay at this stage.

The order allows the authority to pursue collection of the debt by:

- a payment arrangement; *or*
- a distress warrant (see Chapter 11); *or*
- an attachment of earnings order in accordance with the scales set out in the regulations (the costs of unsuccessful distress or applications for committal to prison can also be included in the order); *or*
- deductions from the client's income support (IS), pension credit (PC), income-related employment and support allowance (ESA) or jobseeker's allowance (JSA) at the rate of £3.05 a week;
- a charging order in the county court, provided there is at least £1,000 outstanding under one or more liability orders (see p258); *or*
- bankruptcy (see Chapter 12).

The local authority can also request that information about the client's means be supplied.

Enforcement of a liability order is done by the local authority, unless it chooses to return to the magistrates' court to seek the imprisonment of the client.

Local authorities can only use one of the above enforcement methods for one liability order at a time.

Although, in theory, once the local authority has obtained a liability order there is no time limit on enforcement, in practice, if the client disputes the existence of a liability order, the local authority will either have to produce a copy or some evidence from the magistrates' court that one has been made. Its own internal computer records should not be accepted as sufficient.[39]

Setting aside a liability order

Since 22 April 2004, local authorities (but not council tax payers) have had the power to apply to the magistrates' court to quash the liability order on the ground that it should not have been made.[40] If the magistrates' court is satisfied that the liability order should not have been made it must quash the order.

In addition, if the magistrates' court is satisfied that the local authority is entitled to a liability order for a lesser amount, the magistrates' court must make a liability order for:

- that lesser amount; *plus*
- any sum included in the quashed order in respect of the costs reasonably incurred by the local authority in obtaining that order.

In *Liverpool City Council v Pleroma Distribution,* the Administrative Court held that magistrates' courts have the power to re-open matters where they have acted in excess of jurisdiction (in this case the magistrates had not been informed of Pleroma Distribution's application for an adjournment to enable them to contest the application).[41] In addition to a genuine and arguable dispute about liability, there must have been a substantial procedural error (as in *Pleroma*) and the client must apply promptly – ie, in days or weeks, not months or years.[42]

The application is made by letter requesting the magistrates' court to re-list the local authority's application for the liability order and setting out the grounds on which it is being argued that the original liability order should not have been made. This is appropriate in cases where the local authority does not accept there are grounds for a set-aside and refuses to apply itself.

If the summons for the liability order was not properly served (see p332), the Administrative Court has recommended a procedure for setting aside the liability order to avoid expensive litigation.

- On discovering the existence of the liability order, the client should promptly inform both the local authority and the magistrates' court that the summons was not properly served.
- The local authority should then satisfy itself as to whether or not the client's assertion is correct.
- If this is established, the client and the local authority should co-operate in making a joint application to the magistrates' court to have the liability order set aside.[43]

If the local authority accepts that the order should not have been made, but refuses to apply to set it aside, the client can consider making a complaint to the Local Government Ombudsman, particularly if s/he is out of time to apply her/himself.

Committal to prison

If an application to commit someone to prison is made, the court must arrange a hearing and hold a means enquiry.[44] These proceedings can only begin once a distress warrant has been issued and returned because insufficient or no goods of the client could be found (for whatever reason, including in the case of local taxes because the bailiffs could not gain entry).[45]

The adviser should not rely on the court to produce paperwork and must prepare a full statement of income, expenditure and debts, as well as a clear explanation of any particular difficulties facing the client.

The court must decide whether the client has shown 'wilful refusal' or 'culpable neglect' in failing to pay (see p338). The magistrates should consider the issue for the whole period up to the date of the committal hearing. In all cases, the magistrates must also consider the client's ability to pay at the date of the actual committal hearing. Courts often equate failure to pay with refusal or neglect to pay regardless of the client's financial situation. For this reason, a debt adviser who acts as a representative in the magistrates' court should ensure that the court understands that poverty, rather than politics, is the cause of the non-payment, by producing evidence about the client's income and spending and other priority debts. Free legal representation is available to assist clients at these hearings as well as at committal hearings regarding financial penalties. The number of people committed to prison for non-payment of local taxes has steadily fallen over the past ten years.

Committal hearing

If the court decides there has not been either 'wilful refusal' or 'culpable neglect', it can either remit (write off) all or some of the arrears,[46] or make no order at all. **Note:** since 18 November 2003 local authorities have had the power to write off council tax arrears themselves (see p197). Although there is no time limit in which a local authority must enforce a liability order, the High Court has said that magistrates should consider remitting the debt on their own initiative where more than six years have elapsed between the date of the original default and the committal hearing.[47]

If the magistrates decide there has been 'wilful refusal' or 'culpable neglect', they can issue a warrant committing the client to prison for up to three months. They can (and usually do initially) suspend this warrant on payment of regular instalments. This means that so long as the agreed payments are kept, the client will not be imprisoned. However, unlike financial penalties, the court no longer has the option to remit the debt. If the client fails to comply with the terms of the suspended order, the magistrates must satisfy themselves that s/he had the ability to pay before they can activate the committal order by arranging a further means enquiry.[48]

If a client is committed to prison, no further enforcement action can be taken for those particular arrears. They are still owed, but cease to be priority debts.

The High Court has repeatedly advised magistrates that the purpose of committal in such cases is to obtain payment and not to punish the client. Therefore, although there is no statutory obligation to do so, local authorities, as well as magistrates, should consider alternative viable methods of enforcement and not refuse reasonable offers of payment.[49] However, a suspended committal order is regarded as a method of enforcement in its own right.[50] Orders should not be suspended for more than two to three years and partial remission should be considered in order to reduce the sum in respect of which the order is being made.[51] The magistrates must have regard to the principle of proportionality, with the maximum term being reserved for the most serious cases. The magistrates should use the tables of sentences provided for fines as a guide to the appropriate level of sentences (see *Anthony and Berryman's Magistrates' Court Guide,* Appendix 2).[52] The magistrates must consider the question of wilfulness/culpability separately from the question of how they are going to deal with the case.

When representing a council tax defaulter, it is helpful to begin by presenting a financial statement and evidence relating to her/his debts and social circumstances before asking the court to make a specific decision on the question of wilfulness or culpability. After the court has decided this, the debt adviser can argue about an affordable instalment arrangement, if necessary. It is useful to secure the court's agreement to conduct proceedings in this format because it encourages the court to think about wilfulness and because it allows the debt adviser to rescue something if the initial decision is unfavourable. The financial argument about the payment of a weekly amount by the client should be based on the scales in the regulations for attachment of earnings, although as these make no allowances for dependants or other commitments they will often require modification.

Many magistrates' courts do not allow lay representatives in council tax hearings. If the magistrates do not accept a debt adviser as a representative, s/he can act as a 'McKenzie Friend' (see p314).

The increasing reluctance of magistrates' courts to make committal orders has led many local authorities to resort to bankruptcy proceedings as an enforcement method if the client is a homeowner – in many cases for debts that are only just above the £750 bankruptcy limit (due to increase to £1,500 on 1 October 2009). For more details, see p202.

4. Maintenance

If a maintenance order is made by the magistrates' court for a child or adult dependant or is registered by a magistrates' court for collection after being made in the county court or High Court, the debt is collected by the court exactly as though it were a financial penalty.[53]

Once a maintenance order is in arrears, either a summons or warrant can be issued for a means enquiry. If the client is required to attend a means enquiry, the debt adviser should prepare a financial statement, list of debts and a supporting letter to request a variation in the order and remission of the arrears. The court can:

- suspend the operation of the order temporarily; *or*
- adjourn the hearing to enable the client to clear the arrears; *or*
- direct that payment be made by standing order or direct debit (including directing the client to open a suitable account, if necessary); *or*
- issue a distress warrant (see p321); *or*
- make an attachment of earnings order (see p318) if the client is employed (but not a deductions from benefits order).

If the court is satisfied that an attachment of earnings order is not appropriate and that the client has failed to pay the arrears because of 'wilful refusal' or 'culpable neglect', it can issue a committal warrant, either suspended or for the client's immediate imprisonment. The maximum period of imprisonment is six weeks. Serving a term of imprisonment does not discharge the arrears, but the client cannot be imprisoned again for the same arrears.[54]

A debt adviser should ensure that the client makes an immediate application for a variation of a maintenance order if debts arise.[55] If there are existing arrears, the court can be asked to remit these, although the person entitled to the maintenance must be given the opportunity to make representations. It is usual to remit all but the previous 12 months' arrears.

An application to vary an order should first be made in writing to the clerk, stating the reason for the application and providing financial details. The application should explain any change in the client's circumstances and give details of her/his reduction in income or increase in spending.

The court is likely to be sympathetic to varying a maintenance order as soon as financial problems arise, or to remitting unpaid maintenance, if this has not been paid as a result of a change in circumstances since the order was made or because the client clearly could not afford to make the payments in the first place.

5. Tax debts

Magistrates' courts have powers to deal with some tax debts. These include amounts of income tax and national insurance contributions of less than £2,000. HM Revenue and Customs (the Revenue) makes a 'complaint' to the magistrates' court, which issues a summons to a hearing. There is a 12-month time limit. At the first hearing, the court may make an order for payment if it is satisfied that the tax is due. The order for payment can be by instalments, but the client must attend court and apply for this, and so a financial statement will be required.[56] As the Revenue has the power to use bailiffs without a court order, a distress warrant will not usually be applied for. If the initial order for payment is not obeyed, the Revenue may issue a judgment summons for the client to 'show cause why s/he should not be sent to prison'. At this 'committal hearing' the court will proceed exactly as for unpaid financial penalties by conducting a means enquiry, then assessing whether or not the client has 'wilfully refused' or 'culpably neglected' to pay (see below). Although the court could decide not to imprison the client, it cannot remit these debts. Imprisonment does not write off the debt.

6. Wilful refusal and culpable neglect

There are a number of situations in which magistrates acting as debt collectors are required to decide whether non-payment is due to 'wilful refusal' or 'culpable neglect'.

Although magistrates' courts have been making decisions based on their interpretation of this important phrase for many years, the two phrases are not defined by statute or regulation. There is little guidance on what factors should be taken into account when making a decision, but the client's conduct must be 'blameworthy' in some way.

The client should only be found guilty of **'wilful refusal'** if s/he has made a deliberate decision not to pay the amount due, even though s/he is able to do so – eg, on a point of principle. However, a finding of 'wilful refusal' does not automatically justify a sentence of imprisonment; the two questions must be considered separately.

'Culpable neglect' is more difficult. It means a reckless disregard of the court order and usually involves the situation where the client spends any available income on non-essential items rather than on paying the financial penalty. It is not sufficient for the magistrates to find the client had available income and did not pay; they must also find out why it has not been paid.[57] If a couple are in receipt of benefits intended for them both, the non-claimant client can be found guilty of 'culpable neglect' if there has been a 'household' decision not to pay.[58]

To prove 'culpable neglect', the prosecuting authorities must show that:

- money was available, but was not paid to t he court or local authority; *and*
- this was due to a failure which demonstrates an avoidable choice to use the money for other purposes.

Evidence in the form of a financial statement should demonstrate to the court that the client's 'choices' were impossible and that a failure to pay was not 'culpable'.

Most courts assume that if a person has ignored reminders or suspended committals, they have culpably neglected payment. This assumption should be challenged. The debt adviser should argue that a person:

- did not have any money available after paying for essential items; *or*
- was too stressed to be culpable; *or*
- did not understand the need to pay; *or*
- was not skilful enough to balance a very difficult budget; *or*
- was wrongly advised not to pay.

Notes

1. **Financial penalties**

1 s128(5) Powers of Criminal Courts (Sentencing) Act 2000, as amended by s95 CA 2003
2 *R v Olliver & Olliver* [1989] 11 Cr App R (Sentencing) 10
3 *R v Newark Justices ex parte Keenaghan, The Times,* 3 January 1997
4 s142 MCA 1980, as amended by CAA 1995
5 s14 MCA 1980
6 s76 MCA 1980
7 s77(1) MCA 1980
8 *R v Hereford Magistrates ex parte MacRae, The Times,* 31 December 1998
9 *R v Birmingham Justices ex parte Bennett* [1983] 1 WLR 114
10 s27 and Sch 4 Domestic Violence, Crime and Victims Act 2004 was brought into force by SI 1821/2005
11 *Crossland v Crossland* [1992] 2 FLR 45, confirmed in *R v Hereford Magistrates' Court ex parte MacRae, The Times,* 31 December 1998
12 *R v Sheffield City Justices ex parte Foster, The Times,* 2 December 1999
13 s87(1) MCA 1980
14 s82(3)(b) MCA 1980
15 *R v Corby Magistrates' Court ex parte Mott, The Times,* 12 March 1998
16 s85 MCA 1980
17 ss56(2) and 88 MCA 1980
18 s76 MCA 1980, restricted by s82
19 s88(5) MCA 1980 and ss1(5) and 5A CJA 1982
20 s76(2) MCA 1980
21 s82 MCA 1980
22 *R v Stockport Justices ex parte Conlon, The Times,* 3 January 1997
23 s79 MCA 1980
24 s77 MCA 1980
25 *R v Doncaster Justices ex parte Harrison* [1998] 163 JP 182
26 ss135 and 136 MCA 1980
27 s60 Powers of Criminal Courts (Sentencing) Act 2000
28 Sch 6 CA 2003
29 s89 MCA 1980

2. **Compensation orders**

30 ss1(1) and 35(1) PCCA 1973
31 s37 PCCA 1973
32 s35(1)(a) PCCA 1973

3. **Council tax and community charge**
33 Reg 34(3) CT(AE) Regs; *Regentford Ltd v Thanet DC* [2004] EWHC 246 Admin (*Adviser* 103, abstracts)
34 Reg 35(2) and (2A) CT(AE) Regs, as amended
35 *R v Bristol Justices ex parte Wilson and Young* [1991] 156 JP 409
36 *Hardy v Sefton MBC* [2006] EWHC 1928 (Admin) (*Adviser* 125, abstracts)
37 For a discussion on the role and jurisdiction of valuation tribunals, see A Murdie, 'Computer Says No!', *Adviser* 118. Since 1 April 2008, the new 'appeals direct' system means clients have to appeal direct to the tribunal. See A Murdie, 'Local Taxation Update', *Legal Action*, April 2008
38 Reg 34(5)(b) and (8) CT(AE) Regs
39 See *Adviser* 104, letters
40 Reg 36A CT(AE) Regs, as inserted by Reg 5 CT(AE)(A) Regs
41 *Liverpool City Council v Pleroma Distributio* [2002] EWHC 2467 Admin (*Adviser* 96, abstracts)
42 *R (on the application of Brighton & Hove Justices) v Hamdan* [2004] EWHC 1800 Admin (*Adviser* 106, abstracts)
43 *R (on the application of Tull) v (1) Camberwell Green Magistrates' Court (2) Lambeth LBC* [2004] EWHC 2780, Admin (*Adviser* 113, abstracts). If the magistrates refuse the application, the court pointed out they will have acted unreasonably and could have a costs order made against them if an application for judicial review were necessary.
44 Regs 41(2) CC(AE) Regs; reg 44(2) CT(AE) Regs
45 Reg 41(1) CC(AE) Regs; reg 44(1) CT(AE) Regs
46 Reg 42(2) CC(AE) Regs; reg 48(2) CT(AE) Regs
47 *R v Warrington Borough Council ex parte Barrett,* 18 November 1999, unreported; *R v Gloucestershire Justices ex parte Daldry,* 12 January 2000, unreported
48 *R v Felixstowe Justices ex parte Herridge* [1993] Rating Appeals 83
49 *R v Sandwell Justices ex parte Lynn,* 5 March 1993, unreported; *R v Alfreton Justices ex parte Gratton, The Times,* 17 December 1993
50 *R v Preston Justices ex parte McCosh, The Times,* 30 January 1995
51 *R v Newcastle upon Tyne Justices ex parte Devine,* 23 April 1998, QBD; *R v Doncaster Justices ex parte Jack & Christison, The Times,* 26 May 1999
52 *R v Warrington Borough Council ex parte Barrett,* 18 November 1999, unreported

4. **Maintenance**
53 s76 MCA 1980
54 s94 MCA 1980
55 s60 MCA 1980

5. **Tax debts**
56 s58 MCA 1980

6. **Wilful refusal and culpable neglect**
57 *R v Watford Justices ex parte Hudson,* 21 April 1999, unreported
58 *R v Ramsgate Magistrates ex parte Haddow* (1992) 157 JP 545

Chapter 11

Bailiffs

This chapter covers:

Future changes

In July 2007 the Tribunals, Courts and Enforcement Act 2007 received Royal Assent. The Act makes major changes to the process of seizure of goods by enforcement agents. The procedure will be re-named 'taking control of goods' and will apply to all debts. The process of distress for rent will be abolished for domestic tenancies and replaced by a new procedure for commercial tenancies. Although the Act has been passed, it will be some time before it comes into force. All the details – eg, of protected goods and charges, will follow in regulations. These have yet to be drafted.

A bailiff is someone who acts on behalf of creditors or courts to collect debts, repossess homes or goods, and execute certain arrest warrants. This chapter looks mainly at the role of bailiffs in the seizure of goods to enforce debt and also outlines their powers of arrest (see p360). Because of their widened powers, the Government now prefers to refer to bailiffs as 'enforcement agents'. Advisers should bear in mind two points. Firstly, bailiffs are employed to seize goods, not to collect debts by instalments. Arranging affordable repayments on behalf of a client in multiple debt may, therefore, be very difficult. Secondly, bailiffs seldom have to remove or sell goods, as it is the threat of this that is effective in eliciting payments from a client.

1. Types of bailiff and the seizure of goods

There are several different types of bailiff operating in England and Wales. The most meaningful distinction that can be made between them is on the basis of their powers to seize goods ('distress' or 'distraint'). This determines both their duties and liabilities as enforcement agents, and their powers as bailiffs. The main areas of business for bailiffs, and the main areas for abuse and dispute, are enforcement of council tax, road traffic penalties and fines. Particular attention is given to these in this chapter.

Common law distress

There has always been a power in English law for a landowner to levy distress in respect of certain liabilities arising from, or associated with, her/his land. The surviving forms today are as follows.

Distress for rent

Arrears of unpaid rent can be collected by means of distress, either by the landlord personally or by using a private 'certificated' bailiff. Many private bailiffs hold a certificate, although firms described as certificated bailiffs often employ other staff who are not certificated to undertake most of their work.

In order to be certificated, an individual bailiff must apply to a county court. Applicants must have a bond of £10,000 lodged either with the court or in a bank (or indemnity insurance for the same amount), must know the law of distress sufficiently, and must be a 'fit and proper person to hold a certificate'. In practice, certification means very little as the courts do not investigate a person's suitability or check the information submitted on the application form. There is no monitoring of certificated bailiffs and although most certificates are renewable every two years, this process is largely a formality. The certification system does, however, allow for complaints to be heard by the court. It is the view of the Courts Service that complaints may be made not only against individual bailiffs levying distress for rent, but also against those levying other forms of distraint and execution, and their managers (see p364).

'Distress damage feasant'

'Distress damage feasant' is a remedy that permits the seizure and impounding of 'trespassing chattels'. The power was generally regarded as obsolete until recently, when it was revived to provide a legal justification for the practice of private wheel clamping of wrongfully parked cars.

Execution

'Execution' is the enforcement of civil court judgments by the seizure and sale of goods. There are three different types of execution an adviser may encounter.

High Court execution

The High Court uses bailiffs (High Court enforcement officers) to enforce the following judgments by seizing and selling the defendant's goods:

- High Court judgments of any amount;
- any county court judgment of over £5,000 where the debt has not arisen from an agreement regulated by the Consumer Credit Act 1974;
- county court judgments of between £600 and £5,000 that do not arise from an agreement regulated by the Consumer Credit Act 1974 if the creditor chooses to transfer them.

High Court enforcement officers are private bailiffs, organised on a county basis. Their day-to-day instructions come from the county's under-sheriff, who can be a useful contact for negotiation. High Court enforcement officers have similar powers to county court bailiffs, but are preferred by some creditors because, being private bailiffs, they are considered more effective.

County court execution

The Courts Service employs bailiffs in each county court, responsible for enforcing all warrants in that court's area. The bailiff may enforce the following judgments by seizing and selling the defendant's goods:

- all judgments based on agreements regulated by the Consumer Credit Act 1974;
- all judgments for under £600;
- any other judgment for up to £5,000, unless the creditor chooses to transfer to the High Court for enforcement by execution.

Road traffic penalties

Local authorities may use private bailiffs to enforce unpaid orders for road traffic penalties (decriminalised parking fines). Any sum payable for a parking offence is recoverable by a form of warrant of execution as if payable under a county court order. Road traffic execution is a complex amalgam of county court execution, distress for rent and special provisions of its own, but is essentially county court execution levied by a private certificated bailiff.

Statutory distraint

Many public bodies have a statutory power to seize and sell goods if money is owed to them. There are many forms of 'statutory distraint', but debt advisers will most often encounter the following.

Local taxes

Both council tax and business rates are enforceable by the seizure and sale of goods. Distraint may be levied by either local authority officers or by private bailiffs, provided in both cases they are certificated.

Income tax

HM Revenue and Customs (the Revenue) can levy distraint to collect any unpaid taxes and Class 1 and 4 national insurance contributions. A private bailiff may attend a levy, but only to assist and advise the Revenue's staff. The power of distraint is generally only used against businesses still trading, although occasionally it is used to collect tax or national insurance contributions from someone who is no longer trading, but who has property in the home being levied against.

VAT

The Revenue may use its own officers or private bailiffs to levy for arrears of VAT. About 75 per cent of its collection work is now in private hands.

Magistrates' court orders

Distraint may be used by magistrates' courts to collect unpaid civil debts (ie, tax and national insurance contributions), damages, compensation orders and fines, including those from the Crown Court, Court of Appeal and House of Lords. Many courts restrict distress for fines to fixed penalty offences (eg, fines for motoring offences) or to sums under £100 to £150.

Magistrates' courts use either their own 'civilian enforcement officers' or firms of private bailiffs to collect unpaid fines. These bailiffs are appointed by the court.

Child support maintenance

The Secretary of State for Social Security has the power to levy distraint to collect arrears of maintenance due to the Child Support Agency under a magistrates' court liability order. Private bailiffs are employed.

2. How bailiffs become involved

Whatever the type of bailiff or debt involved, the process of seizure is initiated by the issue of a warrant to the bailiff for the specific sum due from the client. The details of how warrants are issued (and how they may be stopped, if that is possible) depend on the type of warrant.

Distress for rent

How a warrant is issued depends on the tenancy of the person against whom the levy is to be directed. Landlords of assured and protected or statutory tenants cannot levy distress without first obtaining permission from the county court. Generally, the courts are reluctant to grant permission. In addition, the court has at this stage the power to suspend or adjourn the order (see Chapter 9).

Landlords of secure or commercial tenants or of long leaseholders can seize goods without a court order. If the landlord is not an individual, a certificated bailiff must be used, although this could be a member of staff of a local authority.

A warrant may be issued, and distress levied, the day after a rent payment falls due. There need be no prior demand.

This remedy can be used only for the collection of rent and sums collectable as rent, such as service charges. Housing benefit overpayments or council tax arrears, which may appear on a tenant's rent account, should not be enforced in this way.

County court warrants of execution

A warrant of execution (see p257) may be issued by a creditor when a person has defaulted on the terms of payment of a judgment debt. A warrant may be issued for the whole of the balance due under the judgment, or just the arrears (known as a part-warrant). If the judgment was payable by instalments, the bailiff may be asked to levy for one-monthly instalments (or four-weekly instalments, as appropriate) or for not less than £50, whichever is the greater. Consumer credit lenders often prefer to issue part-warrants, as these are considered more likely to be effective. As a result, lenders may repeatedly use execution to threaten the client following default on an instalment order.

The client does not have an opportunity to oppose the issue of a warrant, but the bailiff must deliver a warning notice telling the client that a warrant has been issued. Levy upon the warrant is then delayed for seven days to allow payment to be made. A warrant is valid for 12 months and may be executed at any time within that period.

At any time after the issue of the warrant, the court can suspend or 'stay' its execution. The client should apply to the court on Form N245 (see p302).

High Court execution

If a judgment of the High Court (and some county court judgments – see p257) is unpaid, it may be enforced by execution by the issue of a writ of *fieri-facias* (commonly known as '*fi-fa*'). This instructs the High Court enforcement officers to seize sufficient goods to cover the full amount of the judgment debt, plus interest and the costs of execution. Unlike in the county court (see above), no part-warrants are possible. The client should receive a warning note from the High Court enforcement officer that the writ has been issued, although this is not compulsory and does not always happen.

The client should apply immediately on Form N244 for a stay of execution in order to suspend the writ. See p305 for how to do this.

Road traffic penalties

If a penalty imposed by a parking attendant is not paid, the relevant local authority can obtain an order from the Traffic Enforcement Centre at Northampton County Court, confirming liability. The local authority can enforce this by issuing a warrant to private certificated bailiffs with whom it has a contract.

It can often be difficult to negotiate, as the bailiffs' instructions will usually be to collect the whole debt and not to accept instalments. Although the order is made by the county court, it cannot intervene to suspend the warrant. Normally, the only way of challenging the warrant is to challenge the original charge or order. Various means of appeal exist, initially through the Traffic Enforcement Centre, and then through the Parking Appeals Service. **Note:** the Civil Procedure Rules specify that, if the order is cancelled, the bailiff's warrant 'shall cease to have effect'. Further enforcement is, therefore, not permitted, although it is less clear whether a previous levy and costs are rendered null and void. However, threatening to sue for a refund of these sums may persuade the bailiffs to reimburse the client.

Income tax

The use of distraint for income tax arrears does not have to be sanctioned by a court. Initially, demands for payment are made from the computer collection centres and then by the local collector. If the taxpayer is still seen to be 'neglecting or refusing' to pay, a warrant is issued internally by a senior HM Revenue and Customs (the Revenue) officer.

If dealing with the threat of bailiffs for unpaid tax, the debt adviser should contact the relevant tax office. If the offer is accompanied by a financial statement, the collector will probably accept a reasonable offer to clear the debt (though possibly only over a period of between six and 12 months) and stay the warrant. The collector may also be persuaded to take no action where a debt is clearly unrecoverable.

VAT

The Revenue may use distraint for two reasons – to recover the debt and to close down a business to prevent the problem reoccurring. Little warning is given once the final demand for payment has been ignored, and it is often difficult to negotiate anything but the severest terms of repayment.

The distress process is activated when a VAT return is made by a trader without enclosing full payment of the VAT due or, if a return has not been made, s/he has been assessed as owing over the prescribed figure of £200. At this stage, the Revenue officer collecting VAT arrears will often try to negotiate directly with the client. If this fails, a final demand notice is issued. If the trader still neglects, or refuses, to pay and at least £200 is still due, a warrant is issued. In either case, the adviser may be able to agree a stay on enforcement while instalment payments are made, although the timescale allowed to negotiate may be quite short.

Magistrates' court orders

If a client defaults on a magistrates' court order for payment, the whole sum ordered to be paid falls due and may be enforced by distraint. In the case of fines (which are most commonly enforced by distraint), if the court allowed time to pay or set instalments, or if the defendant was absent at the hearing, a warrant cannot be issued until the court serves written notice on the client stating the total balance due, the instalments ordered and the date when payment begins. Once these conditions have been satisfied, a warrant may be issued on default.

If there is a hearing before the issue of a warrant, either because a review date has been set by the court or because, as with maintenance, an opportunity for the client to appear is required by the legislation, the client may have a chance to prevent distraint. S/he can apply to have the warrant postponed by the magistrates' court at the hearing. This may be done upon further terms of payment. It is, however, almost impossible to suspend or withdraw a warrant once it is with the bailiffs (see p366). However, the bailiff has the power to postpone the sale of goods.

The bailiffs are normally instructed to collect the whole debt forthwith and not to agree to instalment payments.

Local taxes

The magistrates' court issues a 'liability order' that enables the local authority to use a variety of enforcement measures (see p332), including distraint. The court has no power to intervene in the enforcement, either at this stage or later, nor can it set terms of payment.

A warrant is then issued by the local authority to bailiffs to levy the sums due. The debt adviser can either come to an agreement directly with the bailiffs or persuade the local authority to withdraw its warrant. Many local authorities will wish to come to reasonable arrangements with clients if these result in regular payment (see p183). Bear in mind the local authority's own code of practice on local tax enforcement (see p362) when negotiating on these debts, especially when seeking to have the warrant withdrawn.

3. Bailiffs' powers

In addition to bailiffs' specific legal powers, in April 2002 the Lord Chancellor's Department produced a *National Standards for Enforcement Agents* (NSEA). This provides minimum standards of business management and best practice in enforcement work. Copies can be downloaded from the Ministry of Justice website at www.justice.gov.uk. Unfortunately, NSEA does not include a mechanism for monitoring or enforcing its application. Complaints may be made to the Ministry, but will not be followed up. However, it would be appropriate to raise a failure to comply with NSEA in any complaint to the Ombudsman or against a bailiff's county court certificate (see p363).

People who are exempt

Certain people may be protected from the seizure of goods because of their personal status. They include the following.

- **Third parties**. In most cases (rent is the main exception) the warrant only entitles the bailiff to take goods owned solely or jointly by the debtor. Goods that are the property of a third party (including those leased or subject to hire purchase) should not be seized.
- **Children**. Property belonging to a child is protected, as children count as third parties. This is confirmed by NSEA, which also extends protection to goods 'for the exclusive use of a child.'
- **Vulnerable people**. NSEA requires bailiffs and creditors to protect vulnerable and socially excluded people, and to have procedures to deal with cases where it appears that a debtor may fall into such a category. NSEA lists older people, lone parents, people with a disability, people who are seriously ill, recently bereaved or unemployed, and people who have difficulty speaking or understanding English as all potentially vulnerable. This is not an exhaustive list and advisers should always raise suitable cases with bailiffs to consider whether it is appropriate to proceed with enforcement.

Entering premises

The first crucial stage in the procedure is for the bailiff to enter the client's premises. In most cases, it is upon this that success hangs. The client has a number of legal rights. If the bailiff breaches one of these basic principles, the whole levy may be illegal. See p361 for remedies.

Time

The rules on the time of levy are as follows.

- Most forms of distraint and execution can be levied at any time of day and on any day of the week.
- Distress for rent cannot be carried out between sunset and sunrise, nor on a Sunday.
- VAT distraint levies may only be begun between 8am and 8pm. Where the debtor trades partly (or wholly) outside these times, the levy may be commenced at any time and on any day when the business is trading.
- Execution cannot be levied on Sundays, Good Friday or Christmas Day.

Codes of practice may further restrict when distraint may be levied. The NSEA requires that levies should generally not occur outside the hours of 6am and 9pm, nor on Sundays and public holidays. Bailiffs tend to call at varying times and on different days in order to have a good chance of finding a person at home. **Note:** many bailiffs enforcing fines and road traffic penalties habitually call on clients very early in the morning in an effort to seize their car. Pay special attention to the above rules in such cases.

Place

In theory, bailiffs may go anywhere in England and Wales where the client's goods may be found. In practice, they will have either a business or home address on the warrant and this will be the only place they will visit. Matters are more restricted for landlords, who may only levy at the rented premises for which the arrears are due (although there is a right to pursue goods they know have been removed to avoid distress).

Method

Most bailiffs do not have the right to force their way into a property to execute a warrant: they may only enter *peaceably* and *with the permission* of the occupier. 'Permission' can be an express invitation to enter, or may be implied. For example, the courts have said that there is a general right for people on lawful business to come onto premises, and this principle has also been used to explain why bailiffs may open closed doors or climb through open windows (see below).

People can refuse entry to their homes and ask an enforcement agent to leave. The agent must comply promptly with this request, provided s/he has not actually started listing goods. This rule applies to the vast majority of warrants but there are a few exceptions.

- HM Revenue and Customs (the Revenue) can obtain a warrant to force initial entry, but this is very rare.
- Civil court bailiffs can force initial entry to non-domestic premises in order to levy execution – this too is rare.
- Since July 2005, bailiffs and officers executing arrest and distress warrants issued for magistrates' court fines have the power to force entry.[1] These powers should only be exercised where it is 'reasonable' and 'necessary' and advisers should monitor bailiffs acting for magistrates' courts to ensure this is so. Check with your local magistrates' court committee to see if it is permitting its bailiffs to use this provision – not all are.

Any other use of force by a bailiff makes a levy illegal. 'Force' may be as little as placing a foot in the door to prevent it being closed. In theory, therefore, a well-informed debtor may simply deny most bailiffs access and that will be the end of the matter. Bailiffs are, of course, well aware of the limitations on their powers and will try various tactics to get round a determined debtor. They may attempt to walk straight into a house as soon as a door is opened to them, or they may simply decide not to try to enter the house itself but to seize goods outside, such as a car parked on the driveway. Bailiffs may also use one of the wide range of entry rights they have – eg, entering through doors, windows and skylights that are left open, and using ladders to climb in windows or over back walls. It is not normally necessary for bailiffs to use any of these possible entry routes as they are frequently admitted by debtors to avoid embarrassment or confrontation.

Once entry has been gained, a bailiff may break open internal doors. This may be to open cupboards or attics or, if they have entered a house shared by a group of people with no single 'householder' (ie, in multiple occupation), the bailiff is entitled to use force to enter parts of the house that may be exclusively used by the debtor even if they are locked. Once again, the exercise of these powers is usually unnecessary.

Note: bailiffs *cannot* call the police to assist them to enter a debtor's home. The police can only be called to prevent a breach of the peace that is either taking place or is genuinely feared. A breach may be caused by either the bailiff or the debtor. In the latter case, the bailiff may summon police support in advance if s/he has a genuine expectation of difficulty, or may call for help while conducting the levy. A bailiff acting unlawfully may well be in breach of the peace and could be arrested. A bailiff acting lawfully is not liable to arrest.

Identification

The rules on identification are as follows.

- Bailiffs levying distress for rent and for road traffic penalties must produce their certificate to the tenant or other person responsible for the house.
- A bailiff collecting local taxes must carry written authority from the collecting council.
- Enforcement agents acting for magistrates' courts in the execution of warrants of distress and arrest must carry identity cards at all times. These must be shown to the debtor when executing the warrant and to any other person on demand. Warrants should also be shown to the defendant upon request.

No rules are laid down for other bailiffs, though it would be normal to expect them to produce the warrant, and NSEA requires that agents should always produce identification and a copy of their warrant/instruction. If a bailiff falsely identifies her/himself to gain entry, it should be argued that the entry is illegal – s/he has been given permission to enter for a specific purpose and has no right to be there for other reasons.

Levying goods

The power to levy is the power of bailiffs to seize, secure and, if necessary, sell goods in order to discharge the debt due. The levy process can generate many disputes.

Seizure

Seizure involves a bailiff selecting certain specified goods with a view to taking and selling them later. If the goods to be seized are household items, it is essential that the bailiff has first entered the home (see p348). However, once this has been achieved, little in the way of a physical act of seizure is necessary for the bailiff to assert the creditor's rights.

A mere verbal declaration of intent may be enough to constitute seizure, but an inventory is usually taken. This lists the goods that have been seized. Ideally, it should specify items individually, but a statement of 'all goods on the property', although very bad practice and possibly excessive, has been held to be legal. However, the decision pre-dates the introduction of statutory classes of exempt basic items, so it may be argued now that this form of inventory makes a levy unlawful. Inventories that seize 'all goods except those exempt' are illegal.[2] This is because the purpose of an inventory is to inform the debtor and others exactly what has been seized and what has been exempted, so that proceedings may be taken to contest that seizure if necessary. Seizures of 'all goods except those exempt' are too vague to be acceptable; a specific list of the items seized should ideally be provided.

Note: bailiffs may claim to be able to levy without entry and formal seizure. This process is sometimes known as a 'constructive levy'. Often a notice is put through a person's door saying that certain goods have been levied, presumably merely by looking through the window. The courts have rejected levies of household goods by such means. Advisers should assume that seizure requires the bailiff to be physically capable of removing the goods. The emphasis on having had this physical ability at some time indicates that seizure without being in the building in which goods are kept is a nonsense and that such an alleged seizure gives the bailiffs no rights or claim over the goods.

Sometimes bailiffs merely enter and discuss the debt with a client. There is no levy – ie, no change in the status of the goods and no right to make charges, unless steps are taken to list or seize goods, or there is a declaration that this has been done. It is important for advisers to check exactly what has taken place and to see what documentation has been given to the client by the bailiff.

Impounding

Impounding is when goods are placed in the 'custody of the law'. This legal custody is important as it gives the bailiff the right to return at a later date (forcing entry to the debtor's premises if necessary) and remove and sell them. It also protects the goods from seizure or interference by others, whether this is the debtor or another bailiff seeking to levy on the goods.

There are a number of ways in which the goods may be impounded.

- The bailiff leaves the goods with the debtor, subject to a '**walking possession agreement**'. This is an agreement in which the debtor acknowledges that the property is now in the control of the bailiff and is liable to be removed if the debt is not paid. The debtor is allowed to continue to use the goods while s/he arranges payment. A nominal fee is usually charged for walking possession. Bailiffs prefer to have a written agreement to secure their rights and fees, although a verbal agreement could be adequate to impound the goods. Any 'responsible person' in the property may sign an agreement – eg, a spouse or adult dependant. **Note:** if an agreement is one for which a fee may be charged under local tax regulations, it must be signed by the debtor at the time of the levy.

If the bailiff is claiming 'constructive seizure' it is not advisable to sign a walking possession agreement. In other cases, if the bailiff has gained entry, the debtor will have to sign a walking possession order if s/he does not want to risk the goods being removed immediately. In addition, county court bailiffs often require a walking possession agreement as security before they allow time to make an application to suspend the warrant and to vary a payment order. In these cases, although this procedure may not be strictly correct, it may be advisable to agree to walking possession if it is the only way to avoid seizure of property. In either case, signing the agreement gives the debtor a few days to negotiate instalments, to raise a lump sum of money to pay the debt, or to try to have the warrant withdrawn or suspended. If a bailiff cannot obtain a signature and is not in a position to remove immediately, s/he will often hand over a notice of distress and then leave the goods in the property. This constitutes a lawful seizure of the goods, but only for a temporary period of a week or so. If this seizure is not followed up by regular and frequent visits (ie, every few days), the seizure will be 'abandoned' and the bailiffs' rights and costs lost. Their only option is to start again from the beginning. Advisers should remember that impounding on the premises (eg, by walking possession) is only permissible where the relevant legislation gives the bailiffs that power. In the absence of such a provision, walking possession or other methods cannot be used.

- In the case of magistrates' court distraint, unless the warrant specifies otherwise, household goods can only be removed from the debtor's property on the day of sale, having been seized and impounded by means of a **'conspicuous mark'**. There is no provision for 'walking possession' in magistrates' court cases and if advisers encounter walking possession being used in respect of magistrates' court levies, they should argue that the levy is ineffective – ie, no seizure has taken place, the bailiff has no right to remove and sell, no costs may be charged and the bailiffs' only option is to give up and start again.
- **Wheel clamps** are frequently used by bailiffs to impound motor vehicles. Some seek to justify this as an intermediate stage between seizure and removal, to 'immobilise' the vehicle while waiting for a removal truck. It is debatable whether this practice is lawful. Clients faced with such a situation need urgent specialist advice to consider their options, which may include simply removing the clamp from the vehicle if this can be done without damaging it.
- **Immediate removal**. This is most common with vehicles or with easily disposable business assets. Walking possession is preferred in almost every other case.

- **Close possession**. It is lawful to leave a bailiff as a 'possession man' on the premises in 'close possession' of the goods, guarding them against interference. A charge can be made for this activity. It is, however, extremely rare.
- **Securing in a room** or other location on the premises. This is only lawful for distress for rent, but might in that context justify the use of clamps.

Note: advisers should always check any walking possession agreement signed by the client and investigate the circumstances in which seizure and impounding took place in order to satisfy themselves that a legal levy has occurred. If it appears this is not the case, see p361.

Goods

The general rule is that a bailiff may seize any property belonging to the debtor. Certain goods are exempt from seizure and it is important for advisers to go through any inventory with the client to establish which (and whose) goods have been seized.

In most forms of distraint and execution the following cannot be seized:

- 'such tools, books, vehicles and other items of equipment as are necessary to that person for use *personally* by him in his employment, business or vocation'; *and*
- 'such clothing, bedding, furniture, household equipment and provisions as are necessary for satisfying the basic domestic needs of that person and his family'.

A self-employed trader's essential and basic tools are thus protected, but only if these are not used by an employee or partner. A motor vehicle is only protected as a 'tool of the trade' if it is absolutely essential to the continuation of the business. Guidance issued in the past to county court bailiffs suggested that a three-piece suite may be seized in a home if dining chairs remained, or a microwave may be taken if an oven was also available. Furthermore, a couple of recent county court decisions have caused the Insolvency Service to revise its position on the treatment of motor vehicles for domestic purposes in bankruptcies. As the same categories of exemption apply in both distress and execution and in bankruptcy, it may be possible to apply this guidance to cases of seizure of vehicles by bailiffs (see p401 for more details). Remember that these are *subjective* categories of exemption and the adviser should establish the debtor's exact domestic or business circumstances and whether the different exemptions apply to her/him.

In **distress for VAT** a different list of exemptions applies, which is generous in protecting the home, but exempts little at a business.

- Household items that are reasonably required to meet the domestic needs of any person living in the home are exempt. The exempt goods are:
  - beds and bedding;
  - household linen;

  - chairs and settees;
  - tables;
  - food;
  - lights and light fittings;
  - heating appliances;
  - curtains;
  - floor coverings;
  - furniture, equipment and utensils used for cooking, storing and eating food;
  - refrigerators;
  - articles for cleaning, pressing and mending clothes;
  - articles for cleaning the home;
  - furniture used for storing clothing, bedding or household linen, cleaning articles or utensils for cooking and eating food;
  - articles used for safety in the home;
  - toys for the use of any child in the household;
  - medical aids and equipment.
- In business premises, the only exempt goods are fire fighting equipment and medical aids for use on the premises.

In **magistrates' court distraint** the following goods are exempt:
- clothing, beds, bedding; *and*
- tools of the trade in line with the general statutory exemption (see p353).

In **distress for rent** the general rule is that everything on the rented premises may be seized, but this is subject to a wide range of exemptions, including:
- things in use at the time of distress (eg, electrical goods that are turned on);
- perishable items.

These categories of exemptions are known as 'privileges' and are lengthy and, in some cases, complex. If dealing with a client facing distress for rent, especially at business premises, it is important to seek specialist advice.

In addition to the statutory exemptions, other general rules on seizable goods apply to most forms of distress and execution.
- Fixtures and fittings from a property cannot be seized in either distress or execution because they are part of the property itself. The definition is difficult, and is complicated by modern building techniques and materials, but basically a fixture is not merely something fixed, but something that has become part of the property and without which the home would be incomplete. Light fittings are fixtures, whereas shades are not; kitchen units are fixtures, but shelf units may not be.
- Goods belonging to third parties cannot generally be seized (except in some circumstance for distress for rent – see p344). This includes goods belonging to

partners, spouses and relatives as well as to hire and hire purchase companies. In practice, many bailiffs attempt to seize any goods at a particular property, irrespective of their ownership, and will deal with adverse claims to ownership later. If receipts of purchase can be produced, these should be enough to prove the ownership of goods. If there is a possibility that another person's goods may be seized, the debtor or the owner of the goods could draw up an inventory and threaten legal action if any goods are wrongly taken and retained. Bailiffs may decide not to risk seizing goods where there is serious claim to their ownership. Such an inventory could also be drawn up as a statutory declaration, made on oath by the owner in the presence of a commissioner for oaths. Items that are hired, or subject to hire purchase or conditional sale agreements, are not the property of the debtor and should not be seized – a copy of the relevant agreement should be sufficient to satisfy the bailiff. NSEA also requires that goods belonging to *or used by* a child should not be taken.

- Items of no value. The bailiffs should not list goods whose value is so low that it does not cover the cost of their seizure and removal. Nevertheless, this does happen, as it enables the bailiffs to charge fees and to collect money from the debtor. Sometimes these seizures are part of a so-called 'two-tier levy'. Some firms claim they will make an initial cursory levy of a few visible items to secure the creditor's position (but avoiding disturbance for the debtor) but this may be revised later if it is necessary to remove. This procedure is not lawful. Only a first levy is possible – the bailiff may take fewer goods than listed on a later occasion, but never more. Furthermore, initial levies often include seizure of exempt goods, such as all forms of seating in a property. These levies require careful scrutiny and often need to be challenged with the bailiffs.

If goods have been wrongfully seized, the owner of the goods has a number of remedies (see p361). Initially, the matter should be taken up informally with the bailiff or creditor, if necessary backed with the threat of court action.

Always check inventories to confirm what has been seized. In particular, check whether the bailiffs have seized any exempt goods, or only a few items inadequate to cover the costs, or whether they have claimed to levy 'all goods except those exempt'. See p351 for more on inventories.

Selling goods

The purpose of seizure is to give the creditor security over the debtor's goods and to put the debtor under pressure to settle the debt. The ultimate conclusion of the process is to sell the goods, but this is seldom reached because of the costs, inconvenience and low returns. Except perhaps for motor vehicles, most second-hand goods are of no, or negligible, value and it is the threat of sale that is effective, not the remedy itself.

If sale becomes necessary the bailiff must remove the goods seized previously and can, at this stage, use force to re-enter the debtor's property to gain access to the goods. Prior warning is generally given of an intended visit to remove, and entry can only be forced if the debtor has received such prior notice. If this is the case, failure to permit access may be construed as deliberate obstruction. Only what was previously seized can be removed. The NSEA requires bailiffs to handle goods with reasonable care and have insurance in place to cover against damage in transit. A receipt for goods removed should be left at the premises.

Note: the power to force re-entry depends on there having already been a valid seizure of goods. Bailiffs cannot force entry if they did not previously take an inventory and walking possession agreement (or the equivalent in the form of a valid verbal seizure and impounding of goods).

The goods are stored for a few days while the sale is arranged. At this stage, the debtor has the opportunity to pay the sums due.

Normally there must be at least five days before sale. In most cases, this is by public auction. The bailiffs are expected to raise the best price possible, although returns from auction sales tend to be very low. In most forms of distress and execution the debtor may request that the goods be 'appraised' or valued before the sale. This may lead to a slightly higher reserved price being set, but as fees are charged for the process, any gain may be offset by the extra expense incurred.

It is usual for the bailiff to deduct her/his fees from any sale proceeds (or payments made to her/him) before passing the sums on to the instructing creditor. Goods cannot be sold merely to cover the bailiffs' fees if the debt is paid direct to the creditor. Creditors normally try to avoid receiving payments directly from a debtor, which bypasses the bailiffs and circumvent their fees, but in cases where a debt *is* cleared in full with the creditor, and/or the warrant is withdrawn from the bailiffs, the latter will be left without any recourse against the debtor for any unpaid fees.

If the bailiff damages the goods whilst removing or selling them, or could be shown to have mishandled the sale so that the goods were sold for too little, s/he could be sued for damages in the county court.

Fees

Bailiffs are allowed to recover money from the debtor to cover the cost of their action. The charges can inflate the sum due considerably and are the cause of much complaint. Some bailiffs add charges that are not allowed and advisers should, therefore, examine bailiffs' bills carefully to ensure that the burden of debt on a client is not being added to improperly.

The rules for charging for distress are varied, but in most cases the amount bailiffs are allowed to charge is regulated by legislation. The exception is magistrates' courts, in which no scale is laid down. Fees are negotiated separately between each magistrates' court committee and its bailiffs. Advisers should request a copy of the scale in operation.

Note: under the NSEA, bailiffs are required to issue a notice every time a fee is incurred and must provide a breakdown of their fees if they are asked in writing for one. Advisers should request a detailed breakdown of the fees charged to a client, check the fees against the appropriate scale and compare the dates given with the actual events of a case. The fee scale is often reproduced on the bailiffs' notice of seizure and all fee scales are available at www.advisernet.org.uk.

All scales tend to include the same sorts of elements. Fees are charged for certain actions such as visits, seizure and removal, and reasonable disbursements for storage and advertising are permitted. Charges tend to be a mixture of flat-rate fees, sums calculated as a percentage of the sum due, and 'reasonable' amounts. **Note:** the fees charged in the county court, though set by legislation, are much lower than those found in the private sector. There is a standard charge for the issue of the warrant, which is added to the debt. This covers all visits made by bailiffs, plus seizure and possession. Only if the matter reaches the stage of removal and sale are any other fees charged.

Disputed fees

Any charges that the adviser does not consider reasonable may be reviewed by the county court. The court has a power to examine and reassess, if necessary, disputed bailiffs' charges. The process was formerly called 'taxation', but is now known as 'detailed assessment'. The debtor disputing the fees can apply to the court under Part 8 Civil Procedure Rules for a district judge to review the sums demanded by, or paid to, the bailiff. **Note**: this power only extends to charges made under the scales set by statute. As magistrates' bailiffs charges are established by their contract with the court, these fees are not 'taxable', although the legislation permits the magistrates' court to fine bailiffs whose fees are 'improper or undue'. Another legal remedy could be for the debtor to pay the disputed fees and then use the county court to recover the balance by issuing a small claim. The debtor would protect her/his goods from seizure or even removal and sale, but would have to be able to pay up front the whole sum due.

Although legal remedies are available, a more accessible and useful method of redress is to use the bailiffs' trade body complaints procedure. This is valuable if the level or necessity of the fee is being challenged, but is not suitable if the interpretation of the fees regulations is being questioned.

A 'reasonable' fee recoverable by a bailiff is one that is calculated correctly, is applied at the correct stage of the process, is for a fair amount and is legal. Some bailiffs' bills contain fees that may be questioned on all these points. Again, close comparison should be made between the sums demanded and the sums permitted on the statutory scale. Advisers should be aware of the following.

- Fees made too early in the process, before the proper point for making them has been reached – eg, charges for attending with a vehicle when none was present or the costs of preparing for a sale when goods had not even been seized or removed.

- Fees for a sum disproportionate to the work done or debt due. The meaning of 'reasonable' charges was examined in a case in Birmingham County Court in the mid-1980s. The judge decided that any question about 'reasonableness' should be resolved in favour of the payer. A reasonable charge must be related to the value of goods taken. Thus, it cannot be reasonable to remove goods if their sale value is unlikely to cover the costs of removal and sale. The amount charged for bailiffs' services must also be spread across all those against whom they hold warrants issued by a particular creditor. In the case in question, a charge for a removal van was 'taxed down' on the basis that a van could be hired privately for considerably less than the billed sum, and any overheads incurred by the bailiffs could be spread across all those subject to removals on that day.
- Fees for work that is not actually or necessarily undertaken. For example, if a bailiff conducts only one actual levy for a debt, but produces three or four identical inventories for each sum due and makes a separate charge for each, this could be challenged on the basis that only one set of fees should be allowed. Similarly, clients often allege they have been billed for visits that never took place. The bailiff is under a duty to deliver a notice whenever a charge is incurred. Ask for copies of these and challenge the failure to supply them.
- Fees not allowed for on the scale – eg, fees for administering accounts, for negotiating with the debtor or collecting payments from her/him and for clamping vehicles.

In levies for council tax, advisers should also bear in mind the following.

- The use by bailiff's firms of their right to charge for 'attendance to remove' at premises. In the council tax regulations these charges are only allowed *after* a levy has been made – ie, there has been an entry and seizure of goods. Some firms appear to charge *before* there has been any levy. What seems to happen is that the statutory fees allowed for visits are used to cover basic administrative overheads and are added on as soon as an instruction is received, so that the bailiff has then to use the 'attendance' charge to cover initial visits to premises. In road traffic enforcement there is no clear limit on when and how often these charges can be applied. As a result, multiple and substantial charges are often added to an account. Advisers should examine accounts carefully. In council tax cases, challenge attendance fees that are made too early or more than once. In road traffic and fines cases, challenge charges made for attendances to remove when no levy has been made (or walking possession has been taken). Although the context in which these fees can be charged is not as well defined as in council tax distraint, separate fees are allowed in the scale for visits. This implies it was intended that attendance fees should apply to separate and later calls to the premises.

- Redemption fees. The fee scale allows a charge of £24.50 (or 5 per cent of the balance) to be made where 'no sale takes place by reason of payment or tender' of the debt due. Some firms seem to charge this fee in every case where a levy takes place. The regulations, however, envisage a situation where goods have been removed for sale, but where the sale is cancelled at the last minute because the debtor comes up with the full council tax arrears plus the costs: they refer to the goods being made 'available for collection'. Charging this sum earlier in the process, especially where payment of the full debt has neither been made nor offered, seems unjustifiable. The bailiffs' industry has a different interpretation of this fee, but having obtained counsel's opinion on its meaning they have accepted that it can only be charged once the debt has been cleared in full. The bailiffs argue that the fee could be added to the final instalment payable on an account, rather than being deducted from a lump-sum settlement of the debt; this may not be correct as the regulations refer to the 'tender' of the debt, which is usually understood to mean an offer of full payment of the sum outstanding. The bailiffs also believe that this fee should be charged where nothing more than walking possession has been taken. It is difficult to reconcile this with the reference to goods being made available for collection, which implies some change in their location.

Codes of practice

The powers described on pp347–358 are those laid down in law. In addition, some creditors (mostly local authorities) operate codes of practice. These regulate the conduct of their bailiffs and specify the circumstances in which it is considered inappropriate to levy distraint – eg, if a debtor is on means-tested benefits, has a disability or is recently bereaved.

As warrants are often issued against those whom the local authority has voluntarily exempted from distress, it is important for advisers to be familiar with any code the local authority operates and to lobby for warrants to be withdrawn in cases where they should not have been issued. Some local authorities, however, are reluctant to release their codes, stating they are part of their contract with their bailiffs and are, therefore, confidential. This argument should not be accepted. Compliance with the European Convention on Human Rights requires that any measure governing the interference with individuals' rights should be made accessible to them. Codes dealing with bailiffs' rights to enter property and seize goods fall into this category and must be made public.

The Child Support Agency used to operate a comprehensive code of practice that gave extensive additional protection to debtors facing distraint. This document is now largely incorporated into the contracts and service-level agreements agreed with the three enforcement agencies it uses. Other creditors, though not having explicit codes, will often be prepared to withdraw warrants in cases of severe personal and/or financial hardship.

The Freedom of Information Act can be used to obtain copies of codes of practice, as well as copies of a public body's contracts and service-level agreements with the enforcement agencies used. Often an adviser may discover there is no written agreement in place, but nonetheless the Act can be a useful tool for finding out the local criteria within which bailiffs are expected to work.

The NSEA requires enforcement agents to ensure that all information and documentation supplied to debtors is clear and unambiguous, that bailiffs act without any form of discrimination, that they are aware of potentially vulnerable individuals, taking special care when proceeding against them, and that they treat debtors' information confidentially. Bailiffs' firms are required to operate complaints procedures and to make details of these readily available. It is sometimes argued by bailiffs that NSEA is only a guideline. It is, however, more significant than this, as all the main bailiff trade bodies, plus the Local Government Association, are signatories. Bailiffs must have very good reasons for failing to comply – and should be able to justify their decision.

Bailiffs' companies holding a consumer credit licence must also comply with the Office of Fair Trading (OFT) *Debt Collection Guidance*. Many of the larger firms are licensed, but if you are not sure ring the OFT on 020 7211 8608 to check. The OFT guidelines complement and reinforce the NSEA in many areas of practice. A copy can be downloaded from the OFT's website at www.oft.gov.uk.

4. **Powers of arrest**

Since April 2001 private bailiffs have the power to enforce a range of magistrates' court warrants previously executed by the police. These include warrants of arrest to ensure attendance at means enquiries following default in payment of fines and local taxes, and warrants of commitment made following such means enquiries.

When choosing the firm to work for the court, possession of a distress for rent certificate from a county court, convictions and being the subject of complaints, damages claims and insolvency proceedings are all considered. Advisers should note that as part of this scheme, bailiffs and courts are required to operate and publish complaints procedures.

Bailiffs' powers when executing these warrants are broadly similar to those for distress. Warrants may be executed anywhere in England and Wales at any time of day. Under the Domestic Violence, Crimes and Victims Act 2004 an officer has a right to enter premises in search of a person against whom an arrest warrant has been issued, provided there are reasonable grounds for believing that person to be on the premises. Reasonable force may be used to gain entry. A person may be physically seized or touched, and informed that s/he is under arrest, or arrest may be by words alone (provided the person submits to these). The arresting officer is also entitled to search an arrested person for items that could be used either to cause harm to her/himself or to others, or to escape from custody. The arresting officer must have reasonable grounds for conducting a search, and any items found may be seized and retained. As soon as possible after being arrested, a person must be given full and clear details of the reason for her/his arrest and how to complain. Defendants are not liable for any fees for the execution of these warrants.

Resisting a lawful arrest can be an offence. While it may be lawful to resist an unlawful arrest, it will generally be more advisable for clients to make a civil claim for damages for false imprisonment and/or assault after the event, and they should be encouraged to seek legal advice.

5. Complaints against bailiffs

In recent years, the action of bailiffs has been subject to increasing public scrutiny. It is possible that this may lead to changes in certification and regulation. Meanwhile, media interest remains high and such pressure may be effective. The media, however, often wants stories of gross wrongdoing, especially physical violence, by bailiffs – which are rare.

Wrongful seizure

Broadly speaking, the law recognises three categories of bailiffs' offence.

- **Illegal levies**, where the bailiffs do something (generally at the outset of the levy) that they have no power to do – eg, to force entry on a first visit or to seize exempt goods. Because the whole action is rendered unlawful as a result, the debtor can often recover appreciable damages, and the bailiff will have to give up and start again.
- **Irregular levies**, which are seizures where something is done incorrectly later in the process. Most forms of enforcement have regulations stating that such mistakes are *not* to be treated as illegalities. In other words, an error in the conduct of a sale or in leaving a required notice does not invalidate the whole procedure and only entitles the client to recover her/his loss.
- **Excessive levies**, where the bailiff takes far more than is necessary to cover the debt and costs by sale at auction. The debtor can sue to recover the value of the excess. Excessive levies are rare. Many clients believe they have been the victims of such levies because they do not appreciate that bailiffs value their goods at auction value, which may only be 10 per cent of their face value. However, in the case of seizures of cars it may be possible to claim an excessive seizure. Cars are worth more than household goods and hold their value better at auction. They are often seized for fines and road traffic penalties, which are relatively small debts (at least before charges are added). Bailiffs should

establish if other goods are available first, but they tend to take cars because they are available and valuable. Such a procedure is open to challenge.

Except in the case of excessive levies, it is usually only worthwhile taking action against illegal acts.

Threatening court action

If there has been a procedural error, threatening county court action could help a debtor negotiate or have the levy withdrawn. Bailiffs may be reluctant to have their procedures tested in court and may, in any event, find it more advantageous to settle the matter than be involved in the expense of litigation. If negotiations are not progressing, it can be effective to draft a claim form, send it to the bailiffs and threaten to issue in the county court unless payment is made within a set time scale. Frequently a 'commercial decision' will be taken to settle the case at this stage.

Complaining to the bailiffs

If there is a problem, you should also complain to the bailiff's firm itself. Direct contact with the bailiff is seldom fruitful, other than to agree a stay on recovery, and you should find out who the complaints manager is and write to her/him directly. Firms have a duty to deal with complaints promptly under their trade body complaints procedures (see p363). In addition, if they are acting for a public authority such as a local authority or government department, the bailiffs should also be treated as 'public authorities', with all the duties this implies. For example, they should give reasons for their decisions, so that if they refuse to treat a person as vulnerable under a code of practice, they should explain why.

Complaining to creditors

While it is always worthwhile contacting the bailiffs to complain about their actions, it may be unproductive if the point at issue is whether they should have been instructed at all or if the terms of repayment set by the contract with the creditor are impossible for the debtor to meet (council tax contracts, for example, often require the bailiff to collect within three months). In such cases, the bailiffs are bound by the contract with the instructing creditor to enforce the warrant issued to them, and other than asking them to stay the action whilst negotiations are conducted, little else may be possible.

Creditors should always be notified about wrongful acts by their agents, as this may help bring pressure to bear in individual cases and may lead to improved monitoring more generally, but direct contact with a creditor is particularly important where matters such as the personal circumstances of the debtor are at issue. Complaints may be made about either the incorrect use of legal powers or a failure to follow a code of practice (see p347). If the complaint is not properly dealt with, it may be possible to use the organisation's internal complaints procedure. If this is unsatisfactory, it may be possible to complain to an independent adjudicator, such as the Local Government or Parliamentary Ombudsman.

Complaining to trade and professional bodies

If a complaint to a firm of bailiffs is not dealt with satisfactorily, a complaint could be made to the bailiffs' professional or trade organisation. When making such a complaint it should be remembered that these bodies exist to promote their members' interests and are not entirely independent or impartial. Several bodies may be responsible, depending on the type of enforcement agent involved. The relevant bodies to which advisers may turn are the High Court Enforcement Officers Association, the Enforcement Services Association (ESA) and the Association of Civil Enforcement Agencies (ACEA) (see Appendix 2). All operate disciplinary codes linked to complaints procedures. Serious breaches of professional ethics or of procedure may lead to investigation and the imposition of penalties, such as being excluded from membership and, as a result, from the profession (although this is rare). A complaint can also lead to at least an apology and perhaps compensation, such as a refund of fees. ESA and ACEA also have codes of practice regulating members' business practices, which may be of some assistance. These and their complaints procedures can be found on their websites. The complaints procedures can be particularly effective in cases of poor administration and customer care by bailiffs' firms and where fees are disputed as unnecessary or incorrect.

Complaining to the Ombudsman

There is not yet a regulator for the enforcement industry (although this may change). However, most creditors for whom bailiffs act are public sector bodies and are subject to supervision by an Ombudsman. The creditors themselves operate their own complaints procedures, but if this fails to produce a satisfactory outcome for the client, a complaint can be made to the Local Government or Parliamentary Ombudsman or to HM Revenue and Customs Adjudicator.

In the case of local authorities, before a complaint is made to the Ombudsman (or applying for judicial review in the High Court), the case can be taken up by the council's monitoring officer. This person is usually the chief legal officer and must consider whether there has been maladministration or whether the council has acted unlawfully. It can sometimes be helpful to refer a case to the monitoring officer if the department in question is unwilling to intervene or negotiate, but where the adviser believes its bailiffs have acted unlawfully.

Court proceedings

If non-judicial action or pressure fails, court proceedings can be initiated against the bailiffs in order to recover seized goods or gain financial redress. The form of action taken depends on the bailiff's offence (see p361). However, in most cases the value of the claim involved will be well within the small claims limit and so legal action can be taken for relatively little expense and at little risk of legal costs.

If threatened with legal action or having received a claim form, bailiffs will often choose to settle the matter to avoid the expense of litigation or the scrutiny of the court.

An injunction can also be made by the county court to prevent a bailiff's re-entry and removal of goods or their subsequent sale. Injunctions can be applied for at the same time as issuing a claim form, or in advance in urgent cases.

The debtor or owner of the seized goods may be able to start one of the following claims. **Note:** there are detailed procedural requirements for all of these, plus court fees and the risk of substantial legal costs if a case is lost.

- **Sue for wrongful interference with goods.** The owner of goods may be able to get an order for their return if they were illegally seized – although an award of damages for their value is more likely – plus an award of damages for any other losses incurred, such as loss of use. As the courts rarely order the return of the goods themselves, other remedies may be preferable.
- **Sue for the recovery of sums already paid to the bailiffs.** This could be a payment made by the debtor in order to prevent an illegal seizure of goods or for the recovery of disputed fees. This may seem an unlikely occurrence for debt clients, but it often arises in levies on motor vehicles – the debtor will raise the money to continue to have use of her/his car.
- **Start 'replevin'.** This is an obscure and ancient remedy where the goods are immediately ordered to be returned to the debtor, who then takes court action to prove the levy was illegal and s/he was consequently entitled to have her/his goods back. It is not recommended except to use as a threat, as it is not covered by the costs protection of the small claims procedure. (The same is true for complaints about local tax or child support levies to the magistrates' court, unless the client can get legal aid.)
- **Challenge the certificate.** If the bailiff is certificated, it is possible to apply to the court that granted the certificate for it to be revoked on the grounds that the bailiff no longer appears to be a fit or proper person to hold such an authorisation. The complaint must be on the prescribed form. An officer at the court is then required to send a copy to the bailiff. The bailiff must respond within 14 days and, if the judge is dissatisfied that the bailiff has adequately explained the incident and remains fit to hold a certificate, s/he is summonsed to show why the certificate should not be cancelled. At this hearing the judge can proceed as s/he thinks fit – generally the court allows the complainant to make representations. If a certificate is revoked, the debtor may also be awarded

compensation, generally by forfeiture of all or part of the indemnity insurance or bond which the bailiff is required to hold. Unfortunately, there is very limited experience of complaints against certification. Another problem that advisers may encounter is that the rules on certification complaints relate solely to distress for rent. Some judges question whether they have any jurisdiction either to hear complaints at all, or to award any compensation, where the complaint relates to the bailiffs' activities in other fields, whether or not they require a certificate. As a result, the procedure is under-used. It can, however, provide a quick and effective means of redress for an aggrieved person and is worth considering as a threat if a bailiff has acted badly – eg, ignoring codes of practice. If you know the bailiff's name, you can check the certificate details by ringing the Courts Service on 020 7189 2491. If unsure whether a particular bailiff is certificated, the adviser should ask the firm to provide full details.

- **Interpleader.** If a third party's goods have been seized in execution, a special remedy know as 'interpleader' exists to enable the third party to prove ownership and recover them. Specialist help should be sought.

6. Emergency action

People often seek advice only when the 'crunch' comes, such as a visit from a bailiff. In order to buy time for a client's finances to be investigated and an overall repayment strategy devised, it may be necessary to consider some of the emergency measures described here.

Refuse the bailiffs access

Often a debt adviser is first consulted when a client hears from bailiffs. The best advice to protect goods from seizure is to ensure that bailiffs are not given access to property and for the client to remove any goods that are outside the home (especially cars) to a place where they will not be seen. However, in cases of distress for rent, removing goods in this way is an offence.

Bailiffs will try to visit more than once to gain access, so clients should be advised to be vigilant, and keep doors and windows locked. If the bailiffs are unable to gain entry, they will eventually return the warrant to the court, indicating whether or not there are sufficient goods to satisfy the debt. They rely on what they can see through a window to decide this.

If the bailiff fails to raise the sums due, this will not be the end of the debt's recovery; other means are tried. With fines and local taxes the debt often goes back to the court to consider committal to prison (see p328). A person may be committed for 'wilful refusal' or 'culpable neglect' to pay (see p338) and may be threatened that failure to give access to the bailiffs will be construed by the court as wilful refusal. There are no reported instances of a person being committed on this ground.

If bailiffs have already gained access, they can subsequently force their way in for the same debt (see p351).

Get the warrant withdrawn from the bailiffs

In every case, the aim of the debt adviser should be to remove the matter from the hands of the bailiffs and place it back for consideration by the creditor.

In the civil courts, the client should make an immediate application to suspend the warrant. For county court action, this is done on Form N245 (see p302). For High Court action, an application for a stay of execution should be made (see p302). Magistrates' courts do not have such a power. However, since April 2001 magistrates' court bailiffs can postpone the removal and sale of seized goods from the previous period of six days to a maximum period of 60 days where instalment payments have been agreed. This is approved by a court clerk without the need for a hearing to take place.

In situations where there is no power to suspend through the courts and the client cannot afford to pay a lump sum, the only option may be to persuade the issuing creditor that the warrant should be withdrawn because of the client's personal or financial circumstances. This may also be because the person falls into one of the categories of people exempt from distraint by the code of practice operated by that creditor (see p362). In many cases, terms of payment will have to be negotiated at the same time, and often these will be for instalments of sums much lower than it would have been economic for the bailiff to collect.

Threaten court action

If there has been an error in procedure, a lever for negotiation or withdrawal may be to threaten court action (see p364). Bailiffs may be reluctant to have their procedures tested in court and may find it more advantageous to settle the matter than be involved in the expense of litigation.

Raise a lump sum to clear the debt

If the above tactics have been unsuccessful, or if the goods have been seized already, it may be necessary for the client to pay the debt to avoid goods being sold (see Chapter 6 for ways of maximising income). This may be in violation of certain basic principles of money advice, but will often be the only option that the client is prepared to consider. It may also make financial sense as the replacement cost of the items in question may be much more than the total required by the bailiffs.

Note: the Court of Appeal has clarified a debtor's rights to make payments to a bailiff. This may happen either before a levy (or removal) takes place, or afterwards, but payment cannot be offered during a levy or removal, as the sums due cannot be calculated.[3]

Notes

3. **Bailiffs' powers**
   1 s27 Domestic Violence, Crime and Victims Act 2004 and Sch 4 MCA 1981
   2 *Ambrose v Nottingham City Council* [2004] (*Adviser* 107 abstracts)

6. **Emergency action**
   3 *Wilson v South Kesteven District Council* [2000] EWCA Civ 218

12

Chapter 12

Personal insolvency

This chapter covers:

1. Last resort or fresh start?

Someone is said to be 'insolvent' if s/he is unable to pay her/his debts as they fall due. In many cases, people are able to resolve their financial problems by coming to the informal arrangements with their creditors discussed earlier in this *Handbook*. Apart from these arrangements, there are currently three ways in which a client can reach a formal arrangement with her/his creditors through the courts.

- **Administration orders** (see p370). For someone with total unsecured debts exceeding £5,000, however, they are not a viable option under current legislation.
- **Individual voluntary arrangement (IVA).** An IVA is a formal arrangement made between the client and the majority of her/his creditors that creates a legally binding agreement between them (although secured creditors cannot be included unless they agree). The arrangement provides either for the client to defer payment of her/his debts and/or for the creditors to accept less than 100 per cent of their debts. On completion of the IVA, the balance of the debts is written off. The arrangement is set up by a nominee (usually an insolvency practitioner who is an approved accountant or solicitor) who is likely to be appointed as supervisor to oversee the arrangement (see p384). An IVA is normally made as an alternative to bankruptcy, but can be made post-bankruptcy, although this rarely happens in practice. The Official Receiver, a government official employed by the Insolvency Service , can act as nominee and supervisor of a post-bankruptcy IVA (see p416).

- **Bankruptcy** (see p387). Either the Official Receiver or an insolvency practitioner is appointed to handle the client's financial affairs for the benefit of her/his creditors. This person is known as the 'trustee in bankruptcy' (the trustee). This can be done by a request from the client, by one or more creditors or by the supervisor of a failed IVA.

The law on IVAs and bankruptcy is contained in the Insolvency Act 1986, as amended by Part 10 of the Enterprise Act 2002. The detailed rules and forms are contained in the Insolvency Rules 1986, as amended by secondary legislation. The Civil Procedure Rules (which include an Insolvency Practice Direction) apply so long as they are consistent with the bankruptcy rules.

Bankruptcy and IVAs are only available to individuals. Individual insolvency increasingly involves consumer debt rather than individuals facing business failure, and there has been a similar increase in individuals presenting their own bankruptcy petitions. In 2007, nearly 85 per cent of all petitions were debtor's petitions (in 1998 the figure was just over 50 per cent). In 2007, there were 64,480 bankruptcy orders compared with 62,956 in 2006. The number of IVAs entered into almost doubled in 2005 from 10,752 the previous year to 20,293 and have doubled again over the following two years (there were 42,165 in 2007). IVAs are currently being entered into at the rate of about 3,000 a month. Although the rate of failures is falling, however, according to the Insolvency Practices Council, it is still around the 30 per cent mark. There is also evidence of IVAs being set up for people whose only income is incapacity or disability benefits who clearly cannot meet the repayments required by the IVA. The protocol agreed earlier this year for straightforward consumer IVAs may help address these issues (see p379).

In 2006, the Insolvency Service published *Going Bankrupt in England and Wales* as part of its evaluation of the insolvency changes introduced by the Enterprise Act. This was a study of the bankruptcy experience from the individuals' perspective. The report concluded that the causes and effects of bankruptcy are varied and complex, with almost half of the respondents citing inability to manage credit as the reason for their financial failure. Business failure, relationship breakdown, illness and redundancy were the next most common causes given. The advertisement of the bankruptcy order is seen as the main reason for the existence of stigma, as well as difficulties obtaining even a bank account and the effect on an individual's credit rating.

The Enterprise Act changes seem to have had very little impact on individuals' decisions about bankruptcy, with many feeling they had few, if any, practical alternatives. The substantial increase in the number of IVAs (unaffected by the Enterprise Act changes) would seem to confirm this. Indeed, it could be argued that the increase in bankruptcy levels has been caused by irresponsible or over-generous lending practices by financial institutions.

2. Administration orders

An administration order (AO) is a county court order which prevents individual creditors taking enforcement action without permission from the court and which requires that all a person's debts be treated together.[1] It is applied for by the client, who must have at least one judgment against her/him in either the county court or High Court. The client makes a single monthly payment to the court, which then distributes it equitably among the creditors. Chapter 8 describes when an AO is appropriate. An AO is applied for on Form N92. There is no fee for the application, but costs will be added to the sum the client repays, at 10p per pound repaid.

Perhaps because of the low financial limit for AOs, the number of orders made fell steadily from 7,472 in 2000 to 3,700 in 2005, but despite an upward trend in 2006, the number of orders made in 2007 fell to 3,658. Reform of the existing scheme together with other options was put forward by the Department for Constitutional Affairs in *A Choice of Paths* (July 2004), which concluded that AOs are mostly used by those who are living on a low income over a long term and/or are unemployed, are largely unsuccessful in securing repayments to creditors (with 66 per cent of AOs failing), and are not cost-effective for the Courts Service to operate.

The existing AO scheme is due to be replaced in October 2010 (see p418).

Making the application

County court Form N92 requires a list of all the debts proposed to be subject to the order. These must not exceed £5,000. This limit has been the subject of much criticism. AOs can only be given to individuals, but debts that are jointly owed must be included. If a person is jointly and severally liable, s/he should include the whole value of such a debt. Even if finances are shared, couples cannot apply together and should make individual applications if both want to repay their debts in this way. If a couple applies for an AO at the same time and there is a joint debt, it may be acceptable to divide the debt between the two applications.

Guidance on completing Form N92 requires the applicant to list in Part B (list of creditors) arrears only of:

- rent/mortgage;
- council tax (community charge);
- maintenance;
- hire purchase;
- consumer credit debts (including cards).

This does not appear to fit with the legal requirement that the AO should cover the 'whole indebtedness'. Courts' practice on this matter appears to differ and it may be advantageous (for instance, to stay within the £5,000 limit) to apply for an order on the basis of arrears alone if this will be granted by a local court (and another strategy is available for the rest of the indebtedness). In addition, the guidance appears to require arrears of priority debts to be included in Part A (statement of means) as part of the client's expenditure, even when it is intended that the debt should be included in the AO. It is suggested that such debts should not be listed both in Part A and Part B. They should be listed in Part A only where the client is asking the court not to include the debt(s) in the AO, and should be listed in Part B where the client is asking the court to include the debt(s) in the AO.

In most cases, the whole indebtedness should be included on the form. Some courts have queried the inclusion of some debts (eg, council tax arrears and fines) but, following *Preston Borough Council v Riley*,[2] these debts should all be included. Although social fund loans and benefit overpayments can be included in an AO, if the client is in receipt of a benefit from which deductions can be made, those deductions will continue until the AO is completed. At this point, any outstanding balance will no longer be payable and so deductions should stop. The Department for Work and Pensions usually objects to being included, but, for example, if the client is seeking a composition order, it is usually worth trying to include these debts, unless the deductions will clear the debt before the AO is completed.

For employed applicants, an attachment of earnings order will be made unless the client indicates otherwise on the N92. See p264 for more on the advantages and disadvantages of attachment of earnings orders. Most clients prefer not to have an attachment of earnings order.

AOs are registered at the Registry Trust and will probably affect a person's ability to get credit.

The proposed order

Most AOs should be decided by court officers without a hearing. A notice of the application and a calculation are sent to creditors explaining what they can expect to receive (the proposed order). It is only necessary for a district judge to become involved if the amount offered is insufficient to repay the debts in a 'reasonable time'. Guidance to court staff suggests this is three years.

If court staff cannot make an order, a district judge will decide the matter. S/he can either propose a longer repayment period or make a composition order (see p372). S/he can do this with or without a hearing. Debt advisers should explain in a covering letter what they are requesting if, for example, debts are listed on the form, but the client is asking for them to be excluded. **Note:** the rules allow a district judge to make an order without a hearing, but do not permit a district judge to either dismiss an application for an AO or exclude any debts from the AO without a hearing.[3] If a court hearing is required, the client and all the creditors will be sent notice of the hearing, and the creditors will be advised of the balance owing and the proposed terms of the order. The creditors must send a corrected balance to the court, if required. See below for details about the hearing.

If the court staff prepare the order, a copy is sent to the client and all the creditors who then have 14 days in which to object to the granting of an AO. This is an opportunity for the client to object to the level of instalments, as well as for the creditors to object to being included. If no objections are received, a 'final order' is made. If objections are received, a hearing must be arranged to consider them.

Composition orders

A district judge can order that a client pays only a proportion of her/his debts (a composition order). This should be considered if the debts cannot be cleared in a 'reasonable time' (see above).

The debt adviser should help the client to work out the monthly amount available to offer creditors. If this amount will not clear the debts plus the 10 per cent charge made by the court in three years, s/he should suggest a composition order in the box under Section C of the N92.

The percentage of each debt offered is calculated by establishing the total time available for payments (ie, 36 – the number of months in three years) multiplied by the monthly payment offered, deducting 10 per cent from this total, and then dividing the resulting figure by the total of the debts owed, and finally showing this as a percentage.

Example

A person has £75 a month available income and owes a total of £4,500. A sensible composition would be to offer:

36 x £75 = £2,700 total amount to be paid (less 10% handling (£270)) = £2,430

2,430 divided by 4,500 = 0.54 (the proportion to be paid)

0.54 = 54% (the percentage to be paid)

In this case, the following wording can be inserted in the box: 'I would ask that the court considers making a composition order at the rate of 54 pence in the pound.' The client should also use this box to explain her/his reasons for not wanting an attachment of earnings order.

In many cases, the actual order will not be opposed, but a composition may be. However, provided the debt adviser is prepared with facts and figures to justify the financial necessity of what s/he argues, such orders are increasingly acceptable to courts. An application for a composition order can only be decided by a district judge (and not court officers) and cannot be rejected without a hearing.

The court hearing

There will be a court hearing if a judge thinks one is necessary – eg, if s/he may refuse the application, or either the client or a creditor objects to the terms of the proposed order. Creditors may attend the hearing (but rarely do), at which a district judge will decide whether or not to grant the order. The court will normally grant an AO unless the information given is incorrect or it appears that the order would unreasonably deny a creditor another type of remedy. If creditors object merely because they want to take action in pursuit of their debt, the debt adviser should argue that this would result in other creditors being treated less fairly. Some local authorities object to the inclusion of council tax arrears in an AO on the ground that they have an attachment of earnings order and that this will continue regardless. This is incorrect and should be challenged.[4]

Once an AO is granted, it is unlawful for any creditor to approach the client for individual payment. Interest and charges are effectively frozen on all debts included in the order. The court charges a percentage handling fee (currently 10 per cent) for all the money collected and distributes this quarterly. Provided the client makes all the payments required by the AO, s/he is discharged from all the debts in it.

Reviewing an administration order

An AO can be reviewed at any time by the court. The client, any creditor included in the order or the court itself can request a review. Some orders contain provision for periodic reviews. If the client applies, a letter should be used explaining why the review is being requested (usually because of a change in circumstances) and enclosing a financial statement. The court will then arrange a hearing.

On review, the court may:

- reduce the payments;
- suspend all payments for a specified amount of time;
- add or vary a composition order, including theoretically varying it to 0 pence in the pound;
- reinstate a revoked order (but see p374);
- make an attachment of earnings order to secure payments due under the order.[5]

Although creditors are allowed to apply to be added to an AO, there is no specific provision allowing clients to add a creditor. New creditors can sometimes be included by a review on the basis of a 'material change of circumstances', although some courts apply the rules strictly and only allow the creditors to apply. Once made, an AO is not invalidated because the debts are found to exceed the £5,000 limit, but the court can cancel the AO. The court might take this step if it thought the client had 'abused' the AO by obtaining further credit.[6] If a client misses two consecutive payments or persistently fails to pay on time, the court should send a notice requiring either:

- payment;
- an explanation;
- an application for a variation;
- a proposal for payment of arrears.

If the client fails to do one of the above, the AO is revoked in 14 days. If the client replies, the matter is referred to the district judge who may either order a hearing or revoke, suspend or vary the AO. If the order is revoked, suspended or varied without a hearing, creditors or the client can object within 14 days and a hearing must be held.

At a hearing, the district judge will consider all circumstances of the case and make one of the decisions listed above.

If the district judge decides to revoke the order, the court will no longer collect and distribute payments. The creditors will be informed that they are free to pursue their debts individually. In practice, only a small proportion of creditors contact clients following the revocation of an AO.

3. When to use bankruptcy and voluntary arrangements

The possibility and implications of obtaining an individual voluntary arrangement (IVA) should always be considered before deciding on bankruptcy. Bankruptcy is likely to be the preferred option only if a client has a number of debts, no assets (or little or no equity in her/his home), low available income for payment to creditors so that it would take more than three years to clear her/his debts, and it is unlikely that her/his situation will change in the foreseeable future. S/he must also have no need for credit in the medium term.

An IVA is likely to be the preferred option if the client has a number of debts plus a particular reason for wanting to avoid bankruptcy – eg, the possible loss of the family home, and is able to make a substantial offer, but s/he is either unable to persuade her/his creditors to accept an informal arrangement or the only informal arrangement they will accept is open-ended and likely to take many years to complete. However, IVAs do not end in automatic discharge, as bankruptcy does (usually after a maximum of 12 months) (see p413). If the client fails to keep to the arrangement, s/he could still face bankruptcy.

Advisers should take the following factors into account.

Risk to current assets

Property solely owned by a client is directly put at risk in bankruptcy. In practice, many things which a person uses may be owned by someone else (eg, a partner). Jointly owned property or property in which the client has a beneficial interest, particularly the family home, will be indirectly at risk because the trustee may be able to sell it in order to realise the bankrupt's share (see p405). In bankruptcy, any transactions involving gifts of property or transfers where the client did not receive the market value in return will be investigated by the trustee who may be able to reclaim the property (see p410). Similarly, if payments have been made to some creditors but not to others, the trustee may be able to reclaim the money (see p411). This may particularly affect members of the client's family or friends).

There is more flexibility with an IVA, as creditors are usually offered regular payments. However, IVAs increasingly require the client to obtain a valuation of the family home in the final year of the IVA, with a view to raising a lump sum by borrowing against the equity in the property.

Risk to future assets

When considering either bankruptcy or an IVA, the client should bear in mind the potential risk to any future assets, particularly if s/he expects to inherit property in the near future or already owns assets, which may have no or little value now, but which are likely to have a realisable value within the next few years.

IVAs usually contain 'windfall' clauses, although it is possible to make arrangements with potential donors – eg, by asking them to change their wills. Bankruptcy usually lasts for a maximum of only 12 months, whereas IVAs tend to last for around five years.

Effect on future credit

Both bankruptcy and IVAs are a matter of public record. The Individual Insolvency Register contains details of bankruptcies, IVAs (including post-bankruptcy IVAs) and bankruptcy restriction orders (BROs) and undertakings (BRUs – see p399). Bankruptcy records remain on the Register for three months after the date of the client's discharge. IVA records remain until the IVA ends (see p385). Records of BROs (which last for between two and 15 years) remain on the Register until they come to an end. Credit reference agencies keep details on file for six years.

It is unlikely that a lender will give credit to a bankrupt person and it is likely to be more expensive to obtain credit after discharge. In addition, it is an offence for either an undischarged bankrupt, or a person who has been discharged from bankruptcy but is subject to a BRO/BRU, to obtain credit of £500 or more without disclosing her/his status (including ordering goods on credit).[7] This declaration may make it impossible for a person to run her/his own businesses because s/he is unlikely to be given further credit.

Although utilities cannot insist on payment of pre-bankruptcy arrears as a condition of continuing to supply services, they may well require a security deposit or insist on the installation of a pre-payment meter. It may, therefore, be necessary to transfer the accounts to a non-bankrupt member of the family. The policies of a client's utility suppliers should be checked before petitioning for bankruptcy so that the client knows what to expect.

Effect on employment or office

Being an undischarged bankrupt prohibits someone from:

- engaging in business in a name other than that in which s/he was judged bankrupt without disclosing that name to people with whom s/he has business dealings;[8]
- acting as a director of, or directly or indirectly promoting, forming or managing a limited company without permission from the court;[9]
- acting as an insolvency practitioner.[10]

These restrictions end on discharge unless a BRO/BRU is made. The BRO/BRU regime (see p397) is intended to enable the court to continue those restrictions for a minimum of two years and a maximum of 15 years from the date of the BRO/BRU. An MP, local councillor, or a member of the Welsh/Northern Ireland Assembly or the Scottish Parliament, who is made bankrupt in England or Wales and is made the subject of a BRO/BRU must vacate her/his seat immediately. Likewise, a peer is disqualified from sitting and voting in the House of Lords if a BRO/BRU is made against her/him. A bankruptcy order does not automatically disqualify someone from acting as a justice of the peace (JP), but s/he is subject to the Lord Chancellor's general power to appoint and remove JPs if it is thought appropriate. A person subject to a BRO/BRU is unable to exercise her/his right to buy a council house, but because of the restrictions on obtaining credit while a BRO/BRU is in force, it is unlikely that s/he would be able to do this even if this restriction did not apply.

The professional rules of solicitors and accountants make it virtually impossible for people who have been made bankrupt to work in these professions. Other employers may be unwilling to employ a bankrupt person, especially if s/he is responsible for handling money. Charity law limits the ability of people who have been made bankrupt and subject to BROs/BRUs to serve on management committees. The bankruptcy of a sole trader does not necessarily mean the business will close, but it will be difficult for it to continue in view of the above restrictions and the following factors.

- If there are items of business equipment used by the person's employees rather than by her/him personally in the business, s/he will not be able to claim exemption for them (see p401) and the trustee may insist on a sale. Stock in trade is not exempt from sale by the trustee.

- The bankruptcy will be advertised (and any BRO/BRU may be) and publicised locally, and this may damage the reputation of the business as well as of its proprietor.
- The person will find it extremely difficult to operate a bank account, not only because of the credit restrictions, but also because of the possibility of the trustee making a claim against any credit balance in the account.

These restrictions do not apply to someone with an IVA.

Effect on housing

Bankruptcy may well result in the loss of the family home (see p405). Many tenancy agreements contain provisions allowing the landlord to end the tenancy and repossess the property in the event of the tenant's bankruptcy. In the case of a bankrupt homeowner, if there is sufficient equity, the trustee will usually be able to force a sale unless the family can raise a sufficient amount to buy out the trustee's interest (see p407).

In the case of an IVA, although creditors expect the value of the person's interest in the family home to be brought into account, there is less likelihood of the property having to be sold. The recently agreed protocol for consumer IVAs says that clients should not be required to sell their property instead of releasing equity.

Effect on reputation and stress

Although one of the objectives of the Enterprise Act 2002 was to reduce the stigma of bankruptcy, it can still be a humiliating experience for many people. There is a possibility of a public examination of the client's conduct and financial affairs in open court, although this is now rare. There will be an advertisement in the local paper. If the client's conduct is considered blameworthy, s/he may be made the subject of a BRO/BRU with the possibility of further local publicity. Bankruptcy has the potential to add considerably to a person's stress. On the other hand, there is a certainty about bankruptcy, which can reduce stress – most creditors are forced to accept the situation and can no longer pursue the client for payment.

According to *Going Bankrupt*, although some people found bankruptcy a great relief, individuals' perception of being stigmatised is still very strong, with many people reporting they felt 'unworthy' or 'humiliated'. Even after discharge, individuals reported being treated differently, particularly by financial institutions.

IVAs do not carry any stigma, but can be time consuming to draw up and gain agreement for, which could add to stress. In addition, the situation is not finally resolved until the last payment is actually made.

Are there resources available?

If a client wants to petition for her/his own bankruptcy, s/he must pay a deposit (currently £345) in addition to a court fee (currently £150). It may be possible to have the court fee waived (see p237). Lack of resources sometimes prevents someone from obtaining a bankruptcy order, although if the client is unable to raise the court fee/deposit, a charity or trust fund may help.

Although some insolvency practitioners require payment of at least part of their fees in advance, a free initial interview may be available and some insolvency practitioners collect their fees out of the payments made into the IVA. A person may pay more for the 'privilege' of avoiding bankruptcy. The fee for arranging the IVA and supervising it will probably be in the region of £4,000 and could be as high as £5,000 – £7,500. Some IVA providers argue that the client does not actually pay the fees because they come out of the total 'pot' paid into the IVA. In practice, however, only part of the money paid into an IVA actually goes to creditors. However, creditors – particularly the banks – have increasingly expressed their dissatisfaction with the level of fees and the fact they go to the IVA provider out of clients' payments into IVAs. This has been one of the reasons for the higher level of rejection of proposals over the past couple of years, which in turn has led to downward pressure on fees. Creditors increasingly insist that fees are based on the amount actually paid into the IVA rather than on an hourly rate for work done.

4. Individual voluntary arrangements

Who can make individual voluntary arrangements

Only an individual can enter into an individual voluntary arrangement (IVA), including an undischarged bankrupt for whom an IVA is a more attractive option (see p416). At the hearing of a debtor's petition (see p387), the court is required to consider whether an IVA might be a more appropriate option.

An IVA should be explored as an alternative to bankruptcy if the client has at least £100 to £200 a month available to pay her/his creditors, whether or not s/he also has assets. An IVA lasts for a fixed period (usually not more than five years) and so should also be considered where an informal payment arrangement is likely to last longer. If a client has no assets that are at risk in bankruptcy s/he may want to consider bankruptcy, because monthly payments will only last for a maximum of three years (see p403).

There is no maximum or minimum level of debt for an IVA, but, in view of the costs involved, it is unlikely to be appropriate unless the client has a number of debts totalling at least £15,000.

A client faced with being made bankrupt by a creditor should always consider an IVA as an alternative option if s/he does not want to become bankrupt and is not in a position to challenge the creditor (see p391).

The process of individual voluntary arrangements

The first step is to find an insolvency practitioner prepared to act. Many advice agencies have referral arrangements with insolvency practitioners and can arrange an initial free consultation. If the adviser has no contacts, the local Official Receiver's office keeps a rota of insolvency practitioners to whom they refer cases. The local county court may also be able to supply advisers with a list. Otherwise, details of insolvency practitioners in the area can be obtained from the Association of Business Recovery Professionals (R3), Halton House, 20-23 Holborn, London EC1N 2JD (www.r3.org.uk). Avoid companies who say they can refer clients to an insolvency practitioner in return for a fee. Insolvency practitioners are required by their regulators to give a leaflet (*Is a Voluntary Arrangement Right For Me?*) to everyone who consults them about an IVA. This is available at www.r3.org.uk. The insolvency practitioner's fees are agreed as part of the IVA. A typical fee will be in excess of £4,000, but could be as high as £5,000 to £7,500. Many insolvency practitioners do not charge up-front fees, but are paid as they go.

Straightforward consumer individual voluntary arrangements

Over the past few years, faced with rising levels of unaffordable debt, the banks have hardened their attitude to IVAs, which they see as being used more by consumers as a solution to over-indebtedness, than the business people in financial difficulties for whom IVAs were originally developed. The banks say that heavy and misleading media advertising by some IVA providers has created the impression that people are entitled to walk away from the majority of their debts. The banks also claim that in many cases they see very little return, as most of the money paid by consumers is swallowed up by the IVA providers' fees. They have responded by setting arbitrary dividend levels – ie, the pence in the pound they are prepared to accept and caps on the level of fees IVA providers are allowed to charge. Many of them now outsource IVA proposals to a small number of firms known as 'voting houses' (such as TIX), which scrutinise the proposals to ensure they are compliant with the criteria and vote accordingly.

Faced with this, the Insolvency Service and the British Bankers' Association set up the IVA Forum, which has agreed a protocol for creditors and IVA providers. The protocol provides a standard framework for straightforward consumer IVAs (SCIVAs) (not to be confused with simple IVAs, described on p418) and includes standard documentation and standard terms. These can be found at:

www.insolvency.gov.uk/insolvencyprofessionandlegislation/policychange/foum2007/plenarymeeting.htm.

Creditors are expected to accept a protocol-compliant IVA, not propose modifications and, if they do vote against, to disclose their reasons to the IVA provider.

Clients are likely to be suitable for a SCIVA if they:

- are receiving a regular income, either from employment or a pension; *and*
- have at least three debts with two or more creditors.

A SCIVA is unlikely to be suitable for clients who:

- have more than 20–25 per cent of their income from benefits (not including tax credits);
- have more than 20 per cent of their income from bonuses or commission;
- are unemployed;
- have insufficient surplus income to pay a dividend of at least 20 per cent of their debts and there is significant equity in their home (equity release should be proposed at the outset of any IVA);
- are self-employed unless the self-employment produces a regular income.

In order to give creditors confidence that the proposed IVA is the most appropriate solution to the client's debt problems, IVA providers carry out a 'due diligence' process. This means the client is given appropriate advice, including information on the advantages and disadvantages of the various options available for resolving her/his particular debt problem. The protocol also reassures creditors that the IVA provider has verified the information contained in the proposal.

Creditors generally accept financial statements drawn up in accordance with the Consumer Credit Counselling Services and the Common Financial Statement (see p44) guidelines. The insolvency practitioner carries out a review of the client's income and expenditure every 12 months and the client is expected to increase her/his contributions to the IVA by 50 per cent of any net surplus. The insolvency practitioner can also reduce the dividend payable by up to 15 per cent without referring back to creditors to reflect changes in the client's income and expenditure. The insolvency practitioner has discretion to extend the IVA for up to six months initially and then for up to a further three months to enable the arrangement to be completed. IVAs usually last for five years.

The protocol applies whether or not the client is a homeowner. If the client is a homeowner, the IVA must deal with the equity in the home. Six months before the end of the IVA, the client is expected to re-mortgage to release any equity above £5,000 up to a maximum of 85 per cent of the 'loan-to-value' – ie, 85 per cent of the valuation less any outstanding mortgage, provided the increased re-mortgage payments are not more than 50 per cent of the monthly payment into the IVA. If, as a result of a re-mortgage, the client's payments into the IVA fall to below £50 a month, the IVA will be concluded. If the client is unable to re-mortgage, the IVA is extended for up to 12 months.

In addition to the protocol, there are standard terms and conditions. If an IVA proposal is 'protocol compliant', it is expected that creditors will accept it without putting forward unnecessary modifications. Many IVAs provide that, if the client defaults, the arrangement automatically comes to an end and/or the insolvency practitioner must make the client bankrupt. Standard SCIVA terms state that the insolvency practitioner should give the client one to three months (at her/his discretion) to remedy or explain any default and, if the client fails to do this, the matter will be referred to the creditors to:

- vary the terms of the IVA; *or*
- bring the arrangement to an end; *or*
- make the client bankrupt.

The SCIVA protocol and the standard terms do not stipulate the level of dividend or the IVA provider's fees, so it is not yet known how well the new arrangements work in practice.

The proposal

The insolvency practitioner draws up a 'proposal' for the client's creditors and the court. S/he has a duty to ensure a fair balance between the interests of the client and the creditors. In the proposal, the client makes a repayment offer to the creditors. The proposal has to be accepted by creditors owed more than 75 per cent of the total amount of the client's debts. Only the debts of the creditors who actually vote, however, are counted. For example, if the client has total creditors of £20,000, but only £10,000 worth vote, the proposal can be approved, provided more than £7,500 worth of creditors vote in favour. To gain acceptance, a proposal should contain a more attractive financial offer than the creditors could expect to receive in a bankruptcy. This means paying a higher dividend to creditors and the proposal sets out how the client intends to achieve this. It is an offence for a client to make any false representations or to act (or fail to act) in a fraudulent manner in connection with an IVA proposal.[11]

If both members of a couple want to enter into IVAs covering debts in their sole and joint names, they could make separate proposals but this involves higher fees. Alternatively, they could make one proposal between them. However, in order to obtain approval of their IVAs, each proposal must be considered separately and each member of the couple must obtain the required majority of her/his own creditors in favour.

The client should take as much information on her/his financial affairs as possible to the insolvency practitioner. Advisers can assist by preparing a financial statement as well as a list of debts and assets. The proposal must include:

- details of the proposed arrangements, including why an IVA is the appropriate solution and likely to be accepted by creditors. IVAs do not usually provide for

payment of the client's debts in full. They normally provide for her/his available income and the proceeds of the sale of any assets to be distributed to creditors on a *pro rata* basis, with the balances being written off – ie, a composition;
- the anticipated level of the person's income during the period of the IVA;
- details of all assets (and their estimated value) and of any assets available from third parties, such as a relative or friend;
- details of any charges on property in favour of creditors and of any assets that the client proposes to exclude from the IVA. It is usual to make some arrangement for realising the client's share in any equity in the family home and, if this provision is included in the IVA, the client should be aware of its significance;
- details of the client's debts and of any guarantees given for them by third parties;
- the proposed duration of the IVA and the arrangements for payments to creditors, including the estimated amounts and frequency. IVAs do not normally last longer than five years;
- details of the supervisor, and of the fees to be paid to the nominee and the supervisor.

In the case of a SCIVA, the proposal should also contain details of any previous attempts to deal with the client's financial problems and the reasons why these were unsuccessful. The IVA provider should give the client advice and information on the advantages and disadvantages of all available debt solutions. The proposal may contain details of any recommendations made to the client and the reasons s/he has decided to propose an IVA.

An experienced insolvency practitioner will be aware of the proposals likely to be acceptable to creditors and the court, and will ensure the proposal complies with the requirements of the Insolvency Act. The insolvency practitioner is required to endorse the notice of the proposal to indicate s/he is prepared to act and will not do so unless s/he is satisfied that the proposal is viable. Once the insolvency practitioner has signed the proposal, s/he becomes the client's 'nominee'. Once the proposal is made, the client must prepare a statement of affairs, containing details of the matters contained in the proposal.

Within 14 days, the nominee must file a report to the court stating in her/his opinion:
- whether the proposed IVA has a reasonable prospect of being approved and implemented;
- whether a meeting of the client's creditors should be held to consider the proposal; *and*
- if so, the date, time and place proposed.

At the same time, the nominee should also file:

- a copy of the proposal;
- a copy of the statement of affairs;
- a copy of the endorsed notice of proposal;
- a list of the documents filed containing a statement confirming whether or not the client intends to apply for an interim order (see below);
- the fee (currently £30).[12]

The report should be filed to the county court for the district in which the client lives (unless s/he is an undischarged bankrupt, in which case the report should be filed in the court that conducted the bankruptcy). Any application in relation to the IVA is made to the court where the nominee's report was filed.

Interim orders

Until the IVA is approved, the client is vulnerable to enforcement action by creditors. To avoid this, once the insolvency practitioner has become the nominee, the client can apply to the court for an 'interim order'.[13] If an interim order is granted:

- a creditor cannot attempt to make the client bankrupt;
- a landlord cannot repossess the client's property (with or without a court order);
- court proceedings or other enforcement action (including the levy of distress) cannot commence or continue against the client or her/his property without the permission of the court.[14]

The application is made to the county court for the insolvency district in which the client lives (or if the client is an undischarged bankrupt, the court which has conduct of the bankruptcy). It must be accompanied by an affidavit (a sworn statement) and a copy of the endorsed notice of the proposal. A court fee of £150 is payable.

The court sets a hearing date to consider the matter and gives two days' notice. The court can freeze (or 'stay') any other court proceedings or enforcement action against the client pending consideration of the application, and usually does so. If the client is an undischarged bankrupt, notice must be given to the Official Receiver and any trustee.

The court can make an interim order provided that:

- it is satisfied that the proposal is 'serious' and viable – ie, that it has not been made just to delay making a bankruptcy order and with no benefit to creditors;
- the insolvency practitioner is prepared to act as the nominee;
- there has been no application for an interim order in the previous 12 months; *and*
- the client is either an undischarged bankrupt or could petition for her/his own bankruptcy (see p387).

An interim order initially lasts for only 14 days but is usually extended to allow sufficient time for the creditors' meeting to take place and for the nominee to report back to the court.

In most cases, the nominee's report is presented at the same time as any application for an interim order. Provided the court is satisfied that the proposals should be put to the creditors, the court will usually endorse the recommendation and extend the interim order for seven weeks after the proposed date of the meeting. (If the matters are dealt with together, the order is known as a 'concertina order'.)

If the court rejects the nominee's recommendations, the interim order is discharged and any proceedings or enforcement action can continue. The client cannot apply for another interim order for 12 months.[15]

The client can, however, put forward her/his proposal without applying for an interim order, but will be vulnerable to any enforcement action by a creditor until the IVA is actually agreed.

The creditors' meeting

The nominee must inform all creditors of the date and time of the meeting, which is normally held in the nominee's offices and chaired by her/him. The client is usually required to attend. **Note:** in the case of the SCIVA procedure, there is no creditors' meeting. The creditors consider the proposal and vote on it. Although the proposal can be amended, the client must consent to any modifications. It is not unusual for IVAs to contain provisions for any 'windfall' payments received by the client during the period of the IVA to be taken into account. It is also usual to include specific proposals about any beneficial interest the client may have in the family home.

The proposal must be approved by more than 75 per cent of the creditors who vote on the proposal. Many creditors do not attend the meeting, but instead send their vote to the nominee. Certain creditors, such as banks and HM Revenue and Customs, always vote at meetings and, as they also tend to be the largest creditors, any proposal is unlikely to be approved unless these creditors agree. The practice of some banks of referring all proposals they receive to a voting house (which will recommend an acceptance or refusal) means these firms are in a strong position to influence the content of the proposal and its eventual outcome, even if, taken individually, the creditor would not be in position to block the IVA.

The nominee may discuss the proposal with creditors prior to the meeting to obtain agreement. The meeting cannot approve a proposal that would affect the rights of a preferential creditor in bankruptcy (such as arrears of wages owed to employees of the client) or the rights of secured creditors (such as a mortgage lender) without their consent.[16] Unless the IVA specifically excludes a secured lender's right to enforce its security, it may still be able to do so even if it has agreed to being included in the IVA.[17]

Usually, the nominee's appointment is approved at the meeting and s/he becomes the 'supervisor' of the IVA. If the proposal is approved, it takes effect immediately and is binding not only on every creditor who had notice of the meeting and was entitled to vote, but also on any other creditor who would have been entitled to vote if s/he had received notice of the meeting. Such creditors are entitled to claim from the client the amounts they would have received under the IVA and the client will have to make these payments in addition to those made under the IVA. Alternatively, such creditors may challenge the IVA (see below).[18] The outcome of the meeting must be reported to the court within four days. The court records the effect of the report and discharges any interim order.

Challenging an individual voluntary arrangement

The client, or any creditor, can appeal to the court against the IVA within 28 days of the report of the creditors' meeting being made to the court (including those who did not receive notice of the meeting, who have 28 days from when they found out about it), but only on the grounds that:

- there were irregularities in the way the meeting was held – eg, the proposal contained misleading or inaccurate information; *or*
- the arrangement unfairly prejudiced the rights of a creditor – eg, if the meeting approved a proposal to include a debt which is not provable in bankruptcy, such as a student loan, thus preventing the creditor from taking action to recover full payment.

Because an IVA is an agreement between the client and her/his creditors, in theory any debt can be included (apart from secured creditors who can only be included if they specifically agree). However, in the case of other debts which cannot be proved in bankruptcy and/or are still payable by the client after discharge from bankruptcy (see p413), it may be necessary to replicate their treatment in bankruptcy in order to avoid creditors successfully challenging the approval of an IVA in which they find themselves unwilling participants. This can be done either by agreeing to exclude them altogether and leaving them to be paid outside the IVA or by including them with their agreement.

If a creditor challenges an IVA and the court considers the challenge is justified, it may:

- revoke (or suspend) the IVA; *or*
- direct that a fresh creditors' meeting is held to consider a new agreement or reconsider the existing agreement (and renew any interim order).[19]

Completion of the individual voluntary arrangement

The insolvency practitioner's role as 'supervisor' of the IVA is to implement it and ensure the client carries out her/his side of the arrangement as agreed, seeking guidance from the court, if necessary. The supervisor arranges the sale of any assets that need to be sold, and collects the payments due from the client and distributes them to the creditors. If the client's circumstances change, s/he should be advised to contact the supervisor immediately, as it may be possible for the original agreement to be 'modified' at a creditors' meeting. The supervisor may be able to extend the period of the IVA to enable the client to complete the payments. IVAs often make provision for such eventualities either by giving the supervisor a degree of discretion and/or by making specific provision for variation/extension of the IVA. If the IVA contains no such provisions, even though more than a 75 per cent majority was needed for its original approval, it is thought that all the creditors included in the IVA would have to agree to any variation.

Provided the client complies with the IVA, s/he will be discharged from her/his liability to all creditors covered by it at the end of the period. The IVA will not, however, automatically discharge any co-debtor, including the person's spouse or partner, and provision for this will have to be specifically included and agreed. However, unless the joint income is used to fund the IVA (or the partner/spouse has no income), creditors may challenge the IVA.

If the terms of the IVA are not complied with, the supervisor will usually be able to petition for the client's bankruptcy. If the supervisor decides it is not worth doing this – eg, because there are insufficient funds paid into the IVA, individual creditors may decide to do so instead. The client will have to negotiate with them separately if s/he wants to avoid bankruptcy.

Advantages and disadvantages

The advantages of an IVA include the following.

- The client avoids the stigma or publicity that is attached to bankruptcy.
- An IVA can be drawn up to meet the client's situation, so that assets such as the family home are not automatically lost if the creditors agree – eg, because, overall, they will be better off than in bankruptcy.
- Creditors should receive higher payments than they would in a bankruptcy.
- Unsecured creditors who voted against the IVA are still bound by it.
- The client is not subject to the restrictions imposed in bankruptcy and so can still be a company director without the court's permission, and may find it easier to obtain credit for the business than s/he would following bankruptcy.
- The client could be in a profession where s/he could lose her/his job in the event of bankruptcy – eg, accountancy, police or armed forces.

The disadvantages include the following.

- The client should have at least three unsecured creditors and unsecured debts of at least £15,000 for an IVA to be a suitable option.
- If creditors reject the proposal, the client cannot apply for a further interim order for 12 months and may lose any up-front fee paid to the insolvency practitioner.

- The client will generally be required to make higher payments over a longer period than in a bankruptcy.
- The costs of an IVA are relatively high and may have to be paid in advance (although it should be possible to find an insolvency practitioner who does not require up-front fees).
- Assets are at risk if the creditors do not agree to exclude them.
- The client may still be made bankrupt if the IVA fails and the costs of the unsuccessful IVA will be added to the debts.
- The client will be closely monitored by the supervisor during the period of the IVA and will have to report any changes of circumstances.
- If the client's circumstances change, the IVA may fail if the supervisor cannot persuade the creditors to agree to a new arrangement.
- IVAs are a matter of public record and future applications for credit could be affected.

5. Bankruptcy

How a client becomes bankrupt

There are three ways in which a client may become bankrupt.

- A creditor is owed at least £750 (or two or more creditors are owed a total of at least £750 between them). **Note:** the £750 limit is due to be increased to £1,500 on 1 October 2009.
- A client is unable to pay her/his debts.
- The supervisor of an individual voluntary arrangement (IVA) where the client has defaulted applies to the court for her/his bankruptcy.

People who are 'domiciled' in England and Wales, or who are personally present in England or Wales on the day the bankruptcy petition is presented to the court, or who have been resident or carried out a business in England and Wales at some time in the three years before the presentation of the bankruptcy petition, are subject to bankruptcy law. People who live in another European Union (EU) member state (apart from Denmark) and who do not administer their financial affairs on a regular basis in England and Wales are only subject to bankruptcy law if they have an 'establishment' in England or Wales. An 'establishment' is the place where the client carries out her/his business. Business carried out on an occasional basis does not count, nor does merely having a property, such as a holiday home, in England or Wales.[20]

The bankruptcy process

The debtor's petition

In order to make her/himself bankrupt, a client must 'petition' the court on the grounds that s/he is 'unable to pay her/his debts' (although it is possible to become bankrupt for only one debt which the client is unable to pay).[21] This involves completing a court form, called the debtor's bankruptcy petition (Form 6.27), together with a statement of affairs (Form 6.28). These can be obtained from the county court or downloaded from the Insolvency Service website (www.insolvency.gov.uk). Although these can be completed online, they cannot be submitted online and so must be printed off for filing at the court.

The petition and statement of affairs, together with three copies of the petition and one copy of the statement of affairs, must be presented to the client's local county court with bankruptcy jurisdiction. From 1 October 2009, the court will be able to allow the client to present her/his petition to a different court. From 1 October 2009, the court will be able to allow the client to present her/his own petition to a different court in certain circumstances. If the client does not live in England or Wales, the petition must be presented to the High Court in London.[22] If the client administers her/his financial affairs on a regular basis in another EU member state (other than Denmark), s/he must usually petition for bankruptcy in that member state.[23] According to the Insolvency Service: 'The court will usually regard the country where you carry on a business or otherwise earn your living as your centre of main interests. If you are not employed or self-employed your centre of main interests will be the country you normally live in at the date of the petition. Therefore, if you do not live or work in the UK you cannot go bankrupt here.'

A person who only has an 'establishment' in England or Wales but lives in another EU member state (other than Denmark) cannot petition for her/his own bankruptcy in England or Wales, but can be made bankrupt by a UK creditor in some circumstances.

If a client wants to petition for her/his own bankruptcy, a court fee of £150 is payable together with a deposit of £345. The court can waive/remit the fee (see p237) but not the deposit.

The statement of affairs

The statement of affairs requires a considerable amount of information to be supplied, much of which may not be readily available – eg, asset valuations. Although there are guidance notes, these are not comprehensive. If not typed, the statement of affairs should be completed in capital letters. All amounts should be to the nearest pound. The following points should be borne in mind when assisting the client to complete the statement of affairs.

- **Section 1** asks for personal details. Question 1.14 does not require information to be included about any informal attempts to come to a payment arrangement with creditors. Details of any pending court action should be included in the answer to question 1.15, including magistrates' court proceedings.
- **Section 2** only needs to be completed if the client is or has been self-employed at any time in the previous two years.

- **Section 3** asks for details of assets and their valuation. Examples of assets are listed at the start of the section. Approximate values only should be given, using the figure they would fetch at auction rather than their new or replacement value. If any valuable items are listed, they are likely to be claimed by the trustee. Perishable items or items which will diminish in value if not disposed of quickly are likely to be claimed by the Official Receiver before a trustee is appointed.[24] There does not appear to be any particular significance in the reference to life, endowment or pension policies in Question 3.2 and, if the client has disposed of any of these and is unaware of their market value at the time, s/he should either leave that box blank or mark it appropriately – eg, 'unsure of value'. Question 3.3 should be answered for each motor vehicle owned and each motor vehicle disposed of during the previous six months (there does not appear to be any particular significance in that period). The box in Question 3.6 should be ticked if the bailiff has visited. If the bailiff has visited but not levied, the subsequent boxes should be left blank.
- **Section 4** asks for details of secured and unsecured creditors. Again, examples of creditors are listed at the start of the section. If the client is unsure who all her/his creditors are, it may be helpful to obtain a copy of her/his credit reference file.
- **Section 5** asks for details of bank accounts and credit cards. There is no particular significance in the two-year periods referred to in Questions 5.2 and 5.4. Accounts and/or credit cards which the client no longer has must be disclosed. Any bank or building society accounts which the client has may be frozen and so any money needed to cover everyday living expenses should be withdrawn before the application for a bankruptcy order is made.
- **Section 6** asks for details of employment and income. Only details of regular income should be included. All benefit income coming into the household should be included in question 6.6 even if the client is not the claimant. Question 6.7 asks for the amount of contribution to the household expenses (listed at Question 7.1) and this should be worked out on a proportionate basis where it is not possible to identify an exact figure. Question 6.8 asks for 'total household income' calculated as the total of the client's income, income from benefits and contributions. Because of the way income payment orders are calculated (see p403), total income of other household members should be included here. No pence should be included. Any attachment of earnings orders referred to in Question 6.10 should be 'stayed' – ie, halted once the petition is presented.
- **Section 7** asks for details of the client's outgoings, but the total household expenditure should be shown to correspond with the response to Question 6.7 (contributions). The list given only contains the usual household expenses. Any other essential items should also be included.
- **Section 8** asks for details of current properties owned or rented by the client, either solely or jointly. If the client lives in rented accommodation, there are

unlikely to be any issues for the trustee. Advisers should be aware that, where an owner-occupied property is in the sole name of the client's partner, this does not necessarily mean that the client does not have an interest in it. If the client has made a direct contribution to the purchase price, either by paying a deposit or making mortgage repayments, s/he may have an interest in the property and the adviser should seek specialist advice.

- **Section 9** asks for details of property disposed of in the previous five years. If the client has either given property away or has transferred it but not received the cash value or equivalent in return, the trustee may be able to re-open the transaction to restore the position to what it was before the disposal took place (see p416).
- **Section 10** asks for details of members of the client's household and dependants. In deciding the amount of any income payments order, the trustee is required to take into account the reasonable domestic needs of the client and her/his family (see p403).
- **Section 11** is headed 'Causes of Bankruptcy' and asks the client when s/he first had difficulty paying her/his debts, the reasons why s/he is unable to pay her/his debts and whether s/he has lost money through betting or gambling in the previous two years. Great care needs to be taken in completing this section as the replies may lead the Official Receiver to consider applying for a bankruptcy restriction order (BRO – see p397).
- **Section 12** is a declaration that all the information provided is true and accurate to the best of the client's knowledge and belief.
- **Section 13** is a continuation sheet.

Once the forms are completed, they must be taken to the court to be sworn and filed, together with the fee (or an application for exemption or remission on Form EX160) and the deposit. The court will arrange for the papers to be put before a district judge. Some courts arrange a hearing either immediately or later in the day; other courts insist on a prior appointment being made. Advisers should find out the local practice.

Is an individual voluntary arrangement more appropriate?

In some cases, the court is required to refer the case to an insolvency practitioner for a report. This happens if:

- the client's unsecured debts are less than £40,000;
- the client has money and/or property worth at least £4,000;
- the client has not been the subject of bankruptcy proceedings in the previous five years;
- the court considers an IVA might be a more appropriate option.[25]

The client does not have to pay the fee for this report. In practice, there are usually insufficient assets for the insolvency practitioner to recommend an IVA and the bankruptcy proceeds.

Even if the case is not referred to an insolvency practitioner, the court will still not automatically make a bankruptcy order. If it appears, for example, that the client's assets exceed her/his liabilities or that the client is otherwise able to pay her/his debts, the district judge can dismiss the petition and the bankruptcy deposit will be returned to the client. Sometimes, petitions are adjourned for the client to take advice on alternatives to bankruptcy – eg, a repayment arrangement. Otherwise, the bankruptcy order is made.

The creditor's petition

Creditors who are considering making a client bankrupt need to bear in mind that the process is intended to benefit all creditors, not just themselves. They could bear all the costs of obtaining a bankruptcy order only to find that other creditors receive more and they could even end up with nothing at all if the client has no income or assets.

Who can apply

A creditor can apply for someone to be made bankrupt if s/he is owed at least £750 (due to be increased to £1,500 on 1 October 2009), which the person 'appears' unable to pay. Two or more creditors who are owed a total of at least £750 between them can petition together. The creditor must satisfy the court of the client's inability to pay:

- by serving a 'statutory demand' on the client with which s/he fails to comply; *or*
- by unsuccessfully attempting to enforce a court judgment against the client by the use of bailiffs or other enforcement process.[26]

In the case of bailiffs, they must have made serious attempts to enter the client's home and seize property. It is not enough that the bailiff has merely visited the client's home and been unable to gain access.[27]

Essentially, if the enforcement method chosen by the creditor produces no or insufficient money, the creditor can petition for bankruptcy.[28]

Serving a statutory demand

Serving a statutory demand is the most common method used by creditors to satisfy the court of the client's inability to pay. This is a document demanding that the client either pays the debt in full or in part (by instalments or a lump sum) in a manner acceptable to the creditor, or offers security for the debt which is acceptable to the creditor. Form 6.1 is used where there is no judgment; Form 6.2 is used where there is a judgment.

The statutory demand does not have to be issued by the court or even seen by it at this stage. If the client does not comply with the statutory demand within 21 days, the creditor can issue a creditor's petition and ask the court to make a bankruptcy order. A creditor does not need a judgment in order to be able to serve a statutory demand for the debt. However, without a judgment the creditor might find the client is able to challenge the existence of the debt (see below). A creditor who has a judgment is not required to attempt to enforce it; the creditor can serve a statutory demand instead.

Responding to a statutory demand

Some creditors use statutory demands as a method of debt collection. The courts have said that this is only an abuse of process if the creditor is aware the debt is reasonably disputed.[29] Although the creditor may have no intention of making the client bankrupt, statutory demands should never be ignored. On receipt of a statutory demand, the client should consider the following options if s/he does not want to become bankrupt.

- Apply for an administration order or propose an IVA as an alternative to bankruptcy.
- Make payment(s) either to clear the debt in full or reduce it below the £750 bankruptcy limit (or £1,500 after 1 October 2009).
- Make an offer of payment in full and final settlement of the debt or payment in full. This could either be in a lump sum or by instalments. If the debt is subject to a judgment, as well as trying to negotiate with the creditor, the client should apply to the court to vary the judgment to enable payment by instalments with a view to arranging this before the creditor can obtain a bankruptcy order. In appropriate circumstances, the client could apply for a time order (see p283).
- Apply for a time order (if the debt is regulated by the Consumer Credit Act 1974) (see p283).
- Offer a voluntary charge over her/his property as security for the debt (see p192).
- Apply to set aside the statutory demand within 18 days of service.[30]

Setting aside a statutory demand

If the statutory demand has been 'set aside' (ie, cancelled) the creditor cannot apply for a bankruptcy order. The client can apply for the demand to be set aside on the grounds that:

- there is dispute about the money said to be owed. If the creditor has obtained a judgment, the court will not at this stage enquire into the validity of the debt. If this is an issue the client should be advised to consider applying to set aside or appeal the judgment (see pp298 and 307);[31]
- the client has a cross-claim against the creditor, which equals or exceeds the amount of the debt;
- the creditor holds security, which equals or exceeds the amount of the debt;
- on 'other grounds' – eg, the debt is 'statute-barred' (see p124) or the demand has not been signed.[32] A statutory demand based on a judgment debt is not statute-barred even if the judgment was made more than six years ago.[33]

The application is made on Form 6.4, supported by an affidavit on Form 6.5. There is no court fee. The application will be put before a district judge. If s/he considers there are no grounds for the application, s/he can dismiss it without a hearing. Otherwise, a hearing will be arranged at which the district judge will consider the application.

The court will not set aside a statutory demand on the grounds that the creditor has unreasonably refused an offer of payment or security, or even on the grounds that the creditor has refused to consider such an offer. Nor will the court set aside a demand on the grounds that it is for an excessive amount. In such a case, the client is supposed to pay the amount admitted to be due and only apply to set aside the amount in dispute. The court will not 'do a deal' with the client to set the statutory demand aside on condition that s/he makes a payment. The court can set aside a statutory demand in respect of a disputed debt provided it is satisfied there are reasonable grounds of success.

If the application to set aside the statutory demand is dismissed, the creditor will be given leave to present her/his bankruptcy petition.

The petition

The next step is for the creditor to present a bankruptcy petition on the appropriate form to the court. There are different forms depending on whether the creditor is an unsatisfied judgment creditor or has served a statutory demand. Together with the petition, the creditor must file at court:

- an affidavit that the facts stated in the petition are true;
- a court fee of £190; *and*
- the deposit of £415.

Responding to the petition

The petition must be served personally on the client. It is still not too late to prevent a bankruptcy order being made, but the client must give at least seven days' notice to the court and to the creditor of her/his intention to oppose the bankruptcy order. The client can still raise any 'genuine triable issue' even if s/he did not apply to set aside the statutory demand, but s/he cannot put forward any matter on which the court has already ruled against her/him unless there has been a relevant change of circumstances.

The bankruptcy hearing

The hearing will be before a district judge. At the hearing, the creditor must prove s/he has delivered the petition to the client (and, where relevant, that the statutory demand has been brought to the client's attention) and file a certificate to the effect that the debt is still outstanding. If the client has paid the debt (excluding any creditor's costs) in full prior to the date of hearing of the petition it will be dismissed, but the district judge may still order the client to pay the creditor's costs. If not paid, these would have to be the subject of fresh enforcement proceedings (which could be bankruptcy proceedings if the costs order is for £750 or more, or £1,500 after 1 October 2009).

The court has discretion to refuse to make a bankruptcy order in certain circumstances, including where execution on a judgment has been stayed (including an instalment order for payment), or where the creditor has, in the court's opinion, unreasonably refused to accept an offer to pay the debt by instalments or a reduced sum in full and final settlement of the debt, or where it has unreasonably refused an offer to secure the debt.[34] If the client has reduced the debt (excluding any creditor's costs) to less than £750 in between the issue of the petition and the hearing date, the court has the discretion to make a bankruptcy order, taking into account any previous conduct of the client.[35] Even if the petition is dismissed, the client could be ordered to pay the creditor's costs.[36]

It is not unusual for the parties to reach agreement about payment of the debt and the hearing of the petition can be adjourned, but repeated adjournments should not be allowed unless there is a reasonable prospect of payment within a reasonable time.[37] If an agreement is reached and the creditor does not want to proceed with the bankruptcy, the petition can be dismissed with the permission of the court.

The individual voluntary arrangement supervisor's petition

If the client is subject to an IVA, the supervisor can petition for a bankruptcy order on the grounds that:

- the arrangement was based on false or misleading information supplied by the client; *or*
- the client has failed to comply with the terms of the IVA.[38]

If this happens, the supervisor will generally become the client's trustee in bankruptcy.

After a bankruptcy order is made

The Official Receiver

When a bankruptcy order is made (either because the client has petitioned for her/his own bankruptcy or a creditor has successfully petitioned), the court will notify the Official Receiver. Soon after the bankruptcy order is made, which could be on the same day, the client will be contacted by the Official Receiver. The Official Receiver's primary functions are to:

- investigate the client's conduct and financial affairs, and report to the court; *and*
- obtain control of the client's property and any relevant documents.

The client may be asked to complete a questionnaire (Form B40.01). This replicates many of the questions in the client's statement of affairs (Form 6.28) and so the client should keep a copy of this document to assist in completing the questionnaire. If the bankruptcy order has been made because a client has petitioned for her/his own bankruptcy (unless s/he has recently traded or been bankrupt previously), s/he will usually be offered a telephone interview with an examiner (a member of the Official Receiver's staff). The examiner will check the client's answers and ask questions to obtain any additional information. In other cases, the client will be required to attend an interview at the Official Receiver's office.

The client is required to co-operate with the Official Receiver. S/he must give up possession of her/his assets (with limited exceptions) and hand over any papers that are reasonably required.[39] Failure to do so could result in her/his discharge being delayed. The Official Receiver can arrange for her/him to be examined in public by the court about her/his financial affairs and the causes of her/his bankruptcy, although this rarely happens if the client has co-operated fully with the Official Receiver. The Official Receiver can arrange for her/his mail to be re-directed, if appropriate.[40] In appropriate cases, the Official Receiver can apply to the court to impound the client's passport to prevent her/him leaving the country. It is a bankruptcy offence for the client to leave (or attempt to leave) with assets of £1,000 or more which should have been given up to the Official Receiver.[41]

The Official Receiver registers the bankruptcy at the Land Registry, advertises it in the *London Gazette* and one local paper and inserts details in the Insolvency Register (the court can order that this does not happen in some circumstances).[42]

From 1 October 2009, the court will have specific power to prevent the disclosure of the client's current address or whereabouts if this might reasonably be expected to lead to violence (or threats of violence) to the client or other members of the family who live with her/him.[43]

The client's bank account may be frozen. The Official Receiver has a duty to investigate every bankruptcy unless s/he considers such investigation is unnecessary.[44] Any criminal offences revealed must be reported to the authorities (see p396). S/he will usually visit any business premises and may also visit the client's home, but this is rare. If the Official Receiver does visit, s/he may remove any items of value.

Within 12 weeks of making the bankruptcy order, the Official Receiver must decide whether or not to call a meeting of creditors to appoint a trustee in bankruptcy. If no trustee is appointed, the Official Receiver will become the trustee.[45]

The Official Receiver will contact her/his creditors and invite them to 'prove' their debts – ie, submit claims.

Role of the trustee

Once a trustee is appointed, or the Official Receiver becomes the trustee, the client is deprived of ownership of all her/his 'estate' – ie, all her/his property (except certain items – see p401). The estate 'vests' in the trustee – ie, ownership passes automatically to the trustee. The client cannot sell anything, but if arrangements have already been made to sell something (eg, the home), the trustee will almost certainly approve, provided it is a proper commercial deal. The proceeds will then be used to satisfy creditors. The trustee becomes responsible for handling the client's affairs and getting as much money as possible for her/his creditors. The trustee is charged with gathering together and selling all of the property previously owned by the client and distributing the proceeds among her/his creditors.

The client may have property which either cannot be disposed of and/or is subject to obligations which would involve expenditure to the detriment of the estate, and hence creditors. The trustee can dispose of such 'onerous property' – eg, a business lease.[46]

If the client attempts to give away or sell 'her/his' property after the petition but before it passes to the trustee, this transfer is void – ie, of no effect. The court can confirm a sale, but in the absence of this, the property still forms part of the client's estate and can be recovered and sold by the trustee.

Where the client's bank honours a cheque after the date of the bankruptcy order, the transaction will not be void if either:

- the bank did not have notice of the bankruptcy order before honouring the cheque; *or*
- it is not reasonably practicable to recover the payment from the person to whom it was made.[47]

The sale of jointly owned property requires the consent of the co-owner or a court order. If a client acquires any property before discharge, s/he must inform the trustee within 21 days. The trustee then has 42 days (during which the client must not dispose of the property) in which to claim the property for the estate.[48]

Offences

It is an offence for the client to do anything that intentionally conceals information or property from the Official Receiver or trustee, or to deliberately mislead the Official Receiver or trustee about property which s/he had either before or after the bankruptcy. Criminal charges can be brought against a client, leading to a fine and/or imprisonment. However, if the client can show that there was no intention to mislead or defraud, this counts as a valid defence. Other so-called 'bankruptcy offences' include obtaining credit of £500 or more without telling the creditor s/he is bankrupt, and trading under a different business name without informing people with whom s/he comes into contact through the business the name under which s/he was made bankrupt (see pre-discharge restrictions on p397).[49] The majority of convictions are for these two offences.

Bankruptcy restrictions

In addition to revealing possible criminal offences (including bankruptcy offences), it is possible that an investigation could lead to a BRO or bankruptcy restriction undertaking (BRU).

Pre-discharge restrictions

A client who is an undischarged bankrupt cannot:

- obtain credit of £500 or more (in total, not per transaction) without disclosing her/his status as an undischarged bankrupt;
- engage in business in a name other than that in which s/he was made bankrupt without disclosing that name to people with whom s/he has business dealings;
- act as a director of, or directly or indirectly promote, form or manage a limited company without leave of the court;
- act as an insolvency practitioner or an intermediary for debt relief orders (see p419);
- act as a charity trustee (unless s/he is a director of the charity and has obtained leave of the court).

Breach of any of these is a criminal offence, but the restrictions usually end on discharge. On the other hand, people who are regarded as 'culpable' because they have acted recklessly, irresponsibly or dishonestly may be made subject to an extended period of restrictions through a BRO or BRU.

Post-discharge restrictions

The BRO/BRU regime (which mirrors the above restrictions) is intended to enable the court to continue these restrictions for a minimum of two years and a maximum of 15 years from the date of the court order. The court is able to make a BRO/BRU if it thinks it 'appropriate having regard to the conduct of the bankrupt'.

When considering an application for a BRO the court must take into account whether the client has:

- failed to keep records which account for a loss of property by the client, or by a business carried out by her/him. The loss must have occurred in the period beginning two years before petition and ending with the date of the application;
- failed to produce records of this kind on demand by the Official Receiver or the trustee;
- entered into a transaction at an 'under-value' (see p410);
- made an excessive pension contribution;
- failed to supply goods or services which were wholly or partly paid for and which gave rise to a provable claim in the bankruptcy;
- traded before the commencement of the bankruptcy when s/he knew, or ought to have known, that s/he would be unable to pay her/his debts;

- incurred before the commencement of the bankruptcy a debt which s/he did not reasonably expect to be able to pay (which appears to include increasing the amount of debt on a credit card);
- failed to account satisfactorily for a loss of property or for an insufficiency of property to meet bankruptcy debts;
- carried on any gambling, 'rash and hazardous speculation' or 'unreasonable extravagance', which may have contributed to or increased the extent of the bankruptcy or which took place between the presentation of the petition and the commencement of the bankruptcy;
- neglected her/his business affairs, which may have contributed to or increased the extent of the bankruptcy;
- been fraudulent;
- failed to co-operate with the Official Receiver or the trustee.[50]

The conduct that the court is required to take into account addresses behaviour by consumers as well as by traders, and behaviour both before and after the bankruptcy order. Where no period is specified, it is likely that the more serious the misconduct, the longer the period over which it will be taken into account.

The court is also required to consider in particular whether the client was an undischarged bankrupt at some time during the period of six years ending with the date of the bankruptcy to which the application relates. However, it is understood that the existence of two bankruptcies is not considered to be misconduct in itself, but it allows the court to put misconduct in context.

Only conduct on or after 1 April 2004 (the date the BRO regime came into force) can be taken into account.[51] The application can only be made by the Secretary of State or by the Official Receiver acting on the direction of the Secretary of State. The application must normally be made within one year from the date of the bankruptcy order, even if the client is discharged before this. The BRO comes into force on the day it is made and must be for a specified period of:

- at least two years; *but*
- no more than 15 years.[52]

A BRO continues the restrictions set out above in relation to obtaining credit and engaging in business, involvement in a limited company and acting as an insolvency practitioner. Breach of the BRO is punishable as a bankruptcy offence.[53] In addition, being subject to a BRO/BRU may affect a client's employment or her/his ability to hold certain offices. For example, a person subject to a BRO/BRU cannot:

- serve as an MP, local councillor, a national Assembly member or sit in the House of Lords;
- act as a school governor;
- exercise any 'right to buy' under the Housing Act.

It may also affect her/his ability to belong to a professional body. This should always be checked before proceeding with bankruptcy. If it appears there is a risk that post-bankruptcy restrictions may be imposed, a client should be advised to consider whether any of these restrictions would affect her/him.

Application for a bankruptcy restriction order

An application for a BRO must be supported by a report and evidence from the Secretary of State.

The hearing date must be fixed for no earlier than eight weeks from when the court decides on the venue. Since the application is made as part of the bankruptcy proceedings – rather than in separate proceedings – the hearing takes place in the client's local bankruptcy court. The hearing is in public. The Secretary of State must serve the application on the client not more than 14 days after the application was filed at court, together with:

- at least six weeks' notice of the hearing;
- a copy of the Secretary of State's report;
- any further evidence in support of the application; *and*
- an acknowledgement of service.

The client must:

- return the acknowledgement of service to the court, indicating whether or not s/he intends to contest the application, not more than 14 days after the application is served. Otherwise, s/he may attend the hearing, but cannot take part unless the court agrees;
- file at court any evidence opposing the application which s/he wishes the court to consider, within 28 days of being served with the application and supporting evidence;
- serve copies on the Secretary of State within a further three days.

Within 14 days the Secretary of State must file at court any further evidence and serve a copy on the client as soon as reasonably practicable.

The court may make a BRO regardless of whether or not the client attends the hearing or has filed any evidence.[54]

This is an application within the bankruptcy proceedings and is a civil, not a criminal, procedure. The Secretary of State only needs to satisfy the court on the (lower) civil standard of proof – ie, 'on the balance of probabilities' – rather than the (higher) criminal standard – ie, 'satisfied beyond a reasonable doubt'.

Bankruptcy restriction undertakings

In order to avoid the need for court proceedings, the Secretary of State may instead accept the client's offer of a BRU, which has the same effect as a BRO (including the consequences of a breach) from the date it is accepted by the Secretary of State. As with a BRO, it must be entered into:

- for at least two years; *but*
- no more than 15 years.

The Official Receiver informs the client of the period s/he thinks the court will make the BRO for and the client will have to decide:

- whether or not s/he accepts there is a case for a BRO; *and*
- whether or not s/he wants to avoid going to court and risk a longer period.

There are provisions that allow the client to apply to the court to annul the BRU or for an order that it should cease to have effect from an earlier date than originally agreed.[55]

Interim bankruptcy restriction orders

Because the client must be given at least six weeks' notice of the application for a BRO and an application must be made within 12 months of the bankruptcy order (unless the court gives leave to apply later), there may be a gap of several months between the date of discharge and the date of hearing when the client is not subject to any restrictions. The Secretary of State can apply to the court to make an interim BRO.

An interim BRO has the same effect as a full BRO and lasts from when it is made until either:

- the application for the BRO is determined; *or*
- the Secretary of State accepts a BRU; *or*
- it is revoked.[56]

Only two days' notice of the application is required and the hearing will be in public. The Secretary of State must file a report and evidence.[57]

The Secretary of State maintains a register of BROs, interim BROs and BRUs, open to public inspection at no charge at www.insolvency.gov.uk. It may also be in the client's local press.

According to the Insolvency Service, in 2006/07 1,867 people were made the subject of BROs/BRUs (out of around 60,000 bankruptcy orders), the vast majority being for two to five years. BROs/BRUs are most commonly made on the basis of:

- contributing to the bankruptcy by extravagance or gambling;
- incurring debts with no reasonable prospect of being able to repay them;
- entering into transactions either to prefer friends or relatives ahead of other creditors or at an undervalue.[58]

Example

In May 2005 a 34-year-old man was running a music business and had debts estimated by the Official Receiver of around £38,298. He received £300 a week from the business, which fell to £200 and then to nothing when the business ceased trading in July 2005. Despite this, he spent at least £14,284 between May and September 2005 (after which he filed his petition), which he had no reasonable prospect of being able to repay. Of this, £10,728 went on credit cards, £1,767 on a widescreen TV and he increased his overdraft by £1,789. The credit card spending included a payment towards his wedding in Florida, a holiday to Greece, jewellery and designer goods, gym membership, home improvements and driving lessons. He took out a £12,000 bank loan in May 2005, which he said was used to pay a £5,000 gambling debt and repay a £7,000 loan from his partner made the previous year. By the time he went bankrupt, his debts were £52,582. He admitted he spent £120 a week on cocaine and then subsidised his income with credit cards. He was made the subject of a six-year BRU.

Effects of bankruptcy

Protected goods

Some goods do not pass to the trustee and cannot be taken. These include:[59]

- tools of the trade, including a vehicle, which are necessary and used personally by the client in her/his 'employment, business or vocation'. Stock is not protected, which will almost certainly mean that the business has to close down if it is dependent on stock;
- household equipment necessary to the basic domestic needs of the client and her/his family. This should include all clothing, bedding, furniture and household equipment and provisions, except perhaps particularly valuable items (eg, antiques and works of art) or luxury goods with a high re-sale value (eg, video cameras or expensive hi-fi systems).

If the value of any protected goods exceeds the cost of a 'reasonable replacement', the trustee can require the goods to be sold for the benefit of the creditors. In practice, this rarely happens, but if so, the trustee must provide the funds to enable the client to replace the goods.

The trustee can visit bankrupted people and remove goods or close businesses. In practice, however, this is mainly done in cases of businesses or domestic properties where there may be valuable goods. Generally, trustees do not dispose of items unless there will be at least £500 benefit to the estate, as it is not usually economical to do so. If the client acquires any asset which is not protected in the period between the dates of the bankruptcy order and the client's discharge, the trustee may claim it within 42 days of becoming aware of it.[60]

Motor vehicles

The trustee must deal with any motor vehicle owned by, or in the possession of, the client as a matter of urgency, as it is a potential source of liability for the trustee. If the client claims the vehicle is exempt, s/he must complete Form B50.01. If a car is essential for work – eg, if there is no reasonable alternative transport to and from work, the client may be allowed to keep it, although if it is particularly valuable the trustee may order it to be sold to allow a cheaper replacement to be bought (a maximum figure of £2,000 is usually allowed for a replacement vehicle, but could be more depending on the circumstances). The trustee does not usually do this unless there will be at least £500 profit for the benefit of creditors.

Recent guidance from the Insolvency Service has widened the definition of 'employment, business or vocation' to include bankrupt clients who are informal, full-time carers of a disabled friend or relative (including a child) who use the motor vehicle in connection with that role. Although receipt by the client of carer's allowance is not essential, the Insolvency Service regards this as indicative that the client is pursuing a 'vocation' as a carer.

Previous Insolvency Service guidance said that a motor vehicle could never be regarded as an item of 'household equipment'. New guidance now allows the Official Receiver to consider claims from bankrupt clients that a motor vehicle is necessary to meet basic domestic needs. 'Necessary' in this context means that no reasonably practical alternative exists to meet a genuine need. The test of necessity is not satisfied just because use of a motor vehicle is more convenient than the alternatives, unless these are likely to be more expensive. According to the Insolvency Service, the people most likely to come within the guidance are clients who are disabled and need a motor vehicle for mobility. The vehicle must be used personally by the client. If s/he requires assistance to travel in the vehicle, it will not fall within the guidance. Clients who live in urban areas with reasonable public transport are unlikely to be able to benefit from the 'domestic needs' guidance (other than as a result of disability). Even in an urban area, it might be possible to claim exemption on the grounds that a vehicle is necessary to transport children to school where there is no public transport alternative or if children attend different schools and the distance to travel would make walking or cycling an impractical alternative. If the motor vehicle is of high value, the trustee can still require a cheaper replacement be acquired.

If a motor vehicle is not exempt, a member of the client's family may be able to negotiate to buy the vehicle to enable the client to retain it.

If the motor vehicle is subject to a hire purchase or conditional sale agreement, the finance company may be able to terminate the agreement and repossess the vehicle if the client becomes bankrupt. The trustee will always contact the finance company and so, even if the trustee agrees that the vehicle is exempt, the finance company may seek to repossess it. In other cases where there is insufficient equity to make it worth the trustee's while selling the vehicle her/himself, s/he may invite the finance company to repossess the vehicle.[61] Any other asset can be treated in the same way if the trustee regards it as a 'luxury' item.

A mobile home that is not parked on a protected site – ie, a site registered by the local authority under the Caravan Sites Act 1968, but under an informal arrangement, is more likely to be regarded as a 'motor vehicle' than a 'house' even if it is the client's permanent residence. The question of whether it is exempt under the 'domestic needs' category therefore arises. A mobile home parked on a registered site with a degree of immobility may be regarded as a 'house'. A caravan used as a permanent residence with a degree of site permanence and immobility is also likely to be regarded as a house.

Earnings

If the client has at least £100 a month available income, the trustee may suggest a weekly or monthly payment from a client's earnings. If payment is not agreed, s/he can apply to the court for an 'income payments order'. This must be applied for before the client is discharged and the order must specify the period for which it is to last. This must be no longer than three years from the date of the order. These payments will be ordered to be paid to the trustee by the court and can be required of either the client or employer under an attachment of earnings order.[62] Either the client or the trustee can apply to vary the order (both before and after discharge). The court must leave sufficient money for the reasonable domestic needs of the client and her/his family – the client is not restricted to basic income support levels.

The trustee should calculate the client's available income by deducting from her/his actual income the household outgoings (less contributions from other members of the household, either actual or assumed). Any surplus is available income and, provided this is at least £100 a month, the payment is assessed at between 50 per cent and 70 per cent of this figure (minimum £50 a month). In practice, single people are assessed at the higher figure. An income payments order in force on 1 April 2004 will continue to have effect until either:

- any date specified in the order; *or*
- if there is no date, the client is discharged.

The client may apply to the court to either vary the income payments order or for it to cease prior to such specified date.[63]

Income payments agreements

The client can come to an agreement with the trustee over a payment arrangement and incorporate it into a written income payments agreement without applying to the court. An income payments agreement is enforceable as a court order just like an income payments order and can be varied by either:

- a further written agreement; *or*
- the court, on the application of either the client or the trustee.[64]

In the first instance, clients are offered an income payments agreement. In one-fifth of bankruptcy cases, people make payments from their income.

Pensions

If the bankruptcy order was made on a petition presented to the court before 29 May 2000, personal pensions are part of the bankrupt client's estate and must be paid to the trustee by the pension company. This is the case whether the payments fall due during or after the bankruptcy.[65] In the case of occupational pensions, this depends on whether or not the scheme contains a 'forfeiture clause' – ie, the pension is forfeited on bankruptcy and payments are at the discretion of the scheme, usually to another member of the client's household. If there is no forfeiture clause, the pension vests in the trustee.[66] Trustees may argue that pensions pass to them as a matter of course, and so the position should be checked with the pension company. However, although an occupational pension cannot normally be claimed directly by the trustee, the income could be made the subject of an income payments order. In *Kilvert v Flackett* it was held that a lump-sum payment made to the client out of his occupational pension scheme during the bankruptcy was income and could be made the subject of an income payments order where the client already had sufficient other income.[67]

If the bankruptcy order was made on a petition presented on or after 29 May 2000, all rights under an 'HMRC approved pension arrangement' are excluded from the client's estate (ie, they do not vest in the trustee), including personal pension plans. However, if the client becomes entitled to the pension (including a lump sum) during the period of the bankruptcy, it could be made the subject of an income payments order, as above.[68]

From 6 April 2002 the client can:

- apply to the court for an order (an 'exclusion order'); *or*
- agree with her/his trustee in bankruptcy (a 'qualifying agreement') that part or all of her/his rights under an unapproved pension arrangement should be excluded from her/his estate.

A qualifying agreement must be made by deed and can be revoked by the trustee if:

- the client fails to disclose fully all material facts relating to the pension; *and*
- the client has done so to enable her/his rights to be excluded where otherwise they would not have been.

In deciding whether or not to make an exclusion order and, if so, on what terms, the court must consider:

- the future likely needs of the client and her/his family; *and*
- the extent to which those needs are likely to be adequately met out of any other pension (other than retirement pension or an income-related benefit).

The client must apply to the court for an exclusion order:

- within 13 weeks of the bankrupt's estate vesting in the trustee – ie, the date of her/his appointment; *or*
- within 30 days of a qualifying agreement being revoked.

The court can extend the above time limits if there is good cause.[69]

Insurance policies

Ordinary term life assurance policies or endowment policies are not exempt and will usually pass to the trustee in the normal way. If a policy has been assigned or charged to the lender in connection with a mortgage or secured loan, it will be treated as part of the security and will not vest in the trustee (see p395). If a third party is named as beneficiary under the policy, the policy does not normally vest in the trustee. If client was originally the beneficiary under the policy and the transfer of the right to receive the proceeds is a transaction at an under-value (see p410), however, the trustee will claim the benefit of the policy.

Student loans

Loans under the Student Loans Act 1990, whether made before or after the bankruptcy order, are not part of the client's estate and so cannot be claimed by the trustee. On the other hand, they are not bankruptcy debts unless the bankruptcy order was made before 1 July 2004 and so the client will only be released from liability to repay the loan on discharge if the bankruptcy order was made before 1 July 2004 (see p414).

Loans made under the Teaching and Higher Education Act 1998 are not part of the client's estate and cannot be part of an income payments order, but they are not bankruptcy debts unless the bankruptcy order was made before 1 September 2004. The client will only be released from liability on discharge if the bankruptcy order was made before 1 September 2004 (see Chapter 14).

Owner-occupied homes

If the client has a beneficial interest in her/his home (either solely or jointly), that interest automatically becomes the property of the trustee in bankruptcy on her/his appointment. The trustee protects her/his interest by registering either a notice or a restriction at the Land Registry. If it is solely owned by the client, the legal title vests in the trustee and the client's interest, which passes to the trustee, is the whole value of the property. If the home is jointly owned, only the client's share vests in the trustee, but this does not prevent the trustee from taking action to realise that share. The trustee can realise the value of that interest (eg, by selling it to a joint owner or forcing a sale of the property) and this does not have to be done during the period of the bankruptcy.

For bankruptcy orders made on and after 1 April 2004, the trustee has three years from the date of the bankruptcy order to deal with the client's interest in a property which, at the date of the bankruptcy order, is the sole or principal residence of the client, or her/his spouse/civil partner or former spouse/civil partner. If not, the interest will no longer form part of the client's estate and will revert to her/him. It will, therefore, no longer be available to pay the client's bankruptcy debts. However, this will not happen if, during the three-year period, the trustee either:

- realises the interest – eg, by selling her/his interest to the client's partner or some other third party; *or*
- applies for an order for sale or possession of the dwelling house; *or*
- applies for a charging order in respect of the client's interest; *or*
- comes to an agreement with the client regarding her/his interest.[70]

If the trustee decides to take the third option, the charging order is for the value of the client's interest in the property at the date of the charging order plus interest at the prescribed rate (currently 8 per cent a year). The client will, therefore, retain the benefit of any subsequent increase in the value of the property. Since a charging order only secures the value of the client's interest at the date of the order, there is an incentive for the trustee to either realise her/his interest or, if this is not possible, sell the property. It is likely that trustees will only seek charging orders if a sale is undesirable or unlikely to be ordered by the court. The trustee will not be successful in an attempt at the second or third options if the value of the client's interest is less than £1,000 (see below).

Low value exemption

If the value of the client's interest is less than the prescribed amount (£1,000) the court *must* dismiss any application by the trustee in bankruptcy for:

- an order for the sale or possession of the property; *or*
- a charging order on the client's interest in the property.[71]

In valuing the client's interest in the property the court must disregard:

- any loans secured by mortgage or other charge against the property;
- any other third-party interest – eg, a joint owner's share of equity;
- the reasonable costs of sale.[72]

If an endowment policy is in place for payment of a mortgage, it may vest in the trustee who can arrange for it to be sold. In cases where:

- the policy has been formally assigned to the lender; *or*
- the policy document is held by the mortgage lender; *or*
- the mortgage lender's interest in the policy for repayment of the mortgage has been noted with the insurance company; *or*
- there has been a specific agreement between the mortgage lender and the client that the policy would be used to pay the mortgage,

the policy is treated as an asset and taken into account when valuing the client's interest in the property. This may result in there being sufficient equity for the trustee to realise the property.

If another person shares ownership of the home, the trustee will try to sell the client's share to that person. S/he will have to obtain an up-to-date valuation, plus details of any outstanding mortgages or secured loans, and pay her/his own legal costs (at least £250). If the property is jointly owned, the trustee will require 50 per cent of the equity plus her/his legal costs, but will allow some discount to take account of the savings made from not having to take possession of the property and conduct the sale. Any increase in the value of the property as a result of expenditure by either party after the date of bankruptcy should also be taken into account. If there is negative, or very little, equity it will usually be possible to buy out the trustee for a nominal sum (£1) plus her/his legal costs (if the Official Receiver is the trustee, the costs are £211). Similarly, if the property is solely owned by the client, s/he may be able to buy back her/his interest from the trustee. If there is equity, the purchase money will have to come from a third party – eg, a friend or relative. Mortgage lenders are reluctant to agree to people buying an interest in property, unless they take some responsibility for the mortgage. In the case of jointly owned properties, the co-owner(s) is already responsible for the mortgage. In the case of solely owned properties, however, before agreeing to transfer her/his interest to a partner or third party, the trustee must ensure that arrangements have been made between the proposed transferee and the mortgage lender(s) for future payment of the mortgage.

Because of the three-year time limit, if it has not been possible to realise the client's share prior to discharge, it will be reviewed in sufficient time to enable the trustee to deal with the client's interest before it automatically re-vests.

The trustee will probably seek a court order for the sale of a jointly owned property if the non-bankrupt owner will not/cannot purchase the whole and there is sufficient equity. If there is a partner and/or children, their interests should be considered, but after a year these are overridden by the interests of the creditors unless the circumstances of the case are exceptional. This means that, in practice, homes are not sold for at least a year after the bankruptcy.

In deciding whether to order the sale of a house, the court must consider:

- the creditors' interests;
- whether the spouse/civil partner contributed to the bankruptcy;
- the needs and resources of the children and spouse/civil partner;
- other relevant circumstances (but not the client's needs).[73]

If the trustee has obtained a charging order on the client's interest in the property, the trustee is not subject to any limitation period for seeking an order for the sale of the property.[74] If the client's interest remains vested in the trustee, the time limit is three years from the date of the bankruptcy order.

If a property is sold, the trustee will send any money due to the co-owner or other person with an interest in the property on completion. It is important that people who share homes with a bankrupt person are independently advised by a solicitor, particularly if they have made direct contributions to the purchase price, because they may have an equitable or beneficial interest in the property for which they should be paid, even if they are not an 'owner' on the deeds.

Exceptional circumstances

Pre-Human Rights Act caselaw held that circumstances could only be exceptional if they were unusual. In *Barca v Mears* the High Court held that in order to comply with the European Convention on Human Rights 'exceptional circumstances' should now be regarded as circumstances in which the consequences of bankruptcy were of the usual kind but nevertheless were exceptionally severe.

However, even if the court does decide that the circumstances are 'exceptional' so that it is not appropriate to make an immediate order for sale, this does not mean that there can never be an order for sale. The court has the power to defer the sale of the property to a future date which it considers 'fair and reasonable'.[75]

Beneficial interest

If the property is in the sole name of the bankrupt client, the non-bankrupt partner could argue that s/he has a beneficial interest in the property – ie, s/he is entitled to a share in the proceeds of sale of the property. If this can be established, the trustee will have no claim against the non-bankrupt's share of the property so that:

- if the property is sold, the partner will be entitled to be paid the value of her/his share;
- the partner will not have to make any payment to the trustee in respect of her/his share in order to buy out the trustee.

On the other hand, if the property is in the sole name of the non-bankrupt partner, the trustee may try to establish that the client has a beneficial interest. The trustee will also investigate whether the property was put into the partner's sole name in circumstances that amount to a transaction at an under-value (see p410).

The general rule is that the beneficial interest is presumed to be the same as the legal interest. The onus of proving that the parties intended their beneficial interests to be different from their legal interests is on the party seeking to establish this.

If a property is in the sole name of one of the partners, the other partner may have acquired a beneficial interest by making some identifiable contribution to the cost of the property – eg, by:

- contributing to the purchase price with her/his own money; *or*
- helping pay the deposit with her/his own money; *or*

- making direct contributions to the mortgage repayments; *or*
- instead of making direct contributions to the mortgage repayments, contributing to the joint household expenses with her/his own money.

Looking after the property and bringing up children do not entitle the other partner to a beneficial interest.

Assuming the other partner does have a beneficial interest, the value of her/his share depends on the value of her/his contributions, any agreement between the parties and any inferences that can be drawn from their conduct.[76]

Even if the trustee is dealing with a jointly owned property, there may be a question as to whether one of the parties has more than a 50 per cent share in it. The conveyance of a property into joint names as joint tenants is considered to be conclusive evidence of an intention to hold the property in equal shares, unless one of the parties can demonstrate fraud or mistake in the conveyance, or that there has been undue influence (see p104) or a declaration of trust of the beneficial interests. If Land Registry Form TR1 has been used (compulsory for all transfers since 1 April 2008), there is a specific declaration of trust tick box. In *Stack v Dowden*, the House of Lords said that, where there is no declaration of trust, the presumption should be that properties in joint names are owned in equal shares rather than in proportion to the parties' financial contributions to its purchase. If a party seeks to argue otherwise, the onus is on her/him and unequal contributions to the purchase will not be sufficient on its own.

Specialist advice should always be sought if the adviser has grounds for believing that either the client or someone else may have a beneficial interest in a property which could be the subject of a claim by the trustee.[77]

Rented accommodation

Assured, protected and secure tenancies do not automatically vest in the trustee, but can be claimed within the 42-day period, if they have a value, but this is relatively rare.

Pre-bankruptcy rent arrears are a 'bankruptcy debt', which cannot be excluded from the bankruptcy and are provable like any other bankruptcy debt. The landlord has no 'remedy' in respect of that debt.[78] As a creditor in respect of a bankruptcy debt, the landlord would have to obtain the leave of the court to commence such proceedings even for post-bankruptcy rent arrears.[79] The Insolvency Service's view is that a landlord could not rely on pre-bankruptcy rent arrears to commence possession proceedings on the grounds of non-payment of rent. However, if the tenancy is an assured tenancy, the landlord has the option to repossess under Ground 11 ('whether or not the tenant is in arrears on the date on which proceedings for possession are begun, the tenant has persistently delayed paying rent which has become lawfully due'). In the case of assured and secure tenancies, the landlord can also use some other breach of the tenancy not involving rent arrears as a ground for possession. For example, if the tenancy contains a forfeiture clause on bankruptcy, the landlord could obtain a possession order on that ground.[80] Before the client petitions for bankruptcy, the tenancy agreement should be checked for such a clause and enquiries made about the landlord's policy on enforcing it.[81]

In relation to suspended possession orders already in force when the tenant goes bankrupt, the court in *Harlow DC v Hall* said it made no difference whether the date for possession stated in the order was before or after the date of the bankruptcy order, the landlord could still apply for a warrant if the order was not complied with. Trustees should, therefore, allow clients to comply with suspended possession orders provided the overall cost of the accommodation is reasonable.

The safest course of action for a tenant with rent arrears or subject to a possession order who is considering bankruptcy is to make enquiries about the policies and practice of the landlord and the local district judge(s). If rent arrears are accrued after the date of the bankruptcy order, the position depends on whether or not there are pre-bankruptcy rent arrears. If there are, the landlord cannot take proceedings of any description without leave of the court.[82] If there are no pre-bankruptcy rent arrears, there are no restrictions on the landlord taking proceedings.

Transactions at an under-value

A transaction is said to be made at an 'under-value' if it is an exchange of property (including money) for less than its market value. This may be quite innocent with everyone acting in good faith, but if a trustee considers that such a transaction has reduced the assets available to creditors, s/he can apply to the court, which can set the transaction aside.[83]

The trustee can apply to the court to have any transaction set aside if:

- it was carried out in the five years before the date of the bankruptcy order; *and*
- the client was insolvent at the time or the transaction led to her/his insolvency; *or*
- the transaction was carried out within two years of the date of the bankruptcy order, regardless of whether or not the client was insolvent.[84]

If the transaction was with an 'associate' – eg, partner, relative, partner's relative, business partner or employer, it is assumed that the client was insolvent at the time of the transaction. Such transactions could be:

- gifts;
- working or selling goods for nothing or for an amount significantly less than the value of the labour or goods;
- giving security over assets for no benefit in return;
- transferring an interest in property to a former partner (but not under a court order on divorce unless there are exceptional circumstances, such as fraud[85]).

Preferences

If, prior to the bankruptcy, the client has done something which has put a creditor or a guarantor of one of her/his debts into a better position than they would have been in the event of the client's bankruptcy – eg, giving a voluntary charge or paying them in full, this may be a 'preference'. In addition:

- the client must have intended putting them in a better position; *and*
- the client must have been insolvent at the time or the action must have led to her/his insolvency;[86] *and*
- the payment must have been made within six months before the date of the bankruptcy order (or within two years if the preference was to an 'associate' – eg, spouse, partner or other relative, business partner or employer/employee).[87]

If the preference was to an 'associate', it is assumed that the client intended putting them in a better position, unless it can be shown otherwise. An exception to this is if the person is only an associate because s/he is an employee.

The Official Receiver will contact her/his creditors and invite them to 'prove' their debts – ie, submit claims.

Trustee's remedy

In the case of either transactions at an under-value or preferences, the court can restore the position of the parties by, for example, requiring any property or money to be returned to the trustee, ordering the release of any security, or ordering payment to the trustee for goods or services. Protection is given to third parties who act in good faith without notice of the circumstances.[88]

Enforcement action by creditors

Once a bankruptcy petition has been presented to the court or a bankruptcy order has been made, the court can order any existing court or enforcement action being taken by creditors to be discontinued in order to preserve the client's property for the benefit of all of her/his creditors. Once the bankruptcy order has been made, anyone who is a creditor of the client with a debt provable in the bankruptcy (see p412):

- is prohibited from exercising any remedy against the property or person of the client in order to enforce payment of the debt; *and*
- is not allowed to start any new court action against the client before her/his discharge without the permission of the court – eg, for a post-bankruptcy debt.[89]

A creditor who has attempted to enforce a judgment debt prior to the bankruptcy is allowed to retain the benefit of that enforcement if:

- in the case of execution against goods, the goods have either been sold or money paid to the creditor to avoid execution before the date of the bankruptcy order;

- in the case of attachment of earnings orders, the payment has actually been received by the creditor before the date of the bankruptcy order (any existing attachment of earnings order should be revoked as the creditor will not be allowed to retain any future payments in any event);
- in the case of charging orders, the order was made final before the date of the bankruptcy order.

For the purpose of recovery of social fund loans, a client's income support (IS), jobseeker's allowance (JSA), employment and support allowance (ESA) or pension credit (PC) is not treated as the client's 'property' and the Secretary of State can continue making deductions from the client's IS, JSA, ESA or PC to recover the social fund loan. Similarly, if the client has a benefit overpayment, the Secretary of State can carry on making deductions from benefit to recover it.[90] If the client is not entitled to a relevant benefit, the Secretary of State must 'prove' for the debt in the usual way (see below). However, if the client becomes entitled to a benefit prior to her/his discharge, deductions can only be made to recover a social fund loan until the client is discharged. Whether or not the Secretary of State can continue to make deductions to recover an overpayment after the client has been discharged depends on when the overpayment occurred and when the decision to recover was made (see p414).

For the position on rent arrears, see p409. Bankruptcy does not affect the rights of secured creditors (see below).

How money is paid

Once a bankruptcy order is made, the trustee takes over many of the functions of the debt adviser. The client may need considerable personal support, and the debt adviser may need to ensure the trustee acts correctly. However, until discharge, the debt adviser is largely powerless to affect decisions.

Creditors must contact the trustee and are required to 'prove' their claims – ie, demonstrate they are owed the money. This must be done on a prescribed form.[91] The court can prevent any creditor who is entitled to prove in the bankruptcy from attempting to recover the debt in any other way. This power arises as soon as the bankruptcy petition is presented and continues until discharge.[92]

The only debts which cannot be proved are:[93]

- fines;
- maintenance orders (other than orders for payment of a lump sum or costs) and Child Support Agency orders;
- debts arising from certain other orders of the criminal courts;
- student loans under the 1990 and 1998 Acts.

Secured loans do not need to be proved because the rights of a secured creditor is not affected by bankruptcy.

Secured creditors can, theoretically, remove their security and ask to be included in the list of creditors. If they have already forced a sale of the home, they can be included as creditors for any balance due.

The trustee will work out the value of the debts and any assets. S/he will list the following, which are priorities to be paid first:[94]

- bankruptcy expenses (including amounts due to the trustee, the court or the Insolvency Service, which charges for the Official Receiver's services). This often accounts for over 50 per cent of the payments;
- expenses of, for instance, estate agents to realise assets;
- contributions owed by the client to occupational pension schemes;
- arrears of wages to employees for four months before the bankruptcy (up to a maximum of £800 each);
- other ('ordinary') creditors. These creditors receive nothing until the other 'preferential' creditors have been paid in full. If paid at all, these creditors generally receive only a percentage of the value of their debt;
- deferred debts – eg, debts due to the client's spouse;
- interest on any of the above from the date of the bankruptcy order.

Any surplus will be returned to the client.

Discharge

Clients made bankrupt on or after 1 April 2004 are discharged after a maximum period of 12 months, unless the court is satisfied on the application of the Official Receiver or the trustee in bankruptcy that the client is failing, or has failed, to comply with her/his obligations under the Insolvency Act 1986 – eg, she has not co-operated with the Official Receiver/trustee. In this case, the court may order the suspension of the 12-month period either for a set time or until a specified condition is fulfilled.[95] According to the Insolvency Service, about 50 per cent of clients get early discharge, the average period being after seven months.

If the Official Receiver files a notice at court within the 12-month period stating that no investigation of the client's conduct and affairs is necessary or that such an investigation has been concluded, the client will be discharged when the notice is filed.[96]

Pre-April 2004 bankruptcies

People who were bankrupt before 1 April 2004 should have been discharged by 1 April 2005 (unless their discharge period was extended – eg, for non-co-operation). If, however, the client was an undischarged bankrupt at any time during the period of 15 years ending with the day before the pre-commencement bankruptcy order was made, s/he will be discharged either on 1 April 2009 or an earlier date ordered by the court on the client's application for discharge.[97] (The client cannot apply for discharge until s/he has been bankrupt for at least five years.[98])

A client who has been bankrupt before and goes bankrupt again on or after 1 April 2004 is subject to the same discharge rules as other clients who go bankrupt after 1 April 2004, and will automatically be discharged after 12 months (subject to the exceptions discussed above). However, if the Official Receiver is considering a BRO, the fact that the client has been bankrupt before may be relevant (see p397).

Effect of discharge

After discharge, the court issues a certificate to the client on request. There is a £60 fee. All the bankruptcy debts remain unenforceable, except:[99]

- secured creditors. If the home was sold, but insufficient equity raised to pay the secured lender, this debt is no longer secured, but the unsecured part remains unenforceable provided the mortgage or secured loan was taken out prior to the bankruptcy even if the home was not sold until after discharge. Any jointly liable person remains liable for the whole debt;
- benefit and tax credit overpayments where, although the overpayment was made before the date of the bankruptcy order, the decision to recover was not made until after that date. If both the overpayment and the decision to recover were made before the bankruptcy, the client will be released from the overpayment on discharge unless the overpayment was incurred through fraud.[100] However, on discharge from bankruptcy there is no power to make deductions from benefit (or to reduce an existing award of tax credit) in order to recover an overpayment if the decision to recover was made prior to the client becoming bankrupt;[101]
- council tax for the remainder of the current year if the local authority has not obtained a liability order nor served a final demand;[102]
- possibly student loans, depending on the date the bankruptcy order was made (see p405);
- fines (but the client will be released from parking and other charges enforced through the Traffic Enforcement Centre at Northampton County Court);
- maintenance orders and other family court orders, child support and debts from personal injury claims (although the court does have the power to release liability for these in full or in part);
- debts incurred through fraud;
- debt arising from certain other orders of the criminal court.

Occasionally, the trustee is still working on something (eg, the sale of a home) when discharge is granted. In this case, that asset can still be realised and distributed after discharge despite the fact that the recipients of funds could not otherwise pursue payment. The duties to co-operate with, and to provide information to, the Official Receiver and/or trustee continue after discharge for so long as it is reasonably required.[103] The Insolvency Service has now set up regional trustee and liquidator units in order to deal with such long-term matters.

Credit reference agencies record bankruptcies, but it is not necessarily impossible to obtain credit again after discharge.

Annulment

A bankruptcy order can be annulled (cancelled) at any time by the court if the client has either repaid the debts and bankruptcy expenses in full,[104] or has provided full security for them, or if there were insufficient grounds for making the order in the first place.[105] The client then becomes liable once again for all the bankruptcy debts. A bankruptcy order can also be annulled if a creditors' meeting has approved an IVA proposal.[106]

The court has power to rescind a bankruptcy order where there has been a change of circumstances since the order was made and this will benefit the creditors.[107]

Advantages and disadvantages

The advantages of bankruptcy include the following.

- It can remove the uncertainty and anxiety caused by negotiating with a large number of creditors simultaneously.
- There can be a sense of relief for the client.
- The client usually pays less. There is one payment to the trustee rather than individual payments to creditors (payments will usually last for three years).
- It can be a fresh start; the process is intended to rehabilitate the client.
- Creditors have to accept the situation and contact with the client will stop. Most creditors are unable to take further action against the client (see p377).
- The process is certain.
- After discharge, most types of debt are written off and can no longer be pursued by creditors (see p414).

There are also many potential disadvantages of bankruptcy, including the following.

- The client will almost certainly lose any assets of value that can be sold, unless they are exempt (although even then the client may have to accept a replacement of lower value).
- If there is equity in the family home (ie, it is worth more than the mortgage), the trustee will want to realise the client's share of this. This may lead to the home being sold (although this cannot happen if the value of the client's share (after sale costs) does not exceed £1,000).
- If the client owns a business and employs people, or the business has a value, the employees may have to be dismissed and the business sold.
- If the client has mortgage or rent arrears, the home will still be at risk. Bankruptcy does not prevent a secured lender from taking possession proceedings. A landlord may be able to enforce a suspended possession order if the arrears are not paid or find some ground other than rent arrears to start possession proceedings – eg, persistent delay in paying rent.

- The client cannot obtain credit of £500 or more without disclosing her/his status if s/he is an undischarged bankrupt or subject to a BRO or BRU and s/he may find it more difficult to open a bank account.
- The process is expensive. A client who wishes to pay off the debts in order to preserve an asset – eg, the family home, will also have to pay post-bankruptcy costs and these could be substantial.
- The client must allow her/his financial affairs to be scrutinised by officials who may take criminal action if irregularities are found. S/he may also become subject to a BRO/BRU (although, apart from the restriction on obtaining credit, this may have no effect on her/him).
- The client may be barred from certain public offices or may be unable to practise certain professions – eg, accountant, solicitor.
- The client's credit rating will continue to be adversely affected after discharge and this will probably make running a business or buying a home in future very difficult.
- The client may feel judged and humiliated. Some clients may feel there is still a stigma attached to bankruptcy and this could be reinforced in cases where a BRO/BRU is made.
- The client's immigration status may be affected (specialist immigration advice should be obtained.
- While undischarged or subject to a BRO, the client cannot be a company director without the leave of the court (which may be granted on condition that the client makes payments from her/his income for the benefit of creditors) and cannot trade under any name other than the one used at the date of the bankruptcy order without disclosing the name under which s/he went bankrupt to everyone with whom s/he does business.
- The names of people who are made bankrupt are published in the *London Gazette* and also in the local press. BROs/BRUs may also attract local publicity and friends and neighbours may find out about the client's financial difficulties and, if a BRO is made, that s/he has been found to have acted irresponsibly in relation to her/his financial affairs.
- Not all debts will be written off, at the end of bankruptcy – eg, fines, maintenance/child support.
- Secured creditors are not affected by bankruptcy and can still enforce their security.
- Joint debts are not written off, as creditors can still pursue the non-bankrupt co-client. If s/he is the client's partner, the family will still be in financial difficulties.

Post-bankruptcy individual voluntary arrangements

Before 1 April 2004 there were little-used provisions in the Insolvency Act 1986 for an undischarged bankrupt to enter into an IVA with her/his creditors. Very few were made, even though they could have resulted in the bankruptcy order being annulled. An insolvency practitioner was required to act as nominee and supervisor.

Fast-track voluntary arrangements

Section 264 and Schedule 22 Enterprise Act 2002 contain provisions allowing the Official Receiver to act as nominee and supervisor in fast-track, post-bankruptcy voluntary arrangements (FTVAs) in return for a fixed fee (£300 plus 15 per cent of all sums realised). One-half (£812) of the Official Receiver's case administration fee in the bankruptcy (£1,625) will be recovered out of the money paid into the FTVA. This procedure is only likely to be relevant to clients who:

- were made bankrupt by a creditor but do not want to be bankrupt;
- made themselves bankrupt without taking any advice and now realise that it was not the most appropriate option.

The client must complete a 'Proposal to Creditors for a Fast Track Voluntary Arrangement in Satisfaction of Debts' form, supplied by the Insolvency Service together with guidance notes. The form is submitted to the Official Receiver, together with the £300 fee plus a £35 registration fee. The only debts that can be included in a FTVA are those provable in the bankruptcy (see p412). The Official Receiver will not agree to a proposal unless the creditors will be better off under the FTVA than they would be under the bankruptcy. Any income payments should be offered over five years and the level of payments are subject to annual review. The Official Receiver can extend the FTVA for up to 12 months to enable any missed payments to be paid. Any other money received by the client during the period of the FTVA must be disclosed to the Official Receiver, who may require it to be paid into the arrangement. Clients are likely to need assistance from an adviser, not only in completing the proposal form, but also in relation to the FTVA generally.

If the Official Receiver does not agree the proposal and the £300 fee was paid by the client, it will be retained by the Official Receiver in the bankruptcy. If it was paid by a third party, it will be returned. Otherwise, the proposal is filed at court. There is no creditors' meeting. The Official Receiver sends out the proposal to creditors by post. It is not possible to modify it. If the proposal is accepted, the Official Receiver becomes the supervisor and notifies the court, which automatically annuls the bankruptcy order (likely to be the main objective of a client proposing an FTVA).

If the FTVA fails – eg, because the client does not maintain the agreed payments, the arrangement will terminate and:

- the Official Receiver can still realise any assets and distribute any funds in her/his possession in accordance with the arrangement;
- creditors are no longer bound by the arrangement and are free to pursue the client as they see fit.

There is no provision for the Official Receiver to apply for a bankruptcy order. FTVAs have not proved a success – to date, only 22 have been made.

6. Reform of insolvency law

The Insolvency Act 1986 was a landmark piece of legislation, marking a complete break with previous bankruptcy law and practice. It created the current bankruptcy framework and introduced individual voluntary arrangements as an alternative to bankruptcy. The Enterprise Act 2002 was another major reform.

Future changes

In July 2004, the Department for Constitutional Affairs (now the Ministry of Justice) published a consultation paper, *A Choice of Paths*, proposing a number of options to help deal with over-indebtedness, in particular, with people in multiple debt (the 'can't pays' and 'could pays').[108] The proposals include the following.

- A **debt relief scheme** administered by the Insolvency Service to assist the 'can't pay' group, aimed at people with no assets, no surplus income and a fairly low level of debt. People will be discharged from the debts scheduled to a debt relief order (DRO) after 12 months. See p419.
- **Enforcement restriction orders** (EROs) to provide temporary enforcement relief for people in the 'could pay' group who have difficulty meeting their commitments in the short to medium term because of a genuine, unforeseen deterioration in their circumstances. Creditors will be prohibited from taking enforcement action without leave of the court for an initial period of up to six months (with a maximum of 12 months). While an order is in force, clients will be expected to negotiate with their creditors whilst making payments, where possible. See p424.
- **Reform of the administration order (AO) scheme** to improve the existing process by limiting entry to the 'could pay' group. There will be no pre-condition of a judgment, but a maximum debt level (proposed at least £10,000). Orders will last for a maximum of five years, with composition available once payments have been completed. See p425
- **Debt repayment plans** set up by approved operators in the private and voluntary sectors for the 'could pay' group. Operators may have the power to include reluctant creditors in a debt management scheme, to set repayments and impose compositions. Disputes may be referred to the court. See p428

In July 2005, the Insolvency Service published a further consultation paper, *Improving Individual Voluntary Arrangements,* containing proposals for simplifying the current **individual voluntary arrangements** (IVA) regime in recognition of the fact that the majority of IVAs are now proposed by consumers rather than by traders, as originally envisaged. The aim is to improve access to IVAs for clients and increase the return to creditors by streamlining the procedure and, therefore, lowering the cost.

Implementation of simple IVAs (SIVAs) will be by amendment of the Insolvency Act via a regulatory reform order. This is a Parliamentary process, enabling legislation to be amended more quickly than if a new Act were required. The remaining proposals above are in Part 5 and Schedules 17–20 of the Tribunals Courts and Enforcement Act 2007. Much of the detail will be in regulations, which have yet to be published. What follows is, therefore, only an outline.

Timetable for implementation

SIVAs: April 2009;

DROs: April 2009;

AOs: October 2010;

EROs: October 2010;

Approved debt management schemes: the Courts Service is currently consulting on whether and, if so when, to implement these provisions, but the earliest date is understood to be October 2010.

Debt relief orders

When DROs come into force, clients who are unable to pay their debts will be able to apply for an order in respect of their 'qualifying debts'. Any secured debt is not a qualifying debt. Otherwise, any debt for an identifiable sum which is not an 'excluded debt' qualifies for a DRO. The list of excluded debts will be prescribed by regulations, but is likely to include any debt which is not provable in bankruptcy – eg, fines. Business debts will be 'qualifying debts' for a DRO, although not for an ERO or AO.

Qualifying conditions

In order to obtain a DRO, the client must either be domiciled in England and Wales at the date of the application or have been ordinarily resident or carried on business in England and Wales during the previous three years *and* on the date the Official Receiver determines the application (the 'determination date') s/he must not:

- be an undischarged bankrupt, or subject to an IVA, or a bankruptcy restriction order/bankruptcy restriction undertaking, or a debt relief restriction order/undertaking (see p422);
- have had a DRO within the previous six years;
- have a bankruptcy petition pending against her/him;
- have debts above a prescribed limit (expected to be £15,000);
- have surplus monthly income above a prescribed limit (expected to be £50);
- have assets valued at above a prescribed limit (expected to be £300);

- have entered into a transaction at an under-value or given a preference to anyone (see pp410 and 411) at any time in the two years before the DRO application was made and the determination date.

The value of assets and the amount of surplus income will be calculated in accordance with regulations, which will permit certain assets or income to be disregarded. This is likely to include those assets exempt in bankruptcy under the business or domestic needs criteria (see p401). Cars that are not exempt may still be disregarded if they are worth less than £1,000. Assets are valued at their gross, rather than net, value and so clients who are homeowners will not qualify.

The application is made to the Official Receiver[109] online through an approved intermediary. It must be made on a prescribed form and contain prescribed information. A fee is payable (expected to be under £100), but there is no fee remission. There are plans to enable the fee to be paid by instalments through Paypoint and Payzone, but clients who are close to the debt ceiling will need to be aware that accruing interest and charges may take them over the limit if they take too long to pay the fee.

In order to reduce the costs and speed up the process, the Official Receiver will make certain assumptions when determining an application, unless s/he has reason to believe otherwise, namely that:
- the client is unable to pay her/his debts;
- the specified debts are qualifying debts; *and*
- the client satisfies the conditions for a DRO (see p419).

On receipt of an application and confirmation that the fee has been paid the Official Receiver may:
- defer consideration of the application to enable her/him to make enquiries;
- refuse the application on the grounds that:
  - the client does not meet the criteria; *or*
  - the client has given false information in connection with the application; *or*
  - the application is not on the prescribed form or does not contain the prescribed information; *or*
  - the client has not answered the questions to the Official Receiver's satisfaction;
- make a DRO containing details of the client's qualifying debts.

If the Official Receiver refuses to make the order, s/he must give her/his reasons to the client. The fee is not refunded. The client can apply to the court and ask it to overrule the decision to refuse the order. If the order is made, details are registered in the Insolvency Register (and, presumably, on the client's credit reference file). Any creditor listed in the order may object to the making of the DRO, or the inclusion or details of their debt(s) on grounds to be prescribed and within the prescribed period (which must be at least 28 days after the creditor has been notified of the order). The Official Receiver must consider every objection and may conduct an investigation if s/he considers it appropriate.

Role of intermediaries

In order to obtain a DRO, a client must apply through an intermediary. Intermediaries will be authorised and will not be able to charge fees in connection with an application. They are, therefore, likely to be from the voluntary and statutory sectors. There is ongoing consultation on the organisations that will be appointed as 'competent authorities' and on the nature of the authorisation process for individual advisers. The duties of intermediaries will be prescribed by regulations but will include:

- assisting clients to make applications;
- checking that applications have been properly completed;
- sending applications to the Official Receiver.

The Insolvency Service expects that the involvement of intermediaries in making DRO applications will mean that most of them will be well founded. However, it is not clear to what extent (if any) intermediaries will be required to satisfy themselves as to the accuracy of applications or what level of verification of information supplied by clients (if any) will be expected. It is the client who will 'sign' the application and, if the client insists on submitting the application against the intermediary's advice, the application will indicate this. The role of intermediary is likely to involve a marked departure from the traditional role of the debt adviser.

The effect of a debt relief order

Once the DRO is entered on the Insolvency Register a moratorium takes effect in respect of the specified debts and the creditors specified in the order have no remedy in respect of their debts. They are also prohibited from issuing proceedings to enforce their debts or from presenting a bankruptcy petition without the leave of the court. Any pending court proceedings may be stayed. The moratorium period is one year. During the moratorium, the client will be subject to the same restrictions as in bankruptcy – eg, on obtaining credit.

Once the application is made, the client must co-operate with the Official Receiver. This includes providing any information that the Official Receiver may require. Once the order is made, the client must inform the Official Receiver as soon as reasonably practicable of any increase in her/his income during the moratorium period, or of any property s/he acquires.

Unless the moratorium period is terminated early, the client is discharged from her/his qualifying debts listed in the order (but not from any debt incurred through fraud).

Role of the Official Receiver

The Official Receiver will be able to amend the DRO during the moratorium period to correct errors or omissions. However, s/he is unable to add any debt(s) not specified in the application. This means that, unlike in bankruptcy (where provable debts are covered by the order even if they are missed off the statement of affairs), if any debt which would have been a qualifying debt for DRO purposes is omitted from the application, it cannot be added at a later date. It is advisable, therefore, for the client to obtain a copy of her/his credit reference report before an application is completed to ensure all qualifying debts are included.

The Official Receiver may revoke the order (but is not required to do so) if:

- information provided by the client is incomplete, inaccurate or misleading;
- the client has failed to co-operate with the Official Receiver or provide the required information;
- a bankruptcy order has been made against the client or s/he has proposed an IVA to her/his creditors;
- the Official Receiver should not have been satisfied that the client met the conditions for making a DRO (see p419);
- at any time after the client applies for the DRO, s/he no longer meets the conditions on the monthly surplus income and/or assets.

The Official Receiver can revoke the DRO either with immediate effect or at a specified date no more than three months ahead. She must consider whether the client should be given the opportunity to make arrangements with her/his creditors for payment of her/his debts.

A creditor or client who is dissatisfied with the Official Receiver's decision can appeal.

Offences and restrictions

As with bankruptcy, it will be an offence to:

- make false representations or omissions in connection with a DRO application;
- fail intentionally to co-operate with the Official Receiver or knowingly or recklessly make false representations or omissions in relation to information supplied in connection with a DRO application or after a DRO is made;
- conceal or falsify documents;
- dispose of property fraudulently;
- deal fraudulently with property obtained on credit;
- obtain credit of £500 or more without revealing her/his status to the lender during either the moratorium period or the period of any subsequent DRO/undertaking;
- trade in a name different to that in which the DRO was made without revealing the name in which the DRO was made to everyone with whom s/he has business dealings during either the moratorium period or the period of any subsequent debt relief restriction order/undertaking.

Debt relief orders and bankruptcy

Of all the new debt remedies, DROs have most in common with bankruptcy, but there are significant differences.

- Making a bankruptcy order is a judicial act; making a DRO will be an administrative act.
- The cost to the client of applying for a DRO will be considerably less than the cost of applying for a bankruptcy order.
- The client can apply for a bankruptcy order on her/his own, but will need the assistance of an intermediary in order to apply for a DRO.
- Creditors will be able to object to the making of a DRO but cannot object to the making of a bankruptcy order on a debtor's petition.
- There is no maximum debt level for a bankruptcy order and no income or asset pre-conditions.
- If the client has entered into a transaction at an under-value or given a preference within the prescribed period, this may be set aside by the trustee in bankruptcy, but will prevent the client even obtaining a DRO.
- There is no provision for revoking a bankruptcy order on the ground that the client's financial circumstances have improved prior to discharge.
- There is no provision for early discharge from a DRO.
- Assets do not vest in the Official Receiver, and so a DRO will not involve any realisation of assets or require clients to make any income payments to their creditors.
- A DRO only releases the client from the debts actually included in the application; bankruptcy releases the client from her/his 'bankruptcy debts' (see p414), whether or not they are listed in the statement of affairs.

The Insolvency Service expects about 14,000 DRO applications in the first year.

Enforcement restriction orders

An ERO will impose restrictions on the ability of certain creditors to take enforcement action against a client while the order is in force. The order may also impose a requirement on the client to make repayments to her/his creditors.

Qualifying conditions

The client can apply to the county court to make an ERO whether or nor a judgment has been obtained against her/him in respect of any of her/his debts. The client must:

- have at least two 'qualifying debts' (see p424) and be unable to pay at least one of them;
- not have any 'business debts' – ie, a debt incurred during the course of her/his business, but, subject to that, there is no maximum level of indebtedness;
- not be 'excluded' from applying for an ERO (see p424);

- be experiencing a sudden and unforeseen deterioration in her/his financial circumstances from which there must be a realistic prospect of improvement in financial terms within six months from the date of the ERO.

It must also be fair and equitable to make the ERO – ie, the court must look at matters from the point of the view of the creditors as well as the client.

The client is excluded from applying for an ERO if:

- s/he currently has an ERO or had an ERO within the last 12 months unless;
  - the previous ERO ceased to have effect because of the making of an AO or DRO; *or*
  - the previous ERO was revoked because the client no longer had any qualifying debts;
- s/he has either entered into an IVA or is subject to an interim order;
- s/he is an undischarged bankrupt.

Qualifying debts

A 'qualifying debt' is any debt (but not a 'business debt') apart from a debt secured against an asset – eg, a mortgage or secured loan, or one specifically excluded in regulations. It is intended to exclude any debt which is not provable in bankruptcy – eg, fines. It is also intended to exclude:

- rent arrears if the client is still in possession of the property; *and*
- future payments of ongoing commitments – eg, utilities, council tax (a proposal to exclude council tax altogether is likely to be dropped).

It is intended that the court should be able to make an ERO without first giving notice of the application to creditors. However, the court will be required to have regard to any objections a creditor may have after the ERO has been made and may, therefore, vary or revoke the ERO as appropriate in the light of those. If made and confirmed, an ERO must impose on every 'qualifying creditor' – ie, a creditor with a qualifying debt, a requirement:

- not to present a bankruptcy petition against the client in respect of a qualifying debt without the permission of the court;
- not to pursue any remedy for the recovery of a qualifying debt;
- if the creditor supplies the client with gas or electricity, not to disconnect that supply on the ground of non-payment for the supply prior to the making of the ERO unless the court gives permission.[110]

The effect of an enforcement restriction order

Any county court proceedings relating to a qualifying debt (other than bankruptcy proceedings) that were pending against the client when the ERO is made must be stayed. Although the client cannot apply for an ERO if a bankruptcy petition has been presented which is awaiting a decision by the court, it would seem to be possible for the court to stay a petition to enable the client to apply to the court for a DRO.

Creditors may not impose any charges (other than interest) while an ERO is in force (unless they relate to a time before or after the ERO is in force). Any charges imposed in breach of this requirement are not recoverable.

The court may order the client to make payments towards one or more of her/his qualifying debts while the ERO is in force, provided s/he has sufficient 'surplus income' and it would be 'fair and equitable' to do so (there is no guidance on how the second part of this test will be applied). Surplus income will be defined in regulations and is likely to be the difference between justifiable everyday expenses and income from all sources, assessed using the Common Financial Statement (see p44) or similar model. However, for the purposes of imposing a payment requirement under an ERO, any assets – eg, the client's savings, may be taken into account. The payment requirement may be imposed at any time during the ERO and the court may vary it (including removing it) on its own initiative or on the application of the client or a qualifying creditor. In connection with this, the client must provide information to the court about her/his earnings, income, assets and liabilities (including any anticipated changes) at intervals to be specified in regulations. In addition, the client must inform the court before s/he disposes of any assets (other than goods exempt from seizure by bailiffs – see p353) above a certain value (expected to be between £300 and £500). Failure to provide this information is punishable as a contempt of court by imprisonment and/or a fine.

An ERO may last for a maximum period of 12 months. The court may vary the duration. The court must revoke an ERO where the qualifying conditions either were not met or are no longer being met (see p423). The court will also be able to revoke an ERO for other reasons, in particular, if the client has failed to comply with a payment requirement or to provide required information.

New administration orders

According to *A Choice of Paths*, the current AO scheme is fundamentally flawed and inappropriate for the 'can't pay' group as they have little or no disposable income or assets and cannot make worthwhile repayments. Many people with multiple debts turn to the current AO scheme to provide debt relief rather than with realistic hopes of repaying their creditors, as evidenced by the low repayment rates and the need to make composition orders in many cases.

Qualifying conditions

A court will be able to make an AO if:

- the client has at least two 'qualifying debts' and is unable to repay at least one of them;
- the client does not have any 'business debts' (see p423);
- the client is not 'excluded' from applying for an AO (see p426);

- the client's total qualifying debts are less than a prescribed amount (expected to be £15,000); *and*
- the client's surplus income is more than a prescribed amount (expected to be £50 a month).

Qualifying debts

A 'qualifying debt' is any debt (but not a 'business debt') apart from one secured against an asset – eg, a mortgage or secured loan or specifically excluded in regulations. It is intended to exclude any debt which is not provable in bankruptcy – eg, fines. It is also intended to exclude:

- rent arrears if the client is still in possession of the property;
- future payments of ongoing commitments – eg, utilities and council tax (a proposal to exclude council tax altogether is likely to be dropped).

The client is excluded from applying for an AO if:

- s/he currently has an AO or had an AO within the last 12 months unless:
  - the previous AO ceased to have effect because an ERO or DRO was made; *or*
  - the previous AO was revoked because the client no longer had any qualifying debts;
- s/he has either entered into an IVA or is subject to an interim order;
- s/he is an undischarged bankrupt.

An AO can only be made on the application of the client and there is no longer a requirement for her/him to have a judgment. The exclusion of debts secured on assets from the definition of 'qualifying debt' means that homeowners can apply for an AO, but cannot include any debts secured on their home in it. It is likely that the current procedure for applying for an AO will continue, including enabling creditors to object to the AO or to their debt being taken into account as a qualifying debt (creditors will not be able to object to any qualifying debt being included in the AO). It appears likely that payment of an upfront fee will be required, along with a handling charge for administering the AO. The client's payments will be appropriated first to the costs and then to the debts.

The client must declare all her/his qualifying debts, including those not yet due for payment at the date of the application. If the court agrees to make an AO, it must schedule all qualifying debts already due for payment. Declared debts falling due after the date of the AO can be added to the AO on the application of either the client or the creditor. New qualifying debts arising after the date of the AO and falling due for payment during the lifetime of the AO can be added to an existing AO on the application of the creditor or the client, provided this does not take the total debts above the prescribed maximum. Undeclared debts can also be added to an AO, provided this does not take the total debts above the prescribed maximum. If they do, the court must revoke the AO.

The effect of an administration order

The AO will require the client to make payments towards the scheduled debts, which may either be repaid in full or to the extent decided by the court (a composition). Different debts may be repaid to different extents. In order to discourage irresponsible lending, the court can order that repayments are not to be made in respect of new debts added to the AO until the repayments in respect of the original debts have been made.

Repayments are by instalments, calculated in accordance with regulations and based on the client's 'surplus income'. The instalments are likely to be set at £50 a month plus either all or a percentage of additional surplus income. 'Surplus income' will be defined in regulations and is likely to be the difference between justifiable everyday expenses and income from all sources as assessed using the Common Financial Statement or similar model. Any assets – eg, the client's savings, may be taken into account when calculating surplus income. Repayments could be ordered to be made by a lump sum or instalments.

The court may vary the AO on its own initiative, or on the application of the client or a creditor. The client must provide information to the court about her/his earnings, income, assets and liabilities (including any anticipated changes) at intervals to be specified in regulations. In addition, s/he must inform the court before s/he disposes of any assets (other than goods exempt from seizure by bailiffs – see p353) above a value to be specified in regulations (expected to be between £300 and £500). Failure to provide this information is punishable as a contempt of court by imprisonment and/or a fine.

The court can also vary an AO by 'de-scheduling' any debt –ie, removing it from the AO, provided it is 'just and equitable' to do so – eg, if a debt has been incorrectly included in the AO.

There is a maximum limit on the duration of an AO. An AO automatically comes to an end after five years unless the court has specified an earlier date (the court can vary the length of the AO within the overall limit). As long as the AO is in force the client must supply information about her/his earnings or income, and her/his assets and expenditure at specified intervals, including anticipated changes.

Creditors must not:

- present a bankruptcy petition against the client in respect of a qualifying debt without the permission of the court;
- pursue any remedy for the recovery of a qualifying debt without the permission of the court;
- charge any interest, fee or other charge in respect of their debt(s);
- disconnect a gas or electricity supply on the ground of non-payment by the client of charges incurred prior to the making of the AO unless the court gives permission.[111]

Any county court proceedings relating to a qualifying debt (other than bankruptcy proceedings) that were pending against the client when the AO was made must be stayed, but it may be possible for the court to stay a bankruptcy petition to enable the client to apply for an AO.

Once a debt has been paid to the extent provided by the AO, the court must order the client to be discharged from the debt and de-schedule the debt. The court must then revoke the AO.

The court must revoke an AO if the qualifying conditions either were not met at the date the AO was made or are no longer being met (see above). The court may also revoke an AO for other reasons, in particular, if the client has failed to make two payments required under the order (not necessarily consecutive) or to provide required information.

Debt repayment plans

Debt management schemes will be operated by bodies such as Citizens Advice, Payplan or the Consumer Credit Counselling Service. Clients with non-business debts will be able to approach a scheme operator and ask it to arrange a debt repayment plan (DRP). DRPs will:

- cover all the client's debts that are allowed to be included under the terms of the scheme;
- give the client protection against enforcement of those debts;
- require the client to make repayments in respect of those debts (which may involve compounding of some or all of the debts);
- result in the client being discharged from these debts, provided s/he makes the payments required under the DRP.

Creditors included in a DRP arranged under an approved scheme can appeal to the county court against:

- the fact that the DRP had been arranged;
- the fact that the creditor's debt had been included in the DRP; *or*
- the terms of the plan, including the repayments, but not the fact that a debt alleged to be due to another creditor had been included.

Scheme operators can charge for their reasonable costs and recover these from the client or the creditors.

Note: at the time of writing, it is not clear whether the Government intends to implement these provisions, but if so, the earliest date will be October 2010.

Notes

2. **Administration orders**
1 s112 CCA 1984
2 *Preston Borough Council v Riley, The Times,* 19 April 1995, CA; see also *Various v Walker,* Walsall CC, 3 January 1997 (*Legal Action,* May 1997); *Various v MM, HW & CE,* Birmingham CC, 23 October 1997 (*Legal Action,* January 1998)
3 r5(6) and (8) CCR 39
4 *Various v MM, HW & CE,* Birmingham CC, 23 October 1997 (*Legal Action,* January 1998); *A v Fenland District Council,* Kings Lynn CC, August 1997 (*Adviser* 64 abstracts). The decision to the contrary in *Lane v Liverpool City Council,* Liverpool CC, 19 May 1997 (*Adviser* 69 abstracts) appears wrongly decided in the light of the decision in *Re Green* [1979] 1 All ER 832 that an attachment of earnings order is not an assignment of the debt. See also *Nolan v Stoke on Trent County Council* (*Adviser* 118 abstracts), where the court held that continuing to receive money under an attachment of earnings order was a 'remedy' and ordered the local authority to refund the sums deducted since making the AO.
5 r14 CCR 39
6 s112(5) CCA 1984

3. **When to use bankruptcy and voluntary arrangements**
7 s360 IA 1986
8 s360 IA 1986
9 s1 Directors Disqualification Act 1986
10 s390 IA 1986

4. **Individual voluntary arrangements**
11 s262A IA 1986
12 s256A IA 1986; r5.14 IR
13 s253 IA 1986
14 s252 IA 1986
15 s255 IA 1986
16 s258 IA 1986
17 *Rey v FNCB* [2006] EWHC 1386, Ch (*Adviser* 117, abstracts)
18 s260 IA 1986
19 s262 IA 1986

5. **Bankruptcy**
20 s265 IA 1986; EC Reg 1346/2000
21 *Re Hancock* [1904] 1 KB 585, CA
22 r6.9 IR
23 See P Madge, 'Centre of Interest', *Adviser* 93
24 s287(2)b) IA 1986
25 s273 IA 1986
26 s268 IA 1986
27 *Re a debtor, The Times,* 6 March 1995, CA
28 *Skarzynski v Chalford Property Co* [2001] BPIR 673, Ch
29 *Griffin v Wakefield MBC,* 24 March 200, CA (*Adviser* 116, abstracts)
30 Where the statutory demand is posted it is deemed to be served seven days after posting (para 11.5 PD CPR). If the 18-day time limit has passed, it can be extended by the court, provided the petition has not been issued (para 12.5 PD CPR).
31 paras 12.3 and 12.4 PD CPR
32 r6.5 IR
33 *Re Ridgeway Motors* [2005] EWCA Civ 92, CA (*Adviser* 109, abstracts)
34 s271 IA 1986
35 *Lilley v American Express* [2000] BPIR 70, Ch (repeated failure to honour promises of payment)
36 For a more detailed discussion on dealing with creditors' petitions, see M Gallagher, 'Demands and Petitions', *Adviser* 111
37 r6.29 IR; see also *Harrison v Segger* [2005] EWHC 411, Ch (adjourning generally for repayment over four years held unreasonable exercise of discretion)
38 s276 IA 1986
39 s291 IA 1986
40 s371 IA 1986
41 s358 IA 1986
42 r6.34 IR, which enables the court to suspend registration until further order
43 The Insolvency Services Case Help Manual says that this can currently be done by invoking the court's power to amend any order by removing the client's details from the bankruptcy order.

44 s289 IA 1986
45 s293 IA 1986
46 s315 IA 1986
47 s284 IA 1986
48 s307 IA 1986
49 ss350-362 IA 1986 deal with 'bankruptcy offences'
50 Sch 4A para 2 IA 1986
51 Art 7 Enterprise Act 2002 (Commencement No.4) Order 2003 No.2093
52 Sch 4A para 4 IA 1986
53 Sch 21 EA 2002 and s389 IA 1986
54 rr6.241–6.244 I(A)R
55 Sch 4A paras 7–9 IA 1986
56 Sch 4A para 5 IA 1986
57 rr6.245 – 6.246 I(A)R
58 Insolvency Service *Annual Report 2007/08*
59 s283(2) IA 1986
60 ss308 and 309 IA 1986
61 see M Gallagher, 'Bankruptcy: keeping the car', *Adviser* 122
62 s310 IA 1986
63 Sch 19 para 7 EA 2002
64 s310A IA 1986
65 *Re Landau (a bankrupt), The Times,* 1 January 1997
66 *Re Stapleford,* 1 April 1998, Chancery Division, *Insolvency Intelligence,* August/September 1998
67 *Kilvert v Flackett*, *The Times,* 3 August 1998
68 s11 and Sch 2 Welfare Reform and Pensions Act 1999
69 Regs 5 and 6 Occupational and Personal Pension Schemes (Bankruptcy) (No.2) Regs 2002 No.836
70 s283A IA 1986
71 s313A IA 1986
72 Art 3 Insolvency Proceedings (Monetary Limits) (Amendment) Order 2004 No.547
73 s335A IA 1986, as inserted by the TLATA 1996
74 *Doodes v Gotham* [2006] EWCA Civ 1080
75 See, for example, *Martin-Sklan v White* [2006] EWHC 3313, Ch and *Nicholls v Lan* [2006] EWHC 1255, Ch (*Adviser* 122, abstracts)
76 *Stack v Dowden* [2007] UKHL 17 (*Adviser* 123, abstracts)
77 For a discussion on this issue, see M Allen, 'Whose House is it Anyway', *Quarterly Account* 8, IMA, Spring 2008
78 s285(3)(a) IA 1986
79 s285(3)(b) IA 1986
80 See for example, *Cadogan Estates v McMahon* [2001] 1 AC 378, HL
81 See *Ezekiel v Orakpo* [1976] 3 All ER 659, CA; *Razzaq v Pala* [1997] 1 WLR 1336, ChD; Heppinstall, 'Flat Broke', *Solicitors Journal*, 7 March 2003, also supports the view that a landlord of a secure or assured tenant can commence possession proceedings for pre-bankruptcy rent arrears, but only with leave of the court. For a contrary view, see J Kruse, 'The Impact of Bankruptcy on Rent Arrears', *Quarterly Account* 70, IMA, Winter 2003/04
82 s285(3)(b) IA 1986
83 s342 IA 1986
84 ss339 and 341(1) IA 1986
85 *Hill v Haines* [2007] EWCA Civ 1284
86 s340 IA 1986
87 s341 IA 1986
88 s342 IA 1986
89 s285 IA 1986
90 *R v Secretary of State for Social Security ex parte Taylor and Chapman, The Times,* 5 February 1996
91 r6.93 IR
92 s285 IA 1986
93 r12.3 IR
94 Sch 6 IA 1986
95 s279 IA 1986
96 s279(2) IA 1986
97 Sch 19 EA 2002
98 s280 IA 1986
99 s281 IA 1986
100 *R (Steele) v Birmingham City Council and Secretary of State for Work and Pensions* [2005] EWCA Civ 1824, CA (*Adviser* 115, abstracts)
101 *Secretary of State for Work & Pensions v Balding* [2007] EWCA Civ 1327
102 *Re Nolton Business Centres Ltd* [1996] BCC 500, ChD (*Adviser* 109, abstracts). If the council has not served a final demand or obtained a liability order, only the arrears at the date of the bankruptcy order are a bankruptcy debt.
103 ss291(5) and 333(3) IA 1986
104 See D Pomeroy, 'Bankruptcy Annulment', *Adviser* 113 and *Halabi v Camden LBC* [2008] WLR (D) 46, where the court held that the practice of annulling bankruptcy orders on the basis of a solicitor's undertaking to make the required payments was not legal and the annulment order should provide for it not to take effect until the trustee confirmed that all the required payments had actually been made.

105 s282 IA 1986
106 s261(1) IA 1986
107 *Fitch v Official Receiver* [1996] 1WLR 242, CA

6. **Reform of insolvency law**

108 The paper applies the term 'can't pay' to people with £50 a month or less per household of surplus income after taking into account their reasonable domestic needs as calculated using the CFS similar guidelines.
109 There will be only one DRO unit, based in Plymouth. The client must sign a hard copy of the DRO application, which the intermediary will send separately.
110 The supplier may disconnect the supply on the groundsof non-payment of charges incurred after the making of the ERO or for reasons unconnected with non-payment.
111 The supplier may disconnect the supply on the groundsof non-payment of charges incurred after the making of the AO or for reasons unconnected with non-payment.

13

Chapter 13

Business debts

This chapter covers:

This chapter deals with certain types of debt that arise during or after running a business. It also looks at ways in which the debts or strategies covered elsewhere in this *Handbook* need different consideration for the small businessperson.

This chapter must be used in conjunction with the rest of the *Handbook*. Provided the adviser is familiar with the processes of debt advice outlined throughout, this chapter will often be a starting point when dealing with someone who has recently run, or is running, a business.

This chapter is not a guide to business credit or business viability, which are both specialist areas in their own right.

Debt advisers often declare themselves unable to deal with a person's debts while s/he is still running a business. The need to refer to other professional specialists (for instance, tax or business advisers) cannot be overstressed. Business Debtline, a free telephone helpline for the self-employed and small businesses has experience in advising clients who are still trading and may be a useful place of referral. However, this chapter assumes that some limited involvement with the debts of a trading business person is possible. In addition, it will be apparent that many ancillary debts (particularly after a person has ceased trading) can be handled by the debt adviser.

1. Types of small business

It is important to understand what type of business a client is involved in because this determines her/his liability.

Sole trader

A person who is self-employed without business partners is described as a sole trader. Typical sole traders might include people like joiners, electricians or taxi drivers and also sales people who work their own patch on a purely self-employed basis. Sole traders can work either in their own name or using a business name.

Sole traders are legally responsible for their business debts in exactly the same way as they are responsible for personal debts.

Partnership

A partnership is the relationship that exists when two or more people carry on a business together in order to make a profit. A partnership can be very informal, as, for instance, where musicians perform together and share their expenses and payment. No formal written agreement is required for a partnership to exist, but this will always be useful where disputes or problems arise. Partnership agreements should cover questions like distribution of profits (which will be equal unless stated otherwise) and how the partnership can be dissolved. In the absence of a partnership agreement, the Partnership Act 1890 will apply.

A partnership is considered a single legal entity. Unless the partnership rules state otherwise, contracts can be entered into by any one of the partners and bind them all. A partner is normally responsible only for those debts accrued during the period in which s/he was a member of the partnership (although sometimes new partners agree to take responsibility for any partnership debts accrued by their predecessors). Partners continue to be responsible for debts accrued during their partnership, unless they all formally agree otherwise, and also gain the agreement of creditors to a transfer of their liability (perhaps to the remaining partners). Partners may even be held liable for debts incurred by the partnership after they have left, unless notice was given to the creditors. Outgoing partners should ideally seek legal advice when leaving a partnership to ensure they take all necessary action to avoid this happening.

Partnerships may trade under a particular business name or the names of the partners.

Partners are normally jointly and severally liable (see Chapter 5) for all their partnership debts. However, this is no longer the case with tax debts, where the liability for tax falls personally on each partner according to their share of the profit.

Limited companies

A limited company is where a separate legal body is set up to trade and make a profit (which is either kept in the company or distributed to its owners – ie, shareholders). Losses fall to the company rather than the individuals who have set it up. A limited company can be public (ie, where the shares can be bought or sold on the stock market) or private (where shares are owned and transferred among a limited number of people allowed by the company's rules). Companies are owned by their shareholders. They are run by their directors who may also be shareholders (and in most small companies they are) but they need not be. Directors are elected by shareholders and are employees of the company. Companies are governed by legislation, much of which is administered by

Companies House, where records of directors and accounts are kept. Company law is complex and outside the scope of this *Handbook* – it is vital to advise clients to get specialist advice where appropriate.

Unlike in a partnership, the directors are not personally responsible for the debts of a company unless:

- they have agreed to act as guarantor for some, or all, of the company's debts. This is often the case with bank loans to small companies; *or*
- they have acted fraudulently and the company has been liquidated; *or*
- they have continued to trade while the company was insolvent and the company subsequently goes into insolvent liquidation.

Companies legislation is intended to encourage entrepreneurship by protecting unsuccessful business people from the individual consequences of corporate debts.

Credit arrangements made in the name of a limited company cannot be regulated under the Consumer Credit Act 1974.

Co-operatives and franchises

These are rare and specialist advice should be sought if liability is in doubt.

Limited liability partnerships

A new kind of business known as a limited liability partnership (LLP) was introduced in April 2000. This has some of the characteristics of a partnership and some of a company. The liability of the 'members' (not partners) to contribute to the debts of the LLP are limited to the assets of the LLP. There is no recourse to personal assets unless the member has been personally negligent.

Queries relating to LLP debts should be referred to a legal specialist or an accountant with expertise in this area.

2. Stages of debt advice

The rest of this chapter highlights factors to be taken into account in the debt advice process, as outlined in Chapter 3, when advising someone who either runs, or has run, her/his own business, whether as a sole trader, a partner or a company director.

Create trust

People who have run their own business may pose particular challenges to the debt adviser's trust-building skills. Being self-employed requires self-confidence and independence, which may make it difficult for a person to ask for help. If an employee becomes unable to pay her/his debts after being made redundant, at least s/he can see that the causes are beyond her/his control. However, someone whose indebtedness arises after the collapse of her/his own business may have to face feelings of personal failure in addition to the ordinary problems associated with serious debt. The client in debt may, therefore, need time to unburden her/himself of these feelings.

The debt adviser should also ensure that as much responsibility as possible for undertaking the tasks necessary to sort things out is carried by the businessperson. If s/he has already run a business (often for many years), s/he will feel both de-skilled and disempowered if the debt adviser takes over simply because the business is no longer successful.

List creditors and minimise debts

Minimise debts by ceasing to trade

If a person is still running a business but is seriously in debt, s/he should consider whether or not to continue trading. There is clearly no point in doing so if this is just increasing indebtedness and the situation is unlikely to alter. This is a highly complex area and specialist help should be sought from a small business adviser, perhaps via the local Learning and Skills Council or the business's own accountants. The process may be helped by drawing up a business plan for a reasonable period ahead (business advisers often recommend a period of between one and five years). This plan is similar to the financial statement drawn up for the client, except that it deals with income and outgoings of the business, not an individual. The plan should include the following.

- All the business's assets. This should include equipment or machinery with its approximate resale value (which will be different from amounts shown in professionally produced accounts, where the 'book value' is based upon the original cost of an item and its theoretical life). The greatest asset of a business may be the work it has in hand and the debts owed to it. These are notoriously difficult to value. The likelihood of a debt owed to the business actually being paid must be assessed and the contractual status of work in hand measured. For instance, a painter and decorator may have agreed in the autumn to paint the exterior of an existing customer's house the following spring. If the customer loses her/his job during the winter, in the (usual) absence of any binding agreement the work may not materialise.

  A realistic value for any premises or leases on premises that are owned should be estimated, perhaps by a local estate agent, although it should be borne in mind that valuations of business premises are not usually free (as they are for domestic premises). The client's estimate of value may, therefore, have to be sufficient. Business premises are particularly susceptible to a fall in value caused by developments elsewhere in the locality. For instance, the opening of a supermarket nearby is likely both to cause a collapse in the business of a corner shop but also a fall in the value of its premises. In this way, a reduction in the market which causes a business to flounder can also reduce the value of its assets, which would otherwise have been its major protection from financial problems. The value of a lease is a complex matter that can only be accurately assessed by a professional. Leased business premises are not valued in the same way as domestic premises. The shorter the period that the lease has left to run, the less likely it is to be of any value. Advisers should note that if there is no one prepared to take over the lease, this might represent a liability rather than an asset (because the client/tenant otherwise remains liable for the rent until expiry of the lease).

Items like cars should always be valued at the price likely to be obtained at auction rather than a price an optimist might expect to get from a private sale. There are various used car price guides available from newsagents (and on the internet) that give a trade price for reasonably modern cars, and these can be used as a guide.

- Likely income to the business. Draw up a list of payments that the business might expect to receive based on a conservative, but realistic, assessment. Note the dates when payments can be expected. The debt adviser can demonstrate respect for the client's business skills by asking her/him to prepare these figures her/himself.
- Expenditure by the business. A similar, dated list of payments that the business is required to make must be drawn up next. This must include, for example, bank interest and charges, lease or rental charges for both property and equipment, regular bills for fuel and other services (eg, telephones and waste disposal), payments required by suppliers, VAT payments, wages to any staff, estimated tax and national insurance.

The excess income over expenditure will give a rough idea of how much is available for the businessperson to pay her/himself in 'drawings'. If there is no foreseeable likelihood of anything being available, an end to trading is strongly indicated. However, it should be stressed again that the client and/or debt adviser must seek expert assistance before taking such a major step, because items like liability for tax or payments due under a lease, which can be very complex, could make the difference between viability and insolvency. A lay adviser will not generally be qualified to make this decision.

If a person is trading as a partner, the decision to cease trading may not be hers/his alone. Where one partner wants to cease but others do not, s/he should ensure that s/he has formally severed her/his partnership agreement in order to limit her/his liability to those debts that have accrued at that time. S/he should try to gain the agreement of creditors and ex-partners, preferably in writing, that s/he will not be liable for any debts which subsequently come to light, but which relate to the period of her/his membership of the partnership. Where a partnership is informal and there is, therefore, no prescribed way of leaving it, legal advice should be sought so that an agreement can be drawn up terminating the informal partnership. If possible, this should include an agreement that those remaining in the business will indemnify (ie, agree to pay instead of) those leaving against claims against them for past actions (or bills).

Sometimes informal business partnerships exist between people who have personal relationships, such as married or co-habiting couples. It is often the custom that either party can enter into contracts on behalf of the partnership (for which both partners become jointly and severely liable). In such a case, it is important that suppliers are informed that the partnership no longer exists if this is desired. This is often the case when a personal relationship ends and thus a couple cease trading together.

Minimise other debts

Business borrowings are often secured by banks against a person's home. Sometimes such a security is not enforceable if the agreement was entered into as a result of undue influence or misrepresentation by the creditor or another client (see p149). This more commonly occurs where a person who is not the borrower is required to agree to a charge being made on a property in which s/he is either a joint owner or has another interest (perhaps because s/he lives with the owner). In one case, it was decided that a charge was not enforceable where a client's wife had signed it but had not been recommended to take separate legal advice and had been told that her husband's business would be closed down by the bank if she did not do so.[1]

If undue influence or other wrongdoing occurred at the time the security was signed, specialist or legal advice should be sought, as the law is complex in this area.

The debts owed by a person who has run a business may include tax debts. See below for ways in which these might be minimised.

List and maximise income

The scope for improving the income of a person running her/his own business is often greater than that of an employee. Specialist business advice can improve profitability, for instance, through better marketing, the lowering of production costs or overheads, or diversification. The debt adviser should, therefore, refer the client to someone who can help with this.

In addition, there are many grants and other facilities (eg, cheap loans) available to small businesses, which should be investigated. The local Learning and Skills Council or Business Link are probably the best places to start. The payment of tax may use up a substantial proportion of income and, therefore, the need to claim all the relevant individual tax allowances, reliefs and expenses that a business can offset against tax should be noted (see p438).

Self-employed people may be able to claim tax credits. The claim will be assessed on the previous year's net profit. If their profits are likely to be different over the coming period they can include a projection. Council tax benefit, housing benefit, income-based jobseeker's allowance and income support may also be available, as well as disability benefits. If national insurance payments are up to date, it may be possible for a self-employed client to claim employment and support allowance if s/he is unable to work because of sickness.

List expenditure

In drawing up a financial statement for a businessperson, the debt adviser will need figures from the business plan. However, the personal financial statement is a different document and should be kept separate. The expenditure required by the business (even of a sole trader) should be listed separately from personal or household expenses. Sometimes this is not easy, particularly with a sole trader, where, for instance, a car might be necessary for work and to provide family transport. The debt adviser may send the draft business plan along with a household financial statement to creditors.

The debt adviser should be careful not to double-count items shown as outgoings on the business account (and, therefore, reduce the available income), but which may also be paid as part of the household budget. For instance, if a car is used for both domestic and business purposes it should be apportioned partly to the business account before the drawings from the business are shown and then only the remaining (domestic) portion should be shown on the financial statement.

Deal with priority debts

Services

If a business has ceased trading and utility debts on commercial premises are outstanding, the gas and electricity bills may need to be treated as a priority. This is because the power to disconnect home premises for non-payment of commercial bills exists for gas and electricity supplies where those supplies are in the same name and provided by the same supplier.[2] It follows that, if someone traded from home, gas and electricity arrears will be priority debts. If s/he traded from part of the same building (eg, from a shop above which s/he lived), s/he should separate the suppliers to the two premises before arrears accrue to avoid the risk of disconnection of the domestic premises.

Water companies cannot disconnect a supply to any premises other than those to which the water was supplied, and since 30 June 1999 can no longer disconnect the supply to residential premises.[3] It is not entirely clear how this will affect mixed-use premises – eg, a flat above a shop. Ofwat has issued guidance stating it believes the disconnection of mixed-use premises could be illegal and reminds customers of their right to take court action if this has happened. In practice, companies will only disconnect mixed-use premises in rare circumstances.

Water companies have the right to disconnect separate non-domestic premises. The environmental risk of a business being without water could lead to the closure of the business.

Business rates

Business rates may not be charged on empty premises, but this may vary between local authorities, so advisers may wish to check local discounts. If the ratepayer has a lease on the premises, s/he will be liable for the business rates for as long as her/his tenancy exists, even if the premises are empty. Business rates are collected and enforced in the same way as council tax, except that, for instance, tools of the trade are not exempt. Advisers should note this means that bailiffs can seize a ratepayer's property from anywhere (including her/his home address) once a liability order has been made. Another difference is that attachment of earnings orders and charging orders are not allowed for business rates, nor are deductions from benefit.

In practice, many local authorities remit, or write off, large amounts of unpaid business rates. They have the power to remit unpaid business rates where there is 'severe hardship' and where it is reasonable to do so. Most local authorities will, in practice, use this power to write off unpaid rates where a business has ceased trading and those responsible for the rates are dependent on benefit, or where a business may close with job losses if rates are pursued. Local councillors should be approached to put pressure on officers if this is not done.[4]

Distress for rent

Distress for rent (see p342) is a possibility that should be borne in mind if a business is behind with its rent. Distress is possible as soon as rent is overdue. No court order is necessary. If a person is continuing to trade, it is probably impossible to stop bailiffs from making a peaceful entry to her/his premises (since they are likely to be open to the public). Some landlords will see the seizure of the whole of a business's stock as the easiest way of recovering rent arrears, but this will almost certainly have the effect of forcing the client to cease trading. The possibility that bailiffs will arrive unannounced, therefore, means that the utmost priority must be given to securing an arrangement with a business's landlord if the client wishes to continue trading. The business landlord cannot use distress at the trader's home address (unless s/he has removed goods there to avoid seizure).

Leased premises

Many businesses lease their work premises. Such arrangements are governed by the Landlord and Tenant Act 1954. In some cases, the unexpired part of a business lease can be a valuable asset that can be realised if the client decides to cease trading or trade from other premises. Professional advice should always be sought on the valuation of such leases. Where a lease is to be 'assigned' to another person, legal advice should be sought and the permission of the landlord will be required. Unfortunately, if the new tenant fails to pay her/his rent, in certain circumstances the earlier tenant can still be held responsible. In order to protect against this future liability, it is sometimes better to agree with a landlord the surrender of a lease, even where the lease may be saleable for a premium.

Landlords may be prepared to accept the surrender of a lease (which ends the tenant's contractual obligations, such as rent and therefore business rates) where it is clear they are unlikely to get any more money from a particular tenant. If they wish to sue for unpaid rent, landlords must be able to show they have mitigated their losses. In the circumstances where a client has ceased trading and is likely to remain unemployed for some time, and has responsibility for a lease, the debt adviser could approach the landlord directly. S/he should explain that the tenant is unlikely to meet her/his contractual obligations and, in some cases, landlords will agree to a surrender. It is important, however, for the adviser to ensure that s/he is not dealing with a lease which is of value (perhaps because it forms a small part of a redevelopment site or because the rent has been fixed at a low rate for many future years) before s/he gives it away. Specialist advice should be sought.

Other leases

Many businesses will have equipment like photocopiers, electronic scales or games machines which are held on a lease from owners. The debt adviser should first check whether or not the lease is a regulated agreement under the Consumer Credit Act (see Chapter 4). Many lease documents are complex and specialist help may be required.

A business lease will run for a number of years, during which time the owner of the goods (which may be a finance company) simply charges the business rent to use them. At the end of the period there can be no automatic transfer of the goods to the lessee but, in practice, items are often not taken back by lessors. A lease will usually contain provision for early settlement. However, in many cases this figure will be almost as high (usually 95 per cent) as continuing to pay rental until the end of the lease period.

Once a lessee is in arrears with the rental, however, the courts can intervene under common law and alter any clause designed to penalise a lessee who is in arrears. Because the courts have this power only when arrears arise, it may be useful to allow business leases to go into arrears if a client has decided to cease trading.

It should be stressed that business leases are very complex and, as the sums of money involved can be substantial, expert advice should be obtained before reaching any agreement with a lessor about early settlement (trading standards departments may be able to provide such advice).

In calculating the amount that should be paid by the lessee who is in arrears, the courts will ensure that the lessor receives only the actual amount of money that it has lost as a result of the termination. This should include either the goods or their full value at the time of termination. Additionally, lessors should receive the amount that would have been paid in interest less an amount (usually 5 per cent a year) in recognition of the fact that they are receiving this money early. If a lease contains charges for service to equipment leased out, the courts may reduce the future service charges that will not be required after the goods are returned.

VAT debts

Value added tax (VAT) is a tax on the increase in the value of most goods or services (some are exempt) between the time they are bought by a business and when they are sold. Businesses with a turnover of less than £64,000 per annum (2008/09) do not have to register for VAT. All others have to submit returns at a frequency agreed with HM Revenue and Customs (the Revenue) to show the difference between the VAT they pay to other suppliers (input tax) and the VAT they charge their customers (output tax). If they have collected more VAT than they have paid, they must enclose this with their return and submit it by a due date (usually a month after the end of the relevant quarter). If a return is late, the amount due is increased by an automatic surcharge. If a return is not made, the Revenue can estimate the amount due and issue its own assessment, which becomes payable immediately.

Local Revenue officers who collect VAT vary greatly in their approach to struggling or failed businesses. In general, it should be noted that they consider themselves as collectors of a tax which has already been paid by a third party to the client and of which the client is only a custodian. While this may bear little relation to the realities of running a small business, it is an attitude that makes them assertive and swift in their recovery process.

Once payment is outstanding, the Revenue officer at a local office will usually use the threat of distress to force payment. This may initially consist of a visit, phone call or letter to state that distress will be used. A formal notice will then warn the client that immediate payment is required and bailiffs will be used in default.

A distress warrant is then signed by a Revenue officer (recourse to the courts is not necessary).[5]

The warrant will usually be executed by a firm of private bailiffs with a Revenue officer in attendance. Although they have no right to force entry (see Chapter 11), most business premises are accessible to the public (including bailiffs) and therefore negotiation is essential. A client who is still trading should always try to give the bailiffs some money and treat this debt with utmost priority. Distress can provoke or escalate the collapse of a business, both by removing necessary stock or equipment and also by reducing confidence in the business.

The adviser who is faced with unpaid VAT should:

- contact the Revenue, explain the position and request a short time to organise the person's affairs;
- get an accountant to check the amount claimed (particularly if it is an assessed amount);
- explain the seriousness to the client – use a small business adviser if necessary to look at the viability of the business – eg, its credit control procedures.

See Chapter 11 for details of how to deal with bailiffs. Advisers should note the detailed list of exempt goods.

Where distress is not appropriate, the Revenue will often use bankruptcy as a means of collection (see Chapter 12).

Income tax debts

Self-employed people and businesses are responsible for making a return to the Revenue, on which tax bills are based. Under the self-assessment system, taxpayers can calculate their own tax and send in a payment to accompany their return for a particular year. A small business should always get specialist help in claiming all the allowances against tax to which it may be entitled and in treating its profits and losses in the most tax-efficient way. The tax bill is based on simple 'three-line accounts' for small businesses with a turnover of less than £30,000 per year. These are required to show:

- total turnover;
- total expenses and costs of purchases;
- net profit (gross profit less all the business expenses).

In addition to the tax due on its profits, a business may also owe tax (and national insurance contributions) on wages paid to employees.

The actual assessment process is outside the scope of this book and the adviser should, where necessary, get specialist help to check the amount of tax demanded. TaxAid is a useful source of help.

If the client fails to file a tax return, the Revenue will make its own 'determination' of how much tax is due and this is enforceable immediately. It can only be overturned by filing a return. The Revenue can impose penalties and surcharges for late filing of returns and/or non-payment of tax. If the client is unable to persuade the Revenue to waive or remit these penalties, the client can appeal on the ground that s/he had a 'reasonable excuse' for the failure. Note that a late filing penalty cannot exceed the amount of any tax due. If when the return is filed there is no tax to pay, the penalty will be reduced to nil. It is therefore important to file returns, however late.

If a tax bill is unpaid, the Revenue may:

- use distress – ie, seize goods (without a court order) – see p346;
- use the magistrates' court (see p338);
- use the county court and follow judgment with a third-party debt order, attachment of earnings, execution, charging order or instalment order (see p239);
- seek a bankruptcy order (see Chapter 12).

As with VAT, the Revenue is likely to be particularly strict where the money owed includes tax already collected by a business from employees and not passed on to the Revenue. It should be noted that the Revenue is not averse to starting bankruptcy proceedings, even if this is unlikely to lead to a payment being made.

A summons to the magistrates' court is usually used to collect unpaid tax of up to £2,000 where the debt is less than 12 months old. The client will be summonsed to appear at a hearing at which the magistrates will make an order that s/he pays the tax. The client should attend the hearing with a financial statement and ask to pay the tax by instalments. The courts are not able to consider arguments that the tax is not owed or the wrong amount is being claimed. If the client still does not pay, the magistrates may summons her/him to a committal hearing. At this, the client will need to show that s/he has not 'wilfully refused' or 'culpably neglected' to pay this tax (see Chapter 10).

If the county court is used, the client can ask for an instalment order in the usual way.

The Revenue is entitled to claim interest (currently 7.5 per cent a year) on any unpaid tax until payment, and enforces this even after a county court judgment.[6] Once a judgment has been made, the possibility of an administration order exists if the debts are below £5,000 (see Chapter 9).

It is possible to negotiate with the Revenue. Although it is generally easier to negotiate after the client has ceased trading, as with all negotiation, the outcome will depend on the circumstances of the individual case. If the taxpayer has been caused problems by maladministration, the Parliamentary Ombudsman can be contacted via the local MP. There is also a Revenue Adjudicator, who may intervene in cases of particular hardship or unreasonableness.

Draw up a personal financial statement

Creating a financial statement for a person who is running her/his own business is no different from that of an employed person, except that expenses may need apportioning, as explained above, and the amount of her/his income may be less predictable. Both these things should be made clear on the financial statement. The figure for earnings ('drawings') net of tax and national insurance contributions should be taken from the business plan produced to help decide the viability of the business. It is important that the business budget is used to extract a figure for drawings, rather than asking clients how much they draw from the business. The client's drawings may well exceed profis.

Choose a strategy for non-priority debts – bankruptcy and individual voluntary arrangements

These are discussed in Chapter 12. Bankruptcy may often be the most satisfactory way out of the large debts that can arise after the failure of a business. Bankruptcy in itself does not necessarily mean the business must cease trading, particularly where there are no assets of significant value. However, it should be remembered that although discharge from bankruptcy may occur after one year (two or three years prior to 1 April 2004), a person's credit rating will be affected for considerably longer, and if s/he wishes to run a business that will require credit in the future, bankruptcy can be an obstacle to this. Someone with an otherwise viable business but serious debts may be well advised to consider an individual voluntary arrangement.

Notes

2. Stages of debt advice

1 *Barclays Bank plc v O'Brien* [1993] 4 All ER 417, HL; see also *Royal Bank of Scotland v Etridge* (No.2) [2001] UKHL 44; [2002] HLR 4
2 Sch 6 para 1(6) EA 1989; Sch 2B para 7(1) and (3) GA 1986
3 s1 and Sch 1 Water Industry Act 1999
4 s49 LGFA 1988
5 Sch 11 para 5(4) Valued Added Tax Act 1994
6 TMA 1970

Chapter 14

Student debt

This chapter covers:

1. Introduction

This chapter covers the significant issues affecting fees and funding for higher education (HE) in England and Wales.

Student finance has changed dramatically in the last twenty years. The introduction of student loans for living costs for full-time undergraduate students in 1990, of tuition fees in 1998, and higher rates of fees rates and loans for tuition fees in 2006, along with the increase in participation in higher education over this time, has resulted in a system in which the vast majority of students now graduate with some level of debt.

Devolution has also resulted in different arrangements in England and Wales (and also in Scotland and Northern Ireland). Presently, universities and colleges in both England and Wales can, under certain conditions, vary the amount of fees they charge students whose course began on or after 1 September 2006 or those who transfer after this date. Students who started their course prior to this date, or who have moved directly on to an 'end-on' course after completing a course for which they received funding under the previous arrangements, are not affected by the changes. However, if they are starting an end-on course after a gap of a year or more, they come under the new system. From September 2006, the amount of fees charged for publicly funded HE courses depends on the institution, its location and whether it has signed an agreement with the Office for Fair Access. The maximum annual amount a publicly funded institution in England or Wales can charge per person is £3,145 (in 2008/09). Although institutions can charge less, almost all have opted for this rate. The maximum fee level rises with inflation each year.

Students who are subject to these fees and who meet the eligibility criteria can apply for a student loan for fees of up to the rate charged. This is non-means tested. Welsh-domiciled students studying in Wales can also apply for a non-means-tested grant to cover part of their fees.

Students in England and Wales can apply for a means-tested maintenance grant (or, if they are eligible to claim certain social security benefits, a special support grant). They can also apply for a student loan for living costs and may be eligible for a bursary from the institution and discretionary help from the Access to Learning Fund (England) or Financial Contingency Fund (Wales).

'Old system' students eligible for support under the pre-2006 system can also apply for a loan to cover any fee liability. No eligible undergraduate students, therefore, should now have to pay their fees before or during their course – although this option is still available.

Part-time undergraduate students have a separate system of funding. Their fees are unregulated and vary widely. They can apply for grants to help with the cost of fees, but this may not cover the full amount. There is also a small course costs grant and, in Wales, extra allowances for students with children.

Students on certain healthcare-related courses such as nursing, midwifery, occupational therapy and the later years of medicine and dentistry courses are funded by the NHS under a separate scheme. They do not pay tuition fees.

With the exception of teacher training students on Postgraduate Certificate in Education courses, postgraduate students have very limited access to statutory government funds. Similarly, students who wish to study for a second (or subsequent) undergraduate course will find their access to funding severely restricted.

At present, local authorities deal with the majority of applications for student support. However, English-domiciled students who apply to start their courses in the 2009/10 academic year must apply to a new national body called Student Finance England (SFE), which is part of the Student Loans Company (SLC). Continuing students and students in Wales still apply to their local authority.

When advising students and ex-students about debt, the adviser may need to adopt some different strategies and should be aware that students expect to owe money prior to, and on completion of, their studies. Most creditors (banks and the SLC) have structured repayment programmes for 'normal' student debt once the student starts earning. Such indebtedness should not adversely affect the student's creditworthiness (eg, for obtaining a mortgage), although any repayments made (or due to be made) will be listed as outgoings in affordability calculations in future credit applications.

Most of this chapter follows the structure of the rest of the book. Issues are discussed only where the position of the students differs from that of other clients. If an issue is not covered in this section, advisers should, therefore, refer to the main text.

Definitions

Home student

This chapter covers only home students in higher education living in England and Wales. A **'home student'** is defined as:

> a person settled in the UK within the meaning of the Immigration Act 1971 and the person is ordinarily resident in England or Wales on the first day of the first academic year of the course and has been ordinarily resident in the UK, the Channel Islands or the Isle of Man throughout the three-year period preceding the first day of the course. The residence must not have been wholly or mainly for the purpose of receiving full-time education.[1]

Ordinary residence was defined in the case of *Shah and others v Barnet and others* in 1982 as: 'habitual and normal residence in the United Kingdom from choice or settled purpose throughout the prescribed period apart from temporary or occasional absences'.[2]

In addition, a student may be regarded as a home student if s/he, or a certain member of her/his family:

- has refugee status;
- is a European Union citizen with right of permanent residence, and who has been resident in the UK for three years or more;
- is a European Economic Area (EEA) or Swiss national who has taken up employment in the UK and was ordinarily resident in the EEA or Switzerland for three years immediately prior to starting the course;
- is the child of a Turkish national who has taken up employment in the UK and was ordinarily resident in the EEA, Switzerland or Turkey for three years immediately prior to starting the course;
- has been granted humanitarian protection or discretionary leave to remain in the UK.

All the above are still required to be ordinarily resident in England and Wales to be treated as a home student. Note that residency rules are complex, and a student may be eligible home student fee rates but still be ineligible for student support. Local authorities or the SLC/SFE determine whether a student is ordinarily resident in England or Wales as this will affect what support is available. The financial position of international students is not discussed in this chapter. Advisers should contact UKCISA (see Appendix 2).

'Old system' students

Students referred to in this chapter as 'old system' or continuing students are those who fall under the 1998–2005 funding system, as long as they began a designated course before 1 September 2006 and continued on that course after 31 August 2006. This includes students who moved directly on to an 'end-on' course after completing a different undergraduate course under the old regulations, and 'gap year' students – ie, those who were offered a place by 1 August 2005 and began their course before 1 September 2007.

It also includes those who transferred to a similar course at the same HE institution before 1 July 2008.

'New system' students

Students referred to in this chapter as 'new system' students are those who start their course on or after 1 September 2006 and do not fall into one of the exceptions above.

Full-time students

A student is eligible for support for a full-time course as long as the course is 'designated'. It must be a full-time course, a sandwich course or a part-time course for the initial training of teachers, at least one year in duration and be wholly provided by a publicly funded educational institution.

A 'designated course' includes:[3]

- a first degree;
- an HE diploma;
- a BTEC higher national certificate or higher national diploma;
- initial teacher training;
- a course for the further training of teachers or youth and community workers;
- a course to prepare for certain professional examinations of a standard higher than 'A' levels or Scottish Highers, BTEC higher national certificate/higher national diploma, where a first degree is not required for entry;
- a course not higher than a first degree, but higher than those described in the above bullet point – eg, a foundation degree.

Part-time students

A student is a part-time student if the course has been designated as part time.

2. Stages of debt advice

The stages of debt advice described in Chapter 3 need to be applied when working with students, as with anyone else. There are, however, some additional issues to be considered at each stage. These are highlighted below.

Stage 1: create trust

Most higher/further education institutions and students' unions/guilds/ associations offer money advice services. The majority of these are experienced in dealing with student debt and have student-specific information resources. Many students may, therefore, prefer to use this service. There can, however, be issues of impartiality, independence, confidentiality and trust arising when advisers work for the educational institution. This situation is further complicated when the institution is the creditor (see p460). It may not always be appropriate or ethical for an adviser employed by the institution to assist a student in this position. Even when the adviser works for the students' union/guild/association the student may need reassurance that the service is confidential and/or impartial.

In order to create a position of trust with a student in need of debt advice, it is important for the adviser to be aware of the different causes of student debt and not to make a judgement about the position in which a client finds her/himself. Very often the student will not seek help for causes of problems, but their effects.

There are many reasons why a student may be in debt. In addition to the causes of indebtedness that apply to the general population, this can be due to: above-average course costs; local authority assessments not being a true reflection of parental disposable income; debts incurred prior to the client becoming a student; aggressive marketing towards the student group; tuition fees; coping with an income paid in irregular instalments.

Some students can cope with increased levels of debt, accepting that a certain level of indebtedness is inevitable and part of the student experience. For others, it can have a more negative impact. The adviser could be faced with a student who may be extremely anxious, ashamed, desperate, worried or confused. The stage at which the student presents may also have an effect on her/his emotional state, as many wait until the situation can no longer be dealt with without external assistance before seeking help. The impact of all of this can be that the student may be experiencing poor health, mental ill health, relationship difficulties and difficulties with her/his course – eg, low marks, missed deadlines and exam failures. Some students may feel forced to withdraw from their course completely.

Stage 2: list creditors and minimise debts

When noting the status of the debt on the creditor list, it is important to consider the sanctions connected with non-payment in order to determine whether the debt should be recorded as a priority or non-priority. In addition to the criteria referred to in Chapter 7 (if non-payment would give the creditor the right to deprive the client of their home, liberty, essential goods and services or place in the community, then that debt will have priority), the adviser needs to consider the sanctions available to and used by the institution where it is the creditor. Outstanding tuition fees correctly attributable to the student can be listed as a priority debt. For some ex-students, outstanding tuition fees can remain a priority debt as the majority of institutions withhold the award until the debt is cleared. Students entering some professions (eg, teaching) need their degree conferring or degree certificate before they can take up employment. Prioritisation needs to be discussed with the student (see also p454).

The adviser needs to be aware of the threats posed to the client by the recovery action, and whether they are appropriate – p462 details what sanctions should be imposed on the different types of debt the student may have with the institution. Advisers need to be aware when negotiating with creditors that some types of student debt will become repayable in the future, and any offers of repayment need to reflect this.

Stage 3: list income

Student loans (for living costs) and some elements of grants are taken into account as income for benefit purposes. It is, therefore, important that loans are listed as such. Most creditors will otherwise suggest that they are used as a means of making repayments. Without them the financial statement will show a hugely unrealistic deficit. However, advisers need to explain that this source of income is a loan used only for living expenses, that interest is accruing, and that repayment will be required at a future date.

Disabled students can receive non-means-tested additional allowances to their loan/grant. These allowances are to help the student with the extra costs of being on a course of study; they are not to help with living expenses. It is not necessary to include them as income as they will have been already allocated.

Students with dependants may also be entitled to additional allowances. These should be included, but need to be balanced by the expenditure incurred – eg, childcare costs.

If a grant or any other additional allowance is paid it must be listed as income.

Parental contributions, if paid regularly, should be listed as income. These are intended to make up for any shortfall in the grant/loan. The local authority/ Student Loans Company (SLC)/Student Finance England (SFE) will assess how much the parent(s) should pay, although it is not able to enforce payment. In reality, many students do not receive the prescribed parental contribution.

Period to be used

Students, institutions and advisers tend to think of students' income within the framework of the instalment periods for which it is paid – ie, termly, quarterly or annually. Creditors are more likely to understand income expressed in weekly or monthly periods. Breaking down income into these periods is also a helpful exercise for students, as the irregular payment periods often reduce their budgeting ability or financial control.

If a grant is paid to a student, the adviser will need to establish the period which it is meant to cover. Where extra weeks' allowances are paid, the payment period should include the total number of weeks.

For final year students, this income will cease to be taken into account once the course has finished.

How income from a student loan is listed depends on the student's personal circumstances. It can be spread over 52 weeks if it is likely to be the student's main source of income over this period, or if the student has an alternative income during the summer vacation it can be listed as spread over the length of the course. The adviser must consider the financial benefit to the student when deciding how to show this income to creditors. The client should be made aware of the distinction between the income calculation for benefit purposes and that shown on a financial statement or part of a budget plan.

Stage 4: list expenditure

In addition to the items outlined in Chapter 3, students will have additional expenditure, which must be included and which may be required by the course. At this stage, the adviser can help the student identify areas where it may be possible to reduce expenditure – eg, by claiming help with health costs. This area is where the adviser can be of most use to the student, as many students will have little or no experience of budgeting and financial planning. This process should also highlight how debts have arisen and, therefore, help prevent further financial difficulty. The adviser should also help the client deal with irregular income, and both regular and irregular expenditure.

Cost	*Period to be attributed*	*Ways of reducing cost*
Tuition fees ('old system')	This needs to mirror the period of time over which the student loan/main source of income is attributed – eg, over the length of the course (43 weeks).	Ensure that liability is correctly attributed to the student. Ensure no (further) assistance is available – old system students are able to apply for a loan to cover any fee liability.
Tuition fees ('new system')	For most students these do not need listing here as repayment is deferred through a loan. The loan for tuition fees is only available to the student to pay the fees and not as general income. In Wales, eligible Welsh-domiciled students can apply for a non-means-tested grant to cover some of their fees and you should ensure they have done so.	

Tuition fees (part-time students)	If a source of income is paid direct to the institution and is available solely to pay tuition fees, it can be ignored in any financial statement (along with the corresponding tuition fee liability). If the income is paid to the student (and s/he then pays her/his own fees), apportion over the length of the course and include the corresponding amount of tuition fees.	Ensure the student has applied for fee support from the local authority or the SLC/SFE. Check to see if any extra help can be provided from the Access to Learning Fund or from an employer.
Tuition fees (postgraduate/'second degree' students)	If a source of income is paid direct to the institution and is available solely to pay tuition fees, it can be ignored in any financial statement (along with the corresponding tuition fee liability). If the income is paid to the student (and s/he then pays her/his own fees), apportion over the length of the course and include the corresponding amount of tuition fees.	Ensure that liability is correctly attributed to the student. Ensure the student has been categorised correctly by the university or college and that no (further) assistance is available.
Books/reading packs	This needs to mirror the period of time over which the student loan/main source of income is attributed – over the length of the course (453 weeks). Advisers should, through experience, be able to attribute a realistic figure for particular courses within the institution. If this figure cannot be quantified the adviser can use the annually set figure for books included in the student loan.	Suggest using the university library; sharing resources with students on the same course; second-hand book stalls or schemes; local libraries. Students in the year above can advise on books that are absolutely necessary. Increasingly, core texts are available online.

Stationery	To be attributed over the length of the course.	Printing facilities should be provided by the institution. Cost needs to be measured against individual printing costs.
Materials – eg, fabrics, photographic equipment, costs related to field trips	As above.	As above. Bulk purchasing may reduce costs if possible.
Room insurance	Over the rental period, which can differ from the length of the course; *or* For the life of the policy/ payment plan.	Advisers should check if this is necessary, as some policies held by parents can cover items temporarily removed from the family home. The amount of cover can be too little or too much depending on the student's personal effects.
Transport costs	Any transport costs the student may have may vary depending on time of year, personal circumstances and whether s/he has any dependants. If these costs cannot be attributed, use the annually set figure for travel in the loan, plus the cost of at least four journeys home per year. Some students on particular courses may have higher travel costs than others – eg, nursing students and those on teacher training courses, in which case this should be made clear.	Season tickets are often available, as are student travel cards.

Telephone	As above.	Most students own a mobile telephone. Some creditors may need convincing that this is a necessity rather than a luxury. However, the student will need guidance on how to ensure telephone costs are kept to a minimum – eg, on the type of contract and service (and internet) providers, and alternatives such as using telephones in rooms, university-provided internet links and landlines.

Advisers will often have local knowledge (eg, shops and services that offer National Union of Students (NUS)-related discounts) that may help students who are new to the area reduce their expenditure. There is an NUS discount card called 'NUS Extra', costing £10, which attracts nationally-agreed discounts and incorporates the International Student Identity Card. There is an option to obtain a free card, the 'democracy card', and it is likely that this card will be accepted by smaller local businesses.

If the student and adviser decide to use a period of 43 weeks to list the main student income and expenditure, it is usually necessary to draw up a new financial statement showing revised figures for the remaining nine weeks, the long summer vacation. This statement does not need to include study-related costs and related funding.

3. **Types of debt**

This section lists some types of debt specific to students (and ex-students) and which are not included in Chapter 4.

Bank overdrafts

For a definition and the legal position, see Chapter 4.

Special features

Student overdrafts have certain features that are different to other clients. Most high street banks offer full-time undergraduate and some postgraduate students special interest-free overdrafts up to a set limit. This facility is only available on student accounts. Packages will, therefore, vary – eg, students in different academic years may have different overdraft limits. If the overdraft limit is exceeded, interest should be charged on the excess only. In these circumstances, the adviser should inform the bank that the student is seeking assistance with her/his finances. The adviser should try to negotiate an increase in the limit at least to reflect the new overdrawn figure. If the bank refuses, challenge the basis on which it is unauthorised – ie, if cheques have been honoured or funds have been released, this would have been authorised. Some banks have specialised student account managers.

Chapter 4 outlines the strategy for opening a new account in order to prevent an existing bank overdraft swallowing income. In the short term, advisers could also advise on the use of 'first right of appropriation'. This is where the client can state how a deposit made into an overdrawn account should be used. The student should inform the bank, preferably in writing, what specific amounts are to be paid and to whom. The bank must carry out these directions from the client. However, the bank may still charge for the use of the overdraft. This facility should only be used on a short-term basis and the adviser should discuss the overdraft with the client in terms of debt advice and maximising income.

Students may not be allowed an interest-free facility on a new account until they can show a closing balance on an existing account. If a student is unable to open an account (eg, because of low credit scoring) the adviser could contact the Financial Services Authority (see Appendix 2) for information about basic bank accounts where basic facilities are available, even if overdrafts are not.

Most banks allow students terms that continue for a period after they have graduated. The length of time varies between banks and can often be extended by negotiation. This is preferable and advisers should negotiate this option rather than agreeing to overdrawn accounts being 'converted' into graduate loans, as it will be more beneficial to the student. Most banks offer preferential graduate terms – eg, free currency exchange and lower mortgage rates for limited periods.

Graduate loans

Personal loans are available to students after they graduate to cover costs related to graduation and starting work (eg, clothing, relocation costs) and to consolidate student debts. They are only usually authorised if the bank has evidence that the student has secured employment.

Legal position

Graduate loans are regulated by the Consumer Credit Act 1974 (see Chapter 4).

Special features

Graduate loans attract a preferential interest rate. Some banks offer a deferred period of repayment.

Postgraduate loans

Postgraduate loans are personal loans offered by certain high street banks to students undertaking postgraduate studies. As with all other personal loans, they are offered at a fixed or variable rate of interest.

Legal position

Personal loans are regulated under the Consumer Credit Act 1974 (see Chapter 4).

Special features

The terms of these loans vary between the different banks and according to the type and duration of the student's course. The most significant common feature of these loans is deferred repayment. Interest usually accrues during this period. Some loans allow for repayment to be deferred until after the course has ended. In other cases, repayment begins part-way through the course.

Career development loans

For the legal position and definition, see the section on personal loans in Chapter 4.

Special features

Repayment is deferred during the course and for up to one month afterwards. During the deferment period, the Learning and Skills Council pays the interest on the loan. This period can be extended by applying to the bank if the borrower:

- is unemployed and claiming related benefits (including credited national insurance contributions); *or*
- is employed and in receipt of one or more of the following benefits:
  - income support;
  - housing benefit;
  - council tax benefit;
  - working tax credit;
- is taking part in a government training programme and in receipt of training allowance; *or*
- has to attend a course longer than expected (because of ill health or special circumstances). Postponement is subject to a maximum of 17 months (the adviser should check which currently apply) or if for reasons beyond the student's control s/he is required to continue attending her/his course or training.

Note: there may be other circumstances in which the period of repayment can be extended – the terms and conditions of the loan should be checked.

Mortgage-style or fixed-term student loans (pre-1998 students)

Full-time students who began their course between September 1990 and September 1998 (or who were treated as a continuing student when they began their course in the 1998/99 academic year) were eligible for mortgage-style or fixed-term loans which differ in several ways to the income-contingent loans available to new students since 1998.

The Secretary of State for Innovation, Universities and Skills is the creditor, the Student Loans Company (SLC)/Student Finance England (SFE) acts as the agent. They are repaid over five or seven years, depending on how many loans were taken out.

Repayment can be deferred if the client's gross income is below 85 per cent of the national average earnings. Only income is taken into account in this calculation; no account is taken of the client's expenditure and financial commitments. An application for deferral should be made when repayment is due to start and applications for deferral must be made each year. Proof of income should be submitted with this – usually payslips for the preceding three months or a letter from an employer will be sufficient. Interest continues to be charged during any period of deferment.

Given this, it is important that the SLC/SFE is aware of any changes of address to prevent default action. Mortgage-style loans cannot be included in a bankruptcy petition.

Legal position

Agreements are regulated under the Consumer Credit Act 1974 (see Chapter 4).

Special features

Interest is at the rate of inflation. Repayment is not required until the April after the student has finished her/his course, either because s/he has completed or abandoned it. Repayments are monthly and are usually by direct debit from the borrower's bank account. The student will have signed an agreement to repay by direct debit at the time of borrowing. If the student begins another eligible course at the same institution immediately after the first course ceases, repayment will not start until the April after the latter course finishes, but s/he may have to apply for deferment.

Repayments are expected to be made over five years (seven years for those who borrow for five years or more). If more than one loan is outstanding, they are repaid concurrently. The amount owed (including interest) is totalled and divided by the number of months (either 60 or 84) to arrive at monthly repayment. This is reviewed annually.

As long as repayments are not in arrears, any amount still due is cancelled after 25 years, or when the borrower reaches the age of 50 (whichever is earlier). If s/he last borrowed at the age of 40 or over, the outstanding amount is cancelled when the borrower reaches the age of 60. They are also cancelled if the borrower dies, or is permanently incapacitated from work through disability (see p000).

As with other agreements regulated under the Consumer Credit Act, repayment of student loans is enforceable through the county court and the SLC has been quick to take court action against large numbers of borrowers. Problems may arise if a student has closed the bank account from which the SLC /SFE expects direct debit repayments and has not made alternative arrangements, or where the account is so overdrawn that the bank will not honour the direct debit arrangement.

Although information about student loan repayments is not passed to credit reference agencies, the Government intends to make an exception for a small number of 'serial defaulters' of mortgage-style loans where other means of debt recovery have been unsuccessful. Details of arrears may, therefore, appear on a borrower's credit record.

The SLC has sold some loans to private companies to recover, but this should not affect the collection of outstanding loans.

Advisers should:

- check the borrower's gross income (and assist her/him to apply for deferment where appropriate);
- prioritise the debt accordingly.

Income-contingent student loans

From 1998 income-contingent loans have been available to help higher education (HE) students meet their living costs. From September 2006, income-contingent loans are also available for tuition fees (see p461).

The Department for Innovation, Universities and Skills or the Welsh Assembly set the rates of loans for living costs. The amount depends on the year of study, type of course, where the student lives and household income. For students funded under the 'new system', it may also depend on the amount of maintenance grant received. Subject to the maximum rate set, the student decides what level of loan is needed and applies to the SLC/SFE.

The tuition fee set by the institution for the student's course determines the maximum rate of a loan for fees. This will not, in any case, exceed £3,145 in the 2008/09 academic year, and £3,145 plus inflation in later years, unless Parliament decides to change the maximum level institutions can charge. Again, within these limits the student decides what level of loan is needed and applies to the SLC/SFE.

Legal position

The Secretary of State for Innovation, Universities and Skills or the Welsh Assembly is the creditor, the SLC/SFE is the agent and repayments are made through HM Revenue and Customs. The loan is 'low cost' and, therefore, not covered by the Consumer Credit Act.

Special features

Interest is at the rate of inflation. Repayment is made at 9 per cent of earnings over the threshold amount (currently £15,000 a year). This may be different if the borrower lives overseas.

As with mortgage-style loans, repayment does not begin until the April after the borrower finishes or otherwise leaves the course. Borrowers paying tax through the PAYE system will have repayments deducted by their employer. As they are calculated over income payment periods, not on yearly income, some employees can overpay if their earnings are erratic. If at the end of the year this is the case, the employee can obtain a refund. Self-employed borrowers will have their repayment calculated through the self-assessment system.

Borrowers living overseas must contact the SLC/SFE directly to arrange repayment. Living overseas for a certain period of time does not cancel liability for student loan repayment.

Tax credits do not count as income for SLC/SFE calculations. Extra repayments can be made, but it is unlikely that a client in debt will be able to consider this.

For those who started their course prior to September 2006, outstanding income-contingent loans will be cancelled when the borrower reaches 65. For those who start on or after 1 September 2006, outstanding loans will be 'written off' after 25 years. Like mortgage-style loans they are also cancelled if the borrower dies, or is permanently incapacitated from work through disability (see below).

Since 1 September 2004 it has not been possible to include income-contingent student loans in a bankruptcy petition. Failure to repay or update the SLC/SFE about changes can result in penalty charges being added to the outstanding loan amount. The rate triples if the client goes overseas and fails to inform the SLC/SFE that s/he is no longer in the UK tax system, or fails to provide information about living overseas.

Note: borrowers living overseas may make payments at a different threshold amount, depending on the cost of living in that country. The SLC/SFE can advise on this.

Advisers should:

- check the borrower's income, taking into account the fact that repayments are being deducted by the employer or through self-assessment;
- note on the financial statement that repayments will automatically be deducted and will, therefore, not be available income from the date repayments start.

Borrowers with disabilities

Any disability benefits received do not count towards the threshold income (even if they are taxable). The Regulations state that if the Secretary of State is satisfied that, because of her/his disability, an ex-student is permanently unfit for work and s/he is receiving a disability-related benefit, liability for the loan is cancelled. There is no further guidance on how this is done and no definition of 'permanently unfit for work'. If the client complies with other benefit definitions of permanently unfit, advisers can use this when negotiating to have the debt cancelled. See CPAG's *Welfare Benefits and Tax Credits Handbook* for further information.

Debts to the institution

Students are often in debt to their institutions for a wide variety of items – eg, library fines, hardship loans made by the institution, rent, tuition fees, accommodation and disciplinary fines. University regulations govern the circumstances in which fines may be imposed and fees are due. Liability should always be checked and appeal mechanisms used, where appropriate.

The main sources of students' indebtedness to their institutions are discussed below.

Accommodation charges

Most institutions provide some accommodation for their students. Charges are made for the rent and services provided. Services usually include items such as fuel and cleaning. These charges may be called 'residence' or 'accommodation' fees.

Legal position

Rent is payable under the tenancy agreement or licence. The terms of these agreements may be in an individual's contract and/or in university regulations.

Special features

The accommodation provided directly by institutions to students varies. Some of this is in halls of residence, some in houses/flats in the locality owned by the university or leased to it by private landlords.

The length of tenancies may vary, but are rarely longer than 52 weeks, especially in halls of residence. Many tenancies will be for the academic year only – excluding the summer vacation. Some tenancies exclude all vacations. The usual practice is to charge three instalments. There may be a financial penalty for late payment. As in the case of tuition fees, students in financial difficulties may be able to negotiate delayed payments or a more flexible instalment arrangement.

The accommodation charge due for a student's current home is a priority debt. While institutions are often reluctant to evict or take/precipitate court action against their own students, they do try and enforce repayment using other means – eg, by refusing to allow the student to return to university-managed accommodation in subsequent years. They may also refuse to allow the student to progress to the next year of study, or graduate from the course. This could be challenged.

Fines and other charges

Certain costs incurred by students arise from fines or charges. If an appeal procedure exists to resolve disputes about liability or amounts, students should be encouraged to use it. Advisers may be able to assist by providing supporting information or representing students. In some cases, institutions will take into account extenuating circumstances and may waive or reduce certain fines or charges.

The consequences of non-payment differs between institutions and according to the circumstances of each student. For instance, if a debt for tuition fees could legally prevent the student from graduating, it could also prevent her/him progressing to a course of further study or employment and, therefore, needs to be treated as a priority debt. However, if withholding qualifications would not impede the student's progress, the debt could be treated as non-priority. A student may consider any outstanding debts to an institution where s/he wishes to continue studying to be a priority. Advisers need to discuss this carefully with her/him, especially if the student has mistaken notions of the consequences of non-payment.

Tuition fees

Most full-time students who began their course on or after 1 September 1998 and before 1 September 2006 were means tested for a contribution to their tuition fees.

This process continues for 'old system' students until the end of their course (unless they transfer). Students are asked to supply their local authority or the SLC/SFE with their household financial details. The household consists of the student and, where appropriate, their parents, step-parents, spouse, civil partner or cohabiting partner of either sex. This information is then used to assess any contribution towards tuition fees. If the local authority or SLC/SFE deems that the student is to make a contribution and s/he subsequently does not make a payment, this will be a debt to the respective university (not to the local authority or SLC/SFE).

From 2006 any student in England or Wales liable to make a contribution to their tuition fees can apply for a student loan for fees (see p458). The maximum rate is equal to the contribution for which they are liable. Students who begin their studies having been assessed to make a contribution and then subsequently leave should be given a date by which they can do so without having to pay anything towards their fees. This date is fixed by the university. Where tuition fee support is to be paid by the local authority and the student starts in the autumn term, the date is fixed at 1 December. Advisers should argue that the date should also be the same for the fee-paying student, although the institution is under no obligation to do so. Beyond that date, there is some scope for negotiation to allow the fee to be divided over the academic year minus holidays, with the student only paying for the period s/he has actually attended. If a student has to pay fees after transferring from one university to another, the two institutions must negotiate with each other about the transfer of the payment. For students who transfer before 1 December, no fees should be paid to the first institution. If a student transfers to a different university (or a course at the same university which cannot be described as broadly similar) s/he is regarded as a 'new' student and the institution will be allowed to charge up to £3,145 fees. The student, however, remains under the 'old system' for funding and, therefore, her/his total support for fees (grants or loans) would be capped at £1,255. Guidance from Universities UK and Guild HE, the umbrella bodies for HE institutions in the UK, advises institutions not to charge these students fees outside of their range of support.

Recovery of debts to the institution

Methods of recovery vary between institutions. Many do not allow a student to continue into the next year of study if debts are outstanding. If the debt is for tuition fees, this procedure is probably legitimate. However, some institutions do not permit continuation where other charges are outstanding (eg, accommodation fees and library fines). This practice should be challenged. Similarly, if debts remain at the end of the student's course, most institutions refuse to give the student a certificate of qualification or allow her/him to collect her/his results. The Office of Fair Trading (OFT) has issued *Unfair Contract Terms Bulletins* (see www.oft.gov.uk) containing examples of where institutions have amended contractual terms. Its view is that institutions cannot threaten, or carry out, sanctions against students if they are able to withhold services provided in another, different, contract. This means that universities will no longer be able to withhold academic services (eg, tuition, use of library facilities, publication of results) if debts remain outstanding for accommodation services, or where other breaches have occurred. Trading standards officers can, however, choose not to enforce the OFT guidance, in which case students will have to take action themselves.

Institutions are required to offer bursaries to the lowest income students as a condition of their being entitled to charge the higher fees, and most offer them more widely. These will only be of significance as debts if it is claimed they have been awarded in error. If the student has provided incorrect information, it is possible the bursary may be recoverable and the adviser should prioritise accordingly. In all other cases, advisers should argue that the bursary awarded to the student informed her/his choice of institution, repayment could cause hardship and, if applicable, that repayment would not be possible for at least the remaining length of the course.

If a student is awarded a bursary and s/he has outstanding debts to the institution, the institution may choose to use the bursary to pay all or part of the debt rather than pay this money to the student. The minimum mandatory bursary must be paid direct to the student. Advisers should argue that other bursaries should be paid in such a way that the student can use them for their specified purpose, rather than simply paying off debts to the institution.

Institutions may make threats that are not legally permissible in order to ensure payment. These practices put students under considerable pressure to pay outstanding charges and may constitute harassment (see p24). However, most students are anxious not to jeopardise their future and are reluctant to take any action other than to clear their debts in full.

Legislation, such as the Freedom of Information Act 2000 and the Data Protection Act 1998, may force institutions to re-evaluate these practices and give the adviser more options to explore when assisting clients who owe debts to the institutions. Likewise, rulings from the Office of the Independent Adjudicator may force institutions to reconsider such practices. Advisers directly employed by the institution need to be aware of the potential conflict of interest when advising a student with debts to the same institution.

Overpaid statutory awards

See also Chapter 6.

Students are required to repay some, or all, of their local authority/SLC/SFE grant for living costs if it has either been overpaid or if they leave their course (both temporarily or permanently) during a period for which a grant instalment has been paid in advance. In this latter case, the amount of grant for the weeks after the student has left her/his course will be calculated and repayment of only this amount is required.

Legal position

Local authorities and the SLC/SFE have a statutory duty to recover overpaid awards. The legislation requires them to do so during the period of the award where possible – ie, before the student completes her/his course. They have discretionary powers not to pursue recovery, but the circumstances in which they would do this are not defined.

Special features

Practices vary between individual local authorities and the SLC/SFE, but normally the authority attempts to recover the amount in full by deducting it from the next instalment.

Advisers need to negotiate with the local authority/SLC/SFE in the usual way, arriving at an affordable level of repayment. However, if a student continues to receive a grant, the local authority/SLC/SFE is in a powerful position, as it holds the instrument of recovery in its own hands – the next instalment. Advisers should be aware that, while it is the local authority/SLC's/SFE's statutory duty to recover during the period of the award, reductions of each future grant instalment are permissible within the legislation. If the local authority/SLC/SFE remains unwilling to extend the repayment period, evidence of hardship needs to be presented, perhaps to elected members of the authority concerned as well as officers, or to higher levels of SLC/SFE management. Regulations state that the recovery action to be taken should be appropriate to the circumstances and so the adviser should ensure that the local authority/SLC/SFE is fully aware of the student's situation.

Overpaid income-contingent student loans

See p458 for definition and legal position.

Special features

This type of student loan is not regulated by the Consumer Credit Act. If the loan has been made properly (ie, the student is eligible but the amount is classed as an overpayment), it can be recovered from the amount of loan for which the student is eligible for the following academic year. If the student has completed her/his studies, recovery should be through the normal repayment process, although advisers may need to negotiate with the SLC/SFE for this to happen.

4. Minimising debt

See also Chapter 5.

Reducing council tax bills

Advisers must examine the student's liability for council tax. Any dwelling solely occupied by full-time students is exempt for council tax purposes.

A student is not jointly or severally liable to pay council tax if s/he lives in a house/dwelling in which s/he has an equal legal interest with others.

For non-students or part-time students who are liable, the bill may be reduced because full-time students attract a 'status discount'. Thus, if there is only one non-student or part-time student living in the property with one or more full-time student, a 25 per cent discount should be awarded.

Institutions may provide local authorities with lists of full-time students attending courses and, where requested, will issue a letter to a student establishing her/his status. Some institutions charge the student for this letter. Advisers should argue that this is not appropriate. Students should inform council tax offices of their status in order to obtain exemption from, or reduction of, council tax.

See CPAG's *Council Tax Handbook* for more information.

5. Maximising income

Information on student finance is now widely available on the internet, or in CPAG's *Student Support and Benefits Handbook*.

Student funding arrangements have gone though a number of changes and the information required to maximise income and check eligibility is complex. What follows is a guide to the likely sources of income for students in higher education (HE). Legislation for support and fees differs between England, Scotland, Wales and Northern Ireland. English and Welsh support arrangements are broadly similar, but there are differences.

Students seeking debt advice may be doing so as a result of not being able to manage irregular payments effectively when they have regular expenditure. Therefore, great care must be taken to establish future budgeting and financial management to prevent the situation worsening in future payment periods.

It may be appropriate for advisers to deal directly with some creditors and in certain circumstances to request they overpay to assist the client with budgeting. Creditors need a detailed explanation of the student's funding situation to appreciate fully the request being made and to dispel some myths or misinformation they may have about money available to HE students.

Where the available help is means tested, the test will normally be carried out on the student's parental income, unless the student has independent status – ie:

- s/he is 25 or over at the start of the academic year for which s/he is applying; *or*
- s/he married or entered a civil partnership before the start of the academic year for which s/he is applying; *or*
- s/he has supported her/himself for at least three years before the start of the first year of the course; *or*
- s/he has no living parents; *or*
- s/he has care of at least one child on the first day of the academic year for which s/he is applying; *or*
- s/he is a part-time student.

If a student has independent status, her/his parents' (or step-parents') income will not be taken into account when the local authority/Student Loans Company (SLC) /Student Finance England (SFE)assesses her/his entitlement to means-tested support.

If none of the above applies, the student could still be treated as an independent student, if:

- her/his parents cannot be traced; *or*
- her/his parents live abroad and trying to trace them may put them in danger; *or*
- s/he is permanently estranged from her/his parents; *or*
- s/he is in the care of a local authority or voluntary organisation under a custodianship order on her/his18th birthday, or immediately before the course if s/he was not 18 when it began.

Income could be maximised by the student or adviser approaching the local authority or the SLC /SFE and detailing her/his particular circumstances.

If a student is married or in a civil partnership, and is not separated, their spouse's or civil partner's income is included in the means test. Students aged 25 or over who started their course in September 2000 or later and who are living with a cohabiting partner of the opposite sex, and students aged 25 or over who started their course in September 2005 or later and live with a cohabiting partner of the same or opposite sex, also have their partner's income included.

In general, student support is available for the length of the course, plus a year, less any years of previously supported HE study. (Additional years of support may be available if there are compelling personal reasons. Applications are made to the local authority or SLC/SFE, usually in a letter ideally written by the adviser. This would state the compelling personal reasons and their detrimental impact on the client's studies.)

With the exception of supplementary grants (see p469) further support is not generally available for students who have used up their entitlement to funding. However, income-contingent loans for maintenance continue to be available to students who do not already have an honours degree from a UK institution, and to graduate students on courses leading to a professional qualification such as medical doctor, veterinary doctor, dentist or architect. These rules also apply to students thinking of withdrawing or transferring their course.

Bursaries

New full-time, home and European Union students who begin their first degree or Postgraduate Certificate in Education course on or after 1 September 2006 may be eligible for bursaries or scholarships from their university or college. Mandatory bursaries are available when fees are over £2,835 a year (not all universities charge the full £3,145) and the student receives a full special support grant or maintenance grant (household income of £18,360 or less for students who started in the 2006/07 or 2007/08 academic years; £25,000 for those who start in 2008/09). Bursaries are paid separately from the standard student finance package, and amounts vary from institution to institution. If an institution chooses to charge more than £2,835 a year in fees, the minimum mandatory bursary it can offer is the fee charged less £2,835. Thus, where £3,145 a year is charged, the minimum bursary is £310.

There is no set upper limit and institutions can decide on the amounts they offer and some are several thousand pounds or more, although high rates are very rare. The mandatory bursary must be paid in cash, but any bursary amount above this can be paid in cash or, for example, through the provision of accommodation or course-related equipment. The criteria for these higher bursaries vary from place to place: some bursaries and scholarships are awarded on the basis of income/geographical location only; others have an application process and some are awarded on the basis of, for example, academic or sporting achievement or potential. All institutions should publicise their bursaries or scholarships on their websites and the Universities and Colleges Admissions Service has a section on its website devoted to each institution's funding opportunities (see Appendix 2).

Any HE institution bursary should not be treated as income for benefit purposes, provided the student is in receipt of the special support grant (see p470) and the bursary is not for living costs. The institution should provide the student with a letter confirming her/his bursary is for course-related costs.

Students on health-related courses may be eligible for bursaries from the NHS (see p473).

Help with tuition fees

'Old system' students are still able to apply for help to meet the cost of tuition fees. This is assessed on the student's income and that of her/his family (if s/he does not qualify for independent status). The local authority/SLC/SFE assesses eligibility (full-time students and those on a sandwich courses or a part-time course of initial teacher training are eligible) and income. The student may be liable for all, part or none of the tuition fee. Advisers need to check the assessment has been done correctly. If the student has had a change of circumstances or the family income has decreased s/he may be able to request that the local authority/SLC/SFE reassess the level of help given.

Full-time students who depend financially on their parents will not have to pay fees if their parents' residual income is less than £23,660 a year. If income is between £23,660 and £35,535, they pay part of the fees. If it is £35,535 or more they pay the full fee.

The maximum fee currently payable is £1,255. From September 2006 no student has to pay fees upfront; 'old system' students who have to make a contribution can apply for a tuition fee loan (see below).

'New system' Welsh-domiciled students studying at Welsh institutions can also apply for a grant to help pay their fees. This grant is not means tested, and is worth up to £1,890 a year. It is paid at whatever level will bring the fee charged to no more than £1,255. Students can apply for a loan to cover this amount.

Part-time students in both England and Wales may be eligible for a means-tested grant to cover all or part of their fees.

There are no age limits for help with tuition fees or for tuition fee loans. Payment is made directly to the institution by the SLC/SFE. If tuition fee help is received under the old system, it does not have to be repaid. Tuition fee loans, however, are repayable. The arrangements are the same as for income-contingent student loans.

Income-contingent student loans

Students are required to meet the personal eligibility requirements (where the student lives, previous attendance, funding and age).[4] Students under 60 may also be eligible for a student loan for maintenance.

In order to support themselves, students are able to get support from loans, grants (for certain groups of students), bursaries and hardship funds.

Full-time, sandwich and part-time initial teacher training students who are aged up to 60 are eligible for a student loan for maintenance. Previous study affects eligibility. Students with an honours degree are not eligible for a maintenance loan unless their course carries an exemption. The Department for Innovation, Universities and Skills (DIUS) and the Welsh Assembly set the maximum loan available. The amount depends on the year of study, type of course, where the student is living and household income. Within these limits the student decides what level of loan is needed and applies to the SLC/SFE. The amount can be changed up to the maximum set by the local authority – students apply for this on a loan adjustment form.

In addition to the basic (75 per cent) non-means-tested loan, students can get an extra amount, equivalent to 25 per cent of the maximum loan available. This element of the loan is means tested on household income. This includes the student's income and that of her/his parents, spouse, civil partner or cohabiting partner, as appropriate.

Students can also apply for student loans for tuition fees, provided they are eligible. The amount of the loan available is the fee the student is charged (for 'old system'/existing students this is capped at £1,255; for new students institutions can charge variable fees of up to £3,145). Repayment begins in the April after the student leaves or completes the course (see p454).

Long courses loans

Students can apply for a set amount for each additional week they have to attend the course on top of the basic academic year. The amount of the long courses loan (previously, the extra weeks' allowance) depends on whether the student is living in the parental home, away from home or in London. The loans are made in addition to the student loan and have to be repaid in the same way.

Studying abroad

Additional support is available to students who spend time studying abroad for at least eight weeks as part of a UK-based course (the period abroad does not have to be a compulsory part of the course). Students studying abroad for at least eight consecutive weeks who have to take out medical insurance also get help to cover these costs. Help is means tested and paid by the SLC/SFE. Insurance grants are equal to the policy. Travel costs are only paid if the local authority or SLC/SFE considers them reasonable and less than £295 of any claim.

Change in circumstances

If a student has a change in circumstances during the year, s/he should inform the local authority in order to have the level of loan s/he can take out reassessed.

Supplementary grants

Certain 'supplementary' grants are available for full-time students with additional support requirements. Most are not available to part-time students in England, with the exception of the disabled students' allowance. All these grants are available to part-time Welsh-domiciled students, on a *pro rata* basis, assuming their course takes no longer than twice the time of the equivalent full-time course to complete.

Except for disabled students' allowance, these grants are also means tested, both as part of the main means test for support and on the income of any dependants the student has.

Disabled students' allowance

Part-time, full-time, distance learners (including Open University students), postgraduate or undergraduate students who have a disability which makes it more expensive for them to take their course, may be entitled to a number of extra allowances for equipment, non-medical personal support, miscellaneous expenses and travel. Part-time students must complete the course in no more than twice the time it takes to complete the full-time equivalent course. Postgraduate students in receipt of awards from research councils (see p481), NHS bursaries (see p473), or help from their institutions that includes allowances for disability are not eligible for a disabled students' allowance from the local authority or SLC/SFE, but receive similar grants from those funders. The allowance is a non-repayable grant, unaffected by the previous study rules, is not means tested, and is paid by the SLC/SFE, usually direct to any provider of approved specialist equipment or personal support.

Adult dependants' grant

Full-time students who have a spouse, partner or adult member of the family who is financially dependent on them may be eligible for a means-tested, non-repayable adult dependants' grant of up to £2,575 a year, paid by the SLC/SFE in three instalments with the maintenance loan.

Childcare grant

Full-time students with independent status and with dependent children in registered, approved childcare can get a childcare grant. Payments are up to a maximum of 85 per cent of £175 a week for one child and £300 a week for two. This grant is non-repayable and is paid in three instalments by the SLC/SFE. It is not taken into account when calculating entitlement to means-tested benefits and tax credits.

Students cannot get this grant if they or their partner receives the childcare element of working tax credit.

Parents' learning allowance

Means-tested help with course-related costs can be paid to students with dependent children

The maximum grant available is £1,470 a year. It is paid by the SLC/SFE in three instalments and is non-repayable. This grant is not taken into account when calculating entitlement to means-tested benefits and tax credits.

Other grants

Higher education grant

Full-time, 'old system', sandwich, and part-time initial teacher training students who started their course in September 2004 or after may be entitled to this means-tested grant. The amount available is up to £1,000. Those with a family income of £16,750 or less get the full amount, part of the amount if income is between £16,750 and £22,735, and none if income is above £22,735. The grant is paid in three instalments by the SLC/SFE. A student will not qualify for the grant in respect of an academic year unless s/he qualifies for fee support for that year (except if s/he is a student overseas on Erasmus or on a postgraduate flexible initial teacher training course).

Maintenance grant

The grant is available for 'new system' full-time students from September 2006. It is means tested on the student's household income.

The means-test thresholds depend on the year in which the student started her/his course. For those who started in 2006/07 or 2007/08, the full £2,835 grant is payable if household income is below £18,360. A partial grant is payable if income is between £18,361 and £39,305. If a student started in the 2008/09 academic year, the full amount is payable if household income is £25,000 or below, with a partial amount payable for income of up to £60,005.

If there is a change in the student's or family circumstances affecting income, the local authority/SLC/SFE should be notified so the amount of the award can be recalculated. Students receiving the maintenance grant can also apply for the student loan for maintenance. However, loan entitlement will be reduced, pound for pound of maintenance grant entitlement up to £1,260. These grants are paid in three instalments. The maintenance grant is non-repayable.

Special support grant

A means-tested special support grant is available for 'new system' students who start their course on or after 1 September 2006 and who are eligible for means-tested benefits (such as income support, housing benefit and council tax benefit).[5] The grant is intended to cover additional course costs such as books, equipment, travel or childcare. The amount of the grant, the income assessment arrangements and the payment arrangements are the same as the maintenance grant (see above). The amount of special support grant paid does not affect the amount of maintenance loan to which a student may be entitled. Students receiving the special support grant are not eligible for the maintenance grant. The special support grant is non-repayable. It is not taken into account when calculating entitlement to means-tested benefits and tax credits.

Travel allowances

Students who attend an institution outside the UK for at least eight weeks (whether obligatory or optional) and have taken out medical insurance, and those who must attend a placement in the UK away from their main college as part of a medical or dental course, are entitled to help with their travelling expenses, above the normal allowance paid in their loan. Students studying abroad can also claim help to cover the cost of medical insurance. Help is paid by the SLC/SFE but usually assessed by the local authority.

Disabled students may also qualify for help with travel in the disabled students' allowance (see p469).

Care leavers' grant

The care leavers' grant is no longer available for students studying in England or Wales. Local authorities in England and Wales are now responsible for providing support in all vacations for care leavers who left care on or after 1 October 2000. Any individual student who could be worse off as a result of this change should be considered a priority by the Access to Learning Fund (in England) or the Financial Contingency Fund (in Wales) (see p481).

Welsh Assembly learning grant

Students who normally live in Wales and who started their course in 2006/07 or later may be entitled to additional support from the Welsh Assembly. The Welsh Assembly learning grant provides financial support to help meet general living costs. Those with a household income of £18,370 or less receive the full £2,835 grant, between £18,370 and £39,300 receive a partial grant and those over £39,300 no grant. The grant is non-repayable and it is paid in three instalments, one at the start of each term.

'Old system' students may also be entitled to extra help from the Welsh Assembly (also, confusingly, known as a Welsh Assembly learning grant). The maximum payable is £1,500, and it is means tested.

Social work courses

Bursaries are available for students on degree or diploma courses in England, paid by the NHS Business Services Authority. Students are required to meet the residency eligibility criteria. To be eligible, students must be on an approved course, must not already hold an HE social work qualification and must not be receiving support from a social care employer. Undergraduates in England who are not subject to variable fees ('old system') will receive an allowance depending on where they study – in London £3,475; elsewhere £3,075. Students' tuition fees are paid direct to the institution by 1 December. Students who are subject to variable fees ('new system' students) receive higher amounts, as these include an element towards their tuition fee. Again, the amount depends on where they study – in London £4,975; elsewhere £4,575. These bursaries are non-means tested and paid in three instalments. Undergraduate students can also access the standard HE student support package from their local authority

Undergraduate students who normally live in Wales and who are studying for a social work degree are entitled to the standard package of support for undergraduates. They are also eligible for a non-means-tested payment of £1,255 from the Care Council for Wales to cover or contribute to their tuition fee. Both new and existing students are eligible for this. 'Old system' students should apply for the tuition fee grant from Student Finance Wales, the Care Council's Social Work Bursary Scheme makes up any difference between the fee grant and the tuition fee charged. Similarly, 'new system' students studying in Wales should be advised to apply for the fee grant available to other undergraduates to pay for any additional liability.

New students studying outside Wales should apply for a tuition fee loan to cover the difference between the £1,255 paid by the Social Work Bursary Scheme and the fee charged.

In addition, students receive a non-means-tested bursary of £2,500, and a further £500 towards travel costs for placements.

Full-time eligible postgraduates living in England receive the same bursary as undergraduate students from the Business Services Authority, and can also apply for an additional mean-tested bursary of up to £3,928 in London and £2,544 elsewhere. They also receive up to £3,300 for tuition fees, paid directly to the institution and a contribution to practice learning (placement) opportunity expenses. A childcare grant, adults' dependant allowance and parents' learning allowance are also available, paid on the same basis as for undergraduates.

Eligible postgraduate students in Wales funded by the Social Work Bursary Scheme receive up to £3,300 towards their fees, as well as a non-means-tested bursary of £2,500, and £500 towards travel costs for placements. They can also apply for a means-tested bursary of up to £2,510 and additional allowances such as the childcare grant, adult dependant's allowance and parents' learning allowance.

Part-time fee grant and course grant

Part-time students on undergraduate courses in England and Wales which are 50 per cent or more than an equivalent full-time course can apply for a means-tested grant for fees of between £785 and £1,180 (£620 and £930 in Wales). The amount depends on how intensive the course is. They can also get a course grant of up to £255 (£1,050 in Wales). This is to help with travel, book and other course-related costs. The student's income must be less than £16,090 for full support. Students will receive partial support if their income is between £16,090 and £26,825. Applications are assessed by the local authority or SLC/SFE. Forms are available from the DIUS. They are subject to a maximum number of eight academic years.

NHS bursaries

NHS bursaries are available for full-time or part-time pre-registration courses in England (for a current list of prescribed courses and up-to-date information, see www.nhsstudentgrants.co.uk). Bursary applicants are subject to residence conditions. Bursaries are administered and paid by the NHS Student Grants Unit. NHS students are also eligible to apply to the Access to Learning Fund (see p481). Bursaries are awarded for each year of study; they are non-taxable and are paid in monthly instalments (the first instalment covers the first two months of training).

There are two types of NHS bursary. In both cases, the NHS pays the tuition fees. Students studying on a nursing, midwifery and operating department practitioner diploma course are paid a non-means-tested bursary covering 45 weeks. This is a flat-rate basic maintenance grant. Additional allowances may also be payable for:

- disabled students;
- practice placement costs;
- students entering training from care;
- extra weeks' attendance;
- childcare (similar to the DIUS childcare grants, except that the allowance is up to 85 per cent of actual childcare costs to a maximum of £114.75 a week for one child and £170 a week for two or more children;
- adults and children who are financially dependent on the student; *and*
- a parents' learning allowance.

Holders of non-means-tested bursaries are not eligible for the NHS hardship grant, but can apply to the Access to Learning Fund (see p481). Diploma-level students are not eligible for student loans, and this type of funding is not available in Wales.

Students following a degree-level or postgraduate-level course are eligible to receive a means-tested bursary. Additional allowances are available, as with the non-means-tested bursary (see above). Undergraduate-level means-tested bursary holders can apply for student loans and should consider doing so in order to maximise their income while training. They can also apply to the Access to Learning Fund (see p481).

There are also maternity, paternity and adoption allowances. The NHS Student Grants Unit has details.

Arrangements for students in Wales are broadly the same. For information, contact the NHS Wales Student Awards Unit on 029 2019 6167.

Undergraduate medical and dental students living in England and Wales on standard five- or six-year courses in any UK country (starting after 1998) are eligible for NHS bursaries and help with their tuition fees in their fifth and sixth year of study. Those students in England and Wales on the four-year graduate-entry medical programmes are also eligible for NHS bursaries and help with tuition fees in years two to four of the course. Medical and dental students can also apply for NHS hardship funds through the NHS Student Grants Unit. Advisers should help clients to present their case, as there is no prescribed form or process. It is, therefore, advisable that the adviser adds a covering letter explaining the circumstances and the nature of the claim.

Teacher training incentives

These vary between England and Wales.

In England, there are training bursaries of £4,000 for primary school teaching, £6,000 for students taking non-priority secondary school subjects, and £9,000 for students taking priority secondary school subjects (modern foreign languages, ICT, design and technology, music and religious education). The bursaries are paid monthly over nine months and are available for home students undertaking postgraduate courses that lead to qualified teacher status at colleges in England (Postgraduate Certificate in Education (PGCE) courses), but who are not currently employed as teachers. Students on a flexible postgraduate course receive half the bursary after registration for the first assessment module and the remainder after achieving qualified teacher status.

In addition to these bursaries, there is a 'golden hello' scheme. Graduates who took maths, science or applied science receive a £5,000 grant after completing their induction year; those taking other shortage subjects receive £2,500. PGCE students in England can also apply for the full undergraduate package of support, in addition to which the first £1,260 of the maintenance or special support grant is not means tested. In Wales, home students on postgraduate courses leading to qualified teacher status at institutions in Wales (except those already qualified as teachers or employed as teachers) receive a training grant of £7,200 for those studying secondary maths, science, modern foreign languages, design and technology, ICT, religious education, and Welsh as a second language. Students studying all other secondary courses receive a teaching grant of £4,200; students on primary courses receive £2,200. The institution arranges for this to be paid by monthly instalments (usually over nine months). There is also an additional teaching grant, payable on successful completion of the first year:

- £5,000 for graduates teaching maths and science;
- £2,500 for other priority secondary subjects (see above).

Application is to the Welsh Assembly. Payment is by lump sum directly into a bank account.

Undergraduates can apply for secondary undergraduate placement grants, paid by the institution in two instalments. The rate payable depends on whether the subject is a priority subject or not. Additional hardship funding is available from the Financial Contingency Fund (see p481). It can also be available to both undergraduate and postgraduate students who experience financial difficulties that could prevent them finishing their course. Some students studying in Welsh can apply for Welsh medium incentive supplements. Application is to the institution.

Bank overdrafts

Most of the major banks and some building societies offer interest-free overdraft facilities on students' current accounts, up to a set limit. These limits change each year and vary between banks. This special facility is essential to most students in maximising income, both to cover temporary periods of cash-flow shortage (eg, between payments of funding instalments) and for long-term financial management.

Prospective students with existing bank accounts should change to a student account with either their own or a different bank, in order to benefit from the facilities offered. When choosing a bank, students need to consider the following factors, rather than any 'free gifts' on offer:

- which bank offers the largest interest-free overdraft, and the period for which it is offered – generally these extend beyond the end of the course, but can vary;
- the proximity of the bank to where the student lives or studies;
- the availability of telephone and internet banking;
- the interest rates and charges imposed for exceeding the interest-free facility;
- the attitude of campus bank managers or student advisers in local banks – debt advisers in institutions or students' unions can be consulted on these matters.

Managers of campus banks are usually more familiar with student finance issues and, therefore, more sympathetic and realistic when difficulties arise.

A student's credit rating is checked when s/he opens a new account. S/he may be refused the usual student deal if there is a recorded history of credit problems. A student requires an account that will accept direct credits in order to receive her/his student loan. If a student has no bank account and is refused one because of her/his credit rating, the money adviser in the institution or students' union may be able to negotiate with the local or campus bank manager.

Bank loans

Banks will sometimes offer loans to students at competitive rates. A student should be advised, however, that the interest rates on loans from the SLC/SFE make them a cheaper form of long-term borrowing. A bank loan is usually offered towards the end of the student's course. If overdraft facilities appear no longer appropriate, the bank may offer to convert the overdraft to a loan. This offers the advantages of a lower interest rate than the excess overdraft and allows the student access to additional funds. However, unless the loan has a deferred repayment arrangement, the repayments are usually much greater than can be met from the student's income, and may create an overdraft in the student's current account that will result in her/him paying interest on two accounts. In this way, it can become a very expensive, usually unmanageable, option. Advisers should be aware that most banks will now allow student terms on their overdraft to extend to graduation and beyond (in some cases for a number of years) and this may, therefore, be a cheaper option.

Students often feel pressured into accepting loan arrangements, as the banks present them as a positive alternative and are reluctant to allow further borrowing on any other terms. The student will often be better off by ceasing to use the existing bank account and using an ordinary building society savings account. Advisers can then negotiate with the bank as with any other creditor. This strategy will, however, result in the loss of the interest-free overdraft facility to the student.

See also p477 for information on postgraduate loans.

Career development loans

Career development loans are deferred repayment personal loans available through a partnership between the DIUS and three high street banks. Interest on the loan is paid by the Learning and Skills Council during the period of the course and for up to one month after. Repayment is deferred for the same period – longer periods of deferment are available (see p456).

In practice, loans are usually only available for certain types of postgraduate courses (full-time, part-time or distance learning). This is because the course must last no longer than two years (although career development loans can be considered for up to two years of a longer course or a three-year course that includes work experience). Applicants must be 18 or over and must not have reasonable and adequate access to funds for their course or statutory funding. A student must intend to work in the European Union (EU) (or Iceland, Norway or Liechtenstein) after completing the course. Applicants must be ordinarily resident in England, Scotland or Wales with an unlimited right to remain in the UK. (Students will not qualify for a career development loan if their right to remain in the UK is subject to restrictions.) While non-EU nationals are eligible to apply for a loan, they must seek permission from the Home Office in order to study, train or work in the UK after their studies. Refer to UKCISA for advice (see Appendix 2). Career development loans are only available for vocational courses. Students can borrow between £300 and £8,000 to pay for up to 80 per cent of course fees, plus the full cost of travel, books, materials and other related expenses. If the student has been out of work for three months or longer s/he can apply for 100 per cent of the course fees and, if the course is full time, living expenses. Banks will consider applications after the course has already started.

Further information about career development loans can be obtained from participating high street banks or from an information line 0800 585 505. There is also a website at www.direct.gov.uk/cdl

Advisers can assist students to make a realistic assessment of all non-course costs to ensure an adequate loan is requested. Also, students should be advised to compare career development loans with postgraduate loans from banks (see below), as the interest rates and repayment terms of the latter can be more favourable. If a student receiving means-tested benefits obtains a career development loan to fund her/his course, the career development loan is treated as income. If this reduces benefit entitlement, the student should consider paying her/his tuition fees in full at the beginning of the course instead of by the more usual instalment methods.

Postgraduate loans

Some of the major banks make personal loans available to postgraduate (and sometimes also 'second degree') students to cover their course fees and living costs. The loans usually offer deferred repayments, which begin only after the course has finished. Some of these loans are available for specific courses, especially those leading to professional qualifications. The terms and amounts of loans vary between different banks and students need to check which is most suitable for them, and how the terms offered compare with those available from a career development loan if they are pursuing a course for which either might be payable. Students also need to consider whether they can afford the amount of indebtedness involved, which could exceed £5,000 a year.

Postgraduate bursaries

A variety of bodies make awards, but usually only one is appropriate to a particular area of study. It can be difficult to obtain an offer of grant aid to fund postgraduate study, especially in the arts and social sciences.

Postgraduate students can apply for studentships from research councils (see Appendix 2). Competition for these is usually very strong, and students normally need to have at least a degree classification of 2:1 at undergraduate level.

Disabled postgraduate students are eligible for a disabled students' allowance (see p469) if they have to pay extra costs in their postgraduate study as a result of their disability. Details of the levels and type of support available, and information on how to apply, are on each research council's website.

A student can obtain appropriate information and assistance from the department in which s/he intends to study and the university careers service. Students should begin their enquiries well in advance of the start of their course – applications may need to be made at the start of the academic year before the year in which they intend to study. There are organisations which offer awards for vocational courses. A limited number of companies offer assistance to postgraduates. Sponsorship is usually linked to particular courses and institutions, rather than individual students. Students should be advised to contact the appropriate careers/advice centres at the relevant institution.

Benefits

This section is intended as a general guide to eligibility. Advisers should refer to CPAG's *Welfare Benefits and Tax Credits Handbook* or *Student Support and Benefits Handbook* for full details. Most full-time students are not eligible to claim social security benefits. There are a few groups of full-time students who are not excluded from the means-tested benefits system. These are:

- lone parents, including lone foster parents (if the child is under 16 years old);
- disabled students who satisfy certain conditions;
- pensioners;
- students from abroad entitled to urgent cases payment because they are temporarily without funds for a period of up to six weeks (seek further advice on this from UKCISA – see Appendix 2);
- people who have refugee status and who are learning English;
- one of two full-time students with responsibility for a child under 16 years old (or under 20 and still in full-time non-advanced education, although only eligible for help during the summer vacation);
- students waiting to return to their course after taking time out because of illness or caring responsibilities.

Advisers need to highlight the rules on entitlement to benefit, and advise students not to accept automatically Department for Work and Pensions (DWP) or local authority statements that students cannot claim benefit.

The DWP and local authorities find the calculation of students' entitlement highly complex. In many offices it is rare for the first decision to be correct. Students must be advised to have their claims checked by an expert in the institution, students' union or local advice centre.

Advisers need to check that decision makers do not include the student loan as income for students who are ineligible for loans. Advisers also need to inform students who are entitled to benefits but reluctant to take out a loan or a full loan that the full loan will be taken into account whether or not it is taken out.

Career development loans are also taken into account as income. However, most of this income is ignored. Only that part of the loan paid and used for certain living costs is taken into account. For full details, see CPAG's *Welfare Benefits and Tax Credits Handbook*.

In general, grants or loans paid specifically for tuition fees or course costs are disregarded. If a student receives allowances towards extra expenses because of a disability (see p469), these are disregarded in full when calculating her/his benefit entitlement. The childcare grant and parents' learning grant are also disregarded.

Council tax benefit

Full-time students are not liable for council tax if they live in accommodation occupied solely by students on a full-time course (or other people who are exempt).

Those who are liable for council tax are entitled to council tax benefit (CTB) during their period of study if they fall into one of a small number of categories. Advisers need to check whether their client falls into one of these categories, or if s/he has a partner who is eligible to claim CTB on her/his behalf. The period of study applicable in each case should also be checked as, in most cases (and unlike for income support – IS), this excludes the summer vacation and, therefore, the student may be able to claim during this period.

For further details, see CPAG's *Welfare Benefits and Tax Credits Handbook*.

Child tax credit

Students are eligible to apply for child tax credit. Those getting the maximum amount (and no working tax credit) are entitled to free school meals. Help is means tested and paid by direct debit by HM Revenue and Customs, which has a calculator facility on its website to help work out eligibility and amount available (www.taxcredits.inlandrevenue.gov.uk).

Health benefits

See also Chapter 6.

Students under 19 and those on IS, income-based jobseeker's allowance (JSA) and some tax credit claimants, qualify for health benefits. Otherwise, students must apply for assistance on the grounds of low income using Form HC1. These forms are often held by student services departments in institutions, students' unions/guilds/associations or health centres.

For further details, see CPAG's *Welfare Benefits and Tax Credits Handbook*.

Housing benefit

Advisers need to check whether their client is exempt from the rule that full-time students are not entitled to housing benefit (HB), or whether they have a partner who is eligible to claim on their behalf.

The period of study applicable should be checked as, in most cases (and unlike for IS), this excludes the summer vacation and, therefore, the student may be eligible to claim during this period.

Some students who need to maintain two homes may be eligible for payment of housing costs on both.

For further details, see CPAG's *Welfare Benefits and Tax Credits Handbook*.

Income support

Advisers should check whether their client is exempt from the rule that full-time students are not entitled to IS, or whether s/he has a partner who is eligible to claim on her/his behalf.

If a student works during the vacations and her/his IS includes an amount for her/his housing costs, the adviser needs to check that the hours and/or level of earnings do not result in a loss of entitlement to IS for housing costs.

Under certain circumstances, a student or her/his partner may be entitled to housing costs for two homes.

For further details, see CPAG's *Welfare Benefits and Tax Credits Handbook*.

Income-based jobseeker's allowance

If the student has a partner who is able to claim income-based JSA, s/he should be aware that working in the vacations may result in a loss of benefit.

For further details, see CPAG's *Welfare Benefits and Tax Credits Handbook*.

Students taking time out (intercalating students)

Some students need to leave their course temporarily – eg, because of ill health, exam failure, or family or personal problems. Benefit regulations state that full-time students are excluded from IS, HB and CTB for the whole duration of their period of study. For precise definitions of this period for each benefit, see CPAG's *Welfare Benefits and Tax Credits Handbook*. Students who are exempt from the full-time student rule are entitled to those benefits during a period of temporary absence from their course.

Students cannot get IS or JSA while they are ill (unless they are classed as a 'disabled student'), but they can claim JSA, HB, and CTB once the illness or caring responsibilities have come to an end. They can claim from this point until they restart the course or up to the day before they start the new academic year. They can only qualify if they are not eligible for student support during this period.

For other students, the definition of student in the regulations results in 'intercalating students' still being treated as though they were on a full-time course and therefore not entitled to IS, HB and CTB. Students in this situation should obtain advice from their students' union or institution on alternative means of support.

Charities

There are many charities which provide assistance to students. However, most of these are unable to meet the level of demand placed upon them since the reduction in mainstream funding to students.

Applications are more likely to succeed if the student is close to completing her/his course, and/or where funding arrangements have broken down. There are a number of fund-finding vehicles specialising in helping students access money from trusts and charities, such as the Educational Grants Advisory Service and Funderfinder.

Research councils

There are eight research councils that fund postgraduate study:

- Biotechnology and Biological Sciences Research Council (www.bbsrc.ac.uk);
- Engineering and Physical Science Research Council (www.epsrc.ac.uk);
- Economic and Social Research Council (www.esrc.ac.uk);
- Medical Research Council (www.mrc.ac.uk);
- Natural Environment Research Council (www.nerc.ac.uk);
- Science and Technology Facilities Council;
- Arts and Humanities Research Council (www.ahrc.ac.uk);
- Council for the Central Laboratory of the Research Councils (www.cclrc.ac.uk).

Access to Learning Fund

The Access to Learning Fund makes annual allocations from central government to higher education institutions (via the funding councils). In Wales the fund is called the Financial Contingency Fund and the rules are broadly similar. Students' eligibility is based on the satisfaction of residency and immigration conditions, as for statutory support.

The Access to Learning Fund can be used by institutions to help students who are surviving on a low income who may need additional financial help to continue their higher education. Funds can be allocated when the student needs to meet a particular cost not being funded from elsewhere, to ease financial hardship, when emergency help is needed and where a payment would prevent a student from discontinuing her/his course of study. It can only be used to help home students on a full-time or part-time (studying at least half of an equivalent full-time course or those undertaking 'taster' modules of at least 10 per cent of a full-time course) course of higher education (including NHS students).

Priority groups for funding are:

- students with children, especially lone parents;
- mature students, particularly those with existing financial commitments;
- students from low-income families;
- disabled students;
- students entering higher education from care;
- students in their final year of study.

Funds cannot be used to help pay tuition fees for full-time students, but part-time students may be able to receive help for their fees.

Institutions are encouraged to set aside money to assist with financial difficulties arsing during the summer vacation, and students who have temporarily suspended their studies are still eligible to apply for hardship funds.

If a student is entitled to a student loan, s/he must usually have taken out the full amount to which s/he was entitled in the current academic year before being eligible for help from the Access to Learning Fund (or, at least, any payment will be calculated as if s/he had). Institutions decide eligibility and how much to allocate.

Payments are usually grants, although loans can be issued in certain circumstances (loans should be interest-free, but if they remain unpaid can be classed as a debt to the institution – see p460). Advisers can help students to make successful applications by identifying the criteria and priorities of a particular institution's funds, and providing evidence or a supporting letter to show how the particular student meets the criteria.

Hardship funds may be used for emergency payments/loans to help students who have not yet received their loan cheque at the start of the year.

Universities are required to have a Fund allocation appeals procedure. Thus, if a student has been refused a payment, or paid too little, advisers should assist her/him use this. Even successful applicants should be advised to re-apply if their circumstances change during the year, as further assistance could be forthcoming.

Many Fund administrators have a great deal of discretion in deciding or recommending grants, and have to process vast numbers of applications. Intervention by an adviser on behalf of a student could be most effective in improving her/his prospects.

Fund administrators have the power to make third-party payments, including payments direct to creditors. Creditors who are pressing for payment are often willing to allow more time is a payment is to be made directly by an institution.

For the purpose of means-tested benefits, payments from the hardship fund are treated as voluntary and charitable payments (see CPAG's *Welfare Benefits and Tax Credits Handbook*).

Access to Leaning Fund allocations to institutions have reduced this year and it is likely they will continue to reduce in the future.

Additional funds to assist students

Most institutions and some students' unions/guilds/associations and religious groups have a number of small funds available to meet specific circumstances, as well as general hardship funds. Some funds will make grants, others will make interest-free loans available. Students should consult the student services department or students' union/guild/association at their own institution for advice.

Employment

See also the section on benefits (p478) for the impact on benefits of working and p483 for information on tax refunds.

Traditionally, undergraduate students have worked during their vacation periods; many now also work part time through the term time. Income from part-time or casual work is disregarded for the purposes of assessing student support. Advisers need to warn students of the danger of relying on vacation work to supplement their mainstream income. Annual budgeting based on the expectation of an income from vacation work will falter if a job fails to materialise or is offered for fewer hours or weeks than anticipated.

Increasingly, institutions and students' unions provide information on jobs available to students. The institution may have regulations restricting the number of hours students are allowed to work. Aside from these, advisers need to help clients to balance their time between employment and study, and to check that the student is profiting financially from the work after travel and other expenses are taken into account.

Tax refunds

A student who has been working prior to her/his course, or for part of the year, should be advised to claim a refund of income tax when the employment ceases by filling out Form P50 (usually available from students' unions/guilds or tax offices). The form should be submitted to the tax office of her/his last employer, along with the student's P45.

Tax concessions

In order to gain the maximum benefit from term-time and vacation employment, a student who is working and earning under the appropriate tax allowance can arrange for no income tax to be deducted from her/his wages. The student will need to declare that her/his total taxable income in the whole of that financial year will not exceed her/his personal allowance for the same period. For vacation employment the employer needs to complete Form P38(S) and submit it to the tax office. At any other time, a P46 will need to be completed.

6. Dealing with priority debts

See Chapter 7.

Deciding on priority debts to the institution

Certain debts to the institution may need to be treated as priorities because of the consequences of non-payment. Wherever non-payment carries a legitimate threat of loss of accommodation, the debt should be treated as a priority (as outlined in Chapter 7). However, in addition, there are some cases where the legitimate threat of not being able to continue with study or not being allowed to graduate will lead to prioritisation. See p462 for those debts that could lead to this. 'New system' student loans should be prioritised, given that repayments are taken directly from wages when they become due.

Notes

1. **Introduction**
 1 Sch 1 E(SS) Regs
 2 For the extract of the judgment, see notes for guidance in Sch 1 E(SS) Regs

5. **Maximising income**
 3 Sch 2 E(SS) Regs
 4 E(SS) Regs
 5 ss124(1)(e) and 130(2) SSCBA 1992

Appendices

Appendix 1

Useful organisations

Trade bodies

Arts and Humanities Research Council
Whitefriars
Lewins Mead
Bristol BS1 2AE
Tel: 0117 9876 500
www.ahrc.ac.uk

Association of British Insurers
51 Gresham Street
London EC2V 7HQ
Tel: 020 7600 3333
www.abi.org.uk

Association of Chartered Certified Accountants
29 Lincoln's Inn Fields London
WC2A 3EE
Tel: 020 7059 5000
www.accaglobal.com

Association of Civil Enforcement Agencies
513 Bradford Road
Batley
West Yorkshire WF16 8LL
Tel: 01924 350 090

Biotechnology and Biological Sciences Research Council
Polaris House
North Star Avenue
Swindon SN2 1UH
Tel: 01793 413 200
www.bbsrc.ac.uk

British Bankers' Association
Pinners Hall
105-108 Old Broad Street
London EC2N 1EX
Tel: 020 7216 8800
www.bba.org.uk

British Cheque Cashers Association
PO Box 3414
Chester CH1 9BF
Tel: 01244 505 904
www.bcca.co.uk

British Insurance Brokers' Association
14 Bevis Marks
London EC3A 7NT
Tel (members): 0844 77 00 266
Consumer helpline: 0870 950 1790
www.biba.org.uk

Consumer Credit Association
Queens House
Queens Road
Chester CH1 3BQ
Tel: 01244 312 044
www.ccauk.org

Consumer Credit Trade Association
Suite 4, The Wave
1 View Croft Road
Shipley BD17 7DU
Tel: 01274 714 959
www.ccta.co.uk

Council of Mortgage Lenders
Bush House, North West Wing
Aldwych London WC2B 4PJ
Tel: 0845 373 6771
www.cml.org.uk

Credit Services Association
Wingrove House
Ponteland Road
Newcastle-upon-Tyne NE5 3AJ
Tel: 0191 286 5656
www.csa-uk.com

Economic and Social Research Council
Polaris House
North Star Avenue
Swindon SN2 1UJ
Tel: 01793 413 000
www.esrc.ac.uk

Enforcement Services Association
(formerly Certificated Bailiffs Association)
Park House
10 Park Street
Bristol BS1 5HX
Tel: 0117 907 4771
www.ensas.org.uk

Engineering and Physical Sciences Research Council
Polaris House
North Star Avenue
Swindon SN2 1ET
Tel: 01793 444 000
www.epsrc.ac.uk

Finance and Leasing Association
Imperial House
15-19 Kingsway
London WC2B 6UN
Tel: 020 7836 6511
www.fla.org.uk

Insolvency Practitioners Association
Valiant House
4-10 Heneage Lane
London EC3A 5DQ
Tel: 020 7623 5108
www.insolvency-practitioners.org.uk

Institute of Chartered Accountants in England and Wales
Chartered Accountants' Hall
PO Box 433
London EC2P 2BJ
Tel: 020 7920 8100

Level 1, Metropolitan House
321 Avebury Boulevard
Milton Keynes MK9 2FZ
Tel: 01908 248 100
www.icaew.co.uk

Institute of Insurance Brokers
Higham Business Centre
Midland Road
Higham Ferrers NN10 8DW
Tel: 01933 410 003
www.iib-uk.com

Medical Research Council
20 Park Crescent
London W1B 1AL
Tel: 020 7636 5422
www.mrc.ac.uk

Natural Environment Research Council
Polaris House
North Star Avenue
Swindon SN2 1EU
Tel: 01793 411 500
www.nerc.ac.uk

Science and Technology Facilities Council
Polaris House
North Star Avenue
Swindon SN2 1SZ
Tel: 01793 442 000
www.stfc.ac.uk

Ombudsmen and regulatory bodies

Department for Children, Schools and Families
Sanctuary Buildings
Great Smith Street
London SW1P 3BT
Tel: 0870 000 2288
www.dfes.gov.uk

Energy Ombudsman
PO Box 966
Warrington WA4 9DF
Tel: 01925 530 263 or
0845 055 0760
www.energy-ombudsman.org.uk

Financial Ombudsman Service
South Quay Plaza
183 Marsh Wall
London E14 9SR
Tel: 020 7964 1000
www.financial-ombudsman.org.uk

Financial Services Authority
25 The North Colonnade
Canary Wharf
London E14 5HS
Tel: 020 7066 1000
Helpline: 0845 606 1234
www.fsa.gov.uk

Information Commissioner's Office
(formerly Office of the Data Protection Registrar)
Wycliffe House
Water Lane
Wilmslow SK9 5AF
Tel: 01625 545 745
www.informationcommissioner.gov.uk
(for complaints concerning out-of-date or inaccurate personal information)

The Law Society (England and Wales)
113 Chancery Lane
London WC2A 1PL
Tel: 020 7242 1222
www.lawsociety.org.uk

Office for the Supervision of Solicitors
Victoria Court
8 Dormer Place
Leamington Spa CV32 5AE
Tel: 0192 682 0082
Helpline: 0845 608 6565
www.lawsociety.org.uk

Office of Communications (Ofcom)
Riverside House
2a Southwark Bridge Road
London SE1 9HA
Tel: 020 7981 3000
www.ofcom.org.uk

Office of Fair Trading
Fleetbank House
2-6 Salisbury Square
London EC4Y 8JX
Tel: 020 7211 8000
www.oft.gov.uk

Office of Gas and Electricity Markets (Ofgem)
9 Millbank
London SW1P 3GE
Tel: 020 7901 7000
www.ofgem.gov.uk

Office of the Legal Services Ombudsman
3rd Floor, Sunlight House
Quay Street
Manchester M3 3JZ
Tel: 0161 839 7262
Lo Call: 0845 601 0794 (charged at local rates, available nationally)
www.olso.org

Office of the Pensions Ombudsman
11 Belgrave Road
London SW1V 1RB
Tel: 020 7834 9144
www.pensions-ombudsman.org.uk

Office of Water Services (Ofwat)
Centre City Tower
7 Hill Street
Birmingham B5 4UA
Tel: 0121 625 1300
www.ofwat.gov.uk

Parliamentary and Health Service Ombudsman (England)
Millbank Tower
Millbank
London SW1P 4QP
Tel: 0845 015 4033
www.ombudsman.org.uk

Public Services Ombudsman for Wales
1 Ffordd yr Hen Gae
Pencoed CF35 5LJ
Tel 01656 641 150
www.ombudsman-wales.org

The Adjudicator's Office
8th Floor, Euston Tower
286 Euston Road
London NW1 3US
Tel: 0300 057 1111 or
020 7667 1832
www.adjudicatorsoffice.gov.uk

The Commission for Local Administration in England (Local Government Ombudsman)
PO Box 4771
Coventry CV4 0EH
Tel: 0845 602 1983 or 024 7682 1960
www.lgo.org.uk

Welsh Assembly Government
Cathays Park
Cardiff CF10 3NQ
Tel: 0845 010 3300
www.wales.gov.uk

Organisations giving advice or representing advice networks

AdviceUK (formerly Federation of Information and Advice Centres)
12th Floor,
New London Bridge House
25 London Bridge Street
London SE1 9SG
Tel: 020 7407 4070
www.adviceuk.org.uk

Association of British Credit Unions Ltd
Holyoake House
Hanover Street
Manchester M60 0AS
Tel: 0161 832 3694
www.abcul.org

Business Debtline
Tel: 0800 197 6026
www.bdl.org.uk

Citizens Advice
Myddelton House
115-123 Pentonville Road
London N1 9LZ
Tel: 020 7833 2181
www.citizensadvice.org.uk

Consumer Focus (formerly National Consumer Council)
4th Floor, Artillery House
Artillery Row
London SW1P 1RT
Tel: 020 7799 7900
www.consumerfocus.org.uk/

Institute of Money Advisers
Stringer House
34 Lupton Street
Leeds LS10 2QW
Tel: 0113 270 8444
www.i-m-a.org.uk

Law Centres Federation
Third Floor
293-299 Kentish Town Road
London NW5 2TJ
Tel: 020 7428 4400
www.lawcentres.org.uk

Money Advice Trust
21 Garlick Hill
London EC4V 2AU
Tel: 020 7489 7796
www.moneyadvicetrust.org

National Debtline
Tel: 0808 808 4000
www.nationaldebtline.co.uk

National Union of Students
Centro 3
Mandela Street
London NW1 0DU
Tel: 020 7380 6600
www.nusonline.co.uk

TaxAid
Room 304, Linton House
164-180 Union Street
London SE1 0LH
Tel (advisers only, 9am-5pm): 020 7803 4950
Tel (clients, 10am-12pm Mon-Thurs): 0845 120 3779
www.taxaid.org.uk

UCAS (Universities and Colleges Admission Service)
Rosehill
New Barn Lane
Cheltenham GL52 3LZ
Tel: 01242 222 444
www.ucas.com

UKCISA: UK Council for International Student Affairs

9-17 St Albans Place
London N1 0NX
Tel (advice line, 1pm-4pm Mon-Fri):
020 7107 9922
www.ukcisa.org.uk

Appendix 2

Useful publications

A debt adviser should have access to the latest edition of most of the following books:

Debt

Cheshire, Fifoot and Furmston's Law of Contract, Michael Furmston and others, LexisNexis

Consumer Credit Act 2006, Julia Smith and Sandra McCalla, The Law Society

Consumer Law and Practice, Robert Lowe and Geoffrey Woodroffe, Sweet and Maxwell

Consumer Credit Law and Practice, D Rosenthal, Butterworths

Fisher and Lightwood's Law of Mortgage, Falcon Chambers, Butterworths Lexis Nexis

Tolleys Tax Guide, Tolley Publishing Company Ltd

* *Council Tax Handbook,* A Murdie, CPAG, £16 (7th edition, November 2007)

* *Fuel Rights Handbook,* A Murdie, CPAG, £17 (14th edition, March 2008)

Manual of Housing Law, Arden and Hunter, Sweet and Maxwell

* *Guide to Housing Benefit and Council Tax Benefit*, Zebedee, Ward and Lister, CIH/Shelter, £24 (2008/09 edition, June 2008)

* *Personal Finance Handbook*, CPAG, £15 (2nd edition, October 2007)

Personal Insolvency, Stephen Schaw Miller & Edward Bailey, Butterworths Lexis Nexis

Increasing resources

* *Welfare Benefits and Tax Credits Handbook*, CPAG, £36/8.50 for claimants (2008/09, April 2008). Also available as part of *CPAG's Welfare Benefits and Tax Credits Law Online*.

* *CPAG's Welfare Benefits and Tax Credits Law Online*.
Online service via the internet includes the *Handbook* linked to consolidated social security legislation, commissioners' decisions and court cases. All content is updated throughout the year. £56.40 (inc VAT) annual subscription for one user (2008 price)

* *Child Support Handbook*, CPAG, £25 (16th edition, September 2008)

* *Social Security Legislation Volume I: non-means-tested benefits*, Bonner, Hooker and White, Sweet & Maxwell.
£86 for the main volume (2008/09 edition, October 2008)

* *Social Security Legislation Volume II: income support, jobseeker's allowance, state pension credit and the social fund*, Mesher, Wood, Poynter, Wikely and Bonner, Sweet & Maxwell.
£86 for the main volume (2008/09 edition, October 2008)

* *Social Security Legislation Volume III: administration, adjudication and the European dimension*, Rowland and White, Sweet and Maxwell.
£86 for the main volume (2008/09 edition, October 2008)

* *Social Security Legislation Volume IV: tax credits, child trust funds and employer-paid social security benefits*, Wikely and Williams, Sweet and Maxwell.
£86 for the main volume (2008/09 edition, October 2008)

* *Social Security Legislation – updating supplement to Volumes I, II, III & IV*, Sweet and Maxwell.
£58 for the updating supplement (2008/09 edition, spring 2009)

* *CPAG's Housing Benefit and Council Tax Benefit Legislation*, Findlay, Poynter, Stagg, Wright and George.
£97 for the main volume plus updating supplement (2008/09 edition, main volume December 2008)

* *Child Support: the legislation*, Jacobs, Sweet and Maxwell
£85 for the main volume (8th edition, September 2007)

* *Disability Rights Handbook*, Disability Alliance, £21 (2008/09 edition, May 2008)

A Guide to Grants for Individuals in Need, The Directory of Social Change

Voluntary Agencies Directory, available from Harper Row Distribution Ltd, Estover Road, Plymouth PL6 7PZ

Charities Digest, Family Welfare Enterprises Ltd

Tolley's Employment Law Handbook, Slade and Giffin, Tolley Publishing Company Ltd

Student Loans: a guide for students, available from Student Loans Company Ltd, 100 Bothwell Street, Glasgow G2 7JD

Courts and the law

Anthony and Berryman's Magistrates' Court Guide, Butterworths

The Civil Court Practice (The Green Book), Butterworths Lexis Nexis

Dictionary of Law, Collin, Bloomsbury

Defending Possession Proceedings, Luba, Madge and McConnell, Legal Action Group

Insolvency Legislation Annotations and Commentary, Doyle and Keay, Jordans

Muir Hunter on Personal Insolvency, Briggs & others, Thomson Sweet and Maxwell

Practical Banking and Building Society Law, Arora, Blackstone Press

Charging Orders Against Land, Walker and Buckley, Barry Rose Law Publishers

Enforcement of Local Taxation, Murdie and Wise, Legal Action Group

Manual of Housing Law, Andrew Arden and others, Sweet and Maxwell

The Law of Seizure of Goods: debtors' rights and remedies, J Kruse, Barry Rose Law Publishers

Transfer of Powers of Arrest by Magistrates' Courts, J Kruse, ACEA

Skills

Client Interviewing for Lawyers, Avrom Sherr, Sweet and Maxwell

* Indicates that books are available from CPAG. For a full publications list and order form see www.cpag.org.uk/publications; write to CPAG, 94 White Lion Street, London N1 9PF; or call 020 7837 7979.

Appendix 3

Abbreviations used in the notes

AC	Appeal Cases
All ER	All England Reports
Art(s)	Article(s)
CA	Court of Appeal
CC	County court
EWCA	England and Wales Court of Appeal
EWHC	England and Wales High Court
FLR	Family Law Reports
HC	High Court
HL	House of Lords
HLR	Housing Law Reports
JPR	Justice of the Peace Reports
KB	King's Bench Reports
para(s)	Paragraph(s)
PD	Practice Direction
QB	Queen's Bench Reports
QBD	Queen's Bench Division
r(s)	Rule(s)
reg(s)	Regulation(s)
s(s)	Section(s)
Sch(s)	Schedule(s)
UKHL	United Kingdom House of Lords
WLR	Weekly Law Reports

Acts of Parliament

AEA 1971	Attachment of Earnings Act 1971
AJA 1970	Administration of Justice Act 1970
AJA 1973	Administration of Justice Act 1973
CA 2003	Courts Act 2003
CCA 1974	Consumer Credit Act 1974
CCA 2006	Consumer Credit Act 2006

CCA 1984	County Courts Act 1984
CJA 1982	Criminal Justice Act 1982
CLSA 1990	Courts and Legal Services Act 1990
CSPSSA 2000	Child Support, Pensions and Social Security Act 2000
EA 1989	Electricity Act 1989
EA 2002	Enterprise Act 2002
ETA 1973	Employment and Training Act 1973
FSMA 2000	Financial Services and Markets Act 2000
GA 1986	Gas Act 1986
GA 1995	Gas Act 1995
IA 1986	Insolvency Act 1986
IAA 1999	Immigration and Asylum Act 1999
JA 1838	Judgments Act 1838
JSA 1995	Jobseekers Act 1995
LA 1980	Limitation Act 1980
LGA 2003	Local Government Act 2003
LGFA 1988	Local Government Finance Act 1988
LPA 1925	Law of Property Act 1925
MCA 1980	Magistrates' Court Act 1980
MOA 1958	Maintenance Orders Act 1958
PCCA 1973	Powers of Criminal Courts Act 1973
RA 1977	Rent Act 1977
SCA 1981	Supreme Court Act 1981
SGA 1979	Sale of Goods Act 1979
SGSA 1982	Supply of Goods and Services Act 1982
SPCA 2002	State Pension Credit Act 2002
SSAA 1992	Social Security Administration Act 1992
SSCBA 1992	Social Security Contributions and Benefits Act 1992
TCA 2002	Tax Credits Act 2002
TC&EA 2007	Tribunals, Courts and Enforcement Act 2007
TLATA 1996	Trusts of Land and Appointment of Trustees Act 1996
TMA 1970	Taxes Management Act 1970
UA 2000	Utilities Act 2000
WRA 2007	Welfare Reform Act 2007

Regulations and other statutory instruments

Each set of Regulations or Order has a statutory instrument (SI) number and a date. Ask for them by giving that date and number.

CC(AE) Regs	The Community Charge (Administration and Enforcement) Regulations 1989 No.438
CC(IJD)O 1991	The County Court (Interest on Judgment Debts) Order 1991 No.1184

CC(IR) Regs	The Consumer Credit (Information Requirements and Duration of Licences and Charges) Regulations 2007 No.1167
CP Regs	The Consumer Protection from Unfair Trading Regulations 2008 No.1277
CT(AE) Regs	The Council Tax (Administration and Enforcement) Regulations 1992 No.613
CTB Regs	The Council Tax Benefit (General) Regulations 1992 No.1814
CTB(SPC) Regs	The Council Tax Benefit (Persons who have Attained the Qualifying Age for State Pension Credit) Regulations 2006 No.216
CTC Regs	The Child Tax Credit Regulations 2002 No.2007
DFA Regs	The Discretionary Financial Assistance Regulations 2001 No.1167
E(SS) Regs	The Education (Student Support) Regulations 2008 No.529
ESA Regs	The Employment and Support Allowance Regulations 2008 No.794
E(SS) Regs	The Education (Student Support) Regulations 2008 No.529
HB Regs	The Housing Benefit (General) Regulations 1987 No.1971
HB(SPC) Regs	The Housing Benefit (Persons who have Attained the Qualifying Age for State Pension Credit) Regulations 2006 No.214
HCCCJO 1991	The High Court and County Courts Jurisdiction Order 1991 No.724
HSS&WF(A) Regs	The Healthy Start Scheme and Welfare Food (Amendment) Regulations 2005 No.3262
I(A)R	The Insolvency (Amendment) Rules 2003 No.1730
IR	The Insolvency Rules 1986 No.1925
IS Regs	The Income Support (General) Regulations 1987 No.1967
JSA Regs	The Jobseeker's Allowance Regulations 1996 No.207
SFCWP Regs	The Social Fund Cold Weather Payments (General) Regulations 1988 No.1724
SFM&FE Regs	The Social Fund Maternity and Funeral Expenses (General) Regulations 1987 No.481
SFWFP Regs	The Social Fund Winter Fuel Payment Regulations 2000 No.729
SPC Regs	The State Pension Credit Regulations 2002 No.1792
SS(CMB) Regs	The Social Security (Child Maintenance Bonus) Regulations 1996 No.3195
SS(CMPMA) Regs	The Social Security (Child Maintenance Premium and Miscellaneous Amendments) Regulations 2000 No.3176
SS(C&P) Regs	The Social Security (Claims and Payments) Regulations 1987 No.1968
SS(IFW) Regs	The Social Security (Incapacity for Work) (General) Regulations 1995 No.311
TC(Imm) Regs	The Tax Credits (Immigration) Regulations 2003 No.653

TC(PC) Regs	The Tax Credits (Payments by the Commissioners) Regulations 2002 No.2173
TC(R) Regs	The Tax Credits (Residence) Regulations 2003 No.654
UTCC Regs	The Unfair Terms in Consumer Contracts Regulations 1994 No.2083
WTC(EMR) Regs	The Working Tax Credit (Entitlement and Maximum Rate) Regulations 2002 No.2005

Other information

CCR	County Court Rules or Rules of the County Court
CCLR	Consumer Credit Law Reports
CPR	Civil Procedure Rules
DCG	Debt Collection Guidance
DMG	Debt Management Guidance

Index

How to use this Index

Entries against the bold headings direct you to the general information on the subject, or where the subject is covered most fully. Sub-entries are listed alphabetically and direct you to specific aspects of the subject.

F

ORDER FORM

for more copies of this or other CPAG *Handbooks*

DEBT ADVICE HANDBOOK, 8th edition

The only comprehensive one-volume practitioner's guide to the processes and practice of money advice in England and Wales. This is the first revised and updated edition since 2006.

November 2008 978 1 906076 21 4 £20.00

PERSONAL FINANCE HANDBOOK, 2nd edition

Fully updated for general advisers, teachers, consumers and anyone involved in financial literacy work, this *Handbook* is an accessible guide to everyday financial products and services – eg, savings, loans, pensions, tax and insurance.

October 2007 978 1 906076 01 6 £15.00

WELFARE BENEFITS AND TAX CREDITS HANDBOOK, 2008/09 edition

The definitive comprehensive guide to all benefits and tax credits. See overleaf for details of how to access this *Handbook* online.

April 2008 978 1 906076 12 2 £36.00

(£8.50 post-free for individual benefit claimants – direct from CPAG)

FUEL RIGHTS HANDBOOK, 14th edition

This standard practical guide to coping with fuel bills, debt and related problems with fuel supply. Fully updated with all major changes since the previous (2005) edition.

March 2008 978 1 906076 05 4 £17.00

COUNCIL TAX HANDBOOK, 7th edition

This authoritative guide to all aspects of the tax is fully updated with all changes since the previous (2005) edition.

November 2007 978 1 906076 06 1 £16.00

CHILD SUPPORT HANDBOOK, 2008/09 edition

Fully updated to cover the latest information on the child support scheme.

September 2008 978 1 906076 14 6 £25.00

(£6.50 post-free for individual claimants – direct from CPAG)

PAYING FOR CARE HANDBOOK, 6th edition

The standard guide to services, charges and welfare benefits for adults in need of care in the community or in care homes. This is the first revised and updated edition since 2005.

Late 2008 978 1 906076 20 7 £19.50

Payment with order

_______ Debt Advice Handbook @ £20.00 each £_______
_______ Personal Finance Handbook @ £15.00 each £_______
_______ Welfare Benefits and Tax Credits Handbook @ £36.00 each £_______
_______ Fuel Rights Handbook @ £17.00 each £_______
_______ Council Tax Handbook @ £16.00 each £_______
_______ Child Support Handbook @ £25.00 each £_______
_______ Paying for Care Handbook @ £19.50 each £_______

Postage & packing: For orders up to £100 in value, add £3.99 flat fee;
£100.01–£400 add £5.99;
over £400, add £9.99. P&P: £_______
Total: £_______

I enclose a cheque/PO for £_______ payable to Child Poverty Action Group

Title _______ First Name _______ Last Name _______

Organisation _______ Dept _______

Address _______

_______ Postcode _______

***Return form with payment to:* CPAG, Dept HBK, 94 White Lion Street, London N1 9PF**

For details of ordering by credit/debit card or for other information, see www.cpag.org.uk

Money advice courses at CPAG

Dealing with debt

Many community groups and public sector workers have clients with debt problems. This essential two-day course helps generalist advisers, community workers, local authority benefits and housing staff, social workers, health sector staff and others to advise and support clients with debt or money problems. This is a practical course, which takes a rights approach to maximising income, dealing with debts and other related issues. No previous knowledge of money advice techniques is needed. Participants will receive a free copy of the *Debt Advice Handbook*.

Students and debt

This two-day course will look at dealing with debt with specific reference to the needs of students. It will include dealing with debts that students may already have when they join an institution, as well as those debts they incur as a student. It will look at income and expenditure, budgeting issues, and liability issues as they commonly affect students in debt, as well as negotiation with creditors, strategies and legal procedures.

Voluntary bankruptcy: what it means for clients*

This introductory level half-day course is designed to increase the awareness of bankruptcy for those who are not money advisers, but whose work brings them into contact with clients in multiple debt. The course will consider the effects and risks of bankruptcy. At the end of the course, trainees should be able to explain to a client the advantages and disadvantages of bankruptcy and make an appropriate referral if necessary.

Outline of bankruptcy procedure and responding to proceedings*

Creditors are increasingly turning to the use of bankruptcy proceedings, often using statutory demands either to pressurise debtors or as the first step towards having a person declared bankrupt. This half-day course provides an outline of bankruptcy procedures, looking particularly at statutory demands, which are used at the initial stages.

**These two half-day courses are held on the same day and can be booked as a one-day event.*

Coming soon

Tactics for student debt advisers

A new one-day course aimed at experienced student debt advisers.

For dates, prices and more information on any of the above, or to see the complete range of welfare benefits training courses provided by CPAG, please visit www.cpag.org.uk/training or telephone the training department on 020 7812 5228/ 5217 for a brochure to be sent to you.

In-house debt training is also provided. Phone 0207 812 5217 for more details.

CPAG's website – www.cpag.org.uk

Visit our site to find out more about CPAG – its activities and policies. And to find out about other CPAG publications, training courses and membership schemes.

Welfare Rights Bulletin

The ***Bulletin*** is essential reading for welfare rights advisers. One of its unique roles is to provide a cross-referenced bi-monthly update to the *Welfare Benefits and Tax Credits Handbook*.

Contents in 2008/09 will include the fullest coverage of: the new employment and support allowance and the work capability assessment; the new housing allowance for housing benefit; developments regarding overpayments of benefits and tax credits; right to reside issues; social security commissioners' decisions; court decisions, including the latest test cases.

The ***Welfare Rights Bulletin*** is the best value in the field – and compulsory reading for any adviser needing the very latest benefits and tax credits information.

£30.00 for a full year's subscription (six issues)
ISSN 0263 2098

Sent to CPAG Rights and Comprehensive members as well as Bulletin subscribers.

For quick and easy access to the Handbook – become a CPAG 'Rights' or 'Rights Online' member

As a 'Rights' member (£57 per year) you receive automatically:

- The *Welfare Benefits and Tax Credits Handbook*, mailed to you as soon as it's published.
- Six issues of the *Welfare Rights Bulletin* – keeping you up-to-date with benefit and tax credit developments and caselaw throughout the year.

You will save £9 on the retail price of these publications, and postage is free. Your membership entitles you to further benefits:

- Regular mailings, including CPAG's *Poverty* journal and newsletter, training brochures and other useful information.
- Special offers on social security, tax credits and child support legislation – potentially saving nearly £50 this year.

'The easiest way to obtain (the Handbook) annually is to become a member of CPAG and receive the equally valuable bi-monthly Welfare Rights Bulletin' – ***FAMILY LAW***

Or become a 'Rights Online' member (£72 per year inc £7 VAT), with all the benefits shown above except that instead of a printed *Handbook* you get a single user subscription to *Welfare Benefits and Tax Credits Law Online* (see previous page for details).

Send cheques/POs payable to Child Poverty Action Group to:
CPAG, Dept HBK, 94 White Lion Street, London N1 9PF
(This is for new members only – if you are already a Rights member, please wait for your renewal form from CPAG)

Help CPAG to make a difference: make a donation

Child Poverty Action Group is an independent registered charity (Nos. 294841, SC039339) providing advice and support to ensure families have access to their full benefit entitlement. We campaign to bring about positive change for families with children in poverty in the UK. Please add a donation to your order: your support (as an individual or an organisation) allows us to continue to speak up for vulnerable families and fight the injustice of poverty. Thank you.